Why Do You Need this New Edition?

If you're wondering why you should buy this new edition of *Drama: A Pocket Anthology*, here are three good reasons!

1. **Yasmina Reza's Tony-winning comedy *The God of Carnage*,** produced on Broadway with a cast including James Gandolfini and Jeff Daniels, reflects the robust strength of today's Broadway and of contemporary comedy.

2. **Shakespeare's *Twelfth Night*** brings a classic comedy to this collection for the first time.

3. And as always, ***Drama: A Pocket Anthology*** offers a diverse and remarkably comprehensive collection of drama at an affordable price and an attractive length.

W9-AAC-084

about the author

R.S. GWYNN has edited several other books, including *Literature: A Pocket Anthology; Poetry: A Pocket Anthology; Fiction: A Pocket Anthology; Inside Literature: Reading, Responding, Writing* (with Steven Zani); *The Art of the Short Story* (with Dana Gioia); and *Contemporary American Poetry: A Pocket Anthology* (with April Lindner). He has also authored five collections of poetry, including *No Word of Farewell: Selected Poems, 1970–2000.* He has been awarded the Michael Braude Award for verse from the American Academy of Arts and Letters. Gwynn is University Professor of English and Poet-in-Residence at Lamar University in Beaumont, Texas.

DRAMA

A POCKET ANTHOLOGY

FIFTH EDITION

Edited by

R. S. Gwynn
Lamar University

PEARSON

Boston   Columbus   Indianapolis   New York   San Francisco
Upper Saddle River   Amsterdam   Cape Town   Dubai   London   Madrid
Milan   Munich   Paris   Montreal   Toronto   Delhi   Mexico City
São Paulo   Sydney   Hong Kong   Seoul   Singapore   Taipei   Tokyo

Senior Sponsoring Editor: Virginia L. Blanford
Senior Marketing Manager: Joyce Nilsen
Assistant Editor: Rebecca Gilpin
Project Coordination, Text Design, and Electronic Page Makeup: Nitin
    Agarwal, Aptara®, Inc
Creative Art Director : Jayne Conte
Cover Designer: Bruce Kenselaar
Cover Illustration/Photo: Fotolia
Production Project Manager: Clara Bartunek
Printer and Binder: LSC Communications
Cover Printer: LSC Communications

For permission to use copyrighted material, grateful acknowledgment is
made to the copyright holders on appropriate page within text, which are
hereby made part of this copyright page.

Library of Congress Cataloging-in-Publication Data
Drama: a pocket anthology / edited by R.S. Gwynn.—5th ed.
      p. cm.
    Includes index.
    ISBN-13: 978-0-13-396172-0 (alk. paper)
    ISBN-10: 0-13-396172-9 (alk. paper)
    1. Drama—Collections. I. Gwynn, R. S.
PN6112.D68 2010
808.2—dc22   2010043752

10   17

ISBN–13: 978-0-13-396172-0
ISBN–10:   0-13-396172-9

contents

When the *Pocket Anthology* series first appeared, our primary aim was to offer a clear alternative to the anthologies of fiction, poetry, and drama that were available at the time. *Drama: A Pocket Anthology*, is here updated and revised for a fifth edition. Designed to be used in a wide range of courses, *Drama* is published concurrently with two companion volumes, *Fiction* and *Poetry*, as well as in a combined edition, *Literature: A Pocket Anthology*, which comprises most of the selections found in the three independent volumes, as well as introductions to all three genres. Your Pearson representative can supply full details about these books.

What's New in This Edition

As with earlier editions of *Drama*, our goal has been to provide variety and flexibility in the selections offered. In response to calls for a Shakespeare comedy, we have included *Twelfth Night*. Contemporary playwright Yasmina Reza is new to this anthology with the contemporary comedy of manners *The God of Carnage*. While trying to balance classical and contemporary drama in a brief anthology, we have also tried to ensure the representation of women and writers of color, as well as a range of dramatic forms.

Goals of This Anthology

Drama addresses the four wishes and concerns most commonly expressed by both instructors and students. First, of course, is the variety of selections it contains. Admittedly, a pocket anthology has to be very selective in its contents, so we are especially proud that the twelve plays in this book include both established canonical writers from Sophocles and Shakespeare to Ibsen and Tennessee Williams, and contemporary playwrights such as August Wilson, David Ives, and Milcha Sanchez-Scott, who reflect the diversity that is essential to any study of contemporary theater. The range of dramatic genres in *Drama* includes a Greek tragedy, a Shakespearean comedy, a problem play by Ibsen, and eight modern and contemporary plays ranging from one-act comedy and drama to modern tragedy to poetic realism to contemporary comedy of manners. We strongly believe that the plays in *Drama* will provide a reading experience that is thought-provoking and enjoyable, as well as a strong introduction to drama and dramatic conventions overall.

Our second goal was flexibility. We wanted a book that could be used as both a primary and a supplemental text in a wide range of courses, from introduction to drama to advanced classes in theatre or playwriting to creative writing workshops. When combined with one of its companion volumes, *Fiction* or *Poetry*, or with novels, collections of short stories or poems by individual authors, or plays, *Drama* may also be used in introductory literature courses. *Drama* contains, in addition to its generous selection of plays, biographical headnotes about authors, an introduction that covers the techniques and terminology of the genre, and a concise section on writing about drama and research procedures.

Third, we wanted an affordable book. Full-size introductory literature books—and even comprehensive anthologies of drama—now cost well over $70. Pearson Education is committed to keeping the price of the *Pocket Anthology* series reasonable without compromising on design or typeface. We hope that readers will find the attractive layout of *Drama* preferable to the cramped margins and minuscule fonts found in many literature textbooks. Because of its relatively low cost, this volume may be easily supplemented in individual courses with works of criticism, handbooks of grammar and usage, or manuals of style.

Finally, we stressed portability. Many instructors have expressed concern for students who must carry literature books comprising 2,000 or more pages in backpacks already laden with books and materials for other courses. A semester is a short time, and few courses can cover more than a fraction of the material that many full-sized collections contain. Because many instructors focus on a single genre at a time, *Drama* and its companion volumes, *Fiction* and *Poetry*, remain compact yet self-contained volumes that are reasonably easy to handle and carry.

Acknowledgments

No book is ever created in a vacuum. We would like to express our gratitude to the instructors who reviewed the current edition of this volume and offered invaluable recommendations for improvement. They are: Mark G. Aune, California University of Pennsylvania; Elizabeth M. Sloan, Northeast State Community College; E. Bert Wallace, Campbell University; and Royal Ward, Albion College.

We are also grateful to those who reviewed earlier editions, including Ruth Anne Baumgartner, Fairfield University; Paul Castagno, University of North Carolina/Wilmington; Thomas C. Crochunis, Shippensburg University; Laura Early, University of Louisville; and Randy Hendricks, University of West Georgia. Melanie Abrams, California State University/San Bernardino; Francis G. Babcock, Louisiana State University; Maryam Barrie, Washtenaw Community College; Paul Bawek, Florida Southern College; Jeff Gofer, Bellevue Community College; Marla K. Dean, University of Montevallo; Verna Foster, Loyola University (Chicago); Janet Gardner, University of Massachusetts/Dartmouth; Christine Gilmore, University of Toledo; Paul Graharm, West Virginia University; Dennis G. Jerz, University of Wisconsin/Eau Claire; Kevin Kerrane, University of Delaware; Bethany Larson, Buena Vista University; Donna Long, Fairmount State University; James F. Scott, St. Louis University; Jeffrey P. Stephens, Oklahoma State University; James Stick, Des Moines Area Community College; and Karin Westman, Kansas State University.

The editor also acknowledges the invaluable assistance of Rachel Klauss in assembling this edition.

R. S. Gwynn
Lamar University

Introduction

The Play's the Thing

The theater, located in the heart of a rejuvenated downtown business district, is a relic of the silent movie era that has been restored to something approaching its former glory. While only a few members of tonight's audience can actually remember it in its prime, the expertise of the organist seated at the antique Wurlitzer instills a sense of false nostalgia in the crowd, now settling by twos and threes into red, plush-covered seats and looking around in search of familiar faces. Just as the setting is somewhat out of the ordinary, so is this group. Unlike movie audiences, they are for the most part older and less casually dressed. There are few small children present, and even the teenagers seem to be on their best behavior. Oddly, no one is eating popcorn or noisily drawing on a soda straw. A mood of seriousness and anticipation hovers over the theater, and those who have lived in the town long enough can spot the spouse or partner of one of the principal actors nervously folding a program or checking a watch.

As the organ magically descends into the recesses of the orchestra pit, the lights dim, a hush falls over the crowd, and the curtain creakily rises. There is a general murmur of approval at the ingenuity and many hours of hard work that have transformed empty space into a remarkable semblance of an upper-class drawing room in the early 1900s. Dressed as a domestic servant, a young woman, known to the audience from her frequent appearances in local television commercials, enters and begins to dust a table. She hums softly to herself. A tall young man, in everyday life a junior partner in a local law firm, wanders in carrying a tennis racket. The maid turns, sees him, and catches her breath, startled. "Why Mr. Fenton!" she exclaims. . . .

And the world begins.

The full experience of drama—whether at an amateur production like the little theater performance described here or at a huge Broadway playhouse—is much more complex than that of any other form of literature. The word **drama** itself comes from a Greek word meaning "a thing that is done," and the roots of both **theater** and **audience** call to mind the acts of seeing and hearing, respectively. Like other communal public activities—religious services, sporting events, meetings of political or fraternal organizations—drama has evolved, over many centuries, its own set of customs, rituals, and rules. The exact shape of these characteristics—**dramatic conventions**—may differ from country to country or from period to period, but they all have one aim in common, namely to define and govern an art form whose essence is to be found in public performances of written texts. No other form of literature shares this primary goal. Before we can discuss drama purely as literature, we should first ponder some aspects of its unique status as "a thing that is done."

It is worth noting that dramatists are also called playwrights. Note the spelling—a "wright" is a maker, as old family names like Cartwright or Boatwright attest. If a play is in fact *made* rather than written, then a playwright is similar to an architect who has designed a unique building. The concept may be his or hers, but the construction project requires the contributions of many other hands before the sparkling steel and glass tower alters the city's skyline. In the case of a new play, money will have to be raised by a producer, a director chosen, a cast found, a crew assembled, a set designed and built, and many hours of rehearsal completed before the curtain can be raised for the first time. Along the way, modifications to the original play may become necessary, and it is possible that the author will listen to advice from the actors, director, or stage manager and incorporate their opinions into any revisions. Professional theater is, after all, a branch of show business, and no play will survive its premiere for long if it does not attract paying crowds. The dramatists we read and study so reverently today managed to reach large popular audiences in their time. Even ancient Greek playwrights like Sophocles and Euripides must have stood by surreptitiously "counting the house" as the open-air seats slowly filled, and Shakespeare prospered as part-owner of the Globe Theatre to the extent that he was able to retire to his hometown at the ripe old age of forty-seven.

Set beside this rich communal experience, the solitary act of reading a play seems a poor substitute, contrary to the play's very nature (only a small category known as **closet drama** comprises plays intended to be read instead of acted). Yet dramatists like Shakespeare and Ibsen are counted among the giants of world literature, and their works are annually read by far more people than actually see their plays performed. In reading a play, we are forced to pay close attention to such matters as **set description,** particularly with a playwright like Ibsen, who lavishes great attention on the design of his set; references to **properties** or "props" that will figure in the action of the play; physical description of characters and costumes; **stage directions** indicating the movements and gestures made by actors in scenes; and any other **stage business,** that is, action without dialogue. Many modern dramatists are very scrupulous in detailing these matters; writers of earlier periods, however, provided little or no instruction. Reading Sophocles or Shakespeare, we are forced to concentrate on the characters' words to envision how actions and other characters were originally conceived. Reading aloud, alone or in a group, or following along in the text while listening to or watching an audio or video performance is particularly recommended for verse plays such as *Antigone* or *Twelfth Night.* Also, versions of many of the plays contained in this book are currently available on videotape or DVD. While viewing a film is an experience of a different kind from seeing a live performance, film versions obviously provide a convenient insight into the ways in which great actors have interpreted their roles.

Origins of Drama

No consensus exists about the exact date of the birth of drama, but according to most authorities, it originated in Greece over 2500 years ago, an outgrowth of rites of worship of the god Dionysus, who was associated with male fertility, agriculture (especially the cultivation of vineyards), and seasonal renewal. In these Dionysian festivals a group of fifty citizens of Athens, known as a **chorus,** outfitted and trained by a leader, or *choragos,* would perform hymns of praise to the god, known as **dithyrambic poetry.** The celebration concluded with the ritual sacrifice of a goat, or *tragos.* The two main genres of drama originally took their names from these rituals; comedy comes from *kômos,* the Greek word for a festivity. These primitive revels were invariably accompanied with a union of the sexes (*gamos* in Greek, a word that survives in English words like "monogamy") celebrating fertility and continuance of the race, an ancient custom still symbolically observed in the "fade-out kiss" that concludes most comedies. Tragedy, on the other hand, literally means "song of the goat," taking its name from the animal that was killed on the altar **(thymele),** cooked, and shared by the celebrants with their god.

Around 600 B.C. certain refinements took place. In the middle of the sixth century B.C. an official springtime festival, known as the Greater or City Dionysia, was established in Athens, and prizes for the best dithyrambic poems were first awarded. At about the same time a special **orchestra,** or "dancing place," was constructed, a circular area surrounding the altar, and permanent seats, or a **theatron** ("seeing place"), arranged in a semicircle around the orchestra were added. At the back of the orchestra the façade of a temple (the **skene**) and a raised "porch" in front of it (the **proskenion,** in later theaters the **proscenium**) served as a backdrop, usually representing the palace of the ruler; walls extending to either side of the *skene,* the **parodoi,** served to conceal backstage activity from the audience. A wheeled platform, or **eccyclema,** could be pushed through the door of the *skene* to reveal the tragic consequences of a play's climax (there was no onstage "action" in Greek tragedy). Behind the *skene* a crane-like device called a **mechane** (or **deus ex machina**) could be used to lower a god from the heavens or represent a spectacular effect like the flying chariot drawn by dragons at the conclusion of Euripides' *Medea.*

In 535 B.C. a writer named Thespis won the annual competition with a startling innovation. Thespis separated one member of the chorus (called a *hypocrites,* or "actor") and had him engage in **dialogue,** spoken lines representing conversation, with the remaining members. If we define drama primarily as a story related through live action and recited dialogue, then Thespis may rightly be called the father of drama, and his name endures in "thespian," a synonym for actor.

The century after Thespis, from 500–400 B.C., saw many refinements in the way tragedies were performed and is considered the golden age of Greek drama. In this century, the careers of the three great tragic playwrights—Aeschylus (525–456 B.C.), Sophocles (496?–406 B.C.), and Euripides (c. 480–406 B.C.)—and the greatest comic playwright, Aristophanes (450?–385? B.C.) overlapped. It is no coincidence that in this remarkable period Athens, under the leadership of the general Pericles (495–429 B.C.), reached the height of its wealth, influence, and cultural development and was home to the philosophers Socrates (470–399 B.C.) and Plato (c. 427–347 B.C.). Aristotle (384–322 B.C.), the third of the great Athenian philosophers, was also a literary critic who wrote the first extended analysis of drama.

Aristotle on Tragedy

The earliest work of literary criticism in Western civilization is Aristotle's *Poetics,* an attempt to define and classify the different literary **genres** that use rhythm, language, and harmony. Aristotle identifies four genres—epic poetry, dithyrambic poetry, comedy, and tragedy—which have in common their attempts at imitation, or *mimesis,* of various types of human activity.

Aristotle comments most fully on tragedy, and his definition of the genre demands close examination:

> A tragedy, then, is the imitation of an action that is serious and also, as having magnitude, complete in itself; in language with pleasurable accessories, each kind brought in separately in the parts of the work; in a dramatic, not in a narrative form; with incidents arousing pity and fear, wherewith to accomplish its catharsis of such emotions.

First we should note that the imitation here is of *action.* Later in the passage, when Aristotle differentiates between narrative and dramatic forms of literature, it is clear that he is referring to tragedy as a type of literature written primarily for public performance. Furthermore, tragedy must be serious and must have magnitude. By this, Aristotle implies that issues of life and death must be involved and that these issues must be of public import. In many Greek tragedies, the fate of the *polis,* or city, of which the chorus is the voice, is bound up with the actions taken by the main character in the play. Despite their rudimentary form of democracy, the people of Athens would have been perplexed by a tragedy with an ordinary citizen at its center; magnitude in tragedy demands that only the affairs of persons of high rank are of sufficient importance for tragedy. Aristotle further requires that this imitated action possess a sense of completeness. At no point does he say that a tragedy has to end with a death or even in a state of unhappiness; he does require, however, that the audience sense that after the last words are spoken no further story cries out to be told.

The next part of the passage may confuse the modern reader. By "language with pleasurable accessories" Aristotle means the poetic devices of rhythm and, in the choral parts of the tragedy, music and dance as well. Reading the choral passages in a Greek tragedy, we are likely to forget that these passages were intended to be chanted or sung ("chorus" and "choir" share the same root) and danced as well ("choreography" comes from this root as well).

The rest of Aristotle's definition dwells on the emotional effects of tragedy on the audience. Pity and fear are to be evoked—pity because we must care for the characters and to some extent empathize with them, fear because we come to realize that the fate they endure involves acts—of which murder and incest are only two—that civilized men and women most abhor. Finally, Aristotle's word *catharsis* has proved controversial over the centuries. The word literally means "a purging," but readers have debated whether Aristotle is referring to a release of harmful emotions or a transformation of them. In either case, the implication is that viewing a tragedy has a beneficial effect on an audience, perhaps because the viewers' deepest fears are brought to light in a make-believe setting. How many of us, at the end of some particularly wrenching film, have turned to a companion and said, "Thank god, it was only a movie"? The sacrificial animal from whom tragedy took its name was, after all, only a stand-in whose blood was offered to the gods as a substitute for a human subject. The protagonist of a tragedy remains, in many ways, a "scapegoat" on whose head we project our own unconscious terrors.

Aristotle identifies six elements of a tragedy, and these elements are still useful in analyzing not only tragedies but other types of plays as well. In order of importance they are **plot, characterization, theme, diction, melody,** and **spectacle.** Despite the fact that the *Poetics* is over two thousand years old, Aristotle's elements still provide a useful way of understanding how plays work.

Plot

Aristotle considers plot the chief element of a play, and it is easy to see this when we consider that in discussing a film with a friend we usually give a brief summary, or **synopsis,** of the plot, stopping just short of "giving it away" by telling how the story concludes. Aristotle defines plot as "the combination of incidents, or things done in the story," and goes on to give the famous formulation that a plot "is that which has a beginning, middle, and end." Aristotle notes that the best plots are selective in their use of material and have an internal coherence and logic. Two opposite terms that Aristotle introduced are still in use, although with slightly different meanings. By a **unified plot** we generally mean one that takes place in roughly a twenty-four hour period; in a short play with a unified plot like Susan Glaspell's *Trifles,* the action is continuous. By **episodic plot** we mean one that spreads its action out over a longer period of time. A play which has a unified plot, a single setting, and no subplots is said to observe the **three unities,** which critics in some eras have virtually insisted on as ironclad rules. Although most plots are chronological, playwrights in the last half-century have experimented, sometimes radically, with such straightforward progression through time. Some plays effectively blend **flashbacks** to past events with the action, and David Ives's *Sure Thing* plays havoc with chronology, allowing his protagonist to "replay" his previous scenes until he has learned the way to the "sure thing" of the title.

Two other important elements of most successful plots that Aristotle mentions are **reversal** (*peripeteia* in Greek, also known as **peripety**), and **recognition** (*anagnorisis* in Greek, also known as **discovery**). By reversal he means a change "from one state of things within the play to its opposite." Aristotle cites one example from *Oedipus the King,* the tragedy he focuses on: "the Messenger, who, coming to gladden Oedipus and to remove his fears as to his mother, reveals the secret of his birth"; but an earlier reversal in the same play occurs when Jocasta, attempting to alleviate Oedipus's fears of prophecies, inadvertently mentions the "place where three roads meet" where Oedipus killed a man he took to be a stranger. Most plays have more than a single reversal; each episode or act builds on the main character's hopes that his or her problems will be solved, only to dash those expectations as the play proceeds. Recognition, the second term, is perhaps more properly an element of characterization because it involves a character's "change from ignorance to knowledge." If the events of the plot have not served to illuminate the character about his or her failings, then the audience is likely to feel that the story has lacked depth. The kind of self-knowledge that tragedies provide is invariably accompanied by suffering and won at great emotional cost. In comedy, on the other hand, reversals may bring relief to the characters, and recognition may bring about the happy conclusion of the play.

A typical plot may be broken down into several components. First comes the **exposition,** which provides the audience with essential information—who, what, when, where—that it needs to know before the play can continue. A novelist or short story writer can present information directly with some sort of variation on the "Once upon a time" opening. But dramatists have particular problems with exposition because facts must be presented in the form of dialogue and action. Greek dramatists used the first two parts of a tragedy, relying on the audience's familiarity with the myths being retold, to set up the initial situation of the play. Other types of drama use a single character to provide expository material. Medieval morality plays often use a "heavenly messenger" to deliver the opening speech, and some of Shakespeare's plays employ a single character named "Chorus" who speaks an introductory prologue and "sets the scene" for later portions of the plays as well. In *The Glass Menagerie,* Tom Wingfield fulfills this role in an unusual manner, telling the audience at the beginning, "I am the narrator of the play, and also a character in it." Occasionally, we even encounter the least elegant solution to the problem of dramatic exposition, employing minor characters whose sole function is to provide background information in the play's opening scene. Countless drawing-room comedies have raised the curtain on a pair of servants in the midst of a gossipy conversation which catches the audience up on the doings of the family members who comprise the rest of the cast.

The second part of a plot is called the **complication,** the interjection of some circumstance or event that shakes up the stable situation that has existed before the play's opening and begins the **rising action** of the play, during which the audience's tension and expectations become tightly intertwined and involved with the characters and the events they experience. Complication in a play may be both external and internal. A plague, a threatened invasion, or a conclusion of a war are typical examples of external complication, outside events which affect the characters' lives. Many other plays rely primarily on an internal complication, a single character's failure in business or love that comes from a weakness in his or her personality. Often the complication is heightened by **conflict** between two characters whom events have forced into collision with each other. Whatever the case, the complication of the plot usually introduces a problem that the characters cannot avoid. The rising action, which constitutes the body of the play, usually contains a number of moments of **crisis,** when solutions crop up momentarily but quickly disappear. These critical moments in the scenes may take the form of the kinds of reversals discussed above, and the audience's emotional involvement in the plot generally hinges on the characters' rising and falling hopes.

The central moment of crisis in the play is the **climax,** or the moment of greatest tension, which initiates the **falling action** of the plot. Perhaps "moments" of greatest tension would be a more exact phrase, for skillful playwrights know how to wring as much tension as possible from the audience. In the best plots, everything in earlier parts of the play has pointed to this scene. In tragedy, the climax is traditionally accompanied with physical action and violence—a duel, a suicide, a murder—and the play's highest pitch of emotion.

The final part of a plot is the **dénouement,** or **resolution.** The French word literally refers to the untying of a knot, and we might compare the emotional effects of climax and dénouement to a piece of cloth twisted tighter and tighter as the play progresses and then untwisted as the action winds down. The dénouement returns the play and its characters to a stable situation, although not the same one that existed at the beginning of the play, and gives some indication of what the future holds for them. A dénouement may be either closed or open. A **closed dénouement** ties up everything neatly and explains all unanswered questions the audience might have; an **open dénouement** leaves a few tantalizing loose ends.

Several other plot terms should also be noted. Aristotle mentions, not altogether favorably, plots with "double issues." The most common word for this is **subplot,** a less important story involving minor characters that may mirror the main plot of the play. Some plays may even have more than one subplot. Occasionally, a playwright finds it necessary to drop hints about coming events in the plot, perhaps to keep the audience from complaining that certain incidents have happened "out of the blue." This is called **foreshadowing.** If a climactic incident that helps to resolve the plot has not been adequately prepared for, the playwright may be accused of having resorted to a **deus ex machina** ending, which takes its name from the *mechane* that once literally lowered a god or goddess into the midst of the dramatic proceedings. An ending of this sort, like that of an old western movie in which the cavalry arrives out of nowhere just as the wagon train is about to be annihilated, is rarely satisfactory.

Finally, the difference between **suspense** and **dramatic irony** should be addressed. Both of these devices generate tension in the audience, although through opposite means—suspense when the audience does not know what is about to happen; dramatic irony, paradoxically, when it does. Much of our pleasure in reading a new play lies in speculating about what will happen next, but in Greek tragedy the original audience would be fully familiar with the basic outlines of the mythic story before the action even began. Thus, dramatic irony occurs at moments when the audience is more knowledgeable about events than the onstage characters are. In some plays, our foreknowledge of certain events is so strong that we may want to cry out a warning to the characters.

Characterization

The Greek word **agon** means "debate" and refers to the central issue or conflict of a play. From *agon* we derive two words commonly used to denote the chief characters in a play: **protagonist,** literally the "first speaker," and **antagonist,** one who speaks against him. Often the word *hero* is used as a synonym for protagonist, but we should be careful in its application; indeed, in many modern plays it may be more appropriate to speak of the protagonist as an **anti-hero** because she or he may possess few, if any, of the traditional attributes of a hero. Similarly, the word *villain* brings to mind a black-mustached, sneering character in a top hat and opera cloak from an old-fashioned **melodrama** (a play whose complications are solved happily at the last minute by the "triumph of good over evil"), and usually has little application to the complex characters one encounters in a serious play.

Aristotle, in his discussion of characterization, stresses the complexity that marks the personages in the greatest plays. Nothing grows tiresome more quickly than a perfectly virtuous man or woman at the center of a play, and nothing is more offensive to the audience than seeing absolute innocence despoiled. Although Aristotle stresses that a successful protagonist must be better than ordinary men and women, he also insists that the protagonist be somewhat less than perfect:

> There remains, then, the intermediate kind of personage, a man not preeminently virtuous and just, whose misfortune, however, is brought upon him not by vice and depravity but by some error of judgment. . . .

Aristotle's word for this error is **hamartia,** which is commonly translated as "tragic flaw" but might more properly be termed a "great error." Whether he means some innate flaw, like a psychological defect, or simply a great mistake is open to question, but writers of tragedies have traditionally created deeply flawed protagonists. In ordinary circumstances, the protagonist's strength of character may allow him to prosper, but under the pressure of events he may crack when one small chink in his armor widens and leaves him vulnerable. A typical flaw in tragedies is **hubris,** arrogance or excessive pride, which leads the protagonist into errors that might have been avoided if he or she had listened to the advice of others. Although he does not use the term himself, Aristotle touches on the concept of **poetic justice,** the audience's sense that virtue and vice have been fairly dealt with in the play and that the protagonist's punishment is to some degree deserved.

We should bear in mind that the greatest burden of characterization in drama falls on the actor or actress who undertakes a role. No matter how well written a part is, in the hands of an incompetent or inappropriate performer the character will not be credible. Vocal inflection, gesture, and even the strategic use of silence are the stock in trade of actors, for it is up to them to convince us that we are involved in the sufferings and joys of real human beings. No two actors will play the same part in the same manner. We are lucky to have two excellent film versions of Shakespeare's *Henry the Fifth* available. Comparing the cool elegance of Laurence Olivier with the rough and ready exuberance of Kenneth Branagh is a wonderful short course in the equal validity of two radically different approaches to the same role.

In reading, there are several points to keep in mind about main characters. Physical description, while it may be minimal at best, is worth paying close attention to. Sometimes an author will give a character a name that is an indicator of his or her personality and appearance a device called a **characternym.** "Malvolio," for example, means "ill will" in Italian.

Character motivation is another point of characterization to ponder. Why do characters act in a certain manner? What do they hope to gain from their actions? In some cases these motives are clear enough and may be discussed openly by the characters. In other plays, motivation is more elusive, as the playwright deliberately mystifies the audience by presenting characters who perhaps are not fully aware of the reasons for their compulsions. Modern dramatists, influenced by advances in psychology, have often refused to reduce characters' actions to simple equations of cause and effect.

Two conventions that the playwright may employ in revealing motivation are **soliloquy** and **aside.** A soliloquy is a speech made by a single character on stage alone. Hamlet's soliloquies, among them some of the most famous passages in all drama, show us the process of his mind as he toys with various plans of revenge but delays putting them into action. The aside is a brief remark (traditionally delivered to the side of a raised hand) that an actor makes directly to the audience and that the other characters on stage cannot hear. Occasionally, an aside reveals a reason for a character's behavior in a scene. Neither of these devices is as widely used in today's theater as in earlier periods, but they remain part of the dramatist's collection of techniques.

Minor characters are also of great importance in a successful play, and there are several different traditional types. A **foil,** a minor character (often a comic one) with whom a major character sharply contrasts, is used primarily as a sounding board for ideas. A **confidant** is a trusted friend or servant to whom a major character speaks frankly and openly; confidants fulfill in some respects one role that the chorus plays in Greek tragedy. **Stock characters** are stereotypes that are useful for advancing the plot and fleshing out the scenes, particularly in comedies. Hundreds of plays have employed pairs of innocent young lovers, sharp-tongued servants, and meddling mothers-in-law as part of their casts. **Allegorical characters** in morality plays like *Everyman* are clearly labeled by their names and, for the most part, are personifications of human attributes (Beauty, Good Deeds) or of theological concepts (Confession). **Comic relief** in a tragedy may be provided by minor characters like Shakespeare's fools or clowns.

Theme

Aristotle has relatively little to say about the theme of a play, simply noting, "Thought of the personages is shown in everything to be effected by their language." Because he focuses to such a large degree on the emotional side of tragedy—its stimulation of pity and fear—he seems to give less importance to the role of drama as a serious forum for the discussion of ideas, referring his readers to another of his works, *The Art of Rhetoric,* where these matters have greater prominence. Nevertheless, **theme,** the central idea or ideas that a play discusses, is important in Greek tragedy and in the subsequent history of the theater. The trilogies of early playwrights were thematically unified around an *aition,* a Greek word for the origin of a custom, just as a typical elementary school Thanksgiving pageant portrays how the holiday traditions were first established in the Plymouth Colony.

Some dramas are explicitly **didactic** in their intent, existing with the specific aim of instructing the audience in ethical, religious, or political areas. A **morality play,** a popular type of drama in the late Middle Ages, is essentially a sermon on sin and redemption rendered in dramatic terms. More subtle in its didacticism is the **problem play** of the late nineteenth century, popularized by Ibsen, which uses the theater as a forum for the serious debate of social issues like industrial pollution or women's rights. The **drama of ideas** of playwrights like George Bernard Shaw does not merely present social problems; it goes further, actually advancing programs of reform. In the United States during the Great Depression of the 1930s, Broadway theaters featured a great deal of **social drama,** in which radical social and political programs were openly propagandized. In the ensuing decades, the theater has remained a popular site for examining issues of race, class, sexual orientation, and gender.

Keep in mind, however, that plays are not primarily religious or political forums. If we are not entertained and moved by a play's language, action, and plot, then it is unlikely that we will respond to its message. The author who has to resort to long sermons from a *raisonneur,* the French word for a character who serves primarily as the voice of reason (i.e., the mouthpiece for the playwright's opinions), is not likely to hold the audience's sympathy or attention for long. The best plays are complex enough that they cannot be reduced to simple "thesis statements" that sum up their meaning in a few words.

Diction

Aristotle was also the author of the first important manual of public speaking, *The Art of Rhetoric,* so it should come as no surprise that he devotes considerable attention in the *Poetics* to the precise words, either alone or in combinations, that playwrights use. Instead of "diction," we would probably speak today of a playwright's "style," or discuss his or her handling of various levels of idiom in the dialogue. Much of what Aristotle has to say about parts of speech and the sounds of words in Greek is of little interest to us; of chief importance is his emphasis on clarity and originality in the choice of words. For Aristotle, the language of tragedy should be "poetic" in the best sense, somehow elevated above the level of ordinary speech but not so ornate that it loses the power to communicate feelings and ideas to an audience. Realism in speech is largely a matter of illusion, and close inspection of the actual lines of modern dramatists like Miller and Williams reveals a discrepancy between the carefully chosen words that characters speak in plays, often making up lengthy **monologues,** and the halting, often inarticulate ("Ya know what I mean?") manner in which we express ourselves in everyday life. The language of the theater has always been an artificial one. The idiom of plays, whether by Shakespeare or by August Wilson, *imitates* the language of life; it does not duplicate it.

Ancient Greek is a language with a relatively small vocabulary and, even in translation, we encounter a great deal of repetition of key words. *Polis,* the Greek word for city, appears many times in Sophocles' *Antigone,* stressing the communal fate that the protagonist and the chorus, representing the citizens, share. The repetition of key words or phrases represents the use of a **motif** in a play; motifs often have a symbolic presence in the work. Shakespeare's use of the full resources of the English language has been the standard against which all subsequent writers in the language can measure themselves. Shakespeare's language presents some special difficulties to the modern reader. His vocabulary is essentially the same as ours, but many words have changed in meaning or become obsolete over the last four hundred years. Shakespeare is also a master of different **levels of diction.** In the space of a few lines he can range from self-consciously flowery heights ("If after every tempest come such calms, / May the winds blow till they have waken'd death! / And let the labouring bark climb hills of seas / Olympus-high and duck again as low / As hell's to heaven!" exults Othello on being reunited with his bride in Cyprus) to the slangy level of the streets—he is a master of the off-color joke and the sarcastic put-down. We should remember that Shakespeare's poetic drama lavishly uses figurative language; his lines abound with similes, metaphors, personifications, and hyperboles, all characteristic devices of the language of poetry. Shakespeare's theater had little in the way of scenery and no "special effects," so a passage from *Hamlet* like "But, look, the morn, in russet mantle clad / Walks o'er the dew of yon high eastward hill" is not merely pretty or picturesque; it has the dramatic function of helping the audience visualize the welcome end of a long, fearful night.

It is true that playwrights since the middle of the nineteenth century have striven for more fidelity to reality, more verisimilitude, in the language their characters use, but even realistic dramatists often rise to rhetorical peaks that have little relationship to the way people actually speak.

Melody

Greek tragedy was accompanied by music. None of this music survives, and we cannot be certain how it was integrated into the drama. Certainly the choral parts of the play were sung and danced, and it is likely that even the dialogue involved highly rhythmical chanting, especially in passages employing **stichomythia,** rapid alternation of single lines between two actors, a device often encountered during moments of high dramatic tension. In the original language, the different poetic rhythms used in Greek tragedy are still evident, although these are for the most part lost in English translation. At any rate it is apparent that the skillful manipulation of a variety of **poetic meters,** combinations of line lengths and rhythms, for different types of scenes was an important part of the tragic poet's repertoire.

Both tragedies and comedies have been written in verse throughout the ages, often employing rhyme as well as rhythm. *Antigone* is written in a variety of poetic meters, some of which are appropriate for dialogue between actors and others for the choral odes. Shakespeare's *Othello* is composed, like all of his plays, largely in **blank verse,** that is, unrhymed lines of iambic pentameter (lines of ten syllables, alternating unstressed and stressed syllables). He also uses rhymed couplets, particularly for emphasis at the close of scenes; songs; and even prose passages, especially when dealing with comic or "low" characters. A study of Shakespeare's versification is beyond the scope of this discussion, but suffice it to say that a trained actor must be aware of the rhythmical patterns that Shakespeare utilized if she or he is to deliver the lines with anything approaching accuracy.

Of course, not only verse drama has rhythm. The last sentences of Tennessee Williams's prose drama *The Glass Menagerie* can be easily re-cast as blank verse that would not have embarrassed Shakespeare himself:

> Then all at once my sister touches my shoulder.
> I turn around and look into her eyes . . .
> Oh, Laura, Laura, I tried to leave you behind me,
> but I am more faithful than I intended to be!
> I reach for a cigarette, I cross the street,
> I run into the movies or a bar,
> I buy a drink, I speak to the nearest stranger—
> anything that can blow your candles out!
> —for nowadays the world is lit by lightning!
> Blow your candles out, Laura—and so good-bye . . .

The ancient verse heritage of tragedy lingers on in the modern theater and has proved resistant to even the prosaic rhythms of what Williams calls a "world lit by lightning."

Spectacle

Spectacle (sometimes called *mise en scène,* French for "putting on stage") is the last of Aristotle's elements of tragedy and, in his view, the least important. By spectacle we mean the purely visual dimension of a play; in ancient Greece, this meant costumes, a few props, and effects carried out by the use of the *mechane*. Costumes in Greek tragedy were simple but impressive. The tragic mask, or **persona,** and a high-heeled boot (**cothurnus**) were apparently designed to give characters a larger-than-life appearance. Historians also speculate that the mask might have additionally served as a crude megaphone to amplify the actors' voices, a necessary feature when we consider that the open-air theater in Athens could seat over 10,000 spectators.

Other elements of set decoration were kept to a minimum, although playwrights occasionally employed a few well-chosen spectacular effects like the triumphant entrance of the victorious king in Aeschylus's *Agamemnon*. Elizabethan drama likewise relied little on spectacular stage effects. Shakespeare's plays call for few props, and little attempt was made at historical accuracy in costumes, with a noble patron's cast-off clothing dressing Caesar one week, Othello the next.

Advances in technology since Shakespeare's day have obviously facilitated more elaborate effects in what we now call **staging** than patrons of earlier centuries could have envisioned. In the nineteenth century, first gas and then electric lighting not only made effects like sunrises possible but also, through the use of different combinations of color, added atmosphere to certain scenes. By Ibsen's day, realistic **box sets** were designed to resemble, in the smallest details, interiors of houses and apartments with an invisible "fourth wall" nearest the audience. Modern theater has experimented in all directions with set design, from the bare stage to barely suggested walls and furnishings, from revolving stages to scenes that "break the plane" by involving the audience in the drama. Tennessee Williams's *The Glass Menagerie* employs music, complicated lighting and sound effects, and semitransparent **scrims** onto which images are projected, all to enhance the play's dream-like atmosphere. The most impressive uses of spectacle in today's Broadway productions may represent anything from a huge falling chandelier (*Phantom of the Opera*) to giant puppets (*The Lion King*) to flying ballet dancers (*Billy Elliott*). Modern technology can create virtually any sort of stage illusion; the only limitations in today's professional theater are imagination and budget.

Before we leave our preliminary discussion, one further element should be mentioned—**setting.** Particular locales—Thebes, Corinth, and Mycenæ—are the sites of different tragedies, and each city has its own history; in the case of Thebes, this history involves a family curse that touches the members of three generations. But for the most part, specific locales in the greatest plays are less important than the universal currents that are touched. If we are interested in the particular features of Norwegian civic government in the late nineteenth century, we would perhaps do better going to history texts than to Ibsen's *An Enemy of the People.*

Still, every play implies a larger sense of setting, a sense of history that is called the **enveloping action.** The "southern belle" youth of Amanda Wingfield, in Williams's *The Glass Menagerie*, is a fading dream as anachronistic as the "gentlemen callers" she still envisions knocking on her daughter's door. Even though a play from the past may still speak eloquently today, it also provides a "time capsule" whose contents tell us how people lived and what they most valued during the period when the play was written and first performed.

Brief History and Description of Dramatic Conventions

Greek Tragedy

By the time of Sophocles, tragedy had evolved into an art form with a complex set of conventions. Each playwright would submit a **tetralogy,** or set of four plays, to the yearly competition. The first three plays, or **trilogy,** would be tragedies, perhaps unified like those of Aeschylus's *Oresteia,* which deals with Agamemnon's tragic homecoming from the Trojan War. The fourth, called a **satyr-play,** was comic, with a chorus of goatmen engaging in bawdy revels that, oddly, mocked the serious content of the preceding tragedies. Only one complete trilogy, the *Oresteia* by Aeschylus, and one satyr-play, *The Cyclops* by Euripides, have survived. Three plays by Sophocles derived from the myths surrounding Oedipus and his family—*Oedipus the King, Oedipus at Colonus,* and *Antigone*—are still performed and read, but they were written at separate times and accompanied by other tragedies that are now lost. As tragedy developed during this period, it seems clear that playwrights thought increasingly of individual plays as complete in themselves; *Antigone* does not leave the audience with the feeling that there is more to be told, even though Creon is still alive at the end of the play.

Each tragedy was composed according to a prescribed formula, as ritualized as the order of worship in a contemporary church service. The tragedy begins with a **prologue** *(prologos),* "that which is said first." The prologue is an introductory scene that tells the audience important information about the play's setting, characters, and events immediately preceding the opening of the drama. The second part of the tragedy is called the *parodos,* the first appearance of the chorus in the play. As the members of the chorus enter the orchestra, they dance and sing more generally of the situation in which the city finds itself. Choral parts in some translations are divided into sections called **strophes** and **antistrophes,** indicating choral movements to left and right, respectively. The body of the play is made up of two types of alternating scenes. The first, an **episode** *(episodos)* is a passage of dialogue between two or more actors or between the actors and the chorus. Each of these "acts" of the tragedy is separated from the rest by a choral **ode** *(stasimon;* pl. *stasima)* during which the chorus is alone on the orchestra, commenting, as the voice of public opinion, about the course of action being taken by the main characters. Typically there are four pairs of episodes and odes in the play. The final scene of the play is called the *exodos*. During this part the climax occurs out of sight of the audience and a vivid description of this usually violent scene is sometimes delivered by a messenger or other witness. After the messenger's speech, the main character reappears and the resolution of his fate is determined. In some plays a wheeled platform called an *eccyclema* was used to move this fatal tableau into view of the spectators. A tragedy concludes with the exit of the main characters, sometimes leaving the chorus to deliver a brief speech or **epilogue,** a final summing up of the play's meaning.

While we may at first find such complicated rituals bizarre, we should keep in mind that dramatic conventions are primarily customary and artificial and have little to do with "reality" as we usually experience it. The role of the chorus (set by the time of Sophocles at fifteen members) may seem puzzling to modern readers, but in many ways, the conventions of Greek tragedy are no stranger than those of contemporary musical comedy, in which a pair of lovers burst into a duet and dance in the middle of a stroll in the park, soon to be joined by a host of other cast members. What is most remarkable about the history of drama is not how much these conventions have changed but how remarkably similar they have remained for over twenty-five centuries.

Medieval Drama

Drama flourished during Greek and Roman times, but after the fall of the Roman Empire (A.D. 476) it declined during four centuries of eclipse, and was kept alive throughout Europe only by wandering troupes of actors performing various types of **folk drama.** The "Punch and Judy" puppet show, still popular in parts of Europe, is a late survivor of this tradition, as are the ancient slapstick routines of circus clowns. Even though drama was officially discouraged by the Church for a long period, when it did reemerge it was as an outgrowth of the Roman Catholic mass, in the form of **liturgical drama.** Around the ninth century, short passages of sung dialogue between the priest and choir, called **tropes,** were added on special holidays to commemorate the event. These tropes grew more elaborate over the years until full-fledged religious pageants were being performed in front of the altar. In 1210, Pope Innocent III, wishing to restore the dignity of the services, banned such performances from the interior of the church. Moving them outside, first to the church porch and later entirely off church property, provided greater opportunity for inventiveness in action and staging.

In the fourteenth and fifteenth centuries, much of the work of putting on plays passed to the guilds, organizations of skilled craftsmen, and their productions became part of city-wide festivals in many continental and British cities. Several types of plays evolved. **Mystery plays** were derived from holy scripture. **Passion plays** (some of which survive unchanged today) focused on the crucifixion of Christ. **Miracle plays** dramatized the lives of the saints. The last and most complex, **morality plays,** were dramatized sermons with allegorical characters (e.g., Everyman, Death, Good Deeds) representing various generalized aspects of human life.

Elizabethan Drama

While the older morality plays were still performed throughout the sixteenth century, during the time of Queen Elizabeth I (b. 1533, reigned 1558–1603) a new type of drama, typical in many ways of other innovative types of literature developed during the Renaissance, began to be produced professionally by companies of actors not affiliated with any religious institutions. This **secular drama,** beginning in short pieces called **interludes** that may have been designed for entertainment during banquets or other public celebrations, eventually evolved into full-length tragedies and comedies designed for performance in large outdoor theaters like Shakespeare's famous Globe.

A full history of this fertile period would take many pages, but a few of its dramatic conventions are worth noting. We have already mentioned blank verse, the poetic line perfected by Shakespeare's contemporary Christopher Marlowe (1564–1593). Shakespeare wrote tragedies, comedies, and historical dramas with equal success, all characterized by passages that remain the greatest examples of poetic expression in English.

The raised platform stage in an Elizabethan theater used little or no scenery, with the author's descriptive talents setting the scene and indicating lighting and weather. The stage itself had two supporting columns, which might be used to represent trees or hiding places; a raised area at the rear, which could represent a balcony or upper story of a house; a small curtained alcove at its base; and a trap door, which could serve as a grave or hiding place. In contrast to the relatively bare stage, costumes were elaborate and acting was highly stylized. Female roles were played by young boys, and the same actor might play several different minor roles in the same play. The Oscar-winning film *Shakespeare in Love* reveals a great amount of information about Elizabethan staging.

A few more brief words about Shakespeare's plays are in order. First, drama in Shakespeare's time was intended for performance, with publication being of only secondary importance. The text of many of Shakespeare's plays were published in cheap editions called **quartos** which were full of misprints and often contained different versions of the same play. Any play by Shakespeare contains words and passages that different editors have trouble agreeing on. Second, originality, in the sense that we value it, meant little to a playwright in a time before copyright laws; virtually every one of Shakespeare's plays is derived from an earlier source—Greek myth, history, another play or, in the case of *Twelfth Night*, a contemporary prose tale of questionable literary merit. The true test of Shakespeare's genius rests in his ability to transform these raw materials into art. Finally, we should keep in mind that Shakespeare's plays were designed to appeal to a wide audience—educated aristocrats and illiterate "groundlings" filled the theater—and this fact may account for the great diversity of tones and levels of language in the plays. Purists of later eras may have been dismayed by some of Shakespeare's wheezy clowns and bad puns, but for us the mixture of "high" and "low" elements gives his plays their remarkable texture.

The Comic Genres

Shakespeare's ability to move easily between "high" and "low," between tragic and comic, should be a reminder that comedy has developed along lines parallel to tragedy and has never been wholly separate from it. Most of Aristotle's remarks on comedy are lost, but he does make the observation that comedy differs from tragedy in that comedy depicts men and women as worse than they are, whereas tragedy generally stresses their best qualities. During the great age of Greek tragedy, comedies were regularly performed at Athenian festivals. The greatest of the early comic playwrights was Aristophanes (450?–385? B.C.). The plays of Aristophanes are classified as **Old Comedy** and share many of the same structural elements as tragedy. Old Comedy was always satirical and usually obscene; in *Lysistrata*, written during the devastating Athenian wars with Sparta, the men of both sides are brought to their knees by the women of the two cities, who engage in a sex strike until the men relent. Features of Old Comedy included the use of two semi-choruses (in *Lysistrata*, old men and old women); an *agon*, an extended debate between the protagonist and an authority figure; and a *parabasis*, an ode sung by the chorus at an intermission in the action which reveals the author's own views on the play's subject. **New Comedy,** which evolved in the century after Aristophanes, tended to observe more traditional moral values and stressed romance. The New Comedy of Greece greatly influenced the writings of Roman playwrights like Plautus (254–184 B.C.) and Terence (190–159 B.C.). Plautus's *Pseudolus* (combined with elements from two of his other comedies) still finds favor in its modern musical adaptation *A Funny Thing Happened on the Way to the Forum.*

Like other forms of drama, comedy virtually vanished during the early Middle Ages. Its spirit was kept alive primarily by roving companies of actors who staged improvisational dramas in the squares of towns throughout Europe. The popularity of these plays is evidenced by certain elements in the religious dramas of the same period; the *Second Shepherd's Play* (c. 1450) involves a sheep-rustler with three shepherds in an uproarious parody of the Nativity that still evokes laughter today. Even a serious play such as *Everyman* contains satirical elements in the involved excuses that gods and other characters contrive for not accompanying the protagonist on his journey with Death.

On the continent, a highly stylized form of improvisational drama appeared in sixteenth-century Italy, apparently an evolution from earlier types of folk drama. **Commedia dell'arte** involved a cast of masked stock characters (the miserly old man, the young wife, the ardent seducer) in situations involving mistaken identity and cuckoldry. *Commedia dell'arte*, because it is an improvisational form, does not survive, but its popularity influenced the direction that comedy would take in the following century. The great French comic playwright Molière (1622–1673) incorporated many of its elements into his own plays, which combine elements of **farce,** a type of comedy which hinges on broadly drawn characters and embarrassing situations usually involving sexual misconduct, with serious social satire. Comedy such as Molière's, which exposes the hypocrisy and pretensions of people in social situations, is called **comedy of manners;** as Molière put it, the main purpose of his plays was "the correction of mankind's vices," words with which Yasmin Raza would doubtless agree.

Other types of comedy have also been popular in different eras. Shakespeare's comedies begin with the farcical complications of *The Comedy of Errors*, progress through romantic **pastoral** comedies such as *As You Like It*, which present an idealized view of rural life, and end with the philosophical comedies of his final period, of which *The Tempest* is the greatest example. His contemporary Ben Jonson (1572–1637) favored a type known as **comedy of humours,** a type of comedy of manners in which the conduct of the characters is determined by their underlying dominant trait (the four humours were thought to be bodily fluids whose proportions determined personality). English plays of the late seventeenth and early eighteenth centuries tended to combine the hard-edged satire of comedy of manners with varying amounts of sentimental romance. A play of this type, usually hinging on matters of inheritance and marriage, is known as a **drawing-room comedy,** and its popularity, while peaking in the mid-nineteenth century, endures today.

Modern comedy in English can be said to begin with Oscar Wilde (1854–1900) and George Bernard Shaw (1856–1950). Wilde's brilliant wit and skillful incorporation of paradoxical **epigrams,** witty sayings that have made him one of the most quoted authors of the nineteenth century, have rarely been equaled. Shaw, who began his career as a drama critic, admired both Wilde and Ibsen, and succeeded in combining the best elements of the comedy of manners and the problem play in his works. *Major Barbara* (1905), a typical **comedy of ideas,** frames serious discussion of war, religion, and poverty with a search for an heir to a millionaire's fortune and a suitable husband for one of his daughters. Most subsequent writers of comedy, from Neil Simon to Wendy Wasserstein, reveal their indebtedness to Wilde and Shaw.

One striking development of comedy in recent times lies in its deliberate harshness. So-called **black humor,** an extreme type of satire in which barriers of taste are assaulted and pain seems the constant companion of laughter, has characterized much of the work of playwrights like Samuel Beckett (1906–1989), Eugene Ionesco (1912–1994), and Edward Albee (b. 1928).

Realistic Drama, the Modern Stage, and Beyond

Realism is a term that is loosely employed as a synonym for "true to life," but in literary history it denotes a style of writing that developed in the mid-nineteenth century, first in the novels of such masters as

Charles Dickens, Gustave Flaubert, and Leo Tolstoy, and later in the dramas of Ibsen and Anton Chekhov. Many of the aspects of dramatic realism have to do with staging and acting. The box set, with its invisible "fourth wall" facing the audience, could, with the added subtleties of artificial lighting, successfully mimic the interior of a typical middle-class home. Realistic prose drama dropped devices like the soliloquy in favor of more natural methods of acting such as that championed by Konstantin Stanislavsky (1863–1938), the Russian director who worked closely with Chekhov (1860–1904) to perfect a process whereby actors learned to identify with their characters' psychological problems from "inside out." This "method" acting often tries, as is the case in Chekhov's plays and, later, in those of Williams and Miller, to develop a play's **subtext,** the crucial issue in the play that no one can bear to address directly. Stanislavsky's theories have influenced several generations of actors and have become standard throughout the world of the theater. Ibsen's plays, which in fact ushered in the modern era of the theater, are often called **problem plays** because they deal with serious, even controversial or taboo, issues in society. Shaw said that Ibsen's great originality as a playwright lay in his ability to shock the members of the audience into thinking about their own lives. As the barriers of censorship have fallen over the years, the capacity of the theater to shock has perhaps been diminished, but writers still find it a forum admirably suited for debating the controversial issues which divide society.

American and world Drama in the twentieth and the present centuries has gone far beyond realism to experiment with the dream-like atmosphere of **expressionism** (which may employ distorted sets to mirror the troubled, perhaps even unbalanced, psyches of the play's characters) or **theater of the absurd,** which depicts a world, like that of Samuel Beckett's *Waiting for Godot* or the early plays of Edward Albee, without meaning in which everything seems ridiculous. Nevertheless, realism is still the dominant style of today's theater, even if our definition of it has to be modified to take into account plays as diverse as *The Glass Menagerie*, *The Piano Lesson* and *God of Carnage*.

Writing About Drama

WRITING ASSIGNMENTS VARY WIDELY AND YOUR TEACHER'S instructions may range from general ("Discuss any two scenes in the plays we have read") to very specific ("Write an explication, in not less than 1,000 words, of Shakespeare's use of imagery and figurative language in the exchange between Orsino and Viola at the end of 2:4."). Such processes as choosing, limiting, and developing a topic; "brainstorming" by taking notes on random ideas and refining those ideas further through group discussion or conferences with your instructor; using the library and the Internet to locate supporting secondary sources; and revising a first draft in light of critical remarks are undoubtedly techniques you have practiced in other composition classes. Basic types of organizational schemes learned in expository or argumentative writing courses can also be applied to writing about drama. Formal assignments of these types should avoid contractions and jargon, and should be written in a clear, straightforward style. Most literary essays are not of the personal experience type, and you should follow common sense in avoiding the first person and slang. It goes without saying that you should carefully proofread your rough and final drafts to eliminate errors in spelling, punctuation, usage, and grammar.

Typical writing assignments on plays may fall into four main categories: reviews, explication or close reading, analysis, and comparison-contrast. A review, an evaluation of an actual performance of a play, will focus less on the play itself, particularly if it is a well-known one, than on the actors' performances, the overall direction of the production, and the elements of staging. Because reviews are primarily news stories, basic information about the time and place of production should be given at the beginning of the review. A short summary of the play's plot may follow, with perhaps some remarks on its stage history, and subsequent paragraphs will evaluate the performers and the production. Remember that a review is both a *report* and a *recommendation*, either positive or negative, to readers. You should strive for accuracy in such matters as spelling the actors' names correctly, and you should also try to be fair in pointing out the strong and weak points of the production. It is essential to support any general statements about the play's successes or shortcomings with specific references to the production, so it is a good idea to take notes during the performance. Because film versions of most of the plays in this book, sometimes in several different versions, are available on video, you might also be asked to review one of these films, paying attention perhaps to the innovative ways in which directors like Orson Welles or Volker Schlöndorff have "opened up" the action of the plays by utilizing the more complex technical resources of motion pictures. Two good reference sources providing examples of professional drama and film reviews, respectively, are the *New York Times Theater Reviews* (available in several volumes) and the *New York Times Film Reviews;* of course, the *New York Times* and other big-city newspapers may be searched online for reviews of recent productions or archival material. Popular magazines containing drama reviews include *Time, Newsweek, The New Yorker,* and others, and these reviews are indexed in the venerable *Readers' Guide to Periodical Literature* (now available online, along with contemporary electronic databases like Ebscohost). Also, yearbooks like *Theatre World* provide useful information about New York productions of plays, and official websites of recent productions can be found on the Internet.

An explication assignment, on the other hand, requires that you pay close attention to selected passages, giving a detailed account of all the nuances of a speech from a play you have read. Because Shakespeare's poetry is often full of figurative language that may not be fully understood until it has been subjected to an "unfolding" (the literal meaning of explication), individual sections of *Twelfth Night*—speeches, scenes, soliloquies—would be likely choices for writing assignments.

Analysis assignments typically turn on definition and illustration, focusing on only one of the main elements of the play such as plot or characterization. You might be required to explain Aristotle's statements about peripety and then apply his terminology to a contemporary play. Here you would attempt to locate relevant passages from the play to support Aristotle's contentions about the importance of these reversals in the best plots. Or you might be asked to provide a summary of his comments about the tragic hero and then apply this definition to a character. In doing so, you might use other supporting materials such as critical essays from scholarly journals.

Comparison and contrast assignments are also popular. You might be assigned to compare two or more characters in a single play (the two husbands in *The God of Carnage*, for example, or male and female attitudes expressed by the two characters in David Ives's *Sure Thing*), or to contrast characters in two different plays (Antigone and Thomas Stockmann as idealists who sacrifice their personal happiness because of their beliefs). Comparison and contrast assignments require careful planning, and it is essential to find both significant similarities and differences to support your thesis. Obviously, a proposed topic about two characters who have almost nothing in common.

Supporting your statements about a play is necessary, either by quoting directly from the play or, if you are required, to use outside sources for additional critical opinion. You may be required to use secondary sources from the library or Internet in writing your paper. A subject search through your library's books is a good starting place, especially for older playwrights who have attracted extensive critical attention. Reference books and online reference sources like *Twentieth Century Authors*, *Contemporary Authors*, and the *Dictionary of Literary Biography* provide compact overviews of playwrights' careers. *Contemporary Literary Criticism*, *Critical Survey of Drama*, and *Drama Criticism* contain both original evaluations and excerpts from critical pieces on published works, and the *MLA Index* will direct you to articles on drama in scholarly journals. We have already mentioned the reference books from the *New York Times* as an excellent source of drama reviews. One scholarly journal that focuses on individual passages from literary works, the *Explicator*, is also worth inspecting. In recent years, the Internet has facilitated the chores of research, and many online databases, reference works, and periodicals may be quickly located using search engines like Yahoo! (www.yahoo.com) and Google (www.google.com) or online databases such as JSTOR or EbscoHost. The Internet also holds a wealth of information, ranging from corporate websites promoting play productions to sites on individual authors, many of which are run by universities or organizations.

Students should be aware, however, that websites vary widely in quality. Some are legitimate academic sources displaying sound scholarship; others are little more that "fan pages" that may contain erroneous or misleading information or "free paper" sites where the quality matches the price.

Careful documentation of your sources is essential; if you use any material other than what is termed "common knowledge," you must cite it in your paper. Common knowledge includes biographical information, an author's publications, prizes and awards received, and other information that can be found in more than one reference book. Anything else—direct quotes or material you have put in your own words by paraphrasing—requires both a parenthetical citation in the body of your paper and an entry on your works cited pages. Doing less than this is to commit an act of plagiarism, for which the penalties are usually severe. Internet materials, which are so easily cut and pasted into a manuscript, provide an easy temptation but are immediately noticeable. Nothing is easier to spot in a paper than an uncited "lift" from a source; in most cases the vocabulary and sentence structure will be radically different from the rest of the paper.

The 7th edition of the *MLA Handbook for Writers of Research Papers*, which is available in the reference section of almost any library and online at www.mla.org and which, if you plan to write papers for other English or drama courses, is a good addition to your personal library, contains formats for bibliographies and manuscript form that most instructors consider standard; indeed, most of the handbooks of grammar and usage commonly used in college courses follow MLA style and may be sufficient for your needs. If you have doubts, ask your instructor about what format is preferred. The type of parenthetical citation used today is simple to learn and dispenses with such time-consuming and repetitive chores as footnotes and endnotes. In using parenthetical citations remember that your goal is to direct your reader from the quoted passage in the paper to its source in your bibliography and from there, if necessary, to the book or periodical from which the quote is taken. A good parenthetical citation gives only the *minimal* information needed to accomplish this. Here are a few examples from student papers on Shakespeare's *Othello*:

> In a disarming display of modesty before the Venetian senators,
> Othello readily admits that his military background has not prepared him to

act as an eloquent spokesman in his own defense: "[...] little of this great world can I speak / More than pertains to feats of broils and battle; / And therefore little shall I grace my cause / In speaking for myself" (1.3.86-89).

Quotations from Shakespeare's plays are cited by act, scene, and line numbers instead of by page numbers. Note that short quotes from poetic dramas require that line breaks be indicated by the virgule (/) or slash; quotes longer than five lines should be indented ten spaces and formatted to duplicate the line breaks of the original. Here, the reader knows that Shakespeare is the author, so the citation here will simply direct him or her to the anthology or the collected or single edition of Shakespeare listed in the works cited section at the end of the paper:

Shakespeare, William. *The Complete Works of Shakespeare*. Ed. Hardin Craig. New York: Scott, 1961. Print.
Shakespeare, William. *Othello*. Ed. David Bevington. New York: Bantam, 1988.
Shakespeare, William. *The Tragedy of Othello. the Moor of Venice*. *Literature: An Introduction to Fiction. Poetry. and Drama*. 11th ed. Ed. X. J. Kennedy and Dana Gioia. New York: Longman, 2010. 1248–348. Print.

If, on the other hand, you are quoting from a prose drama, you would probably indicate a page number.

Unlike the mature relationship between Dr. and Mrs. Stockmann in *An Enemy of the People*, in *A Doll's House* Ibsen wants to demonstrate immediately that Nora and Helmer share almost child-like attitudes toward each other. "Is that my little lark twittering out there?" is Helmer's initial line in the play (43).

The citation directs the reader to the works cited entry:

Ibsen, Henrik. *Four Major Plays*. Trans. Rolf Fjelde. New York: Signet, 1965. Print.

Similarly, quotes from secondary critical sources should follow the same rules of common sense.

One critic, providing a classic estimate of Shakespeare's skill in conceiving Othello's antagonist, notes, "Evil has nowhere else been portrayed with such mastery as in the character of Iago" (Bradley 173).

In this case, the critic is not named in the paper, so his name must be included in the parenthetical citation. The reader knows where to look in the works cited:

Bradley, A. C. *Shakespearean Tragedy*. New York: Fawcett, 1967. Print.

If the writer provides the critic's name ("A. C. Bradley, providing a classic estimate . . ."), then the parentheses should contain only the page number.

Of course, different types of sources—reference book entries, articles in periodicals, newspaper reviews of plays—require different bibliographical information, so be sure to check the *MLA Handbook* if you have questions. Here are a few more of the most commonly used formats:

An Edited Collection of Essays

Snyder, Susan, ed. *Othello: Critical Essays*. New York: Garland, 1988. Print.

A Casebook

Dean, Leonard Fellows, ed. *A Casebook on Othello*. New York: Crowell, 1961. Print.

Play Reprinted in an Anthology or Textbook

Wilson, August. *Fences*. *Inside Literature*. Ed. R. S. Gwynn and Steven J. Zani. New York: Penguin Academics, 2007. 412–90. Print.

Article in a Reference Book

"Othello." *The Oxford Companion to English Literature*. Ed. Margaret Drabble. 5th ed. New York: Oxford UP, 1985. Print.

Article in a Scholarly Journal

Berry, Edward. "Othello's Alienation." *Studies in English Literature. 1500-1900* 30 (1990) 315–33. Web. 2 Mar. 2011.

Review in a Newspaper

Evans, Everett. "Sturdy Staging of 'Equus' Raises Intriguing Issues." *Houston Chronicle* 19 Jan. 2008: D1+. Print.

Play Production Website

"Sophocles's *Antigone*." 2007. Web. 29 Jan. 2011.

Online Article or Review

Brantley, Ben. "A 'Menagerie' Full of Stars, Silhouettes and Weird Sounds." 23 Mar. 2005. *New York Times*. Web. 12 Feb. 2011.

Online Author Website

"Sophocles." 2008. Literature Online. Web. 8 Mar. 2011.

Online Reference Work

"August Wilson." 2007. *Britannica Online*. Encyclopedia Britannica. Web. 14 Feb. 2011.

DRAMA

Sophocles lived in Athens in the age of Pericles, during the city's greatest period of culture, power, and influence. Sophocles distinguished himself as an athlete, a musician, a military advisor, a politician and, most important, a dramatist. At sixteen, he was chosen to lead a chorus in reciting a poem on the Greek naval victory over the Persians at Salamis, and he won his first prizes as a playwright before he was thirty. Although both Aeschylus, his senior, and Euripides, his younger rival, have their champions, Sophocles, whose career spanned so long a period that he competed against both of them, is generally considered to be the most important Greek writer of tragedies; his thirty victories in the City Dionysia surpass the combined totals of his two great colleagues. Of his 123 plays, only seven survive intact, including three plays relating to Oedipus and his children, Oedipus the King, Antigone, and Oedipus at Colonus, which was produced after Sophocles' death by his grandson. He is generally credited with expanding the technical possibilities of drama by introducing a third actor in certain scenes (Aeschylus used only two) and by both reducing the number of lines given to the chorus and increasing its integration into his plays. Sophocles was intimately involved in both civic and military affairs, twice serving as a chief advisor to Pericles, and his sense of duty to the polis (Greek for "city") is apparent in many of his plays. Sophocles' importance can be judged by the many references that Aristotle makes to his works in his discussion of tragedy in the Poetics.

Antigone

Translated by Robert Fagles

Characters

Antigone, *daughter of Oedipus and Jocasta*
Ismene, *sister of Antigone*
A chorus, *of old Theban citizens and their leader*
Creon, *king of Thebes, uncle of Antigone and Ismene*
A sentry
Haemon, *son of Creon and Eurydice*
Tiresias, *a blind prophet*
A messenger

Eurydice, *wife of Creon*
Guards, attendants, and a boy

> **Time and Scene:** *The royal house of Thebes. It is still night, and the invading armies of Argos have just been driven from the city. Fighting on opposite sides, the sons of Oedipus, Eteocles and Polynices, have killed each other in combat. Their uncle, Creon, is now king of Thebes.*
>
> *Enter Antigone, slipping through the central doors of the palace. She motions to her sister, Ismene, who follows her cautiously toward an altar at the center of the stage.[1]*

ANTIGONE: My own flesh and blood—dear sister, dear Ismene,
    how many griefs our father Oedipus handed down!
    Do you know one, I ask you, one grief
    that Zeus will not perfect for the two of us
    while we still live and breathe! There's nothing,   5
    no pain—our lives are pain—no private shame,
    no public disgrace, nothing I haven't seen
    in your griefs and mine. And now this:
    an emergency decree, they say, the Commander[1]
    has just declared for all of Thebes.   10
    What, haven't you heard? Don't you see?
    The doom reserved for enemies
    marches on the ones we love the most.
ISMENE: Not I, I haven't heard a word, Antigone.
    Nothing of loved ones,   15
    no joy or pain has come my way, not since
    the two of us were robbed of our two brothers,
    both gone in a day, a double blow—
    not since the armies of Argos vanished,
    just this very night. I know nothing more,   20
    whether our luck's improved or ruin's still to come.
ANTIGONE: I thought so. That's why I brought you out here,
    past the gates, so you could hear in private.
ISMENE: What's the matter? Trouble, clearly . . .
    you sound so dark, so grim.   25
ANTIGONE: Why not? Our own brothers' burial!
    Hasn't Creon graced one with all the rites,

[1]Creon. In the original he is given a military title; Antigone will not defer to him as King.

disgraced the other? Eteocles, they say,
has been given full military honors,
rightly so—Creon has laid him in the earth   30
and he goes with glory down among the dead.
But the body of Polynices, who died miserably—
why, a city-wide proclamation, rumor has it,
forbids anyone to bury him, even mourn him.
He's to be left unwept, unburied, a lovely treasure   35
for birds that scan the field and feast to their heart's content.
Such, I hear, is the martial law our good Creon
lays down for you and me—yes, me, I tell you—
and he's coming here to alert the uninformed
in no uncertain terms,   40
and he won't treat the matter lightly. Whoever
disobeys in the least will die, his doom is sealed:
stoning to death inside the city walls!

There you have it. You'll soon show what you are,
worth your breeding, Ismene, or a coward—   45
for all your royal blood.
ISMENE: My poor sister, if things have come to this,
who am I to make or mend them, tell me,
what good am I to you?
ANTIGONE: Decide.
Will you share the labor, share the work?   50
ISMENE: What work, what's the risk? What do you mean?
ANTIGONE: [*Raising her hands.*]
Will you lift up his body with these bare hands
and lower it with me?
ISMENE: What? You'd bury him—
when a law forbids the city?
ANTIGONE: Yes!
He is my brother and—deny it as you will—   55
your brother too.
No one will ever convict me for a traitor.
ISMENE: So desperate, and Creon has expressly—
ANTIGONE: No,
he has no right to keep me from my own.
ISMENE: Oh my sister, think—   60

think how our own father died, hated,[2]
his reputation in ruins, driven on
by the crimes he brought to light himself
to gouge out his eyes with his own hands—
then mother . . . his mother and wife, both in one,   65
mutilating her life in the twisted noose—
and last, our two brothers dead in a single day,
both shedding their own blood, poor suffering boys,
battling out their common destiny hand-to-hand.
Now look at the two of us, left so alone . . .   70
think what a death we'll die, the worst of all
if we violate the laws and override
the fixed decree of the throne, its power—
we must be sensible. Remember we are women,
we're not born to contend with men. Then too,   75
we're underlings, ruled by much stronger hands,
so we must submit in this, and things still worse.

I, for one, I'll beg the dead to forgive me—
I'm forced, I have no choice—I must obey
the ones who stand in power. Why rush to extremes?   80
It's madness, madness.
ANTIGONE: I won't insist,
no, even if you should have a change of heart,
I'd never welcome you in the labor, not with me.
So, do as you like, whatever suits you best—
I will bury him myself.   85
And even if I die in the act, that death will be a glory.
I will lie with the one I love and loved by him—
an outrage sacred to the gods! I have longer
to please the dead than please the living here:
in the kingdom down below I'll lie forever.   90
Do as you like, dishonor the laws
the gods hold in honor.
ISMENE: I'd do them no dishonor . . .
but defy the city? I have no strength for that.

[2] This play was written before *Oedipus the King* and *Oedipus at Colonnus*; the latter gives us a
different picture of Oedipus's end.

ANTIGONE: You have your excuses. I am on my way,
     I'll raise a mound for him, for my dear brother.   95
ISMENE: Oh Antigone, you're so rash—I'm so afraid for you!
ANTIGONE: Don't fear for me. Set your own life in order.
ISMENE: Then don't, at least, blurt this out to anyone.
     Keep it a secret. I'll join you in that, I promise.
ANTIGONE: Dear god, shout it from the rooftops. I'll hate you   100
     all the more for silence—tell the world!
ISMENE: So fiery—and it ought to chill your heart.
ANTIGONE: I know I please where I must please the most.
ISMENE: Yes, if you can, but you're in love with impossibility.
ANTIGONE: Very well then, once my strength gives out   105
     I will be done at last.
ISMENE: You're wrong from the start,
     you're off on a hopeless quest.
ANTIGONE: If you say so, you will make me hate you,
     and the hatred of the dead, by all rights,
     will haunt you night and day.   110
     But leave me to my own absurdity, leave me
     to suffer this—dreadful thing. I will suffer
     nothing as great as death without glory.

                                              [*Exit to the side.*]

ISMENE: Then go if you must, but rest assured,
     wild, irrational as you are, my sister,   115
     you are truly dear to the ones who love you.

[*Withdrawing to the palace. Enter a chorus*[3], *the old citizens of
Thebes, chanting as the sun begins to rise.*]

CHORUS: Glory!—great beam of sun, brightest of all
     that ever rose on the seven gates of Thebes,
          you burn through night at last!
               Great eye of the golden day,   120
     mounting the Dirce's[4] banks you throw him back—
     the enemy out of Argos, the white shield[5], the man of bronze—

---

[3]The chorus of old men celebrates the victory won over the Argive forces and Polynices.
[4]A river of the Theban plain.
[5]The Argive soldiers' shields were painted white.

he's flying headlong now
    the bridle of fate stampeding him with pain!

      And he had driven against our borders,   125
      launched by the warring claims of Polynices—
      like an eagle screaming, winging havoc
      over the land, wings of armor
      shielded white as snow,
      a huge army massing,   130
      crested helmets bristling for assault.

He hovered above our roofs, his vast maw gaping
closing down around our seven gates,
    his spears thirsting for the kill
      but now he's gone, look,   135
before he could glut his jaws with Theban blood
or the god of fire put our crown of towers to the torch.
He grappled the Dragon[6] none can master—Thebes—
    the clang of our arms like thunder at his back!

      Zeus hates with a vengeance all bravado,   140
      the mighty boasts of men. He watched them
      coming on in a rising flood, the pride
      of their golden armor ringing shrill—
      and brandishing his lightning
      blasted the fighter[7] just at the goal,   145
      rushing to shout his triumph from our walls.

Down from the heights he crashed, pounding down on the earth!
And a moment ago, blazing torch in hand—
    mad for attack, ecstatic
he breathed his rage, the storm   150
    of his fury hurling at our heads!
But now his high hopes have laid him low
and down the enemy ranks the iron god of war

---

[6]According to legend the Thebans sprang from the dragon's teeth sown by Cadmus.
[7]Capaneus, the most violent of the Seven against Thebes. He had almost scaled the wall when the lightning of Zeus threw him down.

deals his rewards, his stunning blows—Ares[8]
rapture of battle, our right arm in the crisis.   155

        Seven captains marshaled at seven gates
        seven against their equals, gave
        their brazen trophies[9] up to Zeus,
        god of the breaking rout of battle,
        all but two: those blood brothers,   160
        one father, one mother—matched in rage,
        spears matched for the twin conquest—
        clashed and won the common prize of death.

But now for Victory! Glorious in the morning,
joy in her eyes to meet our joy   165
        she is winging[10] down to Thebes,
our fleets of chariots wheeling in her wake—
        Now let us win oblivion from the wars,
thronging the temples of the gods
in singing, dancing choirs through the night!   170
        Lord Dionysus,[11] god of the dance
        that shakes the land of Thebes, now lead the way!

[*Enter Creon from the palace, attended by his guard.*]

        But look, the king of the realm is coming
        Creon, the new man for the new day,
        whatever the gods are sending now . . .   175
        what new plan will he launch?
        Why this, this special session?
        Why this sudden call to the old men
        summoned at one command?

CREON: My countrymen,
        the ship of state is safe. The gods who rocked her,   180
        after a long, merciless pounding in the storm,
        have righted her once more.

---

[8]Not only the god of war but also one of the patron deities of Thebes.
[9]The victors in Greek battle set up a trophy consisting of the armor of one of the enemy dead,
fixed to a post and set up at the place where the enemy turned to run away.
[10]Victory is portrayed in Greek painting and sculpture as a winged young woman.
[11]A god of the vine and of revel; his father was Zeus, and his mother, Semele, was a Theban princess.

Out of the whole city
I have called you here alone. Well I know,
first, your undeviating respect
for the throne and royal power of King Laius.   185
Next, while Oedipus steered the land of Thebes,
and even after he died, your loyalty was unshakable,
you still stood by their children. Now then,
since the two sons are dead—two blows of fate
in the same day, cut down by each other's hands,   190
both killers, both brothers stained with blood—
as I am next in kin to the dead,
I now possess the throne and all its powers.

Of course you cannot know a man completely,
his character, his principles, sense of judgment,   195
not till he's shown his colors, ruling the people,
making laws. Experience, there's the test.
As I see it, whoever assumes the task,
the awesome task of setting the city's course,
and refuses to adopt the soundest policies   200
but fearing someone, keeps his lips locked tight,
he's utterly worthless. So I rate him now,
I always have. And whoever places a friend
above the good of his own country, he is nothing:
I have no use for him. Zeus my witness,   205
Zeus who sees all things, always—
I could never stand by silent, watching destruction
march against our city, putting safety to rout,
nor could I ever make that man a friend of mine
who menaces our country. Remember this: 210
our country *is* our safety.
Only while she voyages true on course
can we establish friendships, truer than blood itself.
Such are my standards. They make our city great.

Closely akin to them I have proclaimed,   215
just now, the following decree to our people
concerning the two sons of Oedipus.
Eteocles, who died fighting for Thebes,

excelling all in arms: he shall be buried,
crowned with a hero's honors, the cups we pour[12]   220
to soak the earth and reach the famous dead.

But as for his blood brother, Polynices,
who returned from exile, home to his father-city
and the gods of his race, consumed with one desire—
to burn them roof to roots—who thirsted to drink   225
his kinsmen's blood and sell the rest to slavery:
that man—a proclamation has forbidden the city
to dignify him with burial, mourn him at all.
No, he must be left unburied, his corpse
carrion for the birds and dogs to tear,   230
an obscenity for the citizens to behold!

These are my principles. Never at my hands
will the traitor be honored above the patriot.
But whoever proves his loyalty to the state—
I'll prize that man in death as well as life.   235
LEADER: If this is your pleasure, Creon, treating
our city's enemy and our friend this way . . .
The power is yours, I suppose, to enforce it
with the laws, both for the dead and all of us,
the living.
CREON: Follow my orders closely then,   240
be on your guard.
LEADER: We're too old.
Lay that burden on younger shoulders.
CREON: No, no,
I don't mean the body—I've posted guards already.
LEADER: What commands for us then? What other service?
CREON: See that you never side with those who break my orders.   245
LEADER: Never. Only a fool could be in love with death.
CREON: Death is the price—you're right. But all too often
the mere hope of money has ruined many men.

[*A sentry enters from the side.*]

---

[12]Libations (liquid offerings—wine, honey, etc.) poured on the grave.

SENTRY: My lord,
    I can't say I'm winded from running, or set out
    with any spring in my legs either—no sir,   250
    I was lost in thought, and it made me stop, often,
    dead in my tracks, heeling, turning back,
    and all the time a voice inside me muttering,
    "Idiot, why? You're going straight to your death."
    Then muttering, "Stopped again, poor fool?   255
    If somebody gets the news to Creon first,
    what's to save your neck?"
                    And so,
    mulling it over, on I trudged, dragging my feet,
    you can make a short road take forever . . .
    but at last, look, common sense won out,   260
    I'm here, and I'm all yours,
    and even though I come empty-handed
    I'll tell my story just the same, because
    I've come with a good grip on one hope,
    what will come will come, whatever fate—   265
CREON: Come to the point!
    What's wrong—why so afraid?
SENTRY: First, myself, I've got to tell you,
    I didn't do it, didn't see who did—
    Be fair, don't take it out on me.   270
CREON: You're playing it safe, soldier,
    barricading yourself from any trouble.
    It's obvious, you've something strange to tell.
SENTRY: Dangerous too, and danger makes you delay
    for all you're worth.   275
CREON: Out with it—then dismiss!
SENTRY: All right, here it comes. The body—
    someone's just buried it, then run off . . .
    sprinkled some dry dust on the flesh,[13]
    given it proper rites.
CREON: What?   280
    What man alive would dare—
SENTRY: I've no idea, I swear it.

---

[13]A symbolic burial, all Antigone could do alone, without Ismene's help.

There was no mark of a spade, no pickaxe there,
no earth turned up, the ground packed hard and dry,
unbroken, no tracks, no wheelruts, nothing,
the workman left no trace. Just at sunup   285
the first watch of the day points it out—
it was a wonder! We were stunned . . .
a terrific burden too, for all of us, listen:
you can't see the corpse, not that it's buried,
really, just a light cover of road-dust on it,   290
as if someone meant to lay the dead to rest
and keep from getting cursed.
Not a sign in sight that dogs or wild beasts
had worried the body, even torn the skin.

But what came next! Rough talk flew thick and fast,   295
guard grilling guard—we'd have come to blows
at last, nothing to stop it; each man for himself
and each the culprit, no one caught red-handed,
all of us pleading ignorance, dodging the charges,
ready to take up red-hot iron in our fists,   300
go through fire,[14] swear oaths to the gods—
"I didn't do it, I had no hand in it either,
not in the plotting, not in the work itself!"

Finally, after all this wrangling came to nothing,
one man spoke out and made us stare at the ground,   305
hanging our heads in fear. No way to counter him,
no way to take his advice and come through
safe and sound. Here's what he said:
"Look, we've got to report the facts to Creon,
we can't keep this hidden." Well, that won out,   310
and the lot fell to me, condemned me,
unlucky as ever, I got the prize. So here I am,
against my will and yours too, well I know—
no one wants the man who brings bad news.

[14]Both traditional assertions of truthfulness, derived perhaps from some primitive ritual of ordeal—only the liar would get burned.

LEADER: My king,
    ever since he began I've been debating in my mind,   315
    could this possibly be the work of the gods?
CREON: Stop—
    before you make me choke with anger—the gods!
    You, you're senile, must you be insane?
    You say—why it's intolerable—say the gods
    could have the slightest concern for the corpse?   320
    Tell me, was it for meritorious service
    they proceeded to bury him, prized him so? The hero
    who came to burn their temples ringed with pillars,
    their golden treasures—scorch their hallowed earth
    and fling their laws to the winds.   325
    Exactly when did you last see the gods
    celebrating traitors? Inconceivable!
    No, from the first there were certain citizens
    who could hardly stand the spirit of my regime,
    grumbling against me in the dark, heads together,   330
    tossing wildly, never keeping their necks beneath
    the yoke, loyally submitting to their king.
    These are the instigators, I'm convinced—
    they've perverted my own guard, bribed them
    to do their work.
              Money! Nothing worse   335
    in our lives, so current, rampant, so corrupting.
    Money—you demolish cities, root men from their homes,
    you train and twist good minds and set them on
    to the most atrocious schemes. No limit,
    you make them adept at every kind of outrage,   340
    every godless crime—money!
               Everyone—
    the whole crew bribed to commit this crime,
    they've made one thing sure at least:
    sooner or later they will pay the price.

[*Wheeling on the sentry.*]

               You—
    I swear to Zeus as I still believe in Zeus,   345
    if you don't find the man who buried that corpse,

the very man, and produce him before my eyes,
simple death won't be enough for you,
not till we string you up alive
and wring the immorality out of you.   350
Then you can steal the rest of your days,
better informed about where to make a killing.
You'll have learned, at last, it doesn't pay
to itch for rewards from every hand that beckons.
Filthy profits wreck most men, you'll see—   355
they'll never save your life.

SENTRY: Please,
    may I say a word or two, or just turn and go?
CREON: Can't you tell? Everything you say offends me.
SENTRY: Where does it hurt you, in the ears or in the heart?
CREON: And who are you to pinpoint my displeasure?   360
SENTRY: The culprit grates on your feelings,
    I just annoy your ears.
CREON: Still talking?
    You talk too much! A born nuisance—
SENTRY: Maybe so,
    but I never did this thing, so help me!
CREON: Yes you did—
    what's more, you squandered your life for silver!   365
SENTRY: Oh it's terrible when the one who does the judging
    judges things all wrong.
CREON: Well now,
    you just be clever about your judgments—
    if you fail to produce the criminals for me,
    you'll swear your dirty money brought you pain.   370

[*Turning sharply, reentering the palace.*]

SENTRY: I hope he's found. Best thing by far.
    But caught or not, that's in the lap of fortune:
    I'll never come back, you've seen the last of me.
    I'm saved, even now, and I never thought,
    I never hoped—   375
    dear gods, I owe you all my thanks!

[*Rushing out.*]

CHORUS: Numberless wonders
        terrible wonders walk the world but none the match for man—
        that great wonder crossing the heaving gray sea,
                driven on by the blasts of winter
        on through breakers crashing left and right,   380
                holds his steady course
        and the oldest of the gods he wears away—
        the Earth, the immortal, the inexhaustible—
        as his plows go back and forth, year in, year out
                with the breed of stallions[15] turning up the furrows.   385

        And the blithe, lightheaded race of birds he snares,
        the tribes of savage beasts, the life that swarms the depths—
                with one fling of his nets
        woven and coiled tight, he takes them all,
                man the skilled, the brilliant!   390
        He conquers all, taming with his techniques
        the prey that roams the cliffs and wild lairs,
        training the stallion, clamping the yoke across
                his shaggy neck, and the tireless mountain bull.
        And speech and thought, quick as the wind   395
        and the mood and mind for law that rules the city—
                all these he has taught himself
        and shelter from the arrows of the frost
        when there's rough lodging under the cold clear sky
        and the shafts of lashing rain—   400
                ready, resourceful man!
                Never without resources
        never an impasse as he marches on the future—
        only Death, from Death alone he will find no rescue
        but from desperate plagues he has plotted his escapes.   405

        Man the master, ingenious past all measure
        past all dreams, the skills within his grasp—
                he forges on, now to destruction
        now again to greatness. When he weaves in
        the laws of the land, and the justice of the gods   410

---

[15]Mules—the working animal of a Greek farmer.

that binds his oaths together
    he and his city rise high—
        but the city casts out
that man who weds himself to inhumanity
thanks to reckless daring. Never share my hearth   415
never think my thoughts, whoever does such things.

[*Enter Antigone from the side, accompanied by the sentry.*]

Here is a dark sign from the gods—
what to make of this? I know her,
how can I deny it? That young girl's Antigone!
Wretched, child of a wretched father,   420
Oedipus. Look, is it possible?
They bring you in like a prisoner—
why? did you break the king's laws?
Did they take you in some act of mad defiance?

SENTRY: She's the one, she did it single-handed—   425
we caught her burying the body. Where's Creon?

[*Enter Creon from the palace.*]

LEADER: Back again, just in time when you need him.
CREON: In time for what? What is it?
SENTRY: My king,
there's nothing you can swear you'll never do—
second thoughts make liars of us all.   430
I could have sworn I wouldn't hurry back
(what with your threats, the buffeting I just took),
but a stroke of luck beyond our wildest hopes,
what a joy, there's nothing like it. So,
back I've come, breaking my oath, who cares?   435
I'm bringing in our prisoner—this young girl—
we took her giving the dead the last rites.
But no casting lots this time, this is *my* luck,
my prize, no one else's.
                    Now, my lord,
here she is. Take her, question her,   440
cross-examine her to your heart's content.
But set me free, it's only right—
I'm rid of this dreadful business once for all.

CREON: Prisoner! Her? You took her—where, doing what?

SENTRY: Burying the man. That's the whole story.

CREON: What?   445
    You mean what you say, you're telling me the truth?

SENTRY: She's the one. With my own eyes I saw her
    bury the body, just what you've forbidden.
    There. Is that plain and clear?

CREON: What did you see? Did you catch her in the act?   450

SENTRY: Here's what happened. We went back to our post,
    those threats of yours breathing down our necks—
    we brushed the corpse clean of the dust that covered it,
    stripped it bare ... it was slimy, going soft,
    and we took to high ground, backs to the wind   455
    so the stink of him couldn't hit us;
    jostling, baiting each other to keep awake,
    shouting back and forth—no napping on the job,
    not this time. And so the hours dragged by
    until the sun stood dead above our heads,   460
    a huge white ball in the noon sky, beating,
    blazing down, and then it happened—
    suddenly, a whirlwind!
    Twisting a great dust-storm up from the earth,
    a black plague of the heavens, filling the plain,   465
    ripping the leaves off every tree in sight,
    choking the air and sky. We squinted hard
    and took our whipping from the gods.

    And after the storm passed—it seemed endless—
    there, we saw the girl!   470
    And she cried out a sharp, piercing cry,
    like a bird come back to an empty nest,
    peering into its bed, and all the babies gone ...
    Just so, when she sees the corpse bare
    she bursts into a long, shattering wail   475
    and calls down withering curses on the heads
    of all who did the work. And she scoops up dry dust,
    handfuls, quickly, and lifting a fine bronze urn,
    lifting it high and pouring, she crowns the dead
    with three full libations.

we rushed her, closed on the kill like hunters,
and she, she didn't flinch. We interrogated her,
charging her with offenses past and present—
she stood up to it all, denied nothing. I tell you,
it made me ache and laugh in the same breath. 485
It's pure joy to escape the worst yourself,
it hurts a man to bring down his friends.
But all that, I'm afraid, means less to me
than my own skin. That's the way I'm made.

CREON: [Wheeling on Antigone.] You,
with your eyes fixed on the ground—speak up. 490
Do you deny you did this, yes or no?

ANTIGONE: I did it. I don't deny a thing.

CREON: [To the sentry.] You, get out, wherever you please—
you're clear of a very heavy charge.

[He leaves; Creon turns back to Antigone.]

You, tell me briefly, no long speeches— 495
were you aware a decree had forbidden this?

ANTIGONE: Well aware. How could I avoid it? It was public.

CREON: And still you had the gall to break this law?

ANTIGONE: Of course I did. It wasn't Zeus, not in the least,
who made this proclamation—not to me. 500
Nor did that Justice, dwelling with the gods
beneath the earth, ordain such laws for men.
Nor did I think your edict had such force
that you, a mere mortal, could override the gods,
the great unwritten, unshakable traditions. 505
They are alive, not just today or yesterday:
they live forever, from the first of time,
and no one knows when they first saw the light.

These laws—I was not about to break them,
not out of fear of some man's wounded pride, 510
and face the retribution of the gods.
Die I must, I've known it all my life—
how could I keep from knowing?—even without
your death-sentence ringing in my ears.

And if I am to die before my time   515
I consider that a gain. Who on earth,
alive in the midst of so much grief as I,
could fail to find his death a rich reward?
So for me, at least, to meet this doom of yours
is precious little pain. But if I had allowed   520
my own mother's son to rot, an unburied corpse—
that would have been an agony! This is nothing.
And if my present actions strike you as foolish,
let's just say I've been accused of folly
by a fool.

LEADER:

            Like father like daughter,   525
passionate, wild . . .
she hasn't learned to bend before adversity.

CREON: No? Believe me, the stiffest stubborn wills
fall the hardest; the toughest iron,
tempered strong in the white-hot fire,   530
you'll see it crack and shatter first of all.
And I've known spirited horses you can break
with a light bit—proud, rebellious horses.
There's no room for pride, not in a slave
not with the lord and master standing by.   535

This girl was an old hand at insolence
when she overrode the edicts we made public.
But once she had done it—the insolence,
twice over—to glory in it, laughing,
mocking us to our face with what she'd done.   540
I'm not the man, not now: she is the man
if this victory goes to her and she goes free.

Never! Sister's child or closer in blood
than all my family clustered at my altar
worshipping Guardian Zeus—she'll never escape,   545
she and her blood sister, the most barbaric death.
Yes, I accuse her sister of an equal part
in scheming this, this burial.

[*To his attendants.*]

Bring her here!

I just saw her inside, hysterical, gone to pieces.
It never fails: the mind convicts itself   550
in advance, when scoundrels are up to no good,
plotting in the dark. Oh but I hate it more
when a traitor, caught red-handed,
tries to glorify his crimes.

ANTIGONE: Creon, what more do you want   555
than my arrest and execution?

CREON: Nothing. Then I have it all.

ANTIGONE: Then why delay? Your moralizing repels me,
every word you say—pray god it always will.
So naturally all I say repels you too.

Enough.   560

Give me glory! What greater glory could I win
than to give my own brother decent burial?
These citizens here would all agree,

[*To the Chorus.*]

they would praise me too
if their lips weren't locked in fear.   565

[*Pointing to Creon.*]

Lucky tyrants—the perquisites of power!
Ruthless power to do and say whatever pleases *them*.

CREON: You alone, of all the people in Thebes,
see things that way.

ANTIGONE: They see it just that way
but defer to you and keep their tongues in leash.   570

CREON: And you, aren't you ashamed to differ so from them?
So disloyal!

ANTIGONE: Not ashamed for a moment,
not to honor my brother, my own flesh and blood.

CREON: Wasn't Eteocles a brother too—cut down, facing him?

ANTIGONE: Brother, yes, by the same mother, the same father.   575

CREON: Then how can you render his enemy such honors,
such impieties in his eyes?

ANTIGONE: He'll never testify to that,
Eteocles dead and buried.

CREON: He will—
if you honor the traitor just as much as him. 580
ANTIGONE: But it was his brother, not some slave that died—
CREON: Ravaging our country!—
but Eteocles died fighting in our behalf.
ANTIGONE: No matter—Death longs for the same rites for all.
CREON: Never the same for the patriot and the traitor. 585
ANTIGONE: Who, Creon, who on earth can say the ones below
don't find this pure and uncorrupt?
CREON: Never. Once an enemy, never a friend,
not even after death.
ANTIGONE: I was born to join in love, not hate— 590
that is my nature.
CREON: Go down below and love,
if love you must—love the dead! While I'm alive,
no woman is going to lord it over me.

[*Enter Ismene from the palace, under guard.*]

CHORUS: Look,
Ismene's coming, weeping a sister's tears,
loving sister, under a cloud . . . 595
her face is flushed, her cheeks streaming.
Sorrow puts her lovely radiance in the dark.
CREON: You—
in my own house, you viper, slinking undetected,
sucking my life-blood! I never knew
I was breeding twin disasters, the two of you 600
rising up against my throne. Come, tell me,
will you confess your part in the crime or not?
Answer me. Swear to me.
ISMENE: I did it, yes—
if only she consents—I share the guilt,
the consequences too.
ANTIGONE: No, 605
Justice will never suffer that—not you,
you were unwilling. I never brought you in.
ISMENE: But now you face such dangers . . . I'm not ashamed
to sail through trouble with you,
make your troubles mine.

ANTIGONE: Who did the work?   610
  Let the dead and the god of death bear witness!
  I have no love for a friend who loves in words alone.
ISMENE: Oh no, my sister, don't reject me, please,
  let me die beside you, consecrating
  the dead together.
ANTIGONE: Never share my dying,   615
  don't lay claim to what you never touched.
  My death will be enough.
ISMENE: What do I care for life, cut off from you?
ANTIGONE: Ask Creon. Your concern is all for him.
ISMENE: Why abuse me so? It doesn't help you now.
ANTIGONE: You're right— 620
  if I mock you, I get no pleasure from it,
  only pain.
ISMENE: Tell me, dear one,
  what can I do to help you, even now?
ANTIGONE: Save yourself. I don't grudge you your survival.
ISMENE: Oh no, no, denied my portion in your death?   625
ANTIGONE: You chose to live, I chose to die.
ISMENE: Not, at least,
  without every kind of caution I could voice.
ANTIGONE: Your wisdom appealed to one world—mine, another.
ISMENE: But look, we're both guilty, both condemned to death.
ANTIGONE: Courage! Live your life. I gave myself to death,   630
  long ago, so I might serve the dead.
CREON: They're both mad, I tell you, the two of them.
  One's just shown it, the other's been that way
  since she was born.
ISMENE: True, my king,
  the sense we were born with cannot last forever . . .   635
  commit cruelty on a person long enough
  and the mind begins to go.
CREON: Yours did,
  when you chose to commit your crimes with her.
ISMENE: How can I live alone, without her?
CREON: Her?
  Don't even mention her—she no longer exists.   640
ISMENE: What? You'd kill your own son's bride?

CREON: Absolutely:
   there are other fields for him to plow.
ISMENE: Perhaps,
   but never as true, as close a bond as theirs.
CREON: A worthless woman for my son? It repels me.
ISMENE: Dearest Haemon, your father wrongs you so!   645
CREON: Enough, enough—you and your talk of marriage!
ISMENE: Creon—you're really going to rob your son of Antigone?
CREON: Death will do it for me—break their marriage off.
LEADER: So, it's settled then? Antigone must die?
CREON: Settled, yes—we both know that.   650

   [*To the guards.*]

   Stop wasting time. Take them in.
   From now on they'll act like women.
   Tie them up, no more running loose;
   even the bravest will cut and run,
   once they see Death coming for their lives.   655

   [*The guards escort Antigone and Ismene into the palace. Creon
   remains while the old citizens form their chorus.*]

CHORUS: Blest, they are the truly blest who all their lives
   have never tasted devastation. For others, once
   the gods have rocked a house to its foundations
      the ruin will never cease, cresting on and on
   from one generation on throughout the race—   660
   like a great mounting tide
   driven on by savage northern gales,
      surging over the dead black depths
   rolling up from the bottom dark heaves of sand
   and the headlands, taking the storm's onslaught full-force,   665
   roar, and the low moaning
                              echoes on and on
                                 and now
   as in ancient times I see the sorrows of the house,
   the living heirs of the old ancestral kings,
   piling on the sorrows of the dead
      and one generation cannot free the next—   670
   some god will bring them crashing down,

the race finds no release.
And now the light, the hope
    springing up from the late last root
in the house of Oedipus, that hope's cut down in turn   675
by the long, bloody knife swung by the gods of death
by a senseless word
        by fury at the heart.
                Zeus,
yours is the power, Zeus, what man on earth
can override it, who can hold it back?
Power that neither Sleep, the all-ensnaring   680
    no, nor the tireless months of heaven
can ever overmaster—young through all time,
mighty lord of power, you hold fast
    the dazzling crystal mansions of Olympus.
And throughout the future, late and soon   685
as through the past, your law prevails:
no towering form of greatness
    enters into the lives of mortals
      free and clear of ruin.
             True,
our dreams, our high hopes voyaging far and wide   690
bring sheer delight to many, to many others
    delusion, blithe, mindless lusts
and the fraud steals on one slowly . . . unaware
till he trips and puts his foot into the fire.
    He was a wise old man who coined   695
the famous saying: "Sooner or later
foul is fair, fair is foul
to the man the gods will ruin"—
    He goes his way for a moment only   700
      free of blinding ruin.

[*Enter Haemon from the palace.*]

Here's Haemon now, the last of all your sons.
Does he come in tears for his bride,
his doomed bride, Antigone—
bitter at being cheated of their marriage?
CREON: We'll soon know, better than seers could tell us.   705

[Turning to Haemon.]

Son, you've heard the final verdict on your bride?
Are you coming now, raving against your father?
Or do you love me, no matter what I do?

HAEMON: Father, I'm your *son* . . . you in your wisdom
set my bearings for me—I obey you.   710
No marriage could ever mean more to me than you,
whatever good direction you may offer.

CREON: Fine, Haemon.
That's how you ought to feel within your heart,
subordinate to your father's will in every way.
That's what a man prays for: to produce good sons—   715
a household full of them, dutiful and attentive,
so they can pay his enemy back with interest
and match the respect their father shows his friend.
But the man who rears a brood of useless children,
what has he brought into the world, I ask you?   720
Nothing but trouble for himself, and mockery
from his enemies laughing in his face.
                                          Oh Haemon,
never lose your sense of judgment over a woman.
The warmth, the rush of pleasure, it all goes cold
in your arms, I warn you . . . a worthless woman   725
in your house, a misery in your bed.
What wound cuts deeper than a loved one
turned against you? Spit her out,
like a mortal enemy—let the girl go.
Let her find a husband down among the dead.   730
Imagine it: I caught her in naked rebellion,
the traitor, the only one in the whole city.
I'm not about to prove myself a liar,
not to my people, no, I'm going to kill her!
That's right—so let her cry for mercy, sing her hymns   735
to Zeus who defends all bonds of kindred blood.
Why, if I bring up my own kin to be rebels,
think what I'd suffer from the world at large.
Show me the man who rules his household well:
I'll show you someone fit to rule the state.   740

That good man, my son,
I have every confidence he and he alone
can give commands and take them too. Staunch
in the storm of spears he'll stand his ground,
a loyal, unflinching comrade at your side.   745

But whoever steps out of line, violates the laws
or presumes to hand out orders to his superiors,
he'll win no praise from me. But that man
the city places in authority, his orders
must be obeyed, large and small,   750
right and wrong.
              Anarchy—
show me a greater crime in all the earth!
She, she destroys cities, rips up houses,
breaks the ranks of spearmen into headlong rout.
But the ones who last it out, the great mass of them   755
owe their lives to discipline. Therefore
we must defend the men who live by law,
never let some woman triumph over us.
Better to fall from power, if fall we must,
at the hands of a man—never be rated   760
inferior to a woman, never.

LEADER: To us,
unless old age has robbed us of our wits,
you seem to say what you have to say with sense.

HAEMON: Father, only the gods endow a man with reason,
the finest of all their gifts, a treasure.   765
Far be it from me—I haven't the skill,
and certainly no desire, to tell you when,
if ever, you make a slip in speech . . . though
someone else might have a good suggestion.

Of course it's not for you,   770
in the normal run of things, to watch
whatever men say or do, or find to criticize.
The man in the street, you know, dreads your glance,
he'd never say anything displeasing to your face.
But it's for me to catch the murmurs in the dark,   775

the way the city mourns for this young girl.
"No woman," they say, "ever deserved death less,
and such a brutal death for such a glorious action.
She, with her own dear brother lying in his blood—
she couldn't bear to leave him dead, unburied,   780
food for the wild dogs or wheeling vultures.
Death? She deserves a glowing crown of gold!"
So they say, and the rumor spreads in secret,
darkly . . .
        I rejoice in your success, father—
nothing more precious to me in the world.   785
What medal of honor brighter to his children
than a father's growing glory? Or a child's
to his proud father? Now don't, please,
be quite so single-minded, self-involved,
or assume the world is wrong and you are right.   790
Whoever thinks that he alone possesses intelligence,
the gift of eloquence, he and no one else,
and character too . . . such men, I tell you,
spread them open—you will find them empty.
                               No,
it's no disgrace for a man, even a wise man,   795
to learn many things and not to be too rigid.
You've seen trees by a raging winter torrent,
how many sway with the flood and salvage every twig,
but not the stubborn—they're ripped out, roots and all.
Bend or break. The same when a man is sailing: 800
haul your sheets too taut, never give an inch,
you'll capsize, and go the rest of the voyage
keel up and the rowing-benches under.

Oh give way. Relax your anger—change!
I'm young, I know, but let me offer this: 805
it would be best by far, I admit,
if a man were born infallible, right by nature.
If not—and things don't often go that way,
it's best to learn from those with good advice.

LEADER: You'd do well, my lord, if he's speaking to the point,   810
to learn from him.

[*Turning to Haemon.*]

and you, my boy, from him.
You both are talking sense.

CREON: So,
men our age, we're to be lectured, are we?—
schooled by a boy his age?

HAEMON: Only in what is right. But if I seem young,   815
look less to my years and more to what I do.

CREON: Do? Is admiring rebels an achievement?

HAEMON: I'd never suggest that you admire treason.

CREON: Oh?—
isn't that just the sickness that's attacked her?

HAEMON: The whole city of Thebes denies it, to a man.   820

CREON: And is Thebes about to tell me how to rule?

HAEMON: Now, you see? Who's talking like a child?

CREON: Am I to rule this land for others—or myself?

HAEMON: It's no city at all, owned by one man alone.

CREON: What? The city *is* the king's—that's the law!   825

HAEMON: What a splendid king you'd make of a desert island—
you and you alone.

CREON: [*To the chorus.*] This boy, I do believe,
is fighting on her side, the woman's side.

HAEMON: If you are a woman, yes;
my concern is all for you.   830

CREON: Why, you degenerate—bandying accusations,
threatening me with justice, your own father!

HAEMON: I see my father offending justice—wrong.

CREON: Wrong?
To protect my royal rights?

HAEMON: Protect your rights?   835
When you trample down the honors of the gods?

CREON: You, you soul of corruption, rotten through—
woman's accomplice!

HAEMON: That may be,
but you'll never find me accomplice to a criminal.

CREON: That's what *she* is,   840
and every word you say is a blatant appeal for her—

HAEMON: And you, and me, and the gods beneath the earth.

CREON: You will never marry her, not while she's alive.

HAEMON: Then she'll die . . . but her death will kill another.

CREON: What, brazen threats? You go too far!

HAEMON: What threat?   845
Combating your empty, mindless judgments with a word?

CREON: You'll suffer for your sermons, you and your empty wisdom!

HAEMON: If you weren't my father, I'd say you were insane.

CREON: Don't flatter me with Father—you woman's slave!

HAEMON: You really expect to fling abuse at me   850
and not receive the same?

CREON: Is that so!
Now, by heaven, I promise you, you'll pay—
taunting, insulting me! Bring her out,
that hateful—she'll die now, here,
in front of his eyes, beside her groom!   855

HAEMON: No, no, she will never die beside me—
don't delude yourself. And you will never
see me, never set eyes on my face again.
Rage your heart out, rage with friends
who can stand the sight of you.   860

[*Rushing out.*]

LEADER: Gone, my king, in a burst of anger.
A temper young as his . . . hurt him once,
he may do something violent.

CREON: Let him do—
dream up something desperate, past all human limit!
Good riddance. Rest assured,   865
he'll never save those two young girls from death.

LEADER: Both of them, you really intend to kill them both?

CREON: No, not her, the one whose hands are clean—
you're quite right.

LEADER: But Antigone—
what sort of death do you have in mind for her?   870

CREON: I'll take her down some wild, desolate path
never trod by men, and wall her up alive
in a rocky vault, and set out short rations,
just the measure piety demands

to keep the entire city free of defilement.[16]
There let her pray to the one god she worships:
Death—who knows?—may just reprieve her from death.
Or she may learn at last, better late than never,
what a waste of breath it is to worship Death.

[*Exit to the palace.*]

CHORUS: Love, never conquered in battle
Love the plunderer laying waste the rich!   880
Love standing the night-watch
     guarding a girl's soft cheek,
you range the seas, the shepherds' steadings off in the wilds—
not even the deathless gods can flee your onset,
nothing human born for a day—   885
whoever feels your grip is driven mad.
                         Love!—
you wrench the minds of the righteous into outrage,
swerve them to their ruin—you have ignited this,
this kindred strife, father and son at war
     and Love alone the victor—   890
warm glance of the bride triumphant, burning with desire!
Throned in power, side-by-side with the mighty laws!
Irresistible Aphrodite,[17] never conquered—
Love, you mock us for your sport.   895

[*Antigone is brought from the palace under guard.*]

          But now, even I'd rebel against the king,
          I'd break all bounds when I see this—
          I fill with tears, I cannot hold them back,
          not any more ... I see Antigone make her way
          to the bridal vault where all are laid to rest.   900
ANTIGONE: Look at me, men of my fatherland,
          setting out on the last road

---

[16]The penalty originally proclaimed was death by stoning. But this demands the participation of
the citizens, and it may be that Creon, after listening to Haemon's remarks, is not as sure as he
once was of popular support. Creon proposed imprisonment in a tomb with a ration of food. Since
Antigone would die of starvation but not actually by anyone's hand, Creon seems to think that the
city will not be "defiled," that is, will not incur blood guilt.
[17]Goddess of sexual love.

looking into the last light of day
the last I will ever see . . .
the god of death who puts us all to bed   905
takes me down to the banks of Acheron[18] alive—
    denied my part in the wedding-songs,
no wedding-song in the dusk has crowned my marriage—
I go to wed the lord of the dark waters.

CHORUS: Not crowned with glory,[19] or with a dirge,   910
    you leave for the deep pit of the dead.
    No withering illness laid you low,
    no strokes of the sword—a law to yourself,
    alone, no mortal like you, ever, you go down
    to the halls of Death alive and breathing.   915

ANTIGONE: But think of Niobe[20]—well I know her story—
think what a living death she died,
Tantalus' daughter, stranger queen from the east:
there on the mountain heights, growing stone
binding as ivy, slowly walled her round   920
and the rains will never cease, the legends say
the snows will never leave her . . .
    wasting away, under her brows the tears
showering down her breasting ridge and slopes—
a rocky death like hers puts me to sleep.   925

CHORUS: But she was a god, born of gods,
    and we are only mortals born to die.
    And yet, of course, it's a great thing
    for a dying girl to hear, just to hear
    she shares a destiny equal to the gods,   930
    during life and later, once she's dead.

[18]A river in the underworld.

[19]The usual version of this line is "crowned with glory." The Greek word *oukoun* can be negative or positive, depending on the accent, which determines the pronunciation; because written accents were not yet in use in Sophocles' time, no one will ever know for sure which meaning he intended. The present version is based on the belief that the chorus is expressing pity for Antigone's ignominious and abnormal death; she has no funeral at which her fame and praise are recited; she will not die by either of the usual causes—violence and disease—but by a living death. It is as they say, her own choice: she is "a law to [herself]" (line 913).

[20]A Phrygian princess married to Amphion, king of Thebes. She boasted that she had borne more children than Leto, mother of Apollo and Artemis. As vengeance, Apollo and Artemis killed all of Niobe's children. She fled to Phrygia, where she was turned into a rock on Mount Sipylus; the melting of the snow on the mountain caused "tears" to flow down the rock formation, which resembles a woman's face. See *Iliad* 24.651–69.

ANTIGONE: O you mock me!
   Why, in the name of all my fathers' gods
   why can't you wait till I am gone—
        must you abuse me to my face?
   O my city, all your fine rich sons!   935
   And you, you springs of the Dirce,
   holy grove of Thebes where the chariots gather,
        you at least, you'll bear me witness, look,
   unmourned by friend and forced by such crude laws
   I go to my rockbound prison, strange new tomb—   940
        always a stranger, O dear god,
        I have no home on earth and none below,
           not with the living, not with the breathless dead.
CHORUS: You went too far, the last limits of daring—
              smashing against the high throne of Justice!   945
              Your life's in ruins, child—I wonder . . .
                 do you pay for your father's terrible ordeal?
ANTIGONE: There—at last you've touched it, the worst pain
   the worst anguish! Raking up the grief for father
           three times over, for all the doom   950
   that's struck us down, the brilliant house of Laius.
   O mother, your marriage-bed
   the coiling horrors, the coupling there—
           you with your own son, my father—doomstruck mother!
   Such, such were my parents, and I their wretched child.   955
   I go to them now, cursed, unwed, to share their home—
           I am a stranger! O dear brother, doomed
           in your marriage—your marriage murders mine,[21]
               your dying drags me down to death alive!

   [*Enter Creon.*]

CHORUS: Reverence asks some reverence in return—   960
   but attacks on power never go unchecked,
           not by the man who holds the reins of power.
   Your own blind will, your passion has destroyed you.

---

[21]Polynices had married the daughter of Adrastus of Argos, to seal the alliance that enabled him to march against Thebes.

ANTIGONE: No one to weep for me, my friends,
no wedding-song—they take me away   965
in all my pain . . . the road lies open, waiting.
Never again, the law forbids me to see
the sacred eye of day. I am agony!
No tears for the destiny that's mine,
no loved one mourns my death.

CREON: Can't you see?   970
If a man could wail his own dirge *before* he dies,
he'd never finish.

[*To the guards.*]

                    Take her away, quickly!
Wall her up in the tomb, you have your orders.
Abandon her there, alone, and let her choose—
death or a buried life with a good roof for shelter.   975
As for myself, my hands are clean. This young girl—
dead or alive, she will be stripped of her rights,
her stranger's rights,[22] here in the world above.

ANTIGONE: O tomb, my bridal-bed—my house, my prison
cut in the hollow rock, my everlasting watch!   980
I'll soon be there, soon embrace my own,
the great growing family of our dead
Persephone[23] has received among her ghosts.
                                           I,
the last of them all, the most reviled by far,
go down before my destined time's run out.   985
But still I go, cherishing one good hope:
my arrival may be dear to father,
dear to you, my mother,
dear to you, my loving brother, Eteocles—
When you died I washed you with my hands,   990
I dressed you all, I poured the sacred cups
across your tombs. But now, Polynices,
because I laid your body out as well,

---

[22]The Greek words suggest that he sees her not as a citizen but as a resident alien; by her action
she has forfeited citizenship. But now she will be deprived even of that inferior status.
[23]Queen of the underworld.

this, this is my reward. Nevertheless
I honored you—the decent will admit it—   995
well and wisely too.
                    Never, I tell you,
if I had been the mother of children
or if my husband died, exposed and rotting—
I'd never have taken this ordeal upon myself,
never defied our people's will. What law,   1000
you ask, do I satisfy with what I say?
A husband dead, there might have been another.
A child by another too, if I had lost the first.
But mother and father both lost in the halls of Death,
no brother could ever spring to light again.[24]   1005
For this law alone I held you first in honor.
For this, Creon, the king, judges me a criminal
guilty of dreadful outrage, my dear brother!
And now he leads me off, a captive in his hands,
with no part in the bridal-song, the bridal-bed,
denied all joy of marriage, raising children—   1010
deserted so by loved ones, struck by fate,
I descend alive to the caverns of the dead.

What law of the mighty gods have I transgressed?
Why look to the heavens any more, tormented as I am?   1015
Whom to call, what comrades now? Just think,
my reverence only brands me for irreverence!
Very well: if this is the pleasure of the gods,
once I suffer I will know that I was wrong.
But if these men are wrong, let them suffer   1020
nothing worse than they mete out to me—
these masters of injustice!
LEADER: Still the same rough winds, the wild passion
     raging through the girl.

---

[24]This strange justification for her action has been considered unacceptable by many critics, and they have suspected that it was an interpolation by some later producer of the play. But Aristotle quotes it in the next century and appears to have no doubt of its authenticity. If genuine, it means that Antigone momentarily abandons the law she championed against Creon—that all people have a right to burial—and sees her motive as exclusive devotion to her dead brother. For someone facing the prospect of a slow and hideous death, such a self-examination and realization is not impossible. And it makes no difference to the courage and tenacity of her defiance of state power.

CREON: [*To the guards.*] Take her away.
> You're wasting time—you'll pay for it too. 1025

ANTIGONE: Oh god, the voice of death. It's come, it's here.

CREON: True. Not a word of hope—your doom is sealed.

ANTIGONE: Land of Thebes, city of all my fathers—
> O you gods, the first gods of the race!²⁵
> They drag me away, now, no more delay. 1030
> Look on me, you noble sons of Thebes—
> the last of a great line of kings,
> I alone, see what I suffer now
> at the hands of what breed of men—
> all for reverence, my reverence for the gods! 1035

[*She leaves under guard; the chorus gathers.*]

CHORUS: Danaë,²⁶ Danaë—
> even she endured a fate like yours,
>> in all her lovely strength she traded
> the light of day for the bolted brazen vault—
> buried within her tomb, her bridal-chamber, 1040
> wed to the yoke and broken.
>> But she was of glorious birth
>> my child, my child
> and treasured the seed of Zeus within her womb,
> the cloudburst streaming gold! 1045
>> The power of fate is a wonder,
>> dark, terrible wonder—
>> neither wealth nor armies
>> towered walls nor ships
>> black hulls lashed by the salt 1050
> can save us from that force.

The yoke tamed him too
> young Lycurgus flaming in anger

---

²⁵The Theban royal house traced its ancestry through Harmonia, wife of Cadmus, to Aphrodite and Ares, her parents. Cadmus's daughter was Semele.
²⁶Daughter of Acrisius, king of Argos. It was prophesied that he would be killed by his daughter's son; so he shut her up in a bronze tower. But Zeus came to her in the form of a golden rain shower and she bore a son, Perseus, who did in the end accidentally kill his grandfather.

king of Edonia,[27] all for his mad taunts
Dionysus clamped him down, encased   1055
in the chain-mail of rock
    and there his rage
      his terrible flowering rage burst—
sobbing, dying away . . . at last that madman
came to know his god—   1060
    the power he mocked, the power
    he taunted in all his frenzy
    trying to stamp out
    the women strong with the god—
    the torch, the raving sacred cries—   1065
    enraging the Muses who adore the flute.

And far north[28] where the Black Rocks
    cut the sea in half
and murderous straits
split the coast of Thrace   1070
    a forbidding city stands
where once, hard by the walls
the savage Ares thrilled to watch
a king's new queen, a Fury rearing in rage
    against his two royal sons—   1075
    her bloody hands, her dagger-shuttle
stabbing out their eyes—cursed, blinding wounds—
their eyes blind sockets screaming for revenge!

They wailed in agony, cries echoing cries
    the princes doomed at birth . . .   1080
and their mother doomed to chains,
walled up in a tomb of stone[29]—

---

[27]Thrace Lycurgus opposed the introduction of Dionysiac religion into his kingdom and was imprisoned by the god.

[28]The whole story is difficult to follow, and its application to the case of Antigone is obscure. Cleopatra, the daughter of the Athenian princess Orithyia (whom Boreas, the North Wind, carried off to his home in Thrac), was married to Phineus, the Thracian king, and bore him two sons. He tired of her, abandoned her, and married Eidothea ("a king's new queen," line 1074), who put out the eyes of Cleopotra's two sons. Ares watched the savage act.

[29]Lines 1081–82 have no equivalent in the Greek text. They represent a belief that Sophocles' audience knew a version of the legend in which Cleopatra was imprisoned in a stone tomb (which is found in a later source). This would give a point of comparison to Antigone as did the imprisonment of Danaë and Lycurgus.

but she traced her own birth back
to a proud Athenian line and the high gods
and off in caverns half the world away,   1085
born of the wild North Wind
    she sprang on her father's gales,
       racing stallions up the leaping cliffs—
child of the heavens. But even on her the Fates
the gray everlasting Fates rode hard   1090
my child, my child.

[*Enter Tiresias, the blind prophet, led by a boy.*]

TIRESIAS: Lords of Thebes,
I and the boy have come together,
hand in hand. Two see with the eyes of one . . .
so the blind must go, with a guide to lead the way.
CREON: What is it, old Tiresias? What news now?
TIRESIAS: I will teach you. And you obey the seer.
CREON: I will,   1095
I've never wavered from your advice before.
TIRESIAS: And so you kept the city straight on course.
CREON: I owe you a great deal, I swear to that.
TIRESIAS: Then reflect, my son: you are poised,   1100
once more, on the razor-edge of fate.
CREON: What is it? I shudder to hear you.
TIRESIAS: You will learn
when you listen to the warnings of my craft.
As I sat on the ancient seat of augury,
in the sanctuary where every bird I know   1105
will hover at my hands[30]—suddenly I heard it,
a strange voice in the wingbeats, unintelligible,
barbaric, a mad scream! Talons flashing, ripping,
they were killing each other—that much I knew—
the murderous fury whirring in those wings   1110
made that much clear!
              I was afraid,
I turned quickly, tasted the burnt-sacrifice,
ignited the altar at all points—but no fire,

---

[30]A place where the birds gathered and Tiresias waited for omens.

the god in the fire never blazed.
Not from those offerings . . . over the embers   1115
slid a heavy ooze from the long thighbones,
smoking, sputtering out, and the bladder
puffed and burst—spraying gall into the air—
and the fat wrapping the bones slithered off
and left them glistening white. No fire!   1120
The rites failed that might have blazed the future
with a sign. So I learned from the boy here:
he is my guide, as I am guide to others.

                        And it is you—
your high resolve that sets this plague on Thebes.
The public altars and sacred hearths are fouled,   1125
one and all, by the birds and dogs with carrion
torn from the corpse, the doomstruck son of Oedipus!
and so the gods are deaf to our prayers, they spurn
the offerings in our hands, the flame of holy flesh.
No birds cry out an omen clear and true—   1130
they're gorged with the murdered victim's blood and fat.
Take these things to heart, my son, I warn you.
All men make mistakes, it is only human.
But once the wrong is done, a man
can turn his back on folly, misfortune too,   1135
if he tries to make amends, however low he's fallen,
and stops his bullnecked ways. Stubbornness
brands you for stupidity—pride is a crime.
No, yield to the dead!
Never stab the fighter when he's down.   1140

Where's the glory, killing the dead twice over?
I mean you well. I give you sound advice.
It's best to learn from a good adviser
when he speaks for your own good:
it's pure gain.
CREON: Old man—all of you! So,   1145
    you shoot your arrows at my head like archers at the target—
    I even have *him* loosed on me, this fortune-teller.
    Oh his ilk has tried to sell me short
    and ship me off for years. Well,

drive your bargains, traffic—much as you like—   1150
in the gold of India, silver-gold of Sardis.[31]
You'll never bury that body in the grave,
not even if Zeus's eagles rip the corpse
and wing their rotten pickings off to the throne of god!
Never, not even in fear of such defilement   1155
will I tolerate his burial, that traitor.
Well I know, we can't defile the gods—
no mortal has the power.
                              No,
reverend old Tiresias, all men fall,
it's only human, but the wisest fall obscenely   1160
when they glorify obscene advice with rhetoric—
all for their own gain.

TIRESIAS: Oh god, is there a man alive
who knows, who actually believes . . .

CREON: What now?
What earth-shattering truth are you about to utter?   1165

TIRESIAS: . . . just how much a sense of judgment, wisdom
is the greatest gift we have?

CREON: Just as much, I'd say,
as a twisted mind is the worst affliction known.

TIRESIAS: You are the one who's sick, Creon, sick to death.

CREON: I am in no mood to trade insults with a seer.   1170

TIRESIAS: You have already, calling my prophecies a lie.

CREON: Why not?
You and the whole breed of seers are mad for money!

TIRESIAS: And the whole race of tyrants lusts for filthy gain.

CREON: This slander of yours—
are you aware you're speaking to the king?   1175

TIRESIAS: Well aware. Who helped you save the city?

CREON: You—
you have your skills, old seer, but you lust for injustice!

TIRESIAS: You will drive me to utter the dreadful secret in my heart.

CREON: Spit it out! Just don't speak it out for profit.

TIRESIAS: Profit? No, not a bit of profit, not for you.   1180

[31]In Asia Minor. Electrum, a natural alloy of gold and silver, was found in a nearby river.

CREON: Know full well, you'll never buy off my resolve.
TIRESIAS: Then know this too, learn this by heart!
     The chariot of the sun will not race through
     so many circuits more, before you have surrendered
     one born of your own loins, your own flesh and blood,   1185
     a corpse for corpses given in return, since you have thrust
     to the world below a child sprung from the world above,
     ruthlessly lodged a living soul within the grave—
     then you've robbed the gods below the earth,
     keeping a dead body here in the bright air,   1190
     unburied, unsung, unhallowed by the rites.

     You, you have no business with the dead,
     nor do the gods above—this is violence
     you have forced upon the heavens.
     And so the avengers, the dark destroyers late   1195
     but true to the mark, now lie in wait for you,
     the Furies sent by the gods and the god of death
     to strike you down with the pains that you perfected!

     There. Reflect on that, tell me I've been bribed.
     The day comes soon, no long test of time, not now,   1200
     when the mourning cries for men and women break
     throughout your halls. Great hatred rises against you—
     cities in tumult, all whose mutilated sons
     the dogs have graced with burial, or the wild beasts
     or a wheeling crow that wings the ungodly stench of carrion   1205
     back to each city, each warrior's heart and home.

     These arrows for your heart! Since you've raked me
     I loose them like an archer in my anger,
     arrows deadly true. You'll never escape
     their burning, searing force.   1210

     [*Motioning to his escort.*]

     Come, boy, take me home.
     So he can vent his rage on younger men,
     and learn to keep a gentler tongue in his head
     and better sense than what he carries now.

LEADER: The old man's gone, my king—   1215
    terrible prophecies. Well I know,
    since the hair on this old head went gray,
    he's never lied to Thebes.

CREON: I know it myself—I'm shaken, torn.
    It's a dreadful thing to yield . . . but resist now?   1220
    Lay my pride bare to the blows of ruin?
    That's dreadful too.

LEADER: But good advice,
    Creon, take it now, you must.

CREON: What should I do? Tell me . . . I'll obey.

LEADER: Go! Free the girl from the rocky vault   1225
    and raise a mound for the body you exposed.

CREON: That's your advice? You think I should give in?

LEADER: Yes, my king, quickly. Disasters sent by the gods
    cut short our follies in a flash.

CREON: Oh it's hard,
    giving up the heart's desire . . . but I will do it—   1230
    no more fighting a losing battle with necessity.

LEADER: Do it now, go, don't leave it to others.

CREON: Now—I'm on my way! Come, each of you,
    take up axes, make for the high ground,
    over there, quickly! I and my better judgment   1235
    have come round to this—I shackled her,
    I'll set her free myself. I am afraid . . .
    it's best to keep the established laws
    to the very day we die.

[*Rushing out, followed by his entourage. The chorus clusters around the altar.*]

CHORUS: God of a hundred names!
                    Great Dionysus—   1240
    Son and glory of Semele! Pride of Thebes—
    Child of Zeus whose thunder rocks the clouds—
    Lord of the famous lands of evening—
    King of the Mysteries!

King of Eleusis, Demeter's[32] plain
her breasting hills that welcome in the world—   1245
Great Dionysus!
      Bacchus, living in Thebes
the mother-city of all your frenzied women—
                    Bacchus
living along the Ismenus'[33] rippling waters
standing over the field sown with the Dragons' teeth!
You—we have seen you through the flaring smoky fires,   1250
    your torches blazing over the twin peaks[34]
where nymphs of the hallowed cave climb onward
    fired with you, your sacred rage—
we have seen you at Castalia's running spring
and down from the heights of Nysa[35] crowned with ivy   1255
the greening shore rioting vines and grapes
    down you come in your storm of wild women
      ecstatic, mystic cries—
            Dionysus—
down to watch and ward the roads of Thebes!

First of all cities, Thebes you honor first   1260
you and your mother, bride of the lightning—
come, Dionysus! now your people lie
in the iron grip of plague,
come in your racing, healing stride
    down Parnassus'[36] slopes   1265
or across the moaning straits.
              Lord of the dancing—
dance, dance the constellations breathing fire!
Great master of the voices of the night!
Child of Zeus, God's offspring, come, come forth!
Lord, king, dance with your nymphs, swirling, raving   1270

[32]The grain and harvest goddess. Eleusis, the site of the mysteries and the worship of Demeter, is near Athens.
[33]A river at Thebes. Dionysus (or Bacchus) was among the divinities worshipped by the initiates.
[34]The two cliffs above Delphi, where Dionysus was thought to reside in the winter months.
[35]A mountain associated with Dionysiac worship; several mountains are so named, but the reference here is probably to the one on the island of Euboea, off the Attic coast.
[36]Mountain in central Greece just north of the Gulf of Corinth; an important cult of Dionysus was located there, as was Apollo's oracle at Delphi.

arm-in-arm in frenzy through the night
they dance you, Iacchus[37]—

Dance, Dionysus
giver of all good things!

[*Enter a messenger from the side.*]

MESSENGER: Neighbors,
friends of the house of Cadmus and the kings,
there's not a thing in this mortal life of ours   1275
I'd praise or blame as settled once for all.
Fortune lifts and Fortune fells the lucky
and unlucky every day. No prophet on earth
can tell a man his fate. Take Creon:
there was a man to rouse your envy once,   1280
as I see it. He saved the realm from enemies;
taking power, he alone, the lord of the fatherland,
he set us true on course—flourished like a tree
with the noble line of sons he bred and reared . . .
and now it's lost, all gone.

Believe me,   1285
when a man has squandered his true joys,
he's good as dead, I tell you, a living corpse.
Pile up riches in your house, as much as you like—
live like a king with a huge show of pomp,
but if real delight is missing from the lot,   1290
I wouldn't give you a wisp of smoke for it,
not compared with joy.

LEADER: What now?
What new grief do you bring the house of kings?

MESSENGER: Dead, dead—and the living are guilty of their death!

LEADER: Who's the murderer? Who is dead? Tell us.   1295

MESSENGER: Haemon's gone, his blood spilled by the very hand—

LEADER: His father's or his own?

MESSENGER: His own . . .
raging mad with his father for the death—

LEADER: Oh great seer,
you saw it all, you brought your word to birth!

---

[37]Dionysus.

MESSENGER: Those are the facts. Deal with them as you will.

[*As he turns to go, Eurydice enters from the palace.*]

LEADER: Look, Eurydice. Poor woman, Creon's wife,
so close at hand. By chance perhaps,
unless she's heard the news about her son.

EURYDICE: My countrymen,
all of you—I caught the sound of your words
as I was leaving to do my part,   1305
to appeal to queen Athena with my prayers.
I was just loosing the bolts, opening the doors,
when a voice filled with sorrow, family sorrow,
struck my ears, and I fell back, terrified,
into the women's arms—everything went black.   1310
Tell me the news, again, whatever it is . . .
sorrow and I are hardly strangers;
I can bear the worst.

MESSENGER: I—dear lady,
I'll speak as an eye-witness. I was there.
And I won't pass over one word of the truth.   1315
Why should I try to soothe you with a story,
only to prove a liar in a moment?
Truth is always best.

                    So,
I escorted your lord, I guided him
to the edge of the plain where the body lay,   1320
Polynices, torn by the dogs and still unmourned.
And saying a prayer to Hecate of the Crossroads,
Pluto[38] too, to hold their anger and be kind,
we washed the dead in a bath of holy water
and plucking some fresh branches, gathering . . .   1325
what was left of him, we burned them all together
and raised a high mound of native earth, and then
we turned and made for that rocky vault of hers,
the hollow, empty bed of the bride of Death.
And far off, one of us heard a voice,   1330

---

[38]Or Hades, god of the underworld. Hecate is a goddess associated with darkness and burial grounds; offerings to her were left at crossroads.

a long wail rising, echoing
out of that unhallowed wedding-chamber,
he ran to alert the master and Creon pressed on,
closer—the strange, inscrutable cry came sharper,
throbbing around him now, and he let loose   1335
a cry of his own, enough to wrench the heart,
"Oh god, am I the prophet now? going down
the darkest road I've ever gone? My son—
it's *his* dear voice, he greets me! Go, men,
closer, quickly! Go through the gap,   1340
the rocks are dragged back—
right to the tomb's very mouth—and look,
see if it's Haemon's voice I think I hear,
or the gods have robbed me of my senses."

The king was shattered. We took his orders,   1345
went and searched, and there in the deepest,
dark recesses of the tomb we found her . . .
hanged by the neck in a fine linen noose,
strangled in her veils—and the boy,
his arms flung around her waist,   1350
clinging to her, wailing for his bride,
dead and down below, for his father's crimes
and the bed of his marriage blighted by misfortune.
When Creon saw him, he gave a deep sob,
he ran in, shouting, crying out to him,   1355
"Oh my child—what have you done? what seized you,
what insanity? what disaster drove you mad?
Come out, my son! I beg you on my knees!"
But the boy gave him a wild burning glance,
spat in his face, not a word in reply,   1360
he drew his sword—his father rushed out,
running as Haemon lunged and missed!—
and then, doomed, desperate with himself,
suddenly leaning his full weight on the blade,
he buried it in his body, halfway to the hilt.   1365
And still in his senses, pouring his arms around her,
he embraced the girl and breathing hard,
released a quick rush of blood,

bright red on her cheek glistening white.
And there he lies, body enfolding body . . . 1370
he has won his bride at last, poor boy,
not here but in the houses of the dead.

Creon shows the world that of all the ills
afflicting men the worst is lack of judgment.

[*Eurydice turns and reenters the palace.*]

LEADER: What do you make of that? The lady's gone, 1375
   without a word, good or bad.
MESSENGER: I'm alarmed too
   but here's my hope—faced with her son's death,
   she finds it unbecoming to mourn in public.
   Inside, under her roof, she'll set her women
   to the task and wail the sorrow of the house. 1380
   She's too discreet. She won't do something rash.
LEADER: I'm not so sure. To me, at least,
   a long heavy silence promises danger,
   just as much as a lot of empty outcries.
MESSENGER: We'll see if she's holding something back, 1385
   hiding some passion in her heart.
   I'm going in. You may be right—who knows?
   Even too much silence has its dangers.

[*Exit to the palace. Enter Creon from the side, escorted
by attendants carrying Haemon's body on a bier.*]

LEADER: The king himself! Coming toward us,
   look, holding the boy's head in his hands. 1390
   Clear, damning proof, if it's right to say so—
   proof of his own madness, no one else's,
      no, his own blind wrongs.
CREON: Ohhh,
   so senseless, so insane . . . my crimes,
   my stubborn, deadly— 1395
   Look at us, the killer, the killed,
   father and son, the same blood—the misery!
   My plans, my mad fanatic heart,
   my son, cut off so young!

Ai, dead, lost to the world,   1400
not through your stupidity, no, my own.
LEADER: Too late,
too late, you see what justice means.
CREON: Oh I've learned
through blood and tears! Then, it was then,
when the god came down and struck me—a great weight
shattering, driving me down that wild savage path,   1405
ruining, trampling down my joy. Oh the agony,
      the heartbreaking agonies of our lives.

[*Enter the Messenger from the palace.*]

MESSENGER: Master,
what a hoard of grief you have, and you'll have more.
The grief that lies to hand you've brought yourself—

[*Pointing to Haemon's body.*]

the rest, in the house, you'll see it all too soon.   1410
CREON: What now? What's worse than this?
MESSENGER: The queen is dead.
The mother of this dead boy . . . mother to the end—
poor thing, her wounds are fresh.
CREON: No, no,
harbor of Death, so choked, so hard to cleanse!—
why me? why are you killing me?   1415
Herald of pain, more words, more grief?
I died once, you kill me again and again!
What's the report, boy . . . some news for me?
My wife dead? O dear god!
Slaughter heaped on slaughter?

[*The doors open; the body of Eurydice is brought out on her bier.*]

MESSENGER: See for yourself: 1420
now they bring her body from the palace.
CREON: Oh no,
another, a second loss to break the heart.
What next, what fate still waits for me?
I just held my son in my arms and now,
look, a new corpse rising before my eyes—   1425
      wretched, helpless mother—O my son!

MESSENGER: She stabbed herself at the altar,
   then her eyes went dark, after she'd raised
   a cry for the noble fate of Megareus,[39] the hero
   killed in the first assault, then for Haemon,   1430
   then with her dying breath she called down
   torments on your head—you killed her sons.
CREON: Oh the dread,
   I shudder with dread! Why not kill me too?—
   run me through with a good sharp sword?
   Oh god, the misery, anguish—   1435
   I, I'm churning with it, going under.
MESSENGER: Yes, and the dead, the woman lying there,
   piles the guilt of all their deaths on you.
CREON: How did she end her life, what bloody stroke?
MESSENGER: She drove home to the heart with her own hand,   1440
   once she learned her son was dead . . . that agony.
CREON: And the guilt is all mine—
   can never be fixed on another man,
   no escape for me. I killed you,
   I, god help me, I admit it all!   1445

[To his attendants.]

   Take me away, quickly, out of sight.
   I don't even exist—I'm no one. Nothing.
LEADER: Good advice, if there's any good in suffering.
   Quickest is best when troubles block the way.
CREON: [Kneeling in prayer.]
   Come, let it come!—that best of fates for me   1450
   that brings the final day, best fate of all.
   Oh quickly, now—
   so I never have to see another sunrise.
LEADER: That will come when it comes;
   we must deal with all that lies before us.   1455
   The future rests with the ones who tend the future.
CREON: That prayer—I poured my heart into that prayer!

[39]Another son of Creon and Eurydice; he was killed during the siege of the city. Tiresias had
prophesied that his death would save Thebes.

LEADER: No more prayers now. For mortal men
          there is no escape from the doom we must endure.

CREON: Take me away, I beg you, out of sight.   1460
          A rash, indiscriminate fool!
          I murdered you, my son, against my will—
          you too, my wife . . .
                          Wailing wreck of a man,
          whom to look to? where to lean for support?

[*Desperately turning from Haemon to Eurydice on their biers.*]

          Whatever I touch goes wrong—once more   1465
          a crushing fate's come down upon my head.

[*The messenger and attendants lead Creon into the palace.*]

CHORUS: Wisdom is by far the greatest part of joy,
          and reverence toward the gods must be safeguarded.
          The mighty words of the proud are paid in full
          with mighty blows of fate, and at long last   1470
          those blows will teach us wisdom.

                          [*The old citizens exit to the side.*]

William Shakespeare, the supreme writer of English, was born, baptized, and buried in the market town of Stratford-on-Avon, eighty miles from London. Son of a glove maker and merchant who was high bailiff (or mayor) of the town, he probably attended grammar school and learned to read Latin authors in the original. At eighteen, he married Anne Hathaway, twenty-six, by whom he had three children, including twins. By 1592, he had become well known and envied as an actor and playwright in London. From 1594 until he retired, he belonged to the same theatrical company, the Lord Chamberlain's Men (later renamed the King's Men in honor of their patron, James I), for whom he wrote thirty-six plays—some of them, such as Hamlet *and* King Lear, *profound reworkings of old plays. As an actor, Shakespeare is believed to have played supporting roles, such as Hamlet's father's ghost. The company prospered, moved into the Globe Theatre in 1599, and in 1608 bought the fashionable Blackfriars as well; Shakespeare owned an interest in both theaters. When plagues shut down the theaters from 1592 to 1594, Shakespeare turned to story poems; his great sonnets (published only in 1609) probably also date from the 1590s. Plays were regarded as entertainments of little literary merit, and Shakespeare did not bother to supervise their publication. After* The Tempest *(1611), the last play entirely from his hand, he retired to Stratford, where since 1597 he had owned the second largest house in town.*

Twelfth Night; or, What You Will

[Dramatis Personae

ORSINO, *Duke (sometimes called Count) of Illyria*
VALENTINE, *gentleman attending on Orsino*
CURIO, *gentleman attending on Orsino*
VIOLA, *a shipwrecked lady, later disguised as Cesario*
SEBASTIAN, *twin brother of Viola*
ANTONIO, *a sea captain, friend to Sebastian*
CAPTAIN *of the shipwrecked vessel*
OLIVIA, *a rich countess of Illyria*
MARIA, *gentlewoman in Olivia's household*
SIR TOBY BELCH, *Olivia's uncle*
SIR ANDREW AGUECHEEK, *a companion of Sir Toby*
MALVOLIO, *steward of Olivia's household*

FABIAN, *a member of Olivia's household*
FESTE, *a clown, also called FOOL, Olivia's jester*

A PRIEST
FIRST OFFICER
SECOND OFFICER

Lords, Sailors, Musicians, and other Attendants
SCENE: *Illyria*°]

1.1

Enter Orsino Duke of Illyria, Curio, and other lords [with musicians].

ORSINO: If music be the food of love, play on;
    Give me excess of it, that surfeiting,
    The appetite may sicken and so die.
    That strain again! It had a dying fall;°
    Oh, it came o'er my ear like the sweet sound   5
    That breathes upon a bank of violets,
    Stealing and giving odor. Enough, no more.
    'Tis not so sweet now as it was before.
    O spirit of love, how quick and fresh° art thou,
    That, notwithstanding thy capacity   10
    Receiveth as the sea, naught enters there,
    Of what validity° and pitch° soe'er,
    But falls into abatement° and low price
    Even in a minute! So full of shapes° is fancy°
    That it alone is high fantastical.°   15
CURIO: Will you go hunt, my lord?
ORSINO: What, Curio?
CURIO: The hart.
ORSINO: Why, so I do, the noblest that I have.°
    Oh, when mine eyes did see Olivia first,
    Methought she purged the air of pestilence.
    That instant was I turned into a hart,   20

SCENE Illyria Nominally on the east coast of the Adriatic Sea, but with a suggestion also of "illusion" and "delirium."   **4 fall** cadence   **9 quick and fresh** keen and hungry   **12 validity** value. **pitch** superiority. (Literally, the highest point of a falcon's flight.)   **13 abatement** depreciation. (The lover's brain entertains innumerable fantasies but soon tires of them all.)   **14 shapes** imagined forms.   **fancy** love   **15 it ... fantastical** it surpasses everything else in imaginative power.   **17 the noblest . . . have** i.e., my noblest part, my heart. (Punning on *hart*.)

And my desires, like fell° and cruel hounds,
E'er since pursue me.°

Enter Valentine.

                                   How now, what news from her?

VALENTINE: So please my lord, I might not be admitted,
But from her handmaid do return this answer:
The element° itself, till seven years' heat,°   25
Shall not behold her face at ample view;
But like a cloistress° she will veilèd walk,
And water once a day her chamber round
With eye-offending brine—all this to season°
A brother's dead love,° which she would keep fresh   30
And lasting in her sad remembrance.

ORSINO: Oh, she that hath a heart of that fine frame°
To pay this debt of love but to a brother,
How will she love, when the rich golden shaft°
Hath killed the flock of all affections else°   35
That live in her; when liver, brain, and heart,
These sovereign thrones, are all supplied, and filled
Her sweet perfections, with one self king!°
Away before me to sweet beds of flowers.
Love-thoughts lie rich when canopied with bowers.   40

                                            Exeunt.

1.2

Enter Viola, a Captain, and sailors.

VIOLA: What country, friends, is this?

CAPTAIN: This is Illyria, lady.

VIOLA: And what should I do in Illyria?
My brother he is in Elysium.°
Perchance he is not drowned. What think you, sailors?   5

21 fell fierce   **22 pursue me** (Alludes to the story in Ovid of Actaeon, who, having seen Diana bathing, was transformed into a stag and killed by his own hounds.)   **25 element** sky.   **seven years' heat** seven summers   **27 cloistress** nun secluded in a religious community   **29 season** keep fresh. (Playing on the idea of the salt in her tears.)   **30 A brother's dead love** her love for her dead brother and the memory of his love for her   **32 frame** construction   **34 golden shaft** Cupid's golden-tipped arrow, causing love. (His lead-tipped arrow causes aversion.)   **35 affections else** other feelings   **36–8 when … king** i.e., when passion, thought, and feeling all sit in majesty in their proper thrones (liver, brain, and heart), and her sweet perfections are brought to completion by her union with a single lord and husband.
4 Elysium classical abode of the blessed dead.

CAPTAIN: It is perchance that you yourself were saved.

VIOLA: Oh, my poor brother! And so perchance may he be.

CAPTAIN: True, madam, and to comfort you with chance,°
Assure yourself, after our ship did split,
When you and those poor number saved with you   10
Hung on our driving° boat, I saw your brother,
Most provident in peril, bind himself,
Courage and hope both teaching him the practice,
To a strong mast that lived° upon the sea;
Where, like Arion° on the dolphin's back,   15
I saw him hold acquaintance with the waves
So long as I could see.

VIOLA: For saying so, there's gold.   [*She gives money.*]
Mine own escape unfoldeth to my hope,
Whereto thy speech serves for authority,   20
The like of him°. Know'st thou this country?

CAPTAIN: Ay, madam, well, for I was bred and born
Not three hours' travel from this very place.

VIOLA: Who governs here?

CAPTAIN: A noble duke, in nature as in name.   25

VIOLA: What is his name?

CAPTAIN: Orsino.

VIOLA: Orsino! I have heard my father name him.
He was a bachelor then.

CAPTAIN: And so is now, or was so very late;°   30
For but a month ago I went from hence,
And then 'twas fresh in murmur°—as, you know,
What great ones do the less° will prattle of—
That he did seek the love of fair Olivia.

VIOLA: What's she?   35

CAPTAIN: A virtuous maid, the daughter of a count
That died some twelvemonth since, then leaving her
In the protection of his son, her brother,

6-7 **perchance ... perchance** Perhaps ... by mere chance   **8 chance** i.e., what one may hope that chance will bring about   **11 driving** drifting, driven by the seas   **14 lived** i.e., kept afloat   **15 Arion** a Greek poet who so charmed the dolphins with his lyre that they saved him when he leaped into the sea to escape murderous sailors   **19-21 unfoldeth ... him** offers a hopeful example that he may have escaped similarly, to which hope your speech provides support.   **30 late** lately.   **32 murmur** rumor   **33 less** social inferiors

Who shortly also died; for whose dear love,
They say, she hath abjured the sight
And company of men.   40
VIOLA: Oh, that I served that lady,
And might not be delivered° to the world
Till I had made mine own occasion mellow,°
What my estate° is!
CAPTAIN: That were hard to compass,°
Because she will admit no kind of suit,   45
No, not° the Duke's.
VIOLA: There is a fair behavior in thee, Captain,
And though that° nature with a beauteous wall
Doth oft close in pollution, yet of thee
I will believe thou hast a mind that suits   50
With this thy fair and outward character.°
I prithee, and I'll pay thee bounteously,
Conceal me what I am, and be my aid
For such disguise as haply shall become
The form of my intent°. I'll serve this duke.   55
Thou shalt present me as an eunuch° to him.
It may be worth thy pains, for I can sing
And speak to him in many sorts of music
That will allow° me very worth his service.
What else may hap, to time I will commit;   60
Only shape thou thy silence to my wit.°
CAPTAIN: Be you his eunuch, and your mute° I'll be;
When my tongue blabs, then let mine eyes not see.
VIOLA: I thank thee. Lead me on.   *Exeunt.*

1.3

Enter Sir Toby [Belch] and Maria.

SIR TOBY: What a plague means my niece to take the death of
her brother thus? I am sure care's an enemy to life.

---

42 delivered revealed, made known. (With suggestion of "born.")   **43 Till ... mellow** until the time is
ripe for my purpose   **44 estate** social rank.   **compass** encompass, bring about   **46 not** not even
48 though that though   **51 character** face or features as indicating moral qualities.   **54–5 as haply
. . . intent** as may suit the nature of my purpose.   **56 eunuch** castrato, high-voiced singer   **59 allow**
prove   **61 wit** plan, invention.   **62 mute** silent attendant. (Sometimes used of nonspeaking actors.)

MARIA: By my troth, Sir Toby, you must come in earlier o'nights. Your cousin°, my lady, takes great exceptions to your ill hours.

SIR TOBY: Why, let her except before excepted.° 5

MARIA: Ay, but you must confine yourself within the modest° limits of order.

SIR TOBY: Confine? I'll confine myself no finer° than I am. These clothes are good enough to drink in, and so be these boots too. An° they be not, let them hang them-selves in their 10 own straps.

MARIA: That quaffing and drinking will undo you. I heard my lady talk of it yesterday, and of a foolish knight that you brought in one night here to be her wooer.

SIR TOBY: Who, Sir Andrew Aguecheek?

MARIA: Ay, he. 15

SIR TOBY: He's as tall° a man as any's in Illyria.

MARIA: What's that to th' purpose?

SIR TOBY: Why, he has three thousand ducats° a year.

MARIA: Ay, but he'll have but a year in all these ducats.° He's a very fool and a prodigal. 20

SIR TOBY: Fie, that you'll say so! He plays o'th' viol-de-gamboys,° and speaks three or four languages word for word without book,° and hath all the good gifts of nature.

MARIA: He hath indeed, almost natural,° for, besides that he's a fool, he's a great quarreler, and but that he hath the gift° of a 25 coward to allay the gust° he hath in quarreling, 'tis thought among the prudent he would quickly have the gift of a grave.

SIR TOBY: By this hand, they are scoundrels and substractors° that say so of him. Who are they?

MARIA: They that add, moreover, he's drunk nightly in your company. 30

SIR TOBY: With drinking healths to my niece. I'll drink to her as long as there is a passage in my throat and drink in Illyria.

He's a coward and a coistrel° that will not drink to my niece
till his brains turn o'th' toe like a parish top.° What, wench?
Castiliano vulgo!° For here comes Sir Andrew Agueface.°   35

Enter Sir Andrew [Aguecheek].

SIR ANDREW: Sir Toby Belch! How now, Sir Toby Belch?
SIR TOBY: Sweet Sir Andrew!
SIR ANDREW: [*to Maria*] Bless you, fair shrew.°
MARIA: And you too, sir.
SIR TOBY: Accost,° Sir Andrew, accost.   40
SIR ANDREW: What's that?
SIR TOBY: My niece's chambermaid.°
SIR ANDREW: Good Mistress Accost, I desire better acquain-
tance.
MARIA: My name is Mary, sir.
SIR ANDREW: Good Mistress Mary Accost—   45
SIR TOBY: You mistake, knight. "Accost" is front° her, board° her,
woo her, assail her.
SIR ANDREW: By my troth, I would not undertake° her in this
company. Is that the meaning of "accost"?   50
MARIA: Fare you well, gentlemen. [*Going.*]
SIR TOBY: An thou let part° so, Sir Andrew, would thou mightst
never draw sword again.
SIR ANDREW: An you part so, mistress, I would I might never
draw sword again. Fair lady, do you think you have fools in   55
hand?°
MARIA: Sir, I have not you by the hand.
SIR ANDREW: Marry,° but you shall have, and here's my hand.

[He gives her his hand.]

---

33 coistrel horse-groom, base fellow   **34 parish top** a large top provided by the parish to be spun
by whipping, apparently for exercise.   **35 *Castiliano vulgo!*** (Of uncertain meaning. Possibly Sir
Toby is saying "Speak of the devil!" Castiliano is the name adopted by a devil in Haughton's *Grim
the Collier of Croydon*.)   **35 Agueface** (Like *Aguecheek*, this name betokens the thin, pale
countenance of one suffering from an ague or fever.)   **38 shrew** i.e., diminutive creature. (But with
probably unintended suggestion of shrewishness.)   **40 Accost** Go alongside (a nautical term), i.e.,
greet her, address her   **42 chambermaid** lady-in-waiting (a gentlewoman, not one who would do
menial tasks).   **46 front** confront, come alongside.   **46 board** greet, approach (as though
preparing to board in a naval encounter)   **48 undertake** have to do with. (Here with unintended
sexual suggestion, to which Maria mirthfully replies with her jokes about *dry jests, barren,* and
buttery-bar.)   **51 An . . . part** If you let her leave   **54–5 have . . . hand** i.e., have to deal with fools.
(But Maria puns on the literal sense.)   **57 Marry** i.e., Indeed. (Originally, "By the Virgin Mary.")

MARIA: Now, sir, thought is free.° I pray you, bring your hand to th' buttery-bar,° and let it drink.

SIR ANDREW: Wherefore, sweetheart? What's your metaphor? 60

MARIA: It's dry,° sir.

SIR ANDREW: Why, I think so. I am not such an ass but I can keep my hand dry.° But what's your jest?

MARIA: A dry jest, sir.

SIR ANDREW: Are you full of them? 65

MARIA: Ay, sir, I have them at my fingers' ends.° Marry, now I let go your hand, I am barren.°

[She lets go his hand.] Exit Maria.

SIR TOBY: Oh, knight, thou lack'st a cup of canary!° When did I see thee so put down?

SIR ANDREW: Never in your life, I think, unless you see canary 70 put me down.° Methinks sometimes I have no more wit than a Christian or an ordinary man has. But I am a great eater of beef, and I believe that does harm to my wit.

SIR TOBY: No question.

SIR ANDREW: An I thought that, I'd forswear it. I'll ride home tomorrow, Sir Toby. 75

SIR TOBY: *Pourquoi*,° my dear knight?

SIR ANDREW: What is "*pourquoi*"? Do or not do? I would I had bestowed that time in the tongues° that I have in fencing, dancing, and bearbaiting.° Oh, had I but followed the arts!°

SIR TOBY: Then hadst thou had an excellent head of hair. 80

SIR ANDREW: Why, would that have mended° my hair?

SIR TOBY: Past question, for thou see'st it will not curl by nature.

SIR ANDREW: But it becomes me well enough, does't not?

---

58 thought is free i.e., I may think what I like. (Proverbial; replying to *do you think . . . in hand*, above.) **59 buttery-bar** ledge on top of the half-door to the buttery or the wine cellar. (Maria's language is sexually suggestive, though Sir Andrew seems oblivious to that.) **61 dry** thirsty; also dried up, a sign of age and sexual debility **63 dry** (1) ironic (2) dull, barren. (Referring to Sir Andrew.) **66 at my fingers' ends** (1) at the ready (2) by the hand. **66 barren** i.e., empty of jests and of Sir Andrew's hand. **68 thou . . . canary** i.e., you look as if you need a drink. (*Canary* is a sweet wine from the Canary Islands.) **71 put me down** (1) baffle my wits (2) lay me out flat. **76 *Pourquoi*** Why **78 tongues** languages. (Sir Toby then puns on "tongs," curling irons.) **79 bearbaiting** the sport of setting dogs on a chained bear. **the arts** the liberal arts, learning. (But Sir Toby plays on the phrase as meaning "artifice," the antithesis of *nature*.) **81 mended** improved

SIR TOBY: Excellent. It hangs like flax on a distaff;° and I hope to
see a huswife take thee between her legs and spin it off.°   85
SIR ANDREW: Faith, I'll home tomorrow, Sir Toby. Your niece
will not be seen, or if she be, it's four to one she'll none of me.
The Count° himself here hard° by woos her.
SIR TOBY: She'll none o'th' Count. She'll not match above her
degree,° neither in estate,° years, nor wit; I have heard her   90
swear't. Tut, there's life in't,° man.
SIR ANDREW: I'll stay a month longer. I am a fellow o'th' strangest
mind i'th' world; I delight in masques and revels sometimes
altogether.
SIR TOBY: Art thou good at these kickshawses,° knight?   95
SIR ANDREW: As any man in Illyria, whatsoever he be, under the
degree of my betters,° and yet I will not compare with an old
man.°
SIR TOBY: What is thy excellence in a galliard,° knight?
SIR ANDREW: Faith, I can cut a caper.°
SIR TOBY: And I can cut the mutton to't.   100
SIR ANDREW: And I think I have the back-trick° simply as strong
as any man in Illyria.
SIR TOBY: Wherefore are these things hid? Wherefore have
these gifts a curtain before 'em? Are they like to take dust, like
Mistress Mall's picture?° Why dost thou not go to church in a   105
galliard° and come home in a coranto?° My very walk should
be a jig; I would not so much as make water but in a sink-a-
pace.° What dost thou mean? Is it a world to hide virtues° in? I
did think, by the excellent constitution of thy leg, it was
formed under the star of a galliard.°   110

84 **distaff** a staff for holding the flax, tow, or wool in spinning   85 **spin it off** i.e., (1) treat your
flaxen hair as though it were flax on a distaff to be spun (2) cause you to lose hair as a result of
venereal disease (3) make you ejaculate. (*Huswife* suggests "hussy," "whore.")   88 **Count** i.e.,
Duke Orsino, sometimes referred to as Count. **hard** near   90 **degree** social position. **estate**
fortune, social position   91 **there's life in't** i.e., while there's life there's hope   95 **kickshawses**
delicacies, fancy trifles. (From the French, *quelque chose*.)   96–7 **under . . . betters** excepting those
who are above me   97–8 **old man** i.e., one experienced through age.   98 **galliard** lively dance in
triple time   99 **cut a caper** make a lively leap. (But Sir Toby puns on the *caper* used to make a
sauce served with mutton. *Mutton*, in turn, suggests "whore.")   101 **back-trick** backward step in
the galliard. (With sexual innuendo; the back was associated with sexual vigor.)   104 **like to take**
likely to collect   105 **Mistress Mall's picture** i.e., perhaps the portrait of some woman protected
from light and dust, as many pictures were, by curtains. (*Mall* is a diminutive of *Mary*.)   106
coranto lively running dance.   107–8 **sink-a-pace** dance like the galliard. (French *cinquepace*. Sink
also suggests a cesspool into which one might urinate.)   108 **virtues** talents   110 **under . . .
galliard** i.e., under a star favorable to dancing.

SIR ANDREW: Ay, 'tis strong, and it does indifferent well° in a dun-colored stock.° Shall we set about some revels?

SIR TOBY: What shall we do else? Were we not born under Taurus?°

SIR ANDREW: Taurus? That's sides and heart. 115

SIR TOBY: No, sir, it is legs and thighs. Let me see thee caper. [*Sir Andrew capers.*] Ha, higher! Ha, ha, excel-lent! *Exeunt.*

1.4

Enter Valentine, and Viola in man's attire.

VALENTINE: If the Duke continue these favors towards you, Cesario, you are like° to be much advanced. He hath known you but three days, and already you are no stranger.

VIOLA: You either fear his humor° or my negligence, that you call in question the continuance of his love. Is he inconstant, sir, in his favors?

VALENTINE: No, believe me. 5

Enter Duke [Orsino], Curio, and attendants.

VIOLA: I thank you. Here comes the Count.

ORSINO: Who saw Cesario, ho?

VIOLA: On your attendance,° my lord, here.

ORSINO: Stand you awhile aloof.° [*The others stand aside.*] Cesario,
Thou know'st no less but all. I have unclasped 10
To thee the book even of my secret soul.
Therefore, good youth, address thy gait° unto her;
Be not denied access, stand at her doors,
And tell them,° there thy fixèd foot shall grow
Till thou have audience.

VIOLA: Sure, my noble lord, 15
If she be so abandoned to her sorrow
As it is spoke, she never will admit me.

---

111 **indifferent well** well enough. (Said complacently.) 112 **dun-colored stock** mouse-colored stocking. 114 **Taurus** zodiacal sign. (Sir Andrew is mistaken, since Leo governed sides and hearts in medical astrology. Taurus governed legs and thighs, or, more commonly, neck and throat.)
2 **like** likely 3 **humor** changeableness 8 **On your attendance** Ready to do you service 9 **aloof** aside. 12 **address thy gait** go 14 **them** i.e., Olivia's servants

ORSINO: Be clamorous and leap all civil bounds°
          Rather than make unprofited return.
VIOLA: Say I do speak with her, my lord, what then?   20
ORSINO: Oh, then unfold the passion of my love;
          Surprise° her with discourse of my dear° faith.
          It shall become° thee well to act my woes;
          She will attend it better in thy youth
          Than in a nuncio's° of more grave aspect.   25
VIOLA: I think not so, my lord.
ORSINO: Dear lad, believe it;
          For they shall yet belie thy happy years
          That say thou art a man. Diana's lip
          Is not more smooth and rubious;° thy small pipe°   30
          Is as the maiden's organ, shrill and sound,°
          And all is semblative° a woman's part.
          I know thy constellation° is right apt
          For this affair.—Some four or five attend him.
          All, if you will, for I myself am best   35
          When least in company.—Prosper well in this,
          And thou shalt live as freely as thy lord,
          To call his fortunes thine.
VIOLA: I'll do my best
          To woo your lady. [Aside] Yet a barful strife!°   40
          Whoe'er I woo, myself would be his wife.   Exeunt.

1.5

              Enter Maria and Clown [Feste].

MARIA: Nay, either tell me where thou hast been, or I will not
          open my lips so wide as a bristle may enter in way of thy ex-
          cuse. My lady will hang thee for thy absence.
FESTE: Let her hang me. He that is well hanged in this world
          needs to fear no colors.°   5

---

18 civil bounds bounds of civility   **22 Surprise** Take by storm. (A military term.) **dear** heartfelt
23 become suit   **25 nuncio's** messenger's   **30 rubious** ruby red.   **pipe** voice, throat   **31 shrill and
sound** high and clear, uncracked   **32 semblative** resembling, like   **33 constellation** i.e., nature as
determined by your horoscope   **40 barful strife** endeavor full of impediments.
5 fear no colors i.e., fear no foe, fear nothing. (With pun on *colors*, worldly deceptions, and
"collars," halters or nooses.)

MARIA: Make that good.°

FESTE: He shall see none to fear.°

MARIA: A good Lenten° answer. I can tell thee where that saying was born, of "I fear no colors."

FESTE: Where, good Mistress Mary?

MARIA: In the wars,° and that may you be bold to say in your foolery.°   10

FESTE: Well, God give them wisdom that have it; and those that are fools, let them use their talents.°

MARIA: Yet you will be hanged for being so long absent; or to be turned away,° is not that as good as a hanging to you?

FESTE: Many a good hanging° prevents a bad marriage; and for° turning away, let summer bear it out.°   15

MARIA: You are resolute, then?

FESTE: Not so, neither, but I am resolved on two points.°

MARIA: That if one break, the other will hold; or if both break, your gaskins° fall.

FESTE: Apt, in good faith, very apt. Well, go thy way. If Sir Toby would leave drinking, thou wert as witty a piece of Eve's flesh   20
as any in Illyria.°

MARIA: Peace, you rogue, no more o' that. Here comes my lady. Make your excuse wisely, you were best.°   [Exit.]

Enter Lady Olivia with Malvolio, [and attendants].

FESTE: [aside] Wit, an't° be thy will, put me into good fooling! Those wits that think they have thee do very oft prove fools, and I that am sure I lack thee may pass for a wise man. For   25
what says Quinapalus?° "Better a witty fool than a foolish wit."—God bless thee, lady!

WILLIAM SHAKESPEARE

6 **Make that good** Explain that.   7 **He . . . fear** i.e., The hanged man will be dead and unable to see anything.   8 **Lenten** meager, scanty (like Lenten fare), and morbid   9 **In the wars** (Where *colors* would mean "military standards, enemy flags"—the literal meaning of the proverb.)
9–10 **that . . . foolery** that's an answer you may be bold to use in your fool's conundrums. (*Colors* here refer to military banners and insignia used to align rows of fighting men in battle.)
11 **talents** abilities. (Also alluding to the parable of the talents, Matthew 25:14–29, and to "talons," claws.)   13 **turned away** dismissed. (Possibly also meaning "turned off," "hanged.")   14 **good hanging** (With possible bawdy pun on "being well hung.")   14 **for** as for.   15 **let . . . out** i.e., let mild weather make dismissal endurable.   17 **points** (Maria plays on the meaning "laces used to hold up hose or breeches.")   18 **gaskins** wide breeches   20 **thou . . . Illyria** (Feste may be hinting ironically that Maria would be a suitable mate for Sir Toby.)   22 **you were best** it would be best for you.   23 **an't** if it   26 **Quinapalus** (Feste's invented authority.)

OLIVIA: [*to attendants*] Take the fool away.

FESTE: Do you not hear, fellows? Take away the lady.

OLIVIA: Go to,° you're a dry° fool. I'll no more of you. Besides,
            you grow dishonest.   30

FESTE: Two faults, madonna,° that drink and good counsel will
            amend. For give the dry fool drink, then is the fool not dry.
            Bid the dishonest man mend himself; if he mend, he is no
            longer dishonest; if he cannot, let the botcher° mend him.
            Anything that's mended is but patched;° virtue that trans-   35
            gresses is but patched with sin, and sin that amends is but
            patched with virtue. If that this simple syllogism will serve,
            so;° if it will not, what remedy? As there is no true cuckold but
            calamity, so beauty's a flower.° The lady bade take away the
            fool; therefore I say again, take her away.

OLIVIA: Sir, I bade them take away you.   40

FESTE: Misprision° in the highest degree! Lady, *cucullus non facit
            monachum;*° that's as much to say as I wear not motley° in my
            brain. Good madonna, give me leave to prove you a fool.

OLIVIA: Can you do it?

FESTE: Dexteriously, good madonna.

OLIVIA: Make your proof.   45

FESTE: I must catechize you for it, madonna. Good my mouse of
            virtue,° answer me.

OLIVIA: Well, sir, for want of other idleness,° I'll bide° your proof.

FESTE: Good madonna, why mourn'st thou?

OLIVIA: Good fool, for my brother's death.

FESTE: I think his soul is in hell, madonna.   50

OLIVIA: I know his soul is in heaven, fool.

FESTE: The more fool, madonna, to mourn for your brother's
            soul, being in heaven.—Take away the fool, gentlemen.

---

29 Go to (An expression of annoyance or expostulation.) **dry** dull   **31 madonna** my lady
34 botcher mender of old clothes and shoes. (Playing on two senses of *mend:* "reform" and
"repair.")   **34–5 Anything . . . patched** i.e., Life is patched or parti-colored like the Fool's
garment, a mix of good and bad   **37 so** well and good   **38–9 As . . . flower** (Nonsense, yet with a
suggestion that Olivia has wedded calamity but should not be faithful to it, for the natural
course is to seize the moment of youth and beauty before we lose it.)   **41 Misprision** Mistake,
misunderstanding. (A legal term meaning a wrongful action or misdemeanor.)   **41–2 *cucullus . . .
monachum*** the cowl does not make the monk   **42 motley** the many-colored garment of jesters
46–47 Good . . . virtue My good, virtuous mouse. (A term of endearment.)   **48 idleness** pastime.
bide endure

OLIVIA: What think you of this fool, Malvolio? Doth he not mend?°

MALVOLIO: Yes, and shall do till the pangs of death shake him. 55 Infirmity, that decays the wise, doth ever make the better fool.

FESTE: God send you, sir, a speedy infirmity for the better increasing your folly! Sir Toby will be sworn that I am no fox, but he will not pass° his word for two pence that you are no fool.

OLIVIA: How say you to that, Malvolio? 60

MALVOLIO: I marvel Your Ladyship takes delight in such a barren rascal. I saw him put down the other day with° an ordinary fool that has no more brain than a stone. Look you now, he's out of his guard° already. Unless you laugh and minister occasion° to him, he is gagged. I protest° I take these wise men 65 that crow° so at these set° kind of fools no better than the fools' zanies.°

OLIVIA: Oh, you are sick of self-love, Malvolio, and taste with a distempered° appetite. To be generous,° guiltless, and of free° disposition is to take those things for bird-bolts° that you deem cannon bullets. There is no slander in an allowed° fool, 70 though he do nothing but rail; nor no railing in a known discreet man, though he do nothing but reprove.°

FESTE: Now Mercury endue thee with leasing,° for thou speak'st well of fools!

Enter Maria.

MARIA: Madam, there is at the gate a young gentleman much desires to speak with you.

OLIVIA: From the Count Orsino, is it? 75

MARIA: I know not, madam. 'Tis a fair young man, and well attended.

WILLIAM SHAKESPEARE

54 mend i.e., improve, grow more amusing. (But Malvolio uses the word to mean "grow more like a fool.")   **59 pass** give   **62 with** by   **64 out of his guard** defenseless, unprovided with a witty answer   **64–65 minister occasion** provide opportunity (for his fooling)   **65 protest** avow, declare.   **67 crow** laugh stridently   **set** artificial, stereotyped.   **zanies** assistants, aping attendants.   **68 distempered** diseased.   **generous** noble-minded.   **free** magnanimous   **69 bird-bolts** blunt arrows for shooting small birds   **70 allowed** licensed (to speak freely)   **70–72 There . . . reprove** Both a licensed fool and a man known for discretion can criticize freely without being accused of slander in the first instance or railing in the second. (In rebuking Malvolio here, Olivia implies that he is not behaving like a "known discreet man.")   **73 Now . . . leasing** i.e., May Mercury, the god of deception, make you a skillful liar

OLIVIA: Who of my people hold him in delay?

MARIA: Sir Toby, madam,° your kinsman.

OLIVIA: Fetch him off, I pray you. He speaks nothing but madman.° Fie on him! [*Exit Maria.*]
Go you, Malvolio. If it be a suit from the Count, I am   80
sick or not at home; what you will, to dismiss it.

> *Exit Malvolio.* Now you see, sir, how your fooling grows
> old,° and people dislike it.

FESTE: Thou hast spoke for us, madonna, as if thy eldest son
should be a fool; whose skull Jove cram with brains, for—here
he comes—

> *Enter Sir Toby.*

one of thy kin has a most weak *pia mater.*°

OLIVIA: By mine honor, half drunk.—What is he at the gate, cousin?°

SIR TOBY: A gentleman.   85

OLIVIA: A gentleman? What gentleman?

SIR TOBY: 'Tis a gentleman here—[*He belches.*] A plague o' these
pickle-herring! [*To Feste*] How now, sot?°

FESTE: Good Sir Toby.

OLIVIA: Cousin,° cousin, how have you come so early by this
lethargy?

SIR TOBY: Lechery? I defy lechery. There's one at the gate.   90

OLIVIA: Ay, marry, what is he?

SIR TOBY: Let him be the devil an he will, I care not. Give me
faith,° say I. Well, it's all one.° *Exit.*

OLIVIA: What's a drunken man like, Fool?   95

FESTE: Like a drowned man, a fool, and a madman. One draft
above heat° makes him a fool, the second mads him, and a
third drowns him.

OLIVIA: Go thou and seek the crowner,° and let him sit o' my
coz;° for he's in the third degree of drink, he's drowned. Go,
look after him.   100

---

78 madman i.e., the words of madness. **81 old** stale **83** *pia mater* i.e., brain. (Actually the soft
membrane enclosing the brain.) **87 sot** (1) fool (2) drunkard. **89 Cousin** Kinsman. (Here, uncle.)
92–93 Give me faith i.e., to resist the devil. **93 it's all one** it doesn't matter. **96–97 draft above
heat** helping of drink raising his temperature above normal bodily warmth. **98 crowner** coroner
98–99 sit o' my coz hold an inquest on my kinsman (Sir Toby)

FESTE: He is but mad yet, madonna; and the fool shall look to the madman. [*Exit.*]

Enter Malvolio.

MALVOLIO: Madam, yond young fellow swears he will speak with you. I told him you were sick; he takes on him to understand so much, and therefore comes to speak with you. I told him you were asleep; he seems to have a foreknowl- 105 edge of that too, and therefore comes to speak with you. What is to be said to him, lady? He's fortified against any denial.

OLIVIA: Tell him he shall not speak with me.

MALVOLIO: He's been told so; and he says he'll stand at your door like a sheriff's post,° and be the supporter° to a bench, but he'll speak with you.

OLIVIA: What kind o' man is he? 110

MALVOLIO: Why, of mankind.

OLIVIA: What manner of man?

MALVOLIO: Of very ill manner. He'll speak with you, will you or no.

OLIVIA: Of what personage and years is he?

MALVOLIO: Not yet old enough for a man, nor young enough for 115 a boy; as a squash° is before 'tis a peascod,° or a codling° when 'tis almost an apple. 'Tis with him in standing water° between boy and man. He is very well-favored,° and he speaks very shrewishly.° One would think his mother's milk were scarce out of him.

OLIVIA: Let him approach. Call in my gentlewoman. 120

MALVOLIO: Gentlewoman, my lady calls. *Exit.*

Enter Maria.

OLIVIA: Give me my veil. Come, throw it o'er my face.
We'll once more hear Orsino's embassy. [*Olivia veils.*]

Enter Viola.

---

108 sheriff's post post before the sheriff's door to mark a residence of authority, often elaborately carved and decorated. **supporter** prop **116 squash** unripe pea pod. **peascod** ripe pea pod. (The image suggests that the boy's testicles have not yet dropped.) **codling** unripe apple **117 in standing water** at the turn of the tide **118 well-favored** good-looking. **119 shrewishly** sharply.

VIOLA: The honorable lady of the house, which is she?

OLIVIA: Speak to me; I shall answer for her. Your will?

VIOLA: Most radiant, exquisite, and unmatchable beauty—I pray 125
you, tell me if this be the lady of the house, for I never saw her.
I would be loath to castaway my speech; for besides that it is
excellently well penned, I have taken great pains to con° it.
Good beauties, let me sustain no scorn; I am very comptible,°
even to the least sinister° usage.

OLIVIA: Whence came you, sir? 130

VIOLA: I can say little more than I have studied, and that question's out of my part. Good gentle one, give me modest° assurance if you be the lady of the house, that I may proceed in
my speech.

OLIVIA: Are you a comedian?°

VIOLA: No, my profound heart;° and yet, by the very fangs of 135
malice, I swear I am not that I play.° Are you the lady of the
house?

OLIVIA: If I do not usurp myself,° I am.

VIOLA: Most certain, if you are she, you do usurp your-self;° for
what is yours to bestow is not yours to reserve. But this is
from° my commission. I will on with my speech in your
praise, and then show you the heart of my message.

OLIVIA: Come to what is important in't. I forgive you° the praise. 140

VIOLA: Alas, I took great pains to study it, and 'tis poetical.

OLIVIA: It is the more like to be feigned. I pray you, keep it in.
I heard you were saucy at my gates, and allowed your
approach rather to wonder at you than to hear you. If you
be not mad,° begone; if you have reason,° be brief. 'Tis not
that time of moon° with me to make one° in so skipping a
dialogue.

MARIA: Will you hoist sail, sir? Here lies your way. 145

127 con memorize   128 comptible susceptible, sensitive   129 least sinister slightest discourteous
132 modest reasonable   134 comedian actor.   135 my profound heart my most wise lady; or, in all
sincerity 135–6 by . . . I play (Viola hints at her true identity, which malice itself might not detect.)
137 do . . . myself am not an impostor   138 usurp yourself i.e., misappropriate yourself, by
withholding yourself from love and marriage   139 from outside of   140 forgive you excuse you
from repeating   143 not mad i.e., not altogether mad   144 reason sanity.   moon (The moon was
thought to affect lunatics according to its changing phases.)   make one take part.

VIOLA: No, good swabber,° I am to hull° here a little longer.—
Some mollification for° your giant,° sweet lady. Tell me your
mind; I am a messenger.

OLIVIA: Sure you have some hideous matter to deliver, when the
courtesy° of it is so fearful. Speak your office.°

VIOLA: It alone concerns your ear. I bring no overture° of war, no   150
taxation of homage.° I hold the olive° in my hand; my words
are as full of peace as matter.

OLIVIA: Yet you began rudely.° What are you? What would you?

VIOLA: The rudeness that hath appeared in me have I learned
from my entertainment.° What I am and what I would are as
secret as maidenhead°—to your ears, divinity;° to any other's,   155
profanation.

OLIVIA: [to the others] Give us the place here alone. We will hear
this divinity. [Exeunt Maria and attendants.]
Now, sir, what is your text?

VIOLA: Most sweet lady—

OLIVIA: A comfortable° doctrine, and much may be said of it.
Where lies your text?   160

VIOLA: In Orsino's bosom.

OLIVIA: In his bosom? In what chapter of his bosom?

VIOLA: To answer by the method,° in the first of his heart.

OLIVIA: Oh, I have read it. It is heresy. Have you no more to say?

VIOLA: Good madam, let me see your face.   165

OLIVIA: Have you any commission from your lord to negotiate
with my face? You are now out of° your text. But we will draw
the curtain and show you the picture. [Unveiling.] Look you, sir,
such a one I was this present.° Is't not well done?

VIOLA: Excellently done, if God did all.   170

---

146 **swabber** one in charge of washing the decks. (A nautical retort to *hoist sail*.) **hull** lie with
sails furled   147 **Some ... for** i.e., Please mollify, pacify.   **giant** i.e., the diminutive Maria
who, like many giants in medieval romances, is guarding the lady   149 **courtesy** i.e.,
complimentary, "poetical" introduction. (Or Olivia may refer to Cesario's importunate manner
at her gate, as reported by Malvolio.)   **office** commission, business.   150 **overture** declaration.
(Literally, opening.)   151 **taxation of homage** demand for tribute.   **olive** olive-branch
(signifying peace)   153 **Yet ... rudely** i.e., Yet you were saucy at my gates.   154 **entertainment**
reception.   155 **maidenhead** virginity   155 **divinity** sacred discourse   159 **comfortable**
comforting   163 **To ... method** i.e., To continue the metaphor of delivering a sermon, begun
with *divinity* and *what is your text* and continued in *doctrine, heresy*, etc.   167 **out of** straying
from   169 **such ... present** this is a recent portrait of me. (Since it was customary to hang
curtains in front of pictures, Olivia in unveiling speaks as if she were displaying a picture
of herself.)

OLIVIA: 'Tis in grain,° sir; 'twill endure wind and weather.
VIOLA: 'Tis beauty truly blent,° whose red and white
Nature's own sweet and cunning° hand laid on.
Lady, you are the cruel'st she alive
If you will lead these graces to the grave   175
And leave the world no copy.°
OLIVIA: Oh, sir, I will not be so hard hearted. I will give out divers
schedules° of my beauty. It shall be inventoried, and every
particle and utensil° labeled° to my will: as, item, two lips,
indifferent° red; item, two gray eyes, with lids to them; item,   180
one neck, one chin, and so forth. Were you sent hither to
praise° me?
VIOLA: I see you what you are: you are too proud.
But, if° you were the devil, you are fair.
My lord and master loves you. Oh, such love
Could be but recompensed, though you were crowned   185
The nonpareil of beauty!°
OLIVIA: How does he love me?
VIOLA: With adorations, fertile° tears,
With groans that thunder love, with sighs of fire.
OLIVIA: Your lord does know my mind; I cannot love him.   190
Yet I suppose him virtuous, know him noble,
Of great estate, of fresh and stainless youth,
In voices well divulged,° free,° learned, and valiant,
And in dimension and the shape of nature°
A gracious° person. But yet I cannot love him.   195
He might have took his answer long ago.
VIOLA: If I did love you in my master's flame,°
With such a suff'ring, such a deadly° life,
In your denial I would find no sense;
I would not understand it.   200
OLIVIA: Why, what would you?

---

171 **in grain** fast dyed   172 **blent** blended   173 **cunning** skillful   176 **copy** i.e., a child. (But Olivia uses the word to mean "transcript.")   178 **schedules** inventories   179 **utensil** article, item.   **labeled** added as a codicil   180 **indifferent** somewhat   181 **praise** (With pun on "appraise.")   183 **if** even if 184–6 **Oh . . . beauty!** i.e., Even if you were the most beautiful woman alive, that beauty could do no more than repay my master's love for you!   188 **fertile** copious   193 **In . . . divulged** well spoken of. **free** generous   194 **in . . . nature** in his physical form   195 **gracious** graceful, attractive 197 **flame** passion   198 **deadly** deathlike

VIOLA: Make me a willow cabin° at your gate
And call upon my soul° within the house;
Write loyal cantons° of contemnèd° love
And sing them loud even in the dead of night;   205
Hallow° your name to the reverberate hills,
And make the babbling gossip of the air°
Cry out "Olivia!" Oh, you should not rest
Between the elements of air° and earth
But you should pity me!   210
OLIVIA: You might do much.
What is your parentage?
VIOLA: Above my fortunes, yet my state° is well:
I am a gentleman.
OLIVIA: Get you to your lord.   215
I cannot love him. Let him send no more—
Unless, perchance, you come to me again
To tell me how he takes it. Fare you well.
I thank you for your pains. Spend this for me.

[She offers a purse.]

VIOLA: I am no fee'd post,° lady. Keep your purse.   220
My master, not myself, lacks recompense.
Love make his heart of flint that you shall love,°
And let your fervor, like my master's, be
Placed in contempt! Farewell, fair cruelty.   *Exit.*
OLIVIA: "What is your parentage?"   225
"Above my fortunes, yet my state is well:
I am a gentleman." I'll be sworn thou art!
Thy tongue, thy face, thy limbs, actions, and spirit
Do give thee fivefold blazon.° Not too fast! Soft,° soft!
Unless the master were the man.° How now?   230
Even so quickly may one catch the plague?
Methinks I feel this youth's perfections
With an invisible and subtle stealth

---

202 **willow cabin** shelter, hut. (Willow was a symbol of unrequited love.)   203 **my soul** i.e., Olivia
204 **cantons** songs.   **contemnèd** rejected   206 **Hallow** (1) halloo (2) bless   207 **babbling . . .**
air echo   209 **Between . . . air** i.e., anywhere   213 **state** social standing   220 **fee'd post**
messenger to be tipped   223 **Love . . . love** May Cupid make the heart of the man you love as
hard as flint   229 **blazon** heraldic description.   **Soft** Wait a minute   230 **Unless . . . man** i.e.,
Unless Cesario and Orsino changed places.

To creep in at mine eyes. Well, let it be.—
What ho, Malvolio! 235

Enter Malvolio.

MALVOLIO: Here, madam, at your service.
OLIVIA: Run after that same peevish messenger,
The County's° man. He left this ring behind him,

[giving a ring]

Would I or not.° Tell him I'll none of it. 240
Desire him not to flatter with° his lord,
Nor hold him up with hopes; I am not for him.
If that the youth will come this way tomorrow,
I'll give him reasons for't. Hie thee,° Malvolio.
MALVOLIO: Madam, I will. *Exit.*
OLIVIA: I do I know not what, and fear to find 245
Mine eye too great a flatterer for my mind.°
Fate, show thy force. Ourselves we do not owe.°
What is decreed must be; and be this so. *[Exit.]*

2.1

Enter Antonio and Sebastian.

ANTONIO: Will you stay no longer? Nor will you not° that I go
with you?
SEBASTIAN: By your patience,° no. My stars shine darkly over
me. The malignancy° of my fate might perhaps distemper°
yours; therefore I shall crave of you your leave that I may bear
my evils alone. It were a bad recompense for your love to lay
any of them on you. 5
ANTONIO: Let me yet know of you whither you are bound.
SEBASTIAN: No, sooth,° sir; my determinate° voyage is mere extravagancy.° But I perceive in you so excellent a touch of modesty that you will not extort from me what I am willing° to

---

239 County's Count's, i.e., Duke's   **240 Would I or not** whether I wanted it or not.   **241 flatter with**
encourage   **243 Hie thee** Hasten   **246 Mine . . . mind** i.e., that my eyes (through which love
enters the soul) have deceived my reason.   **247 owe** own, control.
1 Nor will you not Do you not wish   **2 patience** leave   **3 malignancy** malevolence (of the stars;
also in a medical sense)   **distemper** infect   **7 sooth** truly.   **determinate** intended, determined
upon   **8 extravagancy** aimless wandering.   **9 am willing . . . in** wish to keep secret

keep in; therefore it charges me in manners° the rather to   10
express° myself. You must know of me then, Antonio, my
name is Sebastian, which I called Roderigo. My father was that
Sebastian of Messaline° whom I know you have heard of. He
left behind him myself and a sister, both born in an hour.° If
the heavens had been pleased, would we had so ended! But   15
you, sir, altered that, for some hour° before you took me from
the breach of the sea° was my sister drowned.

ANTONIO: Alas the day!

SEBASTIAN: A lady, sir, though it was said she much resembled
me, was yet of many accounted beautiful. But though I could   20
not with such estimable wonder° over-far believe that, yet
thus far I will boldly publish° her: she bore a mind that envy°
could not but call fair. She is drowned already, sir, with salt
water, though I seem to drown her remembrance again with
more.

ANTONIO: Pardon me, sir, your bad entertainment.°   25

SEBASTIAN: O good Antonio, forgive me your trouble.°

ANTONIO: If you will not murder° me for my love, let me be your
servant.

SEBASTIAN: If you will not undo what you have done, that is, kill
him whom you have recovered,° desire it not. Fare ye well at
once. My bosom is full of kindness,° and I am yet so near the   30
manners of my mother° that upon the least occasion more
mine eyes will tell tales of me. I am bound to the Count
Orsino's court. Farewell.   *Exit.*

ANTONIO: The gentleness of all the gods go with thee!
I have many enemies in Orsino's court,   35
Else would I very shortly see thee there.
But come what may, I do adore thee so
That danger shall seem sport, and I will go.   *Exit.*

---

10 it . . . manners it is incumbent upon me in all courtesy   **11 express** reveal   **13 Messaline**
possibly Messina, or, more likely, Massila (the modern Marseilles). In Plautus's *Menaechmi*,
Massilians and Illyrians are mentioned together.   **14 in an hour** in the same hour.   **16 some hour**
about an hour   **17 breach of the sea** surf   **21 estimable wonder** admiring judgment   **22 publish**
proclaim   **22 envy** even malice   **25 Pardon . . . entertainment** i.e., I'm sorry I cannot offer you
better hospitality and comfort.   **26 your trouble** the trouble I put you to.   **27 murder . . . love** i.e.,
cause me to die from lacking your love   **29 recovered** rescued, restored   **30 kindness** emotion,
affection   **31 manners of my mother** i.e., womanly inclination to weep

2.2

Enter Viola and Malvolio, at several° doors.

MALVOLIO: Were not you ev'n now with the Countess Olivia?

VIOLA: Even now, sir. On a moderate pace I have since arrived but hither.

MALVOLIO: She returns this ring to you, sir. You might have saved me my pains, to have taken° it away yourself. She adds, moreover, that you should put your lord into a desperate° as-   5 surance she will none of him. And one thing more: that you be never so hardy to come° again in his affairs, unless it be to report your lord's taking of this. Receive it so.

VIOLA: She took the ring of me. I'll none of it.°

MALVOLIO: Come, sir, you peevishly threw it to her, and her will is it   10 should be so returned. [*He throws down the ring.*] If it be worth stooping for, there it lies, in your eye;° if not, be it his that finds it. *Exit.*

VIOLA: [*picking up the ring*]

I left no ring with her. What means this lady?
Fortune forbid my outside have not charmed° her!   15
She made good view of me, indeed so much
That sure methought her eyes had lost her tongue,°
For she did speak in starts, distractedly.
She loves me, sure! The cunning of her passion
Invites me in° this churlish messenger.   20
None of my lord's ring? Why, he sent her none.
I am the man.° If it be so—as 'tis—
Poor lady, she were better love a dream.
Disguise, I see, thou art a wickedness
Wherein the pregnant enemy° does much.   25
How easy is it for the proper false°
In women's waxen° hearts to set their forms!°
Alas, our frailty is the cause, not we,

0.1 several different   **4 to have taken** by taking   **5 desperate** without hope   **7 so hardy to come** so bold as to come   **9 She . . . it** (Viola tells a quick and friendly lie to shield Olivia.)   **12 in your eye** in plain sight   **15 charmed** enchanted   **17 her eyes . . . tongue** i.e., the sight of me had deprived her of speech   **20 in** in the person of   **22 the man** the man of her choice.   **25 the pregnant enemy** the resourceful enemy (either Satan or Cupid)   **26 the proper false** deceptively handsome men   **27 waxen** i.e., malleable, impressionable.   **set their forms** stamp their images (as of a seal).

For such as we are made of, such we be.°
How will this fadge?° My master loves her dearly,   30
And I, poor monster,° fond° as much on him;
And she, mistaken, seems to dote on me.
What will become of this? As I am man,
My state is desperate for my master's love;
As I am woman—now, alas the day!—   35
What thriftless° sighs shall poor Olivia breathe!
O Time, thou must untangle this, not I;
It is too hard a knot for me t'untie.   [*Exit.*]

2.3

Enter Sir Toby and Sir Andrew.

SIR TOBY: Approach, Sir Andrew. Not to be abed after midnight
is to be up betimes;° and *diluculo surgere,*° thou know'st—

SIR ANDREW: Nay, by my troth, I know not, but I know to be up
late is to be up late.

SIR TOBY: A false conclusion. I hate it as an unfilled can.° To be   5
up after midnight and to go to bed then, is early; so that to go
to bed after midnight is to go to bed betimes. Does not our
lives consist of the four elements?°

SIR ANDREW: Faith, so they say, but I think it rather consists of
eating and drinking.   10

SIR TOBY: Thou'rt a scholar; let us therefore eat and drink.—
Marian, I say, a stoup° of wine!

Enter Clown [Feste].

SIR ANDREW: Here comes the Fool, i'faith.

FESTE: How now, my hearts! Did you never see the picture of
"we three"°?

SIR TOBY: Welcome, ass. Now let's have a catch.°   15

SIR ANDREW: By my troth, the Fool has an excellent breast.° I
had rather than forty shillings I had such a leg,° and so sweet a

---

28–9 our . . . be i.e., the fault lies not in us as individuals, but in the frailty of female nature   **30 fadge**
turn out   **31 monster** i.e., being both man and woman. **fond** dote   **36 thriftless** unprofitable
2 betimes early.   *diluculo surgere* (*saluberrimum est*) to rise early is most healthful. (A sentence from
Lilly's *Latin Grammar.*)   **5 can** tankard   **8 four elements** i.e., fire, air, water, and earth, the elements
that were thought to make up all matter.   **12 stoup** drinking vessel   **13–4 picture of "we three"**
picture of two fools or asses inscribed "we three," the spectator being the third   **15 catch** round.
16 breast voice.   **17 leg** (for dancing)

breath to sing, as the Fool has. In sooth, thou wast in very gracious fooling last night, when thou spok'st of Pigrogromitus, of
the Vapians passing the equinoctial of Queubus°. 'Twas very   20
good, i'faith. I sent thee sixpence for thy leman.° Hadst it?

FESTE: I did impeticos thy gratillity;° for Malvolio's nose is no
whipstock.° My lady has a white hand,° and the Myrmidons°
are no bottle-ale houses.°

SIR ANDREW: Excellent! Why, this is the best fooling, when all is
done. Now, a song.   25

SIR TOBY: Come on, there is sixpence for you. [He gives money.]
Let's have a song.

SIR ANDREW: There's a testril° of me too. [He gives money.] If one
knight give a—

FESTE: Would you have a love song, or a song of good life?

SIR TOBY: A love song, a love song.   30

SIR ANDREW: Ay, ay, I care not for good life.°

FESTE: (sings)
O mistress mine, where are you roaming?
Oh, stay and hear, your true love 's coming,
That can sing both high and low.   35
Trip no further, pretty sweeting;
Journeys end in lovers' meeting,
Every wise man's son doth know.

SIR ANDREW: Excellent good, i'faith.

SIR TOBY: Good, good.   40

FESTE: [sings]
What is love? 'Tis not hereafter;
Present mirth hath present laughter;
What's to come is still° unsure.
In delay there lies no plenty.
Then come kiss me, sweet and twenty;°   45
Youth's a stuff will not endure.

19–20 Pigrogromitus . . . Queubus (Feste's mock erudition.) **21 leman** sweetheart. **22 impeticos
thy gratillity** (Suggests "impetticoat, or pocket up, thy gratuity.") **22–3 is no whipstock** is no whip-
handle. (More nonsense, but perhaps suggesting that Malvolio's nose for smelling out faults does
not give him the right to punish, so that he need not be feared.) **23 has a white hand** i.e., is lady-
like. (But Feste's speech may be mere nonsense.) **Myrmidons** followers of Achilles. **23–4 bottle-
ale houses** (Used contemptuously of taverns because they sold low-class drink.) **27 testril** tester,
a coin worth sixpence **31 good life** virtuous living. (Or perhaps Feste means simply "life's
pleasures," but is misunderstood by Sir Andrew to mean "virtuous living.") **43 still** always
45 sweet and twenty i.e., sweet and twenty times sweet, or twenty years old

SIR ANDREW: A mellifluous voice, as I am true knight.

SIR TOBY: A contagious° breath.

SIR ANDREW: Very sweet and contagious, i'faith.   50

SIR TOBY: To hear by the nose, it is dulcet in contagion.° But
shall we make the welkin dance° indeed? Shall we rouse the
night owl in a catch that will draw three souls° out of one
weaver?° Shall we do that?

SIR ANDREW: An you love me, let's do't. I am dog at° a catch.°   55

FESTE: By'r Lady,° sir, and some dogs will catch well.

SIR ANDREW: Most certain. Let our catch be "Thou knave."°

FESTE: "Hold thy peace, thou knave," knight? I shall be
constrained in't to call thee knave, knight.°

SIR ANDREW: 'Tis not the first time I have constrained one to   60
call me knave. Begin, Fool. It begins, "Hold thy peace."

FESTE: I shall never begin if I hold my peace.

SIR ANDREW: Good, i'faith. Come, begin.   *Catch sung.*

    Enter Maria.

MARIA: What a caterwauling do you keep° here! If my lady have
not called up her steward Malvolio and bid him turn you out
of doors, never trust me.   65

SIR TOBY: My lady's a Cataian,° we are politicians,° Malvolio's a
Peg-o'-Ramsey,° and [*he sings*] "Three merry men be we."° Am
not I consanguineous?° Am I not of her blood? Tillyvally!°
Lady!° [*He sings.*] "There dwelt a man in Babylon, lady, lady."°

FESTE: Beshrew° me, the knight's in admirable fooling.   70

SIR ANDREW: Ay, he does well enough if he be disposed, and
so do I too. He does it with a better grace, but I do it more
natural.°

---

49 contagious infectiously delightful   **51 To . . . contagion** i.e., If we were to describe hearing
in olfactory terms, we could say it is sweet in stench.   **52 make . . . dance** i.e., drink till the sky
seems to turn around   **53 draw three souls** (Refers to the threefold nature of the soul—
vegetal, sensible, and intellectual—or to the three singers of the three-part catch; or, just a
comic exaggeration.)   **54 weaver** (Weavers were often associated with psalm singing.)
55 dog at very clever at. (But Feste uses it to   **catch** round. (But Feste uses it to
mean "seize.")   **56 By 'r Lady** (An oath, originally, "by the Virgin Mary.")   **57 "Thou knave"**
(This popular round is arranged so that the three singers repeatedly accost one another with
"Thou knave.")   **58–9 "Hold . . . knight** ("Knight and knave" is a common antithesis, like "rich
and poor.")   **63 keep** keep up   **66 Cataian** Cathayan, i.e., Chinese, a trickster or inscrutable; or,
just nonsense. **politicians** schemers, intriguers   **67 Peg-o'-Ramsey** character in a popular song.
(Used here contemptuously.)   **"Three . . . we"** (A snatch of an old song.)   **68 consanguineous** i.e.,
a blood relative of Olivia.   **Tillyvally!** Nonsense, fiddle-faddle!   **69 "There . . . lady"** (The first
line of a ballad, "The Constancy of Susanna," together with the refrain, "Lady, lady.")   **70 Beshrew**
i.e., The devil take. (A mild curse.)   **73 natural** naturally. (But unconsciously suggesting idiocy.)

SIR TOBY: [*sings*]
"O' the twelfth day of December"°—
MARIA: For the love o' God, peace!

Enter Malvolio.

MALVOLIO: My masters, are you mad? Or what are you? Have 75
you no wit,° manners, nor honesty° but to gabble like tinkers
at this time of night? Do ye make an ale-house of my lady's
house, that ye squeak out your coziers'° catches without any
mitigation or remorse° of voice? Is there no respect of place,
persons, nor time in you?
SIR TOBY: We did keep time, sir, in our catches. Sneck up!° 80
MALVOLIO: Sir Toby, I must be round° with you. My lady bade
me tell you that though she harbors you as her kinsman, she's
nothing allied to your disorders. If you can separate yourself
and your misdemeanors, you are welcome to the house; if not,
an it would please you to take leave of her, she is very willing
to bid you farewell. 85
SIR TOBY: [*sings*]
"Farewell, dear heart, since I must needs be gone."°
MARIA: Nay, good Sir Toby.
FESTE: [*sings*]
"His eyes do show his days are almost done."
MALVOLIO: Is't even so?
SIR TOBY: [*sings*]
"But I will never die." 90
FESTE: "Sir Toby, there you lie."
MALVOLIO: This is much credit to you.
SIR TOBY: [*sings*]
"Shall I bid him go?"
FESTE: [*sings*]
"What an if you do?"
SIR TOBY: [*sings*]
"Shall I bid him go, and spare not?" 95

74 **"O'...December"** (Possibly part of a ballad about the Battle of Musselburgh Field, or Toby's error for the "twelfth day of Christmas," i.e., Twelfth Night.) 76 **wit** common sense. **honesty** decency 78 **coziers'** cobblers' 79 **mitigation or remorse** i.e., considerate lowering 80 **Sneck up!** Go hang! 81 **round** blunt 86 **"Farewell...gone"** (From the ballad "Corydon's Farewell to Phyllis.")

FESTE: [*sings*]
"Oh, no, no, no, no, you dare not."

SIR TOBY: Out o' tune,° sir? Ye lie. Art any more than a steward? Dost thou think, because thou art virtuous, there shall be no more cakes and ale?

FESTE: Yes, by Saint Anne,° and ginger° shall be hot i'th' mouth, too. 100

SIR TOBY: Thou'rt i'the right.—Go, sir, rub your chain with crumbs.°—A stoup of wine, Maria!

MALVOLIO: Mistress Mary, if you prized my lady's favor at any-thing more than contempt, you would not give means° for this uncivil rule.° She shall know of it, by this hand. *Exit.*

MARIA: Go shake your ears.° 105

SIR ANDREW: 'Twere as good a deed as to drink when a man's a-hungry to challenge him the field° and then to break promise with him and make a fool of him.

SIR TOBY: Do't, knight. I'll write thee a challenge, or I'll deliver thy indignation to him by word of mouth.

MARIA: Sweet Sir Toby, be patient for tonight. Since the youth of 110 the Count's was today with my lady, she is much out of quiet. For° Monsieur Malvolio, let me alone with him. If I do not gull° him into a nayword° and make him° a common recre-ation,° do not think I have wit enough to lie straight in my bed. I know I can do it.

SIR TOBY: Possess° us, possess us. Tell us something of him. 115

MARIA: Marry, sir, sometimes he is a kind of Puritan.°

SIR ANDREW: Oh, if I thought that, I'd beat him like a dog.

SIR TOBY: What, for being a Puritan? Thy exquisite reason, dear knight?

---

97 Out o' tune (Perhaps a quibbling reply—"We did too keep time in our tune"—to Malvolio's accusation of having no respect for place or time, line 91. Often emended to *Out o' time,* easily misread in secretary hand.) **99 Saint Anne** mother of the Virgin Mary. (Her cult was derided in the Reformation, much as Puritan reformers also derided the tradition of *cakes and ale* at church feasts.) **ginger** (Commonly used to spice ale.) **101–2 rub . . . crumbs** i.e., scour or polish your steward's chain; attend to your own business and remember your station. **104 give means** i.e., supply drink. **rule** conduct. **105 your ears** i.e., your ass's ears. **107 the field** i.e., to a duel **112 For** As for. **let . . . him** leave him to me. **113 gull** trick. **nayword** byword. (His name will be synonymous with "dupe.") **113–4 recreation** sport **115 Possess** Inform **116 puritan** (Maria's point is that Malvolio is sometimes a *kind* of Puritan, insofar as he is precise about moral conduct and censorious of others for immoral conduct, but that he is nothing consistently except a time-server. He is not, then, simply a satirical type of the Puritan sect. The extent of the resemblance is left unstated.)

SIR ANDREW: I have no exquisite reason for't, but I have reason good enough.

MARIA: The devil a Puritan that he is, or anything constantly,° but a time-pleaser;° an affectioned° ass, that cons state without book° and utters it by great swaths;° the best persuaded° of himself, so crammed, as he thinks, with excellencies, that it is his grounds of faith° that all that look on him love him; and on that vice in him will my revenge find notable cause to work.

SIR TOBY: What wilt thou do?

MARIA: I will drop in his way some obscure epistles° of love, wherein by the color of his beard, the shape of his leg, the manner of his gait, the expressure° of his eye, forehead, and complexion, he shall find himself most feelingly personated.° I can write very like my lady your niece; on a forgotten matter° we can hardly make distinction of our hands.°

SIR TOBY: Excellent! I smell a device.

SIR ANDREW: I have't in my nose too.

SIR TOBY: He shall think, by the letters that thou wilt drop, that they come from my niece, and that she's in love with him.

MARIA: My purpose is indeed a horse of that color.

SIR ANDREW: And your horse now would make him an ass.

MARIA: Ass,° I doubt not.

SIR ANDREW: Oh, 'twill be admirable!

MARIA: Sport royal, I warrant you. I know my physic° will work with him. I will plant you two, and let the Fool make a third, where he shall find the letter. Observe his construction° of it. For this night, to bed, and dream on the event.° Farewell. *Exit.*

SIR TOBY: Good night, Penthesilea.°

SIR ANDREW: Before me,° she's a good wench.

SIR TOBY: She's a beagle° true-bred and one that adores me. What o' that?

120
125
130
135
140
145

TWELFTH NIGHT; OR, WHAT YOU WILL

111

---

120 **constantly** consistently   121 **time-pleaser** time-server, sycophant. **affectioned** affected
122–3 **cons . . . book** learns by heart the phrases and mannerisms of the great   123 **by great swaths** in great sweeps, like rows of mown grain.   **the best persuaded** having the best opinion
124 **grounds of faith** creed, belief   126 **some obscure epistles** an ambiguously worded letter
127 **expressure** expression   128 **personated** represented.   129 **on a forgotten matter** when we've forgotten which of us wrote something or what it was about   130 **hands** handwriting.   136 **Ass, I** (With a pun on "as I.")   138 **physic** medicine   140 **construction** interpretation   141 **event** outcome.   142 **Penthesilea** Queen of the Amazons. (Another ironical allusion to Maria's diminutive stature.)   143 **Before me** i.e., On my soul. (A mild oath.)   144 **beagle** a small, intelligent hunting dog

SIR ANDREW: I was adored once, too.

SIR TOBY: Let's to bed, knight. Thou hadst need send for more money.

SIR ANDREW: If I cannot recover° your niece, I am a foul way out.°

SIR TOBY: Send for money, knight. If thou hast her not i'th' end, call me cut.°

SIR ANDREW: If I do not, never trust me, take it how you will.   150

SIR TOBY: Come, come, I'll go burn some sack.° 'Tis too late to go to bed now. Come, knight; come, knight.

Exeunt.°

2.4

Enter Duke [Orsino], Viola, Curio, and others.

ORSINO: Give me some music. Now, good morrow,° friends.
Now, good Cesario, but° that piece of song,
That old and antique° song we heard last night.
Methought it did relieve my passion much,
More than light airs and recollected terms°   5
Of these most brisk and giddy-pacèd times.
Come, but one verse.

CURIO: He is not here, so please Your Lordship, that should sing it.

ORSINO: Who was it?

CURIO: Feste the jester, my lord, a fool that the Lady Olivia's   10
father took much delight in. He is about the house.

ORSINO: Seek him out, and play the tune the while.

[Exit Curio.] Music plays.

[*To Viola*] Come hither, boy. If ever thou shalt love,
In the sweet pangs of it remember me;
For such as I am, all true lovers are,   15
Unstaid and skittish in all motions else°
Save in the constant image of the creature
That is beloved. How dost thou like this tune?

---

148 recover win. **foul way out** i.e., miserably out of pocket. (Literally, out of my way and in the mire.)   **149 cut** A proverbial term of abuse: literally, a horse with a docked tail; also, a gelding, or the female genital organ.   **151 burn some sack** warm some Spanish wine.   **157.1 Exeunt** (Feste may have left earlier; he says nothing after line 117 and is perhaps referred to without his being present at 172–3.)
1 morrow morning   **2 but** i.e., I ask only   **3 antique** old, quaint, fantastic   **5 recollected terms** studied and artificial expressions   **16 all motions else** all other thoughts and emotions

VIOLA: It gives a very echo to the seat°
    Where Love is throned. 20

ORSINO: Thou dost speak masterly.
    My life upon't, young though thou art, thine eye
    Hath stayed upon some favor° that it loves.
    Hath it not, boy?

VIOLA: A little, by your favor.° 25

ORSINO: What kind of woman is't?

VIOLA: Of your complexion.

ORSINO: She is not worth thee, then. What years, i'faith?

VIOLA: About your years, my lord.

ORSINO: Too old, by heaven. Let still° the woman take 30
    An elder than herself. So wears she° to him;
    So sways she level° in her husband's heart.
    For, boy, however we do praise ourselves,
    Our fancies are more giddy and unfirm,
    More longing, wavering, sooner lost and worn,° 35
    Than women's are.

VIOLA: I think it well, my lord.

ORSINO: Then let thy love be younger than thyself,
    Or thy affection cannot hold the bent;°
    For women are as roses, whose fair flower 40
    Being once displayed,° doth fall that very hour.

VIOLA: And so they are. Alas that they are so,
    To die even when° they to perfection grow!

Enter Curio and Clown [Feste].

ORSINO: Oh, fellow, come, the song we had last night.
    Mark it, Cesario, it is old and plain; 45
    The spinsters° and the knitters in the sun,
    And the free° maids that weave their thread with bones,°
    Do use° to chant it. It is silly sooth,°
    And dallies with° the innocence of love,
    Like the old age.° 50

---

19 the seat i.e., the heart **23 stayed ... favor** rested upon some face **25 by your favor** if you please. (But also hinting at "like you in feature.") **30 still** always **31 wears she** she adapts herself **32 sways she level** she keeps a perfect equipoise and steady affection **35 worn** exhausted. (Sometimes emended to *won*.) **39 hold the bent** hold steady, keep the intensity (like the tension of a bow) **41 displayed** full blown **43 even when** just as **46 spinsters** spinners **47 free** carefree, innocent. **bones** bobbins on which bone-lace was made **48 Do use** are accustomed. **silly sooth** simple truth **49 dallies with** dwells lovingly on, sports with **50 Like ... age** as in the good old times.

FESTE: Are you ready, sir?
ORSINO: Ay, prithee, sing. *Music.*

      The Song.

FESTE: [*sings*]
    Come away,° come away, death,
    And in sad cypress° let me be laid.   55
    Fly away, fly away, breath;
    I am slain by a fair cruel maid.
    My shroud of white, stuck all with yew,°
    Oh, prepare it!
    My part of death, no one so true   60
    Did share it.°
    Not a flower, not a flower sweet
    On my black coffin let there be strown;°
    Not a friend, not a friend greet
    My poor corpse, where my bones shall be thrown.   65
    A thousand thousand sighs to save,
    Lay me, oh, where
    Sad true lover never find my grave,
    To weep there!

ORSINO: [*offering money*] There's for thy pains.   70
FESTE: No pains, sir. I take pleasure in singing, sir.
ORSINO: I'll pay thy pleasure then.
FESTE: Truly, sir, and pleasure will be paid, one time or another.°
ORSINO: Give me now leave to leave° thee.
FESTE: Now, the melancholy god° protect thee, and the tailor   75
make thy doublet° of changeable taffeta,° for thy mind is a
very opal.° I would have men of such constancy put to sea,
that their business might be everything and their intent
everywhere,° for that's it that always makes a good voyage of
nothing.° Farewell.   *Exit.*   80

54 Come away Come hither   **55 cypress** i.e., a coffin of cypress wood, or bier strewn with sprigs of cypress   **58 yew** yew sprigs. (Emblematic of mourning, like cypress.)   **60–1 My . . . it** No one died for love so true to love as I.   **63 strown** strewn   **73 pleasure . . . another** sooner or later one must pay for indulgence. **74 leave to leave** permission to take leave of, dismiss   **75 the melancholy god** i.e., Saturn, whose planet was thought to control the melancholy temperament   **76 doublet** close-fitting jacket.   **changeable taffeta** a silk so woven of various-colored threads that its color shifts with changing perspective   **77 opal** an iridescent precious stone that changes color when seen from various angles or in different lights.   **78–9 that . . . everywhere** i.e., so that in the changeableness of the sea their inconstancy could always be exercised   **79–80 for . . . nothing** because that's the quality that is satisfied with an aimless voyage.

ORSINO: Let all the rest give place.°

[Curio and attendants withdraw.]

Once more, Cesario,
Get thee to yond same sovereign cruelty.
Tell her, my love, more noble than the world,
Prizes not quantity of dirty lands;
The parts° that fortune hath bestowed upon her,   85
Tell her, I hold as giddily as fortune;°
But 'tis that miracle and queen of gems°
That nature pranks° her in attracts° my soul.

VIOLA: But if she cannot love you, sir?

ORSINO: I cannot be so answered.   90

VIOLA: Sooth,° but you must.
Say that some lady—as perhaps there is—
Hath for your love as great a pang of heart
As you have for Olivia. You cannot love her;
You tell her so. Must she not then be answered?°   95

ORSINO: There is no woman's sides
Can bide° the beating of so strong a passion
As love doth give my heart; no woman's heart
So big, to hold° so much. They lack retention.°
Alas, their love may be called appetite,   100
No motion° of the liver, but the palate,°
That suffer surfeit, cloyment,° and revolt;°
But mine is all as hungry as the sea,
And can digest as much. Make no compare°
Between that love a woman can bear me   105
And that I owe° Olivia.

VIOLA: Ay, but I know—

ORSINO: What dost thou know?

VIOLA: Too well what love women to men may owe.
In faith, they are as true of heart as we.   110
My father had a daughter loved a man

---

81 **give place** withdraw.   85 **parts** attributes such as wealth or rank   86 **I ... fortune** I esteem as carelessly as I do fortune, that fickle goddess   87 **that miracle ... gems** i.e., her beauty   88 **pranks** adorns.   **attracts** that attracts   91 **Sooth** In truth   95 **be answered** be satisfied with your answer.   97 **bide** withstand   99 **to hold** as to contain.   **retention** constancy, the power of retaining.   101 **motion** impulse.   **liver ... palate** (Real love is a passion of the liver, whereas fancy, light love, is born in the eye and nourished in the palate.)   102 **cloyment** satiety.   **revolt** revulsion   104 **compare** comparison   106 **owe** have for

As it might be, perhaps, were I a woman,
I should Your Lordship.

ORSINO: And what's her history?

VIOLA: A blank, my lord. She never told her love,
But let concealment, like a worm i'th' bud,
Feed on her damask° cheek. She pined in thought,
And with a green and yellow° melancholy;
She sat like Patience on a monument,°
Smiling at grief. Was not this love indeed?
We men may say more, swear more, but indeed
Our shows° are more than will;° for still° we prove
Much in our vows, but little in our love.

ORSINO: But died thy sister of her love, my boy?

VIOLA: I am all the daughters of my father's house,
And all the brothers too—and yet I know not.
Sir, shall I to this lady?

ORSINO: Ay, that's the theme.
To her in haste; give her this jewel. [*He gives a jewel.*] Say
My love can give no place, bide no denay.°

Exeunt [separately].

2.5

Enter Sir Toby, Sir Andrew, and Fabian.

SIR TOBY: Come thy ways,° Signor Fabian.

FABIAN: Nay, I'll come. If I lose a scruple° of this sport, let me be
boiled° to death with melancholy.

SIR TOBY: Wouldst thou not be glad to have the nig-gardly ras-
cally sheep-biter° come by some notable shame?   5

FABIAN: I would exult, man. You know he brought me out o'favor
with my lady about a bearbaiting° here.

SIR TOBY: To anger him we'll have the bear again, and we will
fool him black and blue.° Shall we not, Sir Andrew?

---

118 damask pink and white like the damask rose   **119 green and yellow** pale and sallow
120 on a monument carved in statuary on a tomb   **124 shows** displays of passion. **more than will**
greater than our determination. **still** always   **131 can . . . denay** cannot yield or endure denial.
1 Come thy ways Come along   **2 a scruple** the least bit   **3 boiled** (With a pun on "biled"; black
bile was the "humor" of melancholy and was thought to be a cold humor.)   **5 sheep-biter** a dog
that bites sheep, i.e., a scoundrel   **7 bearbaiting** (A special target of Puritan disapproval.)
9 fool . . . blue mock him until he is figuratively black and blue.

SIR ANDREW: An° we do not, it is pity of our lives.°   10

Enter Maria [with a letter].

SIR TOBY: Here comes the little villain°.—How now, my metal°
of India!

MARIA: Get ye all three into the boxtree.° Malvolio's coming
down this walk. He has been yonder i' the sun practicing behavior to his own shadow this half hour. Observe him, for the
love of mockery, for I know this letter will make a contempla-   15
tive° idiot of him. Close,° in the name of jesting! [The others
hide.] Lie thou there [throwing down a letter]; for here comes
the trout that must be caught with tickling.°   Exit.

Enter Malvolio.

MALVOLIO: 'Tis but fortune; all is fortune. Maria once told me
she° did affect° me; and I have heard herself come thus near,   20
that should she fancy,° it should be one of my complexion.
Besides, she uses me with a more exalted respect than anyone
else that follows° her. What should I think on't?

SIR TOBY: Here's an overweening rogue!

FABIAN: Oh, peace! Contemplation makes a rare° turkey-cock of
him. How he jets° under his advanced° plumes!   25

SIR ANDREW: 'Slight,° I could so beat the rogue!

SIR TOBY: Peace, I say.

MALVOLIO: To be Count Malvolio.

SIR TOBY: Ah, rogue!

SIR ANDREW: Pistol him, pistol him.   30

SIR TOBY: Peace, peace!

MALVOLIO: There is example° for't. The lady of the Strachy°
married the yeoman of the wardrobe.

SIR ANDREW: Fie on him, Jezebel!°

FABIAN: Oh, peace! Now he's deeply in. Look how imagination
blows° him.

---

10 An If. pity of our lives a pity we should live. 11 villain (Here, a term of endearment.)
metal gold, i.e., priceless one   12 boxtree an evergreen shrub. 15–6 contemplative i.e., from his
musings. 16 Close i.e., Keep close, stay hidden   18 tickling (1) stroking gently about the gills—an
actual method of fishing (2) deception.   20 she Olivia. affect have fondness for 21 fancy fall in
love 23 follows serves 25 rare extraordinary 26 jets struts. advanced prominent 27 'Slight
By His (God's) light 32 example precedent. lady of the Strachy (Apparently a lady who had
married below her station; no certain identification.) 33 Jezebel the proud queen of Ahab, King of
Israel. 34 blows puffs up

MALVOLIO: Having been three months married to her, sitting in
my state°—   35

SIR TOBY: Oh, for a stone-bow,° to hit him in the eye!

MALVOLIO: Calling my officers about me, in my branched° vel-
vet gown; having come from a daybed,° where I have left
Olivia sleeping—

SIR TOBY: Fire and brimstone!

FABIAN: Oh, peace, peace!   40

MALVOLIO: And then to have the humor of state;° and after a
demure travel of regard,° telling them I know my place as I
would they should do theirs, to ask for my kinsman Toby.°

SIR TOBY: Bolts and shackles!

FABIAN: Oh, peace, peace, peace! Now, now.   45

MALVOLIO: Seven of my people, with an obedient start, make out
for him. I frown the while, and perchance wind up my watch,
or play with my°—some rich jewel. Toby approaches; curtsies°
there to me—

SIR TOBY: Shall this fellow live?

FABIAN: Though our silence be drawn from us with cars,° yet
peace.   50

MALVOLIO: I extend my hand to him thus, quenching my famil-
iar° smile with an austere regard of control°—

SIR TOBY: And does not Toby take° you a blow o' the lips then?

MALVOLIO: Saying, "Cousin Toby, my fortunes having cast me on
your niece give me this prerogative of speech—"   55

SIR TOBY: What, what?

MALVOLIO: "You must amend your drunkenness."

SIR TOBY: Out, scab!°

FABIAN: Nay, patience, or we break the sinews of ° our plot.

MALVOLIO: "Besides, you waste the treasure of your time with a
foolish knight—"   60

SIR ANDREW: That's me, I warrant you.

MALVOLIO: "One Sir Andrew."

---

35 **state** chair of state   36 **stone-bow** crossbow that shoots stones   37 **branched** adorned with a
figured pattern suggesting branched leaves or flowers.   38 **daybed** sofa, couch   41 **have . . . state**
adopt the imperious manner of authority   42 **demure . . . regard** grave survey of the company
43 **Toby** (Malvolio omits the title *Sir.*)   48 **play with my** (Malvolio perhaps means his steward's chain
but checks himself in time; as "Count Malvolio," he would not be wearing it. A bawdy meaning of
playing with himself is also suggested.)   **curtsies** bows   50 **with cars** with chariots, i.e., pulling
apart by force   51 **familiar** (1) customary (2) friendly.   52 **regard of control** look of authority
53 **take** deliver   58 **scab** scurvy fellow.   59 **break . . . of** hamstring, disable

SIR ANDREW: I knew 'twas I, for many do call me fool.

MALVOLIO: What employment° have we here?

[Taking up the letter.]

FABIAN: Now is the woodcock° near the gin.°   65

SIR TOBY: Oh, peace, and the spirit of humors° intimate reading
aloud to him!

MALVOLIO: By my life, this is my lady's hand. These beher very
c's, her u's, and her t's;° and thus makes she her great° P's. It is
in contempt of° question her hand.

SIR ANDREW: Her c's, her u's, and her t's. Why that?   70

MALVOLIO: *[reads]* "To the unknown beloved, this, and my good
wishes."—Her very phrases! By your leave, wax.° Soft!° And
the impressure° her Lucrece,° with which she uses° to seal.
'Tis my lady. To whom should this be?   *[He opens the letter.]*

FABIAN: This wins him, liver° and all.   75

MALVOLIO: *[reads]*
"Jove knows I love,
But who?
Lips, do not move;
No man must know."   80
"No man must know." What follows? The numbers altered!°
"No man must know." If this should be thee, Malvolio?

SIR TOBY: Marry, hang thee, brock!°

MALVOLIO: *[reads]*
"I may command where I adore,   85
But silence, like a Lucrece knife,
With bloodless stroke my heart doth gore;
M.O.A.I. doth sway my life."

FABIAN: A fustian° riddle!

SIR TOBY: Excellent wench, say I.   90

MALVOLIO: "M.O.A.I. doth sway my life." Nay, but first, let me
see, let me see, let me see.

---

64 **employment** business 65 **woodcock** (A bird proverbial for its stupidity.) **gin** snare. 66 **humors**
whim, caprice 68 **c's ... t's** i.e., *cut*, slang for the female pudenda. **great** (1) uppercase (2) copious.
(P suggests "pee.") 69 **in contempt of** beyond 72 **By ... wax** (Addressed to the seal on the letter.)
Soft Softly, not so fast. 73 **impressure** device imprinted on the seal. **Lucrece** Lucretia, chaste
matron who, ravished by Tarquin, committed suicide **uses** is accustomed 75 **liver** i.e., the seat of
passion 81 **The numbers altered!** More verses, in a different meter! 83 **brock** badger. (Used
contemptuously.) 89 **fustian** bombastic, ridiculously pompous

FABIAN: What° dish o' poison has she dressed° him!

SIR TOBY: And with what wing° the staniel° checks at it!°

MALVOLIO: "I may command where I adore." Why, she may command me; I serve her, she is my lady. Why, this is evident to any formal capacity.° There is no obstruction in this. And the end—what should that alphabetical position° portend? If I could make that resemble something in me! Softly! "M.O.A.I."— 95

SIR TOBY: Oh, ay,° make up° that. He is now at a cold scent.

FABIAN: Sowter° will cry upon't for all this, though it be as rank as a fox.

MALVOLIO: "M"—Malvolio. "M"! Why, that begins my name! 100

FABIAN: Did not I say he would work it out? The cur is excellent at faults.°

MALVOLIO: "M"—But then there is no consonancy in the sequel that suffers under probation:° "A" should follow, but "O" does.

FABIAN: And "O" shall end,° I hope.

SIR TOBY: Ay, or I'll cudgel him, and make him cry "Oh!" 105

MALVOLIO: And then "I" comes behind.

FABIAN: Ay, an you had any eye° behind you, you might see more detraction at your heels° than fortunes before you.

MALVOLIO: "M.O.A.I." This simulation° is not as the former. And yet, to crush this a little, it would bow to me, for every one of 110 these letters are in my name. Soft! Here follows prose. [*He reads.*] "If this fall into thy hand, revolve.° In my stars° I am above thee, but be not afraid of greatness. Some are born great, some achieve greatness, and some have greatness thrust upon 'em. Thy Fates open their hands;° let thy blood 115 and spirit embrace them; and, to inure° thyself to what thou

120

---

92 What What a. **dressed** prepared for **93 wing** speed. **staniel** kestrel, a sparrow hawk. (The word is used contemptuously because of the uselessness of the staniel for falconry.) **checks at it** turns to fly at it. **95 formal capacity** normal understanding. **96 position** arrangement **97 Oh, ay** (Playing on *O.I.* of *M.O.A.I.*) **make up** work out **98–9 Sowter . . . fox** The hound Sowter (literally, "Cobbler") will bay triumphantly at picking up this false scent, even though the smell is as rank as a fox. ("M.O.A.I." is a false lead that reeks.) **101 at faults** i.e., at maneuvering his way past breaks in the line of scent—in this case, on a false trail. **102–3 no consonancy . . . probation** no pattern in the following letters that stands up under examination. (In fact, the letters "M.O.A.I." represent the first, last, second, and next to last letters of Malvolio's name.) **104 "O" shall end** (1) "O" ends Malvolio's name (2) *omega* ends the Greek alphabet and is thus a symbol for the ending of the world, *alpha* to *omega* (3) Malvolio's cry of pain will end the matter, as Sir Toby suggests in the next line. **107 eye** (punning on the "I" of "Oh, ay" and "M.O.A.I.") **108 detraction . . . heels** defamation pursuing you **109 simulation** disguise, puzzle **112 revolve** consider. **stars** fortune **115 open their hands** offer their bounty **116 inure** accustom.

art like° to be, cast° thy humble slough° and appear fresh. Be opposite° with a kinsman, surly with servants. Let thy tongue tang° arguments of state;° put thyself into the trick of singularity.° She thus advises thee that sighs for thee. 120 Remember who commended thy yellow stockings, and wished to see thee ever cross-gartered.° I say, remember. Go to,° thou art made, if thou desir'st to be so. If not, let me see thee a steward still, the fellow of servants, and not worthy to touch Fortune's fingers. Farewell. She that would alter 125 services° with thee, The Fortunate-Unhappy."

Daylight and champaign° discovers° not more! This is open. I will be proud, I will read politic° authors, I will baffle° Sir Toby, I will wash off gross° acquaintance, I will be point-devise° the very man. I do not now fool myself, to let° imagination jade 130 me;° for every reason excites to this,° that my lady loves me. She did commend my yellow stockings of late, she did praise my leg being cross-gartered; and in this° she manifests herself to my love, and with a kind of injunction drives me to these habits° of her liking. I thank my stars, I am happy.° I will 135 be strange, stout,° in yellow stockings and cross-gartered, even with the swiftness of putting on. Jove and my stars be praised! Here is yet a post-script. [*He reads.*] "Thou canst not choose but know who I am. If thou entertain'st° my love, let it appear in thy smiling; thy smiles become thee well. Therefore in my 140 presence still° smile, dear my sweet, I prithee." Jove, I thank thee. I will smile; I will do everything that thou wilt have me.

Exit.

[*Sir Toby, Sir Andrew, and Fabian come from hiding.*]

FABIAN: I will not give my part of this sport for a pension of thousands to be paid from the Sophy.°

---

117 **like** likely. **cast** cast off. **slough** skin of a snake; hence, former demeanor of humbleness.
118 **opposite** contradictory 119 **tang** sound loud with. **state** politics, statecraft. **trick of singularity** eccentricity of manner. 121 **cross-gartered** wearing garters above and below the knee so as to cross behind it. 122 **Go to** (An expression of remonstrance.) 125–26 **alter services** i.e., exchange place of mistress and servant 127 **champaign** open country. **discovers** discloses 128 **politic** dealing with state affairs. **baffle** deride, degrade. (A technical chivalric term used to describe the disgrace of a perjured knight.) 129 **gross** base. **point-devise** correct to the letter 130 **to let** by letting. 130–1 **jade me** trick me, make me look ridiculous (as an unruly horse might do). 131 **excites to this** prompts this conclusion 133 **this** this letter 135 **these habits** this attire **happy** fortunate. 136 **strange, stout** aloof, haughty 139 **thou entertain'st** you accept 141 **still** continually 143 **Sophy** Shah of Persia.

SIR TOBY: I could marry this wench for this device.

SIR ANDREW: So could I too. 145

SIR TOBY: And ask no other dowry with her but such another jest.

Enter Maria.

SIR ANDREW: Nor I neither.

FABIAN: Here comes my noble gull-catcher.°

SIR TOBY: Wilt thou set thy foot o' my neck?

SIR ANDREW: Or o' mine either? 150

SIR TOBY: Shall I play° my freedom at tray-trip,° and become thy bond slave?

SIR ANDREW: I'faith, or I either?

SIR TOBY: Why, thou hast put him in such a dream that when the image of it leaves him he must run mad. 155

MARIA: Nay, but say true, does it work upon him?

SIR TOBY: Like aqua vitae° with a midwife.

MARIA: If you will then see the fruits of the sport, mark his first approach before my lady. He will come to her in yellow stockings, and 'tis a color she abhors, and cross-gartered, a fashion 160 she detests; and he will smile upon her, which will now be so unsuitable to her disposition, being addicted to a melancholy as she is, that it cannot but turn him into a notable contempt.° If you will see it, follow me.

SIR TOBY: To the gates of Tartar,° thou most excellent devil of wit! 165

SIR ANDREW: I'll make one° too. *Exeunt.*

3.1

Enter Viola, and Clown [Feste, playing his pipe and tabor].

VIOLA: Save° thee, friend, and thy music. Dost thou live by° thy tabor?°

FESTE: No, sir, I live by the church.

VIOLA: Art thou a churchman?

FESTE: No such matter, sir. I do live by the church, for I do live at my house, and my house doth stand by the church. 5

---

148 gull-catcher tricker of *gulls* or dupes.   **151 play** gamble. **tray-trip** a game of dice, success in which depended on throwing a three (*tray*)   **157 aqua vitae** brandy or other distilled liquor   **163 notable contempt** notorious object of contempt.   **165 Tartar** Tartarus, the infernal regions   **166 make one** i.e., tag along

1 Save God save.   **live by** earn your living with. (But Feste uses the phrase to mean "dwell near.")

2 tabor small drum.

VIOLA: So thou mayst say the king lies by° a beggar if a beggar dwell near him, or the church stands by thy tabor if thy tabor stand by° the church.

FESTE: You have said,° sir. To see this age! A sentence° is but a cheveril° glove to a good wit. How quickly the wrong side may be turned outward! 10

VIOLA: Nay, that's certain. They that dally nicely° with words may quickly make them wanton.°

FESTE: I would therefore my sister had had no name, sir.

VIOLA: Why, man?

FESTE: Why, sir, her name's a word, and to dally with that word 15 might make my sister wanton. But indeed, words are very rascals since bonds disgraced them.°

VIOLA: Thy reason, man?

FESTE: Troth, sir, I can yield you none without words, and words are grown so false I am loath to prove reason with them.

VIOLA: I warrant thou art a merry fellow and car'st for nothing.° 20

FESTE: Not so, sir, I do care for something; but in my conscience, sir, I do not care for you. If that be to care for nothing, sir, I would it would make you invisible.°

VIOLA: Art not thou the Lady Olivia's fool?

FESTE: No indeed, sir. The Lady Olivia has no folly. She will keep no fool, sir, till she be married, and fools are as like husbands 25 as pilchers° are to herrings—the husband's the bigger.° I am indeed not her fool but her corrupter of words.

VIOLA: I saw thee late° at the Count Orsino's.

FESTE: Foolery, sir, does walk about the orb° like the sun; it shines everywhere. I would be sorry, sir, but the fool should be 30 as oft with your master as with my mistress.° I think I saw Your Wisdom° there.

TWELFTH NIGHT; OR, WHAT YOU WILL

123

---

6 lies by (1) lies sexually with (2) dwells near   **7–8 stands by . . . stand by** (1) is maintained by (2) is placed near   **9 You have said** You've expressed your opinion.   **sentence** maxim, judgment, opinion   **10 cheveril** kidskin   **11 dally nicely** (1) play subtly (2) toy amorously   **21 wanton** (1) equivocal (2) licentious, unchaste. (Feste then "dallies" with the word in its sexual sense; see line 20.)   **17 since . . . them** i.e., since bonds have been needed to make sworn statements good. (Words cannot be relied on since not even contractual promises are reliable.)   **20 car'st for nothing** are without any worries. (But Feste puns on *care for* in lines 29–30 in the sense of "like.")   **23 invisible** i.e., nothing; absent.   **26 pilchers** pilchards, fish resembling herring but smaller   **the bigger** (1) the larger (2) the bigger fool.   **28 late** recently   **29 orb** earth   **30–1 I would . . . mistress** (1) I should be sorry not to visit Orsino's house often (2) It would be a shame if folly were no less common there than in Olivia's household.   **31 Your Wisdom** i.e., you. (A title of mock courtesy.)

VIOLA: Nay, an thou pass upon me,° I'll no more with thee. Hold, there's expenses for thee.

[She gives a coin.]

FESTE: Now Jove, in his next commodity° of hair, send thee a beard!

VIOLA: By my troth, I'll tell thee, I am almost sick for one°— *[aside]* though I would not have it grow on my chin.—Is thy 35 lady within?

FESTE: Would not a pair of these have bred, sir?

VIOLA: Yes, being kept together and put to use.°

FESTE: I would play Lord Pandarus° of Phrygia, sir, to bring a Cressida to this Troilus.

VIOLA: I understand you, sir. 'Tis well begged.

[She gives another coin.]

FESTE: The matter, I hope, is not great, sir, begging but a beggar; 40 Cressida was a beggar.° My lady is within, sir. I will conster° to them whence you come. Who you are and what you would are out of my welkin°—I might say "element,"° but the word is overworn. *Exit.*

VIOLA: This fellow is wise enough to play the fool,
And to do that well craves a kind of wit. 45
He must observe their mood on whom he jests,
The quality° of persons, and the time,
Not, like the haggard,° check at every feather
That comes before his eye.° This is a practice°
As full of labor as a wise man's art; 50
For folly that he wisely shows is fit,
But wise men, folly-fall'n, quite taint their wit.°

Enter Sir Toby and [Sir] Andrew.

32 **an . . . me** if you fence (verbally) with me, pass judgment on me   33 **commodity** supply
34 **sick for one** (1) eager to have a beard (2) in love with a bearded man   37 **put to use** put out at
interest.   38 **Pandarus** the go-between in the love story of Troilus and Cressida; uncle to
Cressida   40–1 **begging . . . was a beggar** (A reference to Henryson's *Testament of Cresseid* in
which Cressida became a leper and a beggar. Feste desires another coin to be the mate of the
one he has, just as Cressida, the beggar, was mate to Troilus.)   41 **conster** construe, explain
43 **welkin** sky.   **element** (The word can be synonymous with *welkin*, but the common phrase *out
of my element* means "beyond my scope.")   47 **quality** character, rank   48 **haggard** untrained
adult hawk, hence unmanageable   48–9 **check . . . eye** strike at every bird it sees, i.e., dart from
subject to subject.   49 **practice** exercise of skill   51–2 **For . . . wit** for the folly he judiciously
displays is appropriate and clever, whereas when wise men fall into folly they utterly infect their
own intelligence.

SIR TOBY: Save you, gentleman.

VIOLA: And you, sir.

SIR ANDREW: *Dieu vous garde, monsieur.*°   55

VIOLA: *Et vous aussi; votre serviteur.*°

SIR ANDREW: I hope, sir, you are, and I am yours.

SIR TOBY: Will you encounter° the house? My niece is desirous you should enter, if your trade° be to her.

VIOLA: I am bound° to your niece, sir; I mean, she is the list° of   60
my voyage.

SIR TOBY: Taste° your legs, sir. Put them to motion.

VIOLA: My legs do better understand° me, sir, than I understand what you mean by bidding me taste my legs.

SIR TOBY: I mean, to go, sir, to enter.

VIOLA: I will answer you with gait and entrance.°—But we are   65
prevented.°

Enter Olivia and gentlewoman [Maria].

Most excellent accomplished lady, the heavens rain odors on you!

SIR ANDREW: [*to Sir Toby*] That youth's a rare courtier. "Rain odors"—well.

VIOLA: [*to Olivia*] My matter hath no voice,° lady, but to your own most pregnant and vouchsafed° ear.

SIR ANDREW: [*to Sir Toby*] "Odors," "pregnant," and "vouch-   70
safed." I'll get 'em all three all ready.°

OLIVIA: Let the garden door be shut, and leave me to my hearing.
[*Exeunt Sir Toby, Sir Andrew, and Maria.*] Give me your hand, sir.

VIOLA: My duty, madam, and most humble service.

OLIVIA: What is your name?

VIOLA: Cesario is your servant's name, fair princess.   75

OLIVIA: My servant, sir? 'Twas never merry world
Since lowly feigning was called compliment.°
You're servant to the Count Orsino, youth.

---

55 Dieu . . . monsieur God keep you, sir.   **56 Et . . . serviteur** And you, too; (I am) your servant. (Sir Andrew is not quite up to a reply in French.)   **58 encounter** (High-sounding word to express "approach.")   **59 trade** business. (Suggesting also a commercial venture.)   **60 I am bound** (1) I am on a journey. (Continuing Sir Toby's metaphor in *trade*.) (2) I am confined, obligated.   **list** limit, destination   **61 Taste** Try   **62 understand** stand under, support   **65 gait and entrance** going and entering. (With a pun on *gate:*[1] stride [2] entryway.)   **prevented** anticipated.   **68 hath no voice** cannot be uttered   **69 pregnant and vouchsafed** receptive and attentive   **70 all ready** committed to memory for future use.   **75–6 'Twas . . . compliment** Things have never been the same since affected humility (like calling oneself another's servant) began to be mistaken for courtesy.

VIOLA: And he is yours,° and his° must needs be yours;
Your servant's servant is your servant, madam.   80

OLIVIA: For° him, I think not on him. For his thoughts,
Would they were blanks,° rather than filled with me!

VIOLA: Madam, I come to whet your gentle thoughts
On his behalf.

OLIVIA: Oh, by your leave,° I pray you.   85
I bade you never speak again of him.
But, would you undertake another suit,
I had rather hear you to solicit that
Than music from the spheres.°

VIOLA: Dear lady—   90

OLIVIA: Give me leave, beseech you. I did send,
After the last enchantment you did here,
A ring in chase of you; so did I abuse°
Myself, my servant, and, I fear me, you.
Under your hard construction° must I sit,   95
To force that° on you in a shameful cunning
Which you knew none of yours. What might you think?
Have you not set mine honor at the stake°
And baited° it with all th' unmuzzled thoughts
That tyrannous heart can think? To one of your receiving°   100
Enough is shown; a cypress, not a bosom,
Hides my heart.° So, let me hear you speak.

VIOLA: I pity you.

OLIVIA: That's a degree to love.

VIOLA: No, not a grece;° for 'tis a vulgar proof°   105
That very oft we pity enemies.

OLIVIA: Why then, methinks 'tis time to smile° again.
Oh, world, how apt the poor are to be proud!°

79 is yours is your servant.   his those belonging to him   81 For As for   82 blanks blank coins
ready to be stamped or empty sheets of paper   85 by your leave i.e., allow me to interrupt
89 music from the spheres (The heavenly bodies were thought to be fixed in hollow concentric
spheres that revolved one about the other, producing a harmony too exquisite to be heard by
human ears.)   93 abuse wrong, mislead   95 hard construction harsh interpretation   96 To force
that for forcing the ring   98 at the stake (The figure is from bearbaiting.)   99 baited harassed.
(Literally, set the unmuzzled dogs on to bite the bear.)   100 receiving capacity, intelligence
101–2 a cypress . . . heart i.e., I have shown my heart to you, veiled only with thin, gauzelike
cypress cloth rather than the opaque flesh of my bosom.   105 grece step. (Synonymous with
degree in the preceding line.)   vulgar proof common experience   107 smile i.e., cast off love's
melancholy   108 how . . . proud! how ready the unfortunate and rejected (like myself) are to find
something to be proud of in their distress! Or, how apt are persons of comparatively low social
station like yourself to show pride in rejecting love!

If one should be a prey, how much the better
To fall before the lion than the wolf!° *Clock strikes.*   110
The clock upbraids me with the waste of time.
Be not afraid, good youth, I will not have you;
And yet, when wit and youth is come to harvest
Your wife is like° to reap a proper° man.
There lies your way, due west.   115

VIOLA: Then westward ho!°
Grace and good disposition attend Your Ladyship.°
You'll nothing, madam, to my lord by me?

OLIVIA: Stay.
I prithee, tell me what thou think'st of me.   120

VIOLA: That you do think you are not what you are.°

OLIVIA: If I think so, I think the same of you.°

VIOLA: Then think you right. I am not what I am.

OLIVIA: I would you were as I would have you be!

VIOLA: Would it be better, madam, than I am?   125
I wish it might, for now I am your fool.°

OLIVIA: *[aside]*
Oh, what a deal of scorn looks beautiful
In the contempt and anger of his lip!
A murderous guilt shows not itself more soon   130
Than love that would seem hid; love's night is noon.°—
Cesario, by the roses of the spring,
By maidhood, honor, truth, and everything,
I love thee so that, maugre° all thy pride,
Nor° wit nor reason can my passion hide.   135
Do not extort thy reasons from this clause,
For that I woo, thou therefore hast no cause.°
But rather reason thus with reason fetter:°
Love sought is good, but given unsought is better.

---

110 **To fall . . . wolf!** i.e., to fall before a noble adversary rather than to a person like you who
attacks me thus!   114 **like** likely. **proper** handsome, worthy   116 **westward ho** (The cry of Thames
watermen to attract westward-bound passengers.)   117 **Grace . . . Ladyship** May you enjoy God's
blessing and a happy frame of mind.   120–1 **That . . . are** i.e., That you think you are in love with
a man, and you are mistaken.   122 **If . . . you** (Olivia may interpret Viola's cryptic statement as
suggesting that Olivia "does not know herself," i.e., is distracted with passion; she may also hint at
her suspicion that "Cesario" is higher born than he admits.)   126 **fool** butt.   131 **love's . . . noon**
i.e., love, despite its attempt to be secret, reveals itself as plain as day.   134 **maugre** in spite of
135 **Nor** neither   136–7 **Do . . . cause** Do not rationalize your indifference along these lines, that
because I am the wooer you have no cause to reciprocate.   138 **But . . . fetter** But instead control
your reasoning with the following reason

VIOLA: By innocence I swear, and by my youth,   140
          I have one heart, one bosom, and one truth,
          And that no woman has, nor never none
          Shall mistress be of it save I alone.
          And so adieu, good madam. Nevermore
          Will I my master's tears to you deplore.°   145
OLIVIA: Yet come again, for thou perhaps mayst move
          That heart, which now abhors, to like his love.

          Exeunt [separately].

3.2

          Enter Sir Toby, Sir Andrew, and Fabian.

SIR ANDREW: No, faith, I'll not stay a jot longer.
SIR TOBY: Thy reason, dear venom,° give thy reason.
FABIAN: You must needs yield your reason, Sir Andrew.
SIR ANDREW: Marry, I saw your niece do more favors to the
          Count's servingman than ever she bestowed upon me. I saw't   5
          i' th' orchard.°
SIR TOBY: Did she see thee the while, old boy? Tell me that.
SIR ANDREW: As plain as I see you now.
FABIAN: This was a great argument° of love in her toward you.
SIR ANDREW: 'Slight,° will you make an ass o' me?
FABIAN: I will prove it° legitimate, sir, upon the oaths° of judg-   10
          ment and reason.
SIR TOBY: And they have been grand-jurymen since before
          Noah was a sailor.
FABIAN: She did show favor to the youth in your sight only to ex-
          asperate you, to awake your dormouse° valor, to put fire in
          your heart and brimstone in your liver. You should then have   15
          accosted her, and with some excellent jests, fire-new from the
          mint,° you should have banged° the youth into dumbness.
          This was looked for at your hand, and this was balked.° The
          double gilt° of this opportunity you let time wash off, and you

---

145 **deplore** beweep.
2 **venom** i.e., person filled with venomous anger   6 **orchard** garden.   8 **argument** proof
9 **'Slight** By his (God's) light   10 **it** my contention.   **oaths** i.e., testimony under oath   14 **dormouse**
i.e., sleepy and timid   16–7 **fire-new . . . mint** newly coined   17 **banged** struck 18 **balked** missed,
neglected.   19 **double gilt** thick layer of gold, i.e., rare worth

are now sailed into the north of my lady's opinion,° where you 20
will hang like an icicle on a Dutchman's beard° unless you do
redeem it by some laudable attempt either of valor or policy.°

SIR ANDREW: An't be any way, it must be with valor, for policy I
hate. I had as lief be a Brownist° as a politician.°

SIR TOBY: Why, then, build me thy fortunes upon the basis of 25
valor. Challenge me° the Count's youth to fight with him; hurt
him in eleven places. My niece shall take note of it; and assure
thyself, there is no love-broker° in the world can more prevail
in man's commendation with woman than report of valor.

FABIAN: There is no way but this, Sir Andrew. 30

SIR ANDREW: Will either of you bear me a challenge to him?

SIR TOBY: Go, write it in a martial hand. Be curst° and brief; it is
no matter how witty, so it be eloquent and full of invention.
Taunt him with the license of ink.° If thou "thou"-est° him
some thrice, it shall not be amiss; and as many lies° as will lie 35
in thy sheet of paper, although the sheet were big enough for
the bed of Ware° in England, set 'em down. Go, about it. Let
there be gall° enough in thy ink, though thou write with a
goose pen,° no matter. About it.

SIR ANDREW: Where shall I find you? 40

SIR TOBY: We'll call thee° at the cubiculo.° Go.

    Exit Sir Andrew.

FABIAN: This is a dear manikin° to you, Sir Toby.

SIR TOBY: I have been dear° to him, lad, some two thousand
strong or so.

FABIAN: We shall have a rare° letter from him; but you'll not
deliver't? 45

---

20 into . . . opinion i.e., out of the warmth and sunshine of Olivia's favor   **21 icicle . . . beard**
(Alludes to the arctic voyage of William Barents in 1596–1597.)   **22 policy** stratagem.   **24 Brownist**
(An early name of the Congregationalists, from the name of the founder, Robert Browne.)
politician intriguer. (Sir Andrew misinterprets Fabian's more neutral use of *policy,* "clever
stratagem.")   **25–6 build me . . . Challenge me** build . . . Challenge. ("Me" is idiomatic.)   **28 love-
broker** agent between lovers   **32 curst** fierce   **34 with . . . ink** i.e., with all the unfettered
eloquence at your disposal as a writer.   **"thou"-est** ("Thou" was used only between friends or
to inferiors.)   **35 lies** charges of lying   **37 bed of Ware** a famous bedstead capable of holding
twelve persons, about eleven feet square, said to have been at the Stag Inn in Ware, Hertfordshire
38 gall (1) bitterness, rancor (2) a growth found on certain oaks, used as an ingredient of ink
39 goose pen (1) goose quill (2) foolish style   **41 call thee** call for you. **cubiculo** little chamber,
bedchamber.   **42 manikin** puppet   **43 dear** expensive. (Playing on *dear,* "fond," in the previous
speech.)   **45 rare** extraordinary

SIR TOBY: Never trust me, then; and by all means stir on the
youth to an answer. I think oxen and wainropes° cannot hale°
them together. For° Andrew, if he were opened and you find
so much blood in his liver° as will clog the foot of a flea, I'll eat
the rest of th' anatomy.°   50

FABIAN: And his opposite,° the youth, bears in his visage no
great presage of cruelty.

   Enter Maria.

SIR TOBY: Look where the youngest wren of nine° comes.

MARIA: If you desire the spleen,° and will laugh your-selves into
stitches, follow me. Yond gull Malvolio is turned heathen, a   55
very renegado;° for there is no Christian that means to be
saved by believing rightly can ever believe such impossible
passages of grossness.° He's in yellow stockings.

SIR TOBY: And cross-gartered?

MARIA: Most villainously,° like a pedant° that keeps a school i' th'   60
church. I have dogged him like his murderer. He does obey
every point of the letter that I dropped to betray him. He does
smile his face into more lines than is in the new map with the
augmentation of the Indies.° You have not seen such a thing
as 'tis. I can hardly for bear hurling things at him. I know my   65
lady will strike him. If she do, he'll smile and take't for a great
favor.

SIR TOBY: Come, bring us, bring us where he is.

   Exeunt omnes.

3.3

   Enter Sebastian and Antonio.

SEBASTIAN: I would not by my will have troubled you,
But since you make your pleasure of your pains,
I will no further chide you.

---

47 wainropes wagon ropes. **hale** haul. **48 For** As for **49 liver** (A pale and bloodless liver was a
sign of cowardice.) **50 th' anatomy** the cadaver. **51 opposite** adversary **53 youngest . . . nine**
the last hatched and smallest of a nest of wrens **54 the spleen** a laughing fit. (The spleen was
thought to be the seat of immoderate laughter.) **56 renegado** renegade, deserter of his religion
57–8 impossible . . . grossness gross impossibilities (i.e., in the letter). **60 villainously** i.e.,
abominably. **pedant** schoolmaster **63–4 the new . . . Indies** (Probably a reference to a map
made by Emmeric Mollineux in 1599–1600 to be printed in Hakluyt's *Voyages*, showing more of
the East indies, including Japan, than had ever been mapped before.)

ANTONIO: I could not stay behind you. My desire,
More sharp than filèd steel, did spur me forth,   5
And not all° love to see you—though so much°
As might have drawn one to a longer voyage—
But jealousy° what might befall your travel,
Being skilless in° these parts, which to a stranger,
Unguided and unfriended, often prove   10
Rough and unhospitable. My willing love,
The rather° by these arguments of fear,
Set forth in your pursuit.
SEBASTIAN: My kind Antonio,
I can no other answer make but thanks,   15
And thanks; and ever oft good turns°
Are shuffled off° with such uncurrent° pay.
But were my worth,° as is my conscience,° firm,
You should find better dealing.° What's to do?
Shall we go see the relics° of this town?   20
ANTONIO: Tomorrow, sir. Best first go see your lodging.
SEBASTIAN: I am not weary, and 'tis long to night.
I pray you, let us satisfy our eyes
With the memorials and the things of fame
That do renown° this city.   25
ANTONIO: Would you'd pardon me.
I do not without danger walk these streets.
Once in a sea fight 'gainst the Count his° galleys
I did some service, of such note indeed
That were I ta'en here it would scarce be answered.°   30
SEBASTIAN: Belike° you slew great number of his people?
ANTONIO: Th' offense is not of such a bloody nature,
Albeit the quality of the time and quarrel
Might well have given us bloody argument.°
It might have since been answered° in repaying   35
What we took from them, which for traffic's° sake

---

6 all only, merely. **so much** i.e., that was great enough   **8 jealousy** anxiety   **9 skilless in** unacquainted with   **12 The rather** made all the more willing   **16 And . . . turns** (This probably corrupt line is usually made to read, "And thanks and ever thanks; and oft good turns.") **17 shuffled off** turned aside. **uncurrent** worthless (such as mere thanks)   **18 worth** wealth. **conscience** i.e., moral inclination to assist   **19 dealing** treatment, payment.   **20 relics** antiquities **25 renown** make famous   **28 Count his** Count's, i.e., Duke's   **30 it . . . answered** I'd be hard put to offer a defense.   **31 Belike** Perhaps   **34 bloody argument** cause for bloodshed.   **35 answered** compensated   **36 traffic's** trade's

Most of our city did. Only myself stood out,
For which, if I be lapsèd° in this place,
I shall pay dear.

SEBASTIAN: Do not then walk too open. 40

ANTONIO: It doth not fit me. Hold, sir, here's my purse.

[He gives his purse.]

In the south suburbs, at the Elephant,°
Is best to lodge. I will bespeak our diet,°
Whiles you beguile the time and feed your knowledge
With viewing of the town. There shall you have° me. 45

SEBASTIAN: Why I your purse?

ANTONIO: Haply° your eye shall light upon some toy°
You have desire to purchase; and your store°
I think is not for idle markets,° sir.

SEBASTIAN: I'll be your purse-bearer and leave you 50
For an hour.

ANTONIO: To th' Elephant.

SEBASTIAN: I do remember.

Exeunt [separately].

3.4

Enter Olivia and Maria.

OLIVIA: [aside]
I have sent after him; he says he'll come.°
How shall I feast him? What bestow of° him?
For youth is bought more oft than begged or borrowed.
I speak too loud.—
Where's Malvolio? He is sad and civil,° 5
And suits well for a servant with my fortunes.
Where is Malvolio?

MARIA: He's coming, madam, but in very strange manner. He is,
sure, possessed,° madam.

OLIVIA: Why, what's the matter? Does he rave? 10

---

38 lapsèd caught off guard, surprised **42 Elephant** the name of an inn **43 bespeak our diet**
order our food **45 have** find **47 Haply** Perhaps. **toy** trifle **48 store** store of money **49 is not
. . . markets** cannot afford luxuries
1 he . . . come i.e., suppose he says he'll come. **2 of** on **5 sad and civil** sober and decorous
9 possessed (1) possessed with an evil spirit (2) mad

MARIA: No, madam, he does nothing but smile. Your Ladyship were best to have some guard about you if he come, for sure the man is tainted in's° wits.

OLIVIA: Go call him hither. [*Maria summons Malvolio.*] I am as mad as he,

If sad and merry madness equal be.° 15

Enter Malvolio, [cross-gartered and in yellow stockings].

How now, Malvolio?

MALVOLIO: Sweet lady, ho, ho!

OLIVIA: Smil'st thou? I sent for thee upon a sad° occasion.

MALVOLIO: Sad, lady? I could be sad.° This does make some obstruction in the blood, this cross-gartering, but what of that? If 20 it please the eye of one, it is with me as the very true sonnet° is, "Please one and please all."°

OLIVIA: Why, how dost thou, man? What is the matter with thee?

MALVOLIO: Not black° in my mind, though yellow in my legs. It° did come to his° hands, and commands shall be executed. I think we do know the sweet roman hand.° 25

OLIVIA: Wilt thou go to bed,° Malvolio?

MALVOLIO: To bed! "Ay, sweetheart, and I'll come to thee."°

OLIVIA: God comfort thee! Why dost thou smile so and kiss thy hand so oft?

MARIA: How do you, Malvolio?

MALVOLIO: At your request? Yes, nightingales answer daws.° 30

MARIA: Why appear you with this ridiculous boldness before my lady?

MALVOLIO: "Be not afraid of greatness." 'Twas well writ.

OLIVIA: What mean'st thou by that, Malvolio?

MALVOLIO: "Some are born great—"

OLIVIA: Ha? 35

MALVOLIO: "Some achieve greatness—"

---

13 in's in his   **15 If . . . equal be** i.e., if love melancholy and smiling madness are essentially alike. (Love melancholy was regarded as a kind of madness.)   **18 sad** serious   **19 sad** (1) serious (2) melancholy.   **21 sonnet** song, ballad   **22 "Please . . . all"** "To please one special person is as good as to please everybody." (The refrain of a ballad.)   **23 black** i.e., melancholic.   **It** i.e., The letter.   **24 his** Malvolio's   **25 roman hand** fashionable italic or Italian style of handwriting rather than English "secretary" handwriting.   **26 go to bed** i.e., try to sleep off your mental distress. (But Malvolio misinterprets as a sexual invitation.)   **27 "Ay . . . thee"** (Malvolio quotes from a popular song of the day.)   **30 nightingales answer daws** i.e. (to Maria), do you suppose a fine fellow like me would answer a lowly creature (a *daw*, a "jackdaw") like you?

OLIVIA: What say'st thou?

MALVOLIO: "And some have greatness thrust upon them."

OLIVIA: Heaven restore thee!

MALVOLIO: "Remember who commended thy yellow stockings—" 40

OLIVIA: Thy yellow stockings?

MALVOLIO: "And wished to see thee cross-gartered."

OLIVIA: Cross-gartered?

MALVOLIO: "Go to, thou art made, if thou desir'st to be so—"

OLIVIA: Am I made? 45

MALVOLIO: "If not, let me see thee a servant still."

OLIVIA: Why, this is very midsummer madness.°

Enter Servant.

SERVANT Madam, the young gentleman of the Count Orsino's is returned. I could hardly entreat him back. He attends Your Ladyship's pleasure.

OLIVIA: I'll come to him. [*Exit Servant.*] 50
Good Maria, let this fellow be looked to. Where's my cousin Toby? Let some of my people have a special care of him. I would not have him miscarry° for the half of my dowry.

Exeunt [Olivia and Maria, different ways].

MALVOLIO: Oho, do you come near° me now? No worse man than Sir Toby to look to me! This concurs directly with the let- 55
ter. She sends him on purpose that I may appear stubborn to him, for she incites me to that in the letter. "Cast thy humble slough," says she; "be opposite with a kinsman, surly with servants; let thy tongue tang with arguments of state; put thyself into the trick of singularity." And consequently° sets down the 60
manner how: as, a sad° face, a reverend carriage, a slow tongue, in the habit of some sir of note,° and so forth. I have limed° her, but it is Jove's doing, and Jove make me thankful! And when she went away now, "Let this fellow be looked to." "Fellow!"° Not "Malvolio," nor after my degree,° but "fellow." 65
Why, everything adheres together, that no dram° of a scruple,

47 **midsummer madness** (A proverbial phrase; the midsummer moon was supposed to cause madness.) 52 **miscarry** come to harm 53 **come near** understand, appreciate 60 **consequently** thereafter 61 **sad** serious 62 **habit . . . note** attire suited to a man of distinction 63 **limed** caught like a bird with birdlime (a sticky substance spread on branches) 65 **Fellow** (Malvolio takes the basic meaning, "companion.") 65 **after my degree** according to my position 66 **dram** (Literally, one-eighth of a fluid ounce.)

WILLIAM SHAKESPEARE

134

no scruple° of a scruple, no obstacle, no incredulous° or un-
safe° circumstance—what can be said?—nothing that can be
can come between me and the full prospect of my hopes.
Well, Jove, not I, is the doer of this, and he is to be thanked.   70

Enter [Sir] Toby, Fabian, and Maria.

SIR TOBY: Which way is he, in the name of sanctity? If all the
devils of hell be drawn in little,° and Legion° himself possessed him, yet I'll speak to him.
FABIAN: Here he is, here he is.—How is't with you, sir? How is't
with you, man?
MALVOLIO: Go off. I discard you. Let me enjoy my private.° Go   75
off.
MARIA: Lo, how hollow the fiend speaks within him! Did not I
tell you? Sir Toby, my lady prays you to have a care of him.
MALVOLIO: Aha, does she so?
SIR TOBY: Go to, go to! Peace, peace, we must deal gently with
him. Let me alone.°—How do you, Malvolio? How is't with   80
you? What, man, defy° the devil! Consider, he's an enemy to
mankind.
MALVOLIO: Do you know what you say?
MARIA: La you,° an you speak ill of the devil, how he takes it at
heart! Pray God he be not bewitched!
FABIAN: Carry his water° to th' wise woman.°   85
MARIA: Marry, and it shall be done tomorrow morning, if I live.
My lady would not lose him for more than I'll say.
MALVOLIO: How now, mistress?
MARIA: Oh, Lord!
SIR TOBY: Prithee, hold thy peace; this is not the way. Do you   90
not see you move° him? Let me alone with him.
FABIAN: No way but gentleness, gently, gently. The fiend is
rough, and will not be roughly used.
SIR TOBY: Why, how now, my bawcock!° How dost thou, chuck?°
MALVOLIO: Sir!   95

---

67 scruple (Literally, one-third of a dram.)   **incredulous** incredible   **67–8 unsafe** uncertain,
unreliable   **72 drawn in little** (1) portrayed in miniature (2) gathered into a small space.   **Legion**
an unclean spirit. ("My name is Legion, for we are many," Mark 5:9.)   **75 private** privacy.   **80 Let
me alone** Leave him to me.   **81 defy** renounce   **83 La you** Look you   **85 water** urine (for medical
analysis).   **wise woman** sorceress.   **91 move** upset, excite   **94 bawcock** fine fellow. (From the
French *beau-coq*.)   **95 chuck** (A form of "chick," term of endearment.)

SIR TOBY: Ay, biddy,° come with me. What, man, 'tis not for gravity° to play at cherry-pit° with Satan. Hang him, foul collier!°

MARIA: Get him to say his prayers, good Sir Toby, get him to pray.

MALVOLIO: My prayers, minx?

MARIA: No, I warrant you, he will not hear of godliness.   100

MALVOLIO: Go hang yourselves all! You are idle,° shallow things; I am not of your element.° You shall know more° hereafter.

Exit.

SIR TOBY: Is't possible?

FABIAN: If this were played upon a stage, now, I could condemn it as an improbable fiction.   105

SIR TOBY: His very genius° hath taken the infection of the device, man.

MARIA: Nay, pursue him now, lest the device take air and taint.°

FABIAN: Why, we shall make him mad indeed.

MARIA: The house will be the quieter.

SIR TOBY: Come, we'll have him in a dark room and bound.° My   110
niece is already in the belief that he's mad. We may carry° it thus for our pleasure and his penance till our very pastime, tired out of breath, prompt us to have mercy on him, at which time we will bring the device to the bar° and crown thee for a finder of madmen.° But see, but see!   115

Enter Sir Andrew [with a letter].

FABIAN: More matter for a May morning.°

SIR ANDREW: Here's the challenge. Read it. I warrant there's vinegar and pepper in't.

FABIAN: Is't so saucy?°

SIR ANDREW: Ay, is't, I warrant him.° Do but read.   120

SIR TOBY: Give me. [*He reads.*] "Youth, whatsoever thou art, thou art but a scurvy fellow."

FABIAN: Good, and valiant.

---

96 biddy chicken   **96–7 for gravity** suitable for a man of your dignity.   **97 cherry-pit** a children's game consisting of throwing cherry stones into a little hole.   **collier** i.e., Satan. (Literally, a coal vendor.)   **101 idle** foolish   **102 element** sphere.   **know more** i.e., hear about this   **106 genius** i.e., soul, spirit   **107 take . . . taint** become exposed to air (i.e., become known) and thus spoil. **110 have . . . bound** (The standard treatment for insanity at this time.)   **111 carry** manage **114 bar** i.e., bar of judgment   **115 finder of madmen** member of a jury changed with "finding" if the accused is insane.   **116 matter . . . morning** sport for Mayday plays or games.   **119 saucy** (1) spicy (2) insolent.   **120 him** it.

SIR TOBY: [*reads*] "Wonder not, nor admire° not in thy mind, why I do call thee so, for I will show thee no reason for't."

FABIAN: A good note,° that keeps you from the blow of the law. 125

SIR TOBY: [*reads*] "Thou com'st to the Lady Olivia, and in my sight she uses thee kindly. But thou liest in thy throat; that is not the matter I challenge thee for."

FABIAN: Very brief, and to exceeding good sense—less.

SIR TOBY: [*reads*] "I will waylay thee going home, where if it be 130 thy chance to kill me—"

FABIAN: Good.

SIR TOBY: [*reads*] "Thou kill'st me like a rogue and a villain."

FABIAN: Still you keep o' th' windy° side of the law. Good.

SIR TOBY: [*reads*] "Fare thee well, and God have mercy upon one 135 of our souls! He may have mercy upon mine, but my hope is better,° and so look to thyself. Thy friend, as thou usest him, and thy sworn enemy, Andrew Aguecheek." If this letter move° him not, his legs cannot. I'll give't him.

MARIA: You may have very fit occasion for't. He is now in some 140 commerce° with my lady, and will by and by depart.

SIR TOBY: Go, Sir Andrew. Scout me° for him at the corner of the orchard like a bum-baily.° So soon as ever thou see'st him, draw, and as thou draw'st, swear horrible;° for it comes to pass oft that a terrible oath, with a swaggering accent sharply 145 twanged off, gives manhood more approbation° than ever proof° itself would have earned him. Away!

SIR ANDREW: Nay, let me alone for swearing.° *Exit.*

SIR TOBY: Now will not I deliver his letter, for the behavior of the young gentleman gives him out to be of good capacity 150 and breeding; his employment between his lord and my niece confirms no less. Therefore this letter, being so excellently ignorant, will breed no terror in the youth. He will find it comes from a clodpoll.° But, sir, I will deliver his challenge by word of mouth, set upon Aguecheek a notable report of valor, and 155

---

123 admire marvel **125 note** observation, remark **134 windy** windward, i.e., safe, where one is less likely to be driven onto legal rocks and shoals **136-7 my hope is better** (Sir Andrew's comically inept way of saying he hopes to be the survivor; instead, he seems to say, "May I be damned.") **139 move** (1) stir up (2) set in motion **141 commerce** transaction **142 Scout me** Keep watch **143 bum-baily** minor sheriff's officer employed in making arrests. **144 horrible** horribly **146 approbation** reputation (for courage). **147 proof** performance **148 let ... swearing** don't worry about my ability in swearing. **154 clodpoll** blockhead.

drive the gentleman—as I know his youth will aptly receive
it°—into a most hideous opinion of his rage, skill, fury, and
impetuosity. This will so fright them both that they will kill
one another by the look, like cockatrices.°

Enter Olivia and Viola.

FABIAN: Here he comes with your niece. Give them way° till he   160
take leave, and presently° after him.

SIR TOBY: I will meditate the while upon some horrid° message
for a challenge.

[Exeunt Sir Toby, Fabian, and Maria.]

OLIVIA: I have said too much unto a heart of stone
And laid° mine honor too unchary on't.°   165
There's something in me that reproves my fault,
But such a headstrong potent fault it is
That it but mocks reproof.

VIOLA: With the same havior that your passion bears
Goes on my master's griefs.°   170

OLIVIA: *[giving a locket]*
Here, wear this jewel for me. 'Tis my picture.
Refuse it not; it hath no tongue to vex you.
And I beseech you come again tomorrow.
What shall you ask of me that I'll deny,   175
That honor, saved, may upon asking give?°

VIOLA: Nothing but this: your true love for my master.

OLIVIA: How with mine honor may I give him that
Which I have given to you?

VIOLA: I will acquit you.°   180

OLIVIA: Well, come again tomorrow. Fare thee well.
A fiend like thee might bear my soul to hell.°   *[Exit.]*

Enter [Sir] Toby and Fabian.

SIR TOBY: Gentleman, God save thee.

156–7 his . . . it his inexperience will make him all the more ready to believe it   **159 cockatrices**
basilisks, fabulous serpents reputed to be able to kill by a mere look.   **160 Give them way** Stay out
of their way   **161 presently** immediately   **162 horrid** terrifying. (Literally, "bristling.")   **165 laid**
hazarded.   **unchary on't** recklessly on it.   **169–70 With . . . griefs** i.e., Orsino's sufferings in love
are as reckless and uncontrollable as your feelings.   **176 That . . . give?** that can be granted
without compromising my honor?   **180 acquit you** release you of your promise.   **181 A fiend . . .**
hell i.e., You are my torment. (*Like thee* means "in your likeness.")

VIOLA: And you, sir.

SIR TOBY: That defense thou hast, be take thee to't.° Of what na- 185
ture the wrongs are thou hast done him, I know not, but thy
intercepter,° full of despite,° bloody as the hunter,° attends
thee at the orchard end. Dismount thy tuck,° be yare° in thy
preparation, for thy assailant is quick, skillful, and deadly.

VIOLA: You mistake sir. I am sure no man hath any quarrel to° 190
me. My remembrance is very free and clear from any image of
offense done to any man.

SIR TOBY: You'll find it otherwise, I assure you. Therefore, if you
hold your life at any price, be take you to your guard, for your
opposite° hath in him what° youth, strength, skill, and wrath 195
can furnish man withal.°

VIOLA: I pray you, sir, what is he?

SIR TOBY: He is knight, dubbed with unhatched° rapier and on
carpet consideration,° but he is a devil in private brawl. Souls and
bodies hath he divorced three, and his incensement at this moment is so implacable that satisfaction can be none but by pangs 200
of death and sepulchre. Hob, nob° is his word;° give't or take't.

VIOLA: I will return again into the house and desire some con-
duct° of the lady. I am no fighter. I have heard of some kind of
men that put quarrels purposely on others, to taste° their
valor. Belike° this is a man of that quirk.° 205

SIR TOBY: Sir, no. His indignation derives itself out of a very
competent° injury; therefore, get you on and give him his desire. Back you shall not to the house unless you undertake that
with me which with as much safety you might answer him.
Therefore, on, or strip your sword stark naked;° for meddle° 210
you must, that's certain, or for swear to wear iron° about you.

VIOLA: This is as uncivil as strange. I beseech you, do me this
courteous office as to know of° the knight what my offense

---

185 That . . . to't Get ready to deploy whatever skill you have in fencing.   **187 intercepter** he who
lies in wait.   **despite** defiance, ill will.   **bloody as the hunter** bloodthirsty as a hunting dog
188 Dismount thy tuck Draw your rapier.   **yare** ready, nimble   **190 to** with   **195 opposite** opponent.
what whatsoever.   **196 withal** with.   **197 unhatched** unhacked, unused in battle   **198 carpet
consideration** (A carpet knight was one whose title was obtained, not in battle, but through
connections at court.)   **201 Hob, nob** Have or have not, i.e., give it or take it, kill or be killed.   **word**
motto   **202–3 conduct** safe-conduct, escort   **204 taste** test, prove   **205 Belike** Probably.   **quirk**
peculiar humor.   **207 competent** sufficient   **210 strip . . . naked** draw your sword from its sheath.
meddle engage (in conflict)   **211 forswear . . . iron** give up your right to wear a sword   **213 know
of** inquire from

to him is. It is something of my negligence, nothing of my purpose.°

SIR TOBY: I will do so.—Signor Fabian, stay you by this gentle- 215 man till my return. *Exit [Sir] Toby.*

VIOLA: Pray you, sir, do you know of this matter?

FABIAN: I know the knight is incensed against you, even to a mortal arbitrament,° but nothing of the circumstance more.

VIOLA: I beseech you, what manner of man is he? 220

FABIAN: Nothing of that wonderful promise, to read him by his form,° as you are like° to find him in the proof of his valor. He is, indeed, sir, the most skillful, bloody, and fatal opposite that you could possibly have found in any part of Illyria. Will you° walk towards him, I will make your peace with him if I can. 225

VIOLA: I shall be much bound to you for't. I am one that had rather go with° Sir Priest° than Sir Knight. I care not who knows so much of my mettle. *Exeunt.*

Enter [Sir] Toby and [Sir] Andrew.

SIR TOBY: Why, man, he's a very devil; I have not seen such a firago.° I had a pass° with him, rapier, scabbard, and all, and 230 he gives me the stuck-in° with such a mortal motion that it is inevitable; and on the answer,° he pays you as surely as your feet hits the ground they step on. They say he has been fencer to° the Sophy.

SIR ANDREW: Pox on't, I'll not meddle with him.

SIR TOBY: Ay, but he will not now be pacified. Fabian can scarce 235 hold him yonder.

SIR ANDREW: Plague on't, an I thought he had been valiant and so cunning in fence, I'd have seen him damned ere I'd have challenged him. Let him let the matter slip and I'll give him my horse, gray Capilet.°

SIR TOBY: I'll make the motion.° Stand here, make a good show on't. This shall end without the perdition of souls.° [*Aside, as* 240

---

214 **It is ... purpose** It is the result of some oversight, not anything I intended. 219 **mortal arbitrament** trial to the death 221–2 **read ... form** judge him by his appearance 222 **like** likely 224 **Will you** If you will 227 **go with** associate with. **Sir Priest** (*Sir* was a courtesy title for priests.) 230 **firago** virago. **pass** bout 231 **stuck-in** stoccado, a thrust in fencing 232 **answer** return hit 233 **to** in the service of 238 **Capilet** i.e., "little horse." (From "capel," a nag.) 239 **motion** offer. 240 **perdition of souls** i.e., loss of lives.

he crosses to meet Fabian] Marry, I'll ride your horse as well as I ride you.

> *Enter Fabian and Viola.*

[Aside to Fabian] I have his horse to take up° the quarrel. I have persuaded him the youth's a devil.

FABIAN: He is as horribly conceited of him,° and pants and looks pale as if a bear were at his heels.   245

SIR TOBY: *[to Viola]* There's no remedy, sir, he will fight with you for's oath's sake. Marry, he hath better be thought him of his quarrel, and he finds that now scarce to be worth talking of. Therefore draw, for the supportance° of his vow; he protests he will not hurt you.

VIOLA: *[aside]* Pray God defend me! A little thing would make me   250 tell them how much I lack of a man.°

FABIAN: Give ground, if you see him furious.

SIR TOBY: *[crossing to Sir Andrew]* Come, Sir Andrew, there's no remedy. The gentleman will, for his honor's sake, have one bout with you. He cannot by the *duello*° avoid it. But he has promised me, as   255 he is a gentleman and a soldier, he will not hurt you. Come on, to't.

SIR ANDREW: Pray God he keep his oath!

> *Enter Antonio.*

VIOLA: *[to Fabian]* I do assure you, 'tis against my will.

> *[They draw.]*

ANTONIO: *[drawing, to Sir Andrew]*
Put up your sword. If this young gentleman
Have done offense, I take the fault on me;   260
If you offend him, I for him defy you.

SIR TOBY: You, sir? Why, what are you?

ANTONIO: One, sir, that for his love dares yet do more
Than you have heard him brag to you he will.

SIR TOBY: *[drawing]*   265
Nay, if you be an undertaker,° I am for you.°

> *Enter Officers.*

---

242 take up settle, make up   **244 He . . . him** i.e., Cesario has as horrible a conception of Sir Andrew   **249 supportance** upholding   **250–1 A little . . . man** (With bawdy suggestion of the penis.)   **255 *duello*** dueling code   **266 undertaker** one who takes upon himself a task or business; here, a challenger.   **for you** ready for you.

FABIAN: Oh, good Sir Toby, hold! Here come the officers.

SIR TOBY: [*to Antonio*] I'll be with you anon.

VIOLA: [*to Sir Andrew*] Pray, sir, put your sword up, if you please.

SIR ANDREW: Marry, will I, sir; and for that° I promised you, I'll   270
be as good as my word. He° will bear you easily, and reins well.

FIRST OFFICER This is the man. Do thy office.

SECOND OFFICER Antonio, I arrest thee at the suit
Of Count Orsino.

ANTONIO: You do mistake me, sir.   275

FIRST OFFICER No, sir, no jot. I know your favor° well,
Though now you have no sea-cap on your head.—
Take him away. He knows I know him well.

ANTONIO: I must obey. [*To Viola*] This comes with seeking you.
But there's no remedy; I shall answer it.°   280
What will you do, now my necessity
Makes me to ask you for my purse? It grieves me
Much more for what I cannot do for you
Than what befalls myself. You stand amazed,
But be of comfort.   285

SECOND OFFICER Come, sir, away.

ANTONIO: [*to Viola*]
I must entreat of you some of that money.

VIOLA: What money, sir?
For the fair kindness you have showed me here,   290
And part° being prompted by your present trouble,
Out of my lean and low ability
I'll lend you something. My having° is not much;
I'll make division of my present° with you.
Hold, there's half my coffer.°   [*She offers money.*]   295

ANTONIO: Will you deny me now?
Is't possible that my deserts to you
Can lack persuasion?° Do not tempt° my misery,
Lest that it make me so unsound° a man
As to upbraid you with those kindnesses   300
That I have done for you.

---

270 for that as for what   **271 He** i.e., The horse   **276 favor** face   **280 answer it** stand trial and make reparation for it.   **291 part** partly   **293 having** wealth   **294 present** present store **295 coffer** purse. (Literally, strongbox.)   **297–8 deserts . . . persuasion** claims on you can fail to persuade you to help me.   **298 tempt** try too severely   **299 unsound** morally weak, lacking in self-control

VIOLA: I know of none,
  Nor know I you by voice or any feature.
  I hate ingratitude more in a man
  Than lying, vainness,° babbling drunkenness,   305
  Or any taint of vice whose strong corruption
  Inhabits our frail blood.

ANTONIO: Oh, heavens themselves!

SECOND OFFICER   Come, sir, I pray you, go.

ANTONIO: Let me speak a little. This youth that you see here   310
  I snatched one half out of the jaws of death,
  Relieved him with such sanctity of love,°
  And to his image,° which methought did promise
  Most venerable worth,° did I devotion.

FIRST OFFICER   What's that to us? The time goes by. Away!   315

ANTONIO: But, oh, how vile an idol proves this god!
  Thou hast, Sebastian, done good feature shame.°
  In nature there's no blemish but the mind;
  None can be called deformed but the unkind.°
  Virtue is beauty, but the beauteous evil°   320
  Are empty trunks° o'erflourished° by the devil.

FIRST OFFICER   The man grows mad. Away with him! Come,
  come, sir.

ANTONIO: Lead me on.   *Exit [with Officers].*

VIOLA: *[aside]*
  Methinks his words do from such passion fly
  That he believes himself. So do not I.°   325
  Prove true, imagination, oh, prove true,
  That I, dear brother, be now ta'en for you!

SIR TOBY: Come hither, knight. Come hither, Fabian.
  We'll whisper o'er a couplet or two of most sage saws.°

  [They gather apart from Viola.]

---

305 **vainness** vaingloriousness   312 **such ... love** i.e., such veneration as is due to a sacred relic
313 **image** what he appeared to be. (Playing on the idea of a religious icon to be venerated.)
314 **venerable worth** worthiness of being venerated   317 **Thou ... shame** i.e., You have shamed
physical beauty by showing that it does not always reflect inner beauty.   319 **unkind** ungrateful,
unnatural.   320 **beauteous evil** those who are outwardly beautiful but evil within   321 **trunks**
(1) chests (2) bodies.   **o'erflourished** (1) covered with ornamental carvings (2) made outwardly
beautiful 325 **So ... I** i.e., I do not believe myself (in the hope that has arisen in me).   329 **We'll ...**
saws i.e., Let's converse privately. (*Saws* are sayings.)

VIOLA: He named Sebastian. I my brother know   330
Yet living in my glass;° even such and so
In favor° was my brother, and he went
Still° in this fashion, color, ornament,
For him I imitate. Oh, if it prove,°
Tempests are kind, and salt waves fresh in love!   335

     [Exit.]

SIR TOBY: A very dishonest° paltry boy, and more a coward than
a hare. His dishonesty° appears in leaving his friend here in
necessity and denying° him; and for his cowardship, ask
Fabian.

FABIAN: A coward, a most devout coward, religious in it.°

SIR ANDREW: 'Slid,° I'll after him again and beat him.   340

SIR TOBY: Do, cuff him soundly, but never draw thy sword.

SIR ANDREW: An I do not— *[Exit.]*

FABIAN: Come, let's see the event.°

SIR TOBY: I dare lay° any money 'twill be nothing yet.°

     Exeunt.

4.1

     Enter Sebastian and Clown [Feste].

FESTE: Will you make me believe that I am not sent for you?

SEBASTIAN: Go to, go to, thou art a foolish fellow. Let me be
clear of thee.

FESTE: Well held out,° i' faith! No, I do not know you, nor I am
not sent to you by my lady to bid you come speak with her,
nor your name is not Master Cesario, nor this is not my nose,   5
neither. Nothing that is so is so.

SEBASTIAN: I prithee, vent° thy folly somewhere else. Thou
know'st not me.

FESTE: Vent my folly! He has heard that word of° some great
man, and now applies it to a fool. Vent my folly! I am afraid

---

330–1 **I . . . glass** i.e., I know that my brother's likeness lives in me   332 **favor** appearance
333 **Still** always   334 **prove** prove true   336 **dishonest** dishonorable   337 **dishonesty** dishonor
338 **denying** refusing to acknowledge   339 **religious in it** making a religion of cowardice.
340 **'Slid** By his (God's) eyelid   343 **event** outcome.   344 **lay** wager.   **yet** nevertheless, after all.
3 **held out** kept up   6 **vent** (1) utter (2) void, excrete, get rid of   7 **of** from, suited to the diction
of; or, with reference to

this great lubber,° the world, will prove a cockney.° I prithee
now, ungird thy strangeness° and tell me what I shall vent to   10
my lady. Shall I vent to her that thou art coming?

SEBASTIAN: I prithee, foolish Greek,° depart from me. There's
money for thee. [*He gives money.*] If you tarry longer, I shall
give worse payment.

FESTE: By my troth, thou hast an open° hand. These wise men
that give fools money get themselves a good report°—after   15
fourteen years' purchase.°

Enter [Sir] Andrew, [Sir] Toby, and Fabian.

SIR ANDREW: Now, sir, have I met you again? There's for you!
[*He strikes Sebastian.*]

SEBASTIAN: Why, there's for thee, and there, and there!

[*He beats Sir Andrew with the hilt of his dagger.*]

Are all the people mad?

SIR TOBY: Hold, sir, or I'll throw your dagger o'er the house.

FESTE: This will I tell my lady straight.° I would not be in some   20
of your coats° for two pence.   [*Exit.*]

SIR TOBY: Come on, sir, hold!   [*He grips Sebastian.*]

SIR ANDREW: Nay, let him alone. I'll go another way to work with
him. I'll have an action of battery° against him, if there be any
law in Illyria. Though I struck him first, yet it's no matter for that.

SEBASTIAN: Let go thy hand!   25

SIR TOBY: Come, sir, I will not let you go. Come, my young soldier, put up your iron. You are well fleshed.° Come on.

SEBASTIAN: I will be free from thee. [*He breaks free and draws his
sword.*] What wouldst thou now?
If thou dar'st tempt° me further, draw thy sword.   30

SIR TOBY: What, what? Nay, then I must have an ounce or two of
this malapert° blood from you.   [*He draws.*]

Enter Olivia.

9 **lubber** lout.   **cockney** effeminate or foppish fellow. (Feste comically despairs of finding common
sense anywhere if people start using affected phrases like those Sebastian uses.)   **10 ungird thy
strangeness** put off your affectation of being a stranger. (Feste apes the kind of high-flown speech he
has just deplored.)   **12 Greek** (1) one who speaks gibberish (as in "It's all Greek to me") (2) buffoon (as
in "merry Greek")   **14 open** generous. (With money or with blows.)   **15 report** reputation.   **15–6 after
. . . purchase** i.e., at great cost and after long delays. (Land was ordinarily valued at the price of
twelve years' rental; the Fool adds two years to this figure.)   **20 straight** at once.   **20–21 in . . . coats**
i.e., in your shoes   **23 action of battery** lawsuit for physical assault   **27 fleshed** initiated into battle.
30 tempt make trial of   **32 malapert** saucy, impudent

OLIVIA: Hold, Toby! On thy life I charge thee, hold!

SIR TOBY: Madam—

OLIVIA: Will it be ever thus? Ungracious wretch,   35
Fit for the mountains and the barbarous caves,
Where manners ne'er were preached! Out of my sight!—
Be not offended, dear Cesario.—
Rudesby,° begone!

[Exeunt Sir Toby, Sir Andrew, and Fabian.]

I prithee, gentle friend,   40
Let thy fair wisdom, not thy passion, sway
In this uncivil and unjust extent°
Against thy peace. Go with me to my house,
And hear thou there how many fruitless pranks
This ruffian hath botched up,° that thou thereby   45
Mayst smile at this. Thou shalt not choose but go.°
Do not deny.° Beshrew° his soul for me!°
He started one poor heart of mine, in thee.°

SEBASTIAN: *[aside]*
What relish is in this?° How runs the stream?   50
Or° I am mad, or else this is a dream.
Let fancy still my sense in Let he steep;°
If it be thus to dream, still let me sleep!

OLIVIA: Nay, come, I prithee. Would thou'dst be ruled by me!

SEBASTIAN: Madam, I will.   55

OLIVIA: Oh, say so, and so be!   *Exeunt.*

4.2

Enter Maria [carrying a gown and a false beard], and Clown [Feste].

MARIA: Nay, I prithee, put on this gown and this beard; make
him believe thou art Sir° Topas° the curate. Do it quickly. I'll
call Sir Toby the whilst.° *[Exit.]*

39 **Rudesby** Ruffian   42 **extent** attack   45 **botched up** clumsily contrived 46 **Thou . . . go** I insist on your going with me.   47 **deny** refuse.   **Beshrew** Curse. (A mild oath.)   **for me** for my part. 48 **He . . . thee** i.e., He alarmed that part of my heart which lies in your bosom. (To *start* is also to drive an animal such as a *hart [heart]* from its cover.)   50 **What . . . this?** i.e., What am I to make of this? (*Relish* means "taste.")   51 **Or** Either   52 **Let . . . steep** i.e., Let this fantasy continue to steep my senses in forgetfulness. (*Lethe* is the river of forgetfulness in the underworld.) 2 **Sir** (An honorific title for priests.) **Topas** (A name perhaps derived from Chaucer's comic knight in the "Rime of Sir Thopas" or from a similar character in Lyly's *Endymion*. Topaz, a semiprecious stone, was believed to be a cure for lunacy.)   3 **the whilst** in the meantime.

FESTE: Well, I'll put it on, and I will dissemble° myself in't, and I
would I were the first that ever dissembled in such a gown.   5
[*He disguises himself in gown and beard.*] I am not tall enough
to become the function° well, nor lean° enough to be thought
a good student;° but to be said an honest man and a good
housekeeper goes as fairly as to say a careful man and a great
scholar.° The competitors° enter.

    Enter [Sir] Toby [and Maria].

SIR TOBY: Jove bless thee, Master Parson.   10
FESTE: *Bonos dies,*° Sir Toby. For, as the old hermit of Prague,°
that never saw pen and ink, very wittily said to a niece of King
Gorboduc,° "That that is, is"; so I, being Master Parson, am
Master Parson; for what is "that" but "that," and "is" but "is"?
SIR TOBY: To him, Sir Topas.   15
FESTE: What, ho, I say! Peace in this prison!

    *[He approaches the door behind which Malvolio is
    confined.]*

SIR TOBY: The knave counterfeits well; a good knave.
MALVOLIO: (*within*) Who calls there?
FESTE: Sir Topas the curate, who comes to visit Malvolio the lunatic.
MALVOLIO: Sir Topas, Sir Topas, good Sir Topas, go to my lady—   20
FESTE: Out, hyperbolical° fiend!° How vexest thou this man!
Talkest thou nothing but of ladies?
SIR TOBY: Well said, Master Parson.
MALVOLIO: Sir Topas, never was man thus wronged. Good Sir   25
Topas, do not think I am mad. They have laid me here in
hideous darkness.
FESTE: Fie, thou dishonest Satan! I call thee by the most modest°
terms, for I am one of those gentle ones that will use the devil
himself with courtesy. Say'st thou that house° is dark?
MALVOLIO: As hell, Sir Topas.

---

4 dissemble disguise. (With a play on "feign.")   **7 become the function** adorn the priestly office
lean (Scholars were proverbially sparing of diet.)   **8 student** scholar (in divinity)   **8–9 to be . . .
scholar** to be accounted honest and hospitable is as good as being known as a painstaking scholar.
(Feste suggests that honesty and charity are found as often in ordinary men as in clerics.)
9 competitors associates, partners (in this plot)   **11 *Bonos dies*** Good day.   **hermit of Prague**
(Probably another invented authority.)   **12–3 King Gorboduc** a legendary king of ancient Britain,
protagonist in the English tragedy *Gorboduc* (1562)   **21 hyperbolical** vehement, boisterous.
fiend i.e., the devil supposedly possessing Malvolio.   **27 modest** moderate   **29 house** i.e., room

FESTE: Why, it hath bay windows transparent as barricadoes,° 30
and the clerestories° toward the south north are as lustrous as
ebony; and yet complainest thou of obstruction?

MALVOLIO: I am not mad, Sir Topas. I say to you this house is
dark.

FESTE: Madman, thou errest. I say there is no darkness but ignorance, in which thou art more puzzled than the Egyptians 35
in their fog.°

MALVOLIO: I say this house is as dark as ignorance, though ignorance were as dark as hell; and I say there was never man thus
abused. I am no more mad than you are. Make the trial of it in
any constant question.°

FESTE: What is the opinion of Pythagoras concerning wildfowl?° 40

MALVOLIO: That the soul of our grandam might haply° inhabit a
bird.

FESTE: What think'st thou of his opinion?

MALVOLIO: I think nobly of the soul, and no way approve his
opinion.

FESTE: Fare thee well. Remain thou still in darkness. Thou shalt
hold th' opinion of Pythagoras ere I will allow of thy wits,° and 45
fear to kill a woodcock° lest thou dispossess the soul of thy
grandam. Fare thee well.

[He moves away from Malvolio's prison.]

MALVOLIO: Sir Topas, Sir Topas!

SIR TOBY: My most exquisite Sir Topas!

FESTE: Nay, I am for all waters.° 50

MARIA: Thou mightst have done this without thy beard and
gown. He sees thee not.

SIR TOBY: To him in thine own voice, and bring me word how
thou find'st him.—I would we were well rid of this knavery. If
he may be conveniently delivered,° I would he were, for I am 55

---

30 barricadoes barricades. (Which are opaque. Feste speaks comically in impossible paradoxes,
but Malvolio seems not to notice.) **31 clerestories** windows in an upper wall **35 Egyptians . . .
fog** (Alluding to the darkness brought upon Egypt by Moses; see Exodus 10:21–3.) **39 constant
question** problem that requires consecutive reasoning. **40 Pythagoras . . . wildfowl** (An
opening for the discussion of transmigration of souls, a doctrine held by Pythagoras.) **41 haply**
perhaps **45 allow of thy wits** certify your sanity. **46 woodcock** (A proverbially stupid bird,
easily caught.) **50 Nay . . . waters** i.e., Indeed, I can turn my hand to anything. **55 delivered**
i.e., delivered from prison

now so far in offense with my niece that I cannot pursue with any safety this sport to the upshot.° Come by and by to my chamber.

    Exit [with Maria].

FESTE: [*singing as he approaches Malvolio's prison*]
    "Hey, Robin, jolly Robin,
    Tell me how thy lady does."°   60

MALVOLIO: Fool!

FESTE: "My lady is unkind, pardie."°

MALVOLIO: Fool!

FESTE: "Alas, why is she so?"

MALVOLIO: Fool, I say!   65

FESTE: "She loves another—" Who calls, ha?

MALVOLIO: Good Fool, as ever thou wilt deserve well at my hand, help me to a candle, and pen, ink, and paper. As I am a gentleman, I will live to be thankful to thee for't.

FESTE: Master Malvolio?   70

MALVOLIO: Ay, good Fool.

FESTE: Alas, sir, how fell you besides° your five wits?°

MALVOLIO: Fool, there was never man so notoriously abused.° I am as well in my wits, Fool, as thou art.

FESTE: But° as well? Then you are mad indeed, if you be no better in your wits than a fool.   75

MALVOLIO: They have here propertied me,° keep me in darkness, send ministers to me—asses—and do all they can to face me out of my wits.°

FESTE: Advise you° what you say. The minister is here. [*He speaks as Sir Topas.*] Malvolio, Malvolio, thy wits the heavens restore! Endeavor thyself to sleep, and leave thy vain bibble-babble.   80

MALVOLIO: Sir Topas!

FESTE: [*in Sir Topas's voice*] Maintain no words with him, good fellow. [*In his own voice*] Who, I, sir? Not I, sir. God b'wi'you, good

---

57 upshot conclusion.   **59–60 "Hey, Robin . . . does"** (Another fragment of an old song, a version of which is attributed to Sir Thomas Wyatt.)   **62 pardie** i.e., by God, certainly.   **72 besides** out of. **five wits** The intellectual faculties, usually listed as common wit, imagination, fantasy, judgment, and memory.   **73 notoriously abused** egregiously ill treated.   **75 But** Only   **76 propertied me** i.e., treated me as property and thrown me into the lumber-room   **77 face . . . wits** brazenly represent me as having lost my wits.   **78 Advise you** Take care.

Sir Topas. [*In Sir Topas's voice*] Marry, amen. [*In his own voice*] I
will, sir, I will.

MALVOLIO: Fool! Fool! Fool, I say!   85

FESTE: Alas, sir, be patient. What say you, sir? I am shent° for
speaking to you.

MALVOLIO: Good Fool, help me to some light and some paper. I
tell thee I am as well in my wits as any man in Illyria.

FESTE: Welladay° that you were, sir!

MALVOLIO: By this hand, I am. Good Fool, some ink, paper, and   90
light; and convey what I will set down to my lady. It shall advantage thee more than ever the bearing of letter did.

FESTE: I will help you to't. But tell me true, are you not mad indeed, or do you but counterfeit?

MALVOLIO: Believe me, I am not. I tell thee true.   95

FESTE: Nay, I'll ne'er believe a madman till I see his brains. I will
fetch you light and paper and ink.

MALVOLIO: Fool, I'll requite it in the highest degree. I prithee,
begone.

FESTE: [*sings*]
    I am gone, sir,   100
    And anon, sir,
    I'll be with you again,
    In a trice,
    Like to the old Vice,°
    Your need to sustain;   105
    Who, with dagger of lath,°
    In his rage and his wrath,
    Cries, "Aha!" to the devil;
    Like a mad lad,
    "Pare thy nails,° dad?   110
    Adieu, goodman° devil!"   *Exit.*

---

86 shent scolded, rebuked   **89 Welladay** Alas, would that   **104 Vice** comic tempter of the "old"
morality plays   **106 dagger of lath** comic weapon of the Vice in at least some morality plays
110 Pare thy nails (This may allude to the belief that evil spirits could use nail parings to get
control of their victims; cf. Dromio of Syracuse in *The Comedy of Errors*, 4.3.69, "Some devils ask
but the parings of one's nail," and the Boy's characterization of Pistol in *Henry V*, 4.4.72–3, as
"this roaring devil i'th' old play, that everyone may pare his nails with a wooden dagger.")
111 goodman title for a person of substance but not of gentle birth. (This line could be Feste's
farewell to Malvolio and his "devil.")

4.3

Enter Sebastian [with a pearl].

SEBASTIAN: This is the air; that is the glorious sun;
This pearl she gave me, I do feel't and see't;
And though 'tis wonder that enwraps me thus,
Yet 'tis not madness. Where's Antonio, then?
I could not find him at the Elephant;   5
Yet there he was,° and there I found this credit,°
That he did range the town to seek me out.
His counsel now might do me golden service;
For though my soul disputes well with my sense°
That this may be some error, but no madness,   10
Yet doth this accident° and flood of fortune
So far exceed all instance,° all discourse,°
That I am ready to distrust mine eyes
And wrangle with my reason that persuades me
To any other trust° but that I am mad,   15
Or else the lady's mad. Yet if 'twere so,
She could not sway° her house, command her followers,
Take and give back affairs and their dispatch°
With such a smooth, discreet, and stable bearing
As I perceive she does. There's something in't   20
That is deceivable.° But here the lady comes.

Enter Olivia and Priest.

OLIVIA: Blame not this haste of mine. If you mean well,
Now go with me and with this holy man
Into the chantry by.° There, before him,
And underneath that consecrated roof,   25
Plight me the full assurance of your faith,
That my most jealous° and too doubtful° soul
May live at peace. He shall conceal it
Whiles° you are willing it shall come to note,°

---

6 was was previously.   **credit** report   **9 my soul ... sense** i.e., both my rational faculties and my physical senses come to the conclusion   **11 accident** unexpected event   **12 instance** precedent. **discourse** reason   **15 trust** belief   **17 sway** rule   **18 Take ... dispatch** receive reports on matters of household business and see to their execution   **21 deceivable** deceptive.   **24 chantry by** private endowed chapel nearby (where mass would be said for the souls of the dead, including Olivia's brother).   **27 jealous** anxious, mistrustful.   **doubtful** full of doubts   **29 Whiles** until.   **come to note** become known

What time° we will our celebration° keep   30
According to my birth.° What do you say?

SEBASTIAN: I'll follow this good man, and go with you,
And having sworn truth, ever will be true.

OLIVIA: Then lead the way, good father, and heavens so shine
That they may fairly note° this act of mine!   *Exeunt.*   35

5.1

Enter Clown [Feste] and Fabian.

FABIAN: Now, as thou lov'st me, let me see his letter.

FESTE: Good Master Fabian, grant me another request.

FABIAN: Anything.

FESTE: Do not desire to see this letter.

FABIAN: This is to give a dog and in recompense desire my dog
again.°   5

Enter Duke [Orsino], Viola, Curio, and lords.

ORSINO: Belong you to the Lady Olivia, friends?

FESTE: Ay, sir, we are some of her trappings.°

ORSINO: I know thee well. How dost thou, my good fellow?

FESTE: Truly, sir, the better for° my foes and the worse for my
friends.

ORSINO: Just the contrary—the better for thy friends.   10

FESTE: No, sir, the worse.

ORSINO: How can that be?

FESTE: Marry, sir, they praise me, and make an ass of me.° Now
my foes tell me plainly I am an ass, so that by my foes, sir, I
profit in the knowledge of myself, and by my friends I am
abused;° so that, conclusions to be as kisses, if your four nega- 15
tives make your two affirmatives,° why then the worse for my
friends and the better for my foes.

---

30 What time at which time.   **our celebration** i.e., the actual marriage. (What they are about to
perform is a binding betrothal.)   **31 birth** social position.   **35 fairly note** look upon with favor
5 This . . . again (Apparently a reference to a well-known reply of Dr. Bulleyn when Queen
Elizabeth asked for his dog and promised a gift of his choosing in return; he asked to have his dog
back.)   **7 trappings** ornaments, decorations.   **9 for** because of   **13 make an ass of me** i.e., flatter
me into foolishly thinking well of myself.   **15 abused** flatteringly deceived   **15–6 conclusions . . .
affirmatives** i.e., as when a young lady, asked for a kiss, says "no, no" really meaning "yes"; or, as in
grammar, two negatives make an affirmative

ORSINO: Why, this is excellent.

FESTE: By my troth, sir, no, though° it please you to be one of my friends.°

ORSINO: Thou shalt not be the worse for me. There's gold.   20

[He gives a coin.]

FESTE: But° that it would be double-dealing,° sir, I would you could make it another.

ORSINO: Oh, you give me ill counsel.

FESTE: Put your grace in your pocket,° sir, for this once, and let your flesh and blood obey it.°   25

ORSINO: Well, I will be so much a sinner to be° a double-dealer. There's another. *[He gives another coin.]*

FESTE: *Primo, secundo, tertio,*° is a good play,° and the old saying is, the third pays for all.° The triplex,° sir, is a good tripping measure; or the bells of Saint Bennet,° sir, may put you in mind—one, two, three.   30

ORSINO: You can fool no more money out of me at this throw.° If you will let your lady know I am here to speak with her, and bring her along with you, it may awake my bounty further.

FESTE: Marry, sir, lullaby to your bounty till I come again. I go, sir, but I would not have you to think that my desire of having   35 is the sin of covetousness. But as you say, sir, let your bounty take a nap. I will awake it anon.   *Exit.*

Enter Antonio and Officers.

VIOLA: Here comes the man, sir, that did rescue me.

ORSINO: That face of his I do remember well,
Yet when I saw it last it was besmeared   40
As black as Vulcan° in the smoke of war.
A baubling° vessel was he captain of,

---

18 though even though   **19 friends** i.e., those who, according to Feste's syllogism, flatter him.
21 But Except for the fact.   **double-dealing** (1) giving twice (2) deceit, duplicity   **24 Put . . . pocket**
(1) Pay no attention to your honor, put it away (2) Reach in your pocket or purse and show your
customary grace or munificence. (*Your Grace* is also the formal way of addressing a duke.)   **25 it**
i.e., my "ill counsel."   **26 to be** as to be   **27 *Primo . . . tertio*** Latin ordinals: first, second, third.
play (Perhaps a mathematical game or game of dice.)   **28 the third . . . all** the third time is lucky.
(Proverbial.)   **triplex** triple time in music   **29 Saint Bennet** church of St. Benedict   **32 throw**
(1) time (2) throw of the dice.   **41 Vulcan** Roman god of fire and smith to the other gods; his face
was blackened by the fire   **42 baubling** insignificant, trifling

For° shallow draft° and bulk unprizable,°
With which such scatheful° grapple did he make
With the most noble bottom° of our fleet   45
That very envy° and the tongue of loss°
Cried fame and honor on him. What's the matter?

FIRST OFFICER   Orsino, this is that Antonio
That took the *Phoenix* and her freight from Candy,°
And this is he that did the *Tiger* board   50
When your young nephew Titus lost his leg.
Here in the streets, desperate of shame and state,°
In private brabble° did we apprehend him.

VIOLA: He did me kindness, sir, drew on my side,
But in conclusion put strange speech upon me.°   55
I know not what 'twas but distraction.°

ORSINO: Notable° pirate, thou saltwater thief,
What foolish boldness brought thee to their mercies
Whom thou in terms so bloody and so dear°
Hast made thine enemies?   60

ANTONIO: Orsino, noble sir,
Be pleased that I° shake off these names you give me.
Antonio never yet was thief or pirate,
Though, I confess, on base and ground° enough
Orsino's enemy. A witchcraft drew me hither.   65
That most ingrateful boy there by your side
From the rude sea's enraged and foamy mouth
Did I redeem; a wreck° past hope he was.
His life I gave him, and did thereto add
My love, without retention° or restraint,   70
All his in dedication.° For his sake
Did I expose myself—pure° for his love—
Into° the danger of this adverse° town,

---

43 For because of. **draft** depth of water a ship draws. **unprizable** of value too slight to be
estimated, not worth taking as a "prize" **44 scatheful** destructive **45 bottom** ship **46 very envy**
i.e., even those who had most reason to hate him, his enemies. **loss** i.e., the losers **49 from
Candy** on her return from Candia, or Crete **52 desperate . . . state** recklessly disregarding the
disgrace and danger to himself **53 brabble** brawl **55 put . . . me** spoke to me strangely.
56 but distraction unless (it was) madness. **57 Notable** Notorious **59 in terms . . . dear** in so
bloodthirsty and costly a manner **62 Be pleased that I** Allow me to **64 base and ground** solid
grounds **68 wreck** shipwrecked person **70 retention** reservation **71 All . . . dedication** devoted
wholly to him. **72 pure** entirely, purely **73 Into** unto. **adverse** hostile

Drew to defend him when he was beset;
Where being apprehended, his false cunning,   75
Not meaning to partake with me in danger,
Taught him to face me out of his acquaintance°
And grew a twenty years' removèd thing
While one would wink;° denied me mine own purse,
Which I had recommended° to his use   80
Not half an hour before.

VIOLA: How can this be?

ORSINO: When came he to this town?

ANTONIO: Today, my lord; and for three months before,
No interim, not a minute's vacancy,   85
Both day and night did we keep company.

Enter Olivia and attendants.

ORSINO: Here comes the Countess. Now heaven walks on earth.
But for° thee, fellow—fellow, thy words are madness.
Three months this youth hath tended upon me;
But more of that anon.—Take him aside.   90

OLIVIA: [*to Orsino*]
What would my lord—but that he may not have°—
Wherein Olivia may seem serviceable?—
Cesario, you do not keep promise with me.

VIOLA: Madam?   95

ORSINO: Gracious Olivia—

OLIVIA: What do you say, Cesario?—Good my lord°—

VIOLA: My lord would speak. My duty hushes me.

OLIVIA: If it be aught to the old tune, my lord,
It is as fat and fulsome° to mine ear   100
As howling after music.

ORSINO: Still so cruel?

OLIVIA: Still so constant, lord.

ORSINO: What, to perverseness? You uncivil lady,
To whose ingrate and unauspicious° altars   105

---

77 face . . . acquaintance brazenly deny he knew me   **78–9 grew . . . wink** in the twinkling of an
eye acted as though we had been estranged for twenty years   **80 recommended** consigned
88 for as for   **91 but . . . have** except that which he may not have—i.e., my love   **97 Good my lord**
(Olivia urges Orsino to listen to Cesario.)   **100 fat and fulsome** gross and offensive   **105 ingrate**
and unauspicious thankless and unpropitious

My soul the faithfull'st off'rings have breathed out
That e'er devotion tendered! What shall I do?

OLIVIA: Even what it please my lord that shall become° him.

ORSINO: Why should I not, had I the heart to do it,
Like to th' Egyptian thief° at point of death   110
Kill what I love?—a savage jealousy
That sometime savors nobly.° But hear me this:
Since you to nonregardance° cast my faith,
And that° I partly know the instrument
That screws° me from my true place in your favor,   115
Live you the marble-breasted tyrant still.
But this your minion,° whom I know you love,
And whom, by heaven I swear, I tender° dearly,
Him will I tear out of that cruel eye
Where he sits crownèd in his master's spite.°—   120
Come, boy, with me. My thoughts are ripe in mischief.
I'll sacrifice the lamb that I do love,
To spite a raven's heart within a dove.°   [Going.]

VIOLA: And I, most jocund, apt,° and willingly,
To do you rest,° a thousand deaths would die.   125

            [Going.]

OLIVIA: Where goes Cesario?

VIOLA: After him I love
More than I love these eyes, more than my life,
More by all mores° than e'er I shall love wife.
If I do feign, you witnesses above   130
Punish my life for tainting of my love!°

OLIVIA: Ay me, detested!° How am I beguiled!

VIOLA: Who does beguile you? Who does do you wrong?

---

108 **become** suit   110 **th' Egyptian thief** (An allusion to the story of Theagenes and Chariclea
in the *Ethiopica*, a Greek romance by Heliodorus. The robber chief, Thyamis of Memphis,
having captured Chariclea and fallen in love with her, is attacked by a larger band of robbers;
threatened with death, he attempts to slay her first.)   112 **savors nobly** is not without nobility.
113 **nonregardance** neglect   114 **that** since   115 **screws** pries, forces   117 **minion** darling, favorite
118 **tender** regard   119–20 **Him ... spite** I will tear Cesario away from Olivia, in whose cruel
eye he sits like a king to spite me, his true master.   122–3 **I'll ... dove** i.e., I'll kill Cesario, whom
I love, to revenge myself on this seemingly gracious but black-hearted lady.   124 **apt** readily
125 **do you rest** give you ease   129 **by all mores** by all such comparisons   131 **Punish ... love!**
punish me with death for being disloyal to the love I feel!   132 **detested** hated and denounced
by another.

WILLIAM SHAKESPEARE

OLIVIA: Hast thou forgot thyself? Is it so long?
Call forth the holy father. [*Exit an attendant.*]

ORSINO: [*to Viola*] Come, away! 135

OLIVIA: Whither, my lord?—Cesario, husband, stay.

ORSINO: Husband?

OLIVIA: Ay, husband. Can he that deny?

ORSINO: [*to Viola*]
Her husband, sirrah?° 140

VIOLA: No, my lord, not I.

OLIVIA: Alas, it is the baseness of thy fear
That makes thee strangle thy propriety.°
Fear not, Cesario, take thy fortunes up;
Be that° thou know'st thou art, and then thou art 145
As great as that thou fear'st.°

Enter Priest.

Oh, welcome, father!
Father, I charge thee by thy reverence
Here to unfold—though lately we intended
To keep in darkness what occasion° now 150
Reveals before 'tis ripe—what thou dost know
Hath newly passed between this youth and me.

PRIEST A contract of eternal bond of love,
Confirmed by mutual joinder° of your hands,
Attested by the holy close° of lips, 155
Strengthened by interchangement of your rings,
And all the ceremony of this compact
Sealed in my function,° by my testimony;
Since when, my watch hath told me, toward my grave
I have traveled but two hours. 160

ORSINO: [*to Viola*]
Oh, thou dissembling cub! What wilt thou be
When time hath sowed a grizzle° on thy case?°
Or will not else thy craft so quickly grow

___

140 sirrah (The normal way of addressing an inferior.)   **143 strangle thy propriety** i.e., deny what is properly yours, disavow your marriage to me.   **145 that** that which   **146 as that thou fear'st** as him you fear, i.e., Orsino.   **150 occasion** necessity   **154 joinder** joining   **155 close** meeting   **158 Sealed . . . function** ratified through my carrying out of my priestly office   **162 grizzle** scattering of gray hair.   **case** skin.

That thine own trip° shall be thine overthrow?
Farewell, and take her, but direct thy feet   165
Where thou and I henceforth may never meet.

VIOLA: My Lord, I do protest—

OLIVIA: Oh, do not swear!
Hold little faith, though thou hast too much fear.°

Enter Sir Andrew.

SIR ANDREW: For the love of God, a surgeon! Send one presently°
to Sir Toby.   170

OLIVIA: What's the matter?

SIR ANDREW: He's broke° my head across, and has given
Sir Toby a bloody coxcomb° too. For the love of God, your
help! I had rather than forty pound I were at home.

OLIVIA: Who has done this, Sir Andrew?   175

SIR ANDREW: The Count's gentleman, one Cesario. We took him
for a coward, but he's the very devil incardinate.°

ORSINO: My gentleman, Cesario?

SIR ANDREW: 'Od's lifelings,° here he is!—You broke my head
for nothing, and that that I did I was set on to do't by Sir   180
Toby.

VIOLA: Why do you speak to me? I never hurt you.
You drew your sword upon me without cause,
But I bespake you fair,° and hurt you not.   185

SIR ANDREW: If a bloody coxcomb be a hurt, you have hurt me. I
think you set nothing by° a bloody cox-comb.

Enter [Sir] Toby and Clown [Feste].

Here comes Sir Toby, halting.° You shall hear more. But if he
had not been in drink, he would have tickled you othergates°
than he did.

ORSINO: How now, gentleman? How is't with you?   190

SIR TOBY: That's all one.° He's hurt me, and there's th'end
on't.°—Sot,° didst see Dick surgeon, sot?

---

164 **trip** wrestling trick used to throw an opponent. (You'll get overclever and trip yourself up.)
169 **Hold . . . fear** Keep to your oath as well as you can, even if you are frightened by Orsino's
threats.   170 **presently** immediately   173 **broke** broken the skin, cut   174 **coxcomb** fool's cap
resembling the crest of a cock; here, head   178 **incardinate** (For "incarnate.")   180 **'Od's lifelings**
By God's little lives   185 **bespake you fair** addressed you courteously   187 **set nothing by** regard
as insignificant   188 **halting** limping.   189 **othergates** otherwise   191 **That's all one** It doesn't
matter; never mind.   191–2 **there's . . . on't** that's all there is to it.   192 **Sot** (1) Fool (2) Drunkard

FESTE: Oh, he's drunk, Sir Toby, an hour agone;° his eyes were
set° at eight i'th' morning.

SIR TOBY: Then he's a rogue, and a passy measures pavane.° I 195
hate a drunken rogue.

OLIVIA: Away with him! Who hath made this havoc with them?

SIR ANDREW: I'll help you, Sir Toby, because we'll be dressed°
together.

SIR TOBY: Will you help? An ass-head and a coxcomb and a 200
knave, a thin-faced knave, a gull!

OLIVIA: Get him to bed, and let his hurt be looked to.

> [Exeunt Feste, Fabian, Sir Toby, and Sir Andrew.]

Enter Sebastian.

SEBASTIAN: I am sorry, madam, I have hurt your kinsman;
But, had it been the brother of my blood,°
I must have done no less with wit and safety.°—   205
You throw a strange regard upon me,° and by that
I do perceive it hath offended you.
Pardon me, sweet one, even for the vows
We made each other but so late ago.

ORSINO: One face, one voice, one habit,° and two persons,   210
A natural perspective,° that is and is not!

SEBASTIAN: Antonio, O my dear Antonio!
How have the hours racked° and tortured me
Since I have lost thee!

ANTONIO: Sebastian are you?   215

SEBASTIAN: Fear'st thou that,° Antonio?

ANTONIO: How have you made division of yourself?
An apple cleft in two is not more twin
Than these two creatures. Which is Sebastian?

OLIVIA: Most wonderful!   220

SEBASTIAN: [*seeing Viola*]
Do I stand there? I never had a brother;
Nor can there be that deity in my nature

---

193 **agone** ago   194 **set** fixed or closed   195 **passy measures pavane** passe-measure pavane, a
slow-moving, stately dance. (Suggesting Sir Toby's impatience to have his wounds dressed.)
198 **be dressed** have our wounds surgically dressed   204 **the brother ... blood** my own brother
205 **with wit and safety** with intelligent concern for my own safety.   206 **You ... me** You look
strangely at me   210 **habit** dress   211 **A natural perspective** an optical device or illusion created
in this instance by nature   213 **racked** tortured   216 **Fear'st thou that** Do you doubt that

Of here and everywhere.° I had a sister,
Whom the blind° waves and surges have devoured.
Of charity,° what kin are you to me?   225
What countryman? What name? What parentage?

VIOLA: Of Messaline. Sebastian was my father.
Such a Sebastian was my brother, too.
So went he suited° to his watery tomb.
If spirits can assume both form and suit,°   230
You come to fright us.

SEBASTIAN: A spirit I am indeed,
But am in that dimension grossly clad°
Which from the womb I did participate.°
Were you a woman, as the rest goes even,°   235
I should my tears let fall upon your cheek
And say, "Thrice welcome, drownèd Viola!"

VIOLA: My father had a mole upon his brow.

SEBASTIAN: And so had mine.

VIOLA: And died that day when Viola from her birth   240
Had numbered thirteen years.

SEBASTIAN: Oh, that record° is lively in my soul!
He finishèd indeed his mortal act
That day that made my sister thirteen years.

VIOLA: If nothing lets° to make us happy both   245
But this my masculine usurped attire,
Do not embrace me till each circumstance
Of place, time, fortune, do cohere and jump°
That I am Viola—which to confirm
I'll bring you to a captain in this town   250
Where lie my maiden weeds,° by whose gentle help
I was preserved to serve this noble count.
All the occurrence of my fortune since
Hath been between this lady and this lord.

SEBASTIAN: [to Olivia]
So comes it, lady, you have been mistook.   255
But nature to her bias drew in that.°

---

223 here and everywhere omnipresence.   **224 blind** heedless, indiscriminate   **225 Of charity** (Tell me) in kindness   **229 suited** dressed; clad in human form   **230 form and suit** physical appearance and dress   **233 in ... clad** clothed in that fleshly shape **234 participate** possess in common with all humanity.   **235 as ... even** since everything else agrees   **242 record** recollection   **245 lets** hinders **248 jump** coincide, fit exactly   **251 weeds** clothes   **256 nature ... that** nature followed her bent in that. (The metaphor is from the game of bowls.)

You would have been contracted to a maid,°
Nor are you therein, by my life, deceived.
You are betrothed both to a maid and man.
ORSINO: [to Olivia]
Be not amazed; right noble is his blood.   260
If this be so, as yet the glass° seems true,
I shall have share in this most happy wreck.°
[To Viola] Boy, thou hast said to me a thousand times
Thou never shouldst love woman like to me.°
VIOLA: And all those sayings will I over swear,°   265
And all those swearings keep as true in soul
As doth that orbèd continent the fire°
That severs day from night.
ORSINO: Give me thy hand,
And let me see thee in thy woman's weeds.   270
VIOLA: The captain that did bring me first on shore
Hath my maid's garments. He upon some action°
Is now in durance,° at Malvolio's suit,
A gentleman and follower of my lady's.
OLIVIA: He shall enlarge° him. Fetch Malvolio hither.   275
And yet, alas, now I remember me,
They say, poor gentleman, he's much distract.

        Enter Clown [Feste] with a letter, and Fabian.

A most extracting° frenzy of mine own
From my remembrance clearly banished his.°
How does he, sirrah?   280
FESTE: Truly, madam, he holds Beelzebub at the stave's end° as
well as a man in his case may do. He's here writ a letter to you;
I should have given't you today morning. But as a madman's
epistles are no gospels,° so it skills° not much when they are
delivered.°

257 **a maid** i.e., a virgin man   261 **the glass** i.e., the *natural perspective* of line 216   262 **wreck**
shipwreck, accident.   264 **like to me** as well as you love me.   265 **over swear** swear again
267 **As . . . fire** i.e., as the sphere of the sun keeps the fire   272 **action** legal charge   273 **in durance**
imprisoned   275 **enlarge** release   278 **extracting** i.e., that obsessed me and drew all thoughts except
of Cesario from my mind   279 **his** i.e., his madness.   281 **holds . . . end** i.e., keeps the devil at a safe
distance. (The metaphor is of fighting with quarterstaffs or long poles.)   283–4 **a madman's . . .
gospels** i.e., there is no truth in a madman's letters. (An allusion to readings in the church
service of selected passages from the epistles and the gospels.)   284 **skills** matters.   **delivered**
(1) delivered to their recipient (2) read aloud.

OLIVIA: Open't and read it.   285

FESTE: Look then to be well edified when the fool delivers° the
madman. [*He reads loudly.*] "By the Lord, madam—"

OLIVIA: How now, art thou mad?

FESTE: No, madam, I do but read madness. An Your Ladyship
will have it as it ought to be, you must allow *vox.*°   290

OLIVIA: Prithee, read i'thy right wits.

FESTE: So I do, madonna; but to read his right wits° is to read
thus. Therefore perpend,° my princess, and give ear.

OLIVIA: [*to Fabian*] Read it you, sirrah.

FABIAN: (*reads*) "By the Lord, madam, you wrong me, and the   295
world shall know it. Though you have put me in to darkness
and given your drunken cousin rule over me, yet have I the
benefit of my senses as well as Your Ladyship. I have your own
letter that induced me to the semblance I put on, with the
which° I doubt not but to do myself much right or you much   300
shame. Think of me as you please. I leave my duty a little un-
thought of, and speak out of my injury.° The madly used
Malvolio."

OLIVIA: Did he write this?

FESTE: Ay, madam.   305

ORSINO: This savors not much of distraction.

OLIVIA: See him delivered,° Fabian. Bring him hither.

[*Exit Fabian.*]

My lord, so please you, these things further thought on,°
To think me as well a sister as a wife,°
One day shall crown th' alliance on't,° so please you,   310
Here at my house and at my proper° cost.

ORSINO: Madam, I am most apt° t'embrace your offer.
[*To Viola*] Your master quits° you; and for your service done him,
So much against the mettle° of your sex,

---

286 delivers speaks the words of   **290 vox** voice, i.e., an appropriately loud voice.   **292 to read
. . . wits** to express his true state of mind   **293 perpend** consider, attend. (A deliberately lofty
word.)   **299–300 the which** i.e., the letter   **301–2 I leave . . . injury** I leave unsaid the
expressions of duty with which I would normally conclude, and convey instead my sense of
having been wronged.   **307 delivered** released   **308 so . . . on** if you are pleased on further
consideration of all that has happened   **309 To . . . wife** to regard me as favorably as a sister-in-
law as you had hoped to regard me as a wife   **310 crown . . . on't** i.e., serve as occasion for two
marriages confirming our new relationships   **311 proper** own   **312 apt** ready   **313 quits** releases
314 mettle natural disposition

So far beneath your soft and tender breeding,   315
And since you called me master for so long,
Here is my hand. You shall from this time be
Your master's mistress.

OLIVIA: A sister! You are she.

> *Enter [Fabian, with] Malvolio.*

ORSINO: Is this the madman?   320
OLIVIA: Ay, my lord, this same.
How now, Malvolio?
MALVOLIO: Madam, you have done me wrong,
Notorious wrong.
OLIVIA: Have I, Malvolio? No.   325
MALVOLIO: [*showing a letter*]
Lady, you have. Pray you, peruse that letter.
You must not now deny it is your hand.
Write from it,° if you can, in hand or phrase,
Or say 'tis not your seal, not your invention.°   330
You can say none of this. Well, grant it then,
And tell me, in the modesty of honor,°
Why you have given me such clear lights° of favor,
Bade me come smiling and cross-gartered to you,
To put on yellow stockings, and to frown   335
Upon Sir Toby and the lighter° people?
And, acting this in an obedient hope,°
Why have you suffered me to be imprisoned,
Kept in a dark house, visited by the priest,°
And made the most notorious geck° and gull   340
That e'er invention played on?° Tell me why?
OLIVIA: Alas, Malvolio, this is not my writing,
Though, I confess, much like the character;°
But out of° question 'tis Maria's hand.
And now I do bethink me, it was she   345
First told me thou wast mad; then cam'st° in smiling,
And in such forms which here were presupposed°

---

329 from it differently **330 invention** composition.   **332 in . . . honor** in the name of all that is
decent and honorable   **333 clear lights** evident signs   **336 lighter** lesser   **337 acting . . . hope** when
I acted thus out of obedience to you and in hope of your favor   **339 priest** i.e., Feste   **340 geck**
dupe   **341 invention played on** contrivance sported with.   **343 the character** my handwriting
344 out of beyond   **346 cam'st** you came   **347 presupposed** specified beforehand

Upon thee in the letter. Prithee, be content.
This practice° hath most shrewdly passed° upon thee;
But when we know the grounds and authors of it,   350
Thou shalt be both the plaintiff and the judge
Of thine own cause.

FABIAN: Good madam, hear me speak,
And let no quarrel nor no brawl to come°
Taint the condition° of this present hour,   355
Which I have wondered at. In hope it shall not,
Most freely I confess, myself and Toby
Set this device against Malvolio here,
Upon° some stubborn and uncourteous parts°
We had conceived against him.° Maria writ   360
The letter at Sir Toby's great importance,°
In recompense whereof he hath married her.
How with a sportful malice it was followed°
May rather pluck on° laughter than revenge,
If that° the injuries be justly weighed   365
That have on both sides passed.

OLIVIA: [to Malvolio]
Alas, poor fool, how have they baffled° thee!

FESTE: Why, "Some are born great, some achieve greatness, and
some have greatness thrown upon them." I was one, sir, in
this interlude,° one Sir Topas, sir, but that's all one.° "By the   370
Lord, fool, I am not mad." But do you remember? "Madam,
why laugh you at such a barren rascal? An you smile not,
he's gagged." And thus the whirligig° of time brings in his
revenges.

MALVOLIO: I'll be revenged on the whole pack of you!   375

        [Exit.]

OLIVIA: He hath been most notoriously abused.

ORSINO: Pursue him, and entreat him to a peace.
He hath not told us of the captain yet.
When that is known, and golden time convents,°

---

349 **practice** plot.   **shrewdly passed** mischievously been perpetrated   354 **to come** in the future
355 **condition** (happy) nature   359 **Upon** on account of.   **parts** qualities, deeds   360 **conceived against
him** seen and resented in him.   361 **importance** importunity   363 **followed** carried out   364 **pluck on**
induce   365 **If that** if   367 **baffled** disgraced, quelled   370 **interlude** little play.   **that's all one** no
matter for that.   373 **whirligig** spinning top   379 **convents** (1) summons, calls together (2) suits

A solemn combination shall be made   380
Of our dear souls. Meantime, sweet sister,
We will not part from hence. Cesario, come—
For so you shall be, while you are a man;
But when in other habits° you are seen,
Orsino's mistress and his fancy's° queen.   385

      Exeunt [all, except Feste].

FESTE: (*sings*)
   When that I was and a little° tiny boy,
    With hey, ho, the wind and the rain,
   A foolish thing was but a toy,°
    For the rain it raineth every day.
   But when I came to man's estate,   390
    With hey, ho, the wind and the rain,
   'Gainst knaves and thieves men shut their gate,
    For the rain it raineth every day.
   But when I came, alas, to wive,
    With hey, ho, the wind and the rain,   395
   By swaggering could I never thrive,
    For the rain it raineth every day.
   But when I came unto my beds,°
    With hey, ho, the wind and the rain,
   With tosspots° still had drunken heads,   400
    For the rain it raineth every day.
   A great while ago the world begun,
    With hey, ho, the wind and the rain,
   But that's all one, our play is done,
    And we'll strive to please you every day.   405

     [Exit.]

---

384 habits attire   **385 fancy's** love's   **386 and a little** a little   **388 toy** trifle   **398 unto my beds** i.e., (1) drunk to bed, or, perhaps, (2) in the evening of life   **400 tosspots** drunkards

Henrik Ibsen, universally acknowledged as the first of the great modern play-wrights, was born in Skien, a small town in Norway, the son of a merchant who went bankrupt during Ibsen's childhood. Ibsen first trained for a medical career, but drifted into the theater, gaining, like Shakespeare and Molière, important dramatic training through a decade's service as a stage manager and director. Ibsen was unsuccessful in establishing a theater in Oslo, and he spent almost thirty years living and writing in Germany and Italy. The fame he won through early poetic dramas like Peer Gynt (1867), which is considered the supreme exploration of the Norwegian national character, was overshadowed by the realistic prose plays he began writing, starting with Pillars of Society *(1877).* A Doll's House *(1879) and* Ghosts *(1881), which deal, respectively, with a woman's struggle for independence and self-respect and with the taboo subject of venereal disease, made Ibsen an internationally famous, if controversial, figure. In fact, Ibsen wrote* An Enemy of the People *as a response to the public outcry over* Ghosts, *whose subject was considered so controversial that it could not be performed in London until 1891, and then for only a single performance in a private subscription theater. Although Ibsen's type of realism, displayed in "problem plays" such as these and later psychological dramas like* The Wild Duck *(1885) and* Hedda Gabler *(1890), has become so fully assimilated into our literary heritage that now it is difficult to think of him as an innovator, his marriage of the tightly constructed plots of the conventional "well-made play" to serious discussion of social issues was one of the most significant developments in the history of drama. His most influential advocate in English-speaking countries was George Bernard Shaw, whose* The Quintessence of Ibsenism *(1891) is one of the earliest and most influential studies of Ibsen's dramatic methods and ideas.*

An Enemy of the People

Adapted by Arthur Miller

Characters

Morten Kiil
Billing
Mrs. Stockmann
Peter Stockmann

Hovstad
Dr. Stockmann
Morten
Ejlif
Captain Horster
Petra
Aslaksen
The drunk

Synopsis of Scenes

The Action Takes Place in a Norwegian Town

Throughout, in the stage directions, right and left mean stage right and stage left.

Act I

Scene I. Dr. Stockmann's living room

It is evening. Dr. Stockmann's living room is simply but cheerfully furnished. A doorway, upstage right, leads into the entrance hall, which extends from the front door to the dining room, running unseen behind the living room. At the left is another door, which leads to the Doctor's study and other rooms. In the upstage left corner is a stove. Toward the left foreground is a sofa with a table behind it. In the right foreground are two chairs, a small table between them, on which stand a lamp and a bowl of apples. At the back, to the left, an open doorway leads to the dining room, part of which is seen. The windows are in the right wall, a bench in front of them.

As the curtain rises, Billing and Morten Kiil are eating in the dining room. Billing is junior editor of the People's Daily Messenger. *Kiil is a slovenly old man who is feeding himself in a great hurry. He gulps his last bite and comes into the living room, where he puts on his coat and ratty fur hat. Billing comes in to help him.*

BILLING: You sure eat fast, Mr. Kiil. [*Billing is an enthusiast to the point of foolishness.*]

KIIL: Eating don't get you anywhere, boy. Tell my daughter I went home.

Kiil starts across to the front door. Billing returns to his food in the dining room. Kiil halts at the bowl of apples; he takes one, tastes it, likes it, takes another and puts it in his pocket, then continues on toward the door. Again he stops, returns, and takes another apple for his pocket. Then he sees a tobacco can on the table. He covers his action from Billing's possible glance, opens the can, smells it, pours some into his side pocket. He is just closing the can when Catherine Stockman enters from the dining room.

MRS. STOCKMANN: Father! You're not going, are you?

KIIL: Got business to tend to.

MRS. STOCKMANN: Oh, you're only going back to your room and you know it. Stay! Mr. Billing's here, and Hovstad's coming. It'll be interesting for you.

KIIL: Got all kinds of business. The only reason I came over was the butcher told me you bought roast beef today. Very tasty, dear.

MRS. STOCKMANN: Why don't you wait for Tom? He only went for a little walk.

KIIL [*taking out his pipe*]: You think he'd mind if I filled my pipe?

MRS. STOCKMANN: No, go ahead. And here—take some apples. You should always have some fruit in your room.

KIIL: No, no, wouldn't think of it.

The doorbell rings.

MRS. STOCKMANN: That must be Hovstad. [*She goes to the door and opens it.*]

Peter Stockmann, the Mayor, enters. He is a bachelor, nearing sixty. He has always been one of those men who make it their life work to stand in the center of the ship to keep it from overturning. He probably envies the family life and warmth of this house, but when he comes he never wants to admit he came and often sits with his coat on.

MRS. STOCKMANN: Peter! Well, this is a surprise!

PETER STOCKMANN: I was just passing by . . . [*He sees Kiil and smiles, amused.*] Mr. Kiil!

KIIL [*sarcastically*]: Your Honor! [*He bites into his apple and exits.*]

MRS. STOCKMANN: You musn't mind him, Peter, he's getting terribly old. Would you like a bite to eat?

PETER STOCKMANN: No, no thanks. [*He sees Billing now, and Billing nods to him from the dining room.*]

MRS. STOCKMANN [*embarrassed*]:   He just happened to drop in.

PETER STOCKMANN: That's all right. I can't take hot food in the evening. Not with my stomach.

MRS. STOCKMANN: Can't I ever get you to eat anything in this house?

PETER STOCKMANN: Bless you, I stick to my tea and toast. Much healthier and more economical.

MRS. STOCKMANN [*smiling*]:   You sound as though Tom and I throw money out the window.

PETER STOCKMANN: Not you, Catherine. He wouldn't be home, would he?

MRS. STOCKMANN: He went for a little walk with the boys.

PETER STOCKMANN: You don't think that's dangerous, right after dinner? [*There is a loud knocking on the front door.*] That sounds like my brother.

MRS. STOCKMANN: I doubt it, so soon. Come in, please.

Hovstad enters. He is in his early thirties, a graduate of the peas-antry struggling with a terrible conflict. For while he hates au-thority and wealth, he cannot bring himself to cast off a certain desire to partake of them. Perhaps he is dangerous because he wants more than anything to belong, and in a radical that is a withering wish, not easily to be borne.

MRS. STOCKMANN: Mr. Hovstad—

HOVSTAD: Sorry I'm late. I was held up at the printing shop.

[*Surprised*]:   Good evening, Your Honor.

PETER STOCKMANN [*rather stiffly*]:   Hovstad. On business, no doubt.

HOVSTAD: Partly. It's about an article for the paper—

PETER STOCKMANN [*sarcastically*]:   Ha! I don't doubt it. I understand my brother has become a prolific contributor to—what do you call it?—the *People's Daily Liberator?*

HOVSTAD [*laughing, but holding his ground*]:   The *People's Daily Mes-senger,* sir. The Doctor sometimes honors the *Messenger* when he wants to uncover the real truth of some subject.

PETER STOCKMANN: The truth! Oh, yes, I see.

MRS. STOCKMANN [*nervously to Hovstad*]:   Would you like to . . . [*She points to dining room.*]

PETER STOCKMANN: I don't want you to think I blame the Doctor for using your paper. After all, every performer goes for the audience that applauds him most. It's really not your paper I have anything against, Mr. Hovstad.

HOVSTAD: I really didn't think so, Your Honor.

PETER STOCKMANN: As a matter of fact, I happen to admire the spirit of tolerance in our town. It's magnificent. Just don't forget that we have it because we all believe in the same thing; it brings us together.

HOVSTAD: Kirsten Springs, you mean.

PETER STOCKMANN: The springs, Mr. Hovstad, our wonderful new springs. They've changed the soul of this town. Mark my words, Kirsten Springs are going to put us on the map, and there is no question about it.

MRS. STOCKMANN: That's what Tom says too.

PETER STOCKMANN: Everything is shooting ahead—real estate going up, money changing hands every hour, business humming—

HOVSTAD: And no more unemployment.

PETER STOCKMANN: Right. Give us a really good summer, and sick people will be coming here in carloads. The springs will turn into a regular fad, a new Carlsbad. And for once the well-to-do people won't be the only ones paying taxes in this town.

HOVSTAD: I hear reservations are really starting to come in?

PETER STOCKMANN: Coming in every day. Looks very promising, very promising.

HOVSTAD: That's fine. [*To Mrs. Stockmann*]: Then the Doctor's article will come in handy.

PETER STOCKMANN: He's written something again?

HOVSTAD: No, it's a piece he wrote at the beginning of the winter, recommending the water. But at the time I let the article lie.

PETER STOCKMANN: Why, some hitch in it?

HOVSTAD: Oh, no, I just thought it would have a bigger effect in the spring, when people start planning for the summer.

PETER STOCKMANN: That's smart, Mr. Hovstad, very smart.

MRS. STOCKMANN: Tom is always so full of ideas about the springs; every day he—

PETER STOCKMANN: Well, he ought to be, he gets his salary from the springs, my dear.

HOVSTAD: Oh, I think it's more than that, don't you? After all, Doctor Stockmann *created* Kirsten Springs.

PETER STOCKMANN: You don't say! I've been hearing that lately, but I did think I had a certain modest part—

MRS. STOCKMANN: Oh, Tom always says—

HOVSTAD: I only meant the original idea was—

PETER STOCKMANN: My good brother is never at a loss for ideas. All sorts of ideas. But when it comes to putting them into action you need another kind of man, and I did think that at least people in this house would—

MRS. STOCKMANN: But Peter, dear—we didn't mean to— Go get yourself a bite, Mr. Hovstad, my husband will be here any minute.

HOVSTAD: Thank you, maybe just a little something. [*He goes into the dining room and joins Billing at the table*].

PETER STOCKMANN, [*lowering his voice*]:   Isn't it remarkable? Why is it that people without background can never learn tact?

MRS. STOCKMANN: Why let it bother you? Can't you and Thomas share the honor like good brothers?

PETER STOCKMANN: The trouble is that certain men are never satisfied to share, Catherine.

MRS. STOCKMANN: Nonsense. You've always gotten along beautifully with Tom— That must be him now.

She goes to the front door, opens it. Dr. Stockmann is laughing and talking outside. He is in the prime of his life. He might be called the eternal amateur—a lover of things, of people, of sheer living, a man for whom the days are too short, and the future fabulous with discoverable joys. And for all this most people will not like him—he will not compromise for less than God's own share of the world while they have settled for less than Man's.

DR. STOCKMANN [*in the entrance hall*]:   Hey, Catherine! Here's another guest for you! Here's a hanger for your coat, Captain. Oh, that's right, you don't wear overcoats! Go on in, boys. You kids must be hungry all over again. Come here, Captain Horster, I want you to get a look at this roast. [*He pushes Captain Horster along the hallway to the dining room. Ejlif and Morten also go to the dining room*].

MRS. STOCKMANN: Tom, dear . . . [*She motions toward Peter in the living room*].

DR. STOCKMANN [*turns around in the doorway to the living room and sees Peter*]: Oh, Peter . . . [*He walks across and stretches out his hand.*] Say now, this is really nice.

PETER STOCKMANN: I'll have to go in a minute.

DR. STOCKMANN: Oh, nonsense, not with the toddy on the table. You haven't forgotten the toddy, have you, Catherine?

MRS. STOCKMANN: Of course not, I've got the water boiling. [*She goes into the dining room*].

PETER STOCKMANN: Toddy too?

DR. STOCKMANN: Sure, just sit down and make yourself at home.

PETER STOCKMANN: No, thanks, I don't go in for drinking parties.

DR. STOCKMANN: But this is no party.

PETER STOCKMANN: What else do you call it? [*He looks toward the dining room*]. It's extraordinary how you people can consume all this food and live.

DR. STOCKMANN [*rubbing his hands*]: Why? What's finer than to watch young people eat? Peter, those are the fellows who are going to stir up the whole future.

PETER STOCKMANN [*a little alarmed*]: Is that so! What's there to stir up? *He sits in a chair to the left.*

DR. STOCKMANN [*walking around*]: Don't worry, they'll let us know when the time comes. Old idiots like you and me, we'll be left behind like—

PETER STOCKMANN: I've never been called *that* before.

DR. STOCKMANN: Oh, Peter, don't jump on me every minute! You know your trouble, Peter? Your impressions are blunted. You ought to sit up there in that crooked corner of the north for five years, the way I did, and then come back here. It's like watching the first seven days of creation!

PETER STOCKMANN: Here!

DR. STOCKMANN: Things to work and fight for, Peter! Without that you're dead. Catherine, you sure the mailman came today?

MRS. STOCKMANN, [*from the dining room*]: There wasn't any mail today.

DR. STOCKMANN: And another thing, Peter—a good income; *that's* something you learn to value after you've lived on a starvation diet.

PETER STOCKMANN: When did you starve?

DR. STOCKMANN: Damned near! It was pretty tough going a lot of the time up there. And now, to be able to live like a prince! Tonight, for instance, we had roast beef for dinner, and, by God, there was enough left for supper too. Please have a piece—come here.

PETER STOCKMANN: Oh, no, no—please, certainly not.

DR. STOCKMANN: At least let me show it to you! Come in here—we even have a tablecloth. [*He pulls his brother toward the dining room.*]

PETER STOCKMANN: I saw it.

DR. STOCKMANN: Live to the hilt! that's my motto. Anyway, Catherine says I'm earning almost as much as we spend.

PETER STOCKMANN [*refusing an apple*]: Well, you are improving.

DR. STOCKMANN: Peter, that was a joke! You're supposed to laugh! [*He sits in the other chair to the left*].

PETER STOCKMANN: Roast beef twice a day is no joke.

DR. STOCKMANN: Why can't I give myself the pleasure of having people around me? It's a necessity for me to see young, lively, happy people, free people burning with a desire to do something. You'll see. When Hovstad comes in we'll talk and—

PETER STOCKMANN: Oh, yes, Hovstad. That reminds me. He told me he was going to print one of your articles.

DR. STOCKMANN: One of my articles?

PETER STOCKMANN: Yes, about the springs—an article you wrote during the winter?

DR. STOCKMANN: Oh, that one! In the first place, I don't want that one printed right now.

PETER STOCKMANN: No? It sounded to me like it would be very timely.

DR. STOCKMANN: Under normal conditions, maybe so. [*He gets up and walks across the floor*].

PETER STOCKMANN [*looking after him*]: Well, what is abnormal about the conditions now?

DR. STOCKMANN [*stopping*]: I can't say for the moment, Peter—at least not tonight. There could be a great deal abnormal about conditions; then again, there could be nothing at all.

PETER STOCKMANN: Well, you've managed to sound mysterious. Is there anything wrong? Something you're keeping from me? Because I wish once in a while you'd remind yourself that I am chairman of the board for the springs.

DR. STOCKMANN: And I would like *you* to remember that, Peter. Look, let's not get into each other's hair.

PETER STOCKMANN: I don't make a habit of getting into people's hair! But I'd like to underline that everything concerning Kirsten Springs must be treated in a businesslike manner, through the proper channels, and dealt with by the legally constituted authorities. I can't allow anything done behind my back in a roundabout way.

DR. STOCKMANN: When did I ever go behind your back, Peter?

PETER STOCKMANN: You have an ingrained tendency to go your own way, Thomas, and that simply can't go on in a well-organized society. The individual really must subordinate himself to the over-all, or [groping for words, he points to himself] to the authorities who are in charge of the general welfare. *He gets up.*

DR. STOCKMANN: Well, that's probably so. But how the hell does that concern me, Peter?

PETER STOCKMANN: My dear Thomas, this is exactly what you will never learn. But you had better watch out because someday you might pay dearly for it. Now I've said it. Good-bye.

DR. STOCKMANN: Are you out of your mind? You're absolutely on the wrong track.

PETER STOCKMANN: I am usually not. Anyway, may I be excused? [He nods toward the dining room.] Good-by, Catherine. Good evening, gentlemen. [He leaves].

MRS. STOCKMANN, [entering the living room]: He left?

DR. STOCKMANN: And burned up!

MRS. STOCKMANN: What did you do to him now?

DR. STOCKMANN: What does he want from me? He can't expect me to give him an accounting of every move I make, every thought I think, until I am ready to do it.

MRS. STOCKMANN: Why? What should you give him an accounting of?

DR. STOCKMANN [hesitantly]: Just leave that to me, Catherine. Peculiar the mailman didn't come today.

Hovstad, Billing, and Captain Horster have gotten up from the dining-room table and enter the living room. Ejlif and Morten come in a little later. Catherine exits.

BILLING [stretching out his arms]: After a meal like that, by God, I feel like a new man. This house is so—

HOVSTAD [cutting him off]: The Mayor certainly wasn't in a glowing mood tonight.

DR. STOCKMANN: It's his stomach. He has a lousy digestion.

HOVSTAD: I think two editors from the *People's Daily Messenger* didn't help either.

DR. STOCKMANN: No, it's just that Peter is a lonely man. Poor fellow, all he knows is official business and duties, and then all that damn weak tea that he pours into himself. Catherine, may we have the toddy?

MRS. STOCKMANN [*calling from the dining room*]: I'm just getting it.

DR. STOCKMANN: Sit down here on the couch with me, Captain Horster—a rare guest like you—sit here. Sit down, friends.

HORSTER: This used to be such an ugly house. Suddenly it's beautiful!

Billing and Hovstad sit down at the right. Mrs. Stockmann brings a tray with pot, glasses, bottles, etc. on it, and puts it on the table behind the couch.

BILLING [*to Horster, intimately, indicating Stockmann*]: Great man!

MRS. STOCKMANN: Here you are. Help yourselves.

DR. STOCKMANN [*taking a glass*]: We sure will. [*He mixes the toddy.*] And the cigars, Ejlif—you know where the box is. And Morten, get my pipe. [*The boys go out to the left.*] I have a sneaking suspicion that Ejlif is snitching a cigar now and then, but I don't pay any attention. Catherine, you know where I put it? Oh, he's got it. Good boys! [*The boys bring the various things in.*] Help yourselves, fellows. I'll stick to the pipe. This one's gone through plenty of blizzards with me up in the north. Skol! [*He looks around.*] Home! What an invention, heh?

The boys sit down on the bench near the windows.

MRS. STOCKMANN [*who has sat down and is now knitting*]: Are you sailing soon, Captain Horster?

HORSTER: I expect to be ready next week.

MRS. STOCKMANN: And then to America, Captain?

HORSTER: Yes, that's the plan.

BILLING: Oh, then you won't be home for the new election?

HORSTER: Is there going to be another election?

BILLING: Didn't you know?

HORSTER: No, I don't get mixed up in those things.

BILLING: But you are interested in public affairs, aren't you?

HORSTER: Frankly, I don't understand a thing about it.

He does, really, although not very much. Captain Horster is one of the longest silent roles in dramatic literature, but he is not to be thought of as characterless. It is not a bad thing to have a courageous, quiet man for a friend, even if it has gone out of fashion.

MRS. STOCKMANN [*sympathetically*]:   Neither do I, Captain. Maybe that's why I'm always so glad to see you.

BILLING: Just the same, you ought to vote, Captain.

HORSTER: Even if I don't understand anything about it?

BILLING: Understand! What do you mean by that? Society, Captain, is like a ship—every man should do something to help navigate the ship.

HORSTER: That may be all right on shore, but on board a ship it doesn't work out so well.

Petra in hat and coat and with textbooks and notebooks under her arm comes into the entrance hall. She is Ibsen's clear-eyed hope for the future—and probably ours. She is forthright, determined, and knows the meaning of work, which to her is the creation of good on the earth.

PETRA [*from the hall*]:   Good evening.

DR. STOCKMANN, *warmly*:   Good evening, Petra!

BILLING [*to Horster*]:   Great young woman!

There are mutual greetings. Petra removes her coat and hat and places the books on a chair in the entrance hall.

PETRA [*entering the living room*]:   And here you are, lying around like lizards while I'm out slaving.

DR. STOCKMANN: Well, you come and be a lizard too. Come here, Petra, sit with me. I look at her and say to myself, "How did I do it?"

Petra goes over to her father and kisses him.

BILLING: Shall I mix a toddy for you?

PETRA [*coming up to the table*]:   No, thanks, I had better do it myself— you always mix it too strong. Oh, Father, I forgot—I have a letter for you. [*She goes to the chair where her books are.*]

DR. STOCKMANN [*alerted*]:   Who's it from?

PETRA: I met the mailman on the way to school this morning and he gave me your mail too, and I just didn't have time to run back.

DR. STOCKMANN [*getting up and walking toward her*]:   And you don't give it to me until now!

PETRA: I really didn't have time to run back, Father.

MRS. STOCKMANN: If she didn't have time . . .

DR. STOCKMANN: Let's see it—come on, child! [*He takes the letter and looks at the envelope.*] Yes, indeed.

MRS. STOCKMANN: Is that the one you've been waiting for?

DR. STOCKMANN: I'll be right back. There wouldn't be a light on in my room, would there?

MRS. STOCKMANN: The lamp is on the desk, burning away.

DR. STOCKMANN: Please excuse me for a moment. [*He goes into his study and quickly returns. Mrs. Stockmann hands him his glasses. He goes out again.*]

PETRA: What is that, Mother?

MRS. STOCKMANN: I don't know. The last couple of days he's been asking again and again about the mailman.

BILLING: Probably an out-of-town patient of his.

PETRA: Poor Father, he's got much too much to do. [*She mixes her drink.*] This ought to taste good.

HOVSTAD: By the way, what happened to that English novel you were going to translate for us?

PETRA: I started it, but I've gotten so busy—

HOVSTAD: Oh, teaching evening school again?

PETRA: Two hours a night.

BILLING: Plus the high school every day?

PETRA [*sitting down on the couch*]:   Yes, five hours, and every night a pile of lessons to correct!

MRS. STOCKMANN: She never stops going.

HOVSTAD: Maybe that's why I always think of you as kind of breathless and—well, breathless.

PETRA: I love it. I get so wonderfully tired.

BILLING [*to Horster*]:   She looks tired.

MORTEN: You must be a wicked woman, Petra.

PETRA [*laughing*]:   Wicked?

MORTEN: You work so much. My teacher says that work is a punishment for our sins.

EJLIF: And you believe that?

MRS. STOCKMANN: Ejlif! Of course he believes his teacher!

BILLING [smiling]:   Don't stop him . . .

HOVSTAD: Don't you like to work, Morten?

MORTEN: Work? No.

HOVSTAD: Then what will you ever amount to in this world?

MORTEN: Me? I'm going to be a Viking.

EJLIF: You can't! You'd have to be a heathen!

MORTEN: So I'll be a heathen.

MRS. STOCKMANN: I think it's getting late, boys.

BILLING: I agree with you, Morten. I think—

MRS. STOCKMANN [making signs to Billing]:   You certainly don't, Mr. Billing.

BILLING: Yes, by God, I do. I am a real heathen and proud of it. You'll see, pretty soon we're all going to be heathens!

MORTEN: And then we can do anything we want!

BILLING: Right! You see, Morten—

MRS. STOCKMANN, [interrupting]:   Don't you have any homework for tomorrow, boys? Better go in and do it.

EJLIF: Oh, can't we stay in here a while?

MRS. STOCKMANN: No, neither of you. Now run along.

The boys say good night and go off at the left.

HOVSTAD: You really think it hurts them to listen to such talk?

MRS. STOCKMANN: I don't know, but I don't like it.

Dr. Stockmann enters from his study, an open letter in his hand. He is like a sleepwalker, astonished, engrossed. He walks toward the front door.

MRS. STOCKMANN: Tom!

He turns, suddenly aware of them.

DR. STOCKMANN: Boys, there is going to be news in this town!

BILLING: News?

MRS. STOCKMANN: What kind of news?

DR. STOCKMANN: A terrific discovery, Catherine.

HOVSTAD: Really?

MRS. STOCKMANN: That you made?

DR. STOCKMANN: That I made. *He walks back and forth.* Now let the baboons running this town call me a lunatic! Now they'd better watch out. Oh, how the mighty have fallen!

PETRA: What is it, Father?

DR. STOCKMANN: Oh, if Peter were only here! Now you'll see how human beings can walk around and make judgments like blind rats.

HOVSTAD: What in the world's happened, Doctor?

DR. STOCKMANN [*stopping at the table*]: It's the general opinion, isn't it, that our town is a sound and healthy spot?

HOVSTAD: Of course.

MRS. STOCKMANN: What happened?

DR. STOCKMANN: Even a rather unusually healthy spot! Oh, God, a place that can be recommended not only to all people but to sick people!

MRS. STOCKMANN: But, Tom, what are you—

DR. STOCKMANN: And we certainly have recommended it. I myself have written and written, in the *People's Messenger*, pamphlets—

HOVSTAD: Yes, yes, but—

DR. STOCKMANN: The miraculous springs that cost such a fortune to build, the whole Health Institute, is a pesthole!

PETRA: Father! The springs?

MRS. STOCKMANN [*simultaneously*]: Our springs?

BILLING: That's unbelievable!

DR. STOCKMANN: You know the filth up in Windmill Valley? That stuff that has such a stinking smell? It comes down from the tannery up there, and the same damn poisonous mess comes right out into the blessed, miraculous water we're supposed to *cure* people with!

HORSTER: You mean actually where our beaches are?

DR. STOCKMANN: Exactly.

HOVSTAD: How are you so sure about this, Doctor?

DR. STOCKMANN: I had a suspicion about it a long time ago—last year there were too many sick cases among the visitors, typhoid and gastric disturbances.

MRS. STOCKMANN: That did happen. I remember Mrs. Svensen's niece—

DR. STOCKMANN: Yes, dear. At the time we thought that the visitors brought the bug, but later this winter I got a new idea and I started investigating the water.

MRS. STOCKMANN: So that's what you've been working on!

DR. STOCKMANN: I sent samples of the water to the University for an exact chemical analysis.

HOVSTAD: And that's what you have just received?

DR. STOCKMANN [*waving the letter again*]:   This is it. It proves the existence of infectious organic matter in the water.

MRS. STOCKMANN: Well, thank God you discovered it in time.

DR. STOCKMANN: I think we can say that, Catherine.

MRS. STOCKMANN: Isn't it wonderful!

HOVSTAD: And what do you intend to do now, Doctor?

DR. STOCKMANN: Put the thing right, of course.

HOVSTAD: Do you think that can be done?

DR. STOCKMANN: Maybe. If not, the whole Institute is useless. But there's nothing to worry about—I am quite clear on what has to be done.

MRS. STOCKMANN: But, Tom, why did you keep it so secret?

DR. STOCKMANN: What did you want me to do? Go out and shoot my mouth off before I really knew? [*He walks around, rubbing his hands.*] You don't realize what this means, Catherine—the whole water system has got to be changed.

MRS. STOCKMANN: The *whole* water system?

DR. STOCKMANN: The whole water system. The intake is too low, it's got to be raised to a much higher spot. The whole construction's got to be ripped out!

PETRA: Well, Father, at last you can prove they should have listened to you!

DR. STOCKMANN: Ha, she remembers!

MRS. STOCKMANN: That's right, you did warn them—

DR. STOCKMANN: Of course I warned them. When they started the damned thing I told them not to build it down there! But who am I, a mere scientist, to tell politicians where to build a health institute! Well, now they're going to get it, both barrels!

BILLING: This is tremendous! (*To Horster*):   He's a great man!

DR. STOCKMANN: It's bigger than tremendous. [*He starts toward his study.*] Wait'll they see this! (*He stops.*) Petra, my report is on my desk . . . [*Petra goes into his study.*] An envelope, Catherine! [*She goes for it.*] Gentlemen, this final proof from the University [*Petra comes out with the report, which he takes*] and my report [*he flicks the pages*] five solid, explosive pages . . .

MRS. STOCKMANN [*handing him an envelope*]: Is this big enough?

DR. STOCKMANN: Fine. Right to the Board of Directors! [*He inserts the report, seals the envelope, and hands it to Catherine.*] Will you give this to the maid—what's her name again?

MRS. STOCKMANN: Randine, dear, Randine.

DR. STOCKMANN: Tell our darling Randine to wipe her nose and run over to the Mayor right now.

Mrs. Stockmann just stands there looking at him.

DR. STOCKMANN: What's the matter, dear?

MRS. STOCKMANN: I don't know . . .

PETRA: What's Uncle Peter going to say about this?

MRS. STOCKMANN: That's what I'm wondering.

DR. STOCKMANN: What can he say! He ought to be damn glad that such an important fact is brought out before we start an epidemic! Hurry, dear!

Catherine exits at the left.

HOVSTAD: I would like to put a brief item about this discovery in the *Messenger.*

DR. STOCKMANN: Go ahead. I'd really be grateful for that now.

HOVSTAD: Because the public ought to know soon.

DR. STOCKMANN: Right away.

BILLING: By God, you'll be the leading man in this town, Doctor.

DR. STOCKMANN [*walking around with an air of satisfaction*]: Oh, there was nothing to it. Every detective gets a lucky break once in his life. But just the same I—

BILLING: Hovstad, don't you think the town ought to pay Dr. Stockmann some tribute?

DR. STOCKMANN: Oh, no, no . . .

HOVSTAD: Sure, let's all put in a word for—

BILLING: I'll talk to Aslaksen about it!

Catherine enters.

DR. STOCKMANN: No, no, fellows, no fooling around! I won't put up with any commotion. Even if the Board of Directors wants to give me an increase I won't take it—I just won't take it, Catherine.

MRS. STOCKMANN [*dutifully*]: That's right, Tom.

PETRA [*lifting her glass*]: Skol, Father!

EVERYBODY: Skol, Doctor!

HORSTER: Doctor, I hope this will bring you great honor and pleasure.

DR. STOCKMANN: Thanks, friends, thanks. There's one blessing above all others. To have earned the respect of one's neighbors is—is— Catherine, I'm going to dance!

He grabs his wife and whirls her around. There are shouts and struggles, general commotion. The boys in nightgowns stick their heads through the doorway at the right, wondering what is going on. Mrs. Stockmann, seeing them, breaks away and chases them upstairs as the curtain falls.

Scene II. The same, the following morning

Dr. Stockmann's living room the following morning. As the curtain rises, Mrs. Stockmann comes in from the dining room, a sealed letter in her hand. She goes to the study door and peeks in.

MRS. STOCKMANN: Are you there, Tom?

DR. STOCKMANN, [*from within*]: I just got in. [*He enters the living room.*] What's up?

MRS. STOCKMANN: From Peter. It just came. [*She hands him the envelope.*]

DR. STOCKMANN: Oh, let's see. [*He opens the letter and reads*]: "I am returning herewith the report you submitted . . ." [*He continues to read, mumbling to himself.*]

MRS. STOCKMANN: Well, what does he say? Don't stand there!

DR. STOCKMANN [*putting the letter in his pocket*]: He just says he'll come around this afternoon.

MRS. STOCKMANN: Oh. Well, maybe you ought to try to remember to be home then.

DR. STOCKMANN: Oh, I sure will. I'm through with my morning visits anyway.

MRS. STOCKMANN: I'm dying to see how he's going to take it.

DR. STOCKMANN: Why, is there any doubt? He'll probably make it look like he made the discovery, not I.

MRS. STOCKMANN: But aren't you a little bit afraid of that?

DR. STOCKMANN: Oh, underneath he'll be happy, Catherine. It's just that Peter is so afraid that somebody else is going to do something good for this town.

MRS. STOCKMANN: I wish you'd go out of your way and share the honors with him. Couldn't we say that he put you on the right track or something?

DR. STOCKMANN: Oh, I don't mind—as long as it makes everybody happy.

Morten Kiil sticks his head through the doorway. He looks around searchingly and chuckles. He will continue chuckling until he leaves the house. He is the archetype of the little twinkle-eyed man who sneaks into so much of Ibsen's work. He will chuckle you right over the precipice. He is the dealer, the man with the rat's finely tuned brain. But he is sometimes likable because he is without morals and announces the fact by laughing.

KIIL [*slyly*]: Is it really true?

MRS. STOCKMANN [*walking toward him*]: Father!

DR. STOCKMANN: Well, good morning!

MRS. STOCKMANN: Come on in.

KIIL: It better be true or I'm going.

DR. STOCKMANN: What had better be true?

KIIL: This crazy story about the water system. Is it true?

MRS. STOCKMANN: Of course it's true! How did you find out about it?

KIIL: Petra came flying by on her way to school this morning.

DR. STOCKMANN: Oh, she did?

KIIL: Ya. I thought she was trying to make a fool out of me—

MRS. STOCKMANN: Now why would she do that?

KIIL: Nothing gives more pleasure to young people than to make fools out of old people. But this is true, eh?

DR. STOCKMANN: Of course it's true. Sit down here. It's pretty lucky for the town, eh?

KIIL [*fighting his laughter*]: Lucky for the town!

DR. STOCKMANN: I mean, that I made the discovery before it was too late.

KIIL: Tom, I never thought you had the imagination to pull your own brother's leg like this.

DR. STOCKMANN: Pull his leg?

MRS. STOCKMANN: But, Father, he's not—

KIIL: How does it go now, let me get it straight. There's some kind of—like cockroaches in the waterpipes—

DR. STOCKMANN [*laughing*]: No, not cockroaches.

KIIL: Well, some kind of little animals.

MRS. STOCKMANN: Bacteria, Father.

KIIL [*who can barely speak through his laughter*]: Ah, but a whole mess of them, eh?

DR. STOCKMANN: Oh, there'd be millions and millions.

KIIL: And nobody can see them but you, is that it?

DR. STOCKMANN: Yes, that's—well, of course anybody with a micro— [*He breaks off.*] What are you laughing at?

MRS. STOCKMANN [*smiling at Kiil*]: You don't understand, Father. Nobody can actually see bacteria, but that doesn't mean they're not there.

KIIL: Good girl, you stick with him! By God, this is the best thing I ever heard in my life!

DR. STOCKMANN [*smiling*]: What do you mean?

KIIL: But tell me, you think you are actually going to get your brother to believe this?

DR. STOCKMANN: Well, we'll see soon enough!

KIIL: You really think he's that crazy?

DR. STOCKMANN: I hope the whole town will be that crazy, Morten.

KIIL: Ya, they probably are, and it'll serve them right too—they think they're so much smarter than us old-timers. Your good brother ordered them to bounce me out of the council, so they chased me out like a dog! Make jackasses out of all of them, Stockmann!

DR. STOCKMANN: Yes, but, Morten—

KIIL: Long-eared, short-tailed jackasses! [*He gets up.*] Stockmann, if you can make the Mayor and his elegant friends grab at this bait, I will give a couple of hundred crowns to charity, and right now, right on the spot.

DR. STOCKMANN: Well, that would be very kind of you, but I'm—

KIIL: I haven't got much to play around with, but if you can pull the rug out from under him with this cockroach business, I'll give at least fifty crowns to some poor people on Christmas Eve. Maybe this'll teach them to put some brains back in Town Hall!

Hovstad enters from the hall.

HOVSTAD: Good morning! Oh, pardon me . . .

KIIL [*enjoying this proof immensely*]: Oh, this one is in on it, too?

HOVSTAD: What's that, sir?

DR. STOCKMANN: Of course he's in on it.

KIIL: Couldn't I have guessed that! And it's going to be in the papers, I suppose. You're sure tying down the corners, aren't you? Well, lay it on thick. I've got to go.

DR. STOCKMANN: Oh, no, stay a while, let me explain it to you!

KIIL: Oh, I get it, don't worry! Only you can see them, heh? That's the best idea I've ever—damn it, you shouldn't do this for nothing! [*He goes toward the hall.*]

MRS. STOCKMANN [*following him out, laughing*]:   But, Father, you don't understand about bacteria.

DR. STOCKMANN [*laughing*]:   The old badger doesn't believe a word of it.

HOVSTAD: What does he think you're doing?

DR. STOCKMANN: Making an idiot out of my brother—imagine that?

HOVSTAD: You got a few minutes?

DR. STOCKMANN: Sure, as long as you like.

HOVSTAD: Have you heard from the Mayor?

DR. STOCKMANN: Only that he's coming over later.

HOVSTAD: I've been thinking about this since last night—

DR. STOCKMANN: Don't say?

HOVSTAD: For you as a medical man, a scientist, this is a really rare opportunity. But I've been wondering if you realize that it ties in with a lot of other things.

DR. STOCKMANN: How do you mean? Sit down. [*They sit at the right*]. What are you driving at?

HOVSTAD: You said last night that the pollution comes from impurities in the ground—

DR. STOCKMANN: It comes from the poisonous dump up in Windmill Valley.

HOVSTAD: Doctor, I think it comes from an entirely different dump.

DR. STOCKMANN: What do you mean?

HOVSTAD [*with growing zeal*]:   The same dump that is poisoning and polluting our whole social life in this town.

DR. STOCKMANN: For God's sake, Hovstad, what are you babbling about?

HOVSTAD: Everything that matters in this town has fallen into the hands of a few bureaucrats.

DR. STOCKMANN: Well, they're not all bureaucrats—

HOVSTAD: They're all rich, all with old reputable names, and they've got everything in the palm of their hands.

DR. STOCKMANN: Yes, but they happen to have ability and knowledge.

HOVSTAD: Did they show ability and knowledge when they built the water system where they did?

DR. STOCKMANN: No, of course not, but that happened to be a blunder, and we'll clear it up now.

HOVSTAD: You really imagine it's going to be as easy as all that?

DR. STOCKMANN: Easy or not easy, it's got to be done.

HOVSTAD: Doctor, I've made up my mind to give this whole scandal very special treatment.

DR. STOCKMANN: Now wait. You can't call it a scandal yet.

HOVSTAD: Doctor, when I took over the *People's Messenger* I swore I'd blow that smug cabal of old, stubborn, self-satisfied fogies to bits. This is the story that can do it.

DR. STOCKMANN: But I still think we owe them a deep debt of gratitude for building the springs.

HOVSTAD: The Mayor being your brother, I wouldn't ordinarily want to touch it, but I know you'd never let that kind of thing obstruct the truth.

DR. STOCKMANN: Of course not, but . . .

HOVSTAD: I want you to understand me. I don't have to tell you I come from a simple family. I know in my bones what the underdog needs—he's got to have a say in the government of society. That's what brings out ability, intelligence, and self-respect in people.

DR. STOCKMANN: I understand that, but . . .

HOVSTAD: I think a newspaperman who turns down any chance to give the underdog a lift is taking on a responsibility that I don't want. I know perfectly well that in fancy circles they call it agitation, and they can call it anything they like if it makes them happy, but I have my own conscience—

DR. STOCKMANN [*interrupting*]: I agree with you, Hovstad, but this is just the water supply and—[*There is a knock on the door.*] Damn it! Come in!

Mr. Aslaksen, the publisher, enters from the hall. He is simply but neatly dressed. He wears gloves and carries a hat and an umbrella in his hand. He is so utterly drawn it is unnecessary to say anything at all about him.

ASLAKSEN: I beg your pardon, Doctor, if I intrude . . .

HOVSTAD [*standing up*]:   Are you looking for me, Aslaksen?

ASLAKSEN: No, I didn't know you were here. I want to see the Doctor.

DR. STOCKMANN: What can I do for you?

ASLAKSEN: Is it true, Doctor, what I hear from Mr. Billing, that you intend to campaign for a better water system?

DR. STOCKMANN: Yes, for the Institute. But it's not a campaign.

ASLAKSEN: I just wanted to call and tell you that we are behind you a hundred percent.

HOVSTAD [*to Dr. Stockmann*]:   There, you see!

DR. STOCKMANN: Mr. Aslaksen, I thank you with all my heart. But you see—

ASLAKSEN: We can be important, Doctor. When the little businessman wants to push something through, he turns out to be the majority, you know, and it's always good to have the majority on your side.

DR. STOCKMANN: That's certainly true, but I don't understand what this is all about. It seems to me it's a simple straightforward business. The water—

ASLAKSEN: Of course we intend to behave with moderation, Doctor. I always try to be a moderate and careful man.

DR. STOCKMANN: You are known for that, Mr. Aslaksen, but—

ASLAKSEN: The water system is very important to us little businessmen, Doctor. Kirsten Springs are becoming a gold mine for this town, especially for the property owners, and that is why, in my capacity as chairman of the Property Owners Association—

DR. STOCKMANN: Yes.

ASLAKSEN: And furthermore, as a representative of the Temperance Society—You probably know, Doctor, that I am active for prohibition.

DR. STOCKMANN: So I have heard.

ASLAKSEN: As a result, I come into contact with all kinds of people, and since I am known to be a law-abiding and solid citizen, I have a certain influence in this town—you might even call it a little power.

DR. STOCKMANN: I know that very well, Mr. Aslaksen.

ASLAKSEN: That's why you can see that it would be practically nothing for me to arrange a demonstration.

DR. STOCKMANN: Demonstration! What are you going to demonstrate about?

ASLAKSEN: The citizens of the town complimenting you for bringing this important matter to everybody's attention. Obviously it would have to be done with the utmost moderation so as not to hurt the authorities.

HOVSTAD: This could knock the big-bellies right into the garbage can!

ASLAKSEN: No indiscretion or extreme aggressiveness toward the authorities, Mr. Hovstad! I don't want any wild-eyed radicalism on this thing. I've had enough of that in my time, and no good ever comes of it. But for a good solid citizen to express his calm, frank, and free opinion is something nobody can deny.

DR. STOCKMANN [*shaking the publisher's hand*]: My dear Aslaksen, I can't tell you how it heartens me to hear this kind of support. I am happy—I really am—I'm happy. Listen! Wouldn't you like a glass of sherry?

ASLAKSEN: I am a member of the Temperance Society. I—

DR. STOCKMANN: Well, how about a glass of beer?

ASLAKSEN [*considers, then*]: I don't think I can go quite that far, Doctor. I never take anything. Well, good day, and I want you to remember that the little man is behind you like a wall.

DR. STOCKMANN: Thank you.

ASLAKSEN: You have the solid majority on your side, because when the little—

DR. STOCKMANN [*trying to stop Aslaksen's talk*]: Thanks for that, Mr. Aslaksen, and good day.

ASLAKSEN: Are you going back to the printing shop, Mr. Hovstad?

HOVSTAD: I just have a thing or two to attend to here.

ASLAKSEN: Very well. (*He leaves.*)

HOVSTAD: Well, what do you say to a little hypodermic for these fence-sitting deadheads?

DR. STOCKMANN [*surprised*]: Why? I think Aslaksen is a very sincere man.

HOVSTAD: Isn't it time we pumped some guts into these well-intentioned men of good will? Under all their liberal talk they still idolize authority, and that's got to be rooted out of this town. This blunder of the water system has to be made clear to every voter. Let me print your report.

DR. STOCKMANN: Not until I talk to my brother.

HOVSTAD: I'll write an editorial in the meantime, and if the Mayor won't go along with us—

DR. STOCKMANN: I don't see how you can imagine such a thing!

HOVSTAD: Believe me, Doctor, it's possible, and then—

DR. STOCKMANN: Listen, I promise you: he will go along, and then you can print my report, every word of it.

HOVSTAD: On your word of honor?

DR. STOCKMANN [giving Hovstad the manuscript]:   Here it is. Take it. It can't do any harm for you to read it. Return it to me later.

HOVSTAD: Good day, Doctor.

DR. STOCKMANN: Good day. You'll see, it's going to be easier than you think, Hovstad!

HOVSTAD: I hope so, Doctor. Sincerely. Let me know as soon as you hear from His Honor. He leaves.

DR. STOCKMANN [goes to the dining room and looks in]:   Catherine! Oh, you're home already, Petra!

PETRA [coming in]:   I just got back from school.

MRS. STOCKMANN [entering]:   Hasn't he been here yet?

DR. STOCKMANN: Peter? No, but I just had a long chat with Hovstad. He's really fascinated with my discovery, and you know, it has more implications that I thought at first. Do you know what I have backing me up?

MRS. STOCKMANN: What in heaven's name have you got backing you up?

DR. STOCKMANN: The solid majority.

MRS. STOCKMANN: Is that good?

DR. STOCKMANN: Good? It's wonderful. You can't imagine the feeling, Catherine, to know that your own town feels like a brother to you. I have never felt so at home in this town since I was a boy. A noise is heard.

MRS. STOCKMANN: That must be the front door.

DR. STOCKMANN: Oh, it's Peter then. Come in.

PETER STOCKMANN [entering from the hall]:   Good morning!

DR. STOCKMANN: It's nice to see you, Peter.

MRS. STOCKMANN: Good morning. How are you today?

PETER STOCKMANN: Well, so so. [To Dr. Stockmann.] I received your thesis about the condition of the springs yesterday.

DR. STOCKMANN: I got your note. Did you read it?

PETER STOCKMANN: I read it.

DR. STOCKMANN: Well, what do you have to say?

Peter Stockmann clears his throat and glances at the women.

MRS. STOCKMANN: Come on, Petra. [*She and Petra leave the room at the left.*]

PETER STOCKMANN [*after a moment*]: Thomas, was it really necessary to go into this investigation behind my back?

DR. STOCKMANN: Yes. Until I was convinced myself, there was no point in—

PETER STOCKMANN: And now you are convinced?

DR. STOCKMANN: Well, certainly. Aren't you too, Peter? *Pause.* The University chemists corroborated . . .

PETER STOCKMANN: You intend to present this document to the Board of Directors, officially, as the medical officer of the springs?

DR. STOCKMANN: Of course, something's got to be done, and quick.

PETER STOCKMANN: You always use such strong expressions, Thomas. Among other things, in your report you say that we *guarantee* our guests and visitors a permanent case of poisoning.

DR. STOCKMANN: But, Peter, how can you describe it any other way? Imagine! Poisoned internally and externally!

PETER STOCKMANN: So you merrily conclude that we must build a waste-disposal plant—and reconstruct a brand-new water system from the bottom up!

DR. STOCKMANN: Well, do you know some other way out? I don't.

PETER STOCKMANN: I took a little walk over to the city engineer this morning and in the course of conversation I sort of jokingly mentioned these changes—as something we might consider for the future, you know.

DR. STOCKMANN: The future won't be soon enough, Peter.

PETER STOCKMANN: The engineer kind of smiled at my extravagance and gave me a few facts. I don't suppose you have taken the trouble to consider what your proposed changes would cost?

DR. STOCKMANN: No, I never thought of that.

PETER STOCKMANN: Naturally. Your little project would come to at least three hundred thousand crowns.

DR. STOCKMANN [*astonished*]: That expensive!

PETER STOCKMANN: Oh, don't look so upset—it's only money. The worst thing is that it would take some two years.

DR. STOCKMANN: Two years?

PETER STOCKMANN: At the least. And what do you propose we do about the springs in the meantime? Shut them up, no doubt! Because we would have to, you know. As soon as the rumor gets around that the water is dangerous, we won't have a visitor left. So that's the picture, Thomas. You have it in your power literally to ruin your own town.

DR. STOCKMANN: Now look, Peter! I don't want to ruin anything.

PETER STOCKMANN: Kirsten Springs are the blood supply of this town, Thomas—the only future we've got here. Now will you stop and think?

DR. STOCKMANN: Good God! Well, what do you think we ought to do?

PETER STOCKMANN: Your report has not convinced me that the conditions are as dangerous as you try to make them.

DR. STOCKMANN: Now listen; they are even worse than the report makes them out to be. Remember, summer is coming, and the warm weather!

PETER STOCKMANN: I think you're exaggerating. A capable physician ought to know what precautions to take.

DR. STOCKMANN: And what then?

PETER STOCKMANN: The existing water supply for the springs is a fact, Thomas, and has got to be treated as a fact. If you are reasonable and act with discretion, the directors of the Institute will be inclined to take under consideration any means to make possible improvements, reasonably and without financial sacrifices.

DR. STOCKMANN: Peter, do you imagine that I would ever agree to such trickery?

PETER STOCKMANN: Trickery?

DR. STOCKMANN: Yes, a trick, a fraud, a lie! A treachery, a downright crime, against the public and against the whole community!

PETER STOCKMANN: I said before that I am not convinced that there is any actual danger.

DR. STOCKMANN: Oh, you aren't? Anything else is impossible! My report is an absolute fact. The only trouble is that you and your administration were the ones who insisted that the water supply be built where it is, and now you're afraid to admit the blunder you committed. Damn it! Don't you think I can see through it all?

PETER STOCKMANN: All right, let's suppose that's true. Maybe I do care a little about my reputation. I still say I do it for the good of the town—without moral authority there can be no government.

And that is why, Thomas, it is my duty to prevent your report from reaching the Board. Some time later I will bring up the matter for discussion. In the meantime, not a single word is to reach the public.

DR. STOCKMANN: Oh, my dear Peter, do you imagine you can prevent that!

PETER STOCKMANN: It will be prevented.

DR. STOCKMANN: It can't be. There are too many people who already know about it.

PETER STOCKMANN, *angered:*   Who? It can't possibly be those people from the *Daily Messenger* who—

DR. STOCKMANN: Exactly. The liberal, free, and independent press will stand up and do its duty!

PETER STOCKMANN: You are an unbelievably irresponsible man, Thomas! Can't you imagine what consequences that is going to have for you?

DR. STOCKMANN: For me?

PETER STOCKMANN: Yes, for you and your family.

DR. STOCKMANN: What the hell are you saying now!

PETER STOCKMANN: I believe I have the right to think of myself as a helpful brother, Thomas.

DR. STOCKMANN: You have been, and I thank you deeply for it.

PETER STOCKMANN: Don't mention it. I often couldn't help myself. I had hoped that by improving your finances I would be able to keep you from running completely hog wild.

DR. STOCKMANN: You mean it was only for your own sake?

PETER STOCKMANN: Partly, yes. What do you imagine people think of an official whose closest relatives get themselves into trouble time and time again?

DR. STOCKMANN: And that's what I have done?

PETER STOCKMANN: You do it without knowing it. You're like a man with an automatic brain—as soon as an idea breaks into your head, no matter how idiotic it may be, you get up like a sleepwalker and start writing a pamphlet about it.

DR. STOCKMANN: Peter, don't you think it's a citizen's duty to share a new idea with the public?

PETER STOCKMANN: The public doesn't need new ideas—the public is much better off with old ideas.

DR. STOCKMANN: You're not even embarrassed to say that?

PETER STOCKMANN: Now look, I'm going to lay this out once and for all. You're always barking about authority. If a man gives you an order he's persecuting you. Nothing is important enough to respect once you decide to revolt against your superiors. All right then, I give up. I'm not going to try to change you any more. I told you the stakes you are playing for here, and now I am going to give you an order. And I warn you, you had better obey it if you value your career.

DR. STOCKMANN: What kind of an order?

PETER STOCKMANN: You are going to deny these rumors officially.

DR. STOCKMANN: How?

PETER STOCKMANN: You simply say that you went into the examination of the water more thoroughly and you find that you overestimated the danger.

DR. STOCKMANN: I see.

PETER STOCKMANN: And that you have complete confidence that whatever improvements are needed, the management will certainly take care of them.

DR. STOCKMANN [*after a pause*]: My convictions come from the condition of the water. My convictions will change when the water changes, and for no other reason.

PETER STOCKMANN: What are you talking about convictions? You're an official, you keep your convictions to yourself!

DR. STOCKMANN: To myself?

PETER STOCKMANN: As an official, I said. God knows, as a private person that's something else, but as a subordinate employee of the Institute, you have no right to express any convictions or personal opinions about anything connected with policy.

DR. STOCKMANN: Now you listen to me. I am a doctor and a scientist—

PETER STOCKMANN: This has nothing to do with science!

DR. STOCKMANN: Peter, I have the right to express my opinion on anything in the world!

PETER STOCKMANN: Not about the Institute—that I forbid.

DR. STOCKMANN: You forbid!

PETER STOCKMANN: I forbid you as your superior, and when I give orders you obey.

DR. STOCKMANN: Peter, if you weren't my brother—

PETRA [*throwing the door at the left open*]: Father! You aren't going to stand for this! [*She enters.*]

MRS. STOCKMANN [*coming in after her*]: Petra, Petra!

PETER STOCKMANN: What have you two been doing, eavesdropping?

MRS. STOCKMANN: You were talking so loud we couldn't help . . .

PETRA: Yes, I was eavesdropping!

PETER STOCKMANN: That makes me very happy.

DR. STOCKMANN [*approaching his brother*]: You said something to me about forbidding—

PETER STOCKMANN: You forced me to.

DR. STOCKMANN: So you want me to spit in my own face officially—is that it?

PETER STOCKMANN: Why must you always be so colorful?

DR. STOCKMANN: And if I don't obey?

PETER STOCKMANN: Then we will publish our own statement, to calm the public.

DR. STOCKMANN: Good enough! And I will write against you. I will stick to what I said, and I will prove that I am right and that you are wrong, and what will you do then?

PETER STOCKMANN: Then I simply won't be able to prevent your dismissal.

DR. STOCKMANN: What!

PETRA: Father!

PETER STOCKMANN: Dismissed from the Institute is what I said. If you want to make war on Kirsten Springs, you have no right to be on the Board of Directors.

DR. STOCKMANN (*after a pause*): You'd dare to do that?

PETER STOCKMANN: Oh, no, you're the daring man.

PETRA: Uncle, this is a rotten way to treat a man like Father!

MRS. STOCKMANN: Will you be quiet, Petra!

PETER STOCKMANN: So young and you've got opinions already—but that's natural. (*To Mrs. Stockmann.*) Catherine dear, you're probably the only sane person in this house. Knock some sense into his head, will you? Make him realize what he's driving his whole family into.

DR. STOCKMANN: My family concerns nobody but myself.

PETER STOCKMANN: His family and his own town.

DR. STOCKMANN: I'm going to show you who loves his town. The people are going to get the full stink of this corruption, Peter, and then we will see who loves his town!

PETER STOCKMANN: You love your town when you blindly, spitefully, stubbornly go ahead trying to cut off our most important industry?

DR. STOCKMANN: That source is poisoned, man. We are getting fat by peddling filth and corruption to innocent people!

PETER STOCKMANN: I think this has gone beyond opinions and convictions, Thomas. A man who can throw that kind of insinuation around is nothing but a traitor to society!

DR. STOCKMANN [*starting toward his brother in a fury*]:   How dare you to—

MRS. STOCKMANN [*stepping between them*]:   Tom!

PETRA [*grabbing her father's arm*]:   Be careful, Father!

PETER STOCKMANN [*with dignity*]:   I won't expose myself to violence. You have been warned. Consider what you owe yourself and your family! Good day! [*He exits.*]

DR. STOCKMANN [*walking up and down*]:   He's insulted. *He's* insulted!

MRS. STOCKMANN: It's shameful, Tom.

PETRA: Oh, I would love to give him a piece of my mind!

DR. STOCKMANN: It was my own fault! I should have shown my teeth right from the beginning. He called me a traitor to society. Me! Damn it all, that's not going to stick!

MRS. STOCKMANN: Please, think! He's got all the power on his side.

DR. STOCKMANN: Yes, but I have the truth on mine.

MRS. STOCKMANN: Without power, what good is the truth?

PETRA: Mother, how can you say such a thing?

DR. STOCKMANN: That's ridiculous, Catherine. I have the liberal press with me, and the majority. If that isn't power, what is?

MRS. STOCKMANN: But, for heaven's sake, Tom, you aren't going to—

DR. STOCKMANN: What am I not going to do?

MRS. STOCKMANN: You aren't going to fight it out in public with your brother!

DR. STOCKMANN: What the hell else do you want me to do?

MRS. STOCKMANN: But it won't do you any earthly good. If they won't do it, they won't. All you'll get out of it is a notice that you're fired.

DR. STOCKMANN: I am going to do my duty, Catherine. Me, the man he calls a traitor to society!

MRS. STOCKMANN: And how about your duty toward your family— the people you're supposed to provide for?

PETRA: Don't always think of us first, Mother.

MRS. STOCKMANN [*to Petra*]:   You can talk! If worst comes to worst, you can manage for yourself. But what about the boys, Tom, and you and me?

DR. STOCKMANN: What about you? You want me to be the miserable animal who'd crawl up the boots of that damn gang? Will you be happy if I can't face myself the rest of my life?

MRS. STOCKMANN: Tom, Tom, there's so much injustice in the world! You've simply got to learn to live with it. If you go on this way, God help us, we'll have no money again. Is it so long since the north that you've forgotten what it was to live like we lived? Haven't we had enough of that for one lifetime? [*The boys enter.*] What will happen to them? We've got nothing if you're fired!

DR. STOCKMANN: Stop it! [*He looks at the boys.*] Well, boys, did you learn anything in school today?

MORTEN [*looking at them, puzzled*]:   We learned what an insect is.

DR. STOCKMANN: You don't say!

MORTEN: What happened here? Why is everybody—

DR. STOCKMANN: Nothing, nothing. You know what I'm going to do, boys? From now on I'm going to teach you what a man is. [*He looks at Mrs. Stockmann. She cries as the curtain falls.*]

Act II

Scene I. Editorial offices of the *People's Daily Messenger*

The editorial office of the People's Daily Messenger. *At the back of the room, to the left, is a door leading to the printing room. Near it, in the left wall, is another door. At the right of the stage is the entrance door. In the middle of the room there is a large table covered with papers, newspapers, and books. Around it are a few chairs. A writing desk stands against the right wall. The room is dingy and cheerless, the furniture shabby.*

As the curtain rises, Billing is sitting at the desk, reading the manuscript. Hovstad comes in after a moment from the printing room. Billing looks up.

BILLING: The Doctor not come yet?

HOVSTAD: No, not yet. You finish it?

Billing holds up a hand to signal "just a moment." He reads on, the last paragraph of the manuscript. Hovstad comes and stands over him, reading with him. Now Billing closes the manuscript, glances up at Hovstad with some trepidation, then looks off. Hovstad, looking at Billing, walks a few steps away.

HOVSTAD: Well? What do you think of it?

BILLING [*with some hesitation*]:   It's devastating. The Doctor is a brilliant man. I swear, I myself never really understood how incompetent those fat fellows are, on top. [*He picks up the manuscript and waves it a little.*] I hear the rumble of revolution in this.

HOVSTAD [*looking toward the door*]:   Sssh! Aslaksen's inside.

BILLING: Aslaksen's a coward. With all that moderation talk, all he's saying is, he's yellow. You're going to print this, aren't you?

HOVSTAD: Sure, I'm just waiting for the Doctor to give the word. If his brother hasn't given in, we put it on the press anyway.

BILLING: Yes, but if the Mayor's against this it's going to get pretty rough. You know that, don't you?

HOVSTAD: Just let him try to block the reconstruction—the little businessmen and the whole town'll be screaming for his head. Aslaksen'll see to that.

BILLING [*ecstatically*]:   The stockholders'll have to lay out a fortune of money if this goes through!

HOVSTAD: My boy, I think it's going to bust them. And when the springs go busted, the people are finally going to understand the level of genius that's been running this town. Those five sheets of paper are going to put in a liberal administration once and for all.

BILLING: It's a revolution. You know that? [*With hope and fear.*] I mean it, we're on the edge of a real revolution!

DR. STOCKMANN (*entering*):   Put it on the press!

HOVSTAD (*excited*):   Wonderful! What did the Mayor say?

DR. STOCKMANN: The Mayor has declared war, so war is what it's going to be! [*He takes the manuscript from Billing.*] And this is only the beginning! You know what he tried to do?

BILLING [*calling into the printing room*]:   Mr. Aslaksen, the Doctor's here!

DR. STOCKMANN [*continuing*]:   He actually tried to blackmail me! He's got the nerve to tell me that I'm not allowed to speak my mind without his permission! Imagine the shameless effrontery!

HOVSTAD: He actually said it right out?

DR. STOCKMANN: Right to my face! The trouble with me was I kept giving them credit for being our kind of people, but they're dictators!

They're people who'll try to hold power even if they have to poison the town to do it.

Toward the last part of Dr. Stockmann's speech Aslaksen enters.

ASLAKSEN: Now take it easy, Doctor, you—you mustn't always be throwing accusations. I'm with you, you understand, but moderation—

DR. STOCKMANN [*cutting him off*]:   What'd you think of the article, Hovstad?

HOVSTAD: It's a masterpiece. In one blow you've managed to prove beyond any doubt what kind of men are running us.

ASLAKSEN: May we print it now, then?

DR. STOCKMANN: I should say *so!*

HOVSTAD: We'll have it ready for tomorrow's paper.

DR. STOCKMANN: And listen, Mr. Aslaksen, do me a favor, will you? You run a fine paper, but supervise the printing personally, eh? I'd hate to see the weather report stuck into the middle of my article.

ASLAKSEN (*laughing*):   Don't worry, that won't happen this time!

DR. STOCKMANN: Make it perfect, eh? Like you were printing money. You can't imagine how I'm dying to see it in print. After all the lies in the papers, the half-lies, the quarter-lies—to finally see the absolute, unvarnished truth about something important. And this is only the beginning. We'll go on to other subjects and blow up every lie we live by! What do you say, Aslaksen?

ASLAKSEN (*nodding in agreement*):   But just remember . . .

BILLING *and* HOVSTAD *together with* ASLAKSEN: Moderation!

ASLAKSEN [*to Billing and Hovstad*]:   I don't know what's so funny about that!

BILLING (*enthralled*):   Doctor Stockmann, I feel as though I were standing in some historic painting. Goddammit, this is a historic day! Someday this scene'll be in a museum, entitled, "The Day the Truth Was Born."

DR. STOCKMANN [*suddenly*]:   Oh! I've got a patient half-bandaged down the street. [*He leaves.*]

HOVSTAD [*to Aslaksen*]:   I hope you realize how useful he could be to us.

ASLAKSEN: I don't like that business about "this is only the beginning." Let him stick to the springs.

BILLING: What makes you so scared all the time?

ASLAKSEN: I have to live here. It'd be different if he were attacking the national government or something, but if he thinks I'm going to start going after the whole town administration—

BILLING: What's the difference? Bad is bad!

ASLAKSEN: Yes, but there is a difference. You attack the national government, what's going to happen? Nothing. They go right on. But a town administration—they're liable to be overthrown or something! I represent the small property owners in this town—

BILLING: Ha! It's always the same. Give a man a little property and the truth can go to hell!

ASLAKSEN: Mr. Billing, I'm older than you are. I've seen fireeaters before. You know who used to work at that desk before you? Councilman Stensford—*councilman!*

BILLING: Just because I work at a renegade's desk, does that mean—

ASLAKSEN: You're a politician. A politician never knows where he's going to end up. And besides you applied for a job as secretary to the Magistrate, didn't you?

HOVSTAD [*surprised, laughs*]: Billing!

BILLING [*to Hovstad*]: Well, why not? If I get it I'll have a chance to put across some good things. I could put plenty of big boys on the spot with a job like that!

ASLAKSEN: All right, I'm just saying. [*He goes to the printing-room door.*] People change. Just remember when you call me a coward— I may not have made the hot speeches, but I never went back on my beliefs either. Unlike some of the big radicals around here, I didn't change. Of course, I *am* a little more moderate, but moderation is—

HOVSTAD: Oh, God!

ASLAKSEN: I don't see what's so funny about that! [*He glares at Hovstad and goes out.*]

BILLING: If we could get rid of him we—

HOVSTAD: Take it easy—he pays the printing bill, he's not that bad. [*He picks up the manuscript.*] I'll get the printer on this. [*He starts out.*]

BILLING: Say, Hovstad, how about asking Stockmann to back us? Then we could really put out a paper!

HOVSTAD: What would he do for money?

BILLING: His father-in-law.

HOVSTAD: Kiil? Since when has he got money?

BILLING: I think he's loaded with it.

HOVSTAD: No! Why, as long as I've known him he's worn the same overcoat, the same suit—

BILLING: Yeah, and the same ring on his right hand. You ever get a look at that boulder? [*He points to his finger.*]

HOVSTAD: No, I never—

BILLING: All year he wears the diamond inside, but on New Year's Eve he turns it around. Figure it out—when a man has no visible means of support, what is he living on? Money, right?

Petra enters, carrying a book.

PETRA: Hello.

HOVSTAD: Well, fancy seeing you here. Sit down. What—

PETRA [*walking slowly up to Hovstad*]:   I want to ask you a question. [*She starts to open the book.*]

BILLING: What's that?

PETRA: The English novel you wanted translated.

HOVSTAD: Aren't you going to do it?

PETRA [*with deadly seriousness and curiosity*]:   I don't get this.

HOVSTAD: You don't get what?

PETRA: This book is absolutely against everything you people believe.

HOVSTAD: Oh, it isn't that bad.

PETRA: But, Mr. Hovstad, it says if you're good there's a supernatural force that'll fix it so you end up happy. And if you're bad you'll be punished. Since when does the world work that way?

HOVSTAD: Yes, Petra, but this is a newspaper, people like to read that kind of thing. They buy the paper for that and then we slip in our political stuff. A newspaper can't buck the public—

PETRA [*astonished, beginning to be angry*]:   You don't say! [*She starts to go.*]

HOVSTAD [*hurrying after her*]:   Now, wait a minute, I don't want you to go feeling that way. [*He holds the manuscript out to Billing.*] Here, take this to the printer, will you?

BILLING [*taking the manuscript*]:   Sure. (*He goes.*)

HOVSTAD: I just want you to understand something: I never even read that book. It was Billing's idea.

PETRA [*trying to penetrate his eyes*]:   I thought he was a radical.

HOVSTAD: He is. But he's also a—

PETRA [*testily*]:   A newspaperman.

HOVSTAD: Well, that too, but I was going to say that Billing is trying to get the job as secretary to the Magistrate.

PETRA: What?

HOVSTAD: People are—people, Miss Stockmann.

PETRA: But the Magistrate! He's been fighting everything progressive in this town for thirty years.

HOVSTAD: Let's not argue about it, I just didn't want you to go out of here with a wrong idea of me. I guess you know that I—I happen to admire women like you. I've never had a chance to tell you, but I—well, I want you to know it. Do you mind? [*He smiles.*]

PETRA: No, I don't mind, but—reading that book upset me. I really don't understand. Will you tell me why you're supporting my father?

HOVSTAD: What's the mystery? It's a matter of principle.

PETRA: But a paper that'll print a book like this has no principle.

HOVSTAD: Why do you jump to such extremes? You're just like . . .

PETRA: Like what?

HOVSTAD: I simply mean that . . .

PETRA [*moving away from him*]: Like my father, you mean. You really have no use for him, do you?

HOVSTAD: Now wait a minute!

PETRA: What's behind this? Are you just trying to hold my hand or something?

HOVSTAD: I happen to agree with your father, and that's why I'm printing his stuff.

PETRA: You're trying to put something over, I think. Why are you in this?

HOVSTAD: Who're you accusing? Billing gave you that book, not me!

PETRA: But you don't mind printing it, do you? What are you trying to do with my father? You have no principles—what are you up to here?

Aslaksen hurriedly enters from the printing shop, Stockmann's manuscript in his hand.

ASLAKSEN: My God! Hovstad! (*He sees Petra*). Miss Stockmann.

PETRA [*looking at Hovstad*]: I don't think I've been so frightened in my life. [*She goes out.*]

HOVSTAD [*starting after her*]: Please, you mustn't think I—

ASLAKSEN [*stopping him*]: Where are you going? The Mayor's out there.

HOVSTAD: The Mayor!

ASLAKSEN: He wants to speak to you. He came in the back door. He doesn't want to be seen.

HOVSTAD: What does he want? [*He goes to the printing-room door, opens it, calls out with a certain edge of servility.*] Come in, Your Honor!

PETER STOCKMANN [*entering*]: Thank you.

Hovstad carefully closes the door.

PETER STOCKMANN [*walking around*]: It's clean! I always imagined this place would look dirty. But it's clean. [*Commendingly.*] Very nice, Mr. Aslaksen. [*He puts his hat on the desk.*]

ASLAKSEN: Not at all, Your Honor—I mean to say, I always . . .

HOVSTAD: What can I do for you, Your Honor? Sit down?

PETER STOCKMANN [*sits, placing his cane on the table*]: I had a very annoying thing happen today, Mr. Hovstad.

HOVSTAD: That so?

PETER STOCKMANN: It seems my brother has written some sort of—memorandum. About the springs.

HOVSTAD: You don't say.

PETER STOCKMANN [*looking at Hovstad now*]: He mentioned it . . . to you?

HOVSTAD: Yes. I think he said something about it.

ASLAKSEN [*nervously starts to go out, attempting to hide the manuscript*]: Will you excuse me, gentlemen . . .

PETER STOCKMANN [*pointing to the manuscript*]: That's it, isn't it?

ASLAKSEN: This? I don't know, I haven't had a chance to look at it, the printer just handed it to me . . .

HOVSTAD: Isn't that the thing the printer wanted the spelling checked?

ASLAKSEN: That's it. It's only a question of spelling. I'll be right back.

PETER STOCKMANN: I'm very good at spelling. [*He holds out his hand.*] Maybe I can help you.

HOVSTAD: No, Your Honor, there's some Latin in it. You wouldn't know Latin, would you?

PETER STOCKMANN: Oh, yes. I used to help my brother with his Latin all the time. Let me have it.

Aslaksen gives him the manuscript. Peter Stockmann looks at the title on the first page, then glances up sarcastically at Hovstad, who avoids his eyes.

PETER STOCKMANN: You're going to print this?

HOVSTAD: I can't very well refuse a signed article. A signed article is the author's responsibility.

PETER STOCKMANN: Mr. Aslaksen, you're going to allow this?

ASLAKSEN: I'm the publisher, not the editor, Your Honor. My policy is freedom for the editor.

PETER STOCKMANN: You have a point—I can see that.

ASLAKSEN [*reaching for the manuscript*]: So if you don't mind . . .

PETER STOCKMANN: Not at all. [*But he holds on to the manuscript. After a pause.*] This reconstruction of the springs—

ASLAKSEN: I realize, Your Honor—it does mean tremendous sacrifices for the stockholders.

PETER STOCKMANN: Don't upset yourself. The first thing a Mayor learns is that the less wealthy can always be prevailed upon to demand a spirit of sacrifice for the public good.

ASLAKSEN: I'm glad you see that.

PETER STOCKMANN: Oh, yes. Especially when it's the wealthy who are going to do the sacrificing. What you don't seem to understand, Mr. Aslaksen, is that so long as I am Mayor, any changes in those springs are going to be paid for by a municipal loan.

ASLAKSEN: A municipal—you mean you're going to tax the people for this?

PETER STOCKMANN: Exactly.

HOVSTAD: But the springs are a private corporation!

PETER STOCKMANN: The corporation built Kirsten Springs out of its own money. If the people want them changed, the people naturally must pay the bill. The corporation is in no position to put out any more money. It simply can't do it.

ASLAKSEN [*to Hovstad*]:   That's impossible! People will never stand for a new tax. [*To the Mayor.*] Is this a fact or your opinion?

PETER STOCKMANN: It happens to be a fact. Plus another fact— you'll forgive me for talking about facts in a newspaper office—but don't forget that the springs will take two years to make over. Two years without income for your small businessmen, Mr. Aslaksen, and a heavy new tax besides. And all because [*his private emotion comes to the surface; he throttles the manuscript in his hand*] because of this dream, this hallucination, that we live in a pesthole!

HOVSTAD: That's based on science.

PETER STOCKMANN [*raising the manuscript and throwing it down on the table.*]   This is based on vindictiveness, on his hatred of authority and nothing else. [*He pounds on the manuscript.*] This is the mad dream of a man who is trying to blow up our way of life! It has nothing to do with reform or science or anything else, but pure and simple destruction! And I intend to see to it that the people understand it exactly so!

ASLAKSEN [*hit by this*]:   My God! [*To Hovstad.*]   Maybe . . . You sure you want to support this thing, Hovstad?

HOVSTAD [*nervously*]:   Frankly I'd never thought of it in quite that way. I mean . . . [*To the Mayor.*] When you think of it psychologically it's completely possible, of course, that the man is simply out to—I don't know what to say, Your Honor. I'd hate to hurt the town in any way. I never imagined we'd have to have a new tax.

PETER STOCKMANN: You should have imagined it because you're going to have to advocate it. Unless, of course, liberal and radical newspaper readers enjoy high taxes. But you'd know that better than I. I happen to have here a brief story of the actual facts. It proves that, with a little care, nobody need be harmed at all by the water. [*He takes out a long envelope.*] Of course, in time we'd have to make a few minor structural changes and we'd pay for those.

HOVSTAD: May I see that?

PETER STOCKMANN: I want you to *study* it, Mr. Hovstad, and see if you don't agree that—

BILLING [*entering quickly*]:   Are you expecting the Doctor?

PETER STOCKMANN [*alarmed*]:   He's here?

BILLING: Just coming across the street.

PETER STOCKMANN: I'd rather not run into him here. How can I . . .

BILLING: Right this way, sir, hurry up!

ASLAKSEN, [*at the entrance door, peeking*]:   Hurry up!

PETER STOCKMANN, [*going with Billing through the door at the left*]:   Get him out of here right away! [*They exit.*]

HOVSTAD: Do something, do something!

Aslaksen pokes among some papers on the table. Hovstad sits at the desk, starts to "write." Dr. Stockmann enters.

DR. STOCKMANN: Any proofs yet? [*He sees they hardly turn to him.*] I guess not, eh?

ASLAKSEN [*without turning*]:   No, you can't expect them for some time.

DR. STOCKMANN: You mind if I wait?

HOVSTAD: No sense in that, Doctor, it'll be quite a while yet.

DR. STOCKMANN [*laughing, places his hand on Hovstad's back*]:   Bear with me, Hovstad, I just can't wait to see it in print.

HOVSTAD: We're pretty busy, Doctor, so . . .

DR. STOCKMANN [*starting toward the door*]:   Don't let me hold you up. That's the way to be, busy, busy. We'll make this town shine like a jewel! [*He has opened the door, now he comes back.*] Just one thing. I—

HOVSTAD: Couldn't we talk some other time? We're very—

DR. STOCKMANN: Two words. Just walking down the street now, I looked at the people, in the stores, driving the wagons, and suddenly I was—well, touched, you know? By their innocence, I mean. What I'm driving at is, when this exposé breaks they're liable to start making a saint out of me or something, and I—Aslaksen, I want you to promise me that you're not going to try to get up any dinner for me or—

ASLAKSEN [turning toward the Doctor]: Doctor, there's no use concealing—

DR. STOCKMANN: I knew it. Now look, I will simply not attend a dinner in my honor.

HOVSTAD [getting up]: Doctor, I think it's time we—

Mrs. Stockmann enters.

MRS. STOCKMANN: I thought so. Thomas, I want you home. Now come. I want you to talk to Petra.

DR. STOCKMANN: What happened? What are you doing here?

HOVSTAD: Something wrong, Mrs. Stockmann?

MRS. STOCKMANN [leveling a look of accusation at Hovstad]: Doctor Stockmann is the father of three children, Mr. Hovstad.

DR. STOCKMANN: Now look, dear, everybody knows that. What's the—

MRS. STOCKMANN [restraining an outburst at her husband]: Nobody would believe it from the way you're dragging us into this disaster!

DR. STOCKMANN: What disaster?

MRS. STOCKMANN [to Hovstad]: He treated you like a son, now you make a fool of him?

HOVSTAD: I'm not making a—

DR. STOCKMANN: Catherine! (He indicates Hovstad.) How can you accuse—

MRS. STOCKMANN [to Hovstad]: He'll lose his job at the springs, do you realize that? You print the article, and they'll grind him up like a piece of flesh!

DR. STOCKMANN: Catherine, you're embarrassing me! I beg your pardon, gentlemen . . .

MRS. STOCKMANN: Mr. Hovstad, what are you up to?

DR. STOCKMANN: I won't have you jumping at Hovstad, Catherine!

MRS. STOCKMANN: I want you home! This man is not your friend!

DR. STOCKMANN: He is my friend! Any man who shares my risk is my friend! You simply don't understand that as soon as this breaks everybody in this town is going to come out in the streets and drive that gang of—[*He picks up the Mayor's cane from the table, notices what it is, and stops. He looks from it to Hovstad and Aslaksen.*] What's this? [*They don't reply. Now he notices the hat on the desk and picks it up with the tip of the cane. He looks at them again. He is angry, incredulous.*] What the hell is he doing here?

ASLAKSEN: All right, Doctor, now let's be calm and—

DR. STOCKMANN [*starting to move*]: Where is he? What'd he do, talk you out of it? Hovstad! [*Hovstad remains immobile.*] He won't get away with it! Where'd you hide him? [*He opens the door at the left.*]

ASLAKSEN: Be careful, Doctor!

Peter Stockmann enters with Billing through the door Dr. Stockmann opened. Peter Stockmann tries to hide his embarrassment.

DR. STOCKMANN: Well, Peter, poisoning the water was not enough! You're working on the press now, eh? [*He crosses to the entrance door.*]

PETER STOCKMANN: My hat, please. And my stick. [*Dr. Stockmann puts on the Mayor's hat.*] Now what's *this* nonsense! Take that off, that's official insignia!

DR. STOCKMANN: I just wanted you to realize, Peter, [*he takes off the hat and looks at it*] that anyone may wear this hat in a democracy, and that a free citizen is not afraid to touch it. [*He hands him the hat.*] And as for the baton of command, Your Honor, it can pass from hand to hand. [*He hands the cane to Peter Stockmann.*] So don't gloat yet. The people haven't spoken. [*He turns to Hovstad and Aslaksen.*] And I have the people because I have the truth, my friends!

ASLAKSEN: Doctor, we're not scientists. We can't judge whether your article is really true.

DR. STOCKMANN: Then print it under my name. Let *me* defend it!

HOVSTAD: I'm not printing it. I'm not going to sacrifice this newspaper. When the whole story gets out the public is not going to stand for any changes in the springs.

ASLAKSEN: His Honor just told us, Doctor—you see, there will have to be a new tax—

DR. STOCKMANN: Ahhhhh! Yes. I see. That's why you're not scientists suddenly and can't decide if I'm telling the truth. Well. So!

HOVSTAD: Don't take that attitude. The point is—

DR. STOCKMANN: The point, the point, oh, the point is going to fly through this town like an arrow, and I am going to fire it! *To Aslaksen:* Will you print this article as a pamphlet? I'll pay for it.

ASLAKSEN: I'm not going to ruin this paper and this town. Doctor, for the sake of your family—

MRS. STOCKMANN: You can leave his family out of this, Mr. Aslaksen. God help me, I think you people are horrible!

DR. STOCKMANN: My article, if you don't mind.

ASLAKSEN [*giving it to him*]:   Doctor, you won't get it printed in this town.

PETER STOCKMANN: Can't you forget it? [*He indicates Hovstad and Aslaksen.*] Can't you see now that everybody—

DR. STOCKMANN: Your Honor, I can't forget it, and you will never forget it as long as you live. I am going to call a mass meeting, and I—

PETER STOCKMANN: And who is going to rent you a hall?

DR. STOCKMANN: Then I will take a drum and go from street to street, proclaiming that the springs are befouled and poison is rotting the body politic! [*He starts for the door.*]

PETER STOCKMANN: And I believe you really are that mad!

DR. STOCKMANN: Mad? Oh, my brother, you haven't even heard me raise my voice yet. Catherine? [*He holds out his hand, she gives him her elbow. They go stiffly out.*]

Peter Stockmann looks regretfully toward the exit, then takes out his manuscript and hands it to Hovstad, who in turn gives it to Billing, who hands it to Aslaksen, who takes it and exits. Peter Stockmann puts his hat on and moves toward the door. Blackout. The curtain falls.

Act II

Scene II. A room in Captain Horster's house

A room in Captain Horster's house. The room is bare, as though unused for a long time. A large doorway is at the left, two shuttered windows at the back, and another door at the right. Upstage right, packing cases have been set together, forming a platform, on which are a chair and a small table.

There are two chairs next to the platform at the right. One chair stands downstage left.

The room is angled, thus making possible the illusion of a large crowd off in the wing to the left. The platform faces the audience at an angle, thus giving the speakers the chance to speak straight out front and creating the illusion of a large crowd by addressing "people" in the audience.

As the curtain rises the room is empty. Captain Horster enters, carrying a pitcher of water, a glass, and a bell. He is putting these on the table when Billing enters. A crowd is heard talking outside in the street.

BILLING: Captain Horster?

HORSTER [*turning*]: Oh, come in. I don't have enough chairs for a lot of people so I decided not to have chairs at all.

BILLING: My name is Billing. Don't you remember, at the Doctor's house?

HORSTER [*a little coldly*]: Oh, yes, sure. I've been so busy I didn't recognize you. [*He goes to a window and looks out.*] Why don't those people come inside?

BILLING: I don't know, I guess they're waiting for the Mayor or somebody important so they can be sure it's respectable in here. I wanted to ask you a question before it begins, Captain. Why are you lending your house for this? I never heard of you connected with anything political.

HORSTER [*standing still*]: I'll answer that. I travel most of the year and—did you ever travel?

BILLING: Not abroad, no.

HORSTER: Well, I've been in a lot of places where people aren't allowed to say unpopular things. Did you know that?

BILLING: Sure, I've read about it.

HORSTER [*simply*]: Well, I don't like it. [*He starts to go out.*]

BILLING: One more question. What's your opinion about the Doctor's proposition to rebuild the springs?

HORSTER [*turning, thinks, then*]: Don't understand a thing about it.

Three citizens enter.

HORSTER: Come in, come in. I don't have enough chairs so you'll just have to stand. [*He goes out.*]

FIRST CITIZEN: Try the horn.

SECOND CITIZEN: No, let him start to talk first.

THIRD CITIZEN [*a big beef of a man, takes out a horn*]:   Wait'll they hear this! I could blow your mustache off with this!

Horster returns. He sees the horn and stops abruptly.

HORSTER: I don't want any roughhouse, you hear me?

Mrs. Stockmann and Petra enter.

HORSTER: Come in. I've got chairs just for you.

MRS. STOCKMANN [*nervously*]:   There's quite a crowd on the sidewalk. Why don't they come in?

HORSTER: I suppose they're waiting for the Mayor.

PETRA: Are all those people on his side?

HORSTER: Who knows? People are bashful, and it's so unusual to come to a meeting like this, I suppose they—

BILLING [*going over to this group*]:   Good evening, ladies. *They simply look at him.* I don't blame you for not speaking. I just wanted to say I don't think this is going to be a place for ladies tonight.

MRS. STOCKMANN: I don't remember asking your advice, Mr. Billing.

BILLING: I'm not as bad as you think, Mrs. Stockmann.

MRS. STOCKMANN: Then why did you print the Mayor's statement and not a word about my husband's report? Nobody's had a chance to find out what he really stands for. Why, everybody on the street there is against him already!

BILLING: If we printed his report it only would have hurt your husband.

MRS. STOCKMANN: Mr. Billing, I've never said this to anyone in my life, but I think you're a liar.

Suddenly the third citizen lets out a blast on his horn. The women jump, Billing and Horster turn around quickly.

HORSTER: You do that once more and I'll throw you out of here!

Peter Stockmann enters. Behind him comes the crowd. He pretends to be unconnected with them. He goes straight to Mrs. Stockmann, bows.

PETER STOCKMANN: Catherine? Petra?

PETRA: Good evening.

PETER STOCKMANN: Why so coldly? He wanted a meeting and he's got it. [*To Horster.*] Isn't he here?

HORSTER: The Doctor is going around town to be sure there's a good attendance.

PETER STOCKMANN: Fair enough. By the way, Petra, did you paint that poster? The one somebody stuck on the Town Hall?

PETRA: If you can call it painting, yes.

PETER STOCKMANN: You know I could arrest you? It's against the law to deface the Town Hall.

PETRA: Well, here I am. [*She holds out her hands for the handcuffs.*]

MRS. STOCKMANN [*taking it seriously*]:   If you arrest her, Peter, I'll never speak to you!

PETER STOCKMANN [*laughing*]:   Catherine, you have no sense of humor!

He crosses and sits down at the left. They sit right. A drunk comes out of the crowd.

DRUNK: Say, Billy, who's runnin'? Who's the candidate?

HORSTER: You're drunk, Mister, now get out of here!

DRUNK: There's no law says a man who's drunk can't vote!

HORSTER [*pushing the drunk toward the door as the crowd laughs*]:   Get out of here! Get out!

DRUNK: I wanna vote! I got a right to vote!

Aslaksen enters hurriedly, sees Peter Stockmann, and rushes to him.

ASLAKSEN: Your Honor . . . [*He points to the door.*] He's . . .

DR. STOCKMANN [*offstage*]:   Right this way, gentlemen! In you go, come on, fellows!

Hovstad enters, glances at Peter Stockmann and Aslaksen, then at Dr. Stockmann and another crowd behind him, who enter.

DR. STOCKMANN: Sorry, no chairs, gentlemen, but we couldn't get a hall, y'know, so just relax. It won't take long anyway. [*He goes to the platform, sees Peter Stockmann.*] Glad you're here, Peter!

PETER STOCKMANN: Wouldn't miss it for the world.

DR. STOCKMANN: How do you feel, Catherine?

MRS. STOCKMANN (*nervously*):   Just promise me, don't lose your temper . . .

HORSTER [*seeing the drunk pop in through the door*]:   Did I tell you to get out of here!

DRUNK: Look, if you ain't votin', what the hell's going on here? [*Horster starts after him.*] Don't push!

PETER STOCKMANN [*to the drunk*]:   I order you to get out of here and stay out!

DRUNK: I don't like the tone of your voice! And if you don't watch your step I'm gonna tell the Mayor right now, and he'll throw yiz all in the jug! [*To all*]:   What're you, a revolution here?

The crowd bursts out laughing; the drunk laughs with them, and they push him out. Dr. Stockmann mounts the platform.

DR. STOCKMANN [*quieting the crowd*]:   All right, gentlemen, we might as well begin. Quiet down, please. [*He clears his throat.*] The issue is very simple—

ASLAKSEN: We haven't elected a chairman, Doctor.

DR. STOCKMANN: I'm sorry, Mr. Aslaksen, this isn't a meeting. I advertised a lecture and I—

A CITIZEN: I came to a meeting, Doctor. There's got to be some kind of control here.

DR. STOCKMANN: What do you mean, control? What is there to control?

SECOND CITIZEN: Sure, let him speak, this is no meeting!

THIRD CITIZEN: Your Honor, why don't you take charge of this—

DR. STOCKMANN: Just a minute now!

THIRD CITIZEN: Somebody responsible has got to take charge. There's a big difference of opinion here—

DR. STOCKMANN: What makes you so sure? You don't even know yet what I'm going to say.

THIRD CITIZEN: I've got a pretty good idea what you're going to say, and I don't like it! If a man doesn't like it here, let him go where it suits him better. We don't want any troublemakers here!

There is assent from much of the crowd. Dr. Stockmann looks at them with new surprise.

DR. STOCKMANN: Now look, friend, you don't know anything about me—

FOURTH CITIZEN: We know plenty about you, Stockmann!

DR. STOCKMANN: From what? From the newspapers? How do you know I don't like this town? [*He picks up his manuscript.*] I'm here to save the life of this town!

PETER STOCKMANN [*quickly*]:   Now just a minute, Doctor, I think the democratic thing to do is to elect a chairman.

FIFTH CITIZEN: I nominate the Mayor!

Seconds are heard.

PETER STOCKMANN: No, no, no! That wouldn't be fair. We want a neutral person. I suggest Mr. Aslaksen—

SECOND CITIZEN: I came to a lecture, I didn't—

THIRD CITIZEN [*to second citizen*]: What're you afraid of, a fair fight? [*To the Mayor*]: Second Mr. Aslaksen!

The crowd assents.

DR. STOCKMANN: All right, if that's your pleasure. I just want to remind you that the reason I called this meeting was that I have a very important message for you people and I couldn't get it into the press, and nobody would rent me a hall. [*To Peter Stockmann:*] I just hope I'll be given time to speak here. Mr. Aslaksen?

As Aslaksen mounts the platform and Dr. Stockmann steps down, Kiil enters, looks shrewdly around.

ASLAKSEN: I just have one word before we start. Whatever is said tonight, please remember, the highest civic virtue is moderation. [*He can't help turning to Dr. Stockmann, then back to the crowd.*] Now if anybody wants to speak—

The drunk enters suddenly.

DRUNK, *pointing at Aslaksen:* I heard that! Since when you allowed to electioneer at the poles? [*Citizens push him toward the door amid laughter.*] I'm gonna report this to the Mayor, goddammit! [*They push him out and close the door.*]

ASLAKSEN: Quiet, please, quiet. Does anybody want the floor?

Dr. Stockmann starts to come forward, raising his hand, but Peter Stockmann also has his hand raised.

PETER STOCKMANN: Mr. Chairman!

ASLAKSEN [*quickly recognizing Peter Stockmann*]: His Honor the Mayor will address the meeting.

Dr. Stockmann stops, looks at Peter Stockmann, and, suppressing a remark, returns to his place. The Mayor mounts the platform.

PETER STOCKMANN: Gentlemen, there's no reason to take very long to settle this tonight and return to our ordinary, calm, and peaceful life. Here's the issue: Doctor Stockmann, my brother—and believe me, it is not easy to say this—has decided to destroy Kirsten Springs, our Health Institute—

DR. STOCKMANN: Peter!

ASLAKSEN [*ringing his bell*]:   Let the Mayor continue, please. There mustn't be any interruptions.

PETER STOCKMANN: He has a long and very involved way of going about it, but that's the brunt of it, believe me.

THIRD CITIZEN: Then what're we wasting time for? Run him out of town!

Others join in the cry.

PETER STOCKMANN: Now wait a minute. I want no violence here. I want you to understand his motives. He is a man, always has been, who is never happy unless he is badgering authority, ridiculing authority, destroying authority. He wants to attack the springs so he can prove that the administration blundered in the construction.

DR. STOCKMANN [*to Aslaksen*]:   May I speak? I—

ASLAKSEN: The Mayor's not finished.

PETER STOCKMANN: Thank you. Now there are a number of people here who seem to feel that the Doctor has a right to say anything he pleases. After all, we are a democratic country. Now, God knows, in ordinary times I'd agree a hundred per cent with anybody's right to say anything. But these are not ordinary times. Nations have crises, and so do towns. There are ruins of nations, and there are ruins of towns all over the world, and they were wrecked by people who, in the guise of reform, and pleading for justice, and so on, broke down all authority and left only revolution and chaos.

DR. STOCKMANN: What the hell are you talking about!

ASLAKSEN: I'll have to insist, Doctor—

DR. STOCKMANN: I called a lecture! I didn't invite him to attack me. He's got the press and every hall in town to attack me, and I've got nothing but this room tonight!

ASLAKSEN: I don't think you're making a very good impression, Doctor.

Assenting laughter and catcalls. Again Dr. Stockmann is taken aback by this reaction.

ASLAKSEN: Please continue, Your Honor.

PETER STOCKMANN: Now this is our crisis. We know what this town was without our Institute. We could barely afford to keep the streets in condition. It was a dead, third-rate hamlet. Today we're just on the verge of becoming internationally known as a resort. I predict that within five years the income of every man in this room will be immensely greater. I predict that our schools will be bigger and better. And in time this town will be crowded with fine carriages; great homes will be built here; first-class stores will open all along Main Street. I predict that if we are not defamed and maliciously attacked we will someday be one of the richest and most beautiful resort towns in the world. There are your choices. Now all you've got to do is ask yourselves a simple question: Has any one of us the right, the "democratic right," as they like to call it, to pick at minor flaws in the springs, to exaggerate the most picayune faults? [*Cries of No, No!*] And to attempt to publish these defamations for the whole world to see? We live or die on what the outside world thinks of us. I believe there is a line that must be drawn, and if a man decides to cross that line, we the people must finally take him by the collar and declare, "You cannot say that!"

There is an uproar of assent. Aslaksen rings the bell.

PETER STOCKMANN [*continuing*]:   All right then. I think we all understand each other. Mr. Aslaksen, I move that Doctor Stockmann be prohibited from reading his report at this meeting! [*He goes back to his chair, which meanwhile Kiil has occupied.*]

Aslaksen rings the bell to quiet the enthusiasm. Dr. Stockmann is jumping to get up on the platform, the report in his hand.

ASLAKSEN: Quiet, please. Please now. I think we can proceed to the vote.

DR. STOCKMANN: Well, aren't you going to let me speak at all?

ASLAKSEN: Doctor, we are just about to vote on that question.

DR. STOCKMANN: But damn it, man, I've got a right to—

PETRA, *standing up*:   Point of order, Father!

DR. STOCKMANN [*picking up the cue*]:   Yes, point of order!

ASLAKSEN [*turning to him now*]:   Yes, Doctor.

Dr. Stockmann, at a loss, turns to Petra for further instructions.

PETRA: You want to discuss the motion.

DR. STOCKMANN: That's right, damn it, I want to discuss the motion!

ASLAKSEN: Ah . . . [*He glances at Peter Stockmann.*] All right, go ahead.

DR. STOCKMANN, *to the crowd:* Now, listen. [*He points at Peter Stockmann.*] He talks and he talks and he talks, but not a word about the facts! [*He holds up the manuscript.*]

THIRD CITIZEN: We don't want to hear any more about the water!

FOURTH CITIZEN: You're just trying to blow up everything!

DR. STOCKMANN: Well, judge for yourselves, let me read—

Cries of No, No, No! The man with the horn blows it. Aslaksen rings the bell. Dr. Stockmann is utterly shaken. Astonished, he looks at the maddened faces. He lowers the hand holding the manuscript and steps back, defeated.

ASLAKSEN: Please, please now, quiet. We can't have this uproar! [*Quiet returns.*] I think, Doctor, that the majority wants to take the vote before you start to speak. If they so will, you can speak. Otherwise, majority rules. You won't deny that.

DR. STOCKMANN [*turns, tosses the manuscript on the floor, turns back to Aslaksen*]: Don't bother voting. I understand everything now. Can I have a few minutes—

PETER STOCKMANN: Mr. Chairman!

DR. STOCKMANN [*to his brother*]: I won't mention the Institute. I have a new discovery that's a thousand times more important than all the Institutes in the world. [*To Aslaksen*]: May I have the platform.

ASLAKSEN [*to the crowd*]: I don't see how we can deny him that, as long as he confines himself to—

DR. STOCKMANN: The springs are not the subject. [*He mounts the platform, looks at the crowd.*] Before I go into my subject I want to congratulate the liberals and radicals among us, like Mr. Hovstad—

HOVSTAD: What do you mean, radical! Where's your evidence to call me a radical!

DR. STOCKMANN: You've got me there. There isn't any evidence. I guess there never really was. I just wanted to congratulate you on your self-control tonight—you who have fought in every parlor for the principle of free speech these many years.

HOVSTAD: I believe in democracy. When my readers are overwhelmingly against something, I'm not going to impose my will on the majority.

DR. STOCKMANN: You have begun my remarks, Mr. Hovstad. [*He turns to the crowd.*] Gentlemen, Mrs. Stockmann, Miss Stockmann. Tonight

I was struck by a sudden flash of light, a discovery second to none. But before I tell it to you—a little story. I put in a good many years in the north of our country. Up there the rulers of the world are the great seal and the gigantic squadrons of duck. Man lives on ice, huddled together in little piles of stones. His whole life consists of grubbing for food. Nothing more. He can barely speak his own language. And it came to me one day that it was romantic and sentimental for a man of my education to be tending these people. They had not yet reached the stage where they needed a doctor. If the truth were to be told, a veterinary would be more in order.

BILLING: Is that the way you refer to decent hard-working people!

DR. STOCKMANN: I expected that, my friend, but don't think you can fog up my brain with that magic word—the People! Not any more! Just because there is a mass of organisms with the human shape, they do not automatically become a People. That honor has to be earned! Nor does one automatically become a Man by having human shape, and living in a house, and feeding one's face—and agreeing with one's neighbors. That name *also* has to be earned. Now, when I came to my conclusions about the springs—

PETER STOCKMANN: You have no right to—

DR. STOCKMANN: That's a picayune thing, to catch me on a word, Peter. I am not going into the springs. *To the crowd*: When I became convinced of my theory about the water, the authorities moved in at once, and I said to myself, I will fight them to the death, because—

THIRD CITIZEN: What're you trying to do, make a revolution here? He's a revolutionist!

DR. STOCKMANN: Let me finish. I thought to myself: The majority, I have the majority! And let me tell you, friends, it was a grand feeling. Because that's the reason I came back to this place of my birth. I wanted to give my education to this town. I loved it so, I spent months without pay or encouragement and dreamed up the whole project of the springs. And why? Not as my brother says, so that fine carriages could crowd our streets, but so that we might cure the sick, so that we might meet people from all over the world and learn from them, and become broader and more civilized. In other words, more like Men, more like A People.

A CITIZEN: You don't like anything about this town, do you?

ANOTHER CITIZEN: Admit it, you're a revolutionist, aren't you? Admit it!

DR. STOCKMANN: I don't admit it! I proclaim it now! I am a revolutionist! I am in revolt against the age-old lie that the majority is always right!

HOVSTAD: He's an aristocrat all of a sudden!

DR. STOCKMANN: And more! I tell you now that the majority is always wrong, and in this way!

PETER STOCKMANN: Have you lost your mind! Stop talking before—

DR. STOCKMANN: Was the majority right when they stood by while Jesus was crucified? [*Silence.*] Was the majority right when they refused to believe that the earth moved around the sun and let Galileo be driven to his knees like a dog? It takes fifty years for the majority to be right. The majority is never right until it *does* right.

HOVSTAD: I want to state right now, that although I've been this man's friend, and I've eaten at his table many times, I now cut myself off from him absolutely.

DR. STOCKMANN: Answer me this! Please, one more moment! A platoon of soldiers is walking down a road toward the enemy. Every one of them is convinced he is on the right road, the safe road. But two miles ahead stands one lonely man, the outpost. He sees that this road is dangerous, that his comrades are walking into a trap. He runs back, he finds the platoon. Isn't it clear that this man must have the right to warn the majority, to argue with the majority, to fight with the majority if he believes he has the truth? Before many can know something, *one* must know it! [*His passion has silenced the crowd.*] It's always the same. Rights are sacred until it hurts for somebody to use them. I beg you now—I realize the cost is great, the inconvenience is great, the risk is great that other towns will get the jump on us while we're rebuilding—

PETER STOCKMANN: Aslaksen, he's not allowed to—

DR. STOCKMANN: Let me prove it to you! The water is poisoned!

THIRD CITIZEN [*steps up on the platform, waves his fist in Dr. Stockmann's face*]:   One more word about poison and I'm gonna take you outside!

The crowd is roaring; some try to charge the platform. The horn is blowing. Aslaksen rings his bell. Peter Stockmann steps forward, raising his hands. Kiil quietly exits.

PETER STOCKMANN: That's enough. Now stop it! Quiet! There is not going to be any violence here! [*There is silence. He turns to Dr. Stockmann*] Doctor, come down and give Mr. Aslaksen the platform.

DR. STOCKMANN [*staring down at the crowd with new eyes*]: I'm not through yet.

PETER STOCKMANN: Come down or I will not be responsible for what happens.

MRS. STOCKMANN: I'd like to go home. Come on, Tom.

PETER STOCKMANN: I move the chairman order the speaker to leave the platform.

VOICES: Sit down! Get off that platform!

DR. STOCKMANN: All right. Then I'll take this to out-of-town newspapers until the whole country is warned!

PETER STOCKMANN: You wouldn't dare!

HOVSTAD: You're trying to ruin this town—that's all; trying to ruin it.

DR. STOCKMANN: You're trying to build a town on a morality so rotten that it will infect the country and the world! If the only way you can prosper is this murder of freedom and truth, then I say with all my heart, "Let it be destroyed! Let the people perish!"

He leaves the platform.

FIRST CITIZEN [*to the Mayor*]: Arrest him! Arrest him!

SECOND CITIZEN: He's a traitor!

Cries of "Enemy! Traitor! Revolution!"

ASLAKSEN [*ringing for quiet*]: I would like to submit the following resolution: The people assembled here tonight, decent and patriotic citizens, in defense of their town and their country, declare that Doctor Stockmann, medical officer of Kirsten Springs, is an enemy of the people and of his community.

An uproar of assent starts.

MRS. STOCKMANN [*getting up*]: That's not true! He loves this town!

DR. STOCKMANN: You damned fools, you fools!

The Doctor and his family are all standing together, at the right, in a close group.

ASLAKSEN [*shouting over the din*]: Is there anyone against this motion! Anyone against!

HORSTER [*raising his hand*]: I am.

ASLAKSEN: One? [*He looks around.*]

DRUNK [*who has returned, raising his hand*]: Me too! You can't do without a doctor! Anybody'll . . . tell you . . .

ASLAKSEN: Anyone else? With all votes against two, this assembly formally declares Doctor Thomas Stockmann to be the people's enemy. In the future, all dealings with him by decent, patriotic citizens will be on that basis. The meeting is adjourned.

Shouts and applause. People start leaving. Dr. Stockmann goes over to Horster.

DR. STOCKMANN: Captain, do you have room for us on your ship to America?

HORSTER: Any time you say, Doctor.

DR. STOCKMANN: Catherine? Petra?

The three start for the door, but a gantlet has formed, dangerous and silent, except for . . .

THIRD CITIZEN: You'd better get aboard soon, Doctor!

MRS. STOCKMANN: Let's go out the back door.

HORSTER: Right this way.

DR. STOCKMANN: No, no. No back doors. *To the crowd:* I don't want to mislead anybody—the enemy of the people is not finished in this town—not quite yet. And if anybody thinks—

The horn blasts, cutting him off. The crowd starts yelling hysterically: "Enemy! Traitor! Throw him in the river! Come on, throw him in the river! Enemy! Enemy! Enemy!" The Stockmanns, erect, move out through the crowd, with Horster. Some of the crowd follow them out, yelling.

Downstage, watching, are Peter Stockmann, Billing, Aslaksen, and Hovstad. The stage is throbbing with the chant, "Enemy, Enemy, Enemy!" as the curtain falls.

Act III

Dr. Stockmann's living room the following morning. The windows are broken. There is great disorder. As the curtain rises, Dr. Stockmann enters, a robe over shirt and trousers—it's cold in the house. He picks up a stone from the floor, lays it on the table.

DR. STOCKMANN: Catherine! Tell what's-her-name there are still some rocks to pick up in here.

MRS. STOCKMANN [*from inside*]:   She's not finished sweeping up the glass.

As Dr. Stockmann bends down to get at another stone under a chair a rock comes through one of the last remaining panes. He rushes to the window, looks out. Mrs. Stockmann rushes in.

MRS. STOCKMANN [*frightened*]:   You all right?

DR. STOCKMANN [*looking out*]:   A little boy. Look at him run! [*He picks up the stone.*] How fast the poison spreads—even to the children!

MRS. STOCKMANN [*looking out the window*]:   It's hard to believe this is the same town.

DR. STOCKMANN [*adding this rock to the pile on the table*]:   I'm going to keep these like sacred relics. I'll put them in my will. I want the boys to have them in their homes to look at every day. [*He shudders.*] Cold in here. Why hasn't what's-her-name got the glazier here?

MRS. STOCKMANN: She's getting him . . .

DR. STOCKMANN: She's been getting him for two hours! We'll freeze to death in here.

MRS. STOCKMANN [*unwillingly*]: He won't come here, Tom.

DR. STOCKMANN [*stops moving*]: No! The glazier's afraid to fix my windows?

MRS. STOCKMANN: You don't realize—people don't like to be pointed out. He's got neighbors, I suppose, and—[*She hears something.*] Is that someone at the door, Randine?

She goes to the front door. He continues picking up stones. She comes back.

MRS. STOCKMANN: Letter for you.

DR. STOCKMANN [*taking and opening it*]:   What's this now?

MRS. STOCKMANN [*continuing his pick-up for him*]:   I don't know how we're going to do any shopping with everybody ready to bite my head off and—

DR. STOCKMANN: Well, what do you know? We're evicted.

MRS. STOCKMANN: Oh, no!

DR. STOCKMANN: He hates to do it, but with public opinion what it is . . .

MRS. STOCKMANN [*frightened*]:   Maybe we shouldn't have let the boys go to school today.

DR. STOCKMANN: Now don't get all frazzled again.

MRS. STOCKMANN: But the landlord is such a nice man. If he's got to throw us out, the town must be ready to murder us!

DR. STOCKMANN: Just calm down, will you? We'll go to America, and the whole thing'll be like a dream.

MRS. STOCKMANN: But I don't want to go to America— [*She notices his pants.*] When did this get torn?

DR. STOCKMANN [*examining the tear*]: Must've been last night.

MRS. STOCKMANN: Your best pants!

DR. STOCKMANN: Well, it just shows you, that's all—when a man goes out to fight for the truth he should never wear his best pants. [*He calms her*]. Stop worrying, will you? You'll sew them up, and in no time at all we'll be three thousand miles away.

MRS. STOCKMANN: But how do you know it'll be any different there?

DR. STOCKMANN: I don't know. It just seems to me, in a big country like that, the spirit must be bigger. Still, I suppose they must have the solid majority there too. I don't know, at least there must be more room to hide there.

MRS. STOCKMANN: Think about it more, will you? I'd hate to go half around the world and find out we're in the same place.

DR. STOCKMANN: You know, Catherine, I don't think I'm ever going to forget the face of that crowd last night.

MRS. STOCKMANN: Don't think about it.

DR. STOCKMANN: Some of them had their teeth bared, like animals in a pack. And who leads them? Men who call themselves liberals! Radicals! [*She starts looking around at the furniture, figuring.*] The crowd lets out one roar, and where are they, my liberal friends? I bet if I walked down the street now not one of them would admit he ever met me! Are you listening to me?

MRS. STOCKMANN: I was just wondering what we'll ever do with this furniture if we go to America.

DR. STOCKMANN: Don't you ever listen when I talk, dear?

MRS. STOCKMANN: Why must I listen? I know you're right.

Petra enters.

MRS. STOCKMANN: Petra! Why aren't you in school?

DR. STOCKMANN: What's the matter?

PETRA [*with deep emotion, looks at Dr. Stockmann, goes up and kisses him*]: I'm fired.

MRS. STOCKMANN: They wouldn't!

PETRA: As of two weeks from now. But I couldn't bear to stay there.

DR. STOCKMANN [*shocked*]:   Mrs. Busk fired you?

MRS. STOCKMANN: Who'd ever imagine she could do such a thing!

PETRA: It hurt her. I could see it, because we've always agreed so about things. But she didn't dare do anything else.

DR. STOCKMANN: The glazier doesn't dare fix the windows, the landlord doesn't dare let us stay on—

PETRA: The landlord!

DR. STOCKMANN: Evicted, darling! Oh, God, on the wreckage of all the civilizations in the world there ought to be a big sign: "They Didn't Dare!"

PETRA: I really can't blame her, Father. She showed me three letters she got this morning—

DR. STOCKMANN: From whom?

PETRA: They weren't signed.

DR. STOCKMANN: Oh, naturally. The big patriots with their anonymous indignation, scrawling out the darkness of their minds onto dirty little slips of paper—that's morality, and *I'm* the traitor! What did the letters say?

PETRA: Well, one of them was from somebody who said that he'd heard at the club that somebody who visits this house said that I had radical opinions about certain things.

DR. STOCKMANN: Oh, wonderful! Somebody heard that somebody heard that she heard, that he heard . . . ! Catherine, pack as soon as you can. I feel as though vermin were crawling all over me.

Horster enters.

HORSTER: Good morning.

DR. STOCKMANN: Captain! You're just the man I want to see.

HORSTER: I thought I'd see how you all were.

MRS. STOCKMANN: That's awfully nice of you, Captain, and I want to thank you for seeing us through the crowd last night.

PETRA: Did you get home all right? We hated to leave you alone with that mob.

HORSTER: Oh, nothing to it. In a storm there's just one thing to remember: it will pass.

DR. STOCKMANN: Unless it kills you.

HORSTER: You mustn't let yourself get too bitter.

DR. STOCKMANN: I'm trying, I'm trying. But I don't guarantee how I'll feel when I try to walk down the street with "Traitor" branded on my forehead.

MRS. STOCKMANN: Don't think about it.

HORSTER: Ah, what's a word?

DR. STOCKMANN: A word can be like a needle sticking in your heart, Captain. It can dig and corrode like an acid, until you become what they want you to be—really an enemy of the people.

HORSTER: You mustn't ever let that happen, Doctor.

DR. STOCKMANN: Frankly, I don't give a damn any more. Let summer come, let an epidemic break out, then they'll know whom they drove into exile. When are you sailing?

PETRA: You really decided to go, Father?

DR. STOCKMANN: Absolutely. When do you sail, Captain?

HORSTER: That's really what I came to talk to you about.

DR. STOCKMANN: Why? Something happen to the ship?

MRS. STOCKMANN [*happily, to Dr. Stockmann*]: You see! We can't go!

HORSTER: No, the ship will sail. But I won't be aboard.

DR. STOCKMANN: No!

PETRA: You fired too? 'Cause I was this morning.

MRS. STOCKMANN: Oh, Captain, you shouldn't have given us your house.

HORSTER: Oh, I'll get another ship. It's just that the owner, Mr. Vik, happens to belong to the same party as the Mayor, and I suppose when you belong to a party, and the party takes a certain position . . . Because Mr. Vik himself is a very decent man.

DR. STOCKMANN: Oh, they're all decent men!

HORSTER: No, really, he's not like the others.

DR. STOCKMANN: He doesn't have to be. A party is like a sausage grinder: it mashes up clearheads, longheads, fatheads, blockheads—and what comes out? Meatheads!

There is a knock on the hall door. Petra goes to answer.

MRS. STOCKMANN: Maybe that's the glazier!

DR. STOCKMANN: Imagine, Captain! [*He points to the window.*] Refused to come all morning!

Peter Stockmann enters, his hat in his hand. Silence.

PETER STOCKMANN: If you're busy . . .

DR. STOCKMANN: Just picking up broken glass. Come in, Peter. What can I do for you this fine, brisk morning? [*He demonstratively pulls his robe tighter around his throat.*]

MRS. STOCKMANN: Come inside, won't you, Captain?

HORSTER: Yes, I'd like to finish our talk, Doctor.

DR. STOCKMANN: Be with you in a minute, Captain.

Horster follows Petra and Catherine out through the dining-room doorway. Peter Stockmann says nothing, looking at the damage.

DR. STOCKMANN: Keep your hat on if you like, it's a little drafty in here today.

PETER STOCKMANN: Thanks, I believe I will. *He puts his hat on.* I think I caught cold last night—that house was freezing.

DR. STOCKMANN: I thought it was kind of warm—suffocating, as a matter of fact. What do you want?

PETER STOCKMANN: May I sit down? *He indicates a chair near the window.*

DR. STOCKMANN: Not there. A piece of the solid majority is liable to open your skull. Here.

They sit on the couch. Peter Stockmann takes out a large envelope.

DR. STOCKMANN: Now don't tell me.

PETER STOCKMANN: Yes. [*He hands the Doctor the envelope.*]

DR. STOCKMANN: I'm fired.

PETER STOCKMANN: The Board met this morning. There was nothing else to do, considering the state of public opinion.

DR. STOCKMANN [*after a pause*]: You look scared, Peter.

PETER STOCKMANN: I—I haven't completely forgotten that you're still my brother.

DR. STOCKMANN: I doubt that.

PETER STOCKMANN: You have no practice left in this town, Thomas.

DR. STOCKMANN: Oh, people always need a doctor.

PETER STOCKMANN: A petition is going from house to house. Everybody is signing it. A pledge not to call you any more. I don't think a single family will dare refuse to sign it.

DR. STOCKMANN: You started that, didn't you?

PETER STOCKMANN: No. As a matter of fact, I think it's all gone a little too far. I never wanted to see you ruined, Thomas. This will ruin you.

DR. STOCKMANN: No, it won't.

PETER STOCKMANN: For once in your life, will you act like a responsible man?

DR. STOCKMANN: Why don't you say it, Peter? You're afraid I'm going out of town to start publishing about the springs, aren't you?

PETER STOCKMANN: I don't deny that. Thomas, if you really have the good of the town at heart, you can accomplish everything without damaging anybody, including yourself.

DR. STOCKMANN: What's this now?

PETER STOCKMANN: Let me have a signed statement saying that in your zeal to help the town you went overboard and exaggerated. Put it any way you like, just so you calm anybody who might feel nervous about the water. If you'll give me that, you've got your job. And I give you my word, you can gradually make all the improvements you feel are necessary. Now, that gives you what you want . . .

DR. STOCKMANN: You're nervous, Peter.

PETER STOCKMANN [*nervously*]:   I am not nervous!

DR. STOCKMANN: You expect me to remain in charge while people are being poisoned? [*He gets up*].

PETER STOCKMANN: In time you can make your changes.

DR. STOCKMANN: When, five years, ten years? You know your trouble, Peter? You just don't grasp—even now—that there are certain men you can't buy.

PETER STOCKMANN: I'm quite capable of understanding that. But you don't happen to be one of those men.

DR. STOCKMANN [*after a slight pause*]:   What do you mean by that now?

PETER STOCKMANN: You know damned well what I mean by that. Morten Kiil is what I mean by that.

DR. STOCKMANN: Morten Kiil?

PETER STOCKMANN: Your father-in-law, Morten Kiil.

DR. STOCKMANN: I swear, Peter, one of us is out of his mind! What are you talking about?

PETER STOCKMANN: Now don't try to charm me with that professional innocence!

DR. STOCKMANN: What are you talking about?

PETER STOCKMANN: You don't know that your father-in-law has been running around all morning buying up stock in Kirsten Springs?

DR. STOCKMANN [*perplexed*]:   Buying up stock?

PETER STOCKMANN: Buying up stock, every share he can lay his hands on!

DR. STOCKMANN: Well, I don't understand, Peter. What's that got to do with—

PETER STOCKMANN [*walking around agitatedly*]:   Oh, come now, come now, come now!

DR. STOCKMANN: I hate you when you do that! Don't just walk around gabbling "Come now, come now!" What the hell are you talking about?

PETER STOCKMANN: Very well, if you insist on being dense. A man wages a relentless campaign to destroy confidence in a corporation. He even goes so far as to call a mass meeting against it. The very next morning, when people are still in a state of shock about it all, his father-in-law runs all over town, picking up shares at half their value.

DR. STOCKMANN [*realizing, turns away*]:   My God!

PETER STOCKMANN: And you have the nerve to speak to me about principles!

DR. STOCKMANN: You mean you actually believe that I . . . ?

PETER STOCKMANN: I'm not interested in psychology! I believe what I see! And what I see is nothing but a man doing a dirty, filthy job for Morten Kiil. And let me tell you—by tonight every man in this town'll see the same thing!

DR. STOCKMANN: Peter, you, you . . .

PETER STOCKMANN: Now go to your desk and write me a statement denying everything you've been saying, or . . .

DR. STOCKMANN: Peter, you're a low creature!

PETER STOCKMANN: All right then, you'd better get this one straight, Thomas. If you're figuring on opening another attack from out of town, keep this in mind: the morning it's published I'll send out a subpoena for you and begin a prosecution for conspiracy. I've been trying to make you respectable all my life; now if you want to make the big jump there'll be nobody there to hold you back. Now do we understand each other?

DR. STOCKMANN: Oh, we do, Peter! [*Peter Stockmann starts for the door.*] Get the girl—what the hell is her name—scrub the floors, wash down the walls, a pestilence has been here!

Kiil enters. Peter Stockmann almost runs into him. Peter turns to his brother.

PETER STOCKMANN, *pointing to Kiil*:   Ha! [*He turns and goes out.*]

Kiil, humming quietly, goes to a chair.

DR. STOCKMANN: Morten! What have you done? What's the matter with you? Do you realize what this makes me look like?

Kiil has started taking some papers out of his pocket. Dr. Stockmann breaks off on seeing them. Kiil places them on the table.

DR. STOCKMANN: Is that—them?

KIIL: That's them, yes. Kirsten Springs shares. And very easy to get this morning.

DR. STOCKMANN: Morten, don't play with me—what is this all about?

KIIL: What are you so nervous about? Can't a man buy some stock without . . . ?

DR. STOCKMANN: I want an explanation, Morten.

KIIL [*Nodding*]: Thomas, they hated you last night—

DR. STOCKMANN: You don't have to tell me that.

KIIL: But they also believed you. They'd love to murder you, but they believe you. [*Slight pause*]. The way they say it, the pollution is coming down the river from Windmill Valley.

DR. STOCKMANN: That's exactly where it's coming from.

KIIL: Yes. And that's exactly where my tannery is.

Pause. Dr. Stockmann sits down slowly.

DR. STOCKMANN: Well, Morten, I never made a secret to you that the pollution was tannery waste.

KIIL: I'm not blaming you. It's my fault. I didn't take you seriously. But it's very serious now. Thomas, I got that tannery from my father; he got it from his father; and his father got it from my great-grandfather. I do not intend to allow my family's name to stand for the three generations of murdering angels who poisoned this town.

DR. STOCKMANN: I've waited a long time for this talk, Morten. I don't think you can stop that from happening.

KIIL: No, but you can.

DR. STOCKMANN: I?

KIIL [*nudging the shares*]: I've bought these shares because—

DR. STOCKMANN: Morten, you've thrown your money away. The springs are doomed.

KIIL: I never throw my money away, Thomas. These were bought with your money.

DR. STOCKMANN: My money? What . . . ?

KIIL: You've probably suspected that I might leave a little something for Catherine and the boys?

DR. STOCKMANN: Well, naturally, I'd hoped you'd . . .

KIIL [*touching the shares*]: I decided this morning to invest that money in some stock.

DR. STOCKMANN [*slowly getting up*]: You bought that junk with Catherine's money!

KIIL: People call me "badger," and that's an animal that roots out things, but it's also some kind of a pig, I understand. I've lived a clean man and I'm going to die clean. You're going to clean my name for me.

DR. STOCKMANN: Morten . . .

KIIL: Now I want to see if you really belong in a strait jacket.

DR. STOCKMANN: How could you do such a thing? What's the matter with you!

KIIL: Now don't get excited, it's very simple. If you should make another investigation of the water—

DR. STOCKMANN: I don't *need* another investigation, I—

KIIL: If you think it over and decide that you ought to change your opinion about the water—

DR. STOCKMANN: But the water is poisoned! It is poisoned!

KIIL: If you simply go on insisting the water is poisoned [*he holds up the shares*] with these in your house, then there's only one explanation for you—you're absolutely crazy. [*He puts the shares down on the table again.*]

DR. STOCKMANN: You're right! I'm mad! I'm insane!

KIIL [*with more force*]: You're stripping the skin off your family's back! Only a madman would do a thing like that!

DR. STOCKMANN: Morten, Morten, I'm a penniless man! Why didn't you tell me before you bought this junk?

KIIL: Because you would understand it better if I told you after. [*He goes up to Dr. Stockmann, holds him by the lapels. With terrific force, and the twinkle still in his eye*]: And, goddammit, I think you do understand it now, don't you? Millions of tons of water come down that river. How do you know the day you made your tests there wasn't something unusual about the water?

DR. STOCKMANN [*not looking at Kiil*]: Yes, but I . . .

KIIL: How do you know? Why couldn't those little animals have clotted up only the patch of water you souped out of the river? How do you know the rest of it wasn't pure?

DR. STOCKMANN: It's not probable. People were getting sick last summer . . .

KIIL: They were sick when they came here or they wouldn't have come!

DR. STOCKMANN [*breaking away*]: Not intestinal diseases, skin diseases . . .

KIIL [*following him*]: The only place anybody gets a bellyache is here! There are no carbuncles in Norway? Maybe the food was bad. Did you ever think of the food?

DR. STOCKMANN [*with the desire to agree with him*]: No, I didn't look into the food . . .

KIIL: Then what makes you so sure it's the water?

DR. STOCKMANN: Because I tested the water and—

KIIL [*taking hold of him again*]: Admit it! We're all alone here. You have some doubt.

DR. STOCKMANN: Well, there's always a possible . . .

KIIL: Then part of it's imaginary.

DR. STOCKMANN: Well, nothing is a hundred per cent on this earth, but—

KIIL: Then you have a perfect right to doubt the other way! You have a scientific right! And did you ever think of some disinfectant? I bet you never even thought of that.

DR. STOCKMANN: Not for a mass of water like that, you can't . . .

KIIL: Everything can be killed. That's science! Thomas, I never liked your brother either, you have a perfect right to hate him.

DR. STOCKMANN: I didn't do it because I hate my brother.

KIIL: Part of it, part of it, don't deny it! You admit there's some doubt in your mind about the water, you admit there may be ways to disinfect it, and yet you went after your brother as though these doubts didn't exist; as though the only way to cure the thing was to blow up the whole Institute! There's hatred in that, boy, don't forget it. [*He points to the shares*]. These can belong to you now, so be sure, be sure! Tear the hatred out of your heart, stand naked in front of yourself—*are you sure*?

DR. STOCKMANN: What right have you to gamble my family's future on the strength of my convictions?

KIIL: Aha! Then the convictions are not really that strong!

DR. STOCKMANN: I am ready to hang for my convictions! But no man has a right to make martyrs of others; my family is innocent.

Sell back those shares, give her what belongs to her. I'm a penniless man!

KIIL: Nobody is going to say Morten Kiil wrecked this town.

[*He gathers up the shares.*] You retract your convictions—or these go to my charity.

DR. STOCKMANN: Everything?

KIIL: There'll be a little something for Catherine, but not much. I want my good name. It's exceedingly important to me.

DR. STOCKMANN [*bitterly*]: And charity . . .

KIIL: Charity will do it, or you will do it. It's a serious thing to destroy a town.

DR. STOCKMANN: Morten, when I look at you, I swear to God I see the devil!

The door opens, and before we see who is there . . .

DR. STOCKMANN: You!

Aslaksen enters, holding up his hand defensively.

ASLAKSEN: Now don't get excited! Please!

Hovstad enters. He and Aslaksen stop short and smile on seeing Kiil.

KIIL: Too many intellectuals here: I'd better go.

ASLAKSEN [*apologetically*]: Doctor, can we have five minutes of—

DR. STOCKMANN: I've got nothing to say to you.

KIIL [*going to the door*]: I want an answer right away. You hear? I'm waiting. [*He leaves.*]

DR. STOCKMANN: All right, say it quick, what do you want?

HOVSTAD: We don't expect you to forgive our attitude at the meeting, but . . .

DR. STOCKMANN [*groping for the word*]: Your attitude was prone . . . prostrated . . . prostituted!

HOVSTAD: All right, call it whatever you—

DR. STOCKMANN: I've got a lot on my mind, so get to the point. What do you want?

ASLAKSEN: Doctor, you should have told us what was in back of it all. You could have had the *Messenger* behind you all the way.

HOVSTAD: You'd have had public opinion with you now. Why didn't you tell us?

DR. STOCKMANN: Look, I'm very tired, let's not beat around the bush!

HOVSTAD [*gesturing toward the door where Kiil went out*]: He's been all over town buying up stock in the springs. It's no secret any more.

DR. STOCKMANN [*after a slight pause*]: Well, what about it?

HOVSTAD [*in a friendly way*]: You don't want me to spell it out, do you?

DR. STOCKMANN: I certainly wish you would. I—

HOVSTAD: All right, let's lay it on the table. Aslaksen, you want to . . . ?

ASLAKSEN: No, no, go ahead.

HOVSTAD: Doctor, in the beginning we supported you. But it quickly became clear that if we kept on supporting you in the face of public hysteria—

DR. STOCKMANN: Your paper created the hysteria.

HOVSTAD: One thing at a time, all right? [*Slowly, to drive it into Dr. Stockmann's head*]: We couldn't go on supporting you because, in simple language, we didn't have the money to withstand the loss in circulation. You're boycotted now? Well, the paper would have been boycotted too, if we'd stuck with you.

ASLAKSEN: You can see that, Doctor.

DR. STOCKMANN: Oh, yes. But what do you want?

HOVSTAD: *The People's Messenger* can put on such a campaign that in two months you will be hailed as a hero in this town.

ASLAKSEN: We're ready to go.

HOVSTAD: We will prove to the public that you had to buy up the stock because the management would not make the changes required for public health. In other words, you did it for absolutely scientific, public-spirited reasons. Now what do you say, Doctor?

DR. STOCKMANN: You want money from me, is that it?

ASLAKSEN: Well, now, Doctor . . .

HOVSTAD [*to Aslaksen*]: No, don't walk around it. [*To Dr. Stockmann.*] If we started to support you again, Doctor, we'd lose circulation for a while. We'd like you—or Mr. Kiil rather—to make up the deficit. [*Quickly.*] Now that's open and aboveboard, and I don't see anything wrong with it. Do you?

Pause. Dr. Stockmann looks at him, then turns and walks to the windows, deep in thought.

ASLAKSEN: Remember, Doctor, you need the paper, you need it desperately.

DR. STOCKMANN [*returning*]:   No, there's nothing wrong with it at all. I—I'm not at all averse to cleaning up my name—although for myself it never was dirty. But I don't *enjoy* being hated, if you know what I mean.

ASLAKSEN: Exactly.

HOVSTAD: Aslaksen, will you show him the budget . . .

Aslaksen reaches into his pocket.

DR. STOCKMANN: Just a minute. There is one point. I hate to keep repeating the same thing, but the water is poisoned.

HOVSTAD: Now, Doctor . . .

DR. STOCKMANN: Just a minute. The Mayor says that he will levy a tax on everybody to pay for the reconstruction. I assume you are ready to support that tax at the same time you're supporting me.

ASLAKSEN: That tax would be extremely unpopular.

HOVSTAD: Doctor, with you back in charge of the baths, I have absolutely no fear that anything can go wrong.

DR. STOCKMANN: In other words, you will clean up my name—so that I can be in charge of the corruption.

HOVSTAD: But we can't tackle everything at once. A new tax—there'd be an uproar!

ASLAKSEN: It would ruin the paper!

DR. STOCKMANN: Then you don't intend to do anything about the water?

HOVSTAD: We have faith you won't let anyone get sick.

DR. STOCKMANN: In other words, gentlemen, you are looking for someone to blackmail into paying your printing bill.

HOVSTAD [*indignantly*]: We are trying to clear your name, Doctor Stockmann! And if you refuse to cooperate, if that's going to be your attitude . . .

DR. STOCKMANN: Yes? Go on. What will you do?

HOVSTAD [*to Aslaksen*]:   I think we'd better go.

DR. STOCKMANN [*stepping in their way*]:   What will you do? I would like you to tell me. Me, the man two minutes ago you were going to make into a hero—what will you do now that I won't pay you?

ASLAKSEN: Doctor, the public is almost hysterical . . .

DR. STOCKMANN: To my face, tell me what you are going to do!

HOVSTAD: The Mayor will prosecute you for conspiracy to destroy a corporation, and without a paper behind you, you will end up in prison.

DR. STOCKMANN: And you'll support him, won't you? I want it from your mouth, Hovstad. This little victory you will not deny me. [*Hovstad starts for the door. Dr. Stockmann steps into his way*]. Tell the hero, Hovstad. You're going to go on crucifying the hero, are you not? Say it to me! You will not leave here until I get this from your mouth!

HOVSTAD [*looking directly at Dr. Stockmann*]: You are a madman. You are insane with egotism. And don't excuse it with humanitarian slogans, because a man who'll drag his family through a lifetime of disgrace is a demon in his heart! [*He advances on Dr. Stockmann.*] You hear me? A demon who cares more for the purity of a public bath than the lives of his wife and children. Doctor Stockmann, you deserve everything you're going to get!

Dr. Stockmann is struck by Hovstad's ferocious conviction. Aslaksen comes toward him, taking the budget out of his pocket.

ASLAKSEN [*nervously*]: Doctor, please consider it. It won't take much money, and in two months' time I promise you your whole life will change and . . .

Offstage Mrs. Stockmann is heard calling in a frightened voice, "What happened? My God, what's the matter?" She runs to the front door. Dr. Stockmann, alarmed, goes quickly to the hallway. Ejlif and Morten enter. Morten's head is bruised. Petra and Captain Horster enter from the left.

MRS. STOCKMANN: Something happened! Look at him!

MORTEN: I'm all right, they just . . .

DR. STOCKMANN [*looking at the bruise*]: What happened here?

MORTEN: Nothing, Papa, I swear . . .

DR. STOCKMANN [*to Ejlif*]: What happened? Why aren't you in school?

EJLIF: The teacher said we better stay home the rest of the week.

DR. STOCKMANN: The boys hit him?

EJLIF: They started calling you names, so he got sore and began to fight with one kid, and all of a sudden the whole bunch of them . . .

MRS. STOCKMANN [*to Morten*]: Why did you answer!

MORTEN [*indignantly*]: They called him a traitor! My father is no traitor!

EJLIF: But you didn't have to answer!

MRS. STOCKMANN: You should've known they'd all jump on you! They could have killed you!

MORTEN: I don't care!

DR. STOCKMANN [*to quiet him—and his own heart*]:   Morten . . .

MORTEN [*pulling away from his father*]:   I'll kill them! I'll take a rock and the next time I see one of them I'll kill him!

Dr. Stockmann reaches for Morten, who, thinking his father will chastise him, starts to run. Dr. Stockmann catches him and grips him by the arm.

MORTEN: Let me go! Let me . . . !

DR. STOCKMANN: Morten . . . Morten . . .

MORTEN [*crying in his father's arms*]:   They called you traitor, an enemy . . . [*He sobs.*]

DR. STOCKMANN: Sssh. That's all. Wash your face.

Mrs. Stockmann takes Morten. Dr. Stockmann stands erect, faces Aslaksen and Hovstad.

DR. STOCKMANN: Good day, gentlemen.

HOVSTAD: Let us know what you decide and we'll—

DR. STOCKMANN: I've decided. I am an enemy of the people.

MRS. STOCKMANN: Tom, what are you . . . ?

DR. STOCKMANN: To such people, who teach their own children to think with their fists—to them I'm an enemy! And my boy . . . my boys . . . my family . . . I think you can count us all enemies.

ASLAKSEN: Doctor, you could have everything you want!

DR. STOCKMANN: Except the truth. I could have everything but that—that the water is poisoned!

HOVSTAD: But you'll be in charge.

DR. STOCKMANN: But the children are poisoned, the people are poisoned! If the only way I can be a friend of the people is to take charge of that corruption, then I am an enemy! The water is poisoned, poisoned, poisoned! That's the beginning of it and that's the end of it! Now get out of here!

HOVSTAD: You know where you're going to end?

DR. STOCKMANN: I said get out of here! [*He grabs Aslaksen's umbrella out of his hand.*]

MRS. STOCKMANN: What are you doing?

Aslaksen and Hovstad back toward the door as Dr. Stockmann starts to swing.

ASLAKSEN: You're a fanatic, you're out of your mind!

MRS. STOCKMANN: [grabbing Dr. Stockmann to take the umbrella]   What are you doing?

DR. STOCKMANN: They want me to buy the paper, the public, the pollution of the springs, buy the whole pollution of this town! They'll make a hero out of me for that! [Furiously, to Aslaksen and Hovstad:] But I'm not a hero, I'm the enemy—and now you're first going to find out what kind of enemy I am! I will sharpen my pen like a dagger—you, all you friends of the people, are going to bleed before I'm done! Go, tell them to sign the petitions! Warn them not to call me when they're sick! Beat up my children! And never let her [he points to Petra] in the school again or she'll destroy the immaculate purity of the vacuum there! See to all the barricades—the truth is coming! Ring the bells, sound the alarm! The truth, the truth is out, and soon it will be prowling like a lion in the streets!

HOVSTAD: Doctor, you're out of your mind.

He and Aslaksen turn to go. They are in the doorway.

EJLIF, *rushing at them:*   Don't you say that to him!

DR. STOCKMANN [*as Mrs. Stockmann cries out, rushes them with the umbrella*]:   Out of here!

They rush out. Dr. Stockmann throws the umbrella after them, then slams the door. Silence. He has his back pressed against the door, facing his family.

DR. STOCKMANN: I've had all the ambassadors of hell today, but there'll be no more. Now, now listen, Catherine! Children, listen. Now we're besieged. They'll call for blood now, they'll whip the people like oxen— [*A rock comes through a remaining pane. The boys start for the window.*] Stay away from there!

MRS. STOCKMANN: The Captain knows where we can get a ship.

DR. STOCKMANN: No ships.

PETRA: We're staying?

MRS. STOCKMANN: But they can't go back to school! I won't let them out of the house!

DR. STOCKMANN: We're staying.

PETRA: Good!

DR. STOCKMANN: We must be careful now. We must live through this. Boys, no more school. I'm going to teach you, and Petra will. Do you know any kids, street louts, hookey-players—

EJLIF: Oh, sure, we—

DR. STOCKMANN: We'll want about twelve of them to start. But I want them good and ignorant, absolutely uncivilized. Can we use your house, Captain?

HORSTER: Sure, I'm never there.

DR. STOCKMANN: Fine. We'll begin, Petra, and we'll turn out not tax-payers and newspaper subscribers, but free and independent people, hungry for the truth. Oh, I forgot! Petra, run to Grandpa and tell him—tell him as follows: No!

MRS. STOCKMANN [puzzled]: What do you mean?

DR. STOCKMANN [going over to Mrs. Stockmann]: It means, my dear, that we are all alone. And there'll be a long night before it's day—

A rock comes through a paneless window. Horster goes to the window. A crowd is heard approaching.

HORSTER: Half the town is out!

MRS. STOCKMANN: What's going to happen? Tom! What's going to happen?

DR. STOCKMANN [holding his hands up to quiet her, and with a trembling mixture of trepidation and courageous insistence]: I don't know. But remember now, everybody. You are fighting for the truth, and that's why you're alone. And that makes you strong. We're the strongest people in the world . . .

The crowd is heard angrily calling outside. Another rock comes through a window.

DR. STOCKMANN: . . . and the strong must learn to be lonely!

The crowd noise gets louder. He walks upstage toward the windows as a wind rises and the curtains start to billow out toward him. the curtain falls.

—1882

Susan Glaspell was born in Iowa and educated at Drake University. Glaspell was one of the founders, with her husband George Cram Cook, of the Provincetown Players. This company, founded in the Cape Cod resort village, was committed to producing experimental drama, an alternative to the standard fare playing in Broadway theaters. Eventually it was relocated to New York. Along with Glaspell, Eugene O'Neill, America's only Nobel Prize–winning dramatist, wrote plays for this group. Trained as a journalist and the author of short stories and novels, Glaspell wrote Trifles *[1916], her first play, shortly after the founding of the Players, basing her plot on an Iowa murder case she had covered. The one-act play, with both Glaspell and her husband in the cast, premiered during the Players' second season and also exists in a short-story version. Glaspell won the Pulitzer Prize for Drama in 1930 for* Alison's House, *basing the title character on poet Emily Dickinson. A socialist and feminist, Glaspell lived in Provincetown in her last years, writing* The Road to the Temple, *a memoir of her husband's life, and novels.*

Trifles

Characters

George Henderson, *County Attorney*
Mrs. Peters
Henry Peters, *Sheriff*
Lewis Hale, *a neighbor*
Mrs. Hale

The kitchen in the now abandoned farmhouse of John Wright, a gloomy kitchen, and left without having been put in order—unwashed pans under the sink, a loaf of bread outside the breadbox, a dish towel on the table— other signs of incompleted work. At the rear the outer door opens, and the Sheriff comes in, followed by the County Attorney and Hale. The Sheriff and Hale are men in middle life, the County Attorney is a young man; all are much bundled up and go at once to the stove. They are followed by the two women—the Sheriff's Wife first; she is a slight wiry woman, a thin nervous face. Mrs. Hale is larger and would ordinarily be called more comfortable looking, but she is disturbed now and looks fearfully about as she enters. The women have come in slowly and stand close together near the door.

COUNTY ATTORNEY [*rubbing his hands*]:   This feels good. Come up to the fire, ladies.

MRS. PETERS [*after taking a step forward*]:   I'm not—cold.

SHERIFF [*unbuttoning his overcoat and stepping away from the stove as if to the beginning of official business*]:   Now, Mr. Hale, before we move things about, you explain to Mr. Henderson just what you saw when you came here yesterday morning.

COUNTY ATTORNEY: By the way, has anything been moved? Are things just as you left them yesterday?

SHERIFF [*looking about*]:   It's just the same. When it dropped below zero last night, I thought I'd better send Frank out this morning to make a fire for us—no use getting pneumonia with a big case on; but I told him not to touch anything except the stove—and you know Frank.

COUNTY ATTORNEY: Somebody should have been left here yesterday.

SHERIFF: Oh—yesterday. When I had to send Frank to Morris Center for that man who went crazy—I want you to know I had my hands full yesterday. I knew you could get back from Omaha by today, and as long as I went over everything here myself—

COUNTY ATTORNEY: Well, Mr. Hale, tell just what happened when you came here yesterday morning.

HALE: Harry and I had started to town with a load of potatoes. We came along the road from my place; and as I got here, I said, "I'm going to see if I can't get John Wright to go in with me on a party telephone." I spoke to Wright about it once before, and he put me off, saying folks talked too much anyway, and all he asked was peace and quiet—I guess you know about how much he talked himself; but I thought maybe if I went to the house and talked about it before his wife, though I said to Harry that I didn't know as what his wife wanted made much difference to John—

COUNTY ATTORNEY: Let's talk about that later, Mr. Hale. I do want to talk about that, but tell now just what happened when you got to the house.

HALE: I didn't hear or see anything; I knocked at the door, and still it was all quiet inside. I knew they must be up, it was past eight o'clock. So I knocked again, and I thought I heard somebody say, "Come in." I wasn't sure, I'm not sure yet, but I opened the door—this

SUSAN GLASPELL

door [*indicating the door by which the two women are still standing*], and there in that rocker—[*pointing to it*] sat Mrs. Wright. [*They all look at the rocker.*]

COUNTY ATTORNEY: What—was she doing?

HALE: She was rockin' back and forth. She had her apron in her hand and was kind of—pleating it.

COUNTY ATTORNEY: And how did she—look?

HALE: Well, she looked queer.

COUNTY ATTORNEY: How do you mean—queer?

HALE: Well, as if she didn't know what she was going to do next. And kind of done up.

COUNTY ATTORNEY: How did she seem to feel about your coming?

HALE: Why, I don't think she minded—one way or other. She didn't pay much attention. I said, "How do, Mrs. Wright, it's cold, ain't it?" And she said, "Is it?"—and went on kind of pleating at her apron. Well, I was surprised; she didn't ask me to come up to the stove, or to set down, but just sat there, not even looking at me, so I said, "I want to see John." And then she—laughed. I guess you would call it a laugh. I thought of Harry and the team outside, so I said a little sharp: "Can't I see John?" "No," she says, kind o' dull like. "Ain't he home?" says I. "Yes," says she, "he's home." "Then why can't I see him?" I asked her, out of patience. "Cause he's dead," says she. "*Dead?*" says I. She just nodded her head, not getting a bit excited, but rockin' back and forth. "Why—where is he?" says I, not knowing what to say. She just pointed upstairs—like that [*himself pointing to the room above*]. I got up, with the idea of going up there. I walked from there to here—then I says, "Why, what did he die of?" "He died of a rope around his neck," says she, and just went on pleatin' at her apron. Well, I went out and called Harry. I thought I might—need help. We went upstairs, and there he was lyin'—

COUNTY ATTORNEY: I think I'd rather have you go into that upstairs, where you can point it all out. Just go on now with the rest of the story.

HALE: Well, my first thought was to get that rope off. I looked . . . [*Stops, his face twitches.*] . . . but Harry, he went up to him, and he said, "No, he's dead all right, and we'd better not touch anything." So we went back downstairs. She was still sitting that same way.

"Has anybody been notified?" I asked. "No," says she, unconcerned. "Who did this, Mrs. Wright?" said Harry. He said it businesslike— and she stopped pleatin' of her apron. "I don't know," she says. "You don't *know*?" says Harry. "No," says she, "Weren't you sleepin' in the bed with him?" says Harry. "Yes," says she, "but I was on the inside." "Somebody slipped a rope round his neck and strangled him, and you didn't wake up?" says Harry. "I didn't wake up," she said after him. We must 'a looked as if we didn't see how that could be, for after a minute she said, "I sleep sound." Harry was going to ask her more questions, but I said maybe we ought to let her tell her story first to the coroner, or the sheriff, so Harry went fast as he could to Rivers' place, where there's a telephone.

COUNTY ATTORNEY: And what did Mrs. Wright do when she knew that you had gone for the coroner?

HALE: She moved from that chair to this over here . . . [*Pointing to a small chair in the corner.*] . . . and just sat there with her hands held together and looking down. I got a feeling that I ought to make some conversation, so I said I had come in to see if John wanted to put in a telephone, and at that she started to laugh, and then she stopped and looked at me—scared. [*The County Attorney, who has had his notebook out, makes a note.*] I dunno, maybe it wasn't scared. I wouldn't like to say it was. Soon Harry got back, and then Dr. Lloyd came, and you, Mr. Peters, and so I guess that's all I know that you don't.

COUNTY ATTORNEY [*looking around*]:   I guess we'll go upstairs first— and then out to the barn and around there. [*To the Sheriff.*] You're convinced that there was nothing important here—nothing that would point to any motive?

SHERIFF: Nothing here but kitchen things.

[*The County Attorney, after again looking around the kitchen, opens the door of a cupboard closet. He gets up on a chair and looks on a shelf. Pulls his hand away, sticky.*]

COUNTY ATTORNEY: Here's a nice mess.

[*The women draw nearer.*]

MRS. PETERS [*to the other woman*]:   Oh, her fruit; it did freeze. [*To the Lawyer.*] She worried about that when it turned so cold. She said the fir'd go out and her jars would break.

SHERIFF: Well, can you beat the women! Held for murder and wor-
ryin' about her preserves.

COUNTY ATTORNEY: I guess before we're through she may have
something more serious than preserves to worry about.

HALE: Well, women are used to worrying over trifles.

[*The two women move a little closer together.*]

COUNTY ATTORNEY [*with the gallantry of a young politician*]:   And yet,
for all their worries, what would we do without the ladies? [*The
women do not unbend. He goes to the sink, takes a dipperful of water
from the pail and, pouring it into a basin, washes his hands. Starts to
wipe them on the roller towel, turns it for a cleaner place.*] Dirty towels!
[*Kicks his foot against the pans under the sink.*] Not much of a housekeeper, would you say, ladies?

MRS. HALE [*stiffly*]:   There's a great deal of work to be done on a farm.

COUNTY ATTORNEY: To be sure. And yet . . . [*With a little bow to her.*] . . .
I know there are some Dickson county farmhouses which do not
have such roller towels. [*He gives it a pull to expose its full length
again.*]

MRS. HALE: Those towels get dirty awful quick. Men's hands aren't
always as clean as they might be.

COUNTY ATTORNEY: Ah, loyal to your sex, I see. But you and Mrs.
Wright were neighbors. I suppose you were friends, too.

MRS. HALE [*shaking her head*]:   I've not seen much of her of late years.
I've not been in this house—it's more than a year.

COUNTY ATTORNEY: And why was that? You didn't like her?

MRS. HALE: I liked her all well enough. Farmers' wives have their
hands full, Mr. Henderson. And then—

COUNTY ATTORNEY: Yes—?

MRS. HALE [*looking about*]:   It never seemed a very cheerful place.

COUNTY ATTORNEY: No—it's not cheerful. I shouldn't say she had
the homemaking instinct.

MRS. HALE: Well, I don't know as Wright had, either.

COUNTY ATTORNEY: You mean that they didn't get on very well?

MRS. HALE: No, I don't mean anything. But I don't think a place'd be
any cheerfuler for John Wright's being in it.

COUNTY ATTORNEY: I'd like to talk more of that a little later. I want
to get the lay of things upstairs now. [*He goes to the left, where three
steps lead to a stair door.*]

SHERIFF: I suppose anything Mrs. Peters does'll be all right. She was to take in some clothes for her, you know, and a few little things. We left in such a hurry yesterday.

COUNTY ATTORNEY: Yes, but I would like to see what you take, Mrs. Peters, and keep an eye out for anything that might be of use to us.

MRS. PETERS: Yes, Mr. Henderson.

[*The women listen to the men's steps on the stairs, then look about the kitchen.*]

MRS. HALE: I'd hate to have men coming into my kitchen, snooping around and criticizing. [*She arranges the pans under the sink which the Lawyer had shoved out of place.*]

MRS. PETERS: Of course it's no more than their duty.

MRS. HALE: Duty's all right, but I guess that deputy sheriff that came out to make the fire might have got a little of this on. [*Gives the roller towel a pull.*] Wish I'd thought of that sooner. Seems mean to talk about her for not having things slicked up when she had to come away in such a hurry.

MRS. PETERS [*who has gone to a small table in the left rear corner of the room, and lifted one end of a towel that covers a pan*]:   She had bread set. [*Stands still.*]

MRS. HALE [*eyes fixed on a loaf of bread beside the breadbox, which is on a low shelf at the other side of the room. Moves slowly toward it*]:   She was going to put this in there. [*Picks up loaf, then abruptly drops it. In a manner of returning to familiar things.*] It's a shame about her fruit. I wonder if it's all gone. [*Gets up on the chair and looks.*] I think there's some here that's all right, Mrs. Peters. Yes—here; [*Holding it toward the window.*] this is cherries, too. [*Looking again.*] I declare I believe that's the only one. [*Gets down, bottle in her hand. Goes to the sink and wipes it off on the outside.*] She'll feel awful bad after all her hard work in the hot weather. I remember the afternoon I put up my cherries last summer. [*She puts the bottle on the big kitchen table, center of the room, front table. With a sigh, is about to sit down in the rocking chair. Before she is seated realizes what chair it is; with a slow look at it, steps back. The chair, which she has touched, rocks back and forth.*]

MRS. PETERS: Well, I must get those things from the front room closet. [*She goes to the door at the right, but after looking into the other room steps back.*] You coming with me, Mrs. Hale? You could help me carry them. [*They go into the other room; reappear, Mrs. Peters carrying a dress and skirt, Mrs. Hale following with a pair of shoes.*]

MRS. PETERS: My, it's cold in there. [*She puts the cloth on the big table, and hurries to the stove.*]

MRS. HALE [*examining the skirt*]: Wright was close. I think maybe that's why she kept so much to herself. She didn't even belong to the Ladies' Aid. I suppose she felt she couldn't do her part, and then you don't enjoy things when you feel shabby. She used to wear pretty clothes and be lively, when she was Minnie Foster, one of the town girls singing in the choir. But that—oh, that was thirty years ago. This all you was to take in?

MRS. PETERS: She said she wanted an apron. Funny thing to want, for there isn't much to get you dirty in jail, goodness knows. But I suppose just to make her feel more natural. She said they was in the top drawer in this cupboard. Yes, here. And then her little shawl that always hung behind the door. [*Opens stair door and looks.*] Yes, here it is. [*Quickly shuts door leading upstairs.*]

MRS. HALE [*abruptly moving toward her*]: Mrs. Peters?

MRS. PETERS: Yes, Mrs. Hale?

MRS. HALE: Do you think she did it?

MRS. PETERS [*in a frightened voice*]: Oh, I don't know.

MRS. HALE: Well, I don't think she did. Asking for an apron and her little shawl. Worrying about her fruit.

MRS. PETERS [*starts to speak, glances up, where footsteps are heard in the room above. In a low voice*]: Mr. Peters says it looks bad for her. Mr. Henderson is awful sarcastic in speech, and he'll make fun of her sayin' she didn't wake up.

MRS. HALE: Well, I guess John Wright didn't wake when they was slipping that rope under his neck.

MRS. PETERS: No, it's strange. It must have been done awful crafty and still. They say it was such a—funny way to kill a man, rigging it all up like that.

MRS. HALE: That's just what Mr. Hale said. There was a gun in the house. He says that's what he can't understand.

MRS. PETERS: Mr. Henderson said coming out that what was needed for the case was a motive; something to show anger, or—sudden feeling.

MRS. HALE [*who is standing by the table*]: Well, I don't see any signs of anger around here. [*She puts her hand on the dish towel which lies on* the table, stands looking down at the table, one half of which is clean, the other half messy.] It's wiped here. [Makes a move as if to finish work, then turns and looks at loaf of bread outside the breadbox. Drops towel. In that voice of coming back to familiar things.] Wonder how they are finding things upstairs? I hope she had it a little more red-up there. You know, it seems kind of *sneaking.* Locking her up in town and then coming out here and trying to get her own house to turn against her!

MRS. PETERS: But, Mrs. Hale, the law is the law.

MRS. HALE: I s'pose 'tis. [Unbuttoning her coat.] Better loosen up your things, Mrs. Peters. You won't feel them when you go out.

[Mrs. Peters takes off her fur tippet, goes to hang it on a hook at the back of room, stands looking at the under part of the small corner table.]

MRS. PETERS: She was piecing a quilt. [She brings the large sewing basket, and they look at the bright pieces.]

MRS. HALE: It's log cabin pattern. Pretty, isn't it? I wonder if she was goin' to quilt or just knot it?

[Footsteps have been heard coming down the stairs. The Sheriff enters, followed by Hale and the County Attorney.]

SHERIFF: They wonder if she was going to quilt it or just knot it. [The men laugh, the women look abashed.]

COUNTY ATTORNEY [rubbing his hands over the stove]:   Frank's fire didn't do much up there, did it? Well, let's go out to the barn and get that cleared up.

[The men go outside.]

MRS. HALE [resentfully]:   I don't know as there's anything so strange, our takin' up our time with little things while we're waiting for them to get the evidence. [She sits down at the big table, smoothing out a block with decision.] I don't see as it's anything to laugh about.

MRS. PETERS [apologetically]:   Of course they've got awful important things on their minds. [Pulls up a chair and joins Mrs. Hale at the table.]

MRS. HALE [examining another block]:   Mrs. Peters, look at this one. Here, this is the one she was working on, and look at the sewing! All the rest of it has been so nice and even. And look at this! It's all over the place! Why, it looks as if she didn't know what she was about! [*After she has said this, they look at each other, then started to glance back at the door. After an instant Mrs. Hale has pulled at a knot and ripped the sewing.*]

MRS. PETERS: Oh, what are you doing, Mrs. Hale?

MRS. HALE [*mildly*]:   Just pulling out a stitch or two that's not sewed very good. [*Threading a needle.*] Bad sewing always made me fidgety.

MRS. PETERS [*nervously*]:   I don't think we ought to touch things.

MRS. HALE: I'll just finish up this end. [*Suddenly stopping and leaning forward.*] Mrs. Peters?

MRS. PETERS: Yes, Mrs. Hale?

MRS. HALE: What do you suppose she was so nervous about?

MRS. PETERS: Oh—I don't know. I don't know as she was nervous. I sometimes sew awful queer when I'm just tired. [*Mrs. Hale starts to say something, looks at Mrs. Peters, then goes on sewing.*] Well, I must get these things wrapped up. They may be through sooner than we think. [*Putting apron and other things together.*] I wonder where I can find a piece of paper, and string.

MRS. HALE: In that cupboard, maybe.

MRS. PETERS [*looking in cupboard*]:   Why, here's a birdcage. [*Holds it up.*] Did she have a bird, Mrs. Hale?

MRS. HALE: Why, I don't know whether she did or not—I've not been here for so long. There was a man around last year selling canaries cheap, but I don't know as she took one; maybe she did. She used to sing real pretty herself.

MRS. PETERS [*glancing around*]:   Seems funny to think of a bird here. But she must have had one, or why should she have a cage? I wonder what happened to it?

MRS. HALE: I s'pose maybe the cat got it.

MRS. PETERS: No, she didn't have a cat. She's got that feeling some people have about cats—being afraid of them. My cat got in her room, and she was real upset and asked me to take it out.

MRS. HALE: My sister Bessie was like that. Queer, ain't it?

MRS. PETERS [*examining the cage*]:   Why, look at this door. It's broke. One hinge is pulled apart.

MRS. HALE [*looking, too*]:   Looks as if someone must have been rough with it.

MRS. PETERS: Why, yes. [*She brings the cage forward and puts it on the table.*]

MRS. HALE: I wish if they're going to find any evidence they'd be about it. I don't like this place.

MRS. PETERS: But I'm awful glad you came with me, Mrs. Hale. It would be lonesome for me sitting here alone.

MRS. HALE: It would, wouldn't it? [*Dropping her sewing.*] But I tell you what I do wish, Mrs. Peters. I wish I had come over sometimes when *she* was here. I—[*Looking around the room.*]—wish I had.

MRS. PETERS: But of course you were awful busy, Mrs. Hale—your house and your children.

MRS. HALE: I could've come. I stayed away because it weren't cheer-ful—and that's why I ought to have come. I—I've never liked this place. Maybe because it's down in a hollow, and you don't see the road. I dunno what it is, but it's a lonesome place and always was. I wish I had come over to see Minnie Foster sometimes. I can see now—[*Shakes her head.*]

MRS. PETERS: Well, you mustn't reproach yourself, Mrs. Hale. Some-how we just don't see how it is with other folks until—something comes up.

MRS. HALE: Not having children makes less work—but it makes a quiet house, and Wright out to work all day, and no company when he did come in. Did you know John Wright, Mrs. Peters?

MRS. PETERS: Not to know him; I've seen him in town. They say he was a good man.

MRS. HALE: Yes—good; he didn't drink, and kept his word as well as most, I guess, and paid his debts. But he was a hard man, Mrs. Peters. Just to pass the time of day with him. [*Shivers.*] Like a raw wind that gets to the bone. [*Pauses, her eye falling on the cage.*] I should think she would 'a wanted a bird. But what do you suppose went with it?

MRS. PETERS: I don't know, unless it got sick and died. [*She reaches over and swings the broken door, swings it again; both women watch it.*]

MRS. HALE: You weren't raised round here, were you? [*Mrs. Peters shakes her head.*] You didn't know—her?

MRS. PETERS: Not till they brought her yesterday.

MRS. HALE: She—come to think of it, she was kind of like a bird her-self—real sweet and pretty, but kind of timid and—fluttery. How—she—did—change. [*Silence; then as if struck by a happy thought and relieved to get back to everyday things.*] Tell you what,

Mrs. Peters, why don't you take the quilt in with you? It might take up her mind.

MRS. PETERS: Why, I think that's a real nice idea, Mrs. Hale. There couldn't possibly be any objection to it, could there? Now, just what would I take? I wonder if her patches are in here—and her things. [*They look in the sewing basket.*]

MRS. HALE: Here's some red. I expect this has got sewing things in it [*Brings out a fancy box.*] What a pretty box. Looks like something somebody would give you. Maybe her scissors are in here. [*Opens box. Suddenly puts her hand to her nose.*] Why—[*Mrs. Peters bends nearer, then turns her face away.*] There's something wrapped up in this piece of silk.

MRS. PETERS: Why, this isn't her scissors.

MRS. HALE [*lifting the silk*]: Oh, Mrs. Peters—it's—[*Mrs. Peters bends closer.*]

MRS. PETERS: It's the bird.

MRS. HALE [*jumping up*]: But, Mrs. Peters—look at it. Its neck! Look at its neck! It's all—other side *to*.

MRS. PETERS: Somebody—wrung—its neck.

[*Their eyes meet. A look of growing comprehension of horror. Steps are heard outside. Mrs. Hale slips box under quilt pieces, and sinks into her chair. Enter Sheriff and County Attorney. Mrs. Peters rises.*]

COUNTY ATTORNEY [*as one turning from serious things to little pleasantries*]: Well, ladies, have you decided whether she was going to quilt it or knot it?

MRS. PETERS: We think she was going to—knot it.

COUNTY ATTORNEY: Well, that's interesting, I'm sure. [*Seeing the birdcage.*] Has the bird flown?

MRS. HALE [*putting more quilt pieces over the box*]: We think the—cat got it.

COUNTY ATTORNEY [*preoccupied*]: Is there a cat?

[*Mrs. Hale glances in a quick covert way at Mrs. Peters.*]

MRS. PETERS: Well, not now. They're superstitious, you know. They leave.

COUNTY ATTORNEY [*to Sheriff Peters, continuing an interrupted conversation*]: No sign at all of anyone having come from the outside.

Their own rope. Now let's go up again and go over it piece by piece. [*They start upstairs.*] It would have to have been someone who knew just the—

[*Mrs. Peters sits down. The two women sit there not looking at one another, but as if peering into something and at the same time holding back. When they talk now, it is the manner of feeling their way over strange ground, as if afraid of what they are saying, but as if they cannot help saying it.*]

MRS. HALE: She liked the bird. She was going to bury it in that pretty box.

MRS. PETERS [*in a whisper*]: When I was a girl—my kitten—there was a boy took a hatchet, and before my eyes—and before I could get there—[*Covers her face an instant.*] If they hadn't held me back, I would have—[*Catches herself, looks upstairs where steps are heard, falters weakly.*]—hurt him.

MRS. HALE [*with a slow look around her*]: I wonder how it would seem never to have had any children around. [*Pause.*] No, Wright wouldn't like the bird—a thing that sang. She used to sing. He killed that, too.

MRS. PETERS [*moving uneasily*]: We don't know who killed the bird.

MRS. HALE: I knew John Wright.

MRS. PETERS: It was an awful thing was done in this house that night, Mrs. Hale. Killing a man while he slept, slipping a rope around his neck that choked the life out of him.

MRS. HALE: His neck. Choked the life out of him.

[*Her hand goes out and rests on the birdcage.*]

MRS. PETERS [*with a rising voice*]: We don't know who killed him. We don't *know.*

MRS. HALE [*her own feeling not interrupted*]: If there'd been years and years of nothing, then a bird to sing to you, it would be awful—still, after the bird was still.

MRS. PETERS [*something within her speaking*]: I know what stillness is. When we homesteaded in Dakota, and my first baby died—after he was two years old, and me with no other then—

MRS. HALE [*moving*]: How soon do you suppose they'll be through, looking for evidence?

MRS. PETERS: I know what stillness is. [*Pulling herself back.*] The law has got to punish crime, Mrs. Hale.

MRS. HALE [*not as if answering that*]:   I wish you'd seen Minnie Foster when she wore a white dress with blue ribbons and stood up there in the choir and sang. [*A look around the room.*] Oh, I wish I'd come over here once in a while! That was a crime! That was a crime! Who's going to punish that?

MRS. PETERS [*looking upstairs*]:   We mustn't—take on.

MRS. HALE: I might have known she needed help! I know how things can be—for women. I tell you, it's queer, Mrs. Peters. We live close together and we live far apart. We all go through the same things—it's all just a different kind of the same thing. [*Brushes her eyes, noticing the bottle of fruit, reaches out for it.*] If I was you, I wouldn't tell her her fruit was gone. Tell her it *ain't*. Tell her it's all right. Take this in to prove it to her. She—she may never know whether it was broke or not.

MRS. PETERS [*takes the bottle, looks about for something to wrap it in; takes petticoat from the clothes brought from the other room, very nervously begins winding this around the bottle. In a false voice*]:   My, it's a good thing the men couldn't hear us. Wouldn't they just laugh! Getting all stirred up over a little thing like a—dead canary. As if that could have anything to do with—with—wouldn't they *laugh!*

[*The men are heard coming downstairs.*]

MRS. HALE [*under her breath*]:   Maybe they would—maybe they wouldn't.

COUNTY ATTORNEY: No, Peters, it's all perfectly clear except a reason for doing it. But you know juries when it comes to women. If there was some definite thing. Something to show—something to make a story about—a thing that would connect up with this strange way of doing it.

[*The women's eyes meet for an instant. Enter Hale from outer door.*]

HALE: Well, I've got the team around. Pretty cold out there.

COUNTY ATTORNEY: I'm going to stay here awhile by myself. [*To the Sheriff.*] You can send Frank out for me, can't you? I want to go over everything. I'm not satisfied that we can't do better.

SHERIFF: Do you want to see what Mrs. Peters is going to take in?

[*The Lawyer goes to the table, picks up the apron, laughs.*]

COUNTY ATTORNEY: Oh I guess they're not very dangerous things the ladies have picked up. [*Moves a few things about, disturbing the quilt pieces which cover the box. Steps back.*] No, Mrs. Peters doesn't need supervising. For that matter, a sheriff's wife is married to the law. Ever think of it that way, Mrs. Peters?

MRS. PETERS: Not—just that way.

SHERIFF [*chuckling*]:   Married to the law. [*Moves toward the other room.*] I just want you to come in here a minute, George. We ought to take a look at these windows.

COUNTY ATTORNEY [*scoffingly*]:   Oh, windows!

SHERIFF: We'll be right out, Mr. Hale.

[*Hale goes outside. The Sheriff follows the County Attorney into the other room. Then Mrs. Hale rises, hands tight together, look-ing intensely at Mrs. Peters, whose eyes take a slow turn, finally meeting, Mrs. Hale's. A moment Mrs. Hale holds her, then her own eyes point the way to where the box is concealed. Suddenly Mrs. Peters throws back quilt pieces and tries to put the box in the bag she is wearing. It is too big. She opens box, starts to take the bird out, cannot touch it, goes to pieces, stands there helpless. Sound of a knob turning in the other room. Mrs. Hale snatches the box and puts it in the pocket of her big coat. Enter County At-torney and Sheriff.*]

COUNTY ATTORNEY [*facetiously*]:   Well, Henry, at least we found out that she was not going to quilt it. She was going to—what is it you call it, ladies?

MRS. HALE [*her hand against her pocket*]:   We call it—knot it, Mr. Henderson.

CURTAIN

—1917

SUSAN GLASPELL

Tennessee Williams was the first important American playwright to emerge in the post–World War II period. Born Thomas Lanier Williams and raised in St. Louis, he took his professional name from his mother's southern forebears. Williams studied at the University of Missouri and Washington University, ultimately completing a degree in drama at the University of Iowa. After staging some of his early one-act plays with the Group Theater (later known as the Actors Studio), Williams first came to larger public attention with The Glass Menagerie, which won a Drama Critics Circle award in 1945. The Glass Menagerie is clearly autobiographical, drawing on Williams's memories of life with his faded southern belle mother and his tragically disturbed sister, Rose, who ultimately had to be institutionalized. Subsequent plays draw on Williams's life and his southern roots. In 1947, A Streetcar Named Desire received the Pulitzer Prize, the first of two Williams would win in a forty-year career. A Streetcar Named Desire, which starred the young Marlon Brando on stage and film, is, in contrast to The Glass Menagerie, a brutally naturalistic tragedy in which no romantic illusions are allowed to survive. Both Jessica Tandy, who originated the stage role, and Vivien Leigh, who starred in the film, were acclaimed for their portrayals of Blanche DuBois. Williams's plays are constantly revived in little theaters and on Broadway. In the first decade of the twenty-first century, both A Streetcar Named Desire, with Alec Baldwin, and Cat on a Hot Tin Roof, starring Kathleen Turner, completed successful New York engagements, and 2005 saw yet another Broadway revival of The Glass Menagerie, starring Jessica Lange. Some of the film adaptations of Williams's plays, several of which have screenplays written by the author, remain classics, especially Elia Kazan's version of A Streetcar Named Desire. Williams published his autobiography in 1975. A fascinating collection of his correspondence, which gives insight into both his concerns as a writer and his intensely troubled personal life, appeared in 2000.

The Glass Menagerie

> nobody, not even the rain, has such small hands.
> e. e. cummings

Characters

Amanda Wingfield, the mother.—A little woman of great but confused vitality clinging frantically to another time and place. Her characterization must be carefully created, not copied from type. She is not paranoiac, but her life is paranoia. There is much to admire in Amanda, and as much to love and pity as there is to laugh at. Certainly she has endurance and a kind of heroism, and though her foolishness makes her unwittingly cruel at times, there is tenderness in her slight person.

Laura Wingfield, her daughter.—Amanda, having failed to establish contact with reality, continues to live vitally in her illusions, but Laura's situation is even graver. A childhood illness has left her crippled, one leg slightly shorter than the other, and held in a brace. This defect need not be more than suggested on the stage. Stemming from this, Laura's separation increases till she is like a piece of her own glass collection, too exquisitely fragile to move from the shelf.

Tom Wingfield, her son.—And the narrator of the play. A poet with a job in a warehouse. His nature is not remorseless, but to escape from a trap he has to act without pity.

Jim O'Connor, the gentleman caller.—A nice, ordinary young man.

Scene: An alley in St. Louis.

Part 1. Preparation for a Gentleman Caller.

Part 2. The Gentleman Calls.

Part 3. Now and the Past.

Scene I

The Wingfield apartment is in the rear of the building, one of those vast hive-like conglomerations of cellular living-units that flower as warty growths in overcrowded urban centers of lower middle-class population and are symptomatic of the impulse of this largest and fundamentally enslaved section of American society to avoid fluidity and differentiation and to exist and function as one interfused mass of automatism.

The apartment faces an alley and is entered by a fire-escape, a structure whose name is a touch of accidental poetic truth, for all of these huge buildings are always burning with the slow and implacable fires of human desperation. The fire escape is included in the set—that is, the landing of it and steps descending from it.

The scene is memory and is therefore non-realistic. Memory takes a lot of poetic license. It omits some details; others are exaggerated, according to the *emotional value of the articles it touches, for memory is seated predominantly in the heart. The interior is therefore rather dim and poetic.*

At the rise of the curtain, the audience is faced with the dark, grim rear wall of the Wingfield tenement. This building, which runs parallel to the footlights, is flanked on both sides by dark, narrow alleys which run into murky canyons of tangled clotheslines, garbage cans and the sinister latticework of neighboring fire-escapes. It is up and down these side alleys that exterior entrances and exits are made, during the play. At the end of Tom's opening commentary, the dark tenement wall slowly reveals (by means of a transparency) the interior of the ground floor Wingfield apartment.

Downstage is the living room, which also serves as a sleeping room for Laura, the sofa unfolding to make her bed. Upstage, center, and divided by a wide arch or second proscenium with transparent faded portieres (or second curtain), is the dining room. In an old-fashioned what-not in the living room are seen scores of transparent glass animals. A blown-up photograph of the father hangs on the wall of the living room, facing the audience, to the left of the archway. It is the face of a very handsome young man in a doughboy's First World War cap. He is gallantly smiling, ineluctably smiling, as if to say, "I will be smiling forever."

The audience hears and sees the opening scene in the dining room through both the transparent wall of the building and the transparent gauze portieres of the diningroom arch. It is during this revealing scene that the fourth wall slowly ascends, out of sight.

This transparent exterior wall is not brought down again until the very end of the play, during Tom's final speech.

The narrator is an undisguised convention of the play. He takes whatever license with dramatic convention as is convenient to his purposes.

Tom enters dressed as a merchant sailor from alley, stage left, and strolls across the front of the stage to the fire-escape. There he stops and lights a cigarette. He addresses the audience.

TOM: Yes, I have tricks in my pocket, I have things up my sleeve. But I am the opposite of a stage magician. He gives you the illusion that has the appearance of truth. I give you truth in the pleasant disguise of illusion. To begin with, I turn back time. I reverse it to that quaint period, the thirties, when the huge middle class of America was matriculating in a school for the blind. Their eyes had failed them, or they had failed their eyes, and so they were having their fingers pressed forcibly down on the fiery Braille alphabet of a dissolving economy. In Spain there was revolution. Here there was only shouting and confusion. In Spain there was Guernica. Here there were disturbances of labor, sometimes pretty violent, in otherwise peaceful cities such as Chicago, Cleveland, Saint Louis . . . . This is the social background of the play.

[Music.]

The play is memory. Being a memory play, it is dimly lighted, it is sentimental, it is not realistic. In memory everything seems to happen to music. That explains the fiddle in the wings. I am the narrator of the play, and also a character in it. The other characters are my mother, Amanda, my sister, Laura, and a gentleman caller who appears in the final scenes. He is the most realistic character in the play, being an emissary from a world of reality that we were somehow set apart from. But since I have a poet's weakness for symbols, I am using this character also as a symbol; he is the long delayed but always expected something that we live for. There is a fifth character in the play who doesn't appear except in this larger-than-life photograph over the mantel. This is our father who left us a long time ago. He was a telephone man who fell in love with long distances; he gave up his job with the telephone company and skipped the light fantastic out of town . . . . The last we heard of him was a picture post-card from Mazatlan, on the Pacific coast of Mexico, containing a message of two words—"Hello—Good-bye!" and no address. I think the rest of the play will explain itself . . . .

Amanda's voice becomes audible through the portieres.

[Legend on Screen: "Où Sont Les Neiges?"]°

He divides the portieres and enters the upstage area. Amanda and Laura are seated at a drop-leaf table. Eating is indicated by gestures without food or utensils. Amanda faces the audience. Tom and Laura are seated in profile. The interior has lit up softly and through the scrim we see Amanda and Laura seated at the table in the upstage area.

Où Sont Les Neiges refrain from a poem by François Villion [1431–1463?]: "Where are the snows of yesteryear?"

AMANDA [*calling*]: Tom?

TOM: Yes, Mother.

AMANDA: We can't say grace until you come to the table!

TOM: Coming, Mother. [*He bows slightly and withdraws, reappearing a few moments later in his place at the table.*]

AMANDA [*to her son*]: Honey, don't *push* with your *fingers*. If you have to push with something, the thing to push with is a crust of bread. And chew—chew! Animals have sections in their stomachs which enable them to digest food without mastication, but human beings are supposed to chew their food before they swallow it down. Eat food leisurely, son, and really enjoy it. A well-cooked meal has lots of delicate flavors that have to be held in the mouth for appreciation. So chew your food and give your salivary glands a chance to function!

[*Tom deliberately lays his imaginary fork down and pushes his chair back from the table.*]

TOM: I haven't enjoyed one bite of this dinner because of your constant directions on how to eat it. It's you that makes me rush through meals with your hawk-like attention to every bite I take. Sickening—spoils my appetite—all this discussion of animals' secretion—salivary glands—mastication!

AMANDA [*lightly*]: Temperament like a Metropolitan star! [*He rises and crosses downstage.*] You're not excused from the table.

TOM: I am getting a cigarette.

AMANDA: You smoke too much. [*Laura rises.*]

LAURA: I'll bring in the blanc mange.

[*He remains standing with cigarette by the portieres during the following.*]

AMANDA [*rising*]: No, sister, no, sister—you be the lady this time and I'll be the darky.

LAURA: I'm already up.

AMANDA: Resume your seat, little sister—I want you to stay fresh and pretty—for gentlemen callers!

LAURA: I'm not expecting any gentlemen callers.

AMANDA [*crossing out to kitchenette. Airily.*]: Sometimes they come when they are least expected! Why, I remember one Sunday afternoon in the Blue Mountain—[*Enters kitchenette.*]

TOM: I know what's coming!

LAURA: Yes. But let her tell it.

TOM: Again?

LAURA: She loves to tell it.

[*Amanda returns with bowl of dessert.*]

AMANDA: One Sunday afternoon in Blue Mountain—your mother received—*seventeen!*—gentlemen callers! Why sometimes there weren't chairs enough to accommodate them all. We had to send the nigger over to bring in folding chairs from the parish house.

TOM [*remaining at portieres*]: How did you entertain those gentlemen callers?

AMANDA: I understood the art of conversation!

TOM: I bet you could talk.

AMANDA: Girls in those days *knew* how to talk, I can tell you.

TOM: Yes?

[*Image: Amanda as a Girl on a Porch Greeting Callers.*]

AMANDA: They knew how to entertain their gentlemen callers. It wasn't enough for a girl to be possessed of a pretty face and a graceful figure—although I wasn't slighted in either respect. She also needed to have a nimble wit and a tongue to meet all occasions.

TOM: What did you talk about?

AMANDA: Things of importance going on in the world! Never anything coarse or common or vulgar. [*She addresses Tom as though he were seated in the vacant chair at the table though he remains by portieres. He plays this scene as though he held the book.*] My callers were gentlemen—all! Among my callers were some of the most prominent young planters of the Mississippi Delta—planters and sons of planters!

[*Tom motions for music and a spot of light on Amanda. Her eyes lift, her face glows, her voice becomes rich and elegiac.*]

[Screen Legend: "Où Sont Les Neiges?"]

There was young Champ Laughlin who later became vice-president of the Delta Planters Bank. Hadley Stevenson who was drowned in Moon Lake and left his widow one hundred and fifty thousand in Government bonds. There were the Cutrere brothers, Wesley and Bates. Bates was one of my bright particular beaux!

He got in a quarrel with that wild Wainright boy. They shot it out on the floor of Moon Lake Casino. Bates was shot through the stomach. Died in the ambulance on his way to Memphis. His widow was also well provided for, came into eight or ten thousand acres, that's all. She married him on the rebound—never loved her—carried my picture on him the night he died! And there was that boy that every girl in the Delta had set her cap for! That beautiful, brilliant young Fitzhugh boy from Green County!

TOM: What did he leave his widow?

AMANDA: He never married! Gracious, you talk as though all of my old admirers had turned up their toes to the daisies!

TOM: Isn't this the first you mentioned that still survives?

AMANDA: That Fitzhugh boy went North and made a fortune—came to be known as the Wolf of Wall Street! He had the Midas touch, whatever he touched turned to gold! And I could have been Mrs. Duncan J. Fitzhugh, mind you! But—I picked your *father!*

LAURA [*rising*]: Mother, let me clear the table.

AMANDA: No dear, you go in front and study your typewriter chart. Or practice your shorthand a little. Stay fresh and pretty!—It's almost time for our gentlemen callers to start arriving. [*She flounces girlishly toward the kitchenette.*] How many do you suppose we're going to entertain this afternoon?

[*Tom throws down the paper and jumps up with a groan.*]

LAURA [*alone in the dining room*]: I don't believe we're going to receive any, Mother.

AMANDA [*reappearing, airily*]: What? No one—not one? You must be joking! [*Laura nervously echoes her laugh. She slips in a fugitive manner through the half-open portieres and draws them gently behind her. A shaft of very clear light is thrown on her face against the faded tapestry of the curtain.*] [*Music: "The Glass Menagerie" Under Faintly.*] [*Lightly*] Not one gentleman caller? It can't be true! There must be a flood, there must have been a tornado!

LAURA: It isn't a flood, it's not a tornado, Mother. I'm just not popular like you were in Blue Mountain . . . . [*Tom utters another groan. Laura glances at him with a faint, apologetic smile. Her voice catching a little*] Mother's afraid I'm going to be an old maid.

[The Scene Dims Out with "Glass Menagerie" Music.]

On the dark stage the screen is lighted with the image of blue roses. Gradually Laura's figure becomes apparent and the screen goes out. The music subsides. Laura is seated in the delicate ivory chair at the small clawfoot table. She wears a dress of soft violet material for a kimono—her hair tied back from her forehead with a ribbon. She is washing and polishing her collection of glass.

Amanda appears on the fire-escape steps. At the sound of her ascent, Laura catches her breath, thrusts the bowl of ornaments away and seats herself stiffly before the diagram of the typewriter keyboard as though it held her spellbound. Something has happened to Amanda. It is written in her face as she climbs to the landing: a look that is grim and hopeless and a little absurd.

She has one of those cheap or imitation velvety-looking cloth coats with imitation fur collar. Her hat is five or six years old, one of those dreadful cloche hats that were worn in the late twenties, and she is clasping an enormous black patent-leather pocketbook with nickel clasp and initials. This is her full-dress outfit, the one she usually wears to the D.A.R.

Before entering she looks through the door. She purses her lips, opens her eyes wide, rolls them upward and shakes her head. Then she slowly lets herself in the door. Seeing her mother's expression Laura touches her lips with a nervous gesture.

LAURA: Hello, Mother, I was—[*She makes a nervous gesture toward the chart on the wall. Amanda leans against the shut door and stares at Laura with a martyred look.*]

AMANDA: Deception? Deception? [*She slowly removes her hat and gloves, continuing the swift suffering stare. She lets the hat and gloves fall on the floor—a bit of acting.*]

LAURA [*shakily*]:   How was the D.A.R. meeting? [*Amanda slowly opens her purse and removes a dainty white handkerchief which she shakes out delicately and delicately touches to her lips and nostrils.*] Didn't you go to the D.A.R. meeting, Mother?

AMANDA [*faintly, almost inaudibly*]:   —No.—No. [*Then more forcibly*] I did not have the strength—to go to the D.A.R. In fact, I did not have the courage. I waited to find a hole in the ground and hide myself in it forever! [*She crosses slowly to the wall and removes the diagram of the typewriter keyboard. She holds it in front of her for a second, staring at it sweetly and sorrowfully—then bites her lips and tears it in two pieces.*]

LAURA [*faintly*]: Why did you do that, Mother? [*Amanda repeats the same procedure with the chart of the Gregg Alphabet.*] Why are you—

AMANDA: Why? Why? How old are you, Laura?

LAURA: Mother, you know my age.

AMANDA: I thought that you were an adult; it seems that I was mistaken. [*She crosses slowly to the sofa and sinks down and stares at Laura.*]

LAURA: Please don't stare at me, Mother.

[*Amanda closes her eyes and lowers her head. Count ten.*]

AMANDA: What are we going to do, what is going to become of us, what is the future?

[*Count ten.*]

LAURA: Has something happened, Mother? [*Amanda draws a long breath and takes out the handkerchief again. Dabbing process.*] Mother, has—something happened?

AMANDA: I'll be right in a minute. I'm just bewildered—[*count five*] — by life . . . .

LAURA: Mother, I wish you would tell me what's happened.

AMANDA: As you know, I was supposed to be inducted into my office at the D.A.R. this afternoon. [*Image: A Swarm of Typewriters.*] But I stopped off at Rubicam's Business College to speak to your teachers about your having a cold and ask them what progress they thought you were making down there.

LAURA: Oh . . . .

AMANDA: I went to the typing instructor and introduced myself as your mother. She didn't know who you were. Wingfield, she said. We don't have any such student enrolled at the school! I assured her she did, that you had been going to classes since early in January. "I wonder," she said, "if you could be talking about that terribly shy little girl who dropped out of school after only a few days' attendance?" "No," I said, "Laura, my daughter, has been going to school every day for the past six weeks!" "Excuse me," she said. She took the attendance book out and there was your name, unmistakably printed, and all the dates you were absent until they decided that you had dropped out of school. I still said, "No, there must have been some mistake! There must have been some mix-up in the records!" And she said, "No—I remember her perfectly now. Her hand shook so that she couldn't hit the right keys! The first time we gave a speed-test, she broke down completely—was sick at the stomach and almost had to be carried into the washroom! After that morning she never showed up any more. We phoned the house but never got any answer"—while I was working at Famous and Barr, I suppose demonstrating those—Oh! I felt so weak I could barely keep on my feet. I had to sit down while they got me a glass of water! Fifty dollars' tuition, all of our plans—my hopes and ambitions for you—just gone up the spout, just gone up the spout like that. [*Laura draws a long breath and gets awkwardly to her feet. She crosses to the victrola and winds it up.*] What are you doing?

LAURA: Oh! [*She releases the handle and returns to her seat.*]

AMANDA: Laura, where have you been going when you've gone out pretending that you were going to business college?

LAURA: I've just been going out walking.

AMANDA: That's not true.

LAURA: It is. I just went walking.

AMANDA: Walking? Walking? In winter? Deliberately courting pneumonia in that light coat? Where did you walk to, Laura?

LAURA: It was the lesser of two evils, Mother. [*Image: Winter Scene in Park.*] I couldn't go back up. I—threw up—on the floor!

AMANDA: From half past seven till after five thirty every day you mean to tell me you walked around in the park, because you wanted to make me think that you were still going to Rubicam's Business College?

LAURA: It wasn't as bad as it sounds. I went inside places to get warmed up.

AMANDA: Inside where?

LAURA: I went in the art museum and the birdhouses at the Zoo. I visited the penguins every day! Sometimes I did without lunch and went to the movies. Lately I've been spending most of my afternoons in the Jewel-box, that big glass house where they raise the tropical flowers.

AMANDA: You did all this to deceive me, just for the deception? [*Laura looks down.*] Why?

LAURA: Mother, when you're disappointed, you get that awful suffering look on your face. Like the picture of Jesus' mother in the museum!

AMANDA: Hush!

LAURA: I couldn't face it.

[*Pause: A whisper of strings.*]

[Legend: "The Crust of Humility."]

AMANDA [*hopelessly fingering the huge pocketbook*]: So what are we going to do the rest of our lives? Stay home and watch the parades go by? Amuse ourselves with the glass menagerie, darling? Eternally play those worn-out phonograph records your father left as a painful reminder of him? We won't have a business career—we've given that up because it gave us nervous indigestion! [*Laughs wearily.*] What is there left but dependency all our lives? I know so well what becomes of unmarried women who aren't prepared to occupy a position. I've seen such pitiful cases in the South—barely tolerated spinsters living upon the grudging patronage of sister's husband or brother's wife!—stuck away in some little mousetrap of a room—encouraged by one inlaw to visit another—little bird-like women without any nest—eating the crust of humility all their life! Is that the future that we've mapped out for ourselves? I swear it's the only alternative I can think of! It isn't a very pleasant alternative, is it? Of course—some girls *do* marry. [*Laura twists her hands nervously.*] Haven't you ever liked some boy?

LAURA: Yes, I liked one once. [*Rises.*] I came across his picture a while ago.

AMANDA [*with some interest*]: He gave you his picture?

LAURA: No, it's in the year-book.

AMANDA [*disappointed*]: Oh—a high-school boy.

[Screen Image: Jim as a High-School Hero Bearing a Silver Cup.]

LAURA: Yes. His name was Jim. [*Laura lifts the heavy annual from the clawfoot table.*] Here he is in *The Pirates of Penzance*.

AMANDA [*absently*]: The what?

LAURA: The operetta the senior class put on. He had a wonderful voice and we sat across the aisle from each other Mondays, Wednesdays, and Fridays in the Aud. Here he is with the silver cup for debating! See his grin?

AMANDA [*absently*]: He must have had a jolly disposition.

LAURA: He used to call me—Blue Roses.

[Image: Blue Roses.]

AMANDA: Why did he call you such a name as that?

LAURA: When I had that attack of pleurosis—he asked me what was the matter when I came back. I said pleurosis—he thought I said Blue Roses! So that's what he always called me after that. Whenever he saw me, he'd holler, "Hello, Blue Roses!" I didn't care for the girl that he went out with. Emily Meisenbach. Emily was the best-dressed girl at Soldan. She never struck me, though, as being sincere . . . . It says in the Personal Section—they're engaged. That's—six years ago! They must be married by now.

AMANDA: Girls that aren't cut out for business careers usually wind up married to some nice man. [*Gets up with a spark of revival.*] Sister, that's what you'll do!

[*Laura utters a startled, doubtful laugh. She reaches quickly for a piece of glass.*]

LAURA: But, Mother—

AMANDA: Yes? [*Crossing to photograph.*]

LAURA [*in a tone of frightened apology*]:   I'm—crippled!

[Image: Screen.]

AMANDA: Nonsense! Laura, I've told you never, never to use that word. Why, you're not crippled, you just have a little defect— hardly noticeable, even! When people have some slight disadvantage like that, they cultivate other things to make up for it—develop charm—and vivacity—and—*charm!* That's all you have to do! [*She turns again to the photograph.*] One thing your father had *plenty of*—was *charm!*

[*Tom motions to the fiddle in the wings.*]

[The Scene Fades Out with Music.]

Scene III
(Legend on the Screen: "After the Fiasco—")

[*Tom speaks from the fire-escape landing.*]

TOM: After the fiasco at Rubicam's Business College, the idea of getting a gentleman caller for Laura began to play a more important part in Mother's calculations. It became an obsession.

Like some archetype of the universal unconscious, the image of the gentleman caller haunted our small apartment . . . . [*Image: Young Man at Door with Flowers.*] An evening at home rarely passed without some allusion to this image, this specter, this hope . . . . Even when he wasn't mentioned, his presence hung in Mother's preoccupied look and in my sister's frightened, apologetic manner—hung like a sentence passed upon the Wingfields! Mother was a woman of action as well as words. She began to take logical steps in the planned direction. Late that winter and in the early spring—realizing that extra money would be needed to properly feather the nest and plume the bird—she conducted a vigorous campaign on the telephone, roping in subscribers to one of those magazines for matrons called *The Home-maker's Companion*, the type of journal that features the serialized sublimation of ladies of letters who think in terms of delicate cup-like breasts, slim, tapering waists, rich, creamy thighs, eyes like wood-smoke in autumn, fingers that soothe and caress like strains of music, bodies as powerful as Etruscan sculpture.

[Screen Image: Glamour Magazine Cover.]

[*Amanda enters with phone on long extension cord. She is spotted in the dim stage.*]

AMANDA: Ida Scott? This is Amanda Wingfield! We *missed* you at the D.A.R. last Monday! I said to myself: She's probably suffering with that sinus condition! How is that sinus condition? Horrors! Heaven have mercy!—You're a Christian martyr, yes, that's what you are, a Christian martyr! Well, I just now happened to notice that your subscription to the *Companion's* about to expire! Yes, it expires with the next issue, honey!—just when that wonderful new serial by Bessie Mae Hopper is getting off to such an exciting start. Oh, honey, it's something that you can't miss! You remember how *Gone With the Wind* took everybody by storm? You simply couldn't go out if you hadn't read it. All everybody *talked* was Scarlett O'Hara. Well, this is a book that critics already compare to *Gone With the Wind*. It's the *Gone With the Wind* of the post-World War generation!—What?—Burning? Oh, honey, don't let them burn, go take a look in the oven and I'll hold the wire! Heavens—I think she's hung up!

[Dim Out.]

[Legend on Screen: "You Think I'm in Love with Continental Shoemakers?"]

[*Before the stage is lighted, the violent voices of Tom and Amanda are heard. They are quarreling behind the portieres. In front of them stands Laura with clenched hands and panicky expression. A clear pool of light on her figure throughout this scene.*]

TOM: What in Christ's name am I—

AMANDA [*shrilly*]:   Don't you use that—

TOM: Supposed to do!

AMANDA: Expression! Not in my—

TOM: Ohhh!

AMANDA: Presence! Have you gone out of your senses?

TOM: I have, that's true, *driven* out!

AMANDA: What is the matter with you, you—big—big—IDIOT!

TOM: Look—I've got *no thing*, no single thing—

AMANDA: Lower your voice?

TOM: In my life here that I can call my OWN! Everything is—

AMANDA: Stop that shouting!

TOM: Yesterday you confiscated my books! You had the nerve to—

AMANDA: I took that horrible novel back to the library—yes! That hideous book by that insane Mr. Lawrence. [*Tom laughs wildly.*] I cannot control the output of diseased minds or people who cater to them—[*Tom laughs still more wildly.*] BUT I WON'T ALLOW SUCH FILTH BROUGHT INTO MY HOUSE! No, no, no, no, no!

TOM: House, house! Who pays rent on it, who makes a slave of himself to—

AMANDA [*fairly screeching*]:   Don't you DARE to—

TOM: No, no, I musn't say things! *I've* got to just—

AMANDA: Let me tell you—

TOM: I don't want to hear any more! [*He tears the portieres open. The upstage area is lit with a turgid smoky red glow.*]

Amanda's hair is in metal curlers and she wears a very old bathrobe, much too large for her slight figure, a relic of the faithless Mr. Wingfield. An upright typewriter and a mild disarray of manuscripts are on the drop-leaf table. The quarrel was probably precipitated by Amanda's interruption of his creative labor. A

chair lying overthrown on the floor. Their gesticulating shadows
are cast on the ceiling by the fiery glow.

AMANDA: You *will* hear more, you—

TOM: No, I won't hear more, I'm going out!

AMANDA: You come right back in—

TOM: Out, out out! Because I'm—

AMANDA: Come back here, Tom Wingfield! I'm not through talking to you!

TOM: Oh, go—

LAURA [*desperately*]:   Tom!

AMANDA: You're going to listen, and no more insolence from you! I'm at the end of my patience! [*He comes back toward her.*]

TOM: What do you think I'm at? Aren't I supposed to have any patience to reach the end of, Mother? I know, I know. It seems unimportant to you, what I'm *doing*—what I *want* to do—having a little *difference* between them! You don't think that—

AMANDA: I think you've been doing things that you're ashamed of. That's why you act like this. I don't believe that you go every night to movies. Nobody goes to the movies night after night. Nobody in their right minds goes to movies as often as you pretend to. People don't go to the movies at nearly midnight, and movies don't let out at two A.M. Come in stumbling. Muttering to yourself like a maniac! You get three hours' sleep and then go to work. Oh, I can picture the way you're doing down there. Moping, doping, because you're in no condition.

TOM [*wildly*]:   No, I'm in no condition!

AMANDA: What right have you got to jeopardize your job? Jeopardize the security of us all? How do you think we'd manage if you were—

TOM: Listen! You think I'm crazy *about the warehouse?* [*He bends fiercely toward her slight figure.*] You think I'm in love with the Continental Shoemakers? You think I want to spend fifty-five *years* down there in that—*celotex interior!* with—*fluorescent—tubes!* Look! I'd rather somebody picked up a crowbar and battered out my brains than go back mornings! I *go!* Every time you come in yelling that God damn "*Rise and Shine!*" "*Rise and Shine!*" I say to myself "How *lucky dead* people are!" But I get up. I *go!* For sixty-five dollars a month I gave up all that I dream of doing and being *ever!* And you say self—*self's* all I ever think of. Why, listen, if self is what I thought of, Mother, I'd be where he is—GONE! [*Pointing to father's picture.*] As far as the system of transportation reaches! [*He starts past her. She grabs his arm.*] Don't grab at me, Mother!

AMANDA: Where are you going?

TOM: I'm going to the *movies!*

AMANDA: I don't believe that lie!

TOM [*crouching toward her, overtowering her tiny figure. She backs away, gasping*]: I'm going to opium dens! Yes, opium dens, dens of vice and criminals' hang-outs, Mother. I've joined the Hogan gang, I'm a hired assassin, I carry a tommy-gun in a violin case! I run a string of cat-houses in the Valley. They call me Killer, Killer Wingfield, I'm leading a double-life, a simple, honest warehouse worker by day, by night a dynamic *czar* of the *underworld, Mother.* I go to gambling casinos, I spin away fortunes on the roulette table! I wear a patch over one eye and a false mustache, sometimes I put on green whiskers. On those occasions they call me—*El Diablo!* Oh, I could tell you things to make you sleepless! My enemies plan to dynamite this place. They're going to blow us all sky-high some night! I'll be glad, very happy, and so will you! You'll go up, up on a broomstick, over Blue Mountain with seventeen gentlemen callers! You ugly—babbling old—*witch* . . . . [*He goes through a series of violent, clumsy movements, seizing his overcoat, lunging to the door, pulling it fiercely open. The women watch him, aghast. His arm catches in the sleeve of the coat as he struggles to pull it on. For a moment he is pinioned by the bulky garment. With an outraged groan he tears the coat off again, splitting the shoulders of it, and hurls it across the room. It strikes against the shelf of Laura's glass collection, there is a tinkle of shattering glass. Laura cries out as if wounded.*]

[Music Legend: "The Glass Menagerie."]

LAURA [*shrilly*]: My glass! —menagerie . . . . [*She covers her face and turns away.*]

[*But Amanda is still stunned and stupefied by the "ugly witch" so that she barely notices this occurrence. Now she recovers her speech.*]

AMANDA [*in an awful voice*]: I won't speak to you—until you apologize! [*She crosses through the portieres and draws them together behind her. Tom is left with Laura. Laura clings weakly to the mantel with* her face averted. Tom stares at her stupidly for a moment. Then he crosses to shelf. Drops awkwardly to his knees to collect the fallen glass, glancing at Laura as if he would speak but couldn't.]

["The Glass Menagerie" steals in as the Scene Dims Out.]

Scene IV

The interior is dark. Faint light in the alley. A deep-voiced bell in a church is tolling the hour by five as the scene commences.

Tom appears at the top of the alley. After each solemn boom of the bell in the tower, he shakes a little noise-maker or rattle as if to express the tiny spasm of man in contrast to the sustained power and dignity of the Almighty. This and the unsteadiness of his advance make it evident that he has been drinking.

As he climbs the few steps to the fire-escape landing light steals up inside. Laura appears in night-dress, observing Tom's empty bed in the front room.

Tom fishes in his pockets for the door-key, removing a motley assortment of articles in the search, including a perfect shower of movie-ticket stubs and an empty bottle. At last he finds the key, but just as he is about to insert it, it slips from his fingers. He strikes a match and crouches below the door.

TOM [bitterly]: One crack—and it falls through!

[Laura opens the door.]

LAURA: Tom! Tom, what are you doing?

TOM: Looking for a door-key.

LAURA: Where have you been all this time?

TOM: I have been to the movies.

LAURA: All this time at the movies?

TOM: There was a very long program. There was a Garbo picture and a Mickey Mouse and a travelogue and a newsreel and a preview of coming attractions. And there was an organ solo and a collection for the milk-fund—simultaneously—which ended up in a terrible fight between a fat lady and an usher!

LAURA [innocently]: Did you have to stay through everything?

TOM: Of course! And, oh, I forgot! There was a big stage show! The headliner on this stage show was Malvolio the Magician. He performed wonderful tricks, many of them, such as pouring water back and forth between pitchers. First it turned to wine and then it turned to beer and then it turned to whiskey. I know it was whiskey it finally turned into because he needed somebody to come up out of the audience to help him, and I came up—both shows! It was Kentucky Straight Bourbon. A very generous fellow, he gave souvenirs. [*He pulls from his back pocket a shimmering rainbow-colored scarf.*] He gave me this. This is his magic scarf. You can have it, Laura. You wave it over a canary cage and you get a bowl of gold-fish. You wave it over the goldfish bowl and they fly away canaries . . . . But the wonderfulest trick of all was the coffin trick. We nailed him into a coffin and he got out of the coffin without removing one nail. [*He has come inside.*] There is a trick that would come in handy for me—get me out of this 2 by 4 situation! [*Flops onto bed and starts removing shoes.*]

LAURA: Tom—Shhh!

TOM: What you shushing me for?

LAURA: You'll wake up Mother.

TOM: Goody, goody! Pay 'er back for those "Rise an' Shines." [*Lies down, groaning.*] You know it don't take much intelligence to get yourself into a nailed-up coffin, Laura. But who in hell ever got himself out of one without removing one nail?

[*As if in answer, the father's grinning photograph lights up.*]

[Scene Dims Out.]

Immediately following: The church bell is heard striking six. At the sixth stroke the alarm clock goes off in Amanda's room, and after a few moments we hear her calling: "Rise and Shine! Rise and Shine! Laura, go tell your brother to rise and shine!"

TOM [*sitting up slowly*]: I'll rise—but I won't shine.

[*The light increases.*]

AMANDA: Laura, tell your brother his coffee is ready.

[*Laura slips into the front room.*]

LAURA: Tom! it's nearly seven. Don't make Mother nervous. [*He stares at her stupidly. Beseechingly.*] Tom, speak to Mother this morning. Make up with her, apologize, speak to her!

TOM: She won't to me. It's her that started not speaking.

LAURA: If you just say you're sorry she'll start speaking.

TOM: Her not speaking—is that such a tragedy?

LAURA: Please—please!

AMANDA [calling from kitchenette]:   Laura, are you going to do what I asked you to do, or do I have to get dressed and go out myself?

LAURA: Going, going—soon as I get on my coat! [She pulls on a shapeless felt hat with nervous, jerky movement, pleadingly glancing at Tom. Rushes awkwardly for coat. The coat is one of Amanda's, inaccurately made-over, the sleeves too short for Laura.] Butter and what else?

AMANDA [entering upstage]:   Just butter. Tell them to charge it.

LAURA: Mother, they make such faces when I do that.

AMANDA: Sticks and stones may break my bones, but the expression of Mr. Garfinkel's face won't harm me! Tell your brother his coffee is getting cold.

LAURA [at door]:   Do what I asked you, will you, will you, Tom?

[He looks sullenly away.]

AMANDA: Laura, go now or just don't go at all!

LAURA [rushing out]:   Going—going! [A second later she cries out. Tom springs up and crosses to the door. Amanda rushes anxiously in. Tom opens the door.]

TOM: Laura?

LAURA: I'm all right. I slipped, but I'm all right.

AMANDA [peering anxiously after her]:   If anyone breaks a leg on those fire-escape steps, the landlord ought to be sued for every cent he possesses! [She shuts the door. Remembers she isn't speaking and returns to the other room.]

[As Tom enters listlessly for his coffee, she turns her back to him and stands rigidly facing the widow on the gloomy gray vault of the areaway. Its light on her face with its aged but childish features is cruelly sharp, satirical as a Daumier print.]

[Music Under: "Ave Maria."]

[Tom glances sheepishly but sullenly at her averted figure and slumps at the table. The coffee is scalding hot; he sips it and gasps and spits it back in the cup. At his gasp, Amanda catches her breath and half turns. Then catches herself and turns back to the window.

Tom blows on his coffee, glancing sidewise at his mother. She clears her throat. Tom clears his. He starts to rise. Sinks back down again, scratches his head, clears his throat again. Amanda coughs. Tom raises his cup in both hands to blow on it, his eyes *staring over the rim of it at his mother for several moments. Then he slowly sets the cup down and awkwardly and hesitantly rises from the chair.*]

TOM [*hoarsely*]: Mother. I—I apologize. Mother. [*Amanda draws a quick, shuddering breath. Her face works grotesquely. She breaks into childlike tears.*] I'm sorry for what I said, for everything that I said, I didn't mean it.

AMANDA [*sobbingly*]: My devotion has made me a witch and so I make myself hateful to my children!

TOM: No, you *don't*.

AMANDA: I worry so much, don't sleep, it makes me nervous!

TOM [*gently*]: I understand that.

AMANDA: I've had to put up a solitary battle all these years. But you're my right-hand bower! Don't fall down, don't fail!

TOM [*gently*]: I try, Mother.

AMANDA [*with great enthusiasm*]: Try and you will SUCCEED! [*The notion makes her breathless.*] Why, you—you're just *full* of natural endowments! Both of my children—they're *unusual* children! Don't you think I know it? I'm so—*proud*! Happy and—feel I've—so much to be thankful for but—Promise me one thing, son!

TOM: What, Mother?

AMANDA: Promise, son, you'll—never be a drunkard!

TOM [*turns to her grinning*]: I will never be a drunkard!

AMANDA: That's what frightened me so, that you'd be drinking! Eat a bowl of Purina!

TOM: Just coffee, Mother.

AMANDA: Shredded wheat biscuit?

TOM: No. No, Mother, just coffee.

AMANDA: You can't put in a day's work on an empty stomach. You've got ten minutes—don't gulp! Drinking too-hot liquids makes cancer of the stomach . . . . Put cream in.

TOM: No, thank you.

AMANDA: To cool it.

TOM: No! No, thank you, I want it black.

AMANDA: I know, but it's not good for you. We have to do all that we can to build ourselves up. In these trying times we live in, all that we have to cling to is each other . . . . That's why it's so important to— Tom, I—I sent out your sister so I could discuss something with you. If you hadn't spoken I would have spoken to you. [*Sits down.*]

TOM [*gently*]:   What is it, Mother, that you want to discuss?

AMANDA: Laura!

[*Tom puts his cup down slowly.*]

[Legend on Screen: "Laura."]
[Music: "The Glass Menagerie."]

TOM: —Oh.—Laura . . .

AMANDA [*touching his sleeve*]:   You know how Laura is. So quiet but—still water runs deep! She notices things and I think she—broods about them. [*Tom looks up.*] A few days ago I came in and she was crying.

TOM: What about?

AMANDA: You.

TOM: Me?

AMANDA: She has an idea that you're not happy here.

TOM: What gave her that idea?

AMANDA: What gives her any idea? However, you do act strangely. I—I'm not criticizing, understand *that!* I know your ambitions do not lie in the warehouse, that like everybody in the whole wide world—you've had to—make sacrifices, but—Tom—Tom—life's not easy, it calls for—Spartan endurance! There's so many things in my heart that I cannot describe to you! I've never told you but I—*loved* your father . . . .

TOM [*gently*]:   I know that, Mother.

AMANDA: And you—when I see you taking after his ways! Staying out late—and—well, you *had* been drinking the night you were in that—terrifying condition! Laura says that you hate the apartment and that you go out nights to get away from it! Is that true, Tom?

TOM: No. You say there's so much in your heart that you can't describe to me. That's true of me, too. There's so much in my heart that I can't describe to *you!* So let's respect each other's—

AMANDA: But, why—*why*, Tom—are you always so *restless?* Where do you go to, nights?

TOM: I—go to the movies.

AMANDA: Why do you go to the movies so much, Tom?

TOM: I go to the movies because—I like adventure. Adventure is something I don't have much of at work, so I go to the movies.

AMANDA: But, Tom, you go to the movies *entirely too much!*

TOM: I like a lot of adventure.

[*Amanda looks baffled, then hurt. As the familiar inquisition re-sumes he becomes hard and impatient again. Amanda slips back into her querulous attitude toward him.*]

[Image on Screen: Sailing Vessel with Jolly Roger.]

AMANDA: Most young men find adventure in their careers.

TOM: Then most young men are not employed in a warehouse.

AMANDA: The world is full of young men employed in warehouses and offices and factories.

TOM: Do all of them find adventure in their careers?

AMANDA: They do or they do without it! Not everybody has a craze for adventure.

TOM: Man is by instinct a lover, a hunter, a fighter, and none of these instincts are given much play at the warehouse!

ARMANDA: Man is by instinct! Don't quote instinct to me! Instinct is something that people have got away from! It belongs to animals! Christian adults don't want it!

TOM: What do Christian adults want, then, Mother?

AMANDA: Superior things! Things of the mind and the spirit! Only animals have to satisfy instincts! Surely your aims are somewhat higher than theirs! Than monkeys—pigs—

TOM: I reckon they're not.

AMANDA: You're joking. However, that isn't what I wanted to discuss.

TOM [*rising*]:   I haven't much time.

AMANDA [*pushing his shoulders*]:   Sit down.

TOM: You want me to punch in red at the warehouse, Mother?

AMANDA: You have five minutes. I want to talk about Laura.

[Legend: "Plans and Provisions."]

TOM: All right! What about Laura?

AMANDA: We have to be making plans and provisions for her. She's older than you, two years, and nothing has happened. She just drifts along doing nothing. It frightens me terribly how she just drifts along.

TOM: I guess she's the type that people call home girls.

AMANDA: There's no such type, and if there is, it's a pity! That is un-less the home is hers, with a husband!

TOM: What?

AMANDA: Oh, I can see the handwriting on the wall as plain as I see the nose in front of my face! It's terrifying! More and more you remind me of your father! He was out all hours without explanation— Then *left!* *Good-bye!* And me with the bag to hold. I saw that letter you got from the Merchant Marine. I know what you're dreaming of. I'm not standing here blindfolded. Very well, then. Then *do* it! But not till there's somebody to take your place.

TOM: What do you mean?

AMANDA: I mean that as soon as Laura has got somebody to take care of her, married, a home of her own, independent—why, then you'll be free to go wherever you please, on land, on sea, whichever way the wind blows! But until that time you've got to look out for your sister. I don't say me because I'm old and don't matter! I say for your sister because she's young and dependent. I put her in business college—a dismal failure! Frightened her so it made her sick to her stomach. I took her over to the Young People's League at the church. Another fiasco. She spoke to nobody, nobody spoke to her. Now all she does is fool with those pieces of glass and play those worn-out records. What kind of life is that for a girl to lead!

TOM: What can I do about it?

AMANDA: Overcome selfishness! Self, self, self is all that you ever think of! [*Tom springs up and crosses to get his coat. It is ugly and bulky. He pulls on a cap with earmuffs.*] Where is your muffler? Put your wool muffler on! [*He snatches it angrily from the closet and tosses it around his neck and pulls both ends tight.*] Tom! I haven't said what I had in mind to ask you.

TOM: I'm too late to—

AMANDA [*catching his arms very importunately. Then shyly.*]: Down the warehouse, aren't there some—nice young men?

TOM: No!

AMANDA: There *must* be—*some.*

TOM: Mother—

[*Gesture.*]

AMANDA: Find out one that's clean-living—doesn't drink and—ask him out for sister?

TOM: What?

AMANDA: For *sister!* To *meet!* Get acquainted!

TOM [*stamping to door*]: Oh, my *go-osh!*

AMANDA: Will you? [*He opens door. Imploringly*] Will you? [*He starts down.*] Will you? Will you, dear?

TOM [*calling back*]:   YES!

[*Amanda closes the door hesitantly and with a troubled but faintly hopeful expression.*]

[Screen Image: Glamour Magazine Cover.]

[*Spot Amanda at phone.*]

AMANDA: Ella Cartwright? This is Amanda Wingfield! How are you, honey? How is that kidney condition? [*Count five.*] Horrors! [*Count five.*] You're a Christian martyr, yes, honey, that's what you are, a Christian martyr! Well, I just happened to notice in my little red book that your subscription to the *Companion* has just run out! I knew that you wouldn't want to miss out on the wonderful serial starting in this new issue. It's by Bessie Mae Hopper, the first thing she's written since *Honeymoon for Three*. Wasn't that a strange and interesting story? Well, this one is even lovelier, I believe. It has a sophisticated society background. It's all about the horsey set on Long Island!

[Fade Out.]

Scene V

[Legend on Screen: "Annunciation."] Fade With Music.

It is early dusk of a spring evening. Supper has just been finished in the Wingfield apartment. Amanda and Laura in light-colored dresses are removing dishes from the table, in the upstage area, which is shadowy, their movements formalized almost as a dance or ritual, their moving forms as pale and silent as moths. Tom, in white shirt and trousers, rises from the table and crosses toward the fire-escape.

AMANDA [*as he passes her*]:   Son, will you do me a favor?

TOM: What?

AMANDA: Comb your hair! You look so pretty when your hair is combed! [*Tom slouches on the sofa with the evening paper. Enormous caption "Franco Triumphs."*] There is only one respect in which I would like you to emulate your father.

TOM: What respect is that?

AMANDA: The care he always took of his appearance. He never allowed himself to look untidy. [*He throws down the paper and crosses
to the fire-escape.*] Where are you going?

TOM: I'm going out to smoke.

AMANDA: You smoke too much. A pack a day at fifteen cents a pack.
How much would that amount to in a month? Thirty times fifteen
is how much, Tom? Figure it out and you will be astounded at what
you could save. Enough to give you a night-school course in accounting at Washington U! Just think what a wonderful thing that
would be for you, son!

[*Tom is unmoved by the thought.*]

TOM: I'd rather smoke. [*He steps out on the landing, letting the screen
door slam.*]

AMANDA [*sharply*]:   I know! That's the tragedy of it . . . . [*Alone, she
turns to look at her husband's picture.*]

[Dance Music: "All the World Is Waiting for the Sunrise!"]

TOM [*to the audience*]:   Across the alley from us was the Paradise
Dance Hall. On evenings in spring the windows and doors were
open and the music came outdoors. Sometimes the lights were
turned out except for a large glass sphere that hung from the ceiling. It would turn slowly about and filter the dusk with delicate
rainbow colors. Then the orchestra played a waltz or a tango,
something that had a slow and sensuous rhythm. Couples would
come outside, to the relative privacy of the alley. You could see
them kissing behind ashpits and telephone poles. This was the
compensation for lives that passed like mine, without any change
or adventure. Adventure and change were imminent in this year.
They were waiting around the corner for all these kinds. Sus-
pended in the mist over Berchtesgaden, caught in the folds of
Chamberlain's umbrella—In Spain there was Guernica! But here
there was only hot swing music and liquor, dance halls, bars, and
movies, and sex that hung in the gloom like a chandelier and
flooded the world with brief, deceptive rainbows . . . . All the world
was waiting for bombardments!

[*Amanda turns from the picture and comes outside.*]

AMANDA [*sighing*]:   A fire-escape landing's a poor excuse for a porch.
[*She spreads a newspaper on a step and sits down, gracefully and*

demurely as if she were settling into a swing on a Mississippi veranda.]
What are you looking at?

TOM: The moon.

AMANDA: Is there a moon this evening?

TOM: It's rising over Garfinkel's Delicatessen.

AMANDA: So it is! A little silver slipper of a moon. Have you made a wish on it yet?

TOM: Um-hum.

AMANDA: What did you wish for.

TOM: That's a secret.

AMANDA: A secret, huh? Well, I won't tell you mine either. I will be just as mysterious as you.

TOM: I bet I can guess what yours is.

AMANDA: Is my head so transparent?

TOM: You're not a sphinx.

AMANDA: No, I don't have secrets. I'll tell you what I wished for on the moon. Success and happiness for my precious children! I wish for that whenever there's a moon, and when there isn't a moon, I wish for it, too.

TOM: I thought perhaps you wished for a gentleman caller.

AMANDA: Why do you say that?

TOM: Don't you remember asking me to fetch one?

AMANDA: I remember suggesting that it would be nice for your sister if you brought home some nice young man from the warehouse. I think I've made that suggestion more than once.

TOM: Yes, you have made it repeatedly.

AMANDA: Well?

TOM: We are going to have one.

AMANDA: What?

TOM: A gentleman caller!

[The Annunciation Is Celebrated with Music.]

[*Amanda rises.*]

[Image on Screen: Caller with Bouquet.]

AMANDA: You mean you have asked some nice young man to come over?

TOM: Yep. I've asked him to dinner.

AMANDA: You really did?

TOM: I did!

AMANDA: You did, and did he—*accept?*

TOM: He did!

AMANDA: Well, well—well, well! That's—lovely!

TOM: I thought that you would be pleased.

AMANDA: It's definite, then?

TOM: Very definite.

AMANDA: Soon?

TOM: Very soon.

AMANDA: For heaven's sake, stop putting on and tell me some things, will you?

TOM: What things do you want me to tell you?

AMANDA: Naturally I would like to know when he's *coming!*

TOM: He's coming tomorrow.

AMANDA: Tomorrow?

TOM: Yep. Tomorrow.

AMANDA: But, Tom!

TOM: Yes, Mother?

AMANDA: Tomorrow gives me no time!

TOM: Time for what?

AMANDA: Preparations! Why didn't you phone me at once, as soon as you asked him, the minute that he accepted? Then, don't you see, I could have been getting ready!

TOM: You don't have to make any fuss.

AMANDA: Oh, Tom, Tom, Tom, of course I have to make a fuss! I want things nice, not sloppy! Not thrown together. I'll certainly have to do some fast thinking, won't I?

TOM: I don't see why you have to think at all.

AMANDA: You just don't know. We can't have a gentleman caller in a pig-sty! All my wedding silver has to be polished, the monogrammed table linen ought to be laundered! The windows have to be washed and fresh curtains put up. And how about clothes? We have to *wear* something, don't we?

TOM: Mother, this boy is no one to make a fuss over!

AMANDA: Do you realize he's the first young man we've had introduced to your sister? It's terrible, dreadful, disgraceful that poor little sister has never received a single gentleman caller! Tom, come inside! [*She opens the screen door.*]

TOM: What for?

AMANDA: I want to ask you some things.

TOM: If you're going to make such a fuss, I'll call it off, I'll tell him not to come.

AMANDA: You certainly won't do anything of the kind. Nothing offends people worse than broken engagements. It simply means I'll have to work like a Turk! We won't be brilliant, but we'll pass inspection. Come on inside. [*Tom follows, groaning.*] Sit down.

TOM: Any particular place you would like me to sit?

AMANDA: Thank heavens I've got that new sofa! I'm also making payments on a floor lamp I'll have sent out! And put the chintz covers on, they'll brighten things up! Of course I'd hoped to have these walls re-papered . . . . What is the young man's name?

TOM: His name is O'Connor.

AMANDA: That, of course, means fish—tomorrow is Friday! I'll have that salmon loaf—with Durkee's dressing! What does he do? He works at the warehouse?

TOM: Of course! How else would I—

AMANDA: Tom, he—doesn't drink?

TOM: Why do you ask me that?

AMANDA: Your father *did!*

TOM: Don't get started on that!

AMANDA: He *does* drink, then?

TOM: Not that I know of!

AMANDA: Make sure, be certain! The last thing I want for my daughter's a boy who drinks?

TOM: Aren't you being a little premature? Mr. O'Connor has not yet appeared on the scene!

AMANDA: But will tomorrow. To meet your sister, and what do I know about his character? Nothing! Old maids are better off than wives of drunkards!

TOM: Oh, my God.

AMANDA: Be still!

TOM [*leaning forward to whisper*]: Lots of fellows meet girls whom they don't marry!

AMANDA: Oh, talk sensibly, Tom—and don't be sarcastic! [*She has gotten a hairbrush.*]

TOM: What are you doing?

AMANDA: I'm brushing that cow-lick down! What is this young man's position at the warehouse?

TOM [*submitting grimly to the brush and the interrogation*]: This young man's position is that of a shipping clerk, Mother.

AMANDA: Sounds to me like a fairly responsible job, the sort of a job *you* would be in if you just had more *get-up.* What is his salary? Have you got any idea?

TOM: I would judge it to be approximately eighty-five dollars a month.

AMANDA: Well—not princely, but—

TOM: Twenty more than I make.

AMANDA: Yes, how well I know! But for a family man, eighty-five dollars a month is not much more than you can just get by on . . . .

TOM: Yes, but Mr. O'Connor is not a family man.

AMANDA: He might be, mightn't he? Some time in the future?

TOM: I see. Plans and provisions.

AMANDA: You are the only young man that I know of who ignores the fact that the future becomes the present, the present the past, and the past turns into everlasting regret if you don't plan for it!

TOM: I will think that over and see what I can make of it.

AMANDA: Don't be supercilious with your mother! Tell me some more about this—what do you call him?

TOM: James D. O'Connor. The D. is for Delaney.

AMANDA: Irish on *both* sides! *Gracious!* And doesn't drink?

TOM: Shall I call him up and ask him right this minute?

AMANDA: The only way to find out about those things is to make discreet inquiries at the proper moment. When I was a girl in Blue Mountain and it was suspected that a young man drank, the girl whose attentions he had been receiving, if any girl *was,* would sometimes speak to the minister of his church, or rather her father would if her father was living, and sort of feel him out on the young man's character. That is the way such things are discreetly handled to keep a young woman from making a tragic mistake!

TOM: Then how did you happen to make a tragic mistake?

AMANDA: That innocent look of your father's had everyone fooled! He *smiled*—the world was *enchanted!* No girl can do worse than put herself at the mercy of a handsome appearance! I hope that Mr. O'Connor is not too good-looking.

TOM: No, he's not too good-looking. He's covered with freckles and hasn't too much of a nose.

AMANDA: He's not right-down homely, though?

TOM: Not right-down homely. Just medium homely, I'd say.

AMANDA: Character's what to look for in a man.

TOM: That's what I've always said, Mother.

AMANDA: You've never said anything of the kind and I suspect you would never give it a thought.

TOM: Don't be suspicious of me.

AMANDA: At least I hope he's the type that's up and coming.

TOM: I think he really goes in for self-improvement.

AMANDA: What reason have you to think so?

TOM: He goes to night school.

AMANDA [*beaming*]:   Splendid! What does he do, I mean study?

TOM: Radio engineering and public speaking!

AMANDA: Then he has visions of being advanced in the world! Any young man who studies public speaking is aiming to have an executive job some day! And radio engineering? A thing for the future! Both of these facts are very illuminating. Those are the sort of things that a mother should know concerning any young man who comes to call on her daughter. Seriously or—not.

TOM: One little warning. He doesn't know about Laura. I didn't let on that we had dark ulterior motives. I just said, why don't you come have dinner with us? He said okay and that was the whole conversation.

AMANDA: I bet it was! You're eloquent as an oyster. However, he'll know about Laura when he gets here. When we sees how lovely and sweet and pretty she is, he'll thank his lucky stars he was asked to dinner.

TOM: Mother, you mustn't expect too much of Laura.

AMANDA: What do you mean?

TOM: Laura seems all those things to you and me because she's ours and we love her. We don't even notice she's crippled any more.

AMANDA: Don't say crippled! You know that I never allow that word to be used!

TOM: But face facts, Mother. She is and—that's not all—

AMANDA: What do you mean "not all"?

TOM: Laura is very different from other girls.

AMANDA: I think the difference is all to her advantage.

TOM: Not quite all—in the eyes of others—strangers—she's terribly shy and lives in a world of her own and those things make her seem a little peculiar to people outside the house.

AMANDA: Don't say peculiar.

TOM: Face the facts. She is.

[The Dance-Hall Music Changes to a Tango That Has a Minor and
Somewhat Ominous Tone.]

AMANDA: In what way is she peculiar—may I ask?

TOM [*gently*]:   She lives in a world of her own—a world of—little glass ornaments, Mother . . . . [*Gets up, Amanda remains holding the brush, looking at him, troubled.*] She plays old phonograph records and—that's
about all—[*He glances at himself in the mirror and crosses to the door.*]

AMANDA [sharply]:   Where are you going?

TOM: I'm going to the movies. [*Out screen door.*]

AMANDA: Not to the movies, every night to the movies! [*Follows
quickly to screen door.*] I don't believe you always go to the movies!
[*He is gone. Amanda looks worriedly after him for a moment. Then
vitality and optimism return and she turns from the door. Crossing to
portieres.*] Laura! Laura! [*Laura answers from kitchenette.*]

LAURA: Yes, Mother.

AMANDA: Let those dishes go and come in front! [*Laura appears with
dish towel. Gaily*] Laura, come here and make a wish on the moon!

LAURA [*entering*]:   Moon—moon?

AMANDA: A little silver slipper of a moon. Look over your left shoulder, Laura, and make a wish! [*Laura looks faintly puzzled as if called
out of sleep. Amanda seizes her shoulders and turns her at angle by the
door.*] Now! Now, darling, *wish!*

LAURA: What shall I wish for, Mother?

AMANDA [*her voice trembling and her eyes suddenly filling with tears*]:
Happiness! Good Fortune!

[*The violin rises and the stage dims out.*]

Scene VI

[Image: High School Hero.]

TOM: And so the following evening I brought Jim home to dinner. I
had known Jim slightly in high school. In high school Jim was a
hero. He had tremendous Irish good nature and vitality with the
scrubbed and polished look of white chinaware. He seemed to
move in a continual spotlight. He was a star in basketball, captain
of the debating club, president of the senior class and the glee club
and he sang the male lead in the annual light operas. He was always running or bounding, never just walking. He seemed always
at the point of defeating the law of gravity. He was shooting with

such velocity through his adolescence that you would logically expect him to arrive at nothing short of the White House by the time he was thirty. But Jim apparently ran into more interference after his graduation from Soldan. His speed had definitely slowed. Six years after he left high school he was holding a job that wasn't much better than mine.

[Image: Clerk.]

He was the only one at the warehouse with whom I was on friendly terms. I was valuable to him as someone who could remember his former glory, who had seen him win basketball games and the silver cup in debating. He knew of my secret practice of retiring to a cabinet of the washroom to work on poems when business was slack in the warehouse. He called me Shakespeare. And while the other boys in the warehouse regarded me with suspicious hostility, Jim took a humorous attitude toward me. Gradually his attitude affected the others, their hostility wore off and they also began to smile at me as people smile at an oddly fashioned dog who trots across their path at some distance.

I knew that Jim and Laura had known each other at Soldan, and I had heard Laura speak admiringly of his voice. I didn't know if Jim remembered her or not. In high school Laura had been as unobtrusive as Jim had been astonishing. If he did remember Laura, it was not as my sister for when I asked him to dinner, he grinned and said, "You know, Shakespeare, I never thought of you as having folks!" He was about to discover that I did . . . .

[Light upstage.]
[Legend on Screen: "The Accent of a Coming Foot."]

[*Friday evening. It is about five o'clock of a late spring evening which comes "scattering poems in the sky." A delicate lemony light is in the Wingfield apartment. Amanda has worked like a Turk in preparation for the gentleman caller. The results are astonishing. The new floor lamp with its rose-silk shade is in place, a colored paper lantern conceals the broken light fixture in the ceiling, new billowing white curtains are at the windows, chintz covers are on chairs, and sofa, a pair of new sofa pillows make their initial appearance.*

Open boxes and tissue paper are scattered on the floor.

Laura stands in the middle with lifted arms while Amanda crouches before her, adjusting the hem of the new dress, devout and ritualistic. The dress is colored and designed by memory. The arrangement of Laura's hair is changed; it is softer and more becoming. A fragile, unearthly prettiness has come out in Laura: she is like a piece of translucent glass touched by light, given a momentary radiance, not actual, not lasting.]

AMANDA [*impatiently*]: Why are you trembling?

LAURA: Mother, you've made me so nervous!

AMANDA: How have I made you nervous?

LAURA: By all this fuss! You make it seem so important?

AMANDA: I don't understand you, Laura. You couldn't be satisfied with just sitting home, and yet whenever I try to arrange something for you, you seem to resist it. [*She gets up.*] Now take a look at yourself. No, wait! Wait just a moment—I have an idea!

LAURA: What is it now?

[*Amanda produces two powder puffs which she wraps in handkerchiefs and stuffs in Laura's bosom.*]

LAURA: Mother, what are you doing?

AMANDA: They call them "Gay Deceivers"!

LAURA: I won't wear them!

AMANDA: You will!

LAURA: Why should I?

AMANDA: Because, to be painfully honest, your chest is flat.

LAURA: You make it seem like we were setting a trap.

AMANDA: All pretty girls are a trap, a pretty trap, and men expect them to be.

[Legend: "A Pretty Trap."]

Now look at yourself, young lady. This is the prettiest you will ever be! I've got to fix myself now! You're going to be surprised by your mother's appearance.

[*She crosses through portieres, humming gaily.*]

[*Laura moves slowly to the long mirror and stares solemnly at herself. A wind blows the white curtains inward in a slow, graceful motion and with a faint, sorrowful sighing.*]

AMANDA [*offstage*]:   It isn't dark enough yet. [*She turns slowly before the mirror with a troubled look.*]

[Legend on Screen: "This Is My Sister: Celebrate Her with Strings!"
Music.]

AMANDA [*laughing, off*]:   I'm going to show you something. I'm going to make a spectacular appearance!

LAURA: What is it, Mother?

AMANDA: Possess your soul in patience—you will see! Something I've resurrected from that old trunk! Styles haven't changed so terribly much after all . . . . [*She parts the portieres.*] Now just look at your mother! [*She wears a girlish frock of yellowed voile with a blue silk sash. She carries a bunch of jonquils—the legend of her youth is nearly revived. Feverishly*] This is the dress in which I led the cotillion. Won the cakewalk twice at Sunset Hill, wore one spring to the Governor's ball in Jackson! See how I sashayed around the ballroom, Laura? [*She raises her skirt and does a mincing step around the room.*] I wore it on Sundays for my gentleman callers! I had it on the day I met your father—I had malaria fever all that spring. The change of climate from East Tennessee to the Delta—weakened resistance—I had a little temperature all the time—not enough to be serious—just enough to make me restless and giddy! Invitations poured in parties all over the Delta!—"Stay in bed," said Mother, "you have fever!"—but I just wouldn't.—I took quinine but kept on going, going!—Evenings, dances!—Afternoon, long, long rides! Picnics—lovely!—So lovely, that country in May.—All lacy with dogwood, literally flooded with jonquils.—That was the spring I had the craze for jonquils. Jonquils became an absolute obsession. Mother said, "Honey, there's no more room for jonquils." And still I kept bringing in more jonquils. Whenever, wherever I saw them, I'd say, "Stop! Stop! I see jonquils!" I made the young men help me gather the jonquils! It was a joke, Amanda and her jonquils! Finally there were no more vases to hold them, every available space was filled with jonquils. No vases to hold them? All right, I'll hold them myself! And then I—[*She stops in front of the picture.*] [*Music.*] met your father! Malaria fever and jonquils and then—this—boy . . . . [*She switches on the rose-colored lamp.*] I hope they get here before it starts to rain. [*She crosses upstage and places the jonquils in a bowl on the table.*] I gave your brother a little extra change so he and Mr. O'Connor could take the service car home.

LAURA [*with altered look*]:   What did you say his name was?

AMANDA: O'Connor.

LAURA: What is his first name?

AMANDA: I don't remember. Oh, yes, I do. It was—Jim!

[*Laura sways slightly and catches hold of a chair.*]

[Legend on Screen: "Not Jim!"]

LAURA [*faintly*]:   Not—Jim!

AMANDA: Yes, that was it, it was Jim! I've never know a Jim that wasn't nice!

[Music: Ominous.]

LAURA: Are you sure his name is Jim O'Connor?

AMANDA: Yes. Why?

LAURA: Is he the one that Tom used to know in high school?

AMANDA: He didn't say so. I think he just got to know him at the warehouse.

LAURA: There was a Jim O'Connor we both knew in high school— [*Then, with effort.*] If that is the one that Tom is bringing to dinner— you'll have to excuse me, I won't come to the table.

AMANDA: What sort of nonsense is this?

LAURA: You asked me once if I'd ever liked a boy. Don't you remember I showed you this boy's picture?

AMANDA: You mean the boy you showed me in the year book?

LAURA: Yes, that boy.

AMANDA: Laura, Laura, were you in love with that boy?

LAURA: I don't know, Mother. All I know is I couldn't sit at the table if it was him!

AMANDA: It won't be him! It isn't the least bit likely. But whether it is or not, you will come to the table. You will not be excused.

LAURA: I'll have to be, Mother.

AMANDA: I don't intend to humor your silliness, Laura. I've had too much from you and your brother, both! So just sit down and compose yourself till they come. Tom has forgotten his key so you'll have to let them in, when they arrive.

LAURA [*panicky*]:   Oh, Mother—*you* answer the door!

AMANDA [*lightly*]:   I'll be in the kitchen—busy!

LAURA: Oh, Mother, please answer the door, don't make me do it!

AMANDA [*crossing into kitchenette*]:   I've got to fix the dressing for the salmon. Fuss, fuss—silliness!—over a gentleman caller!

[*Door swings shut. Laura is left alone.*]

[Legend: "Terror!"]

[*She utters a low moan and turns off the lamp—sits stiffly on the edge of the sofa, knotting her fingers together.*]

[Legend on Screen: "The Opening of a Door!"]

[*Tom and Jim appear on the fire-escape steps and climb to the landing. Hearing their approach, Laura rises with a panicky gesture. She retreats to the portieres.*

The doorbell. Laura catches her breath and touches her throat. Low drums.]

AMANDA [*calling*]:   Laura, sweetheart! The door!

[*Laura stares at it without moving.*]

JIM: I think we just beat the rain.

TOM: Uh-huh. [*He rings again, nervously, Jim whistles and fishes for a cigarette.*]

AMANDA [*very, very gaily*]:   Laura, that is your brother and Mr. O'Connor! Will you let them in, darling?

[*Laura crosses toward kitchenette door*].

LAURA [*breathlessly*]:   Mother—you go to the door!

[*Amanda steps out of the kitchenette and stares furiously at Laura. She points imperiously at the door.*]

LAURA: Please, please!

AMANDA [*in a fierce whisper*]:   What is the matter with you, you silly thing?

LAURA [*desperately*]:   Please, you answer it, *please!*

AMANDA: I told you I wasn't going to humor you, Laura. Why have you chosen this time to lose your mind?

LAURA: Please, please, please, you go!

AMANDA: You'll have to go to the door because I can't.

LAURA [despairingly]:   I can't either!

AMANDA: Why?

LAURA: I'm sick?

AMANDA: I'm sick, too—of your nonsense! Why can't you and your brother be normal people? Fantastic whims and behavior! [Tom gives a long ring.] Preposterous goings on! Can you give me one reason—[Calls out lyrically.] COMING! JUST ONE SECOND!—why should you be afraid to open a door? Now you answer it, Laura!

LAURA: Oh, oh, oh . . . [She returns through the portieres. Darts to the victrola and winds it frantically and turns it on.]

AMANDA: Laura Wingfield, you march right to that door!

LAURA: Yes—yes, Mother.

[A faraway, scratchy rendition of "Dardanella" softens the air and gives her strength to move through it. She slips to the door and draws it cautiously open. Tom enters with the caller, Jim O'Connor.]

TOM: Laura, this is Jim. Jim, this is my sister, Laura.

JIM [stepping inside]:   I didn't know that Shakespeare had a sister!

LAURA [retreating stiff and trembling from the door]:   How—how do you do?

JIM [heartily extending his hand]:   Okay!

[Laura touches it hesitantly with hers.]

JIM: Your hand's cold, Laura!

LAURA: Yes, well—I've been playing the victrola . . . .

JIM: Must have been playing classical music on it! You ought to play a little hot swing music to warm you up!

LAURA: Excuse me—I haven't finished playing the victrola . . . .

[She turns awkwardly and hurries onto the front room. She pauses a second by the victrola. Then catches her breath and darts through the portieres like a frightened deer.]

JIM [grinning]:   What was the matter?

TOM: Oh—with Laura? Laura is—terribly shy.

JIM: Shy, huh? It's unusual to meet a shy girl nowadays. I don't believe you ever mentioned you had a sister.

TOM: Well, now you know. I have one. Here is the Post Dispatch. You want a piece of it?

JIM: Uh-huh.

TOM: What piece? The comics?

JIM: Sports! [*Glances at it.*] Ole Dizzy Dean is on his bad behavior.

TOM [*disinterest*]: Yeah? [*Lights cigarette and crosses back to fire-escape door.*]

JIM: Where are you going?

TOM: I'm going out on the terrace.

JIM [*goes after him*]: You know, Shakespeare—I'm going to sell you a bill of goods!

TOM: What goods?

JIM: A course I'm taking.

TOM: Huh?

JIM: In public speaking! You and me, we're not the warehouse type.

TOM: Thanks—that's good news. But what has public speaking got to do with it?

JIM: It fits you for—executive positions!

TOM: Awww.

JIM: I tell you it's done a helluva lot for me.

[Image: Executive at Desk.]

TOM: In what respect?

JIM: In every! Ask yourself what is the difference between you an' me in the office down front? Brains?—No!—Ability?—No! Then what? Just one little thing—

TOM: What is that one little thing?

JIM: Primarily it amounts to—social poise! Being able to square up to people and hold your own on any social level!

AMANDA [*off stage*]: Tom?

TOM: Yes, Mother?

AMANDA: Is that you and Mr. O'Connor?

TOM: Yes, Mother.

AMANDA: Well, you just make yourselves comfortable in there.

TOM: Yes, Mother.

AMANDA: Ask Mr. O'Connor if he would like to wash his hands.

JIM: Aw—no—no—thank you—I took care of that at the warehouse. Tom—

TOM: Yes?

JIM: Mr. Mendoza was speaking to me about you.

TOM: Favorably?

JIM: What do you think?

TOM: Well—

JIM: You're going to be out of a job if you don't wake up.

TOM: I am waking up—

JIM: You show no signs.

TOM: The signs are interior.

[Image on Screen: The Sailing Vessel with Jolly Roger Again.]

TOM: I'm planning to change. [*He leans over the rail speaking with quiet exhilaration. The incandescent marquees and signs of the first-run movie houses light his face from across the alley. He looks like a voyager.*] I'm right at the point of committing myself to a future that doesn't include the warehouse and Mr. Mendoza or even a night-school course in public speaking.

JIM: What are you gassing about?

TOM: I'm tired of the movies.

JIM: Movies!

TOM: Yes, movies! Look at them—[*A wave toward the marvels of Grand Avenue.*] All of those glamorous people—having adventures—hogging it all, gobbling the whole thing up! You know what happens? People go to the *movies* instead of *moving!* Hollywood characters are supposed to have all the adventures for everybody in America, while everybody in America sits in a dark room and watches them have them! Yes, until there's a war. That's when adventure becomes available to the masses! *Everyone's* dish, not only Gable's! Then the people in the dark room come out of the dark room to have some adventures themselves—Goody, goody—It's our turn now, to go to the South Sea Island—to make a safari—to be exotic, far-off—But I'm not patient. I don't want to wait till then. I'm tired of the *movies* and I am *about* to move!

JIM [*incredulously*]:   Move?

TOM: Yes.

JIM: When?

TOM: Soon!

JIM: Where? Where?

[*Theme Three: Music Seems to Answer the Question, While Tom Thinks It Over. He Searches Among His Pockets.*]

TOM: I'm starting to boil inside. I know I seem dreamy, but inside—well, I'm boiling! Whenever I pick up a shoe, I shudder a little thinking how short life is and what I am doing!—Whatever that means. I know it doesn't mean shoes—except as something to wear on a traveler's feet! [*Finds paper.*] Look—

JIM: What?

TOM: I'm a member.

JIM [*reading*]:   The Union of Merchant Seamen.

TOM: I paid my dues this month, instead of the light bill.

JIM: You will regret it when they turn the lights off.

TOM: I won't be here.

JIM: How about your mother?

TOM: I'm like my father. The bastard son of a bastard! See how he grins? And he's been absent going on sixteen years!

JIM: You're just talking, you drip. How does you mother feel about it?

TOM: Shhh—Here comes Mother! Mother is not acquainted with my plans.

AMANDA [*enters portiere*]:   Where are you all?

TOM: On the terrace, Mother.

[*They start inside. She advances to them. Tom is distinctly shocked at her appearance. Even Jim blinks a little. He is making his first contact with girlish Southern vivacity and in spite of the night-school course in public speaking is somewhat thrown off the beam by the unexpected outlay of social charm. Certain responses are attempted by Jim but are swept aside by Amanda's gay laughter and chatter. Tom is embarrassed but after the first shock Jim reacts very warmly. Grins and chuckles, is altogether won over.*]

[Image: Amanda as a Girl.]

AMANDA [*coyly smiling, shaking her girlish ringlets*]:   Well, well, well, so this is Mr. O'Connor. Introductions entirely unnecessary. I've heard so much about you from my boy. I finally said to him, Tom—good gracious!—why don't you bring this paragon to supper? I'd like to meet this nice young man at the warehouse!—Instead of just hearing him sing your praises so much! I don't know why my son is so stand-offish—that's not Southern behavior! Let's sit down and—I think we could stand a little more air in here! Tom, leave the door open. I felt a nice fresh breeze a moment ago. Where has it gone? Mmm, so warm already! And not quite summer, even. We're going to burn up when summer really gets started. However, we're having—we're having a very light supper. I think light things are better fo' this time of year. The same as light clothes are. Light clothes an' light food are what warm weather calls fo'. You know our blood gets so thick during th' winter—it takes a while fo' us to *adjust* ou'selves!—when the season changes . . . It's come so quick this year. I wasn't prepared. All of a sudden— heavens! Already summer!—I ran to the trunk an' pulled out this light dress—Terribly old! Historical almost! But feels so good—so good an' co-ol, y'know . . . .

TOM: Mother—

AMANDA: Yes, honey?

TOM: How about—supper?

AMANDA: Honey, you go ask Sister if supper is ready! You know that Sister is in full charge of supper! Tell her you hungry boys are wait-ing for it. [*To Jim*] Have you met Laura?

JIM: She—

AMANDA: Let you in? Oh, good, you've met already! It's rare for a girl as sweet an' pretty as Laura to be domestic! But Laura is, thank heavens, not only pretty but also very domestic. I'm not at all. I never was a bit. I never could make a thing but angel-food cake. Well, in the South we had so many servants. Gone, gone, gone. All vestiges of gracious living! Gone completely! I wasn't prepared for what the future brought me. All of my gentleman callers were sons of planters and so of course I assumed that I would be married to one and raise my family on a large piece of land with plenty of ser-vants. But man proposes—and woman accepts the proposal!—To vary that old, old saying a little bit—I married no planter! I mar-ried a man who worked for the telephone company!—that gal-lantly smiling gentleman over there! [*Points to the picture.*] A tele-phone man who—fell in love with long distance!—Now he travels and I don't even know where!—But what am I going on for about my—tribulations! Tell me yours—I hope you don't have any! Tom?

TOM [*returning*]:   Yes, Mother?

AMANDA: Is supper nearly ready?

TOM: It looks to me like supper is on the table.

AMANDA: Let me look—[*She rises prettily and looks through portieres.*] Oh, lovely—but where is Sister?

TOM: Laura is not feeling well and she says that she thinks she'd bet-ter not come to the table.

AMANDA: What?—Nonsense!—Laura? Oh, Laura!

LAURA [*off stage, faintly*]:   Yes, Mother.

AMANDA: You really must come to the table. We won't be seated until you come to the table! Come in, Mr. O'Connor. You sit over there and I'll—Laura? Laura Wingfield! You're keeping us waiting, honey! We can't say grace until you come to the table!

[*The back door is pushed weakly open and Laura comes in. She is obviously quite faint, her lips trembling, her eyes wide and staring. She moves unsteadily toward the table.*]

[Legend: "Terror!"]

[*Outside a summer storm is coming abruptly. The white curtains billow inward at the windows and there is a sorrowful murmur and deep blue dusk. Laura suddenly stumbles—She catches at a chair with a faint moan.*]

TOM: Laura!

AMANDA: Laura! [*There's a clap of thunder*]. [*Legend: "Ah!"*] [*Despairingly*] Why, Laura, you *are* sick, darling! Tom, help your sister into the living room, dear! Sit in the living room, Laura—rest on the sofa. Well! [*To the gentleman caller*] Standing over the hot stove made her ill! I told her that it was just too warm this evening, but—[*Tom comes back in. Laura is on the sofa.*] Is Laura all right now?

TOM: Yes.

AMANDA: What is that? Rain? A nice cool rain has come up? [*She gives the gentleman caller a frightened look.*] I think we may—have grace—now . . . [*Tom looks at her stupidly.*] Tom, honey—you say grace!

TOM: Oh . . . "For these and all thy mercies—" [*They bow their heads. Amanda stealing a nervous glance at Jim. In the living room Laura, stretched on the sofa, clenches her hands to her lips, to hold back a shuddering sob.*] God's Holy Name be praised—

[The Scene Dims Out.]

Scene VII. A souvenir

Half an hour later. Dinner is just being finished in the upstage area which is concealed by the drawn portieres.

As the curtain rises Laura is still huddled upon the sofa, her feet drawn under her, her head resting on a pale blue pillow, her eyes wide and mysteriously watchful. The new floor lamp with its shade of rose-colored silk gives a soft, becoming light to her face, bringing out the fragile, unearthly prettiness which usually escapes attention. There is a steady murmur of rain, but it is slackening and stops soon after the scene begins; the air outside becomes pale and luminous as the moon breaks out.

A moment after the curtain rises, the lights in both rooms flicker and go out.

JIM: Hey, there, Mr. Light Bulb!

[Amanda laughs nervously.]

[Legend: "Suspension of a Public Service."]

AMANDA: Where was Moses when the lights went out? Ha-ha. Do you know the answer to that one, Mr. O'Connor?

JIM: No, Ma'am, what's the answer?

AMANDA: In the dark! [Jim laughs appreciatively.] Everybody sit still. I'll light the candles. Isn't it lucky we have them on the table? Where's a match. Which of you gentlemen can provide a match?

JIM: Here.

AMANDA: Thank you, sir.

JIM: Not at all, Ma'am!

AMANDA: I guess the fuse has burnt out. Mr. O'Connor, can you tell a burnt-out fuse? I know I can't and Tom is a total loss when it comes to mechanics. [Sound: Getting Up: Voices Recede a Little to Kitchenette.] Oh, be careful, you don't bump into something. We don't want our gentleman caller to break his neck. Now wouldn't that be a fine howdy-do?

JIM: Ha-ha! Where is the fuse-box?

AMANDA: Right there next to the stove. Can you see anything?

JIM: Just a minute.

AMANDA: Isn't electricity a mysterious thing? Wasn't it Benjamin Franklin who tied a key to a kite? We live in such a mysterious universe, don't we? Some people say that science clears up all the mysteries for us. In my opinion it only creates more! Have you found it yet?

JIM: No, Ma'am. All these fuses look okay to me.

AMANDA: Tom!

TOM: Yes, Mother?

AMANDA: That light bill I gave you several days ago. The one I told you we got the notices about?

TOM: Oh.—Yeah.

[Legend: "Ha!"]

AMANDA: You didn't neglect to pay it by any chance.

TOM: Why, I—

AMANDA: Didn't! I might have known it!

JIM: Shakespeare probably wrote a poem on the light bill, Mrs. Wingfield.

AMANDA: I might have known better than to trust him with it! There's such a high price for negligence in this world!

JIM: Maybe the poem will win a ten-dollar prize.

AMANDA: We'll just have to spend the remainder of the evening in the nineteenth century, before Mr. Edison made the Mazda lamp!

JIM: Candlelight is my favorite kind of light.

AMANDA: That shows you're romantic! But that's no excuse for Tom. Well, we got through dinner. Very considerate of them to let us get through dinner before they plunged us into everlasting darkness, wasn't it, Mr. O'Connor?

JIM: Ha-ha!

AMANDA: Tom, as a penalty for your carelessness you can help me with the dishes.

JIM: Let me give you a hand.

AMANDA: Indeed you will not!

JIM: I ought to be good for something.

AMANDA: Good for something? [*Her tone is rhapsodic.*] *You?* Why, Mr. O'Connor, nobody, *nobody's* given me this much entertainment in years—as you have!

JIM: Aw, now, Mrs. Wingfield!

AMANDA: I'm not exaggerating, not one bit! But Sister is all by her lonesome. You go keep her company in the parlor! I'll give you this lovely old candelabrum that used to be on the altar at the church of the Heavenly Rest. It was melted a little out of shape when the church burnt down. Lightning struck it one spring. Gypsy Jones was holding a revival at the time and he estimated that the church was destroyed because the Episcopalians gave card parties.

JIM: Ha-ha.

AMANDA: And how about coaxing Sister to drink a little wine? I think it would be good for her! Can you carry both at once?

JIM: Sure, I'm Superman!

AMANDA: Now, Thomas, get into this apron!

[*The door of the kitchenette swings closed on Amanda's gay laughter; the flickering light approaches the portieres. Laura sits up nervously as he enters. Her speech at first is low and breathless from the almost intolerable strain of being alone with a stranger.*]

[*Legend: "I Don't Suppose You Remember Me at All!"*]

[*In her first speeches in this scene, before Jim's warmth overcomes her paralyzing shyness, Laura's voice is thin and breathless as though she has run up a steep flight of stairs. Jim's attitude is gently humorous. In playing this scene it should be stressed that while the incident is apparently unimportant, it is to Laura the climax of her secret life.*]

JIM: Hello, there, Laura.

LAURA [*faintly*]: Hello. [*She clears her throat.*]

JIM: How are you feeling now? Better?

LAURA: Yes. Yes, thank you.

JIM: This is for you. A little dandelion wine. [*He extends it toward her with extravagant gallantry.*]

LAURA: Thank you.

JIM: Drink it—but don't get drunk! [*He laughs heartily. Laura takes the glass uncertainly; laughs shyly.*] Where shall I set the candles?

LAURA: Oh—oh, anywhere . . .

JIM: How about here on the floor? Any objections?

LAURA: No.

JIM: I'll spread a newspaper under to catch the drippings. I like to sit on the floor. Mind if I do?

LAURA: Oh, no.

JIM: Give me a pillow?

LAURA: What?

JIM: A pillow!

LAURA: Oh . . . [*Hands him one quickly.*]

JIM: How about you? Don't you like to sit on the floor?

LAURA: Oh—yes.

JIM: Why don't you, then?

LAURA: I—will.

JIM: Take a pillow! [*Laura does. Sits on the other side of the candelabrum. Jim crosses his legs and smiles engagingly at her.*] I can't hardly see you sitting way over there.

LAURA: I can—see you.

JIM: I know, but that's not fair, I'm in the limelight. [*Laura moves her pillow closer.*] Good! Now I can see you! Comfortable?

LAURA: Yes.

JIM: So am I. Comfortable as a cow. Will you have some gum?

LAURA: No, thank you.

JIM: I think that I will indulge, with your permission. [*Musingly unwraps it and holds it up.*] Think of the fortune made by the guy that invented the first piece of chewing gum. Amazing, huh? The Wrigley Building is one of the sights of Chicago.—I saw it summer before last when I went up to the Century of Progress. Did you take in the Century of Progress?

LAURA: No, I didn't.

JIM: Well, it was quite a wonderful exposition. What impressed me most was the Hall of Science. Gives you an idea of what the future will be in America, even more wonderful than the present time is! [*Pause. Smiling at her*] Your brother tells me you're shy. Is that right, Laura?

LAURA: I—don't know.

JIM: I judge you to be an old-fashioned type of girl. Well, I think that's a pretty good type to be. Hope you don't think I'm being too personal—do you?

LAURA [*hastily, out of embarrassment*]: I believe I *will* take a piece of gum, if you—don't mind. [*Clearing her throat*] Mr. O'Connor, have you—kept up with your singing?

JIM: Singing? Me?

LAURA: Yes. I remember what a beautiful voice you had.

JIM: When did you hear me sing?

[Voice Offstage in the Pause.]

VOICE [*offstage*]: O blow, ye winds, heigh-ho,
A-roving I will go!
I'm off to my love

With a boxing glove—
Ten thousand miles away!

JIM: You say you've heard me sing?

LAURA: Oh, yes! Yes, very often . . . I—don't suppose you remember me—at all?

JIM [*smiling doubtfully*]: You know I have an idea I've seen you before. I had that idea soon as you opened the door. It seemed almost like I was about to remember your name. But the name that I started to call you—wasn't a name! And so I stopped myself before I said it.

LAURA: Wasn't it—Blue Roses?

JIM [*springs up, grinning*]: Blue Roses! My gosh, yes—Blue Roses! That's what I had on my tongue when you opened the door! Isn't it funny what tricks your memory plays? I didn't connect you with the high school somehow or other. But that's where it was; it was high school. I didn't even know you were Shakespeare's sister! Gosh, I'm sorry.

LAURA: I didn't expect you to. You—barely knew me!

JIM: But we did have a speaking acquaintance, huh?

LAURA: Yes, we—spoke to each other.

JIM: When did you recognize me?

LAURA: Oh, right away!

JIM: Soon as I came in the door?

LAURA: When I heard your name I thought it was probably you. I knew that Tom used to know you a little in high school. So when you came in the door—Well, then I was—sure.

JIM: Why didn't you say something, then?

LAURA [*breathlessly*]: I didn't know what to say, I was—too surprised!

JIM: For goodness' sakes! You know, this sure is funny!

LAURA: Yes! Yes, isn't it, though . . .

JIM: Didn't we have a class in something together?

LAURA: Yes, we did.

JIM: What class was that?

LAURA: It was—singing—Chorus!

JIM: Aw!

LAURA: I sat across the aisle from you in the Aud.

JIM: Aw.

LAURA: Mondays, Wednesdays and Fridays.

JIM: Now I remember—you always came in late.

LAURA: Yes, it was so hard for me, getting upstairs. I had that brace on my leg—it clumped so loud!

JIM: I never heard any clumping.

LAURA [*wincing at the recollection*]:   To me it sounded like—thunder!

JIM: Well, well, well. I never even noticed.

LAURA: And everybody was seated before I came in. I had to walk in front of all those people. My seat was in the back row. I had to go clumping all the way up the aisle with everyone watching!

JIM: You shouldn't have been self-conscious.

LAURA: I know, but I was. It was always such a relief when the singing started.

JIM: Aw, yes. I've placed you now! I used to call you Blue Roses. How was it that I got started calling you that?

LAURA: I was out of school a little while with pleurosis. When I came back you asked me what was the matter. I said I had pleurosis—you thought I said Blue Roses. That's what you always called me after that!

JIM: I hope you didn't mind.

LAURA: Oh, no—I liked it. You see, I wasn't acquainted with many—people . . . .

JIM: As I remember you sort of stuck by yourself.

LAURA: I—I—never had much luck at—making friends.

JIM: I don't see why you wouldn't.

LAURA: Well, I—started out badly.

JIM: You mean being—

LAURA: Yes, it sort of—stood between me—

JIM: You shouldn't have let it!

LAURA: I know but it did, and—

JIM: You were shy with people!

LAURA: I tried not to be but never could—

JIM: Overcome it?

LAURA: No, I—I never could!

JIM: I guess being shy is something you have to work out of kind of gradually.

LAURA [*sorrowfully*]:   Yes—I guess it—

JIM: Takes time!

LAURA: Yes.

JIM: People are not so dreadful when you know them. That's what you have to remember! And everybody has problems, not just you, but practically everybody has got some problems. You think of yourself as having the only problems, as being the only one who is disappointed. But just look around you and you will see lots of people as disappointed as you are. For instance, I hoped when I was going to high school that I would be further along at this time, six years later, than I am now—You remember that wonderful write-up I had in *The Torch?*

LAURA: Yes! [*She rises and crosses to the table.*]

JIM: It said I was bound to succeed in anything I went into! [*Laura returns with the annual.*] Holy Jeez! *The Torch!* [*He accepts it reverently. They smiled across it with mutual wonder. Laura crouches beside him and they begin to turn through it. Laura's shyness is dissolving in his warmth.*]

LAURA: Here you are in *Pirates of Penzance!*

JIM [*wistfully*]:   I sang the baritone lead in that operatta.

LAURA [*rapidly*]:   So—*beautifully!*

JIM [*protesting*]:   Aw—

LAURA: Yes, yes—beautifully—beautifully!

JIM: You heard me?

LAURA: All three times!

JIM: No!

LAURA: Yes!

JIM: All three performances?

LAURA [*looking down*]:   Yes.

JIM: Why?

LAURA: I—wanted to ask you to—autograph my program.

JIM: Why didn't you ask me to?

LAURA: You were always surrounded by your own friends so much that I never had a chance to.

JIM: You should have just—

LAURA: Well, I—thought you might think I was—

JIM: Thought I might think you was—what?

LAURA: Oh—

JIM [*with reflective relish*]:   I was beleaguered by females in those days.

LAURA: You were terribly popular!

JIM: Yeah—

LAURA: You had such a—friendly way—

JIM: I was spoiled in high school.

LAURA: Everybody—liked you!

JIM: Including you?

LAURA: I—yes, I—I did, too—[*She gently closes the book in her lap.*]

JIM: Well, well, well!—Give me that program, Laura. [*She hands it to him. He signs it with a flourish.*] There you are—better late then never!

LAURA: Oh, I—what a—surprise!

JIM: My signature isn't worth very much right now. But some day—maybe—it will increase in value! Being disappointed is one thing and being discouraged is something else. I am disappointed but I'm not discouraged. I'm twenty-three years old. How old are you?

LAURA: I'll be twenty-four in June.

JIM: That's not old age!

LAURA: No, but—

JIM: You finished high school?

LAURA [*with difficulty*]: I didn't go back.

JIM: You mean you dropped out?

LAURA: I made bad grades in my final examinations. [*She rises and replaces the book and the program. Her voice strained.*] How is—Emily Meisenbach getting along?

JIM: Oh, that kraut-head!

LAURA: Why do you call her that?

JIM: That's what she was.

LAURA: You're not still—going with her?

JIM: I never see her.

LAURA: It said in the Personal Section that you were—engaged!

JIM: I know, but I wasn't impressed by that—propaganda!

LAURA: It wasn't—the truth?

JIM: Only in Emily's optimistic opinion!

LAURA: Oh—

[Legend: "What Have You Done Since High School?"]

[*Jim lights a cigarette and leans indolently back on his elbows smiling at Laura with a warmth and charm which light her inwardly with altar candles. She remains by the table and turns in her hands a piece of glass to cover her tumult.*]

JIM [*after several reflective puffs on a cigarette*]: What have you done since high school? [*She seems not to hear him.*] Huh? [*Laura looks up.*] I said what have you done since high school, Laura?

LAURA: Nothing much.

JIM: You must have been doing something these six long years.

LAURA: Yes.

JIM: Well, then, such as what?

LAURA: I took a business course at business college—

JIM: How did that work out?

LAURA: Well, not very—well—I had to drop out, it gave me—indigestion—

[*Jim laughs gently.*]

JIM: What are you doing now?

LAURA: I don't do anything—much. Oh, please don't think I sit around doing nothing! My glass collection takes up a good deal of my time. Glass is something you have to take good care of.

JIM: What did you say—about glass?

LAURA: Collection I said—I have one—[*She clears her throat and turns away again, acutely shy.*]

JIM [*abruptly*]: You know what I judge to be the trouble with you? Inferiority complex! Know what that is? That's what they call it when someone low-rates himself? I understand it because I had it, too. Although my case was not so aggravated as yours seems to be. I had it until I took up public speaking, developed my voice, and learned that I had an aptitude for science. Before that time I never thought of myself as being outstanding in any way whatsoever! Now I've never made a regular study of it, but I have a friend who says I can analyze people better than doctors that make a profession of it. I don't claim that to be necessarily true, but I can sure guess a person's psychology, Laura. [*Takes out his gum.*] Excuse me, Laura. I always take it out when the flavor is gone. I'll use this scrap of paper to wrap it in. I know how it is to get it stuck on a shoe. Yep—that's what I judge to be your principal trouble. A lack of confidence in yourself as a person. You don't have the proper amount of faith in yourself. I'm basing that fact on a number of your remarks and also on certain observations I've made. For instance that clumping you thought was so awful in high school. You say that you even dreaded to walk into class. You see what you did? You dropped out of school, you gave up an education because of a clump, which as far as I know was practically nonexistent! A little physical defect is what you have? Hardly noticeable even! Magnified thousands of times by imagination! You know what my strong advice to you is? Think of yourself as superior in some way!

LAURA: In what way would I think?

JIM: Why, man alive, Laura! Just look about you a little. What do you see? A world full of common people! All of 'em born and all of' em going to die! Which of them has one-tenth of your good points! Or mine! Or anyone else's, as far as that goes—Gosh! Everybody excels in some one thing. Some in many! [*Unconsciously glances at himself in the mirror.*] All you've got to do is discover in what! Take me, for instance. [*He adjusts his tie at the mirror.*] My interest happens to lie in electrodynamics. I'm taking a course in radio engineering at night school, Laura, on top of a fairly responsible job at the warehouse. I'm taking that course and studying public speaking.

LAURA: Ohhhh.

JIM: Because I believe in the future of television! [*Turning back to her.*] I wish to be ready to go up right along with it. Therefore I'm planning to get in on the ground floor. In fact, I've already made the right connections and all that remains is for the industry itself to get under way! Full steam—[*His eyes are starry.*] Knowledge—Zzzzzp! Money—Zzzzzzp! Power! That's the cycle democracy is built on! [*His attitude is convincingly dynamic. Laura stares at him, even her shyness eclipsed in her absolute wonder. He suddenly grins.*] I guess you think I think a lot of myself!

LAURA: No—o-o-o, I—

JIM: Now how about you? Isn't there something you take more interest in than anything else?

LAURA: Well, I do—as I said—have my—glass collection—

[*A peal of girlish laughter from the kitchen.*]

JIM: I'm not right sure I know what you're talking about. What kind of glass is it?

LAURA: Little articles of it, they're ornaments mostly! Most of them are little animals made out of glass, the tiniest little animals in the world. Mother calls them a glass menagerie! Here's an example of one, if you'd like to see it! This one is one of the oldest. It's nearly thirteen. [*He stretches out his hand.*] [*Music: "The Glass Menagerie."*] Oh, be careful—if you breathe, it breaks!

JIM: I'd better not take it. I'm pretty clumsy with things.

LAURA: Go on. I trust you with him! [*Places it in his palm.*] There now—you're holding him gently! Hold him over the light, he loves the light! You see how the light shines through him?

JIM: It sure does shine!

LAURA: I shouldn't be partial, but he is my favorite one.

JIM: What kind of thing is this one supposed to be?

LAURA: Haven't you noticed the single horn on his forehead?

JIM: A unicorn, huh?

LAURA: Mmm-hmmm!

JIM: Unicorns, aren't they extinct in the modern world?

LAURA: I know!

JIM: Poor little fellow, he must feel sort of lonesome.

LAURA [*smiling*]:   Well, if he does he doesn't complain about it. He stays on a shelf with some horses that don't have horns and all of them seem to get along nicely together.

JIM: How do you know?

LAURA [*lightly*]:   I haven't heard any arguments among them!

JIM [*grinning*]:   No arguments, huh? Well, that's a pretty good sign! Where shall I set him?

LAURA: Put him on the table. They all like a change of scenery once in a while!

JIM [*stretching*]:   Well, well, well, well—Look how big my shadow is when I stretch!

LAURA: Oh, oh, yes—it stretches across the ceiling!

JIM [*crossing to door*]:   I think it's stopped raining. [*Opens fire-escape door*] Where does the music come from?

LAURA: From the Paradise Dance Hall across the alley.

JIM: How about cutting the rug a little, Miss Wingfield?

LAURA: Oh, I—

JIM: Or is your program filled up? Let me have a look at it. [*Grasps imaginary card.*] Why, every dance is taken! I'll just have to scratch some out. [*Waltz Music: "La Golondrina."*] Ahhh, a waltz! [*He executes some sweeping turns by himself then holds his arms toward Laura.*]

LAURA [*breathlessly*]:   I—can't dance!

JIM: There you go, that inferiority stuff!

LAURA: I've never danced in my life!

JIM: Come on, try!

LAURA: Oh, but I'd step on you!

JIM: I'm not made out of glass.

LAURA: How—how—how do we start?

JIM: Just leave it to me. You hold your arms out a little.

LAURA: Like this?

JIM: A little bit higher. Right. Now don't tighten up, that's the main thing about it—relax.

LAURA [*laughing breathlessly*]: It's hard not to.

JIM: Okay.

LAURA: I'm afraid you can't budge me.

JIM: What do you bet I can't? [*He swings her into motion.*]

LAURA: Goodness, yes, you can!

JIM: Let yourself go, now, Laura, just let yourself go.

LAURA: I'm—

JIM: Come on!

LAURA: Trying!

JIM: Not so stiff—Easy does it!

LAURA: I know but I'm—

JIM: Loosen th' backbone! There now, that's a lot better.

LAURA: Am I?

JIM: Lots, lots better! [*He moves her about the room in a clumsy waltz.*]

LAURA: Oh, my!

JIM: Ha-ha!

LAURA: Goodness, yes you can!

JIM: Ha-ha-ha! [*They suddenly bump into the table, Jim stops.*] What did we hit on?

LAURA: Table.

JIM: Did something fall off it? I think—

LAURA: Yes.

JIM: I hope that it wasn't the little glass horse with the horn!

LAURA: Yes.

JIM: Aw, aw, aw. Is it broken?

LAURA: Now it is just like all the other horses.

JIM: It's lost its—

LAURA: Horn! It doesn't matter. Maybe it's a blessing in disguise.

JIM: You'll never forgive me. I bet that was your favorite piece of glass.

LAURA: I don't have favorites much. It's no tragedy, Freckles. Glass breaks so easily. No matter how careful you are. The traffic jars the shelves and things fall off them.

JIM: Still I'm awfully sorry that I was the cause.

LAURA [*smiling*]: I'll just imagine he had an operation. The horn was removed to make him feel less—freakish! [*They both laugh.*] Now he will feel more at home with the other horses, the ones that don't have horns . . .

JIM: Ha-ha, that's very funny! [*Suddenly serious.*] I'm glad to see that you have a sense of humor. You know—you're—well—very different! Surprisingly different from anyone else I know! [*His voice becomes soft and hesitant with a genuine feeling.*] Do you mind me telling you that? [*Laura is abashed beyond speech.*] You make me feel sort of—I don't know how to put it! I'm usually pretty good at expressing things, but—This is something that I don't know how to say! [*Laura touches her throat, clears it—turns the broken unicorn in her hands.*] [*Even softer.*] Has anyone ever told you that you were pretty? [*Pause: Music.*] [*Laura looks up slowly, with wonder, and shakes her head.*] Well, you are! In a very different way from anyone else. And all the nicer because of the difference, too. [*His voice becomes low and husky. Laura turns away, nearly faint with the novelty of her emotions.*] I wish that you were my sister. I'd teach you to have some confidence in yourself. The different people are not like other people, but being different is nothing to be ashamed of. Because other people are not such wonderful people. They're one hundred times one thousand. You're one times one! They walk all over the earth. You just stay here. They're common as—weeds, but—you—well, you're—Blue Roses!

[Image on Screen: Blue Roses.]
[Music Changes.]

LAURA: But blue is wrong for—roses . . .

JIM: It's right for you—You're—pretty!

LAURA: In what respect am I pretty?

JIM: In all respects—believe me! Your eyes—your hair—are pretty! Your hands are pretty! [*He catches hold of her hand.*] You think I'm making this up because I'm invited to dinner and have to be nice. Oh, I could do that! I could put on an act for you, Laura, and say lots of things without being very sincere. But this time I am. I'm talking to you sincerely. I happened to notice you had this inferiority complex that keeps you from feeling comfortable with people. Somebody needs to build your confidence up and make you proud instead of shy and turning away and—blushing—Somebody ought to—ought to—*kiss* you, Laura!

[*His hand slips slowly up her arm to her shoulder.*] [*Music Swells Tumultuously.*] [*He suddenly turns her about and kisses her on the* lips. *When he releases her Laura sinks on the sofa with a bright, dazed look. Jim backs away and fishes in his pocket for a cigarette.*] [*Legend on Screen: "Souvenir."*] Stumble-john! [*He lights the cigarette, avoiding her look. There is a peal of girlish laughter from Amanda in the kitchen. Laura slowly raises and opens her hand. It still contains the little broken glass animal. She looks at it with a tender, bewildered expression.*] Stumble-john! I shouldn't have done that—That was way off the beam. You don't smoke, do you? [*She looks up, smiling, not hearing the question. He sits besides her a little gingerly. She looks at him speechlessly—waiting. He coughs decorously and moves a little farther aside as he considers the situation and senses her feelings, dimly, with perturbation. Gently.*] Would you—care for a—mint? [*She doesn't seem to hear him but her look grows brighter even.*] Peppermint—Life Saver? My pocket's a regular drug store— wherever I go . . . [*He pops a mint in his mouth. Then gulps and decides to make a clean breast of it. He speaks slowly and gingerly.*] Laura, you know, if I had a sister like you, I'd do the same thing as Tom. I'd bring out fellows—introduce her to them. The right type of boys of a type to—appreciate her. Only—well—he made a mistake about me. Maybe I've got no call to be saying this. This may not have been the idea in having me over. But what if it was? There's nothing wrong about that. The only trouble is that in my case—I'm not in a situation to—do the right thing. I can't take down your number and say I'll phone. I can't call up next week and—ask for a date. I thought I had better explain the situation in case you misunderstood it and—hurt your feelings . . . . [*Pause. Slowly, very slowly, Laura's look changes, her eyes returning slowly from his to the ornament in her palm.*]

[*Amanda utters another gay laugh in the kitchen.*]

LAURA [*faintly*]:   You—won't—call again?

JIM: No, Laura. I can't. [*He rises from the sofa.*] As I was just explaining, I've—got strings on me, Laura, I've—been going steady! I go out all the time with a girl named Betty. She's a home-girl like you, and Catholic, and Irish, and in a great many ways we—get along fine. I met her last summer on a moonlight boat trip up the river to Alton, on the Majestic. Well—right away from the start it was—

love! [*Legend: "Love!"*] [*Laura sways slightly forward and grips the arm of the sofa. He fails to notice, now enrapt in his own comfortable being.*] Being in love has made a new man of me! [*Leaning stiffly forward, clutching the arm of the sofa, Laura struggles visibly with her storm. But Jim is oblivious, she is a long way off.*] The power of love is really pretty tremendous! Love is something that—changes the whole world, Laura! [*The storm abates a little and Laura leans back. He notices her again.*] It happened that Betty's aunt took sick, she got a wire and had to go to Centralia. So Tom—when he asked me to dinner—I naturally just accepted the invitation, not knowing that you—that he—that I—[*He stops awkwardly.*] Huh—I'm a stumble-john! [*He flops back on the sofa. The holy candles in the altar of Laura's face have been snuffed out! There is a look of almost infinite desolation. Jim glances at her uneasily.*] I wish that you would—say something. [*She bites her lip which was trembling and then bravely smiles. She opens her hand again on the broken glass ornament. Then she gently takes his hand and raises it level to her own. She carefully places the unicorm in the palm of his hand, then pushes his fingers closed upon it.*] What are you—doing that for? You want me to have him?—Laura? [*She nods.*] What for?

LAURA: A—souvenir . . .

[*She rises unsteadily and crouches beside the victrola to wind it up.*]

[Legend on Screen: "Things Have a Way of Turning Out So Badly."]
[Or Image: "Gentleman Caller Waving Good-Bye—Gaily."]

[*At this moment Amanda rushes brightly back in the front room. She bears a pitcher of fruit punch in an old-fashioned cut-glass pitcher and a plate of macaroons. The plate has a gold border and poppies painted on it.*]

AMANDA: Well, well, well! Isn't the air delightful after the shower? I've made you children a little liquid refreshment. [*Turns gaily to the gentleman caller.*] Jim, do you know that song about lemonade?
"Lemonade, lemonade
Made in the shade and stirred with a spade—
Good enough for any old maid!"

JIM [*uneasily*]:   Ha-ha! No—I never heard it.

AMANDA: Why, Laura! You look so serious!

JIM: We were having a serious conversation.

AMANDA: Good! Now you're better acquainted!

JIM [*uncertainly*]: Ha-ha! Yes.

AMANDA: You modern young people are much more serious-minded than my generation. I was so gay as a girl!

JIM: You haven't changed, Mrs. Wingfield.

AMANDA: Tonight I'm rejuvenated! The gaiety of the occasion, Mr. O'Connor! [*She tosses her head with a peal of laughter. Spills lemonade.*] Oooo! I'm baptizing myself!

JIM: Here—let me—

AMANDA [*setting the pitcher down.*]: There now. I discovered we had some maraschino cherries. I dumped them in, juice and all!

JIM: You shouldn't have gone to that trouble, Mrs. Wingfield.

AMANDA: Trouble, trouble? Why it was loads of fun! Didn't you hear me cutting up in the kitchen? I bet your ears were burning! I told Tom how outdone with him I was for keeping you to himself so long a time! He should have brought you over much, much sooner! Well, now that you've found your way, I want you to be a very frequent caller! Not just occasional but all the time. Oh, we're going to have a lot of gay times together! I see them coming! Mmm, just breathe that air! So fresh, and the moon's so pretty! I'll skip back out—I know where my place is when young folks are having a—serious conversation!

JIM: Oh, don't go out, Mrs. Wingfield. The fact of the matter is I've got to be going.

AMANDA: Going, now? You're joking! Why, it's only the shank of the evening, Mr. O'Connor.

JIM: Well, you now how it is.

AMANDA: You mean you're a young workingman and have to keep workingmen's hours. We'll let you off early tonight. But only on the condition that next time you stay later. What's the best night for you? Isn't Saturday night the best night for you workingmen?

JIM: I have a couple of time-clocks to punch, Mrs. Wingfield. One at morning, another one at night.

AMANDA: My, but you are ambitious! You work at night, too?

JIM: No, Ma'am, not work but—Betty! [*He crosses deliberately to pick up his hat. The band at the Paradise Dance Hall goes into a tender waltz.*]

AMANDA: Betty? Betty? Who's—Betty! [*There is an ominous cracking sound in the sky.*]

JIM: Oh, just a girl. The girl I go steady with! [*He smiles charmingly. The sky falls.*]

[Legend: "The Sky Falls"]

AMANDA [*a long-drawn exhalation*]: Ohhhh . . . Is it a serious romance, Mr. O'Connor?

JIM: We're going to be married the second Sunday in June.

AMANDA: Ohhhh—how nice! Tom didn't mention that you were engaged to be married.

JIM: The cat's not out of the bag at the warehouse yet. You know how they are. They call you Romeo and stuff like that. [*He stops at the oval mirror to put on his hat. He carefully shapes the brim and the crown to give a discreetly dashing effect.*] It's been a wonderful evening, Mrs. Wingfield. I guess this is what they mean by Southern hospitality.

AMANDA: It really wasn't anything at all.

JIM: I hope it don't seem like I'm rushing off. But I promised Betty I'd pick her up at the Wabash depot, an' by the time I get my jalopy down there her train'll be in. Some women are pretty upset if you keep 'em waiting.

AMANDA: Yes, I know—The tyranny of women! [*Extends her hand.*] Goodbye, Mr. O'Connor. I wish you luck—and happiness—and success! All three of them, and so does Laura!—Don't you, Laura?

LAURA: Yes!

JIM [*taking her hand*]: Goodbye, Laura. I'm certainly going to treasure that souvenir. And don't you forget the good advice I gave you. [*Raises his voice to a cheery shout.*] So long, Shakespeare! Thanks again, ladies—Good night!

[*He grins and ducks jauntily out. Still bravely grimacing, Amanda closes the door on the gentleman caller. Then she turns back to the room with a puzzled expression. She and Laura don't dare to face each other. Laura crouches beside the victrola to wind it.*]

AMANDA [*faintly*]: Things have a way of turning out so badly. I don't believe that I would play the victrola. Well, well—well—Our gentleman caller was engaged to be married! Tom!

TOM [*from back*]: Yes, Mother?

AMANDA: Come in here a minute. I want to tell you something aw-fully funny.

TOM [*enters with macaroon and a glass of the lemonade*]:   Has the gen-tleman caller gotten away already?

AMANDA: The gentleman caller has made an early departure. What a wonderful joke you played on us!

TOM: How do you mean?

AMANDA: You didn't mention that he was engaged to be married.

TOM: Jim? Engaged?

AMANDA: That's what he just informed us.

TOM: I'll be jiggered! I didn't know about that.

AMANDA: That seems very peculiar.

TOM: What's peculiar about it?

AMANDA: Didn't you call him your best friend down at the warehouse?

TOM: He is, but how did I know?

AMANDA: It seems extremely peculiar that you wouldn't know your best friend was going to be married!

TOM: The warehouse is where I work, not where I know things about people!

AMANDA: You don't know things anywhere! You live in a dream; you manufacture illusions! [*He crosses to door.*] Where are you going?

TOM: I'm going to the movies.

AMANDA: That's right, now that you've had us make such fools of ourselves. The effort, the preparations, all the expense! The new floor lamp, the rug, the clothes for Laura! All for what? To entertain some other girl's fiancé! Go to the movies, go! Don't think about us, a mother deserted, an unmarried sister who's crippled and has no job! Don't let anything interfere with your selfish pleasure! Just go, go, go—to the movies!

TOM: All right, I will! The more you shout about my selfishness to me the quicker I'll go, and I won't go to the movies!

AMANDA: Go, then! Then go to the moon—you selfish dreamer!

Tom smashes his glass on the floor. He plunges out on the fire-escape, slamming the door. Laura screams—cut by door.

Dance-hall music up. Tom goes to the rail and grips it desper-ately, lifting his face in the chill white moonlight penetrating the narrow abyss of the alley.

[Legend on Screen: "And So Good-Bye . . ."]

[*Tom's closing speech is timed with the interior pantomime. The interior scene is played as though viewed through sound-proof glass. Amanda appears to be making a comforting speech to Laura who is huddled upon the sofa. Now that we cannot hear the mother's speech, her silliness is gone and she has dignity and tragic beauty. Laura's dark hair hides her face until at the end of the speech she lifts it to smile at her mother. Amanda's gestures are slow and graceful, almost dancelike, as she comforts her daughter. At the end of her speech she glances a moment at the father's picture—then withdraws through the portieres. At close of Tom's speech, Laura blows out the candles, ending the play.*]

TOM: I didn't go to the moon, I went much further—for time is the longest distance between two places—Not long after that I was fired for writing a poem on the lid of a shoe-box. I left Saint Louis. I descended the steps of this fire-escape for a last time and followed, from then on, in my father's footsteps, attempting to find in motion what was lost in space—I traveled around a great deal. The cities swept about me like dead leaves, leaves that were brightly colored but torn away from the branches. I would have stopped, but I was pursued by something. It always came upon me unawares, taking me altogether by surprise. Perhaps it was a familiar bit of music. Perhaps it was only a piece of transparent glass— Perhaps I am walking along a street at night, in some strange city, before I have found companions. I pass the lighted window of a shop where perfume is sold. The window is filled with pieces of colored glass, tiny transparent bottles in delicate colors, like bits of a shattered rainbow. Then all at once my sister touches my shoulder. I turn around and look into her eyes . . . Oh, Laura, Laura, I tried to leave you behind me, but I am more faithful than I intended to be! I reach for a cigarette, I cross the street, I run into the movies or a bar, I buy a drink, I speak to the nearest stranger— anything that can blow your candles out! [*Laura bends over the candles.*]—for nowadays the world is lit by lightning! Blow out your candles, Laura—and so goodbye . . .

[*She blows the candles out.*]

[The Scene Dissolves.]

—1944

Edward Albee began his career as the author of one-act plays that were performed off-Broadway and in Europe. The Zoo Story was first produced in Berlin on a double bill with another one-act play by Samuel Beckett, and Albee was immediately recognized as one of the earliest American playwrights associated with the theater of the absurd. Albee first came to the attention of mainstream audiences with the 1962 Broadway production of the full-length Who's Afraid of Virginia Woolf?, *which was later made into a successful film by Mike Nichols, starring Elizabeth Taylor and Richard Burton. Since then, Albee's work has been frequently performed, and three plays—*A Delicate Balance *(1966),* Seascape *(1975), and* Three Tall Women *(1994)—have won Pulitzer Prizes. In 1996, Albee was a Kennedy Center Honoree and was awarded a National Medal of the Arts. Now in his 80s, Albee continues teaching at the University of Houston's Edward Albee New Playwrights Workshop and has recently won a Tony Award for best play for* The Goat, or Who Is Sylvia? *(2002).* Who's Afraid of Virginia Woolf? *was successfully revived on Broadway in 2005, starring Kathleen Turner. Now in his 80s, Albee remains a potent force in American drama.*

The Sandbox

Characters

The Young Man, *25, a good-looking, well-built boy in a bathing suit*
Mommy, *55, a well-dressed, imposing woman*
Daddy, *60, a small man; gray, thin*
Grandma, *86, a tiny, wizened woman with bright eyes*
The Musician, *no particular age, but young would be nice*

Note: When, in the course of the play, Mommy and Daddy call each other by these names, there should be no suggestion of regionalism. These names are of empty affection and point up the pre-senility and vacuity of their children.

Scene: *A bare stage, with only the following: Near the footlights, far stage-right, two simple chairs set side by side, facing the audience; near the footlights, far stage-left, a chair facing stage-right with a music stand before it; farther back, and stage-center, slightly elevated and raked, a large child's sandbox with a toy pail and shovel; the background is the sky, which alters from brightest day to deepest night.*

At the beginning, it is brightest day, the Young Man is alone on stage, to the rear of the sandbox, and to one side. He is doing calisthenics; he does calisthenics until quite at the very end of the play. These calisthenics, employing the arms only, should suggest the beating and fluttering of wings. The Young Man is, after all, the Angel of Death.

Mommy and Daddy enter from the stage-left, Mommy first.

MOMMY [*motioning to Daddy*]:   Well, here we are; this is the beach.

DADDY [*whining*]:   I'm cold.

MOMMY [*dismissing him with a little laugh*]:   Don't be silly; it's as warm as toast. Look at that nice young man over there: *he* doesn't think it's cold. [*Waves to the Young Man.*] Hello.

YOUNG MAN [*with an endearing smile*]:   Hi!

MOMMY [*looking about*]:   This will do perfectly . . . don't you think so, Daddy? There's sand there . . . and the water beyond. What do you think, Daddy?

DADDY [*vaguely*]:   Whatever you say, Mommy.

MOMMY [*with the same little laugh*]:   Well, of course . . . whatever I say. Then, it's settled, is it?

DADDY [*shrugs*]:   She's your mother, not mine.

MOMMY: I know she's my mother. What do you take me for? [*A pause.*] All right, now; let's get on with it. [*She shouts into the wings, stage-left.*] You! Out there! You can come in now.

The Musician enters, seats himself in the chair, stage-left, places music on the music stand, is ready to play. Mommy nods approvingly.

MOMMY: Very nice; very nice. Are you ready, Daddy? Let's go get Grandma.

DADDY: Whatever you say, Mommy.

MOMMY [*leading the way out, stage-left*]:   Of course, whatever I say. [*To the Musician.*] You can begin now.

The Musician begins playing; Mommy and Daddy exit; the Musician, all the while playing nods to the Young Man.

YOUNG MAN [*with the same endearing smile*]:   Hi!

After a moment, Mommy and Daddy re-enter, carrying Grandma. She is borne in by their hands under her armpits; she is quite rigid; her legs are drawn up; her feet do not touch the ground; the expression on her ancient face is that of puzzlement and fear.

DADDY: Where do we put her?

MOMMY [*the same little laugh*]: Wherever I say, of course. Let me see ... well ... all right, over there ... in the sandbox. [*Pause.*] Well, what are you waiting for Daddy? ... The sandbox!

Together they carry Grandma over to the sandbox and more or less dump her in.

GRANDMA [*righting herself to a sitting position; her voice a cross between a baby's laugh and cry*]: Ahhhhhh! Graaaaa!

DADDY [*dusting himself*]: What do we do now?

MOMMY [*to the Musician*]: You can stop now. [*The Musician stops.*] [*Back to Daddy.*] What do you mean, what do we do now? We go over there and sit down, of course. [*To the Young Man.*] Hello there.

YOUNG MAN [*again smiling*]: Hi!

Mommy and Daddy move to the chairs, stage-right, and sit down. A pause.

GRANDMA [*same as before*]: Ahhhhhh! Ahhaaaaaa! Graaaaaa!

DADDY: Do you think ... do you think she's ... comfortable?

MOMMY [*impatiently*]: How would I know?

DADDY [*pause*]: What do we do now?

MOMMY [*as if remembering*]: We ... wait. We ... sit here ... and we wait ... that's what we do.

DADDY [*after a pause*]: Shall we talk to each other?

MOMMY [*with that little laugh; picking something off her dress*]: Well, *you* can talk, if you want to ... if you can think of anything to *say* ... if you can think of anything *new*.

DADDY [*thinks*]: No ... I suppose not.

MOMMY [*with a triumphant laugh*]: Of course not!

GRANDMA [*banging the toy shovel against the pail*]: Haaaaaa! Ah-haaaaaa!

MOMMY [*out over the audience*]: Be quiet, Grandma ... just be quiet, and wait.

Grandma throws a shovelful of sand at Mommy.

MOMMY [*still out over the audience*]: She's throwing sand at me! You stop that, Grandma; you stop throwing sand at Mommy! [*To Daddy.*] She's throwing sand at me.

Daddy looks around at Grandma, who screams at him.

GRANDMA: GRAAAAAA!

MOMMY: Don't look at her. Just . . . sit here . . . be very still . . . and wait. [*To the Musician.*] You . . . uh . . . you go ahead and do whatever it is you do.

The Musician plays. Mommy and Daddy are fixed, staring out beyond the audience. Grandma looks at them, looks at the Musician, looks at the sandbox, throws down the shovel.

GRANDMA: Ah-haaaaaa! Graaaaaa! [*Looks for reaction; gets none.*] Now . . . [*directly to the audience.*] Honestly! What a way to treat an old woman! Drag her out of the house . . . stick her in a car . . . bring her out here from the city . . . dump her in a pile of sand . . . and leave her here to set. I'm eighty-six years old! I was married when I was seventeen. To a farmer. He died when I was thirty. [*To the Musician.*] Will you stop that, please?

The Musician stops playing.

I'm a feeble old woman . . . how do you expect anybody to hear me over that peep! peep! peep! [*To herself.*] There's no respect around here. [*To the Young Man.*] There's no respect around here!

YOUNG MAN [*same smile*]: Hi!

GRANDMA [*after a pause, a mild double-take, continues, to the audience*]: My husband died when I was thirty [*indicates Mommy*], and I had to raise that big cow over there all by my lonesome. You can imagine what *that* was like. Lordy! [*To the Young Man.*] Where'd they get *you*?

YOUNG MAN: Oh . . . I've been around for a while.

GRANDMA: I'll bet you have! Heh, heh, heh. Will you look at you!

YOUNG MAN [*flexing his muscles*]: Isn't that something? [*Continues his calisthenics.*]

GRANDMA: Boy, oh boy; I'll say. Pretty good.

YOUNG MAN [*sweetly*]: I'll say.

GRANDMA: Where ya from?

YOUNG MAN: Southern California.

GRANDMA [*nodding*]: Figgers, figgers. What's your name, honey?

YOUNG MAN: I don't know . . .

GRANDMA [*to the audience*]: Bright, too!

YOUNG MAN: I mean . . . I mean, they haven't given me one yet . . . the studio . . .

GRANDMA: [*giving him the once-over*]. You don't say . . . you don't say. Well . . . uh, I've got to talk some more . . . don't you go 'way.

YOUNG MAN: Oh, no.

GRANDMA [*turning her attention back to the audience*]:   Fine; fine. [*Then, once more, back to the Young Man.*] You're ... you're an actor, hunh?

YOUNG MAN [*beaming*]:   Yes. I am.

GRANDMA [*to the audience again; shrugs*]:   I'm smart that way. *Anyhow,* I had to raise ... that over there all by my lonesome; and what's next to her there ... that's what she married. Rich? I tell you ... money, money, money. They took me off the *farm* ... which was real decent of them ... and they moved me into the big town house with *them* ... fixed a nice place for me under the stove ... gave me an army blanket ... and my own dish ... my very own dish! So, what have I got to complain about? Nothing, of course, I'm not complaining. [*She looks up at the sky, shouts to someone offstage.*] Shouldn't it be getting dark now, dear?

The lights dim; night comes on. The Musician begins to play; it becomes deepest night. There are spots on all the players, including the Young Man, who is, of course, continuing his calisthenics.

DADDY [*stirring*]:   It's nighttime.

MOMMY: Shhhh. Be still ... wait.

DADDY [*whining*]:   It's so hot.

MOMMY: Shhhhhh. Be still ... wait.

GRANDMA [*to herself*]:   That's better. Night. [*To the Musician.*] Honey, do you play all through this part?

The Musician nods.

Well, keep it nice and soft; that's a good boy.

The Musician nods again; plays softly.

That's nice.

There is an off-stage rumble.

DADDY [*starting*]:   What was that?

MOMMY [*beginning to weep*]:   It was nothing.

DADDY: It was ... it was ... thunder ... or a wave breaking ... or something.

MOMMY: [*whispering, through her tears*]:   It was an off-stage rumble ... and you know what *that* means ...

DADDY: I forget. . . .

MOMMY [*barely able to talk*]: It means the time has come for poor Grandma . . . and I can't bear it!

DADDY: [*vacantly*]: I . . . I suppose you've got to be brave.

GRANDMA [*mocking*]: That's right, kid; be brave. You'll bear up; you'll get over it.

Another off-stage rumble . . . louder.

MOMMY: Ohhhhhhhhhh . . . poor Grandma . . . poor Grandma. . . .

GRANDMA [*to Mommy*]: I'm fine! I'm all right! It hasn't happened yet!

A violent off-stage rumble. All the lights go out, save the spot on the Young Man; the Musician stops playing.

MOMMY: Ohhhhhhhhhh. . . . Ohhhhhhhhhh. . . .

Silence.

GRANDMA: Don't put the lights up yet . . . I'm not ready; I'm not quite ready. [*Silence.*] All right, dear . . . I'm about done.

The lights come up again, to brightest day; the Musician begins to play. Grandma is discovered, still in the sandbox, lying on her side, propped up on an elbow, half covered, busily shoveling sand over herself.

GRANDMA [*muttering*]: I don't know how I'm supposed to do anything with this goddam toy shovel. . . .

DADDY: Mommy! It's daylight!

MOMMY [*brightly*]: So it is! Well! Our long night is over. We must put away our tears, take off our mourning . . . and face the future. It's our duty.

GRANDMA [*still shoveling; mimicking*]: . . . take off our mourning . . . face the future. . . . Lordy!

Mommy and Daddy rise, stretch. Mommy waves to the young man.

YOUNG MAN [*with that smile*]: Hi!

Grandma plays dead. [!] Mommy and Daddy go over to look at her; she is a little more than half buried in the sand; the toy shovel is in her hands, which are crossed on her breast.

MOMMY [*before the sandbox; shaking her head*]: Lovely! It's . . . it's hard to be sad . . . she looks . . . so happy. [*With pride and conviction.*] It pays to do things well. [*To the Musician.*] All right, you can stop now, if you want to. I mean, stay around for a swim, or something; it's all right with us. [*She sighs heavily.*] Well, Daddy . . . off we go.

DADDY: Brave Mommy!

MOMMY: Brave Daddy!

They exit, stage-left.

GRANDMA [*after they leave; lying quite still*]: It pays to do things well. . . . Boy, oh boy! [*She tries to sit up*] . . . well, kids . . . [*but she finds she can't*] . . . I . . . I can't get up, I . . . I can't move. . . .

The Young Man stops his calisthenics, nods to the Musician, walks over to Grandma, kneels down by the sandbox.

GRANDMA: I . . . can't move. . . .

YOUNG MAN: Shhhhh . . . be very still. . . .

GRANDMA: I . . . I can't move. . . .

YOUNG MAN: Uh . . . ma'am; I . . . I have a line here.

GRANDMA: Oh, I'm sorry, sweetie; you go right ahead.

YOUNG MAN: I am . . . uh . . .

GRANDMA: Take your time, dear.

YOUNG MAN [*prepares; delivers the line like a real amateur*]: I am the Angel of Death. I am . . . uh . . . I am come for you.

GRANDMA: What . . . wha . . . [*Then, with resignation.*] . . . ohhhh . . . ohhhh, I see.

The Young Man bends over, kisses Grandma gently on the forehead.

GRANDMA [*her eyes closed, her hands folded on her breast again, the shovel between her hands, a sweet smile on her face*]: Well . . . that was very nice, dear . . .

YOUNG MAN [*still kneeling*]: Shhhhhh . . . be still. . . .

GRANDMA: What I mean was . . . you did that very well, dear. . . .

YOUNG MAN [*blushing*]: . . . oh . . .

GRANDMA: No; I mean it. You've got that . . . you've got a quality.

YOUNG MAN [*with his endearing smile*]: Oh . . . thank you; thank you very much . . . ma'am.

GRANDMA [*slowly; softly—as the Young Man puts his hands on top of Grandma's*]: You're . . . you're welcome . . . dear.

Tableau. The Musician continues to play as the curtain slowly comes down.

Curtain

Athol Fugard was born in Middelburg, Cape Province, South Africa, and was educated at the University of Cape Town. Growing up during the period of South African apartheid, Fugard both resisted and participated in the segregationist policies of the government, even insisting, at one point, that the family servants call him Master Harold (his given first name) and, in a moment of anger, spitting on one with whom he had been especially close. As he later said to an interviewer, "I think at a fairly early age I became suspicious of what the system was trying to do to me. . . . I became conscious of what attitudes it was trying to implant in me and what prejudices it was trying to pass on to me." Fugard founded the first important black theatrical company in South Africa, and he gained early prominence in his native country by his exploration of racial issues. While Fugard does not consider himself a political writer, his depictions of the interplay of black and white lives made him a controversial figure as a critic of apartheid. "Master Harold". . . and the boys is clearly an autobiographical work, for Fugard's father was a wounded war veteran, and his mother helped to support the family by running a tea room. After leaving college to travel to the Far East as a crew member of a tramp steamer, Fugard at first attempted to write novels but soon turned to the theater. Fugard began to produce his plays in the mid-1950s, and the New York production of The Blood Knot in 1964 established his American reputation. "Master Harold" . . . and the boys was first produced in New Haven, Connecticut, in 1982, and soon enjoyed a successful Broadway run. Since the end of the apartheid era, Fugard has continued to write plays and autobiographical memoirs. He has often been mentioned as a possible recipient of the Nobel Prize.

"Master Harold" . . . and the boys

Characters

Hally
Sam
Willie

Scene: *The St. George's Park Tea Room on a wet and windy Port Elizabeth afternoon.*

Tables and chairs have been cleared and are stacked on one side except for one which stands apart with a single chair. On this table a knife, fork, spoon and side plate in anticipation of a simple meal, together with a pile of comic books.

Other elements: a serving counter with a few stale cakes under glass and a not very impressive display of sweets, cigarettes and cool drinks, etc.; a few cardboard advertising handouts—Cadbury's Chocolate, Coca-Cola—and a blackboard on which an untrained hand has chalked up the prices of Tea, Coffee, Scones, Milkshakes—all flavors—and Cool Drinks; a few sad ferns in pots; a telephone; an old-style jukebox.

There is an entrance on one side and an exit into a kitchen on the other.

Leaning on the solitary table, his head cupped in one hand as he pages through one of the comic books, is Sam. A black man in his mid-forties. He wears the white coat of a waiter. Behind him on his knees, mopping down the floor with a bucket of water and a rag, is Willie. Also black and about the same age as Sam. He has his sleeves and trousers rolled up.

The year: 1950

WILLIE [*Singing as he works*]:
"She was scandalizin' my name,
She took my money
She called me honey
But she was scandalizin' my name.
Called it love but was playin' a game . . ."

He gets up and moves the bucket. Stands thinking for a moment, then, raising his arms to hold an imaginary partner, he launches into an intricate ballroom dance step. Although a mildly comic figure, he reveals a reasonable degree of accomplishment.

Hey, Sam.

Sam, absorbed in the comic book, does not respond.

Hey, Boet Sam!

Sam looks up.

I'm getting it. The quickstep. Look now and tell me. [*He repeats the step*] Well?

SAM [*Encouragingly*]:   Show me again.

WILLIE: Okay, count for me.

SAM: Ready?

WILLIE: Ready.

SAM: Five, six, seven, eight . . . [*Willie starts to dance*] A-n-d one two three four . . . and one two three four . . . [*Ad libbing as Willie dances*] Your shoulders, Willie . . . your shoulders! Don't look down! Look happy, Willie! Relax, Willie!

WILLIE [*Desperate but still dancing*]:   I am relax.

SAM: No, you're not.

WILLIE [*He falters*]:   Ag no man, Sam! Mustn't talk. You make me make mistakes.

SAM: But you're too stiff.

WILLIE: Yesterday I'm not straight . . . today I'm too stiff!

SAM: Well, you are. You asked me and I'm telling you.

WILLIE: Where?

SAM: Everywhere. Try to glide through it.

WILLIE: Glide?

SAM: Ja, make it smooth. And give it more style. It must look like you're enjoying yourself.

WILLIE [*Emphatically*]:   I wasn't.

SAM: Exactly.

WILLIE: How can I enjoy myself? Not straight, too stiff and now it's also glide, give it more style, make it smooth. . . . Haai! Is hard to remember all those things, Boet Sam.

SAM: That's your trouble. You're trying too hard.

WILLIE: I try hard because it *is* hard.

SAM: But don't let me see it. The secret is to make it look easy. Ballroom must look happy, Willie, not like hard work. It must . . . Ja! . . . it must look like romance.

WILLIE: Now another one! What's romance?

SAM: Love story with happy ending. A handsome man in tails, and in his arms, smiling at him, a beautiful lady in evening dress!

WILLIE: Fred Astaire, Ginger Rogers.

SAM: You got it. Tapdance or ballroom, it's the same. Romance. In two weeks' time when the judges look at you and Hilda, they must see a man and a woman who are dancing their way to a happy ending. What I saw was you holding her like you were frightened she was going to run away.

WILLIE: Ja! Because that is what she wants to do! I got no romance left for Hilda anymore, Boet Sam.

SAM: Then pretend. When you put your arms around Hilda, imagine she is Ginger Rogers.

WILLIE: With no teeth? You try.

SAM: Well, just remember, there's only two weeks left.

WILLIE: I know, I know! [*To the jukebox*] I do it better with music. You got sixpence for Sarah Vaughan?

SAM: That's a slow foxtrot. You're practicing the quick-step.

WILLIE: I'll practice slow foxtrot.

SAM [*Shaking his head*]: It's your turn to put money in the jukebox.

WILLIE: I only got bus fare to go home. [*He returns disconsolately to his work*] Love story and happy ending! She's doing it all right, Boet Sam, but is not me she's giving happy endings. Fuckin' whore! Three nights now she doesn't come practice. I wind up gramophone, I get record ready and I sit and wait. What happens? Nothing. Ten o'clock I start dancing with my pillow. You try and practice romance by yourself, Boet Sam. Struesgod, she doesn't come tonight I take back my dress and ballroom shoes and I find me new partner. Size twenty-six. Shoes size seven. And now she's also making trouble for me with the baby again. Reports me to Child Wellfed, that I'm not giving her money. She lies! Every week I am giving her money for milk. And how do I know is my baby? Only his hair looks like me. She's fucking around all the time I turn my back. Hilda Samuels is a bitch! [*Pause*] Hey, Sam!

SAM: Ja.

WILLIE: You listening?

SAM: Ja.

WILLIE: So what you say?

SAM: About Hilda?

WILLIE: Ja.

SAM: When did you last give her a hiding?

WILLIE [*Reluctantly*]: Sunday night.

SAM: And today is Thursday.

WILLIE [*He knows what's coming*]: Okay.

SAM: Hiding on Sunday night, then Monday, Tuesday and Wednesday she doesn't come to practice . . . and you are asking me why?

WILLIE: I said okay, Boet Sam!

SAM: You hit her too much. One day she's going to leave you for good.

WILLIE: So? She makes me the hell-in too much.

SAM [*Emphasizing his point*]: *Too* much and *too* hard. You had the same trouble with Eunice.

WILLIE: Because she also make the hell-in, Boet Sam. She never got the steps right. Even the waltz.

SAM: Beating her up every time she makes a mistake in the waltz? [*Shaking his head*] No, Willie! That takes the pleasure out of ballroom dancing.

WILLIE: Hilda is not too bad with the waltz, Boet Sam. Is the quickstep where the trouble starts.

SAM [*Teasing him gently*]: How's your pillow with the quickstep?

WILLIE [*Ignoring the tease*]: Good! And why? Because it got no legs. That's her trouble. She can't move them quick enough, Boet Sam. I start the record and before halfway Count Basie is already winning. Only time we catch up with him is when gramophone runs down.

Sam laughs.

Haaikona, Boet Sam, is not funny.

SAM [*Snapping his fingers*]: I got it! Give her a handicap.

WILLIE: What's that?

SAM: Give her a ten-second start and then let Count Basie go. Then I put my money on her. Hot favorite in the Ballroom Stakes: Hilda Samuels ridden by Willie Malopo.

WILLIE [*Turning away*]: I'm not talking to you no more.

SAM [*Relenting*]: Sorry, Willie . . .

WILLIE: It's finish between us.

SAM: Okay, okay . . . I'll stop.

WILLIE: You can also fuck off.

SAM: Willie, listen! I want to help you!

WILLIE: No more jokes?

SAM: I promise.

WILLIE: Okay. Help me.

SAM [*His turn to hold an imaginary partner*]: Look and learn. Feet together. Back straight. Body relaxed. Right hand placed gently in the small of her back and wait for the music. Don't start worrying about making mistakes or the judges or the other competitors. It's just you, Hilda and the music, and you're going to have a good time. What Count Basie do you play?

WILLIE: "You the cream in my coffee, you the salt in my stew."

SAM: Right. Give it to me in strict tempo.

WILLIE: Ready?

SAM: Ready.

WILLIE: A-n-d . . . [*Singing*]
"You the cream in my coffee.
You the salt in my stew.

You will always be my necessity.
I'd be lost without
   you. . . ." [etc.]

Sam launches into the quickstep. He is obviously a much more accomplished dancer than Willie. Hally enters. A seventeen-year-old white boy. Wet raincoat and school case. He stops and watches Sam. The demonstration comes to an end with a flourish. Applause from Hally and Willie.

HALLY: Bravo! No question about it. First place goes to Mr. Sam Semela.

WILLIE [*In total agreement*]:   You was gliding with style, Boet Sam.

HALLY [*Cheerfully*]:   How's it, chaps?

SAM: Okay, Hally.

WILLIE [*Springing to attention like a soldier and saluting*]:   At your service, Master Harold!

HALLY: Not long to the big event, hey!

SAM: Two weeks.

HALLY: You nervous?

SAM: No.

HALLY: Think you stand a chance?

SAM: Let's just say I'm ready to go out there and dance.

HALLY: It looked like it. What about you, Willie?

Willie groans.

What's the matter?

SAM: He's got leg trouble.

HALLY [*Innocently*]:   Oh, sorry to hear that, Willie.

WILLIE: Boet Sam! You promised. [*Willie returns to his work*]

Hally deposits his school case and takes off his raincoat. His clothes are a little neglected and untidy: black blazer with school badge, gray flannel trousers in need of an ironing, khaki shirt and tie, black shoes. Sam has fetched a towel for Hally to dry his hair.

HALLY: God, what a lousy bloody day. It's coming down cats and dogs out there. Bad for business, chaps . . . [*Conspiratorial whisper*] . . . but it also means we're in for a nice quiet afternoon.

SAM: You can speak loud. Your Mom's not here.

HALLY: Out shopping?

SAM: No. The hospital.

HALLY: But it's Thursday. There's no visiting on Thursday afternoons. Is my Dad okay?

SAM: Sounds like it. In fact, I think he's going home.

HALLY [*Stopped short by Sam's remark*]: What do you mean?

SAM: The hospital phoned.

HALLY: To say what?

SAM: I don't know. I just heard your Mom talking.

HALLY: So what makes you say he's going home?

SAM: It sounded as if they were telling her to come and fetch him.

Hally thinks about what Sam has said for a few seconds.

HALLY: When did she leave?

SAM: About an hour ago. She said she would phone you. Want to eat?

Hally doesn't respond.

Hally, want your lunch?

HALLY: I suppose so. [*His mood has changed*] What's on the menu? . . . as if I don't know.

SAM: Soup, followed by meat pie and gravy.

HALLY: Today's?

SAM: No.

HALLY: And the soup?

SAM: Nourishing pea soup.

HALLY: Just the soup. [*The pile of comic books on the table*] And these?

SAM: For your Dad. Mr. Kempston brought them.

HALLY: You haven't been reading them, have you?

SAM: Just looking.

HALLY [*Examining the comics*]: Jungle Jim . . . Batman and Robin . . . Tarzan . . . God, what rubbish! Mental pollution. Take them away.

Sam exits waltzing into the kitchen. Hally turns to Willie.

HALLY: Did you hear my Mom talking on the telephone, Willie?

WILLIE: No, Master Hally. I was at the back.

HALLY: And she didn't say anything to you before she left?

WILLIE: She said I must clean the floors.

HALLY: I mean about my Dad.

WILLIE: She didn't say nothing to me about him, Master Hally.

HALLY [*With conviction*]: No! It can't be. They said he needed at least another three weeks of treatment. Sam's definitely made a mistake.

[*Rummages through his school case, finds a book and settles down at the table to read*] So, Willie!

WILLIE: Yes, Master Hally! Schooling okay today?

HALLY: Yes, okay. . . . [*He thinks about it*] . . . No, not really. Ag, what's the difference? I don't care. And Sam says you've got problems.

WILLIE: Big problems.

HALLY: Which leg is sore?

Willie groans.

Both legs.

WILLIE: There is nothing wrong with my legs. Sam is just making jokes.

HALLY: So then you *will* be in the competition.

WILLIE: Only if I can find me a partner.

HALLY: But what about Hilda?

SAM [*Returning with a bowl of soup*]: She's the one who's got trouble with her legs.

HALLY: What sort of trouble, Willie?

SAM: From the way he describes it, I think the lady has gone a bit lame.

HALLY: Good God! Have you taken her to see a doctor?

SAM: I think a vet would be better.

HALLY: What do you mean?

SAM: What do you call it again when a racehorse goes very fast?

HALLY: Gallop?

SAM: That's it!

WILLIE: Boet Sam!

HALLY: "A gallop down the homestretch to the winning post." But what's that got to do with Hilda?

SAM: Count Basie always gets there first.

Willie lets fly with his slop rag. It misses Sam and hits Hally.

HALLY [*Furious*]: For Christ's sake, Willie! What the hell do you think you're doing!

WILLIE: Sorry, Master Hally, but it's him. . . .

HALLY: Act your bloody age! [*Hurls the rag back at Willie*] Cut out the nonsense now and get on with your work. And you too, Sam. Stop fooling around.

Sam moves away.

No. Hang on. I haven't finished! Tell me exactly what my Mom said.

SAM: I have. "When Hally comes, tell him I've gone to the hospital and I'll phone him."

HALLY: She didn't say anything about taking my Dad home?

SAM: No. It's just that when she was talking on the phone . . .

HALLY [Interrupting him]: No, Sam. They can't be discharging him. She would have said so if they were. In any case, we saw him last night and he wasn't in good shape at all. Staff nurse even said there was talk about taking more X-rays. And now suddenly today he's better? If anything, it sounds more like a bad turn to me . . . which I sincerely hope it isn't. Hang on . . . how long ago did you say she left?

SAM: Just before two . . . [His wrist watch] . . . hour and a half.

HALLY: I know how to settle it. [Behind the counter to the telephone. Talking as he dials] Let's give her ten minutes to get to the hospital, ten minutes to load him up, another ten, at the most, to get home and another ten to get him inside. Forty minutes. They should have been home for at least half an hour already. [Pause—he waits with the receiver to his ear] No reply, chaps. And you know why? Because she's at his bedside in hospital helping him pull through a bad turn. You definitely heard wrong.

SAM: Okay.

As far as Hally is concerned, the matter is settled. He returns to his table, sits down and divides his attention between the book and his soup. Sam is at his school case and picks up a textbook.

Modern Graded Mathematics for Standards Nine and Ten. [Opens it at random and laughs at something he sees] Who is this supposed to be?

HALLY: Old fart-face Prentice.

SAM: Teacher?

HALLY: Thinks he is. And believe me, that is not a bad likeness.

SAM: Has he seen it?

HALLY: Yes.

SAM: What did he say?

HALLY: Tried to be clever, as usual. Said I was no Leonardo da Vinci and that bad art had to be punished. So, six of the best, and his are bloody good.

SAM: On your bum?

HALLY: Where else? The days when I got them on my hands are gone forever, Sam.

SAM: With your trousers down!

HALLY: No. He's not quite that barbaric.

SAM: That's the way they do it in jail.

HALLY [*Flicker of morbid interest*]:   Really?

SAM: Ja. When the magistrate sentences you to "strokes with a light cane."

HALLY: Go on.

SAM: They make you lie down on a bench. One policeman pulls down your trousers and holds your ankles, another one pulls your shirt over your head and holds your arms . . .

HALLY: Thank you! That's enough.

SAM: . . . and the one that gives you the strokes talks to you gently and for a long time between each one. [*He laughs*]

HALLY: I've heard enough, Sam! Jesus! It's a bloody awful world when you come to think of it. People can be real bastards.

SAM: That's the way it is, Hally.

HALLY: It doesn't *have* to be that way. There is something called progress, you know. We don't exactly burn people at the stake anymore.

SAM: Like Joan of Arc.

HALLY: Correct. If she was captured today, she'd be given a fair trial.

SAM: And then the death sentence.

HALLY [*A world-weary sigh*]:   I know, I know! I oscillate between hope and despair for this world as well, Sam. But things will change, you wait and see. One day somebody is going to get up and give history a kick up the backside and get it going again.

SAM: Like who?

HALLY [*After thought*]:   They're called social reformers. Every age, Sam, has got its social reformer. My history book is full of them.

SAM: So where's ours?

HALLY: Good question. And I hate to say it, but the answer is: I don't know. Maybe he hasn't even been born yet. Or is still only a babe in arms at his mother's breast. God, what a thought.

SAM: So we just go on waiting.

HALLY: Ja, looks like it. [*Back to his soup and the book*]

SAM [*Reading from the textbook*]:   "Introduction: In some mathematical problems only the magnitude . . ." [*He mispronounces the word "magnitude"*]

HALLY [*Correcting him without looking up*]:   Magnitude.

SAM: What's it mean?

HALLY: How big it is. The size of the thing.

SAM [*Reading*]:   ". . . magnitude of the quantities is of importance. In other problems we need to know whether these quantities are negative or positive. For example, whether there is a debit or credit bank balance . . ."

HALLY: Whether you're broke or not.

SAM: ". . . whether the temperature is above or below Zero . . ."

HALLY: Naught degrees. Cheerful state of affairs! No cash and you're freezing to death. Mathematics won't get you out of that one.

SAM: "All these quantities are called . . ." [*Spelling the word*] . . . s-c-a-l . . .

HALLY: Scalars.

SAM: Scalars! [*Shaking his head with a laugh*] You understand all that?

HALLY [*Turning a page*]:   No. And I don't intend to try.

SAM: So what happens when the exams come?

HALLY: Failing a maths exam isn't the end of the world, Sam. How many times have I told you that examination results don't measure intelligence?

SAM: I would say about as many times as you've failed one of them.

HALLY [*Mirthlessly*]:   Ha, ha, ha.

SAM [*Simultaneously*]:   Ha, ha, ha.

HALLY: Just remember Winston Churchill didn't do particularly well at school.

SAM: You've also told me that one many times.

HALLY: Well, it just so happens to be the truth.

SAM [*Enjoying the word*]:   Magnitude! Magnitude! Show me how to use it.

HALLY [*After thought*]:   An intrepid social reformer will not be daunted by the magnitude of the task he has undertaken.

SAM [*Impressed*]:   Couple of jaw-breakers in there!

HALLY: I gave you three for the price of one. Intrepid, daunted and magnitude. I did that once in an exam. Put five of the words I had to explain in one sentence. It was half a page long.

SAM: Well, I'll put my money on you in the English exam.

HALLY: Piece of cake. Eighty percent without even trying.

SAM [*Another textbook from Hally's case*]:   And history?

HALLY: So-so. I'll scrape through. In the fifties if I'm lucky.

SAM: You didn't do too badly last year.

HALLY: Because we had World War One. That at least had some action. You try to find that in the South African Parliamentary system.

SAM [*Reading from the history textbook*]: "Napoleon and the principle of equality." Hey! This sounds interesting. "After concluding peace with Britain in 1802, Napoleon used a brief period of calm to in-sti-tute . . ."

HALLY: Introduce.

SAM: ". . . many reforms. Napoleon regarded all people as equal before the law and wanted them to have equal opportunities for advancement. All ves-ti-ges of the feu-dal system with its oppression of the poor were abolished." Vestiges, feudal system and abolished. I'm all right on oppression.

HALLY: I'm thinking. He swept away . . . abolished . . . the last remains . . . vestiges . . . of the bad old days . . . feudal system.

SAM: Ha! There's the social reformer we're waiting for. He sounds like a man of some magnitude.

HALLY: I'm not so sure about that. It's a damn good title for a book, though. A man of magnitude!

SAM: He sounds pretty big to me, Hally.

HALLY: Don't confuse historical significance with greatness. But maybe I'm being a bit prejudiced. Have a look in there and you'll see he's two chapters long. And hell! . . . has he only got dates, Sam, all of which you've got to remember! This campaign and that campaign, and then, because of all the fighting, the next thing is we get Peace Treaties all over the place. And what's the end of the story? Battle of Waterloo, which he loses. Wasn't worth it. No, I don't know about him as a man of magnitude.

SAM: Then who would you say was?

HALLY: To answer that, we need a definition of greatness, and I suppose that would be somebody who . . . somebody who benefited all mankind.

SAM: Right. But like who?

HALLY [*He speaks with total conviction*]: Charles Darwin. Remember him? That big book from the library. *The Origin of the Species.*

SAM Him?

HALLY: Yes. For his Theory of Evolution.

SAM: You didn't finish it.

HALLY: I ran out of time. I didn't finish it because my two weeks was up. But I'm going to take it out again after I've digested what I read. It's safe. I've hidden it away in the Theology section. Nobody ever goes in there. And anyway who are you to talk? You hardly even looked at it.

SAM: I tried. I looked at the chapters in the beginning and I saw one called "The Struggle for an Existence." Ah ha, I thought. At last! But what did I get? Something called the mistletoe which needs the apple tree and there's too many seeds and all are going to die except one . . . ! No, Hally.

HALLY [*Intellectually outraged*]:   What do you mean, No! The poor man had to start somewhere. For God's sake, Sam, he revolutionized science. Now we know.

SAM: What?

HALLY: Where we come from and what it all means.

SAM: And that's a benefit to mankind? Anyway, I still don't believe it.

HALLY: God, you're impossible. I showed it to you in black and white.

SAM: Doesn't mean I got to believe it.

HALLY: It's the likes of you that kept the Inquisition in business. It's called bigotry. Anyway, that's my man of magnitude. Charles Darwin! Who's yours?

SAM [*Without hesitation*]:   Abraham Lincoln.

HALLY: I might have guessed as much. Don't get sentimental, Sam. You've never been a slave, you know. And anyway we freed your ancestors here in South Africa long before the Americans. But if you want to thank somebody on their behalf, do it to Mr. William Wilberforce. Come on. Try again. I want a real genius. [*Now enjoying himself, and so is Sam. Hally goes behind the counter and helps himself to a chocolate*]

SAM: William Shakespeare.

HALLY [*No enthusiasm*]:   Oh. So you're also one of them, are you? You're basing that opinion on only one play, you know. You've only read my *Julius Caesar* and even I don't understand half of what they're talking about. They should do what they did with the old Bible: bring the language up to date.

SAM: That's all you've got. It's also the only one *you've* read.

HALLY: I know. I admit it. That's why I suggest we reserve our judgment until we've checked up on a few others. I've got a feeling, though, that by the end of this year one is going to be enough for me, and I can give you the names of twenty-nine other chaps in the Standard Nine class of the Port Elizabeth Technical College who feel the same. But if you want him, you can have him. My turn now. [*Pacing*] This is a damned good exercise, you know! It started off looking like a simple question and here it's got us really probing into the intellectual heritage of our civilization.

SAM: So who is it going to be?

HALLY: My next man . . . and he gets the title on two scores: social reform and literary genius . . . is Leo Nikolaevich Tolstoy.

SAM: That Russian.

HALLY: Correct. Remember the picture of him I showed you?

SAM: With the long beard.

HALLY [*Trying to look like Tolstoy*]: And those burning, visionary eyes. My God, the face of a social prophet if ever I saw one! And remember my words when I showed it to you? Here's a *man*, Sam!

SAM: Those were words, Hally.

HALLY: Not many intellectuals are prepared to shovel manure with the peasants and then go home and write a "little book" called *War and Peace*. Incidentally, Sam, he was somebody else who, to quote, ". . . did not distinguish himself scholastically."

SAM: Meaning?

HALLY: He was also no good at school.

SAM: Like you and Winston Churchill.

HALLY [*Mirthlessly*]: Ha, ha, ha.

SAM [*Simultaneously*]: Ha, ha, ha.

HALLY: Don't get clever, Sam. That man freed his serfs of his own free will.

SAM: No argument. He was a somebody, all right. I accept him.

HALLY: I'm sure Count Tolstoy will be very pleased to hear that. Your turn. Shoot. [*Another chocolate from behind the counter*] I'm waiting, Sam.

SAM: I've got him.

HALLY: Good. Submit your candidate for examination.

SAM: Jesus.

HALLY [*Stopped dead in his tracks*]: Who?

SAM: Jesus Christ.

HALLY: Oh, come on, Sam!

SAM: The Messiah.

HALLY: Ja, but still . . . No, Sam. Don't let's get started on religion. We'll just spend the whole afternoon arguing again. Suppose I turn around and say Mohammed?

SAM: All right.

HALLY: You can't have them both on the same list!

SAM: Why not? You like Mohammed, I like Jesus.

HALLY: I *don't* like Mohammed. I never have. I was merely being hypothetical. As far as I'm concerned, the Koran is as bad as the Bible. No. Religion is out! I'm not going to waste my time again arguing with you about the existence of God. You know perfectly well I'm an atheist . . . and I've got homework to do.

SAM: Okay, I take him back.

HALLY: You've got time for one more name.

SAM [*After thought*]: I've got one I know we'll agree on. A simple straightforward great Man of Magnitude . . . and no arguments. And *he* really *did* benefit all mankind.

HALLY: I wonder. After your last contribution I'm beginning to doubt whether anything in the way of an intellectual agreement is possible between the two of us. Who is he?

SAM: Guess.

HALLY: Socrates? Alexandre Dumas? Karl Marx? Dostoevsky? Nietzsche?

Sam shakes his head after each name.

Give me a clue.

SAM: The letter P is important . . .

HALLY: Plato!

SAM: . . . and his name begins with an F.

HALLY: I've got it. Freud and Psychology.

SAM: No. I didn't understand him.

HALLY: That makes two of us.

SAM: Think of mouldy apricot jam.

HALLY [*After a delighted laugh*]: Penicillin and Sir Alexander Fleming! And the title of the book: *The Microbe Hunters.* [*Delighted*] Splendid, Sam! Splendid. For once we are in total agreement. The major breakthrough in medical science in the Twentieth Century. If it wasn't for him, we might have lost the Second World War. It's deeply gratifying, Sam, to know that I haven't been wasting my time in talking to you. [*Strutting around proudly*] Tolstoy may have educated his peasants, but I've educated you.

SAM: Standard Four to Standard Nine.

HALLY: Have we been at it as long as that?

SAM: Yep. And my first lesson was geography.

HALLY [*Intrigued*]:   Really? I don't remember.

SAM: My room there at the back of the old Jubilee Boarding House. I had just started working for your Mom. Little boy in short trousers walks in one afternoon and asks me seriously: "Sam, do you want to see South Africa?" Hey man! Sure I wanted to see South Africa!

HALLY: Was that me?

SAM: . . . So the next thing I'm looking at a map you had just done for homework. It was your first one and you were very proud of yourself.

HALLY: Go on.

SAM: Then came my first lesson. "Repeat after me, Sam: Gold in the Transvaal, mealies in the Free State, sugar in Natal and grapes in the Cape." I still know it!

HALLY: Well, I'll be buggered. So that's how it all started.

SAM: And your next map was one with all the rivers and the mountains they came from. The Orange, the Vaal, the Limpopo, the Zambezi . . .

HALLY: You've got a phenomenal memory!

SAM: You should be grateful. That is why you started passing your exams. You tried to be better than me.

They laugh together. Willie is attracted by the laughter and joins them.

HALLY: The old Jubilee Boarding House. Sixteen rooms with board and lodging, rent in advance and one week's notice. I haven't thought about it for donkey's years . . . and I don't think that's an accident. God, was I glad when we sold it and moved out. Those years are not remembered as the happiest ones of an unhappy childhood.

WILLIE [*Knocking on the table and trying to imitate a woman's voice*]: "Hally, are you there?"

HALLY: Who's that supposed to be?

WILLIE: "What you doing in there, Hally? Come out at once!"

HALLY [*To Sam*]:   What's he talking about?

SAM: Don't you remember?

WILLIE: "Sam, Willie . . . is he in there with you boys?"

SAM: Hiding away in our room when your mother was looking for you.

HALLY [*Another good laugh*]:   Of course! I used to crawl and hide under your bed! But finish the story, Willie. Then what used to happen?

You chaps would give the game away by telling her I was in there with you. So much for friendship.

SAM: We couldn't lie to her. She knew.

HALLY: Which meant I got another rowing for hanging around the "servants' quarters." I think I spent more time in there with you chaps than anywhere else in that dump. And do you blame me? Nothing but bloody misery wherever you went. Somebody was always complaining about the food, or my mother was having a fight with Micky Nash because she'd caught her with a petty officer in her room. Maud Meiring was another one. Remember those two? They were prostitutes, you know. Soldiers and sailors from the troopships. Bottom fell out of the business when the war ended. God, the flotsam and jetsam that life washed up on our shores! No joking, if it wasn't for your room, I would have been the first certified ten-year-old in medical history. Ja, the memories are coming back now. Walking home from school and thinking: "What can I do this afternoon?" Try out a few ideas, but sooner or later I'd end up in there with you fellows. I bet you I could still find my way to your room with my eyes closed. [He does exactly that]. Down the corridor . . . telephone on the right, which my Mom keeps locked because somebody is using it on the sly and not paying . . . past the kitchen and unappetizing cooking smells . . . around the corner into the backyard, hold my breath again because there are more smells coming when I pass your lavatory, then into that little passageway, first door on the right and into your room. How's that?

SAM: Good. But, as usual, you forgot to knock.

HALLY: Like that time I barged in and caught you and Cynthia . . . at it. Remember? God, was I embarrassed! I didn't know what was going on at first.

SAM: Ja, that taught you a lesson.

HALLY: And about a lot more than knocking on doors, I'll have you know, and I don't mean geography either. Hell, Sam, couldn't you have waited until it was dark?

SAM: No.

HALLY: Was it that urgent?

SAM: Yes, and if you don't believe me, wait until your time comes.

HALLY: No, thank you. I am not interested in girls. [Back to his memories . . . Using a few chairs he recreates the room as he lists the items] A gray little room with a cold cement floor. Your bed against that wall . . . and I now know why the mattress sags so much! . . . Willie's bed . . . it's propped up on bricks because one leg is broken . . . that wobbly little table with the washbasin and jug of water . . . Yes! . . . stuck to the wall above it are some pin-up pictures from magazines. Joe Louis . . .

WILLIE: Brown Bomber. World Title. [*Boxing pose*] Three rounds and knockout.

HALLY: Against who?

SAM: Max Schmeling.

HALLY: Correct. I can also remember Fred Astaire and Ginger Rogers, and Rita Hayworth in a bathing costume which always made me hot and bothered when I looked at it. Under Willie's bed is an old suitcase with all his clothes in a mess, which is why I never hide there. Your things are neat and tidy in a trunk next to your bed, and on it there is a picture of you and Cynthia in your ballroom clothes, your first silver cup for third place in a competition and an old radio which doesn't work anymore. Have I left out anything?

SAM: No.

HALLY: Right, so much for the stage directions. Now the characters. [*Sam and Willie move to their appropriate positions in the bedroom*] Willie is in bed, under his blankets with his clothes on, complaining nonstop about something, but we can't make out a word of what he's saying because he's got his head under the blankets as well. You're on your bed trimming your toenails with a knife—not a very edifying sight—and as for me . . . What am I doing?

SAM: You're sitting on the floor giving Willie a lecture about being a good loser while you get the checker board and pieces ready for a game. Then you go to Willie's bed, pull off the blankets and make him play with you first because you know you're going to win, and that gives you the second game with me.

HALLY: And you certainly were a bad loser, Willie!

WILLIE: Haai!

HALLY: Wasn't he, Sam? And so slow! A game with you almost took the whole afternoon. Thank God I gave up trying to teach you how to play chess.

WILLIE: You and Sam cheated.

HALLY: I never saw Sam cheat, and mine were mostly the mistakes of youth.

WILLIE: Then how is it you two was always winning?

HALLY: Have you ever considered the possibility, Willie, that it was because we were better than you?

WILLIE: Every time better?

HALLY: Not every time. There were occasions when we deliberately let you win a game so that you would stop sulking and go on playing with us. Sam used to wink at me when you weren't looking to show me it was time to let you win.

WILLIE: So then you two didn't play fair.

HALLY: It was for your benefit, Mr. Malopo, which is more than being fair. It was an act of self-sacrifice. [*To Sam*] But you know what my best memory is, don't you?

SAM: No.

HALLY: Come on, guess. If your memory is so good, you must remember it as well.

SAM: We got up to a lot of tricks in there, Hally.

HALLY: This one was special, Sam.

SAM: I'm listening.

HALLY: It started off looking like another of those useless nothing-to-do afternoons. I'd already been down to Main Street looking for adventure, but nothing had happened. I didn't feel like climbing trees in the Donkin Park or pretending I was a private eye and following a stranger . . . so as usual: See what's cooking in Sam's room. This time it was you on the floor. You had two thin pieces of wood and you were smoothing them down with a knife. It didn't look particularly interesting, but when I asked you what you were doing, you just said, "Wait and see, Hally. Wait . . . and see" . . . in that secret sort of way of yours, so I knew there was a surprise coming. You teased me, you bugger, by being deliberately slow and not answering my questions!

Sam laughs.

And whistling while you worked away! God, it was infuriating! I could have brained you! It was only when you tied them together in a cross and put that down on the brown paper that I realized what you were doing. "Sam is making a kite?" And when I asked you and you said "Yes" . . . ! [*Shaking his head with disbelief*] The sheer audacity of it took my breath away. I mean, seriously, what the hell does a black man know about flying a kite? I'll be honest with you, Sam, I had no hopes for it. If you think I was excited and happy, you got another guess coming. In fact, I was shit-scared that we were going to make fools of ourselves. When we left the boarding house to go up onto the hill, I was praying quietly that there wouldn't be any other kids around to laugh at us.

SAM [*Enjoying the memory as much as Hally*]: Ja, I could see that.

HALLY: I made it obvious, did I?

SAM: Ja. You refused to carry it.

HALLY: Do you blame me? Can you remember what the poor thing looked like? Tomato-box wood and brown paper! Flour and water for glue! Two of my mother's old stockings for a tail, and then all those bits and pieces of string you made me tie together so that we could fly it! Hell, no, that was now only asking for a miracle to happen.

SAM: Then the big argument when I told you to hold the string and run with it when I let go.

HALLY: I was prepared to run, all right, but straight back to the boarding house.

SAM [*Knowing what's coming*]: So what happened?

HALLY: Come on, Sam, you remember as well as I do.

SAM: I want to hear it from you.

Hally pauses. He wants to be as accurate as possible.

HALLY: You went a little distance from me down the hill, you held it up ready to let it go. . . . "This is it," I thought. "Like everything else in my life, here comes another fiasco." Then you shouted, "Go, Hally!" and I started to run. [*Another pause*] I don't know how to describe it, Sam. Ja! The miracle happened! I was running, waiting for it to crash to the ground, but instead suddenly there was something alive behind me at the end of the string, tugging at it as if it wanted to be free. I looked back . . . [*Shakes his head*] . . . I still can't believe my eyes. It was flying! Looping around and trying to climb even higher into the sky. You shouted to me to let it have more string. I did, until there was none left and I was just holding that piece of wood we had tied it to. You came up and joined me. You were laughing.

SAM: So were you. And shouting, "It works, Sam! We've done it!"

HALLY: And we had! I was so proud of us! It was the most splendid thing I had ever seen. I wished there were hundreds of kids around to watch us. The part that scared me, though, was when you showed me how to make it dive down to the ground and then just when it was on the point of crashing, swoop up again!

SAM: You didn't want to try yourself.

HALLY: Of course not! I would have been suicidal if anything had happened to it. Watching you do it made me nervous enough. I was quite happy just to see it up there with its tail fluttering behind it. You left me after that, didn't you? You explained how to get it down, we tied it to the bench so that I could sit and watch it, and you went away. I wanted you to stay, you know. I was a little scared of having to look after it by myself.

SAM [*Quietly*]:   I had work to do, Hally.

HALLY: It was sort of sad bringing it down, Sam. And it looked sad again when it was lying there on the ground. Like something that had lost its soul. Just tomato-box wood, brown paper and two of my mother's old stockings! But, hell, I'll never forget that first moment when I saw it up there. I had a stiff neck the next day from looking up so much.

Sam laughs. Hally turns to him with a question he never thought of asking before.

Why did you make that kite, Sam?

SAM [*Evenly*]:   I can't remember.

HALLY: Truly?

SAM: Too long ago, Hally.

HALLY: Ja, I suppose it was. It's time for another one, you know.

SAM: Why do you say that?

HALLY: Because it feels like that. Wouldn't be a good day to fly it, though.

SAM: No. You can't fly kites on rainy days.

HALLY   [*He studies Sam. Their memories have made him conscious of the man's presence in his life*]:   How old are you, Sam?

SAM: Two score and five.

HALLY: Strange, isn't it?

SAM: What?

HALLY: Me and you.

SAM: What's strange about it?

HALLY: Little white boy in short trousers and a black man old enough to be his father flying a kite. It's not every day you see that.

SAM: But why strange? Because the one is white and the other black?

HALLY: I don't know. Would have been just as strange, I suppose, if it had been me and my Dad . . . cripple man and a little boy! Nope!

There's no chance of me flying a kite without it being strange. [*Simple statement of fact—no self-pity*] There's a nice little short story there. "The Kite-Flyers." But we'd have to find a twist in the ending.

SAM: Twist?

HALLY: Yes. Something unexpected. The way it ended with us was too straightforward . . . me on the bench and you going back to work. There's no drama in that.

WILLIE: And me?

HALLY: You?

WILLIE: Yes me.

HALLY: You want to get into the story as well, do you? I got it! Change the title: "Afternoons in Sam's Room" . . . expand it and tell all the stories. It's on its way to being a novel. Our days in the old Jubilee. Sad in a way that they're over. I almost wish we were still in that little room.

SAM: We're still together.

HALLY: That's true. It's just that life felt the right size in there . . . not too big and not too small. Wasn't so hard to work up a bit of courage. It's got so bloody complicated since then.

The telephone rings. Sam answers it.

SAM: St. George's Park Tea Room . . . Hello, Madam . . . Yes, Madam, he's here. . . . Hally, it's your mother.

HALLY: Where is she phoning from?

SAM: Sounds like the hospital. It's a public telephone.

HALLY [*Relieved*]:   You see! I told you. [*The telephone*] Hello, Mom . . . Yes . . . Yes no fine. Everything's under control here. How's things with poor old Dad? . . . Has he had a bad turn? . . . What? . . . Oh, God! . . . Yes, Sam told me, but I was sure he'd made a mistake. But what's this all about, Mom? He didn't look at all good last night. How can he get better so quickly? . . . Then very obviously you must say no. Be firm with him. You're the boss. . . . You know what it's going to be like if he comes home. . . . Well then, don't blame me when I fail my exams at the end of the year. . . . Yes! How am I expected to be fresh for school when I spend half the night massaging his gammy leg? . . . So am I! . . . So tell him a white lie. Say Dr. Colley wants more X-rays of his stump. Or bribe him. We'll sneak in double tots of brandy in future. . . . What? . . . Order him to get back into bed at once! If he's going to behave like a child, treat him like one. . . . All right, Mom! I was just trying to . . . I'm sorry. . . . I said I'm sorry. . . . Quick, give me your number. I'll phone you back. [*He hangs up and waits a few seconds*] Here we go again! [*He dials*] I'm sorry, Mom. . . . Okay . . . But now listen to me carefully. All it needs is for you to put your foot down. Don't take no for an answer. . . . Did you hear me? And whatever you do, don't discuss it with him. . . . Because I'm frightened you'll give in to him. . . . Yes, Sam gave me lunch. . . . I ate all of it! . . . No, Mom not a soul. It's still raining here. . . . Right, I'll tell them. I'll just do some homework and then lock up. . . . But remember now, Mom. Don't listen to anything he says. And phone me back and let me know what happens. . . . Okay. Bye, Mom. [*He hangs up. The men are staring at him*] My Mom says that when you're finished with the floors you must do the windows. [*Pause*] Don't misunderstand me, chaps. All I want is for him to get better. And if he was, I'd be the first person to say: "Bring him home." But he's not, and we can't give him the medical care and attention he needs at home. That's what hospitals are there for. [*Brusquely*] So don't just stand there! Get on with it!

Sam clears Hally's table.

You heard right. My Dad wants to go home.

SAM: Is he better?

HALLY [*Sharply*]: No! How the hell can he be better when last night he was groaning with pain? This is not an age of miracles!

SAM: Then he should stay in hospital.

HALLY [*Seething with irritation and frustration*]: Tell me something I don't know, Sam. What the hell do you think I was saying to my Mom? All I can say is fuck-it-all.

SAM: I'm sure he'll listen to your Mom.

HALLY: You don't know what she's up against. He's already packed his shaving kit and pajamas and is sitting on his bed with his crutches, dressed and ready to go. I know him when he gets in that mood. If she tries to reason with him, we've had it. She's no match for him when it comes to a battle of words. He'll tie her up in knots. [*Trying to hide his true feelings*]

SAM: I suppose it gets lonely for him in there.

HALLY: With all the patients and nurses around? Regular visits from the Salvation Army? Balls! It's ten times worse for him at home. I'm at school and my mother is here in the business all day.

SAM: He's at least got you at night.

HALLY [*Before he can stop himself*]: And we've got him! Please! I don't want to talk about it anymore. [*Unpacks his school case, slamming down books on the table*] Life is just a plain bloody mess, that's all. And people are fools.

SAM: Come on, Hally.

HALLY: Yes, they are! They bloody well deserve what they get.

SAM: Then don't complain.

HALLY: Don't try to be clever, Sam. It doesn't suit you. Anybody who thinks there's nothing wrong with this world needs to have his head examined. Just when things are going along all right, without fail someone or something will come along and spoil everything. Somebody should write that down as a fundamental law of the Universe. The principle of perpetual disappointment. If there is a God who created this world, he should scrap it and try again.

SAM: All right, Hally, all right. What you got for homework?

HALLY: Bullshit, as usual. [*Opens an exercise book and reads*] "Write five hundred words describing an annual event of cultural or historical significance."

SAM: That should be easy enough for you.

HALLY: And also plain bloody boring. You know what he wants, don't you? One of their useless old ceremonies. The commemoration of the landing of the 1820 Settlers, or if it's going to be culture, Carols by Candlelight every Christmas.

SAM: It's an impressive sight. Make a good description, Hally. All those candles glowing in the dark and the people singing hymns.

HALLY: And it's called religious hysteria. [*Intense irritation*] Please, Sam! Just leave me alone and let me get on with it. I'm not in the mood for games this afternoon. And remember my Mom's orders . . . you're to help Willie with the windows. Come on now, I don't want any more nonsense in here.

SAM: Okay, Hally, okay.

Hally settles down to his homework; determined preparations . . .
pen, ruler, exercise book, dictionary, another cake . . . all of which
will lead to nothing.

Sam waltzes over to Willie and starts to replace tables and chairs.
He practices a ballroom step while doing so. Willie watches.
When Sam is finished, Willie tries.

Good! But just a little bit quicker on the turn and only move in to her after she's crossed over. What about this one?

Another step. When Sam is finished, Willie again has a go.

Much better. See what happens when you just relax and enjoy yourself? Remember that in two weeks' time and you'll be all right.

WILLIE: But I haven't got partner, Boet Sam.

SAM: Maybe Hilda will turn up tonight.

WILLIE: No, Boet Sam. [*Reluctantly*] I gave her a good hiding.

SAM: You mean a bad one.

WILLIE: Good bad one.

SAM: Then you mustn't complain either. Now you pay the price for losing your temper.

WILLIE: I also pay two pounds ten shilling entrance fee.

SAM: They'll refund you if you withdraw now.

WILLIE [*Appalled*]: You mean, don't dance?

SAM: Yes.

WILLIE: No! I wait too long and I practice too hard. If I find me new partner, you think I can be ready in two weeks? I ask Madam for my leave now and we practice every day.

SAM: Quickstep non-stop for two weeks. World record, Willie, but you'll be mad at the end.

WILLIE: No jokes, Boet Sam.

SAM: I'm not joking.

WILLIE: So then what?

SAM: Find Hilda. Say you're sorry and promise you won't beat her again.

WILLIE: No.

SAM: Then withdraw. Try again next year.

WILLIE: No.

SAM: Then I give up.

WILLIE: Haaikona, Boet Sam, you can't.

SAM: What do you mean, I can't? I'm telling you: I give up.

WILLIE [*Adamant*]: No! [*Accusingly*] It was you who start me ballroom dancing.

SAM: So?

WILLIE: Before that I use to be happy. And is you and Miriam who bring me to Hilda and say here's partner for you.

SAM: What are you saying, Willie?

WILLIE: You!

SAM: But me what? To blame?

WILLIE: Yes.

SAM: Willie . . . ? [*Bursts into laughter*]

WILLIE: And now all you do is make jokes at me. You wait. When Miriam leaves you is my turn to laugh. Ha! Ha! Ha!

SAM [*He can't take Willie seriously any longer*]:   She can leave me tonight! I know what to do. [*Bowing before an imaginary partner*] May I have the pleasure? [*He dances and sings*]
"Just a fellow with his pillow . . .
Dancin' like a willow . . .
In an autumn breeze . . ."

WILLIE: There you go again!

Sam goes on dancing and singing.

Boet Sam!

SAM: There's the answer to your problem! Judges' announcement in two weeks' time: "Ladies and gentlemen, the winner in the open section . . . Mr. Willie Malopo and his pillow!"

This is too much for a now really angry Willie. He goes for Sam, but the latter is too quick for him and puts Hally's table between the two of them.

HALLY [*Exploding*]:   For Christ's sake, you two!

WILLIE [*Still trying to get at Sam*]:   I donner you, Sam! Struesgod!

SAM [*Still laughing*]:   Sorry, Willie . . . Sorry . . .

HALLY: Sam! Willie! [*Grabs his ruler and gives Willie a vicious whack on the bum*] How the hell am I supposed to concentrate with the two of you behaving like bloody children!

WILLIE: Hit him too!

HALLY: Shut up, Willie.

WILLIE: He started jokes again.

HALLY: Get back to your work. You too, Sam. [*His ruler*] Do you want another one, Willie?

Sam and Willie return to their work. Hally uses the opportunity to escape from his unsuccessful attempt at homework. He struts around like a little despot, ruler in hand, giving vent to his anger and frustration.

Suppose a customer had walked in then? Or the Park Superinten-
dent. And seen the two of you behaving like a pair of hooligans.
That would have been the end of my mother's license, you know.
And your jobs! Well, this is the end of it. From now on there will
be no more of your ballroom nonsense in here. This is a business
establishment, not a bloody New Brighton dancing school. I've
been far too lenient with the two of you. [*Behind the counter for a
green cool drink and a dollop of ice cream. He keeps up his tirade as he
prepares it*] But what really makes me bitter is that I allow you
chaps a little freedom in here when business is bad and what do
you do with it? The foxtrot! Specially you, Sam. There's more to
life than trotting around a dance floor and I thought at least you
knew it.

SAM: It's a harmless pleasure, Hally. It doesn't hurt anybody.

HALLY: It's also a rather simple one, you know.

SAM: You reckon so? Have you ever tried?

HALLY: Of course not.

SAM: Why don't you? Now.

HALLY: What do you mean? Me dance?

SAM: Yes. I'll show you a simple step—the waltz—then you try it.

HALLY: What will that prove?

SAM: That it might not be as easy as you think.

HALLY: I didn't say it was easy. I said it was simple—like in simple-
minded, meaning mentally retarded. You can't exactly say it chal-
lenges the intellect.

SAM: It does other things.

HALLY: Such as?

SAM: Make people happy.

HALLY [*The glass in his hand*]:   So do American cream sodas with ice
cream. For God's sake, Sam, you're not asking me to take ballroom
dancing serious, are you?

SAM: Yes.

HALLY [*Sigh of defeat*]:   Oh, well, so much for trying to give you a decent education. I've obviously achieved nothing.

SAM: You still haven't told me what's wrong with admiring something that's beautiful and then trying to do it yourself.

HALLY: Nothing. But we happen to be talking about a foxtrot, not a
thing of beauty.

SAM: But that is just what I'm saying. If you were to see two champions doing, two masters of the art . . . !

HALLY: Oh, God, I give up. So now it's also art!

SAM: Ja.

HALLY: There's a limit, Sam. Don't confuse art and entertainment.

SAM: So then what is art?

HALLY: You want a definition?

SAM: Ja.

HALLY [*He realizes he has got to be careful. He gives the matter a lot of thought before answering*]: Philosophers have been trying to do that for centuries. What is Art? What is Life? But basically I suppose it's . . . the giving of meaning to matter.

SAM: Nothing to do with beautiful?

HALLY: It goes beyond that. It's the giving of form to the formless.

SAM: Ja, well, maybe it's not art, then. But I still say it's beautiful.

HALLY: I'm sure the word you mean to use is entertaining.

SAM [*Adamant*]: No. Beautiful. And if you want proof, come along to the Centenary Hall in New Brighton in two weeks' time.

The mention of the Centenary Hall draws Willie over to them.

HALLY: What for? I've seen the two of you prancing around in here often enough.

SAM [*He laughs*]: This isn't the real thing, Hally. We're just playing around in here.

HALLY: So? I can use my imagination.

SAM: And what do you get?

HALLY: A lot of people dancing around and having a so-called good time.

SAM: That all?

HALLY: Well, basically it is that, surely.

SAM: No, it isn't. Your imagination hasn't helped you at all. There's a lot more to it than that. We're getting ready for the championships, Hally, not just another dance. There's going to be a lot of people, all right, and they're going to have a good time, but they'll only be spectators, sitting around and watching. It's just the competitors out there on the dance floor. Party decorations and fancy lights all around the walls! The ladies in beautiful evening dresses!

HALLY: My mother's got one of those, Sam, and, quite frankly, it's an embarrassment every time she wears it.

SAM [*Undeterred*]:   Your imagination left out the excitement.

Hally scoffs.

Oh, yes. The finalists are not going to be out there just to have a good time. One of those couples will be the 1950 Eastern Province Champions. And your imagination left out the music.

WILLIE: Mr. Elijah Gladman Guzana and his Orchestral Jazzonions.

SAM: The sound of the big band, Hally. Trombone, trumpet, tenor and alto sax. And then, finally, your imagination also left out the climax of the evening when the dancing is finished, the judges have stopped whispering among themselves and the Master of Ceremonies collects their scorecards and goes up onto the stage to announce the winners.

HALLY: All right. So you make it sound like a bit of a do. It's an occasion. Satisfied?

SAM [*Victory*]:   So you admit that!

HALLY: Emotionally yes, intellectually no.

SAM: Well, I don't know what you mean by that, all I'm telling you is that it is going to be *the* event of the year in New Brighton. It's been sold out for two weeks already. There's only standing room left. We've got competitors coming from Kingwilliamstown, East London, Port Alfred.

Hally starts pacing thoughtfully.

HALLY: Tell me a bit more.

SAM: I thought you weren't interested . . . intellectually.

HALLY [*Mysteriously*]:   I've got my reasons.

SAM: What do you want to know?

HALLY: It takes place every year?

SAM: Yes. But only every third year in New Brighton. It's East London's turn to have the championships next year.

HALLY: Which, I suppose, makes it an even more significant event.

SAM: Ah ha! We're getting somewhere. Our "occasion" is now a "significant event."

HALLY: I wonder.

SAM: What?

HALLY: I wonder if I would get away with it.

SAM: But what?

HALLY [*To the table and his exercise book*]:   "Write five hundred words describing an annual event of cultural or historical significance."

Would I be stretching poetic license a little too far if I called your ballroom championships a cultural event?

SAM: You mean . . . ?

HALLY: You think we could get five hundred words out of it, Sam?

SAM: Victor Sylvester has written a whole book on ballroom dancing.

WILLIE: You going to write about it, Master Hally?

HALLY: Yes, gentlemen, that is precisely what I am considering doing. Old Doc Bromely—he's my English teacher—is going to argue with me, of course. He doesn't like natives. But I'll point out to him that in strict anthropological terms the culture of a primitive black society includes its dancing and singing. To put my thesis in a nutshell: The war-dance has been replaced by the waltz. But it still amounts to the same thing: the release of primitive emotions through movement. Shall we give it a go?

SAM: I'm ready.

WILLIE: Me also.

HALLY: Ha! This will teach the old bugger a lesson. [*Decision taken*] Right. Let's get ourselves organized. [*This means another cake on the table. He sits*] I think you've given me enough general atmosphere, Sam, but to build the tension and suspense I need facts. [*Pencil poised*]

WILLIE: Give him facts, Boet Sam.

HALLY: What you called the climax . . . how many finalists?

SAM: Six couples.

HALLY [*Making notes*]:   Go on. Give me the picture.

SAM: Spectators seated right around the hall. [*Willie becomes a spectator*]

HALLY: . . . and it's a full house.

SAM: At one end, on the stage, Gladman and his Orchestral Jazzonions. At the other end is a long table with the three judges. The six finalists go onto the dance floor and take up their positions. When they are ready and the spectators have settled down, the Master of Ceremonies goes to the microphone. To start with, he makes some jokes to get the people laughing . . .

HALLY: Good touch! [*As he writes*] ". . . creating a relaxed atmosphere which will change to one of tension and drama as the climax is approached."

SAM [*Onto a chair to act out the M.C.*]:   "Ladies and gentlemen, we come now to the great moment you have all been waiting for this evening . . . . The finals of the 1950 Eastern Province Open Ballroom

Dancing Championships. But first let me introduce the finalists! Mr. and Mrs. Welcome Tchabalala from Kingwilliamstown . . ."

WILLIE [*He applauds after every name*]:   Is when the people clap their hands and whistle and make a lot of noise, Master Hally.

SAM: "Mr. Mulligan Njikelane and Miss Nomhle Nkonyeni of Grahamstown; Mr. and Mrs. Norman Nchinga from Port Alfred; Mr. Fats Bokolane and Miss Dina Plaatjies from East London; Mr. Sipho Dugu and Mrs. Mable Magada from Peddie; and from New Brighton our very own Mr. Willie Malopo and Miss Hilda Samuels."

Willie can't believe his ears. He abandons his role as spectator and scrambles into position as a finalist.

WILLIE: Relaxed and ready to romance!

SAM: The applause dies down. When everybody is silent, Gladman lifts up his sax, nods at the Orchestral Jazzonions . . .

WILLIE: Play the jukebox please, Boet Sam!

SAM: I also only got bus fare, Willie.

HALLY: Hold it, everybody. [*Heads for the cash register behind the counter*] How much is in the till, Sam?

SAM: Three shillings. Hally . . . your Mom counted it before she left.

Hally hesitates.

HALLY: Sorry, Willie. You know how she carried on the last time I did it. We'll just have to pool our combined imaginations and hope for the best. [*Returns to the table*] Back to work. How are the points scored, Sam?

SAM: Maximum of ten points each for individual style, deportment, rhythm and general appearance.

WILLIE: Must I start?

HALLY: Hold it for a second, Willie. And penalties?

SAM: For what?

HALLY: For doing something wrong. Say you stumble or bump into somebody . . . do they take off any points?

SAM [*Aghast*]:   Hally . . . !

HALLY: When you're dancing. If you and your partner collide into another couple.

Hally can get no further. Sam has collapsed with laughter. He explains to Willie.

SAM: If me and Miriam bump into you and Hilda . . .

Willie joins him in another good laugh.

Hally, Hally . . . !

HALLY [*Perplexed*]:   Why? What did I say?

SAM: There's no collisions out there, Hally. Nobody trips or stumbles or bumps into anybody else. That's what that moment is all about. To be one of those finalists on that dance floor is like . . . like being in a dream about a world in which accidents don't happen.

HALLY [*Genuinely moved by Sam's image*]:   Jesus, Sam! That's beautiful!

WILLIE [*Can endure waiting no longer*]:   I'm starting! [*Willie dances while Sam talks*]

SAM: Of course it is. That's what I've been trying to say to you all afternoon. And it's beautiful because that is what we want life to be like. But instead, like you said, Hally, we're bumping into each other all the time. Look at the three of us this afternoon: I've bumped into Willie, the two of us have bumped into you, you've bumped into your mother, she bumping into your Dad. . . . None of us knows the steps and there's no music playing. And it doesn't stop with us. The whole world is doing it all the time. Open a newspaper and what do you read? America has bumped into Russia, England is bumping into India, rich man bumps into poor man. Those are big collisions, Hally. They make for a lot of bruises. People get hurt in all that bumping, and we're sick and tired of it now. It's been going on for too long. Are we never going to get it right? . . . Learn to dance life like champions instead of always being just a bunch of beginners at it?

HALLY [*Deep and sincere admiration of the man*]:   You've got a vision, Sam!

SAM: Not just me. What I'm saying to you is that everybody's got it. That's why there's only standing room left for the Centenary Hall in two weeks' time. For as long as the music lasts, we are going to see six couples get it right, the way we want life to be.

HALLY: But is that the best we can do, Sam . . . watch six finalists dreaming about the way it should be?

SAM: I don't know. But it starts with that. Without the dream we won't know what we're going for. And anyway I reckon there are a few people who have got past just dreaming about it and are trying for something real. Remember that thing we read once in the paper about the Mahatma Gandhi? Going without food to stop those riots in India?

HALLY: You're right. He certainly was trying to teach people to get the steps right.

SAM: And the Pope.

HALLY: Yes, he's another one. Our old General Smuts as well, you know. He's also out there dancing. You know, Sam, when you come to think of it, that's what the United Nations boils down to . . . a dancing school for politicians!

SAM: And let's hope they learn.

HALLY [*A little surge of hope*]: You're right. We mustn't despair. Maybe there's some hope for mankind after all. Keep it up, Willie. [*Back to his table with determination*] This is a lot bigger than I thought. So what have we got? Yes, our title: "A World Without Collisions."

SAM: That sounds good! "A World Without Collisions."

HALLY: Subtitle: "Global Politics on the Dance Floor." No. A bit too heavy, hey? What about "Ballroom Dancing as a Political Vision"?

The telephone rings. Sam answers it.

SAM: St. George's Park Tea Room . . . Yes, Madam . . . Hally, it's your Mom.

HALLY [*Back to reality*]: Oh, God, yes! I'd forgotten all about that. Shit! Remember my words, Sam? Just when you're enjoying yourself, someone or something will come along and wreck everything.

SAM: You haven't heard what she's got to say yet.

HALLY: Public telephone?

SAM: No.

HALLY: Does she sound happy or unhappy?

SAM: I couldn't tell. [*Pause*] She's waiting, Hally.

HALLY [*To the telephone*]: Hello, Mom . . . No, everything is okay here. Just doing my homework. . . . What's your news? . . . You've what? . . . [*Pause. He takes the receiver away from his ear for a few seconds. In the course of Hally's telephone conversation, Sam and Willie discretely position the stacked tables and chairs. Hally places the receiver back to his ear*] Yes, I'm still here. Oh, well, I give up now. Why did you do it, Mom? . . . Well, I just hope you know what you've let us in for. . . . [*Loudly*] I said I hope you know what you've let us in for! It's the end of the peace and quiet we've been having. [*Softly*] Where is he? [*Normal voice*] He can't hear us from in there. But for God's sake, Mom, what happened? I told you to be firm with him. . . . Then you and the nurses should have held him down, taken his crutches away. . . . I know only too well he's my father! . . . I'm not being disrespectful, but I'm sick and tired of emptying stinking chamberpots full of phlegm and piss. . . . Yes, I do! When you're not there, he asks *me* to do it. . . . If you really want to know the truth, that's why I've got no appetite for my food. . . . Yes! There's a lot of things you don't know about. For your information, I still haven't got that science textbook I need. And you know why? He borrowed the money you gave me for it. . . . Because I didn't want to start another fight between you two. . . . He says that every time. . . . All right, Mom! [*Viciously*] Then just remember to start hiding your bag away again, because he'll be at your purse before long for money for booze. And when he's well enough to come down here, you better keep an eye on the till as well, because that is also going to develop a leak. . . . Then don't complain to me when he starts his old tricks. . . . Yes, you do. I get it from you on one side and from him on the other, and it makes life hell for me. I'm not going to be the peacemaker anymore. I'm warning you now: when the two of you start fighting again, I'm leaving home. . . . Mom, if you start crying, I'm going to put down the receiver. . . . Okay . . . [*Lowering his voice to a vicious whisper*] Okay, Mom. I heard you. [*Desperate*] No. . . . Because I don't want to. I'll see him when I get home! Mom! . . . [*Pause. When he speaks again, his tone changes completely. It is not simply pretense. We sense a genuine emotional conflict*] Welcome home, chum! . . . What's that? . . . Don't be silly, Dad. You being home is just about the best news in the world. . . . I bet you are. Bloody depressing there with everybody going on about their ailments, hey! . . . How you feeling? . . . Good . . . Here as well, pal. Coming down cats and dogs. . . . That's right. Just the day for a kip and a toss in your old Uncle Ned. . . . Everything's just hunky-dory on my side, Dad. . . . Well, to start with, there's a nice pile of comics for you on the counter. . . . Yes, old Kemple brought them in. *Batman and Robin, Submariner* . . . just your cup of tea . . . I will. . . . Yes, we'll spin a few yarns tonight. . . . Okay, chum, see you in a little while. . . . No, I promise. I'll come straight home. . . . [*Pause—his mother comes back on the phone*] Mom? Okay. I'll lock up now. . . . What? . . . Oh, the brandy . . . Yes, I'll remember! . . . I'll put it in my suitcase now, for God's sake. I know well enough what will happen if he doesn't get it. . . . [*Places a bottle of brandy on the counter*] I *was* kind to him, Mom. I didn't say anything nasty! . . . All right. Bye. [*End of telephone conversation. A desolate Hally doesn't move. A strained silence*]

SAM [*Quietly*]:   That sounded like a bad bump, Hally.

HALLY [*Having a hard time controlling his emotions. He speaks carefully*]: Mind your own business, Sam.

SAM: Sorry. I wasn't trying to interfere. Shall we carry on? Hally? [*He indicates the exercise book. No response from Hally*]

WILLIE [*Also trying*]:   Tell him about when they give out the cups, Boet Sam.

SAM: Ja! That's another big moment. The presentation of the cups after the winners have been announced. You've got to put that in.

Still no response from Hally.

WILLIE: A big silver one, Master Hally, called floating trophy for the champions.

SAM: We always invite some big-shot personality to hand them over. Guest of honor this year is going to be His Holiness Bishop Jabulani of the All African Free Zionist Church.

Hally gets up abruptly, goes to his table and tears up the page he was writing on.

HALLY: So much for a bloody world without collisions.

SAM: Too bad. It was on its way to being a good composition.

HALLY: Let's stop bullshitting ourselves, Sam.

SAM: Have we been doing that?

HALLY: Yes! That's what all our talk about a decent world has been . . . just so much bullshit.

SAM: We did say it was still only a dream.

HALLY: And a bloody useless one at that. Life's a fuck-up and it's never going to change.

SAM: Ja, maybe that's true.

HALLY: There's no maybe about it. It's a blunt and brutal fact. All we've done this afternoon is waste our time.

SAM: Not if we'd got your homework done.

HALLY: I don't give a shit about my homework, so, for Christ's sake, just shut up about it. [*Slamming books viciously into his school case*] Hurry up now and finish your work. I want to lock up and get out of here. [*Pause*] And then go where? Home-sweet-fucking-home. Jesus, I hate that word.

Hally goes to the counter to put the brandy bottle and comics in his school case. After a moment's hesitation, he smashes the bottle of brandy. He abandons all further attempts to hide his feelings. Sam and Willie work away as unobtrusively as possible.

Do you want to know what is really wrong with your lovely little dream, Sam? It's not just that we are all bad dancers. That does happen to be perfectly true, but there's more to it than just that. You left out the cripples.

SAM: Hally!

HALLY [*Now totally reckless*]:   Ja! Can't leave them out, Sam. That's why we always end up on our backsides on the dance floor. They're also out there dancing . . . like a bunch of broken spiders trying to do the quick-step! [*An ugly attempt at laughter*] When you come to think of it, it's a bloody comical sight. I mean, it's bad enough on two legs . . . but one and a pair of crutches! Hell, no, Sam. That's guaranteed to turn that dance floor into a shambles. Why you shaking your head? Picture it, man. For once this afternoon let's use our imaginations sensibly.

SAM: Be careful, Hally.

HALLY: Of what? The truth? I seem to be the only one around here who is prepared to face it. We've had the pretty dream, it's time now to wake up and have a good long look at the way things really are. Nobody knows the steps, there's no music, the cripples are also out there tripping up everybody and trying to get into the act, and it's all called the All-Comers-How-to-Make-a-Fuckup-of-Life Championships. [*Another ugly laugh*] Hang on, Sam! The best bit is still coming. Do you know what the winner's trophy is? A beautiful big chamber-pot with roses on the side, and it's full to the brim with piss. And guess who I think is going to be this year's winner.

SAM [*Almost shouting*]:   Stop now!

HALLY [*Suddenly appalled by how far he has gone*]:   Why?

SAM: Hally? It's your father you're talking about.

HALLY: So?

SAM: Do you know what you've been saying?

Hally can't answer. He is rigid with shame. Sam speaks to him sternly.

No, Hally, you mustn't do it. Take back those words and ask for forgiveness! It's a terrible sin for a son to mock his father with jokes like that. You'll be punished if you carry on. Your father is your father, even if he is a . . . cripple man.

WILLIE: Yes, Master Hally. Is true what Sam say.

SAM: I understand how you are feeling, Hally, but even so . . .

HALLY: No, you don't!

SAM: I think I do.

HALLY: And I'm telling you you don't. Nobody does. [*Speaking carefully as his shame turns to rage at Sam*] It's your turn to be careful, Sam. Very careful! You're treading on dangerous ground. Leave me and my father alone.

SAM: I'm not the one who's been saying things about him.

HALLY: What goes on between me and my Dad is none of your business!

SAM: Then don't tell me about it. If that's all you've got to say about him, I don't want to hear.

For a moment Hally is at loss for a response.

HALLY: Just get on with your bloody work and shut up.

SAM: Swearing at me won't help you.

HALLY: Yes, it does! Mind your own fucking business and shut up!

SAM: Okay. If that's the way you want it, I'll stop trying.

He turns away. This infuriates Hally even more.

HALLY: Good. Because what you've been trying to do is meddle in something you know nothing about. All that concerns you in here, Sam, is to try and do what you get paid for—keep the place clean and serve the customers. In plain words, just get on with your job. My mother is right. She's always warning me about allowing you to get too familiar. Well, this time you've gone too far. It's going to stop right now.

No response from Sam.

You're only a servant in here, and don't forget it.

Still no response. Hally is trying hard to get one.

And as far as my father is concerned, all you need to remember is that he is your boss.

SAM [*Needled at last*]: No, he isn't. I get paid by your mother.

HALLY: Don't argue with me, Sam!

SAM: Then don't say he's my boss.

HALLY: He's a white man and that's good enough for you.

SAM: I'll try to forget you said that.

HALLY: Don't! Because you won't be doing me a favor if you do. I'm telling you to remember it.

A pause. Sam pulls himself together and makes one last effort.

SAM: Hally, Hally . . . ! Come on now. Let's stop before it's too late. You're right. We *are* on dangerous ground. If we're not careful, somebody is going to get hurt.

HALLY: It won't be me.

SAM: Don't be so sure.

HALLY: I don't know what you're talking about, Sam.

SAM: Yes, you do.

HALLY [*Furious*]: Jesus, I wish you would stop trying to tell me what I do and what I don't know.

Sam gives up. He turns to Willie.

SAM: Let's finish up.

HALLY: Don't turn your back on me! I haven't finished talking.

He grabs Sam by the arm and tries to make him turn around. Sam reacts with a flash of anger.

SAM: Don't do that, Hally! [*Facing the boy*] All right, I'm listening. Well? What do you want to say to me?

HALLY [*Pause as Hally looks for something to say*]: To begin with, why don't you also start calling me Master Harold, like Willie.

SAM: Do you mean that?

HALLY: Why the hell do you think I said it?

SAM: And if I don't?

HALLY: You might just lose your job.

SAM [*Quietly and very carefully*]: If you make me say it once, I'll never call you anything else again.

HALLY: So? [*The boy confronts the man*] Is that meant to be a threat?

SAM: Just telling you what will happen if you make me do that. You must decide what it means to you.

HALLY: Well, I have. It's good news. Because that is exactly what Master Harold wants from now on. Think of it as a little lesson in respect, Sam, that's long overdue, and I hope you remember it as well as you do your geography. I can tell you now that somebody who will be glad to hear I've finally given it to you will be my Dad. Yes! He agrees with my Mom. He's always going on about it as well. "You must teach the boys to show you more respect, my son."

SAM: So now you can stop complaining about going home. Everybody is going to be happy tonight.

HALLY: That's perfectly correct. You see, you mustn't get the wrong idea about me and my Dad, Sam. We also have our good times together. Some bloody good laughs. He's got a marvelous sense of humor. Want to know what our favorite joke is? He gives out a big groan, you see, and says: "It's not fair, is it, Hally?" Then I have to ask: "What, chum?" And then he says: "A nigger's arse" . . . and we both have a good laugh.

The men stare at him with disbelief.

What's the matter, Willie? Don't you catch the joke? You always were a bit slow on the uptake. It's what is called a pun. You see, fair means both light in color and to be just and decent. [*He turns to Sam*] I thought *you* would catch it, Sam.

SAM: Oh ja, I catch it all right.

HALLY: But it doesn't appeal to your sense of humor.

SAM: Do you really laugh?

HALLY: Of course.

SAM: To please him? Make him feel good?

HALLY: No, for heaven's sake! I laugh because I think it's a bloody good joke.

SAM: You're really trying hard to be ugly, aren't you? And why drag poor old Willie into it? He's done nothing to you except show you the respect you want so badly. That's also not being fair, you know . . . and I mean just or decent.

WILLIE: It's all right, Sam. Leave it now.

SAM: It's me you're after. You should just have said "Sam's arse" . . . because that's the one you're trying to kick. Anyway, how do you know it's not fair? You've never seen it. Do you want to? [*He drops his trousers and underpants and presents his backside for Hally's inspection*] Have a good look. A real Basuto arse . . . which is about as nigger as they can come. Satisfied? [*Trousers up*] Now you can make your Dad even happier when you go home tonight. Tell him I showed you my arse and he is quite right. It's not fair. And if it will give him an even better laugh next time, I'll also let *him* have a look. Come, Willie, let's finish up and go.

Sam and Willie start to tidy up the tea room. Hally doesn't move.
He waits for a moment when Sam passes him.

HALLY [*Quietly*]:   Sam . . .

Sam stops and looks expectantly at the boy. Hally spits in his
face. A long and heartfelt groan from Willie. For a few seconds
Sam doesn't move.

SAM [*Taking out a handkerchief and wiping his face*]:   It's all right, Willie.

To Hally.

Ja, well, you've done it . . . Master Harold. Yes, I'll start calling you that from now on. It won't be difficult anymore. You've hurt yourself, Master Harold. I saw it coming. I warned you, but you wouldn't listen. You've just hurt yourself *bad*. And you're a coward, Master Harold. The face you should be spitting in is your father's . . . but you used mine, because you think you're safe inside your fair skin . . . and this time I don't mean just or decent. [*Pause, then moving violently towards Hally*] Should I hit him, Willie?

WILLIE [*Stopping Sam*]:   No, Boet Sam.

SAM [*Violently*]:   Why not?

WILLIE: It won't help, Boet Sam.

SAM: I don't want to help! I want to hurt him.

WILLIE: You also hurt yourself.

SAM: And if he had done it to you, Willie?

WILLIE: Me? Spit at me like I was a dog? [*A thought that had not occurred to him before. He looks at Hally*] Ja. Then I want to hit him. I want to hit him hard!

A dangerous few seconds as the men stand staring at the boy.
Willie turns away, shaking his head.

But maybe all I do is go cry at the back. He's little boy, Boet Sam. Little *white* boy. Long trousers now, but he's still little boy.

SAM [*His violence ebbing away into defeat as quickly as it flooded*]: You're right. So go on, then: groan again, Willie. You do it better than me. [*To Hally*] You don't know all of what you've just done . . . Master Harold. It's not just that you've made me feel dirtier than

I've ever been in my life . . . I mean, how do I wash off yours and your father's filth? . . . I've also failed. A long time ago I promised myself I was going to try and do something, but you've just shown me . . . Master Harold . . . that I've failed. [*Pause*] I've also got a memory of a little white boy when he was still wearing short trousers and a black man, but they're not flying a kite. It was the old Jubilee days, after dinner one night. I was in my room. You came in and just stood against the wall, looking down at the ground, and only after I'd asked you what you wanted, what was wrong, I don't know how many times, did you speak and even then so softly I almost didn't hear you. "Sam, please help me to go and fetch my Dad." Remember? He was dead drunk on the floor of the Central Hotel Bar. They'd phoned for your Mom, but you were the only one at home. And do you remember how we did it? You went in first by yourself to ask permission for me to go into the bar. Then I loaded him onto my back like a baby and carried him back to the boarding house with you following behind carrying his crutches. [*Shaking his head as he remembers*] A crowded Main Street with all the people watching a little white boy following his drunk father on a nigger's back! I felt for that little boy . . . Master Harold. I felt for him. After that we still had to clean him up, remember? He'd messed in his trousers, so we had to clean him up and get him into bed.

HALLY [*Great pain*]:   I love him, Sam.

SAM: I know you do. That's why I tried to stop you from saying these things about him. It would have been so simple if you could have just despised him for being a weak man. But he's your father. You love him and you're ashamed of him. You're ashamed of so much! . . . And now that's going to include yourself. That was the promise I made to myself: to try and stop that happening. [*Pause*] After we got him to bed you came back with me to my room and sat in a corner and carried on just looking down at the ground. And for days after that! You hadn't done anything wrong, but you went around as if you owed the world an apology for being alive. I didn't like seeing that! That's not the way a boy grows up to be a man!. . . But the one person who should have been teaching you what that means was the cause of your shame. If you really want to know, that's why I made you that kite. I wanted you to look up, be proud of something, of yourself . . . [*Bitter smile at the memory*] . . . and you certainly were that when I left you with it up there on the hill. Oh, ja . . . something else! . . . If you ever do write it as a short story, there *was* a twist in our ending. I couldn't sit down there and stay with you. It was a "Whites Only" bench. You were too young, too excited to notice then. But not anymore. If you're not careful . . . Master Harold . . . you're going to be sitting up there by yourself for a long time to come, and there won't be a kite in the sky. [*Sam has got nothing more to say. He exits into the kitchen, taking off his waiter's jacket*]

WILLIE: Is bad. Is all all bad in here now.

HALLY [*Books into his school case, raincoat on*]: Willie . . . [*It is difficult to speak*] Will you lock up for me and look after the keys?

WILLIE: Okay.

Sam returns. Hally goes behind the counter and collects the few coins in the cash register. As he starts to leave . . .

SAM: Don't forget the comic books.

Hally returns to the counter and puts them in his case. He starts to leave again.

SAM [*To the retreating back of the boy*]: Stop . . . Hally . . .

Hally stops, but doesn't turn to face him.

Hally . . . I've got no right to tell you what being a man means if I don't behave like one myself, and I'm not doing so well at that this afternoon. Should we try again, Hally?

HALLY: Try what?

SAM: Fly another kite, I suppose. It worked once, and this time I need it as much as you do.

HALLY: It's still raining, Sam. You can't fly kites on rainy days, remember.

SAM: So what do we do? Hope for better weather tomorrow?

HALLY [*Helpless gesture*]: I don't know. I don't know anything anymore.

SAM: You sure of that, Hally? Because it would be pretty hopeless if that was true. It would mean nothing has been learnt in here this afternoon, and there was a hell of a lot of teaching going on . . . one way or the other. But anyway, I don't believe you. I reckon there's one thing you know. You don't *have* to sit up there by yourself. You know what that bench means now, and you can leave it any time you choose. All you've got to do is stand up and walk away from it.

Hally leaves. Willie goes up quietly to Sam.

WILLIE: Is okay, Boet Sam. You see. Is . . . [*He can't find any better words*] . . . is going to be okay tomorrow. [*Changing his tone*] Hey, Boet Sam! [*He is trying hard*] You right. I think about it and you right. Tonight I find Hilda and say sorry. And make promise I won't beat her no more. You hear me, Boet Sam?

SAM: I hear you, Willie.

WILLIE: And when we practice I relax and romance with her from beginning to end. Non-stop! You watch! Two weeks' time: "First prize for promising newcomers: Mr. Willie Malopo and Miss Hilda Samuels." [*Sudden impulse*] To hell with it! I walk home. [*He goes to the jukebox, puts in a coin and selects a record. The machine comes to life in the gray twilight, blushing its way through a spectrum of soft, romantic colors*] How did you say it, Boet Sam? Let's dream. [*Willie sways with the music and gestures for Sam to dance*]

Sarah Vaughan sings.

"Little man you're crying,
I know why you're blue,
Someone took your kiddy car away;
Better go to sleep now,
Little man you've had a busy day." [*etc. etc.*]
You lead. I follow.

The men dance together.

"Johnny won your marbles,
Tell you what we'll do;
Dad will get you new ones right away;
Better go to sleep now,
Little man you've had a busy day."

—1982

August Wilson, whose birth name was Frederick August Kittel, was born in Pittsburgh's predominantly African-American Hill District, the setting of many of his plays. The child of a mixed-race marriage, he grew up fatherless and credits his real education in life and, incidentally, in language to the older men in his neighborhood, whose distinctive voices echo memorably in his plays. A school dropout at fifteen after a teacher unjustly accused him of plagiarism, he joined in the Black Power movement of the 1960s, eventually founding the Black Horizon on the Hill, an African-American theater company. Wilson admits to having had little confidence in his own ability to write dialogue during his early career, and his first publications were poems. A move to St. Paul, Minnesota, led to work with the Minneapolis Playwrights' Center. After his return to Pittsburgh he wrote Jitney *and* Fullerton Street, *which were staged by regional theaters. His career hit full stride with the successful debut of* Ma Rainey's Black Bottom *(1984), which was first produced at the Yale Repertory Theater and later moved to Broadway.* Joe Turner's Come and Gone *(1986) was his next success, and* Fences *(1987) and* The Piano Lesson *(1990) both won Pulitzer Prizes and other major awards, establishing Wilson as the most prominent African-American dramatist. In most of Wilson's plays a historical theme is prominent, as Wilson attempts to piece together the circumstances that led African Americans to northern cities, depicting how they remain united and sometimes divided by a common cultural heritage that transcends even the ties of friendship and family. But to these social concerns Wilson brings a long training in the theater and a poet's love of language. As he said to an interviewer in 1991, "[Poetry] is the bedrock of my playwriting. . . . The idea of metaphor is a very large idea in my plays and something that I find lacking in most contemporary plays. I think I write the kinds of plays that I do because I have twenty-six years of writing poetry underneath all of that."* Two Trains Running *(1992),* Seven Guitars *(1995), and* King Hedley II *(2001) are recent plays.*

The Piano Lesson

Characters

Doaker
Boy Willie
Lymon
Berniece

Maretha
Avery
Wining Boy
Grace

Scene: *The action of the play takes place in the kitchen and parlor of the house where Doaker Charles lives with his niece, Berniece, and her eleven-year-old daughter, Maretha. The house is sparsely furnished, and although there is evidence of a woman's touch, there is a lack of warmth and vigor. Berniece and Maretha occupy the upstairs rooms. Doaker's room is prominent and opens onto the kitchen. Dominating the parlor is an old upright piano. On the legs of the piano, carved in the manner of African sculpture, are mask-like figures resembling totems. The carvings are rendered with a grace and power of invention that lifts them out of the realm of craftsmanship and into the realm of art. At left is a staircase leading to the upstairs.*

Act I

Scene I

The lights come up on the Charles household. It is five o'clock in the morning. The dawn is beginning to announce itself, but there is something in the air that belongs to the night. A stillness that is a portent, a gathering, a coming together of something akin to a storm. There is a loud knock at the door.

BOY WILLIE: [*Off stage, calling.*] Hey, Doaker . . . Doaker! [*He knocks again and calls.*]
Hey, Doaker! Hey, Berniece! Berniece!

Doaker enters from his room. He is a tall, thin man of forty-seven, with severe features, who has for all intents and purposes retired from the world though he works full-time as a railroad cook.

DOAKER: Who is it?
BOY WILLIE: Open the door, nigger! It's me . . . Boy Willie!
DOAKER: Who?
BOY WILLIE: Boy Willie! Open the door!

Doaker opens the door and Boy Willie and Lymon enter. Boy Willie is thirty years old. He has an infectious grin and a boy-ishness that is apt for his name. He is brash and impulsive, talkative and somewhat crude in speech and manner. Lymon is twenty-nine. Boy Willie's partner, he talks little, and then with a straightforwardness that is often disarming.

DOAKER: What you doing up here?

BOY WILLIE: I told you, Lymon. Lymon talking about you might be sleep. This is Lymon. You remember Lymon Jackson from down home? This my Uncle Doaker.

DOAKER: What you doing up here? I couldn't figure out who that was. I thought you was still down in Mississippi.

BOY WILLIE: Me and Lymon selling watermelons. We got a truck out there. Got a whole truckload of watermelons. We brought them up here to sell. Where's Berniece?

Calls.

Hey, Berniece!

DOAKER: Berniece up there sleep.

BOY WILLIE: Well, let her get up.

Calls.

Hey, Berniece!

DOAKER: She got to go to work in the morning.

BOY WILLIE: Well she can get up and say hi. It's been three years since I seen her.

Calls.

Hey, Berniece! It's me . . . Boy Willie.

DOAKER: Berniece don't like all that hollering now. She got to work in the morning.

BOY WILLIE: She can go on back to bed. Me and Lymon been riding two days in that truck . . . the least she can do is get up and say hi.

DOAKER: [*Looking out the window.*] Where you all get that truck from?

BOY WILLIE: It's Lymon's. I told him let's get a load of watermelons and bring them up here.

LYMON: Boy Willie say he going back, but I'm gonna stay. See what it's like up here.

BOY WILLIE: You gonna carry me down there first.

LYMON: I told you I ain't going back down there and take a chance on that truck breaking down again. You can take the train. Hey, tell him Doaker, he can take the train back. After we sell them watermelons he have enough money he can buy him a whole railroad car.

DOAKER: You got all them watermelons stacked up there no wonder the truck broke down. I'm surprised you made it this far with a load like that. Where you break down at?

BOY WILLIE: We broke down three times! It took us two and a half days to get here. It's a good thing we picked them watermelons fresh.

LYMON: We broke down twice in West Virginia. The first time was just as soon as we got out of Sunflower. About forty miles out she broke down. We got it going and got all the way to West Virginia before she broke down again.

BOY WILLIE: We had to walk about five miles for some water.

LYMON: It got a hole in the radiator but it runs pretty good. You have to pump the brakes sometime before they catch. Boy Willie have his door open and be ready to jump when that happens.

BOY WILLIE: Lymon think that's funny. I told the nigger I give him ten dollars to get the brakes fixed. But he thinks that funny.

LYMON: They don't need fixing. All you got to do is pump them till they catch.

Berniece enters on the stairs. Thirty-five years old, with an eleven-year-old daughter, she is still in mourning for her husband after three years.

BERNIECE: What you doing all that hollering for?

BOY WILLIE: Hey, Berniece. Doaker said you was sleep. I said at least you could get up and say hi.

BERNIECE: It's five o'clock in the morning and you come in here with all this noise. You can't come like normal folks. You got to bring all that noise with you.

BOY WILLIE: Hell, I ain't done nothing but come in and say hi. I ain't got in the house good.

BERNIECE: That's what I'm talking about. You start all that hollering and carry on as soon as you hit the door.

BOY WILLIE: Aw hell, woman, I was glad to see Doaker. You ain't had to come down if you didn't want to. I come eighteen hundred miles to see my sister I figure she might want to get up and say hi. Other than that you can go back upstairs. What you got, Doaker? Where your bottle? Me and Lymon want a drink.

To Berniece.

This is Lymon. You remember Lymon Jackson from down home.

LYMON: How you doing, Berniece. You look just like I thought you looked.

BERNIECE: Why you all got to come in hollering and carrying on? Waking the neighbors with all that noise.

BOY WILLIE: They can come over and join the party. We fixing to have a party. Doaker, where your bottle? Me and Lymon celebrating. The Ghosts of the Yellow Dog got Sutter.

BERNIECE: Say what?

BOY WILLIE: Ask Lymon, they found him the next morning. Say he drowned in his well.

DOAKER: When this happen, Boy Willie?

BOY WILLIE: About three weeks ago. Me and Lymon was over in Stoner County when we heard about it. We laughed. We thought it was funny. A great big old three-hundred-and-forty-pound man gonna fall down his well.

LYMON: It remind me of Humpty Dumpty.

BOY WILLIE: Everybody say the Ghosts of the Yellow Dog pushed him.

BERNIECE: I don't want to hear that nonsense. Somebody down there pushing them people in their wells.

DOAKER: What was you and Lymon doing over in Stoner County?

BOY WILLIE: We was down there working. Lymon got some people down there.

LYMON: My cousin got some land down there. We was helping him.

BOY WILLIE: Got near about a hundred acres. He got it set up real nice. Me and Lymon was down there chopping down trees. We was using Lymon's truck to haul the wood. Me and Lymon used to haul wood all around them parts.

To Berniece.

Me and Lymon got a truckload of watermelons out there.

Berniece crosses to the window to the parlor.

Doaker, where your bottle? I know you got a bottle stuck up in your room. Come on, me and Lymon want a drink.

Doaker exits into his room.

BERNIECE: Where you all get that truck from?

BOY WILLIE: I told you it's Lymon's.

BERNIECE: Where you get the truck from, Lymon?

LYMON: I bought it.

BERNIECE: Where he get that truck from, Boy Willie?

BOY WILLIE: He told you he bought it. Bought it for a hundred and twenty dollars. I can't say where he got that hundred and twenty dollars from . . . but he bought that old piece of truck from Henry Porter. [*To* LYMON.] Where you get that hundred and twenty dollars from, nigger?

LYMON: I got it like you get yours. I know how to take care of money.

Doaker brings a bottle and sets it on the table.

BOY WILLIE: Aw hell, Doaker got some of that good whiskey. Don't give Lymon none of that. he ain't used to good whiskey. He liable to get sick.

LYMON: I done had good whiskey before.

BOY WILLIE: Lymon bought that truck so he have him a place to sleep. He down there wasn't doing no work or nothing. Sheriff looking for him. He bought that truck to keep away from the sheriff. Got Stovall looking for him too. He down there sleeping in that truck ducking and dodging both of them. I told him come on let's go up and see my sister.

BERNIECE: What the sheriff looking for you for, Lymon?

BOY WILLIE: The man don't want you to know all his business. He's my company. He ain't asking you no questions.

LYMON: It wasn't nothing. It was just a misunderstanding.

BERNIECE: He in my house. You say the sheriff looking for him, I wanna know what he looking for him for. Otherwise you all can go back out there and be where nobody don't have to ask you nothing.

LYMON: It was just a misunderstanding. Sometimes me and the sheriff we don't think alike. So we just got crossed on each other.

BERNIECE: Might be looking for him about that truck. He might have stole that truck.

BOY WILLIE: We ain't stole no truck, woman. I told you Lymon bought it.

DOAKER: Boy Willie and Lymon got more sense than to ride all the way up here in a stolen truck with a load of watermelons. Now they might have stole them watermelons, but I don't believe they stole that truck.

BOY WILLIE: You don't even know the man good and you calling him a thief. And we ain't stole them watermelons either. Them old man Pitterford's watermelons. He give me and Lymon all we could load for ten dollars.

DOAKER: No Wonder you got them stacked up out there. You must have five hundred watermelons stacked up out there.

BERNIECE: Boy Willie, when you and Lymon planning on going back?

BOY WILLIE: Lymon say he staying. As soon as we sell them watermelons I'm going on back.

BERNIECE: [*Starts to exit up the stairs.*] That's what you need to do. And you need to do it quick. Come in here disrupting the house. I don't want all that loud carrying on around here. I'm surprised you ain't woke Maretha up.

BOY WILLIE: I was fixing to get her now.

Calls.

Hey, Maretha!

DOAKER: Berniece don't like all that hollering now.

BERNIECE: Don't you wake that child up!

BOY WILLIE: You going up there . . . wake her up and tell her her uncle's here. I ain't seen her in three years. Wake her up and send her down here. She can go back to bed.

BERNIECE: I ain't waking that child up . . . and don't you be making all that noise. You and Lymon need to sell them watermelons and go on back.

Berniece exits up the stairs.

BOY WILLIE: I see Berniece still try to be stuck up.

DOAKER: Berniece alright. She don't want you making all that noise. Maretha up there sleep. Let her sleep until she get up. She can see you then.

BOY WILLIE: I ain't thinking about Berniece. You hear from Wining Boy? You know Cleotha died?

DOAKER: Yeah, I heard that. He come by here about a year ago. Had a whole sack of money. He stayed here about two weeks. Ain't offered nothing. Berniece asked him for three dollars to buy some food and he got mad and left.

LYMON: Who's Wining Boy?

BOY WILLIE: That's my uncle. That's Doaker's brother. You heard me talk about Wining Boy. He play piano. He done made some records and everything. He still doing that, Doaker?

DOAKER: He made one or two records a long time ago. That's the only ones I ever known him to make. If you let him tell it he a big recording star.

BOY WILLIE: He stopped down home about two years ago. That's what I hear. I don't know. Me and Lymon was up on Parchman Farm doing them three years.

DOAKER: He don't never stay in one place. Now, he been here about eight months ago. Back in the winter. Now, you subject not to see him for another two years. It's liable to be that long before he stop by.

BOY WILLIE: If he had a whole sack of money you liable never to see him. You ain't gonna see him until he get broke. Just as soon as that sack of money is gone you look up and he be on your doorstep.

LYMON: [*Noticing the piano.*] Is that the piano?

BOY WILLIE: Yeah . . . look here, Lymon. See how it got all those carvings on it. See, that's what I was talking about. See how it's carved up real nice and polished and everything? You never find you another piano like that.

LYMON: Yeah, that look real nice.

BOY WILLIE: I told you. See how it's polished? My mama used to polish it every day. See all them pictures carved on it? That's what I was talking about. You can get a nice price for that piano.

LYMON: That's all Boy Willie talked about the whole trip up here. I got tired of hearing him talk about the piano.

BOY WILLIE: All you want to talk about is women. You ought to hear this nigger, Doaker. Talking about all the women he gonna get when he get up here. He ain't had none down there but he gonna get a hundred when he get up here.

DOAKER: How your people doing down there, Lymon?

LYMON: They alright. They still there. I come up here to see what it's like up here. Boy Willie trying to get me to go back and farm with him.

BOY WILLIE: Sutter's brother selling the land. He say he gonna sell it to me. That's why I come up here. I got one part of it. Sell them watermelons and get me another part. Get Berniece to sell that piano and I'll have the third part.

DOAKER: Berniece ain't gonna sell that piano.

BOY WILLIE: I'm gonna talk to her. When she see I got a chance to get Sutter's land she'll come around.

DOAKER: You can put that thought out your mind. Berniece ain't gonna sell that piano.

BOY WILLIE: I'm gonna talk to her. She been playing on it?

DOAKER: You know she won't touch that piano. I ain't never known her to touch it since Mama Ola died. That's over seven years now. She say it got blood on it. She got Maretha playing on it though. Say Maretha can go on and do everything she can't do. Got her in an extra school down at the Irene Kaufman Settlement House. She want Maretha to grow up and be a schoolteacher. Say she good enough she can teach on the piano.

BOY WILLIE: Maretha don't need to be playing on no piano. She can play on the guitar.

DOAKER: How much land Sutter got left?

BOY WILLIE: Got a hundred acres. Good land. He done sold it piece by piece, he kept the good part for himself. Now he got to give that up. His brother come down from Chicago for the funeral . . . he up there in Chicago got some kind of business with soda fountain equipment. He anxious to sell the land, Doaker. He don't want to be bothered with it. He called me to him and said cause of how long our families done known each other and how we been good friends and all, say he wanted to sell the land to me. Say he'd rather see me with it than Jim Stovall. Told me he'd let me have it for two thousand dollars cash money. He don't know I found out the most Stovall would give him for it was fifteen hundred dollars. He trying to get that extra five hundred out of me telling me he doing me a favor. I thanked him just as nice. Told him what a good man Sutter was and how he had my sympathy and all. Told him to give me two weeks. He said he'd wait on me. That's why I come up here. Sell them watermelons. Get Berniece to sell that piano. Put them two parts with the part I done saved. Walk in there. Tip my hat. Lay my money down on the table. Get my deed and walk on out. This time I get to keep all the cotton. Hire me some men to work it for me. Gin my cotton. Get my seed. And I'll see you again next year. Might even plant some tobacco or some oats.

DOAKER: You gonna have a hard time trying to get Berniece to sell that piano. You know Avery Brown from down there don't you? He up here now. He followed Berniece up here trying to get her to marry him after Crawley got killed. He been up here about two years. He call himself a preacher now.

BOY WILLIE: I know Avery. I know him from when he used to work on the Willshaw place. Lymon know him too.

DOAKER: He after Berniece to marry him. She keep telling him no but he won't give up. He keep pressing her on it.

BOY WILLIE: Avery think all white men is bigshots. He don't know there some white men ain't got as much as he got.

DOAKER: He supposed to come past here this morning. Berniece going down to the bank with him to see if he can get a loan to start his church. That's why I know Berniece ain't gonna sell that piano. He tried to get her to sell it to help him start his church. Sent the man around and everything.

BOY WILLIE: What man?

DOAKER: Some white fellow was going around to all the colored people's houses looking to buy up musical instruments. He'd buy anything. Drums. Guitars. Harmonicas. Pianos. Avery sent him past here. He looked at the piano and got excited. Offered her a nice price. She turned him down and got on Avery for sending him past. The man kept on her about two weeks. He seen where she wasn't gonna sell it, he gave her his number and told her if she ever wanted to sell it to call him first. Say he'd go one better than what anybody else would give her for it.

BOY WILLIE: How much he offer her for it?

DOAKER: Now you know me. She didn't say and I didn't ask. I just know it was a nice price.

LYMON: All you got to do is find out who he is and tell him somebody else wanna buy it from you. Tell him you can't make up your mind who to sell it to, and if he like Doaker say, he'll give you anything you want for it.

BOY WILLIE: That's what I'm gonna do. I'm gonna find out who he is from Avery.

DOAKER: It ain't gonna do you no good. Berniece ain't gonna sell that piano.

BOY WILLIE: She ain't got to sell it. I'm gonna sell it. I own just as much of it as she does.

BERNIECE: [Offstage, hollers.] Doaker! Go on get away. Doaker!

DOAKER: [Calling.] Berniece?

Doaker and Boy Willie rush to the stairs, Boy Willie runs up the stairs, passing Berniece as she enters, running.

DOAKER: Berniece, what's the matter? You alright? What's the matter?

Berniece tries to catch her breath. She is unable to speak.

DOAKER: That's alright. Take your time. You alright. What's the matter?

He calls.

Hey, Boy Willie?

BOY WILLIE: [*Offstage.*] Ain't nobody up here.

BERNIECE: Sutter . . . Sutter's standing at the top of the steps.

DOAKER: [*Calls.*] Boy Willie!

Lymon crosses to the stairs and looks up. Boy Willie enters from the stairs.

BOY WILLIE: Hey Doaker, what's wrong with her? Berniece, what's wrong? Who was you talking to?

DOAKER: She say she seen Sutter's ghost standing at the top of the stairs.

BOY WILLIE: Seen what? Sutter? She ain't seen no Sutter.

BERNIECE: He was standing right up there.

BOY WILLIE: [*Entering on the stairs.*] That's all in Berniece's head. Ain't nobody up there. Go on up there, Doaker.

DOAKER: I'll take your word for it. Berniece talking about what she seen. She say Sutter's ghost standing at the top of the steps. She ain't just make all that up.

BOY WILLIE: She up there dreaming. She ain't seen no ghost.

LYMON: You want a glass of water, Berniece? Get her a glass of water, Boy Willie.

BOY WILLIE: She don't need no water. She ain't seen nothing. Go on up there and look. Ain't nobody up there but Maretha.

DOAKER: Let Berniece tell it.

BOY WILLIE: I ain't stopping her from telling it.

DOAKER: What happened, Berniece?

BERNIECE: I come out my room to come back down here and Sutter was standing there in the hall.

BOY WILLIE: What he look like?

BERNIECE: He look like Sutter. He look like he always look.

BOY WILLIE: Sutter couldn't find his way from Big Sandy to Little Sandy. How he gonna find his way all the way up here to Pittsburgh? Sutter ain't never even heard of Pittsburgh.

DOAKER: Go on, Berniece.

BERNIECE: Just standing there with the blue suit on.

BOY WILLIE: The man ain't never left Marlin County when he was living . . . and he's gonna come all the way up here now that he's dead?

DOAKER: Let her finish. I want to hear what she got to say.

BOY WILLIE: I'll tell you this. If Berniece had seen him like she think she seen him she'd still be running.

DOAKER: Go on, Berniece. Don't pay Boy Willie no mind.

BERNIECE: He was standing there . . . had his hand on top of his head. Look like he might have thought if he took his hand down his head might have fallen off.

LYMON: Did he have on a hat?

BERNIECE: Just had on that blue suit . . . I told him to go away and he just stood there looking at me . . . calling Boy Willie's name.

BOY WILLIE: What he calling my name for?

BERNIECE: I believe you pushed him in the well.

BOY WILLIE: Now what kind of sense that make? You telling me I'm gonna go out there and hide in the weeds with all them dogs and things he got around there . . . I'm gonna hide and wait till I catch him looking down his well just right . . . then I'm gonna run over and push him in. A great big old three-hundred-and-forty-pound man.

BERNIECE: Well, what he calling your name for?

BOY WILLIE: He bending over looking down his well, woman . . . how he know who pushed him? It could have been anybody. Where was you when Sutter fell in his well? Where was Doaker? Me and Lymon was over in Stoner County. Tell her, Lymon. The Ghosts of the Yellow Dog got Sutter. That's what happened to him.

BERNIECE: You can talk all that Ghosts of the Yellow Dog stuff if you want. I know better.

LYMON: The Ghosts of the Yellow Dog pushed him. That's what the people say. They found him in his well and all the people say it must be the Ghosts of the Yellow Dog. Just like all them other men.

BOY WILLIE: Come talking about he looking for me. What he come all the way up here for? If he looking for me all he got to do is wait. He could have saved himself a trip if he looking for me. That ain't nothing but in Berniece's head. Ain't no telling what she liable to come up with next.

BERNIECE: Boy Willie, I want you and Lymon to go ahead and leave my house. Just go on somewhere. You don't do nothing but bring trouble with you everywhere you go. If it wasn't for you Crawley would still be alive.

BOY WILLIE: Crawley what? I ain't had nothing to do with Crawley getting killed. Crawley three time seven. He had his own mind.

BERNIECE: Just go on and leave. Let Sutter go somewhere else looking for you.

BOY WILLIE: I'm leaving. Soon as we sell them watermelons. Other than that I ain't going nowhere. Hell, I just got here. Talking about Sutter looking for me. Sutter was looking for that piano. That's what he was looking for. He had to die to find out where that piano was at . . . If I was you I'd get rid of it. That's the way to get rid of Sutter's ghost. Get rid of that piano.

BERNIECE: I want you and Lymon to go on and take all this confusion out of my house!

BOY WILLIE: Hey, tell her, Doaker. What kind of sense that make? I told you, Lymon, as soon as Berniece see me she was gonna start something. Didn't I tell you that? Now she done made up that story about Sutter just so she could tell me to leave her house. Well, hell, I ain't going nowhere till I sell them watermelons.

BERNIECE: Well why don't you go out there and sell them! Sell them and go on back!

BOY WILLIE: We waiting till the people get up.

LYMON: Boy Willie say if you get out there too early and wake the people up they get mad at you and won't buy nothing from you.

DOAKER: You won't be waiting long. You done let the sun catch up with you. This the time everybody be getting up around here.

BERNIECE: Come on, Doaker, walk up here with me. Let me get Maretha up and get her started. I got to get ready myself. Boy Willie, just go on out there and sell them watermelons and you and Lymon leave my house.

Berniece and Doaker exit up the stairs.

BOY WILLIE: [*Calling after them.*] If you see Sutter up there . . . tell him I'm down here waiting on him.

LYMON: What if she see him again?

BOY WILLIE: That's all in her head. There ain't no ghost up there.

Calls.

Hey, Doaker . . . I told you ain't nothing up there.

LYMON: I'm glad he didn't say he was looking for me.

BOY WILLIE: I wish I would see Sutter's ghost. Give me a chance to put a whupping on him.

LYMON: You ought to stay up here with me. You be down there working his land . . . he might come looking for you all the time.

BOY WILLIE: I ain't thinking about Sutter. And I ain't thinking about staying up here. You stay up here. I'm going back and get Sutter's land. You think you ain't got to work up here. You think this the land of milk and honey. But I ain't scared of work. I'm going back and farm every acre of that land.

Doaker enters from the stairs.

I told you there ain't nothing up there, Doaker. Berniece dreaming all that.

DOAKER: I believe Berniece seen something. Berniece level-headed. She ain't just made all that up. She say Sutter had on a suit. I don't believe she ever seen Sutter in a suit. I believe that's what he was buried in, and that's what Berniece saw.

BOY WILLIE: Well, let her keep on seeing him then. As long as he don't mess with me.

Doaker starts to cook his breakfast.

I heard about you, Doaker. They say you got all the women looking out for you down home. They be looking to see you coming. Say you got a different one every two weeks. Say they be fighting one another for you to stay with them.

To Lymon.

Look at him, Lymon. He know it's true.

DOAKER: I ain't thinking about no women. They never get me tied up with them. After Coreen I ain't got no use for them. I stay up on Jack Slattery's place when I be down there. All them women want is somebody with a steady payday.

BOY WILLIE: That ain't what I hear. I hear every two weeks the women all put on their dresses and line up at the railroad station.

DOAKER: I don't get down there but once a month. I used to go down there every two weeks but they keep switching me around. They keep switching all the fellows around.

BOY WILLIE: Doaker can't turn that railroad loose. He was working the railroad when I was walking around crying for sugartit. My mama used to brag on him.

DOAKER: I'm cooking now, but I used to line track. I pieced together the Yellow Dog stitch by stitch. Rail by rail. Line track all up around there. I lined track all up around Sunflower and Clarksdale. Wining Boy worked with me. He helped put in some of that track. He'd work it for six months and quit. Go back to playing piano and gambling.

BOY WILLIE: How long you been with the railroad now?

DOAKER: Twenty-seven years. Now, I'll tell you something about the railroad. What I done learned after twenty-seven years. See, you got North. You got West. You look over here you got South. Over there you got East. Now, you can start from anywhere. Don't care where you at. You got to go one of them four ways. And whichever way you decide to go they got a railroad that will take you there. Now, that's something simple. You think anybody would be able to understand that. But you'd be surprised how many people trying to go North get on a train going West. They think the train's supposed to go where they going rather than where it's going.

Now, why people going? Their sister's sick. They leaving before they kill somebody . . . and they sitting across from somebody who's leaving to keep from getting killed. They leaving cause they can't get satisfied. They going to meet someone. I wish I had a dollar for every time that someone wasn't at the station to meet them. I done seen that a lot. In between the time they sent the telegram and the time the person get there . . . they done forgot all about them.

They got so many trains out there they have a hard time keeping them from running into each other. Got trains going every whichaway. Got people on all of them. Somebody going where somebody just left. If everybody stay in one place I believe this would be a better world. Now what I done learned after twenty-seven years of railroading is this . . . if the train stays on the track . . . it's going to get where it's going. It might not be where you going. If it ain't then all you got to do is sit and wait cause the train's coming back to get you. The train don't never stop. It'll come back every time. Now I'll tell you another thing . . .

BOY WILLIE: What you cooking over there, Doaker? Me and Lymon's hungry.

DOAKER: Go on down there to Wylie and Kirkpatrick to Eddie's restaurant. Coffee cost a nickel and you can get two eggs, sausage, and grits for fifteen cents. He even give you a biscuit with it.

BOY WILLIE: That look good what you got. Give me a little piece of that grilled bread.

DOAKER: Here . . . go on take the whole piece.

BOY WILLIE: Here you go, Lymon . . . you want a piece?

He gives Lymon a piece of toast. Maretha enters from the stairs.

BOY WILLIE: Hey, sugar. Come here and give me a hug. Come on give Uncle Boy Willie a hug. Don't be shy. Look at her, Doaker. She done got bigger. Ain't she got big?

DOAKER: Yeah, she getting up there.

BOY WILLIE: How you doing, sugar?

MARETHA: Fine.

BOY WILLIE: You was just a little old thing last time I seen you. You remember me, don't you? This your Uncle Boy Willie from down South. That there's Lymon. He my friend. We come up here to sell watermelons. You like watermelons?

Maretha nods.

We got a whole truckload out front. You can have as many as you want. What you been doing?

MARETHA: Nothing.

BOY WILLIE: Don't be shy now. Look at you getting all big. How old is you?

MARETHA: Eleven. I'm gonna be twelve soon.

BOY WILLIE: You like it up here? You like the North?

MARETHA: It's alright.

BOY WILLIE: That there's Lymon. Did you say hi to Lymon?

MARETHA: Hi.

LYMON: How you doing? You look just like your mama. I remember you when you was wearing diapers.

BOY WILLIE: You gonna come down South and see me? Uncle Boy Willie gonna get him a farm. Gonna get a great big old farm. Come down there and I'll teach you how to ride a mule. Teach you how to kill a chicken, too.

MARETHA: I seen my mama do that.

BOY WILLIE: Ain't nothing to it. You just grab him by his neck and twist it. Get you a real good grip and then you just wring his neck and throw him in the pot. Cook him up. Then you got some good eating. What you like to eat? What kind of food you like?

MARETHA: I like everything . . . except I don't like no black-eyed peas.

BOY WILLIE: Uncle Doaker tell me your mama got you playing that piano. Come on play something for me.

Boy Willie crosses over to the piano followed by Maretha.

Show me what you can do. Come on now. Here . . . Uncle Boy Willie give you a dime . . . show me what you can do. Don't be bashful now. That dime say you can't be bashful.

Maretha plays. It is something any beginner first learns.

Here, let me show you something.

Boy Willie sits and plays a simple boogie-woogie.

See that? See what I'm doing? That's what you call the boogie-woogie. See now . . . you can get up and dance to that. That's how good it sound. It sound like you wanna dance. You can dance to that. It'll hold you up. Whatever kind of dance you wanna do you can dance to that right there. See that? See how it go? Ain't nothing to it. Go on you do it.

MARETHA: I got to read it on the paper.

BOY WILLIE: You don't need no paper. Go on. Do just like that there.

BERNIECE: Maretha! You get up here and get ready to go so you be on time. Ain't no need you trying to take advantage of company.

MARETHA: I got to go.

BOY WILLIE: Uncle Boy Willie gonna get you a guitar. Let Uncle Doaker teach you how to play that. You don't need to read no paper to play the guitar. Your mama told you about that piano? You know how them pictures got on there?

MARETHA: She say it just always been like that since she got it.

BOY WILLIE: You hear that, Doaker? And you sitting up here in the house with Berniece.

DOAKER: I ain't got nothing to do with that. I don't get in the way of Berniece's raising her.

BOY WILLIE: You tell your mama to tell you about that piano. You ask her how them pictures got on there. If she don't tell you I'll tell you.

BERNIECE: Maretha!

MARETHA: I got to get ready to go.

BOY WILLIE: She getting big, Doaker. You remember her, Lymon?

LYMON: She used to be real little.

There is a knock on the door. Doaker goes to answer it. Avery enters. Thirty-eight years old, honest and ambitious, he has taken to the city like a fish to water, finding in it opportunities for growth and advancement that did not exist for him in the rural South. He is dressed in a suit and tie with a gold cross around his neck. He carries a small Bible.

DOAKER: Hey, Avery, come on in. Berniece upstairs.

BOY WILLIE: Look at him . . . look at him . . . he don't know what to say. He wasn't expecting to see me.

AVERY: Hey, Boy Willie. What you doing up here?

BOY WILLIE: Look at him, Lymon.

AVERY: Is that Lymon? Lymon Jackson?

BOY WILLIE: Yeah, you know Lymon.

DOAKER: Berniece be ready in a minute, Avery.

BOY WILLIE: Doaker say you a preacher now. What . . . we supposed to call you Reverend? You used to be plain old Avery. When you get to be a preacher, nigger?

LYMON: Avery say he gonna be a preacher so he don't have to work.

BOY WILLIE: I remember when you was down there on the Willshaw place planting cotton. You wasn't thinking about no Reverend then.

AVERY: That must be your truck out there. I saw that truck with them watermelons, I was trying to figure out what it was doing in front of the house.

BOY WILLIE: Yeah, me and Lymon selling watermelons. That's Lymon's truck.

DOAKER: Berniece say you all going down to the bank.

AVERY: Yeah, they give me a half day off work. I got an appointment to talk to the bank about getting a loan to start my church.

BOY WILLIE: Lymon say preachers don't have to work. Where you working at, nigger?

DOAKER: Avery got him one of them good jobs. He working at one of them skyscrapers downtown.

AVERY: I'm working down there at the Gulf Building running an elevator. Got a pension and everything. They even give you a turkey on Thanksgiving.

LYMON: How you know the rope ain't gonna break? Ain't you scared the rope's gonna break?

AVERY: That's steel. They got steel cables hold it up. It take a whole lot of breaking to break that steel. Naw, I ain't worried about nothing like that. It ain't nothing but a little old elevator. Now, I wouldn't get in none of them airplanes. You couldn't pay me to do nothing like that.

LYMON: That be fun. I'd rather do that than ride in one of them elevators.

BOY WILLIE: How many of them watermelons you wanna buy?

AVERY: I thought you was gonna give me one seeing as how you got a whole truck full.

BOY WILLIE: You can get one, get two. I'll give you two for a dollar.

AVERY: I can't eat but one. How much are they?

BOY WILLIE: Aw, nigger, you know I'll give you a watermelon. Go on, take as many as you want. Just leave some for me and Lymon to sell.

AVERY: I don't want but one.

BOY WILLIE: How you get to be a preacher, Avery? I might want to be a preacher one day. Have everybody call me Reverend Boy Willie.

AVERY: It come to me in a dream. God called me and told me he wanted me to be a shepherd for his flock. That's what I'm gonna call my church . . . The Good Shepherd Church of God in Christ.

DOAKER: Tell him what you told me. Tell him about the three hobos.

AVERY: Boy Willie don't want to hear all that.

LYMON: I do. Lots a people say your dreams can come true.

AVERY: Naw. You don't want to hear all that.

DOAKER: Go on. I told him you was a preacher. He didn't want to believe me. Tell him about the three hobos.

AVERY: Well, it come to me in a dream. See . . . I was sitting out in this railroad yard watching the trains go by. The train stopped and these three hobos got off. They told me they had come from Nazareth and was on their way to Jerusalem. They had three candles. They gave me one and told me to light it . . . but to be careful that it didn't go out. Next thing I knew I was standing in front of this house. Something told me to go knock on the door. This old woman opened the door and said they had been waiting on me. Then she led me into this room. It was a big room and it was full of all kinds of different people. They looked like anybody else except they all had sheep heads and was making noise like sheep make. I heard somebody call my name. I looked around and there was these same three hobos. They told me to take off my clothes and they give me a blue robe with gold thread. They washed my feet and combed my hair. Then they showed me these three doors and told me to pick one.

I went through one of them doors and that flame leapt off that candle and it seemed like my whole head caught fire. I looked around and there was four or five other men standing there with these same blue robes on. Then we heard a voice tell us to look out across this valley. We looked out and saw the valley was full of wolves. The voice told us that these sheep people that I had seen in the other room had to go over to the other side of this valley and somebody had to take them. Then I heard another voice say, "Who shall I send?" Next thing I knew I said, "Here I am. Send me." That's when I met Jesus. He say, "If you go, I'll go with you." Something told me to say, "Come on. Let's go." That's when I woke up. My head still felt like it was on fire . . . but I had a peace about myself that was hard to explain. I knew right then that I had been filled with the Holy Ghost and called to be a servant of the Lord. It took me a while before I could accept that. But then a lot of little ways God showed me that it was true. So I became a preacher.

LYMON: I see why you gonna call it the Good Shepherd Church. You dreaming about them sheep people. I can see that easy.

BOY WILLIE: Doaker say you sent some white man past the house to look at that piano. Say he was going around to all the colored people's houses looking to buy up musical instruments.

AVERY: Yeah, but Berniece didn't want to sell that piano. After she told me about it . . . I could see why she didn't want to sell it.

BOY WILLIE: What's this man's name?

AVERY: Oh, that's a while back now. I done forgot his name. He give Berniece a card with his name and telephone number on it, but I believe she throwed it away.

Berniece and Maretha enter from the stairs.

BERNIECE: Maretha, run back upstairs and get my pocketbook. And wipe that hair grease off your forehead. Go ahead, hurry up.

Maretha exits up the stairs.

How you doing, Avery? You done got all dressed up. You look nice. Boy Willie, I thought you and Lymon was going to sell them watermelons.

BOY WILLIE: Lymon done got sleepy. We liable to get some sleep first.

LYMON: I ain't sleepy.

DOAKER: As many watermelons as you got stacked up on that truck out there, you ought to have been gone.

BOY WILLIE: We gonna go in a minute. We going.

BERNIECE: Doaker. I'm gonna stop down there on Logan Street. You want anything?

DOAKER: You can pick up some ham hocks if you going down there. See if you can get the smoked ones. If they ain't got that get the fresh ones. Don't get the ones that got all that fat under the skin. Look for the long ones. They nice and lean.

He gives her a dollar.

Don't get the short ones lessen they smoked. If you got to get the fresh ones make sure that they the long ones. If they ain't got them smoked then go ahead and get the short ones.

Pause.

You may as well get some turnip greens while you down there. I got some buttermilk . . . if you pickup some cornmeal I'll make me some cornbread and cook up them turnip greens.

Maretha enters from the stairs.

MARETHA: We gonna take the streetcar?

BERNIECE: Me and Avery gonna drop you off at the settlement house. You mind them people down there. Don't be going down there showing your color. Boy Willie, I done told you what to do. I'll see you later, Doaker.

AVERY: I'll be seeing you again, Boy Willie.

BOY WILLIE: Hey, Berniece . . . what's the name of that man Avery sent past say he want to buy the piano?

BERNIECE: I knew it. I knew it when I first seen you. I knew you was up to something.

BOY WILLIE: Sutter's brother say he selling the land to me. He waiting on me now. Told me he'd give me two weeks. I got one part. Sell them watermelons get me another part. Then we can sell that piano and I'll have the third part.

BERNIECE: I ain't selling that piano, Boy Willie. If that's why you come
up here you can just forget about it.

To Doaker.

Doaker, I'll see you later. Boy Willie ain't nothing but a whole lot of
mouth. I ain't paying him no mind. If he come up here thinking he
gonna sell that piano then he done come up here for nothing.

Berniece, Avery, and Maretha exit the front door.

BOY WILLIE: Hey, Lymon! You ready to go sell these watermelons.

*Boy Willie and Lymon start to exit. At the door Boy Willie turns to
Doaker.*

Hey, Doaker . . . if Berniece don't want to sell that piano . . . I'm
gonna cut it in half and go on and sell my half.

Boy Willie and Lymon exit.

The lights go down on the scene.

Scene II

*The lights come up on the kitchen. It is three days later. Wining Boy sits at the
kitchen table. There is a half-empty pint bottle on the table. Doaker busies
himself washing pots. Wining Boy is fifty-six years old. Doaker's older brother,
he tries to present the image of a successful musician and gambler, but his
music, his clothes, and even his manner of presentation are old. He is a man
who looking back over his life continues to live it with an odd mixture of zest
and sorrow.*

WINING BOY: So the Ghosts of the Yellow Dog got Sutter. That just go
to show you I believe I always lived right. They say every dog
gonna have his day and time it go around it sure come back to you.
I done seen that a thousand times. I know the truth of that. But I'll
tell you outright . . . if I see Sutter's ghost I'll be on the first thing I
find that got wheels on it.

Doaker enters from his room.

DOAKER: Wining Boy!

WINING BOY: And I'll tell you another thing . . . Berniece ain't gonna
sell that piano.

DOAKER: That's what she told him. He say he gonna cut it in half and
go on and sell his half. They been around here three days trying to

sell them watermelons. They trying to get out to where the white folks live but the truck keep breaking down. They go a block or two and it break down again. They trying to get out to Squirrel Hill and can't get around the corner. He say soon as he can get that truck empty to where he can set the piano up in there he gonna take it out of here and go sell it.

WINING BOY: What about them boys Sutter got? How come they ain't farming that land?

DOAKER: One of them going to school. He left down there and come North to school. The other one ain't got as much sense as that frying pan over yonder. That is the dumbest white man I ever seen. He'd stand in the river and watch it rise till it drown him.

WINING BOY: Other than seeing Sutter's ghost how's Berniece doing?

DOAKER: She doing alright. She still got Crawley on her mind. He been dead three years but she still holding on to him. She need to go out here and let one of these fellows grab a whole handful of whatever she got. She act like it done got precious.

WINING BOY: They always told me any fish will bite if you got good bait.

DOAKER: She stuck up on it. She think it's better than she is. I believe she messing around with Avery. They got something going. He a preacher now. If you let him tell it the Holy Ghost sat on his head and heaven opened up with thunder and lightning and God was calling his name. Told him to go out and preach and tend to his flock. That's what he gonna call his church. The Good Shepherd Church.

WINING BOY: They had that joker down in Spear walking around talking about he Jesus Christ. He gonna live the life of Christ. Went through the Last Supper and everything. Rented him a mule on Palm Sunday and rode through the town. Did everything ... talking about he Christ. He did everything until they got up to that crucifixion part. Got up to that part and told everybody to go home and quit pretending. He got up to the crucifixion part and changed his mind. Had a whole bunch of folks come down there to see him get nailed to the cross. I don't know who's the worse fool. Him or them. Had all them folks come down there ... even carried the cross up this little hill. People standing around waiting to see him get nailed to the cross and he stop everything and preach a little sermon and told everybody to go home. Had enough nerve to tell them to come to church on Easter Sunday to celebrate his resurrection.

DOAKER: I'm surprised Avery ain't thought about that. He trying every little thing to get him a congregation together. They meeting over at his house till he get him a church.

WINING BOY: Ain't nothing wrong with being a preacher. You got the preacher on one hand and the gambler on the other. Sometimes there ain't too much difference in them.

DOAKER: How long you been in Kansas City?

WINING BOY: Since I left here. I got tied up with some old gal down there.

Pause.

You know Cleotha died.

DOAKER: Yeah, I heard that last time I was down there. I was sorry to hear that.

WINING BOY: One of her friends wrote and told me. I got the letter right here.

He takes the letter out of his pocket.

I was down in Kansas City and she wrote and told me Cleotha had died. Name of Willa Bryant. She say she know cousin Rupert.

He opens the letter and reads.

Dear Wining Boy: I am writing this letter to let you know Miss Cleotha Holman passed on Saturday the first of May she departed this world in the loving arms of her sister Miss Alberta Samuels. I know you would want to know this and am writing as a friend of Cleotha. There have been many hardships since last you seen her but she survived them all and to the end was a good woman whom I hope have God's grace and is in His Paradise. Your cousin Rupert Bates is my friend also and he give me your address and I pray this reaches you about Cleotha. Miss Willa Bryant. A friend.

He folds the letter and returns it to his pocket.

They was nailing her coffin shut by the time I heard about it. I never knew she was sick. I believe it was that yellow jaundice. That's what killed her mama.

DOAKER: Cleotha wasn't but forty-some

WINING BOY: She was forty-six. I got ten years on her. I met her when she was sixteen. You remember I used to run around there. Couldn't nothing keep me still. Much as I loved Cleotha I loved to ramble.

Couldn't nothing keep me still. We got married and we used to fight about it all the time. Then one day she asked me to leave. Told me she loved me before I left. Told me, Wining Boy, you got a home as long as I got mine. And I believe in my heart I always felt that and that kept me safe.

DOAKER: Cleotha always did have a nice way about her.

WINING BOY: Man that woman was something. I used to thank the Lord. Many a night I sat up and looked out over my life. Said, well, I had Cleotha. When it didn't look like there was nothing else for me, I said, thank God, at least I had that. If ever I go anywhere in this life I done known a good woman. And that used to hold me till the next morning.

Pause.

What you got? Give me a little nip. I know you got something stuck up in your room.

DOAKER: I ain't seen you walk in here and put nothing on the table. You done sat there and drank up your whiskey. Now you talking about what you got.

WINING BOY: I got plenty money. Give me a little nip.

Doaker carries a glass into his room and returns with it half-filled. He sets it on the table in front of Wining Boy.

WINING BOY: You hear from Coreen?

DOAKER: She up in New York. I let her go from my mind.

WINING BOY: She was something back then. She wasn't too pretty but she had a way of looking at you made you know there was a whole lot of woman there. You got married and snatched her out from under us and we all got mad at you.

DOAKER: She up in New York City. That's what I hear.

The door opens and Boy Willie and Lymon enter.

BOY WILLIE: Aw hell . . . look here! We was just talking about you. Doaker say you left out of here with a whole sack of money. I told him we wasn't going see you till you got broke.

WINING BOY: What you mean broke? I got a whole pocketful of money.

DOAKER: Did you all get that truck fixed?

BOY WILLIE: We got it running and got halfway out there on Centre and it broke down again. Lymon went out there and messed it up some more. Fellow told us we got to wait till tomorrow to get it fixed. Say he have it running like new. Lymon going back down there and sleep in the truck so the people don't take the watermelons.

LYMON: Lymon nothing. You go down there and sleep in it.

BOY WILLIE: You was sleeping in it down home, nigger! I don't know nothing about sleeping in no truck.

LYMON: I ain't sleeping in no truck.

BOY WILLIE: They can take all the watermelons. I don't care. Wining Boy, where you coming from? Where you been?

WINING BOY: I been down in Kansas City.

BOY WILLIE: You remember Lymon? Lymon Jackson.

WINING BOY: Yeah, I used to know his daddy.

BOY WILLIE: Doaker say you don't never leave no address with nobody. Say he got to depend on your whim. See when it strike you to pay a visit.

WINING BOY: I got four or five addresses.

BOY WILLIE: Doaker say Berniece asked you for three dollars and you got mad and left.

WINING BOY: Berniece try and rule over you too much for me. That's why I left. It wasn't about no three dollars.

BOY WILLIE: Where you getting all these sacks of money from? I need to be with you. Doaker say you had a whole sack of money . . . turn some of it loose.

WINING BOY: I was just fixing to ask you for five dollars.

BOY WILLIE: I ain't got no money. I'm trying to get some. Doaker tell you about Sutter? The Ghosts of the Yellow Dog got him about three weeks ago. Berniece done seen his ghost and everything. He right upstairs.

Calls.

Hey Sutter! Wining Boy's here. Come on, get a drink!

WINING BOY: How many that make the Ghosts of the Yellow Dog done got?

BOY WILLIE: Must be about nine or ten, eleven or twelve. I don't know.

DOAKER: You got Ed Saunders. Howard Peterson. Charlie Webb.

WINING BOY: Robert Smith. That fellow that shot Becky's boy . . . say he was stealing peaches . . .

DOAKER: You talking about Bob Mallory.

BOY WILLIE: Berniece say she don't believe all that about the Ghosts of the Yellow Dog.

WINING BOY: She ain't got to believe. You go ask them white folks in Sunflower County if they believe. You go ask Sutter if he believe. I don't care if Berniece believe or not. I done been to where the Southern cross the Yellow Dog and called out their names. They talk back to you, too.

LYMON: What they sound like? The wind or something?

BOY WILLIE: You done been there for real, Wining Boy?

WINING BOY: Nineteen thirty. July of nineteen thirty I stood right there on that spot. It didn't look like nothing was going right in my life. I said everything can't go wrong all the time . . . let me go down there and call on the Ghosts of the Yellow Dog, see if they can help me. I went down there and right there where them two railroads cross each other . . . I stood right there on that spot and called out their names. They talk back to you, too.

LYMON: People say you can ask them questions. They talk to you like that?

WINING BOY: A lot of things you got to find out on your own. I can't say how they talked to nobody else. But to me it just filled me up in a strange sort of way to be standing there on that spot. I didn't want to leave. It felt like the longer I stood there the bigger I got. I seen the train coming and it seem like I was bigger than the train. I started not to move. But something told me to go ahead and get on out the way. The train passed and I started to go back up there and stand some more. But something told me not to do it. I walked away from there feeling like a king. Went on and had a stroke of luck that run on for three years. So I don't care if Berniece believe or not. Berniece ain't got to believe. I know cause I been there. Now Doaker'll tell you about the Ghosts of the Yellow Dog.

DOAKER: I don't try and talk that stuff with Berniece. Avery got her all tied up in that church. She just think it's a whole lot of nonsense.

BOY WILLIE: Berniece don't believe in nothing. She just think she believe. She believe in anything if it's convenient for her to believe. But when that convenience run out then she ain't got nothing to stand on.

WINING BOY: Let's not get on Berniece now. Doaker tell me you talking about selling that piano.

BOY WILLIE: Yeah . . . hey, Doaker, I got the name of that man Avery was talking about. The man what's fixing the truck gave me his name. Everybody know him. Say he buy up anything you can make music with. I got his name and his telephone number. Hey, Wining Boy, Sutter's brother say he selling the land to me. I got one part. Sell them watermelons get me the second part. Then . . . soon as I get them watermelons out that truck I'm gonna take and sell that piano and get the third part.

DOAKER: That land ain't worth nothing no more. The smart white man's up here in these cities. He cut the land loose and step back and watch you and the dumb white man argue over it.

WINING BOY: How you know Sutter's brother ain't sold it already? You talking about selling the piano and the man's liable to sold the land two or three times.

BOY WILLIE: He say he waiting on me. He say he give me two weeks. That's two weeks from Friday. Say if I ain't back by then he might gonna sell it to somebody else. He say he wanna see me with it.

WINING BOY: You know as well as I know the man gonna sell the land to the first one walk up and hand him the money.

BOY WILLIE: That's just who I'm gonna be. Look, you ain't gotta know he waiting on me. I know. Okay. I know what the man told me. Stoval already done tried to buy the land from him and he told him no. The man say he waiting on me . . . he waiting on me. Hey, Doaker . . . . give me a drink. I see Wining Boy got his glass.

Doaker exists into his room.

Wining Boy, what you doing in Kansas City? What they got down there?

LYMON: I hear they got some nice-looking women in Kansas City. I sure like to go down there and find out.

WINING BOY: Man, the women down there is something else.

Doaker enters with a bottle of whiskey. He sets it on the table with some glasses.

DOAKER: You wanna sit up here and drink up my whiskey, leave a dollar on the table when you get up.

BOY WILLIE: You ain't doing nothing but showing your hospitality. I know we ain't got to pay for your hospitality.

WINING BOY: Doaker say they had you and Lymon down on the Parchman Farm. Had you on my old stomping grounds.

BOY WILLIE: Me and Lymon was down there hauling wood for Jim Miller and keeping us a little bit to sell. Some white fellows tried to run us off of it. That's when Crawley got killed. They put me and Lymon in the penitentiary.

LYMON: They ambushed us right there where that road dip down and around that bend in the creek. Crawley tried to fight them. Me and Boy Willie got away but the sheriff got us. Say we was stealing wood. They shot me in my stomach.

BOY WILLIE: They looking for Lymon down there now. They rounded him up and put him in jail for not working.

LYMON: Fined me a hundred dollars. Mr. Stovall come and paid my hundred dollars and the judge say I got to work for him to pay him back his hundred dollars. I told them I'd rather take my thirty days but they wouldn't let me do that.

BOY WILLIE: As soon as Stovall turned his back, Lymon was gone. He down there living in that truck dodging the sheriff and Stovall. He got both of them looking for him. So I brought him up here.

LYMON: I told Boy Willie I'm gonna stay up here. I ain't going back with him.

BOY WILLIE: Ain't nobody twisting your arm to make you go back. You can do what you want to do.

WINING BOY: I'll go back with you. I'm on my way down there. You gonna take the train? I'm gonna take the train.

LYMON: They treat you better up here.

BOY WILLIE: I ain't worried about nobody mistreating me. They treat you like you let them treat you. They mistreat me I mistreat them right back. Ain't no difference in me and the white man.

WINING BOY: Ain't no difference as far as how somebody supposed to treat you. I agree with that. But I'll tell you the difference between the colored man and the white man. Alright. Now you take and eat some berries. They taste real good to you. So you say I'm gonna go out and get me a whole pot of these berries and cook them up to make a pie or whatever. But you ain't looked to see them berries is sitting in the white fellow's yard. Ain't got no fence around them. You figure anybody want something they'd fence it in. Alright. Now the white man come along and say that's my land. Therefore everything that grow on it belong to me. He tell the sheriff, "I want you to put this nigger in jail as a warning to all the other niggers. Otherwise first thing you know these niggers have everything that belong to us."

BOY WILLIE: I'd come back at night and haul off his whole patch while he was sleep.

WINING BOY: Alright. Now Mr. So and So, he sell the land to you. And he come to you and say, "John, you own the land. It's all yours now. But them is my berries. And come time to pick them I'm gonna send my boys over. You got the land . . . but them berries, I'm gonna keep them. They mine." And he go and fix it with the law that them is his berries. Now that's the difference between the colored man and the white man. The colored man can't fix nothing with the law.

BOY WILLIE: I don't go by what the law say. The law's liable to say anything. I go by if it's right or not. It don't matter to me what the law say. I take and look at it for myself.

LYMON: That's why you gonna end up back down there on the Parchman Farm.

BOY WILLIE: I ain't thinking about no Parchman Farm. You liable to go back before me.

LYMON: They work you too hard down there. All that weeding and hoeing and chopping down trees. I didn't like all that.

WINING BOY: You ain't got to like your job on Parchman. Hey, tell him, Doaker, the only one got to like his job is the waterboy.

DOAKER: If he don't like his job he need to set that bucket down.

BOY WILLIE: That's what they told Lymon. They had Lymon on water and everybody got mad at him cause he was lazy.

LYMON: That water was heavy.

BOY WILLIE: They had Lymon down there singing:

Sings.

O Lord Berta Berta O Lord gal oh-ah
O Lord Berta Berta O Lord gal well

[Lymon *and* Wining Boy *join in.*]

Go 'head marry don't you wait on me oh-ah
Go 'head marry don't you wait on me well
Might not want you when I go free oh-ah
Might not want you when I go free well

BOY WILLIE: Come on, Doaker. Doaker know this one.

As Doaker joins in the men stamp and clap to keep time. They sing in harmony with great fervor and style.

O Lord Berta Berta O Lord gal oh-ah
O Lord Berta Berta O Lord gal well

Raise them up higher, let them drop on down oh-ah
Raise them up higher, let them drop on down well
Don't know the difference when the sun go down oh-ah
Don't know the difference when the sun go down well

Berta in Meridan and she living at ease oh-ah
Berta in Meridan and she living at ease well
I'm on old Parchman, got to work or leave oh-ah
I'm on old Parchman, got to work or leave well

O Alberta, Berta, O Lord gal oh-ah
O Alberta, Berta, O Lord gal well

When you marry, don't marry no farming man oh-ah
When you marry, don't marry no farming man well
Everyday Monday, hoe handle in your hand oh-ah
Everyday Monday, hoe handle in your hand well

When you marry, marry a railroad man, oh-ah
When you marry, marry a railroad man, well
Everyday Sunday, dollar in your hand oh-ah
Everyday Sunday, dollar in your hand well

O Alberta, Berta, O Lord gal oh-ah
O Alberta, Berta, O Lord gal well

BOY WILLIE: Doaker like that part. He like that railroad part.

LYMON: Doaker sound like Tangleye. He can't sing a lick.

BOY WILLIE: Hey, Doaker, they still talk about you down on Parchman. They ask me, "You Doaker Boy's nephew?" I say, "Yeah, me and him is family." They treated me alright soon as I told them that. say, "Yeah, he my uncle."

DOAKER: I don't never want to see none of them niggers no more.

BOY WILLIE: I don't want to see them either. Hey, Wining Boy, come on play some piano. You a piano player, play some piano. Lymon wanna hear you.

WINING BOY: I give that piano up. That was the best thing that ever happened to me, getting rid of that piano. That piano got so big and I'm carrying it around on my back. I don't wish that on no-body. See, you think it's all fun being a recording star. Got to carrying that piano around and man did I get slow. Got just like molasses. The world just slipping by me and I'm walking around with that piano. Alright. Now, there ain't but so many places you can go.

Only so many road wide enough for you and that piano. And that piano get heavier and heavier. Go to a place and they find out you play piano, the first thing they want to do is give you a drink, find you a piano, and sit you right down. And that's where you gonna be for the next eight hours. They ain't gonna let you get up! Now, the first three or four years of that is fun. You can't get enough whiskey and you can't get enough women and you don't never get tired of playing that piano. But that only last so long. You look up one day and you hate the whiskey, and you hate the women, and you hate the piano. But that's all you got. You can't do nothing else. All you know how to do is play that piano. Now, who am I? Am I me? Or am I the piano player? Sometime it seem like the only thing to do is shoot the piano player cause he the cause of all the trouble I'm having.

DOAKER: What you gonna do when your troubles get like mine?

LYMON: If I knew how to play it, I'd play it. That's a nice piano.

BOY WILLIE: Whoever playing better play quick. Sutter's brother say he waiting on me. I sell them watermelons. Get Berniece to sell that piano. Put them two parts with the part I done saved . . .

WINING BOY: Berniece ain't gonna sell that piano. I don't see why you don't know that.

BOY WILLIE: What she gonna do with it? She ain't doing nothing but letting it sit up there and rot. That piano ain't doing nobody no good.

LYMON: That's a nice piano. If I had it I'd sell it. Unless I knew how to play like Wining Boy. You can get a nice price for that piano.

DOAKER: Now I'm gonna tell you something, Lymon don't know this . . . but I'm gonna tell you why me and Wining Boy say Berniece ain't gonna sell that piano.

BOY WILLIE: She ain't got to sell it! I'm gonna sell it! Berniece ain't got no more rights to that piano than I do.

DOAKER: I'm talking to the man . . . let me talk to the man. See, now . . . to understand why we say that . . . to understand about that piano . . . you got to go back to slavery time. See, our family was owned by a fellow named Robert Sutter. That was Sutter's grandfather. Alright. The piano was owned by a fellow named Joel Nolander. He was one of the Nolander brothers from down in Georgia. It was coming up on Sutter's wedding anniversary and he was looking to buy his wife . . . Miss Ophelia was her name . . . he was looking to buy her an anniversary present. Only thing with him . . . he ain't had no money. But he had some niggers. So he asked Mr. Nolander to see if maybe he could trade off some of his niggers for that piano. Told him he would give him one and a half niggers for it. That's the way he told him. Say he could have one full grown and one half grown. Mr. Nolander agreed only he say he had to pick them. He didn't want Sutter to give him just any old nigger. He say he wanted to have the pick of the litter. So Sutter lined up his niggers and Mr. Nolander looked them over and out of the whole bunch he picked my grandmother . . . her name was Berniece . . . same like Berniece . . . and he picked my daddy when he wasn't nothing but a little boy nine years old. They made the trade off and Miss Ophelia was so happy with that piano that it got to be just about all she would do was play on that piano.

WINING BOY: Just get up in the morning, get all dressed up and sit down and play on that piano.

DOAKER: Alright. Time go along. Time go along. Miss Ophelia got to missing my grandmother . . . the way she would cook and clean the house and talk to her and what not. And she missed having my daddy around the house to fetch things for her. So she asked to see if maybe she could trade back that piano and get her niggers back. Mr. Nolander said no. Said a deal was a deal. Him and Sutter had a big falling out about it and Miss Ophelia took sick to the bed. Wouldn't get out of the bed in the morning. She just lay there. The doctor said she was wasting away.

WINING BOY: That's when Sutter called our granddaddy up to the house.

DOAKER: Now, our granddaddy's name was Boy Willie. That's who Boy Willie's named after . . . only they called him Willie Boy. Now, he was a worker of wood. He could make you anything you wanted out of wood. He'd make you a desk. A table. A lamp. Anything you wanted. Them white fellows around there used to come up to Mr. Sutter and get him to make all kinds of things for them. Then they'd pay Mr. Sutter a nice price. See, everything my granddaddy made Mr. Sutter owned cause he owned him. That's why when Mr. Nolander offered to buy him to keep the family together Mr. Sutter wouldn't sell him. Told Mr. Nolander he didn't have enough money to buy him. Now . . . am I telling it right, Wining Boy?

WINING BOY: You telling it.

DOAKER: Sutter called him up to the house and told him to carve my grandmother and my daddy's picture on the piano for Miss Ophelia. And he took and carved this . . .

Doaker crosses over to the piano.

See that right there? That's my grandmother, Berniece. She looked just like that. And he put a picture of my daddy when he wasn't nothing but a little boy the way he remembered him. He made them up out of his memory. Only thing . . . he didn't stop there. He carved all this. He got a picture of his mama . . . Mama Esther . . . and his daddy, Boy Charles.

WINING BOY: That was the first Boy Charles.

DOAKER: Then he put on the side here all kinds of things. See that? That's when him and Mama Berniece got married. They called it jumping the broom. That's how you got married in them days. Then he got here when my daddy was born . . . and here he got Mama Esther's funeral . . . and down here he got Mr. Nolander taking Mama Berniece and my daddy away down to his place in Georgia. He got all kinds of things what happened with our family. When Mr. Sutter seen the piano with all them carvings on it he got mad. He didn't ask for all that. But see . . . there wasn't nothing he could do about it. When Miss Ophelia seen it . . . she got excited. Now she had her piano and her niggers too. She took back to playing it and played on it right up till the day she died. Alright . . . now see, our brother Boy Charles . . . that's Berniece and Boy Willie's daddy . . . he was the oldest of us three boys. He's dead now. But he would have been fifty-seven if he had lived. He died in 1911 when he was thirty-one years old. Boy Charles used to talk about that piano all the time. He never could get it off his mind. Two or three months go by and he be talking about it again. He be talking about taking it out of Sutter's house. Say it was the story of our whole family and as long as Sutter had it . . . he had us. Say we was still in slavery. Me and Wining Boy tried to talk him out of it but it wouldn't do any good. Soon as he quiet down about it he'd start up again. We seen where he wasn't gonna get it off his mind . . . so, on the Fourth of July, 1911 . . . when Sutter was at the picnic what the county give every year . . . me and Wining Boy went on down there with him and took that piano out of Sutter's house. We put it on a wagon and me and Wining Boy carried it over into the next county with Mama Ola's people. Boy Charles decided to stay around there and wait until Sutter got home to make it look like business as usual.

Now, I don't know what happened when Sutter came home and found that piano gone. But somebody went up to Boy Charles's house and set it on fire. But he wasn't in there. He must have seen them coming cause he went down and caught the 3:57 Yellow Dog. He didn't know they was gonna come down and stop the train. Stopped the train and found Boy Charles in the boxcar with four of them hobos. Must have got mad when they couldn't find the piano cause they set the boxcar afire and killed everybody. Now, nobody know who done that. Some people say it was Sutter cause it was his piano. Some people say it was Sheriff Carter. Some people say it was Robert Smith and Ed Saunders. But don't nobody know for sure. It was about two months after that that Ed Saunders fell down his well. Just upped and fell down his well for no reason. People say it was the ghost of them men who burned up in the boxcar that pushed him in his well. They started calling them the Ghosts of the Yellow Dog. Now, that's how all that got started and that's why we say Berniece ain't gonna sell that piano. Cause her daddy died over it.

BOY WILLIE: All that's in the past. If my daddy had seen where he could have traded that piano in for some land of his own, it wouldn't be sitting up here now. He spent his whole life farming on somebody else's land. I ain't gonna do that. See, he couldn't do no better. When he come along he ain't had nothing he could build on. His daddy ain't had nothing to give him. The only thing my daddy had to give me was that piano. And he died over giving me that. I ain't gonna let it sit up there and rot without trying to do something with it. If Berniece can't see that, then I'm gonna go ahead and sell my half. And you and Wining Boy know I'm right.

DOAKER: Ain't nobody said nothing about who's right and who's wrong. I was just telling the man about the piano. I was telling him why we say Berniece ain't gonna sell it.

LYMON: Yeah, I can see why you say that now. I told Boy Willie he ought to stay up here with me.

BOY WILLIE: You stay! I'm going back! That's what I'm gonna do with my life! Why I got to come up here and learn to do something I don't know how to do when I already know how to farm? You stay up here and make your own way if that's what you want to do. I'm going back and live my life the way I want to live it.

Wining Boy gets up and crosses to the piano.

WINING BOY: Let's see what we got here. I ain't played on this thing for a while.

DOAKER: You can stop telling that. You was playing on it the last time you was through here. We couldn't get you off of it. Go on and play something.

Wining Boy sits down at the piano and plays and sings. The song is one which has put many dimes and quarters in his pocket, long ago, in dimly remembered towns and way stations. He plays badly, without hesitation, and sings in a forceful voice.

WINING BOY: *Singing.*

I am a rambling gambling man
I gambled in many towns
I rambled this wide world over
I rambled this world around
I had my ups and downs in life
And bitter times I saw
But I never knew what misery was
Till I lit on old Arkansas.

I started out one morning
To meet that early train
He said, "You better work for me
I have some land to drain.
I'll give you fifty cents a day,
Your washing, board and all
And you shall be a different man
In the state of Arkansas."

I worked six months for the rascal
Joe Herrin was his name
He fed me old corn dodgers
They was hard as any rock
My tooth is all got loosened
And my knees begin to knock
That was the kind of hash I got
In the state of Arkansas.

Traveling man
I've traveled all around this world

Traveling man
I've traveled from land to land
Traveling man
I've traveled all around this world
Well it ain't no use
writing no news
I'm a traveling man.

The door opens and Berniece enters with Maretha.

BERNIECE: Is that . . . Lord, I know that ain't Wining Boy sitting there.

WINING BOY: Hey, Berniece.

BERNIECE: You all had this planned. You and Boy Willie had this planned.

WINING BOY: I didn't know he was gonna be here. I'm on my way down home. I stopped by to see you and Doaker first.

DOAKER: I told the nigger he left out of here with that sack of money, we thought we might never see him again. Boy Willie say he wasn't gonna see him till he got broke. I looked up and seen him sitting on the doorstep asking for two dollars. Look at him laughing. He know it's the truth.

BERNIECE: Boy Willie, I didn't see that truck out there. I thought you was out selling watermelons.

BOY WILLIE: We done sold them all. Sold the truck too.

BERNIECE: I don't want to go through none of your stuff. I done told you to go back where you belong.

BOY WILLIE: I was just teasing you, woman. You can't take no teasing?

BERNIECE: Wining Boy, when you get here?

WINING BOY: A little while ago. I took the train from Kansas City.

BERNIECE: Let me go upstairs and change and then I'll cook you something to eat.

BOY WILLIE: You ain't cooked me nothing when I come.

BERNIECE: Boy Willie, go on and leave me alone. Come on, Maretha, get up here and change your clothes before you get them dirty.

Berniece exits up the stairs, followed by Maretha.

WINING BOY: Maretha sure getting big, ain't she, Doaker. And just as pretty as she want to be. I didn't know Crawley had it in him.

Boy Willie crosses to the piano.

BOY WILLIE: Hey, Lymon . . . get up on the other side of this piano and let me see something.

WINING BOY: Boy Willie, what is you doing?

BOY WILLIE: I'm seeing how heavy this piano is. Get up over there, Lymon.

WINING BOY: Go on and leave that piano alone. You ain't taking that piano out of here and selling it.

BOY WILLIE: Just as soon as I get them watermelons out that truck.

WINING BOY: Well, I got something to say about that.

BOY WILLIE: This my daddy's piano.

WINING BOY: He ain't took it by himself. Me and Doaker helped him.

BOY WILLIE: He died by himself. Where was you and Doaker at then? Don't come telling me nothing about this piano. This is me and Berniece's piano. Am I right, Doaker?

DOAKER: Yeah, you right.

BOY WILLIE: Let's see if we can lift it up, Lymon. Get a good grip on it and pick it up on your end. Ready? Lift!

As they start to move the piano, the sound of Sutter's Ghost *is heard.* Doaker *is the only one to hear it. With difficulty they move the piano a little bit so it is out of place.*

BOY WILLIE: What you think?

LYMON: It's heavy . . . but you can move it. Only it ain't gonna be easy.

BOY WILLIE: It wasn't that heavy to me. Okay, let's put it back.

The sound of Sutter's Ghost is heard again. They all hear it as Berniece enters on the stairs.

BERNIECE: Boy Willie . . . you gonna play around with me one too many times. And then God's gonna bless you and West is gonna dress you. Now set that piano back over there. I done told you a hundred times I ain't selling that piano.

BOY WILLIE: I'm trying to get me some land, woman. I need that piano to get me some money so I can buy Sutter's land.

BERNIECE: Money can't buy what that piano cost. You can't sell your soul for money. It won't go with the buyer. It'll shrivel and shrink to know that you ain't taken on to it. But it won't go with the buyer.

BOY WILLIE: I ain't talking about all that, woman. I ain't talking about selling my soul. I'm talking about trading that piece of wood for some land. Get something under your feet. Land the only thing

God ain't making no more of. You can always get you another piano. I'm talking about some land. What you get something out the ground from. That's what I'm talking about. You can't do nothing with that piano but sit up there and look at it.

BERNIECE: That's just what I'm gonna do. Wining Boy, you want me to fry you some pork chops?

BOY WILLIE: Now, I'm gonna tell you the way I see it. The only thing that make that piano worth something is them carvings Papa Willie Boy put on there. That's what make it worth something. That was my great-granddaddy. Papa Boy Charles brought that piano into the house. Now, I'm supposed to build on what they left me. You can't do nothing with that piano sitting up here in the house. That's just like if I let them watermelons sit out there and rot. I'd be a fool. Alright now, if you say to me, Boy Willie, I'm using that piano. I give out lessons on it and that help me make my rent or whatever. Then that be something else. I'd have to go on and say, well, Berniece using that piano. She building on it. Let her go on and use it. I got to find another way to get Sutter's land. But Doaker say you ain't touched that piano the whole time it's been up here. So why you wanna stand in my way? See, you just looking at the sentimental value. See, that's good. That's alright. I take my hat off whenever somebody say my daddy's name. But I ain't gonna be no fool about no sentimental value. You can sit up here and look at the piano for the next hundred years and it's just gonna be a piano. You can't make more than that. Now I want to get Sutter's land with that piano. I get Sutter's land and I can go down and cash in the crop and get my seed. As long as I got the land and the seed then I'm alright. I can always get me a little something else. Cause that land give back to you. I can make me another crop and cash that in. I still got the land and the seed. But that piano don't put out nothing else. You ain't got nothing working for you. Now, the kind of man my daddy was he would have understood that. I'm sorry you can't see it that way. But that's why I'm gonna take that piano out of here and sell it.

BERNIECE: You ain't taking that piano out of my house.

She crosses to the piano.

Look at this piano. Look at it. Mama Ola polished this piano with her tears for seventeen years. For seventeen years she rubbed on it till her hands bled. Then she rubbed the blood in . . . mixed it up with the rest of the blood on it. Every day that God breathed life into her body she rubbed and cleaned and polished and prayed over it. "Play something for me, Berniece. Play something for me, Berniece." Every day. "I cleaned it up for you, play something for me, Berniece." You always talking about your daddy but you ain't never stopped to look at what his foolishness cost your mama. Seventeen years' worth of cold nights and an empty bed. For what? For a piano? For a piece of wood? To get even with somebody? I look at you and you're all the same. You, Papa Boy Charles, Wining Boy, Doaker, Crawley . . . you're all alike. All this thieving and killing and thieving and killing. And what it ever lead to? More killing and more thieving. I ain't never seen it come to nothing. People getting burned up. People getting shot. People falling down their wells. It don't never stop.

DOAKER: Come on now, Berniece, ain't no need in getting upset.

BOY WILLIE: I done a little bit of stealing here and there, but I ain't never killed nobody. I can't be speaking for nobody else. You all got to speak for yourself, but I ain't never killed nobody.

BERNIECE: You killed Crawley just as sure as if you pulled the trigger.

BOY WILLIE: See, that's ignorant. That's downright foolish for you to say something like that. You ain't doing nothing but showing your ignorance. If the nigger was here I'd whup his ass for getting me and Lymon shot at.

BERNIECE: Crawley ain't knew about the wood.

BOY WILLIE: We told the man about the wood. Ask Lymon. He knew all about the wood. He seen we was sneaking it. Why else we gonna be out there at night? Don't come telling me Crawley ain't knew about the wood. Them fellows come up on us and Crawley tried to bully them. Me and Lymon seen the sheriff with them and give in. Wasn't no sense in getting killed over fifty dollars' worth of wood.

BERNIECE: Crawley ain't knew you stole that wood.

BOY WILLIE: We ain't stole no wood. Me and Lymon was hauling wood for Jim Miller and keeping us a little bit on the side. We dumped our little bit down there by the creek till we had enough to make a load. Some fellows seen us and we figured we better get it before they did. We come up there and got Crawley to help us load it. Figured we'd cut him in. Crawley trying to keep the wolf from his door . . . we was trying to help him.

LYMON: Me and Boy Willie told him about the wood. We told him some fellows might be trying to beat us to it. He say let me go back and get my thirty-eight. That's what caused all the trouble.

BOY WILLIE: If Crawley ain't had the gun he'd be alive today.

LYMON: We had it about half loaded when they come up on us. We seen the sheriff with them and we tried to get away. We ducked around near the bend in the creek . . . but they was down there too. Boy Willie say let's give in. But Crawley pulled out his gun and started shooting. That's when they started shooting back.

BERNIECE: All I know is Crawley would be alive if you hadn't come up there and got him.

BOY WILLIE: I ain't had nothing to do with Crawley getting killed. That was his own fault.

BERNIECE: Crawley's dead and in the ground and you still walking around here eating. That's all I know. He went off to load some wood with you and ain't never come back.

BOY WILLIE: I told you, woman . . . I ain't had nothing to do with . . .

BERNIECE: He ain't here, is he? He ain't here!

Berniece hits Boy Willie.

I said he ain't here. Is he?

Berniece continues to hit Boy Willie, who doesn't move to defend himself, other than back up and turning his head so that most of the blows fall on his chest and arms.

DOAKER: [*Grabbing Berniece:*] Come on, Berniece . . . let it go, it ain't his fault.

BERNIECE: He ain't here, is he? Is he?

BOY WILLIE: I told you I ain't responsible for Crawley.

BERNIECE: He ain't here.

BOY WILLIE: Come on now, Berniece . . . don't' do this now. Doaker get her. I ain't had nothing to do with Crawley.

BERNIECE: You come up there and got him!

BOY WILLIE: I done told you now. Doaker, get her. I ain't playing.

DOAKER: Come on, Berniece.

Maretha is heard screaming upstairs. It is a scream of stark terror.

MARETHA: Mama! . . . Mama!

The lights go down to black. End of Act One.

Act II

Scene I

The lights come up on the kitchen. It is the following morning. Doaker is ironing the pants to his uniform. He has a pot cooking on the stove at the same time. He is singing a song. The song provides him with the rhythm for his work and he moves about the kitchen with the ease born of many years as a railroad cook.

DOAKER:

> *Gonna leave Jackson Mississippi*
> *and go to Memphis*
> *and double back to Jackson*
> *Come on down to Hattiesburg*
> *Change cars on the Y.D.*
> *coming through the territory to*
> *Meridian*
> *and Meridian to Greenville*
> *and Greenville to Memphis*
> *I'm on my way and I know where*

> *Change cars on the Katy*
> *Leaving Jackson*
> *and going through Clarksdale*
> *Hello Winona!*
> *Courtland!*
> *Bateville!*
> *Como!*
> *Senitobia!*
> *Lewisberg!*
> *Sunflower!*
> *Glendora!*
> *Sharkey!*
> *And double back to Jackson*
> *Hello Greenwood*
> *I'm on my way Memphis*
> *Clarksdale*
> *Moorhead*
> *Indianola*
> *Can a highball pass through?*

Highball on through sir
Grand Carson!
Thirty First Street Depot
Fourth Street Depot
Memphis!

Wining Boy enters carrying a suit of clothes.

DOAKER: I thought you took that suit to the pawnshop?

WINING BOY: I went down there and the man tell me the suit is too old. Look at this suit. This is one hundred percent silk! How a silk suit gonna get too old? I know what it was he just didn't want to give me five dollars for it. Best he wanna give me is three dollars. I figure a silk suit is worth five dollars all over the world. I wasn't gonna part with it for no three dollars so I brought it back.

DOAKER: They got another pawnshop up on Wylie.

WINING BOY: I carried it up there. He say he don't take no clothes. Only thing he take is guns and radios. Maybe a guitar or two. Where's Berniece?

DOAKER: Berniece still at work. Boy Willie went down there to meet Lymon this morning. I guess they got that truck fixed, they been out there all day and ain't come back yet. Maretha scared to sleep up there now. Berniece don't know, but I seen Sutter before she did.

WINING BOY: Say what?

DOAKER: About three weeks ago. I had just come back from down there. Sutter couldn't have been dead more than three days. He was sitting over there at the piano. I come out to go to work . . . and he was sitting right there. Had his hand on top of his head just like Berniece said. I believe he broke his neck when he fell in the well. I kept quiet about it. I didn't see no reason to upset Berniece.

WINING BOY: Did he say anything? Did he say he was looking for Boy Willie?

DOAKER: He was just sitting there. He ain't said nothing. I went on out the door and left him sitting there. I figure as long as he was on the other side of the room everything be alright. I don't know what I would have done if he had started walking toward me.

WINING BOY: Berniece say he was calling Boy Willie's name.

DOAKER: I ain't heard him say nothing. He was just sitting there when I seen him. But I don't believe Boy Willie pushed him in the well. Sutter here cause of that piano. I heard him playing on it one time. I thought it was Berniece but then she don't play that kind of music. I come out here and ain't seen nobody, but them piano keys was moving a mile a minute. Berniece need to go on and get rid of if. It ain't done nothing but cause trouble.

WINING BOY: I agree with Berniece. Boy Charles ain't took it to give it back. He took it cause he figure he had more right to it than Sutter did. If Sutter can't understand that . . . then that's just the way that go. Sutter dead and in the ground . . . don't care where his ghost is. He can hover around and play on the piano all he want. I want to see him carry it out the house. That's what I want to see. What time Berniece get home? I don't see how I let her get away from me this morning.

DOAKER: You up there sleep. Berniece leave out of here early in the morning. She out there in Squirrel Hill cleaning house for some bigshot down there at the steel mill. They don't like you to come late. You come late they won't give you your carfare. What kind of business you got with Berniece?

WINING BOY: My business. I ain't asked you what kind of business you got.

DOAKER: Berniece ain't got no money. If that's why you was trying to catch her. She having a hard enough time trying to get by as it is. If she go ahead and marry Avery . . . he working every day . . . she go ahead and marry him they could do alright for themselves. But as it stands she ain't got no money.

WINING BOY: Well, let me have five dollars.

DOAKER: I just give you a dollar before you left out of here. You ain't gonna take my five dollars out there and gamble and drink it up.

WINING BOY: Aw, nigger, give me five dollars. I'll give it back to you.

DOAKER: You wasn't looking to give me five dollars when you had that sack of money. You wasn't looking to throw nothing my way. Now you wanna come in here and borrow five dollars. If you going back with Boy Willie you need to be trying to figure out how you gonna get train fare.

WINING BOY: That's why I need the five dollars. If I had five dollars I could get me some money.

Doaker goes into his pocket.

Make it seven.

DOAKER: You take this five dollars . . . and you bring my money back here too.

Boy Willie and Lymon enter. They are happy and excited. They have money in all of their pockets and are anxious to count it.

DOAKER: How'd you do out there?

BOY WILLIE: They was lining up for them.

LYMON: Me and Boy Willie couldn't sell them fast enough. Time we got one sold we'd sell another.

BOY WILLIE: I seen what was happening and told Lymon to up the price on them.

LYMON: Boy Willie say charge them a quarter more. They didn't care. A couple of people give me a dollar and told me to keep the change.

BOY WILLIE: One fellow bought five. I say now what he gonna do with five watermelons? He can't eat them all. I sold him the five and asked him did he want to buy five more.

LYMON: I ain't never seen nobody snatch a dollar fast as Boy Willie.

BOY WILLIE: One lady asked me say, "Is they sweet?" I told her say, "Lady, where we grow these watermelons we put sugar in the ground." You know, she believed me. Talking about she had never heard of that before. Lymon was laughing his head off. I told her, "Oh, yeah, we put the sugar right in the ground with the seed." She say, "Well, give me another one." Them white folks is something else . . . ain't they, Lymon?

LYMON: Soon as you holler watermelons they come right out their door. Then they go and get their neighbors. Look like they having a contest to see who can buy the most.

WINING BOY: I got something for Lymon.

Wining Boy goes to get his suit. Boy Willie and Lymon continue to count their money.

BOY WILLIE: I know you got more than that. You ain't sold all them watermelons for that little bit of money.

LYMON: I'm still looking. That ain't all you got either. Where's all them quarters?

BOY WILLIE: You let me worry about the quarters. Just put the money on the table.

WINING BOY: [*Entering with his suit.*] Look here, Lymon . . . see this? Look at his eyes getting big. He ain't never seen a suit like this. This is one hundred percent silk. Go ahead . . . put it on. See if it fit you.

Lymon tries the suit coat on.

Look at that. Feel it. That's one hundred percent genuine silk. I got
that in Chicago. You can't get clothes like that nowhere but New
York and Chicago. You can't get clothes like that in Pittsburgh.
These folks in Pittsburgh ain't never seen clothes like that.

LYMON: This is nice, feel real nice and smooth.

WINING BOY: That's a fifty-five-dollar suit. That's the kind of suit the
bigshots wear. You need a pistol and a pocketful of money to wear
that suit. I'll let you have it for three dollars. The women will fall
out their windows they see you in a suit like that. Give me three
dollars and go on and wear it down the street and get you a
woman.

BOY WILLIE: That looks nice, Lymon. Put the pants on. Let me see it
with the pants.

Lymon begins to try on the pants.

WINING BOY: Look at that . . . see how it fits you? Give me three dollars
and go on and take it. Look at that, Doaker . . . don't he look nice?

DOAKER: Yeah . . . that's a nice suit.

WINING BOY: Got a shirt to go with it. Cost you an extra dollar. Four
dollars you got the whole deal.

LYMON: How this look, Boy Willie?

BOY WILLIE: That look nice . . . if you like that kind of thing. I don't
like them dress-up kind of clothes. If you like it, look real nice.

WINING BOY: That's the kind of suit you need for up here in the North.

LYMON: Four dollars for everything? The suit and the shirt?

WINING BOY: That's cheap. I should be charging you twenty dollars. I
give you a break cause you a homeboy. That's the only way I let you
have it for four dollars.

LYMON: [*Going into his pocket.*] Okay . . . here go the four dollars.

WINING BOY: You got some shoes? What size you wear?

LYMON: Size nine.

WINING BOY: That's what size I got! Size nine. I let you have them for
three dollars.

LYMON: Where they at? Let me see them.

WINING BOY: They real nice shoes, too. Got a nice tip to them. Got
pointy toe just like you want.

Wining Boy goes to get his shoes.

LYMON: Come on, Boy Willie, let's go out tonight. I wanna see what it looks like up here. Maybe we go to a picture show. Hey, Doaker, they got picture shows up here?

DOAKER: The Rhumba Theater. Right down there on Fullerton Street. Can't miss it. Got the speakers outside on the sidewalk. You can hear it a block away. Boy Willie know where it's at.

Doaker exits into his room.

LYMON: Let's go to the picture show, Boy Willie. Let's go find some women.

BOY WILLIE: Hey, Lymon, how many of them watermelons would you say we got left? We got just under a half a load . . . right?

LYMON: About that much. Maybe a little more.

BOY WILLIE: You think that piano will fit up in there?

LYMON: If we stack them watermelons you can sit it up in the front there.

BOY WILLIE: I'm gonna call that man tomorrow.

WINING BOY: [*Returns with his shoes.*] Here you go . . . size nine. Put them on. Cost you three dollars. That's a Florsheim shoe. That's the kind Staggerlee wore.

LYMON: [*Trying on the shoes.*] You sure these size nine?

WINING BOY: You can look at my feet and see we wear the same size. Man, you put on that suit and them shoes and you got something there. You ready for whatever's out there. But is they ready for you? With them shoes on you be the King of the Walk. Have everybody stop to look at your shoes. Wishing they had a pair. I'll give you a break. Go on and take them for two dollars.

Lymon pays Wining Boy two dollars.

LYMON: Come on, Boy Willie . . . let's go find some women. I'm gonna go upstairs and get ready. I'll be ready to go in a minute. Ain't you gonna get dressed?

BOY WILLIE: I'm gonna wear what I got on. I ain't dressing up for these city niggers.

Lymon exits up the stairs.

That's all Lymon think about is women.

WINING BOY: His daddy was the same way. I used to run around with him. I know his mama too. Two strokes back and I would have been his daddy! His daddy's dead now . . . but I got the nigger out of jail one time. They was fixing to name him Daniel and walk him through the Lion's Den. He got in a tussle with one of them white fellows and the sheriff lit on him like white on rice. That's how the whole thing come about between me and Lymon's mama. She knew me and his daddy used to run together and he got in jail and she went down there and took the sheriff a hundred dollars. Don't get me to lying about where she got it from. I don't know. The sheriff *looked at that hundred dollars and turned his nose up.* Told her, say, "That ain't gonna do him no good. You got to put another hundred on top of that." She come up *there and got me where I was playing at this saloon* . . . said she had all but fifty dollars and asked me if I could help. Now the way I figured it . . . without that fifty dollars the sheriff was gonna turn him over to Parchman. The sheriff turn him over to Parchman it be three years before anybody see him again. Now I'm gonna say it right . . . I will give anybody fifty dollars to keep them out of jail for three years. I give her the fifty dollars and she told me to come over to the house. I ain't asked her. I figure if she was nice enough to invite me I ought to go. I ain't had to say a word. She invited me over just as nice. Say, "Why don't you come over to the house?" She ain't had to say nothing else. Them words rolled off her tongue just as nice. I went on down there and sat about three hours. Started to leave and changed my mind. She grabbed hold to me and say, "Baby, it's all night long." That was one of the shortest nights I have ever spent on this earth! I could have used another eight hours. Lymon's daddy didn't even say nothing to me when he got out. He just looked at me funny. He had a good notion something had happened between me an' her. L. D. Jackson. That was one bad-luck nigger. Got killed at some dance. Fellow walked in and shot him thinking he was somebody else.

Doaker enters from his room.

Hey, Doaker, you remember L. D. Jackson?

DOAKER: That's Lymon's daddy. That was one bad-luck nigger.

BOY WILLIE: Look like you ready to railroad some.

DOAKER: Yeah, I got to make that run.

Lymon enters from the stairs. He is dressed in his new suit and shoes, to which he has added a cheap straw hat.

LYMON: How I look?

WINING BOY: You look like a million dollars. Don't he look good, Doaker? Come on, let's play some cards. You wanna play some cards?

BOY WILLIE: We ain't gonna play no cards with you. Me and Lymon gonna find some women. Hey, Lymon, don't play no cards with Wining Boy. He'll take all your money.

WINING BOY: [*to Lymon.*] You got a magic suit there. You can get you a woman easy with that suit . . . but you got to know the magic words. You know the magic words to get you a woman?

LYMON: I just talk to them to see if I like them and they like me.

WINING BOY: You just walk right up to them and say, "If you got the harbor I got the ship." If that don't work ask them if you can put them in your pocket. The first thing they gonna say is, "It's too small." That's when you look them dead in the eye and say, "Baby, ain't nothing small about me." If that don't work then you move on to another one. Am I telling him right, Doaker?

DOAKER: That man don't need you to tell him nothing about no women. These women these days ain't gonna fall for that kind of stuff. You got to buy them a present. That's what they looking for these days.

BOY WILLIE: Come on, I'm ready. You ready, Lymon? Come on, let's go find some women.

WINING BOY: Here, let me walk out with you. I wanna see the women fall out their window when they see Lymon.

They all exit and the lights go down on the scene.

Scene II

The lights come up on the kitchen. It is late evening of the same day. Berniece has set a tub for her bath in the kitchen. She is heating up water on the stove. There is a knock at the door.

BERNIECE: Who is it?

AVERY: It's me, Avery.

Berniece opens the door and lets him in.

BERNIECE: Avery, come on in. I was just fixing to take my bath.

AVERY: Where Boy Willie? I see that truck out there almost empty. They done sold almost all them watermelons.

BERNIECE: They was gone when I come home. I don't know where they went off to. Boy Willie around here about to drive me crazy.

AVERY: They sell them watermelons . . . he'll be gone soon.

BERNIECE: What Mr. Cohen say about letting you have the place?

AVERY: He say he'll let me have it for thirty dollars a month. I talked him out of thirty-five and he say he'll let me have it for thirty.

BERNIECE: That's a nice spot next to Benny Diamond's store.

AVERY: Berniece . . . I be at home and I get to thinking you up here an' I'm down there. I get to thinking how that look to have a preacher that ain't married. It makes for a better congregation if the preacher was settled down and married.

BERNIECE: Avery . . . not now. I was fixing to take my bath.

AVERY: You know how I feel about you, Berniece. Now . . . I done got the place from Mr. Cohen. I get the money from the bank and I can fix it up real nice. They give me a ten cents a hour raise down there on the job . . . now Berniece, I ain't got much in the way of comforts. I got a hole in my pockets near about as far as money is concerned. I ain't never found no way through life to a woman I care about like I care about you. I need that. I need somebody on my bond side. I need a woman that fits in my hand.

BERNIECE: Avery, I ain't ready to get married now.

AVERY: You too young a woman to close up, Berniece.

BERNIECE: I ain't said nothing about closing up. I got a lot of woman left in me.

AVERY: Where's it at? When's the last time you looked at it?

BERNIECE: [Stunned by his remark.] That's a nasty thing to say. And you call yourself a preacher.

AVERY: Anytime I get anywhere near you . . . you push me away.

BERNIECE: I got enough on my hands with Maretha. I got enough people to love and take care of.

AVERY: Who you got to love you? Can't nobody get close enough to you. Doaker can't half say nothing to you. You jump all over Boy Willie. Who you got to love you, Berniece?

BERNIECE: You trying to tell me a woman can't be nothing without a man. But you alright, huh? You can just walk out of here without me—without a woman—and still be a man. that's alright. Ain't nobody gonna ask you, "Avery, who you got to love you?" That's alright for you. But everybody gonna be worried about Berniece. "How Berniece gonna take care of herself? How she gonna raise that child without a man? Wonder what she do with herself. How she gonna live like that?" Everybody got all kinds of questions for Berniece. Everybody telling me I can't be a woman unless I got a man. Well, you tell me, Avery—you know—how much woman am I?

AVERY: It wasn't me, Berniece. You can't blame me for nobody else. I'll own up to my own shortcomings. But you can't blame me for Crawley or nobody else.

BERNIECE: I ain't blaming nobody for nothing. I'm just stating the facts.

AVERY: How long you gonna carry Crawley with you, Berniece? It's been over three years. At some point you got to let go and go on. Life's got all kinds of twists and turns. That don't mean you stop living. That don't mean you cut yourself off from life. You can't go through life carrying Crawley's ghost with you. Crawley's been dead three years. Three years, Berniece.

BERNIECE: I know how long Crawley's been dead. You ain't got to tell me that. I just ain't ready to get married right now.

AVERY: What is you ready for, Berniece? You just gonna drift along from day to day. Life is more than making it from one day to another. You gonna look up one day and it's all gonna be past you. Life's gonna be gone out of your hands—there won't be enough to make nothing with. I'm standing here now, Berniece—but I don't know how much longer I'm gonna be standing here waiting on you.

BERNIECE: Avery, I told you . . . when you get your church we'll sit down and talk about this. I got too many other things to deal with right now. Boy Willie and the piano . . . and Sutter's ghost. I thought I might have been seeing things, but Maretha done seen Sutter's ghost, too.

AVERY: When this happen, Berniece?

BERNIECE: Right after I came home yesterday. Me and Boy Willie was arguing about the piano and Sutter's ghost was standing at the top of the stairs. Maretha scared to sleep up there now. Maybe if you bless the house he'll go away.

AVERY: I don't know, Berniece. I don't know if I should fool around with something like that.

BERNIECE: I can't have Maretha scared to go to sleep up there. Seem like if you bless the house he would go away.

AVERY: You might have to be a special kind of preacher to do something like that.

BERNIECE: I keep telling myself when Boy Willie leave he'll go on and leave with him. I believe Boy Willie pushed him in the well.

AVERY: That's been going on down there a long time. The Ghosts of the Yellow Dog been pushing people in their wells long before Boy Willie got grown.

BERNIECE: Somebody down there pushing them people in their wells. They ain't just upped and fell. Ain't no wind pushed nobody in their well.

AVERY: Oh, I don't know. God works in mysterious ways.

BERNIECE: He ain't pushed nobody in their wells.

AVERY: He caused it to happen. God is the Great Causer. He can do anything. He parted the Red Sea. He say I will smite my enemies. Reverend Thompson used to preach on the Ghosts of the Yellow Dog as the hand of God.

BERNIECE: I don't care who preached what. Somebody down there pushing them people in their wells. Somebody like Boy Willie. I can see him doing something like that. You ain't gonna tell me that Sutter just upped and fell in his well. I believe Boy Willie pushed him so he could get his land.

AVERY: What Doaker say about Boy Willie selling the piano?

BERNIECE: Doaker don't want no part of that piano. He ain't never wanted no part of it. He blames himself for not staying behind with Papa Boy Charles. He washed his hands of that piano a long time ago. He didn't want me to bring it up here—but I wasn't gonna leave it down there.

AVERY: Well, it seems to me somebody ought to be able to talk to Boy Willie.

BERNIECE: You can't talk to Boy Willie. He been that way all his life. Mama Ola had her hands full trying to talk to him. He don't listen to nobody. He just like my daddy. He get his mind fixed on something and can't nobody turn him from it.

AVERY: You ought to start a choir at the church. Maybe if he seen you was doing something with it—if you told him you was gonna put it in my church—maybe he'd see it different. You ought to put it down in the church and start a choir. The Bible say, "Make a joyful noise unto the Lord." Maybe if Boy Willie see you was doing something with it he'd see it different.

BERNIECE: I done told you I don't play on that piano. Ain't no need in you to keep talking this choir stuff. When my mama died I shut the top on that piano and I ain't never opened it since. I was only playing it for her. When my daddy died seem like all her life went into that piano. She used to have me playing on it . . . had Miss Eula come in and teach me . . . say when I played it she could hear my daddy talking to her. I used to think them pictures came alive and walked through the house. Sometime late at night I could hear my mama talking to them. I said that wasn't gonna happen to me. I don't play that piano cause I don't want to wake them spirits. They never be walking around in this house.

AVERY: You got to put all that behind you, Berniece.

BERNIECE: I got Maretha playing on it. She don't know nothing about it. Let her go on and be a schoolteacher or something. She don't have to carry all of that with her. She got a chance I didn't have. I ain't gonna burden her with that piano.

AVERY: You got to put all of that behind you, Berniece. That's the same thing like Crawley. Everybody got stones in their passway. You got to step over them or walk around them. You picking them up and carrying them with you. All you got to do is set them down by the side of the road. You ain't got to carry them with you. You can walk over there right now and play that piano. You can walk over there right now and God will walk over there with you. Right now you can set that sack of stones down by the side of the road and walk away from it. You don't have to carry it with you. You can do it right now.

Avery crosses over to the piano and raises the lid.

Come on, Berniece . . . set it down and walk away from it. Come on, play "Old Ship of Zion." Walk over here and claim it as an instrument of the Lord. You can walk over here right now and make it into a celebration.

Berniece moves toward the piano.

BERNIECE: Avery . . . I done told you I don't want to play that piano. Now or no other time.

AVERY: The Bible say, "The Lord is my refuge . . . and my strength!" With the strength of God you can put the past behind you, Berniece. With the strength of God you can do anything! God got a bright tomorrow. God don't ask what you done . . . God ask what you gonna do. The strength of God can move mountains! God's got a bright tomorrow for you . . . all you got to do is walk over here and claim it.

BERNIECE: Avery, just go on and let me finish my bath. I'll see you tomorrow.

AVERY: Okay, Berniece. I'm gonna go home. I'm gonna go home and read up on my Bible. And tomorrow . . . if the good Lord give me strength tomorrow . . . I'm gonna come by and bless the house . . . and show you the power of the Lord.

Avery crosses to the door.

It's gonna be alright, Berniece. God say he will soothe the troubled waters. I'll come by tomorrow and bless the house.

The lights go down to black.

Several hours later. The house is dark. Berniece has retired for the night. Boy Willie enters the darkened house with Grace.

BOY WILLIE: Come on in. This my sister's house. My sister live here. Come on, I ain't gonna bite you.

GRACE: Put some light on. I can't see.

BOY WILLIE: You don't need to see nothing, baby. This here is all you need to see. All you need to do is see me. If you can't see me you can feel me in the dark. How's that, sugar?

He attempts to kiss her.

GRACE: Go on now . . . wait!

BOY WILLIE: Just give me one little old kiss.

GRACE: [*Pushing him away.*] Come on, now. Where I'm gonna sleep at?

BOY WILLIE: We got to sleep out here on the couch. Come on, my sister don't mind. Lymon come back he just got to sleep on the floor. He run off with Dolly somewhere he better stay there. Come on, sugar.

GRACE: Wait now . . . you ain't told me nothing about no couch. I thought you had a bed. Both of us can't sleep on that little old couch.

BOY WILLIE: It don't make no difference. We can sleep on the floor. Let Lymon sleep on the couch.

GRACE: You ain't told me nothing about no couch.

BOY WILLIE: What difference it make? You just wanna be with me.

GRACE: I don't want to be with you on no couch. Ain't you got no bed?

BOY WILLIE: You don't need no bed, woman. My granddaddy used to take women on the backs of horses. What you need a bed for? You just want to be with me.

GRACE: You sure is country. I didn't know you was this country.

BOY WILLIE: There's a lot of things you don't know about me. Come on, let me show you what this country boy can do.

GRACE: Let's go to my place. I got a room with a bed if Leroy don't come back there.

BOY WILLIE: Who's Leroy? You ain't said nothing about no Leroy.

GRACE: He used to be my man. He ain't coming back. He gone off with some other gal.

BOY WILLIE: You let him have your key?

GRACE: He ain't coming back.

BOY WILLIE: Did you let him have your key?

GRACE: He got a key but he ain't coming back. He took off with some other gal.

BOY WILLIE: I don't wanna go nowhere he might come. Let's stay here. Come on, sugar.

He pulls her over to the couch.

Let me heist your hood and check your oil. See if your battery needs charged.

He pulls her to him. They kiss and tug at each other's clothing. In their anxiety they knock over a lamp.

BERNIECE: Who's that . . . Wining Boy?

BOY WILLIE: It's me . . . Boy Willie. Go on back to sleep. Everything's alright.

To Grace.

That's my sister. Everything's alright, Berniece. Go on back to sleep.

BERNIECE: What you doing down there? What you done knocked over?

BOY WILLIE: It wasn't nothing. Everything's alright. Go on back to sleep.

To Grace.

That's my sister. We alright. She gone back to sleep.

They begin to kiss. Berniece enters from the stairs dressed in a nightgown. She cuts on the light.

BERNIECE: Boy Willie, what you doing down here?

BOY WILLIE: It was just that there lamp. It ain't broke. It's okay. Everything's alright. Go on back to bed.

BERNIECE: Boy Willie, I don't allow that in my house. You gonna have to take your company someplace else.

BOY WILLIE: It's alright. We ain't doing nothing. We just sitting here talking. This here is Grace. That's my sister Berniece.

BERNIECE: You know I don't allow that kind of stuff in my house.

BOY WILLIE: Allow what? We just sitting here talking.

BERNIECE: Well, your company gonna have to leave. Come back and talk in the morning.

BOY WILLIE: Go on back upstairs now.

BERNIECE: I got an eleven-year-old girl upstairs. I can't allow that around here.

BOY WILLIE: Ain't nobody said nothing about that. I told you we just talking.

GRACE: Come on . . . let's go to my place. Ain't nobody got to tell me to leave but once.

BOY WILLIE: You ain't got to be like that, Berniece.

BERNIECE: I'm sorry, Miss. But he know I don't allow that in here.

GRACE: You ain't got to tell me but once. I don't stay nowhere I ain't wanted.

BOY WILLIE: I don't know why you want to embarrass me in front of my company.

GRACE: Come on, take me home.

BERNIECE: Go on, Boy Willie. Just go on with your company.

Boy Willie and Grace exit. Berniece puts the light on in the kitchen and puts on the teakettle. Presently there is a knock at the door. Berniece goes to answer it. Berniece opens the door. Lymon enters.

LYMON: How you doing, Berniece? I thought you'd be asleep. Boy Willie been back here?

BERNIECE: He just left out of here a minute ago.

LYMON: I went out to see a picture show and never got there. We always end up doing something else. I was with this woman she just wanted to drink up all my money. So I left her there and came back looking for Boy Willie.

BERNIECE: You just missed him. He just left out of here.

LYMON: They got some nice-looking women in this city. I'm gonna like it up here real good. I like seeing them with their dresses on. Got them high heels. I like that. Make them look like they real precious. Boy Willie met a real nice one today. I wish I had met her before he did.

BERNIECE: He come by here with some woman a little while ago. I told him to go on and take all that out of my house.

LYMON: What she look like, the woman he was with? Was she a brown-skinned woman about this high? Nice and healthy? Got nice hips on her?

BERNIECE: She had on a red dress.

LYMON: That's her! That's Grace. She real nice. Laugh a lot. Lot of fun to be with. She don't be trying to put on. Some of these woman act like they the Queen of Sheba. I don't like them kind. Grace ain't like that. She real nice with herself.

BERNIECE: I don't know what she was like. He come in here all drunk knocking over the lamp, and making all kind of noise. I told them to take that somewhere else. I can't really say what she was like.

LYMON: She real nice. I seen her before he did. I was trying not to act like I seen her. I wanted to look at her a while before I said something. She seen me when I come into the saloon. I tried to act like I didn't see her. Time I looked around Boy Willie was talking to her. She was talking to him kept looking at me. That's when her friend Dolly came. I asked her if she wanted to go to the picture show. She told me to buy her a drink while she thought about it. Next thing I knew she done had three drinks talking about she too tired to go. I bought her another drink, then I left. Boy Willie was gone and I thought he might have come back here. Doaker gone, huh? He say he had to make a trip.

BERNIECE: Yeah, he gone on his trip. This is when I can usually get me some peace and quiet, Maretha asleep.

LYMON: She look just like you. Got them big eyes. I remember her when she was in diapers.

BERNIECE: Time just keep on. It go on with or without you. She going on twelve.

LYMON: She sure is pretty. I like kids.

BERNIECE: Boy Willie say you staying . . . what you gonna do up here in this big city? You thought about that?

LYMON: They never get me back down there. The sheriff looking for me. All because they gonna try and make me work for somebody when I don't want to. They gonna try and make me work for Stovall when he don't pay nothing. It ain't like that up here. Up here you more or less do what you want to. I figure I find me a job and try to get set up and then see what the year brings. I tried to do that two or three times down there . . . but it never would work out. I was always in the wrong place.

BERNIECE: This ain't a bad city once you get to know your way around.

LYMON: Up here is different. I'm gonna get me a job unloading boxcars or something. One fellow told me say he know a place. I'm gonna go over there with him next week. Me and Boy Willie finish selling them watermelons I'll have enough money to hold me for a while. But I'm gonna go over there and see what kind of jobs they have.

BERNIECE: You shouldn't have too much trouble finding a job. It's all in how you present yourself. See now, Boy Willie couldn't get no job up here. Somebody hire him they got a pack of trouble on their hands. Soon as they find that out they fire him. He don't want to do nothing unless he do it his way.

LYMON: I know. I told him let's go to the picture show first and see if there was any women down there. They might get tired of sitting at home and walk down to the picture show. He say he wanna look around first. We never did get down there. We tried a couple of places and then we went to this saloon where he met Grace. I tried to meet her before he did but he beat me to her. We left Wining Boy sitting down there running his mouth. He told me if I wear this suit I'd find me a woman. He was almost right.

BERNIECE: You don't need to be out there in them saloons. Ain't no telling what you liable to run into out there. This one liable to cut you as quick as that one shoot you. You don't need to be out there. You start out that fast life you can't keep it up. It makes you old quick. I don't know what them women out there be thinking about.

LYMON: Mostly they be lonely and looking for somebody to spend the night with them. Sometimes it matters who it is and sometimes it don't. I used to be the same way. Now it got to matter. That's why I'm here now. Dolly liable not to even recognize me if she sees me again. I don't like women like that. I like my women to be with me in a nice and easy way. That way we can both enjoy ourselves. The way I see it we the only two people like us in the world. We got to see how we fit together. A woman that don't want to take the time to do that I don't bother with. Used to. Used to bother with all of them. Then I woke up one time with this woman and I didn't know who she was. She was the prettiest woman I had ever seen in my life. I spent the whole night with her and didn't even know it. I had never taken the time to look at her. I guess she kinda knew I ain't never really looked at her. She must have known that cause she ain't wanted to see me no more. If she had wanted to see me I believe we might have got married. How come you ain't married? It seem like to me you would be married. I remember Avery from down home. I used to call him plain old Avery. Now he Reverend Avery. That's kinda funny about him becoming a preacher. I like when he told about how that come to him in a dream about them sheep people and them hobos. Nothing ever come to me in a dream like that. I just dream about women. Can't never seem to find the right one.

BERNIECE: She out there somewhere. You just got to get yourself ready to meet her. That's what I'm trying to do. Avery's alright. I ain't really got nobody in mind.

LYMON: I get me a job and a little place and get set up to where I can make a woman comfortable I might get married. Avery's nice. You ought to go ahead and get married. You be a preacher's wife you won't have to work. I hate living by myself. I didn't want to be no strain on my mama so I left home when I was about sixteen. Everything I tried seem like it just didn't work out. Now I'm trying this.

BERNIECE: You keep trying it'll work out for you.

LYMON: You ever go down there to the picture show?

BERNIECE: I don't go in for all that.

LYMON: Ain't nothing wrong with it. It ain't like gambling and sinning. I went to one down in Jackson once. It was fun.

BERNIECE: I just stay home most of the time. Take care of Maretha.

LYMON: It's getting kind of late. I don't know where Boy Willie went off to. He's liable not to come back. I'm gonna take off these shoes. My feet hurt. Was you in bed? I don't mean to be keeping you up.

BERNIECE: You ain't keeping me up. I couldn't sleep after that Boy Willie woke me up.

LYMON: You got on that nightgown. I likes women when they wear them fancy nightclothes and all. It makes their skin look real pretty.

BERNIECE: I got this at the five-and-ten-cents store. It ain't so fancy.

LYMON: I don't too often get to see a woman dressed like that.

There is a long pause. Lymon takes off his suit coat.

Well, I'm gonna sleep here on the couch. I'm supposed to sleep on the floor but I don't reckon Boy Willie's coming back tonight. Wining Boy sold me this suit. Told me it was a magic suit. I'm gonna put it on again tomorrow. Maybe it bring me a woman like he say.

He goes into his coat pocket and takes out a small bottle of perfume.

I almost forgot I had this. Some man sold me this for a dollar. Say it come from Paris. This is the same kind of perfume the Queen of France wear. That's what he told me. I don't know if it's true or not. I smelled it. It smelled good to me. Here . . . smell it see if you like it. I was gonna give it to Dolly. But I didn't like her too much.

BERNIECE: [*Takes the bottle.*] It smells nice.

LYMON: I was gonna give it to Dolly if she had went to the picture with me. Go on, you take it.

BERNIECE: I can't take it. Here . . . go on you keep it. You'll find some-body to give it to.

LYMON: I wanna give it to you. Make you smell nice.

He takes the bottle and puts perfume behind Berniece's ear.

They tell me you supposed to put it right here behind your ear. Say if you put it there you smell nice all day.

Berniece stiffens at his touch. Lymon bends down to smell her.

There . . . you smell real good now.

He kisses her neck.

You smell real good for Lymon.

He kisses her again. Berniece returns the kiss, then breaks the embrace and crosses to the stairs. She turns and they look silently at each other. Lymon hands her the bottle of perfume. Berniece exits up the stairs. Lymon picks up his suit coat and strokes it lovingly with the full knowledge that it is indeed a magic suit. The lights go down on the scene.

It is late the next morning. The lights come up on the parlor. Lymon is asleep on the sofa. Boy Willie enters the front door.

BOY WILLIE: Hey, Lymon! Lymon, come on get up.

LYMON: Leave me alone.

BOY WILLIE: Come on, get up, nigger! Wake up, Lymon.

LYMON: What you want?

BOY WILLIE: Come on, let's go. I done called the man about the piano.

LYMON: What piano?

BOY WILLIE: [*Dumps Lymon on the floor.*] Come on, get up!

LYMON: Why you leave, I looked around and you was gone.

BOY WILLIE: I come back here with Grace, then I went looking for you. I figured you'd be with Dolly.

LYMON: She just want to drink and spend up your money. I come on back here looking for you to see if you wanted to go to the picture show.

BOY WILLIE: I been up at Grace's house. Some nigger named Leroy come by but I had a chair up against the door. He got mad when he couldn't get in. He went off somewhere and I got out of there before he could come back. Berniece got mad when we came here.

LYMON: She say you was knocking over the lamp busting up the place.

BOY WILLIE: That was Grace doing all that.

LYMON: Wining Boy seen Sutter's ghost last night.

BOY WILLIE: Wining Boy's liable to see anything. I'm surprised he found the right house. Come on, I done called the man about the piano.

LYMON: What he say?

BOY WILLIE: He say to bring it on out. I told him I was calling for my sister, Miss Berniece Charles. I told him some man wanted to buy it for eleven hundred dollars and asked him if he would go any better. He said yeah, he would give me eleven hundred and fifty dollars for it if it was the same piano. I described it to him again and he told me to bring it out.

LYMON: Why didn't you tell him to come and pick it up?

BOY WILLIE: I didn't want to have no problem with Berniece. This way we just take it on out there and it be out the way. He want to charge twenty-five dollars to pick it up.

LYMON: You should have told him the man was gonna give you twelve hundred for it.

BOY WILLIE: I figure I was taking a chance with that eleven hundred. If I had told him twelve hundred he might have run off. Now I wish I had told him twelve-fifty. It's hard to figure out white folks sometimes.

LYMON: You might have been able to tell him anything. White folks got a lot of money.

BOY WILLIE: Come on, let's get it loaded before Berniece come back. Get that end over there. All you got to do is pick it up on that side. Don't worry about this side. You wanna stretch you' back for a minute?

LYMON: I'm ready.

BOY WILLIE: Get a real good grip on it now.

The sound of Sutter's Ghost is heard. They do not hear it.

LYMON: I got this end. You get that end.

BOY WILLIE: Wait till I say ready now. Alright. You got it good? You got a grip on it?

LYMON: Yeah, I got it. You lift up on that end.

BOY WILLIE: Ready? Lift!

The piano will not budge.

LYMON: Man, this piano is heavy! It's gonna take more than me and you to move this piano.

BOY WILLIE: We can do it. Come on—we did it before.

LYMON: Nigger—you crazy! That piano weighs five hundred pounds!

BOY WILLIE: I got three hundred pounds of it! I know you can carry two hundred pounds! You be lifting them cotton sacks! Come on lift this piano!

They try to move the piano again without success.

LYMON: It's stuck. Something holding it.

BOY WILLIE: How the piano gonna be stuck? We just moved it. Slide you' end out.

LYMON: Naw—we gonna need two or three more people. How this big old piano get in the house?

BOY WILLIE: I don't know how it got in the house. I know how it's going out though! You get on this end. I'll carry three hundred and fifty pounds of it. All you got to do is slide your end out. Ready?

They switch sides and try again without success. Doaker enters from his room as they try to push and shove it.

LYMON: Hey, Doaker . . . how this piano get in the house?

DOAKER: Boy Willie, what you doing?

BOY WILLIE: I'm carrying this piano out the house. What it look like I'm doing? Come on, Lymon, let's try again.

DOAKER: Go on let the piano sit there till Berniece come home.

BOY WILLIE: You ain't got nothing to do with this, Doaker. This my business.

DOAKER: This is my house, nigger! I ain't gonna let you or nobody else carry nothing out of it. You ain't gonna carry nothing out of here without my permission!

BOY WILLIE: This is my piano. I don't need your permission to carry my belongings out of your house. This is mine. This ain't got nothing to do with you.

DOAKER: I say leave it over there till Berniece come home. She got part of it too. Leave it set there till you see what she say.

BOY WILLIE: I don't care what Berniece say. Come on, Lymon. I got this side.

DOAKER: Go on and cut it half in two if you want to. Just leave Berniece's half sitting over there. I can't tell you what to do with your piano. But I can't let you take her half out of here.

BOY WILLIE: Go on, Doaker. You ain't got nothing to do with this. I don't want you starting nothing now. Just go on and leave me alone. Come on, Lymon. I got this end.

Doaker goes into his room. Boy Willie and Lymon prepare to move the piano.

LYMON: How we gonna get it in the truck?

BOY WILLIE: Don't worry about how we gonna get it on the truck. You got to get it out the house first.

LYMON: It's gonna take more than me and you to move this piano.

BOY WILLIE: Just lift up on that end, nigger!

Doaker comes to the doorway of his room and stands.

DOAKER: [*Quietly with authority.*] Leave that piano set over there till Berniece come back. I don't care what you do with it then. But you gonna leave it sit over there right now.

BOY WILLIE: Alright . . . I'm gonna tell you this, Doaker. I'm going out of here . . . I'm gonna get me some rope . . . find me a plank and some wheels . . . and I'm coming back. Then I'm gonna carry that piano out of here . . . sell it and give Berniece half the money. See . . . now that's what I'm gonna do. And you . . . or nobody else is gonna stop me. Come on, Lymon . . . let's go get some rope and stuff. I'll be back, Doaker.

Boy Willie and Lymon exit. The lights go down on the scene.

The lights come up. Boy Willie sits on the sofa, screwing casters on a wooden plank. Maretha is sitting on the piano stool. Doaker sits at the table playing solitaire.

BOY WILLIE: [*To Maretha.*] Then after that them white folks down around there started falling down their wells. You ever seen a well? A well got a wall around it. It's hard to fall down a well. You got to be leaning way over. Couldn't nobody figure out too much what was making these fellows fall down their well . . . so everybody says the Ghosts of the Yellow Dog must have pushed them. That's what everybody called them four men what got burned up in the boxcar.

MARETHA: Why they call them that?

BOY WILLIE: Cause the Yazoo Delta railroad got yellow boxcars. Sometime the way the whistle blow sound like an old dog howling so the people call it the Yellow Dog.

MARETHA: Anybody ever see the Ghosts?

BOY WILLIE: I told you they like the wind. Can you see the wind?

MARETHA: No.

BOY WILLIE: They like the wind you can't see them. But sometimes you be in trouble they might be around to help you. They say if you go where the Southern cross the Yellow Dog . . . you go to where them two railroads cross each other . . . and call out their names . . . they say they talk back to you. I don't know, I ain't never done that. But Uncle Wining Boy he say he been down there and talked to them. You have to ask him about that part.

Berniece has entered from the front door.

BERNIECE: Maretha, you go on and get ready for me to do your hair.

Maretha crosses to the steps.

Boy Willie, I done told you to leave my house.

To Maretha.

Go on, Maretha.

Maretha is hesitant about going up the stairs.

BOY WILLIE: Don't be scared. Here, I'll go up there with you. If we see Sutter's ghost I'll put a whupping on him. Come on, Uncle Boy Willie going with you.

Boy Willie and Maretha exit up the stairs.

BERNIECE: Doaker—what is going on here?

DOAKER: I come home and him and Lymon was moving the piano. I told them to leave it over there till you got home. He went out and got that board and them wheels. He say he gonna take that piano out of here and ain't nobody gonna stop him.

BERNIECE: I ain't playing with Boy Willie. I got Crawley's gun upstairs. He don't know but I'm through with it. Where Lymon go?

DOAKER: Boy Willie sent him for some rope just before you come in.

BERNIECE: I ain't studying Boy Willie or Lymon—or the rope. Boy Willie ain't taking that piano out this house. That's all there is to it.

Boy Willie and Maretha enter on the stairs. Maretha carries a hot comb and a can of hair grease. Boy Willie crosses over and continues to screw the wheels on the board.

MARETHA: Mama, all the hair grease is gone. There ain't but this little bit left.

BERNIECE: [*Gives her a dollar.*] Here . . . run across the street and get another can. You come straight back, too. Don't you be playing around out there. And watch the cars. Be careful when you cross the street.

Maretha exits out the front door.

Boy Willie, I done told you to leave my house.

BOY WILLIE: I ain't in you' house. I'm in Doaker's house. If he ask me to leave then I'll go on and leave. But consider me done left your part.

BERNIECE: Doaker, tell him to leave. Tell him to go on.

DOAKER: Boy Willie ain't done nothing for me to put him out of the house. I told you if you can't get along just go on and don't have nothing to do with each other.

BOY WILLIE: I ain't thinking about Berniece.

He gets up and draws a line across the floor with his foot.

There! Now I'm out of your part of the house. Consider me done left your part. Soon as Lymon come back with that rope. I'm gonna take that piano out of here and sell it.

BERNIECE: You ain't gonna touch that piano.

BOY WILLIE: Carry it out of here just as big and bold. Do like my daddy would have done come time to get Sutter's land.

BERNIECE: I got something to make you leave it over there.

BOY WILLIE: It's got to come better than this thirty-two-twenty.

DOAKER: Why don't you stop all that! Boy Willie, go on and leave her alone. You know how Berniece get. Why you wanna sit there and pick with her?

BOY WILLIE: I ain't picking with her. I told her the truth. She the one talking about what she got. I just told her what she better have.

BERNIECE: That's alright, Doaker. Leave him alone.

BOY WILLIE: She trying to scare me. Hell, I ain't scared of dying. I look around and see people dying every day. You got to die to make room for somebody else. I had a dog that died. Wasn't nothing but a puppy. I picked it up and put it in a bag and carried it up there to Reverend C. L. Thompson's church. I carried it up there and prayed and asked Jesus to make it live like he did the man in the Bible. I prayed real hard. Knelt down and everything. Say ask in Jesus' name. Well, I must have called Jesus' name two hundred times. I called his name till my mouth got sore. I got up and looked in the bag and the dog still dead. It ain't moved a muscle! I say, "Well, ain't nothing precious." And then I went out and killed me a cat. That's when I discovered the power of death. See, a nigger that ain't afraid to die is the worse kind of nigger for the white man. He can't hold that power over you. That's what I learned when I killed that cat. I got the power of death too. I can command him. I can call him up. The white man don't like to see that. He don't like for you to stand up and look him square in the eye and say, "I got it too." Then he got to deal with you square up.

BERNIECE: That's why I don't talk to him, Doaker. You try and talk to him and that's the only kind of stuff that comes out his mouth.

DOAKER: You say Avery went home to get his Bible?

BOY WILLIE: What Avery gonna do? Avery can't do nothing with me. I wish Avery would say something to me about this piano.

DOAKER: Berniece ain't said about that. Avery went home to get his Bible. He coming by to bless the house see if he can get rid of Sutter's ghost.

BOY WILLIE: Ain't nothing but a house full of ghosts down there at the church. What Avery look like chasing away somebody's ghost?

Maretha enters the front door.

BERNIECE: Light that stove and set that comb over there to get hot. Get something to put around your shoulders.

BOY WILLIE: The Bible say an eye for an eye, a tooth for a tooth, and a life for a life. Tit for tat. But you and Avery don't want to believe that. You gonna pass up that part and pretend it ain't in there. Everything else you gonna agree with. But if you gonna agree with part of it you got to agree with all of it. You can't do nothing halfway. You gonna go at the Bible halfway. You gonna act like that part ain't in there. But you pull out the Bible and open it and see what it say. Ask Avery. He a preacher. He'll tell you it's in there. He the Good Shepherd. Unless he gonna shepherd you to heaven with half the Bible.

BERNIECE: Maretha, bring me that comb. Make sure it's hot.

Maretha brings the comb. Berniece begins to do her hair.

BOY WILLIE: I will say this for Avery. He done figured out a path to go through life. I don't agree with it. But he done fixed it so he can go right through it real smooth. Hell, he liable to end up with a million dollars that he done got from selling bread and wine.

MARETHA: OWWWWWW!

BERNIECE: Be still, Maretha. If you was a boy I wouldn't be going through this.

BOY WILLIE: Don't you tell that girl that. Why you wanna tell her that?

BERNIECE: You ain't got nothing to do with this child.

BOY WILLIE: Telling her you wished she was a boy. How's that gonna make her feel?

BERNIECE: Boy Willie, go on and leave me alone.

DOAKER: Why don't you leave her alone? What you got to pick with her for? Why don't you go on out and see what's out there in the streets? Have something to tell the fellows down home.

BOY WILLIE: I'm waiting on Lymon to get back with that truck. Why don't you go on out and see what's out there in the streets? You ain't got to work tomorrow. Talking about me . . . why don't you go out there? It's Friday night.

DOAKER: I got to stay around here and keep you all from killing one another.

BOY WILLIE: You ain't got to worry about me. I'm gonna be here just as long as it takes Lymon to get back here with that truck. You ought to be talking to Berniece. Sitting up there telling Maretha she wished she was a boy. What kind of thing is that to tell a child? If you want to tell her something tell her about that piano. You ain't even told her about that piano. Like that's something to be ashamed of. Like she supposed to go off and hide somewhere about that piano. You ought to mark down on the calendar the day that Papa Boy Charles brought that piano into the house. You ought to mark that day down and draw a circle around it . . . and every year when it come up throw a party. Have a celebration. If you did that she wouldn't have no problem in life. She could walk around here with her head held high. I'm talking about a big party! Invite everybody! Mark that day down with a special meaning. That way she know where she at in the world. You got her going out here thinking she wrong in the world. Like there ain't no part of it belong to her.

BERNIECE: Let me take care of my child. When you get one of your own then you can teach it what you want to teach it.

Doaker exits into his room.

BOY WILLIE: What I want to bring a child into this world for? Why I wanna bring somebody else into all this for? I'll tell you this . . . If I was Rockefeller I'd have forty or fifty. I'd make one every day. Cause they gonna start out in life with all the advantages. I ain't got no advantages to offer nobody. Many is the time I looked at my daddy and seen him staring off at his hands. I got a little older I know what he was thinking. He sitting there saying, "I got these big old hands but what I'm gonna do with them? Best I can do is make a fifty-acre crop for Mr. Stovall. Got these big old hands capable of doing anything. I can take and build something with these hands. But where's the tools? All I got is these hands. Unless I go out here and kill me somebody and take what they got . . . it's a long row to hoe for me to get something of my own. So what I'm gonna do with these big old hands? What would you do?"

See now . . . if he had his own land he wouldn't have felt that way. If he had something under his feet that belonged to him he could stand up taller. That's what I'm talking about. Hell, the land is there for everybody. All you got to do is figure out how to get you a piece. Ain't no mystery to life. You just got to go out and meet it square on. If you got a piece of land you'll find everything else fall right into place. You can stand right up next to the white man and talk about the price of cotton . . . the weather, and anything else you want to talk about. If you teach that girl that she living at the bottom of life, she's gonna grow up and hate you.

BERNIECE: I'm gonna teach her the truth. That's just where she living. Only she ain't got to stay there.

To Maretha.

Turn you' head over to the other side.

BOY WILLIE: This might be your bottom but it ain't mine. I'm living at the top of life. I ain't gonna just take my life and throw it away at the bottom. I'm in the world like everybody else. The way I see it everybody else got to come up a little taste to be where I am.

BERNIECE: You right at the bottom with the rest of us.

BOY WILLIE: I'll tell you this . . . and ain't a living soul can put a come back on it. If you believe that's where you at then you gonna act that way. If you act that way then that's where you gonna be. It's as simple as that. Ain't no mystery to life. I don't know how you come to believe that stuff. Crawley didn't think like that. He wasn't living at the bottom of life. Papa Boy Charles and Mama Ola wasn't living at the bottom of life. You ain't never heard them say nothing like that. They would have taken a strap to you if they heard you say something like that.

Doaker enters from his room.

Hey, Doaker . . . Berniece say the colored folks is living at the bottom of life. I tried to tell her if she think that . . . that's where she gonna be. You think you living at the bottom of life? Is that how you see yourself?

DOAKER: I'm just living the best way I know how. I ain't thinking about no top or no bottom.

BOY WILLIE: That's what I tried to tell Berniece. I don't know where she got that from. That sound like something Avery would say. Avery think cause the white man give him a turkey for Thanksgiving that makes him better than everybody else. That's gonna raise him out of the bottom of life. I don't need nobody to give me a turkey. I can get my own turkey. All you have to do is get out my way. I'll get me two or three turkeys.

BERNIECE: You can't even get a chicken let alone two or three turkeys. Talking about get out your way. Ain't nobody in your way.

To Maretha.

Straighten your head, Maretha! Don't be bending down like that. Hold your head up!

To Boy Willie.

All you got going for you is talk. You' whole life that's all you ever had going for you.

BOY WILLIE: See now . . . I'll tell you something about me. I done strung along and strung along. Going this way and that. Whatever way would lead me to a moment of peace. That's all I want. To be as easy with everything. But I wasn't born to that. I was born to a time of fire.

The world ain't wanted no part of me. I could see that since I was about seven. The world say it's better off without me. See, Berniece accept that. She trying to come up to where she can prove something to the world. Hell, the world a better place cause of me. I don't see it like Berniece. I got a heart that beats here and it beats just as loud as the next fellow's. Don't care if he black or white. Sometime it beats louder. When it beats louder, then everybody can hear it. Some people get scared of that. Like Berniece. Some people get scared to hear a nigger's heart beating. They think you ought to lay low with that heart. Make it beat quiet and go along with everything the way it is. But my mama ain't birthed me for nothing. So what I got to do? I got to mark my passing on the road. Just like you write on a tree, "Boy Willie was here."

That's all I'm trying to do with that piano. Trying to put my mark on the road. Like my daddy done. My heart say for me to sell that piano and get me some land so I can make a life for myself to live in my own way. Other than that I ain't thinking about nothing Berniece got to say.

There is a knock at the door. Boy Willie crosses to it and yanks it open thinking it is Lymon. Avery enters. He carries a Bible.

BOY WILLIE: Where you been, nigger? Aw . . . I thought you was Lymon. Hey, Berniece, look who's here.

BERNIECE: Come on in, Avery. Don't you pay Boy Willie no mind.

BOY WILLIE: Hey . . . Hey, Avery . . . tell me this . . . can you get to heaven with half the Bible?

BERNIECE: Boy Willie . . . I done told you to leave me alone.

BOY WILLIE: I just ask the man a question. He can answer. He don't need you to speak for him. Avery . . . if you only believe on half the Bible and don't want to accept the other half . . . you think God let you in heaven? Or do you got to have the whole Bible? Tell Berniece . . . if you only believe in part of it . . . when you see God he gonna ask you why you ain't believed in the other part . . . then he gonna send you straight to Hell.

AVERY: You got to be born again. Jesus say unless a man be born again he cannot come unto the Father and who so ever heareth my words and believeth them not shall be cast into a fiery pit.

BOY WILLIE: That's what I was trying to tell Berniece. You got to believe in it all. You can't go at nothing halfway. She think she going to heaven with half the Bible.

To Berniece.

You hear that . . . Jesus say you got to believe in it all.

BERNIECE: You keep messing with me.

BOY WILLIE: I ain't thinking about you.

DOAKER: Come on in, Avery, and have a seat. Don't pay neither one of them no mind. They been arguing all day.

BERNIECE: Come on in, Avery.

AVERY: How's everybody in here?

BERNIECE: Here, set this comb back over there on that stove.

To Avery.

Don't pay Boy Willie no mind. He been around here bothering me since I come home from work.

BOY WILLIE: Boy Willie ain't bothering you. Boy Willie ain't bothering nobody. I'm just waiting on Lymon to get back. I ain't thinking about you. You heard the man say I was right and you still don't want to believe it. You just wanna go and make up anythin'. Well there's Avery . . . there's the preacher . . . go on and ask him.

AVERY: Berniece believe in the Bible. She been baptized.

BOY WILLIE: What about that part that say an eye for an eye a tooth for a tooth and a life for a life? Ain't that in there?

DOAKER: What they say down there at the bank, Avery?

AVERY: Oh, they talked to me real nice. I told Berniece . . . they say maybe they let me borrow the money. They done talked to my boss down at work and everything.

DOAKER: That's what I told Berniece. You working every day you ought to be able to borrow some money.

AVERY: I'm getting more people in my congregation every day. Berniece says she gonna be the Deaconess. I get me my church I can get married and settled down. That's what I told Berniece.

DOAKER: That be nice. You all ought to go ahead and get married. Berniece don't need to be by herself. I tell her that all the time.

BERNIECE: I ain't said nothing about getting married. I said I was thinking about it.

DOAKER: Avery get him his church you all can make it nice.

To Avery.

Berniece said you was coming by to bless the house.

AVERY: Yeah, I done read up on my Bible. She asked me to come by and see if I can get rid of Sutter's ghost.

BOY WILLIE: Ain't no ghost in this house. That's all in Berniece's head. Go on up there and see if you see him. I'll give you a hundred dollars if you see him. That's all in her imagination.

DOAKER: Well, let her find that out then. If Avery blessing the house is gonna make her feel better . . . what you got to do with it?

AVERY: Berniece say Maretha seen him too. I don't know, but I found a part in the Bible to bless the house. If he is here then that ought to make him go.

BOY WILLIE: You worse than Berniece believing all that stuff. Talking about . . . if he here. Go on up there and find out. I been up there I ain't seen him. If you reading from that Bible gonna make him leave out of Berniece imagination, well, you might be right. But if you talking about . . .

DOAKER: Boy Willie, why don't you just be quiet? Getting all up in the man's business. This ain't got nothing to do with you. Let him go ahead and do what he gonna do.

BOY WILLIE: I ain't stopping him. Avery ain't got no power to do nothing.

AVERY: Oh, I ain't got no power. God got the power! God got power over everything in His creation. God can do anything. God say, "As I commandeth so it shall be." God said, "Let there be light," and there was light. He made the world in six days and rested on the seventh. God's got a wonderful power. He got power over life and death. Jesus raised Lazareth from the dead. They was getting ready to bury him and Jesus told him say, "Rise up and walk." He got up and walked and the people made great rejoicing at the power of God. I ain't worried about him chasing away a little old ghost!

There is a knock at the door. Boy Willie goes to answer it. Lymon enters carrying a coil of rope.

BOY WILLIE: Where you been? I been waiting on you and you run off somewhere.

LYMON: I ran into Grace. I stopped and bought her drink. She say she gonna go to the picture show with me.

BOY WILLIE: I ain't thinking about no Grace nothing.

LYMON: Hi, Berniece.

BOY WILLIE: Give me that rope and get up on this side of the piano.

DOAKER: Boy Willie, don't start nothing now. Leave the piano alone.

BOY WILLIE: Get that board there, Lymon. Stay out of this, Doaker.

Berniece exits up the stairs.

DOAKER: You just can't take the piano. How you gonna take the piano? Berniece ain't said nothing about selling that piano.

BOY WILLIE: She ain't got to say nothing. Come on, Lymon. We got to lift one end at a time up on the board. You got to watch so that the board don't slide up under there.

LYMON: What we gonna do with the rope?

BOY WILLIE: Let me worry about the rope. You just get up on this side over here with me.

Berniece enters from the stairs. She has her hand in her pocket where she has Crawley's gun.

AVERY: Boy Willie . . . Berniece . . . why don't you all sit down and talk this out now?

BERNIECE: Ain't nothing to talk out.

BOY WILLIE: I'm through talking to Berniece. You can talk to Berniece till you get blue in the face, and it don't make no difference. Get up on that side, Lymon. Throw that rope around there and tie it to the leg.

LYMON: Wait a minute . . . wait a minute, Boy Willie. Berniece got to say. Hey, Berniece . . . did you tell Boy Willie he could take this piano?

BERNIECE: Boy Willie ain't taking nothing out of my house but himself. Now you let him go ahead and try.

BOY WILLIE: Come on, Lymon, get up on this side with me.

Lymon stands undecided.

Come on, nigger! What you standing there for?

LYMON: Maybe Berniece is right, Boy Willie. Maybe you shouldn't sell it.

AVERY: You all ought to sit down and talk it out. See if you can come to an agreement.

DOAKER: That's what I been trying to tell them. Seem like one of them ought to respect the other one's wishes.

BERNIECE: I wish Boy Willie would go on and leave my house. That's what I wish. Now, he can respect that. Cause he's leaving here one way or another.

BOY WILLIE: What you mean one way or another? What's that supposed to mean? I ain't scared of no gun.

DOAKER: Come on, Berniece, leave him alone with that.

BOY WILLIE: I don't care what Berniece say. I'm selling my half. I can't help it if her half got to go along with it. It ain't like I'm trying to cheat her out of her half. Come on, Lymon.

LYMON: Berniece . . . I got to do this . . . Boy Willie say he gonna give you half of the money . . . say he want to get Sutter's land.

BERNIECE: Go on, Lymon. Just go on . . . I done told Boy Willie what to do.

BOY WILLIE: Here, Lymon . . . put that rope up over there.

LYMON: Boy Willie, you sure you want to do this? The way I figure it . . . I might be wrong . . . but I figure she gonna shoot you first.

BOY WILLIE: She just gonna have to shoot me.

BERNIECE: Maretha, get on out the way. Get her out the way, Doaker.

DOAKER: Go on, do what your mama told you.

BERNIECE: Put her in your room.

Maretha exits to Doaker's room. Boy Willie and Lymon try to lift the piano. The door opens and Wining Boy enters. He has been drinking.

WINING BOY: Man, these niggers around here! I stopped down there at Seefus . . . . These folks standing around talking about Patchneck Red's coming. They jumping back and getting off the sidewalk talking about Patchneck Red this and Patchneck Red that. Come to find out . . . you know who they was talking about? Old John D. from up around Tyler! Used to run around with Otis Smith. He got everybody scared of him. Calling him Patchneck Red. They don't know I whupped the nigger's head in one time.

BOY WILLIE: Just make sure that board don't slide, Lymon.

LYMON: I got this side. You watch that side.

WINING BOY: Hey, Boy Willie, what you got? I know you got a pint stuck up in your coat.

BOY WILLIE: Wining Boy, get out the way!

WINING BOY: Hey, Doaker. What you got? Gimme a drink. I want a drink.

DOAKER: It look like you had enough of whatever it was. Come talking about "What you got?" You ought to be trying to find somewhere to lay down.

WINING BOY: I ain't worried about no place to lay down. I can always find me a place to lay down in Berniece's house. Ain't that right, Berniece?

BERNIECE: Wining Boy, sit down somewhere. You been out there drinking all day. Come in here smelling like an old polecat. Sit on down there, you don't need nothing to drink.

DOAKER: You know Berniece don't like all that drinking.

WINING BOY: I ain't disrespecting Berniece. Berniece, am I disrespecting you? I'm just trying to be nice. I been with strangers all day and they treated me like family. I come in here to family and you treat me like a stranger. I don't need your whiskey. I can buy my own. I wanted your company, not your whiskey.

DOAKER: Nigger, why don't you go upstairs and lay down? You don't need nothing to drink.

WINING BOY: I ain't thinking about no laying down. Me and Boy Willie fixing to party. Ain't that right, Boy Willie? Tell him. I'm fixing to play me some piano. Watch this.

Wining Boy sits down at the piano.

BOY WILLIE: Come on, Wining Boy! Me and Lymon fixing to move the piano.

WINING BOY: Wait a minute . . . wait a minute. This a song I wrote for Cleotha. I wrote this song in memory of Cleotha.

He begins to play and sing.

Hey little woman what's the matter with you now
Had a storm last night and blowed the line all down

Tell me how long
Is I got to wait
Can I get it now
Or must I hesitate

It takes a hesitating stocking in her hesitating shoe
It takes a hesitating woman wanna sing the blues

Tell me how long
Is I got to wait
Can I kiss you now
Or must I hesitate.

BOY WILLIE: Come on, Wining Boy, get up! Get up, Wining Boy! Me and Lymon's fixing to move the piano.

WINING BOY: Naw . . . Naw . . . you ain't gonna move this piano!

BOY WILLIE: Get out the way, Wining Boy.

Wining Boy, his back to the piano, spreads his arms out over the piano.

WINING BOY: You ain't taking this piano out the house. You got to take me with it!

BOY WILLIE: Get on out the way, Wining Boy! Doaker get him!

There is a knock on the door.

BERNIECE: I got him, Doaker. Come on, Wining Boy. I done told Boy Willie he ain't taking the piano.

Berniece tries to take Wining Boy away from the piano.

WINING BOY: He got to take me with it!

Doaker goes to answer the door. Grace enters.

GRACE: Is Lymon here?

DOAKER: Lymon.

WINING BOY: He ain't taking that piano.

BERNIECE: I ain't gonna let him take it.

GRACE: I thought you was coming back. I ain't gonna sit in that truck all day.

LYMON: I told you I was coming back.

GRACE: [*Sees Boy Willie.*] Oh, hi, Boy Willie. Lymon told me you was gone back down South.

LYMON: I said he was going back. I didn't say he had left already.

GRACE: That's what you told me.

BERNIECE: Lymon, you got to take your company someplace else.

LYMON: Berniece, this is Grace. That there is Berniece. That's Boy Willie's sister.

GRACE: Nice to meet you.

To Lymon.

I ain't gonna sit out in that truck all day. You told me you was gonna take me to the movie.

LYMON: I told you I had something to do first. You supposed to wait on me.

BERNIECE: Lymon, just go on and leave. Take Grace or whoever with you. Just go on get out my house.

BOY WILLIE: You gonna help me move this piano first, nigger!

LYMON: [*To Grace.*] I got to help Boy Willie move the piano first.

Everybody but Grace suddenly senses Sutter's presence.

GRACE: I ain't waiting on you. Told me you was coming right back. Now you got to move a piano. You just like all the other men.

Grace now senses something.

Something ain't right here. I knew I shouldn't have come back up in this house.

Grace exits.

LYMON: Hey, Grace! I'll be right back, Boy Willie.

BOY WILLIE: Where you going, nigger?

LYMON: I'll be back. I got to take Grace home.

BOY WILLIE: Come on, let's move the piano first!

LYMON: I got to take Grace home. I told you I'll be back.

Lymon exits. Boy Willie exits and calls after him.

BOY WILLIE: Come on, Lymon! Hey . . . Lymon! Lymon . . . come on!

Again, the presence of Sutter is felt.

WINING BOY: Hey, Doaker, did you feel that? Hey, Berniece . . . did you get cold? Hey, Doaker . . .

DOAKER: What you calling me for?

WINING BOY: I believe that's Sutter.

DOAKER: Well, let him stay up there. As long as he don't mess with me.

BERNIECE: Avery, go on and bless the house.

DOAKER: You need to bless that piano. That's what you need to bless. It ain't done nothing but cause trouble. If you gonna bless anything go on and bless that.

WINING BOY: Hey, Doaker, if he gonna bless something let him bless everything. The kitchen . . . the upstairs. Go on and bless it all.

BOY WILLIE: Ain't no ghost in this house. He need to bless Berniece's head. That's what he need to bless.

AVERY: Seem like that piano's causing all the trouble. I can bless that. Berniece, put me some water in that bottle.

Avery takes a small bottle from his pocket and hands it to Berniece, who goes into the kitchen to get water. Avery takes a candle from his pocket and lights it. He gives it to Berniece as she gives him the water.

Hold this candle. Whatever you do make sure it don't go out.

O Holy Father we gather here this evening in the Holy Name to cast out the spirit of one James Sutter. May this vial of water be empowered with thy spirit. May each drop of it be a weapon and a shield against the presence of all evil and may it be a cleansing and blessing of this humble abode.

Just as Our Father taught us how to pray so He say, "I will prepare a table for you in the midst of mine enemies," and in His hands we place ourselves to come unto his presence. Where there is Good so shall it cause Evil to scatter to the Four Winds.

He throws water at the piano at each commandment.

AVERY: Get thee behind me, Satan! Get thee behind the face of Righteousness as we Glorify His Holy Name! Get thee behind the Hammer of Truth that breaketh down the Wall of Falsehood! Father. Father. Praise. Praise. We ask in Jesus' name and call forth the power of the Holy Spirit as it is written. . . .

He opens the Bible and reads from it.

I will sprinkle clean water upon thee and ye shall be clean.

BOY WILLIE: All this old preaching stuff. Hell, just tell him to leave.

Avery continues reading throughout Boy Willie's outburst.

AVERY: I will sprinkle clean water upon you and you shall be clean: from all your uncleanliness, and from all your idols, will I cleanse you. A new heart also will I give you, and a new spirit will I put within you: and I will take out of your flesh the heart of stone, and I will give you a heart of flesh. And I will put my spirit within you, and cause you to walk in my statutes, and ye shall keep my judgments, and do them.

Boy Willie grabs a pot of water from the stove and begins to fling it around the room.

BOY WILLIE: Hey Sutter! Sutter! Get your ass out this house! Sutter! Come on and get some of this water! You done drowned in the well, come on and get some more of this water!

Boy Willie is working himself into a frenzy as he runs around the room throwing water and calling Sutter's name. Avery continues reading.

BOY WILLIE: Come on, Sutter!

He starts up the stairs.

Come on, get some water! Come on, Sutter!

The sound of Sutter's Ghost is heard. As Boy Willie approaches the steps he is suddenly thrown back by the unseen force, which is choking him. As he struggles he frees himself, then dashes up the stairs.

BOY WILLIE: Come on, Sutter!

AVERY: [*Continuing.*] A new heart also will I give you and a new spirit will I put within you: and I will take out of your flesh the heart of stone, and I will give you a heart of flesh. And I will put my spirit within you, and cause you to walk in my statutes, and ye shall keep my judgments, and do them.

There are loud sounds heard from upstairs as Boy Willie begins to wrestle with Sutter's Ghost. It is a life-and-death struggle fraught with perils and faultless terror. Boy Willie is thrown down the stairs. Avery is stunned into silence. Boy Willie picks himself up and dashes back upstairs.

AVERY: Berniece, I can't do it.

There are more sounds heard from upstairs. Doaker and Wining Boy stare at one another in stunned disbelief. It is in this moment, from somewhere old, that Berniece realizes what she must do. She crosses to the piano. She begins to play. The song is found piece by piece. It is an old urge to song that is both a commandment and a plea. With each repetition it gains in strength. It is intended as an exorcism and a dressing for battle. A rustle of wind blowing across two continents.

BERNIECE: [*Singing.*]

I want you to help me
I want you to help me
I want you to help me
I want you to help me
I want you to help me
I want you to help me
Mama Berniece
I want you to help me
Mama Esther
I want you to help me
Papa Boy Charles
I want you to help me
Mama Ola
I want you to help me

I want you to help me
I want you to help me
I want you to help me
I want you to help me
I want you to help me
I want you to help me
I want you to help me
I want you to help me

The sound of a train approaching is heard. The noise upstairs subsides.

BOY WILLIE: Come on, Sutter! Come back, Sutter!

Berniece begins to chant:

BERNIECE:

> *Thank you.*
> *Thank you.*
> *Thank you.*

> *A calm comes over the house. Maretha enters from Doaker's room. Boy Willie enters on the stairs. He pauses a moment to watch Berniece at the piano.*

BERNIECE:

> *Thank you.*
> *Thank you.*

BOY WILLIE: Wining Boy, you ready to go back down home? Hey, Doaker, what time the train leave?

DOAKER: You still got time to make it.

> *Maretha crosses and embraces Boy Willie.*

BOY WILLIE: Hey Berniece . . . if you and Maretha don't keep playing on that piano . . . ain't no telling . . . me and Sutter both liable to be back.

> *He exits.*

BERNIECE: Thank you.

> *The lights go down to black.*

*David Ives grew up on Chicago's South Side, the son of working-class par-
ents, and wrote his first play at the age of nine: "But then I realized you had
to have a copy of the script for each person in the play, so that was the end of
it." Impressed by theatrical productions he saw in his teens, Ives entered North-
western University and after graduation attended Yale Drama School. After
several attempts to become a "serious writer," he decided to "aspire to silliness
on a daily basis" and began creating the short comic plays on which his reputation rests. An evening of six one-act comedies,* All in the Timing, *had a
successful off-Broadway production in 1994, running over two years. In 1996
it was the most performed contemporary play in the nation, and* Sure Thing,
*its signature piece, remains popular, especially with student drama groups. A
second collection of one acts,* Mere Mortals, *had a successful run at Primary
Stages in 1997, and a third collection,* Lives of Saints, *was produced in 1999.
A number of his collections—including* All in the Timing *(1995),* Time Flies
(2001), and Polish Joke and Other Plays *(2004)—have been published. Ives's
comedic skills range from a hilarious parody of David Mamet's plays (presented at an event honoring Mamet) to his witty revision of a legendary character in the full-length* Don Juan in Chicago *(1995). His short plays, in many
cases, hinge on brilliant theatrical conceits; in* Mayflies, *a boy mayfly and girl
mayfly must meet, court, and consummate their relationship before their one
day of adult life ends.* Sure Thing, *a piece that plays witty tricks with time,
resembles a scene in the Bill Murray film* Groundhog Day, *the script of
which was written some years after Ives's play. Among many other activities,
Ives has written the books for concert versions of a number of classic American musicals. In an article titled "Why I Shouldn't Write Plays," Ives notes,
among other reasons, "All reviews should carry a Surgeon General's warning.
The good ones turn your head, the bad ones break your heart."*

Sure Thing

Characters

Betty
Bill

Scene: *A café.*

*Betty, a woman in her late twenties, is reading at a café table. An empty
chair is opposite her. Bill, same age, enters.*

BILL: Excuse me. Is this chair taken?

BETTY: Excuse me?

BILL: Is this taken?

BETTY: Yes it is.

BILL: Oh. Sorry.

BETTY: Sure thing.

A bell rings softly.

BILL: Excuse me. Is this chair taken?

BETTY: Excuse me?

BILL: Is this taken?

BETTY: No, but I'm expecting somebody in a minute.

BILL: Oh. Thanks anyway.

BETTY: Sure thing.

A bell rings softly.

BILL: Excuse me. Is this chair taken?

BETTY: No, but I'm expecting somebody very shortly.

BILL: Would you mind if I sit here till he or she or it comes?

BETTY [*glances at her watch*]: They do seem to be pretty late. . . .

BILL: You never know who you might be turning down.

BETTY: Sorry. Nice try, though.

BILL: Sure thing.

Bell.

Is this seat taken?

BETTY: No it's not.

BILL: Would you mind if I sit here?

BETTY: Yes I would.

BILL: Oh.

Bell.

Is this chair taken?

BETTY: No it's not.

BILL: Would you mind if I sit here?

BETTY: No. Go ahead.

BILL: Thanks. [*He sits. She continues reading.*] Everyplace else seems to be taken.

BETTY: Mm-hm.

BILL: Great place.

BETTY: Mm-hm.

BILL: What's the book?
BETTY: I just wanted to read in quiet, if you don't mind.
BILL: No. Sure thing.

   Bell.

BILL: Everyplace else seems to be taken.
BETTY: Mm-hm.
BILL: Great place for reading.
BETTY: Yes, I like it.
BILL: What's the book?
BETTY: *The Sound and the Fury.*
BILL: Oh. Hemingway.

   Bell.

What's the book?
BETTY: *The Sound and the Fury.*
BILL: Oh. Faulkner.
BETTY: Have you read it?
BILL: Not . . . actually. I've sure read *about* it, though. It's supposed to
   be great.
BETTY: It is great.
BILL: I hear it's great. [*Small pause.*] Waiter?

   Bell.

What's the book?
BETTY: *The Sound and the Fury.*
BILL: Oh. Faulkner.
BETTY: Have you read it?
BILL: I'm a Mets fan, myself.

   Bell.

BETTY: Have you read it?
BILL: Yeah, I read it in college.
BETTY: Where was college?
BILL: I went to Oral Roberts University.

   Bell.

BETTY: Where was college?
BILL: I was lying. I never really went to college. I just like to party.

   Bell.

BETTY: Where was college?

BILL: Harvard.

BETTY: Do you like Faulkner?

BILL: I love Faulkner. I spent a whole winter reading him once.

BETTY: I've just started.

BILL: I was so excited after ten pages that I went out and bought everything else he wrote. One of the greatest reading experiences of my life. I mean, all that incredible psychological understanding. Page after page of gorgeous prose. His profound grasp of the mystery of time and human existence. The smells of the earth . . . What do you think?

BETTY: I think it's pretty boring.

Bell.

BILL: What's the book?

BETTY: *The Sound and the Fury.*

BILL: Oh! Faulkner!

BETTY: Do you like Faulkner?

BILL: I love Faulkner.

BETTY: He's incredible.

BILL: I spent a whole winter reading him once.

BETTY: I was so excited after ten pages that I went out and bought everything else he wrote.

BILL: All that incredible psychological understanding.

BETTY: And the prose is so gorgeous.

BILL: And the way he's grasped the mystery of time—

BETTY: —and human existence. I can't believe I've waited this long to read him.

BILL: You never know. You might not have liked him before.

BETTY: That's true.

BILL: You might not have been ready for him. You have to hit these things at the right moment or it's no good.

BETTY: That's happened to me.

BILL: It's all in the timing. [*Small pause.*] My name's Bill, by the way.

BETTY: I'm Betty.

BILL: Hi.

BETTY: Hi. [*Small pause.*]

BILL: Yes I thought reading Faulkner was . . . a great experience.

BETTY: Yes. [*Small pause.*]

BILL: *The Sound and the Fury . . . [Another small pause.]*
BETTY: Well. Onwards and upwards. [*She goes back to her book.*]
BILL: Waiter—?

Bell.

You have to hit these things at the right moment or it's no good.
BETTY: That's happened to me.
BILL: It's all in the timing. My name's Bill, by the way.
BETTY: I'm Betty.
BILL: Hi.
BETTY: Hi.
BILL: Do you come in here a lot?
BETTY: Actually I'm just in town for two days from Pakistan.
BILL: Oh. Pakistan.

Bell.

My name's Bill, by the way.
BETTY: I'm Betty.
BILL: Hi.
BETTY: Hi.
BILL: Do you come in here a lot?
BETTY: Every once in a while. Do you?
BILL: Not so much anymore. Not as much as I used to. Before my nervous breakdown.

Bell.

Do you come in here a lot?
BETTY: Why are you asking?
BILL: Just interested.
BETTY: Are you really interested, or do you just want to pick me up?
BILL: No, I'm really interested.
BETTY: Why would you be interested in whether I come in here a lot?
BILL: I'm just . . . getting acquainted.
BETTY: Maybe you're only interested for the sake of making small talk long enough to ask me back to your place to listen to some music, or because you've just rented this great tape for your VCR, or because you've got some terrific unknown Django Reinhardt record, only all you really want to do is fuck—which you won't do very well—after which you'll go into the bathroom and pee very loudly, then pad into the kitchen and get yourself a beer from the

refrigerator without asking me whether I'd like anything, and then you'll proceed to lie back down beside me and confess that you've got a girlfriend named Stephanie who's away at medical school in Belgium for a year, and that you've been involved with her—*off and on*—in what you'll call a very "intricate" relationship, for the past *seven YEARS*. None of which *interests* me, mister!

BILL: Okay.

Bell.

Do you come in here a lot?

BETTY: Every other day, I think.

BILL: I come in here quite a lot and I don't remember seeing you.

BETTY: I guess we must be on different schedules.

BILL: Missed connections.

BETTY: Yes. Different time zones.

BILL: Amazing how you can live right next door to somebody in this town and never even know it.

BETTY: I know.

BILL: City life.

BETTY: It's crazy.

BILL: We probably pass each other in the street every day. Right in front of this place, probably.

BETTY: Yep.

BILL [*looks around*]:   Well the waiters here sure seem to be in some different time zone. I can't seem to locate one anywhere. . . . Waiter! [*He looks back.*] So what do you—[*He sees that she's gone back to her book.*]

BETTY: I beg pardon?

BILL: Nothing. Sorry.

Bell.

BETTY: I guess we must be on different schedules.

BILL: Missed connections.

BETTY: Yes. Different time zones.

BILL: Amazing how you can live right next door to somebody in this town and never even know it.

BETTY: I know.

BILL: City life.

BETTY: It's crazy.

BILL: You weren't waiting for somebody when I came in, were you?

BETTY: Actually I was.

BILL: Oh. Boyfriend?

BETTY: Sort of.

BILL: What's a sort-of boyfriend?

BETTY: My husband.

BILL: Ah-ha.

Bell.

You weren't waiting for somebody when I came in, were you?

BETTY: Actually I was.

BILL: Oh. Boyfriend?

BETTY: Sort of.

BILL: What's a sort-of boyfriend?

BETTY: We were meeting here to break up.

BILL: Mm-hm . . .

Bell.

What's a sort-of boyfriend?

BETTY: My lover. Here she comes right now!

Bell.

BILL: You weren't waiting for somebody when I came in, were you?

BETTY: No, just reading.

BILL: Sort of a sad occupation for a Friday night, isn't it? Reading here, all by yourself?

BETTY: Do you think so?

BILL: Well sure. I mean, what's a good-looking woman like you doing out alone on a Friday night?

BETTY: Trying to keep away from lines like that.

BILL: No, listen—

Bell.

You weren't waiting for somebody when I came in, were you?

BETTY: No, just reading.

BILL: Sort of a sad occupation for a Friday night, isn't it? Reading here all by yourself?

BETTY: I guess it is, in a way.

BILL: What's a good-looking woman like you doing out alone on a Friday night anyway? No offense, but . . .

BETTY: I'm out alone on a Friday night for the first time in a very long time.

BILL: Oh.

BETTY: You see, I just recently ended a relationship.

BILL: Oh.

BETTY: Of rather long standing.

BILL: I'm sorry. [*Small pause.*] Well listen, since reading by yourself *is* such a sad occupation for a Friday night, would you like to go elsewhere?

BETTY: No . . .

BILL: Do something else?

BETTY: No thanks.

BILL: I was headed out to the movies in a while anyway.

BETTY: I don't think so.

BILL: Big chance to let Faulkner catch his breath. All those long sentences get him pretty tired.

BETTY: Thanks anyway.

BILL: Okay.

BETTY: I appreciate the invitation.

BILL: Sure thing.

Bell.

You weren't waiting for somebody when I came in, were you?

BETTY: No, just reading.

BILL: Sort of a sad occupation for a Friday night, isn't it? Reading here all by yourself?

BETTY: I guess I was trying to think of it as existentially romantic. You know—cappuccino, great literature, rainy night . . .

BILL: That only works in Paris. We *could* hop the late plane to Paris. Get on a Concorde. Find a café . . .

BETTY: I'm a little short on plane fare tonight.

BILL: Darn it, so am I.

BETTY: To tell you the truth, I was headed to the movies after I finished this section. Would you like to come along? Since you can't locate a waiter?

BILL: That's a very nice offer, but . . .

BETTY: Uh-huh. Girlfriend?

BILL: Two, actually. One of them's pregnant, and Stephanie—

Bell.

BETTY: Girlfriend?

BILL: No, I don't have a girlfriend. Not if you mean the castrating bitch I dumped last night.

Bell.

BETTY: Girlfriend?

BILL: Sort of. Sort of.

BETTY: What's a sort-of girlfriend?

BILL: My mother.

Bell.

I just ended a relationship, actually.

BETTY: Oh.

BILL: Of rather long standing.

BETTY: I'm sorry to hear it.

BILL: This is my first night out alone in a long time. I feel a little bit at sea, to tell you the truth.

BETTY: So you didn't stop to talk because you're a Moonie, or you have some weird political affiliation—?

BILL: Nope. Straight-down-the-ticket Republican.

Bell.

Straight-down-the-ticket Democrat.

Bell.

Can I tell you something about politics?

Bell.

I like to think of myself as a citizen of the universe.

Bell.

I'm unaffiliated.

BETTY: That's a relief. So am I.

BILL: I vote my beliefs.

BETTY: Labels are not important.

BILL: Labels are not important, exactly. Take me, for example. I mean, what does it matter if I had a two-point at—

Bell.

three-point at—

Bell.

four-point at college? Or if I did come from Pittsburgh—

Bell.

Cleveland—

Bell.

Westchester County?

BETTY: Sure.

BILL: I believe that a man is what he is.

Bell.

A person is what he is.

Bell.

A person is . . . what they are.

BETTY: I think so too.

BILL: So what if I admire Trotsky?

Bell.

So what if I once had a total-body liposuction?

Bell.

So what if I don't have a penis?

Bell.

So what if I spent a year in the Peace Corps? I was acting on my convictions.

BETTY: Sure.

BILL: You just can't hang a sign on a person.

BETTY: Absolutely. I'll bet you're a Scorpio.

Many bells ring.

Listen, I was headed to the movies after I finished this section. Would you like to come along?

BILL: That sounds like fun. What's playing?

BETTY: A couple of the really early Woody Allen movies.

BILL: Oh.

BETTY: You don't like Woody Allen?

BILL: Sure. I like Woody Allen.

BETTY: But you're not crazy about Woody Allen.

BILL: Those early ones kind of get on my nerves.
BETTY: Uh-huh.

Bell.

BILL: Y'know I was headed to the—
BETTY [*simultaneously*]: I was thinking about—
BILL: I'm sorry.
BETTY: No, go ahead.
BILL: I was going to say that I was headed to the movies in a little while, and . . .
BETTY: So was I.
BILL: The Woody Allen festival?
BETTY: Just up the street.
BILL: Do you like the early ones?
BETTY: I think anybody who doesn't ought to be run off the planet.
BILL: How many times have you seen *Bananas*?
BETTY: Eight times.
BILL: Twelve. So are you still interested? [*Long pause.*]
BETTY: Do you like Entenmann's crumb cake . . . ?
BILL: Last night I went out at two in the morning to get one. Did you have an Etch-a-Sketch as a child?
BETTY: Yes! And do you like Brussels sprouts? [*Pause.*]
BILL: No, I think they're disgusting.
BETTY: They *are* disgusting!
BILL: Do you still believe in marriage in spite of current sentiments against it?
BETTY: Yes.
BILL: And children?
BETTY: Three of them.
BILL: Two girls and a boy.
BETTY: Harvard, Vassar, and Brown.
BILL: And will you love me?
BETTY: Yes.
BILL: And cherish me forever?
BETTY: Yes.
BILL: Do you still want to go to the movies?
BETTY: Sure thing.
BILL AND BETTY [*together*]: Waiter!

Blackout   —1988

MILCHA SANCHEZ-SCOTT ▪ (b. 1953)

Milcha Sanchez-Scott was born in Bali of Indonesian and Colombian parents. She attended school in England and moved to California in her teens. Following college at the University of San Diego, she had her first plays produced in the early 1980s. The Cuban Swimmer, first performed in 1984, displays elements of the "magic realism" practiced in fiction by Colombian Nobel prize—winner Gabriel García Márquez. Her most successful fulllength play is Roosters (1987), which was made into a 1995 film starring Edward James Olmos.

The Cuban Swimmer

Characters

Margarita Suárez, *the swimmer*
Eduardo Suárez, *her father, the coach*
Simón Suárez, *her brother*
Aída Suárez, *the mother*
Abuela, *her grandmother*
Voice of Mel Munson
Voice of Mary Beth White
Voice of Radio Operator

Scene: *The Pacific Ocean between San Pedro and Catalina Island.*

Time: *Summer.*

Live conga drums can be used to punctuate the action of the play.

Scene I

Pacific Ocean. Midday. On the horizon, in perspective, a small boat enters upstage left, crosses to upstage right, and exits. Pause. Lower on the horizon, the same boat, in larger perspective, enters upstage right, crosses and exits upstage left. Blackout.

Scene II

Pacific Ocean. Midday. The swimmer, Margarita Suárez, is swimming. On the boat following behind her are her father, Eduardo Suárez, holding a megaphone, and Simón, her brother, sitting on top of the cabin with his shirt off, punk sunglasses on, binoculars hanging on his chest.

EDUARDO: [*Leaning forward, shouting in time to Margarita's swimming.*]
Uno, dos, uno, dos. Y uno, dos . . . keep your shoulders parallel to the
water.

SIMÓN: I'm gonna take these glasses off and look straight into the sun.

EDUARDO: [*Through megaphone.*] *Muy bien, muy bien* . . . but punch
those arms in, baby.

SIMÓN: [*Looking directly at the sun through binoculars.*] Come on, come
on, zap me. Show me something. [*He looks behind at the shoreline
and ahead at the sea.*] Stop! Stop, *Papi!* Stop!

*Aída Suárez and Abuela, the swimmer's mother and grand-
mother, enter running from the back of the boat.*

AÍDA AND ABUELA: *Qué? Qué es?*

AÍDA: *Es un* shark?

EDUARDO: Eh?

ABUELA: *Que es un* shark *dicen?*

Eduardo blows whistle. Margarita looks up at the boat.

SIMÓN: No, *Papi,* no shark, no shark. We've reached the halfway mark.

ABUELA: [*Looking into the water.*] *A dónde está?*

AÍDA: It's not in the water.

ABUELA: Oh, no? Oh, no?

AÍDA: No! *A poco* do you think they're gonna have signs in the water to
say you are halfway to Santa Catalina? No. It's done very scientific.
A ver, hijo, explain it to your grandma.

SIMÓN: Well, you see, Abuela—[*He points behind.*] There's San Pedro.
[*He points ahead.*] And there's Santa Catalina. Looks halfway to me.

*Abuela shakes her head and is looking back and forth, trying
to make the decision, when suddenly the sound of a helicopter
is heard.*

ABUELA: [*Looking up.*] Virgencita de la Caridad del Cobre. *Qué es eso?*

Sound of helicopter gets closer. Margarita looks up.

MARGARITA: *Papi, Papi!*

*A small commotion on the boat, with Everybody pointing at the
helicopter above. Shadows of the helicopter fall on the boat.
Simón looks up at it through binoculars.*

Papi—*qué es?* What is it?

EDUARDO: [*Through megaphone.*] Uh . . . uh . . . uh, *un momentico . . . mi hija.* . . . Your *papi*'s got everything under control, understand? Uh . . . you just keep stroking. And stay . . . uh . . . close to the boat.

SIMÓN: Wow, *Papi!* We're on TV, man! Holy Christ, we're all over the fucking U.S.A.! It's Mel Munson and Mary Beth White!

AÍDA: *Por Dios!* Simón, don't swear. And put on your shirt.

Aída fluffs her hair, puts on her sunglasses and waves to the helicopter. Simón leans over the side of the boat and yells to Margarita.

SIMÓN: Yo, Margo! You're on TV, man.

EDUARDO: Leave your sister alone. Turn on the radio.

MARGARITA: *Papi! Qué está pasando?*

ABUELA: *Que es la televisión dicen?* [*She shakes her head.*] *Porque como yo no puedo ver nada sin mis espejuelos.*

Abuela rummages through the boat, looking for her glasses. Voices of Mel Munson and Mary Beth White are heard over the boat's radio.

MEL'S VOICE: As we take a closer look at the gallant crew of *La Havana* . . . and there . . . yes, there she is . . . the little Cuban swimmer from Long Beach, California, nineteen-year-old Margarita Suárez. The unknown swimmer is our Cinderella entry . . . a bundle of tenacity, battling her way through the choppy, murky waters of the cold Pacific to reach the Island of Romance . . . Santa Catalina . . . where should she be the first to arrive, two thousand dollars and a gold cup will be waiting for her.

AÍDA: Doesn't even cover our expenses.

ABUELA: *Qué dice?*

EDUARDO: Shhhh!

MARY BETH'S VOICE: This is really a family effort, Mel, and—

MEL'S VOICE: Indeed it is. Her trainer, her coach, her mentor, is her father, Eduardo Suárez. Not a swimmer himself, it says here, Mr. Suárez is head usher of the Holy Name Society and the owner-operator of Suárez Treasures of the Sea and Salvage Yard. I guess it's one of those places—

MARY BETH'S VOICE: If I might interject a fact here, Mel, assisting in this swim is Mrs. Suárez, who is a former Miss Cuba.

MEL'S VOICE: And a beautiful woman in her own right. Let's try and get a closer look.

Helicopter sound gets louder. Margarita, frightened, looks up again.

MARGARITA: *Papi!*

EDUARDO: [*Through megaphone.*] *Mi hija*, don't get nervous . . . it's the press. I'm handling it.

AÍDA: I see how you're handling it.

EDUARDO: [*Through megaphone.*] Do you hear? Everything is under control. Get back into your rhythm. Keep your elbows high and kick and kick and kick and kick . . .

ABUELA [*Finds her glasses and puts them on.*]: *Ay sí, es la televisión* . . . [*She points to helicopter.*] *Qué lindo mira* . . . [*She fluffs her hair, gives a big wave.*] *Aló América! Viva mi Margarita, viva todo los Cubanos en los Estados Unidos!*

AÍDA: *Ay por Dios*, Cecilia, the man didn't come all this way in his helicopter to look at you jumping up and down, making a fool of yourself.

ABUELA: I don't care. I'm proud.

AÍDA: He can't understand you anyway.

ABUELA: *Viva* . . . [*She stops.*] Simón, *cómo se dice viva?*

SIMÓN: Hurray.

ABUELA: Hurray for *mi* Margarita *y* for all the Cubans living *en* the United States, *y un abrazo* . . . Simón, *abrazo* . . .

SIMÓN: A big hug.

ABUELA: *Sí*, a big hug to all my friends in Miami, Long Beach, Union City, except for my son Carlos, who lives in New York in sin! He lives . . . [*She crosses herself.*] in Brooklyn with a Puerto Rican woman in sin! *No decente* . . .

SIMÓN: Decent.

ABUELA: Carlos, *no decente*. This family, *decente*.

AÍDA: Cecilia, *por Dios*.

MEL'S VOICE: Look at that enthusiasm. The whole family has turned out to cheer little Margarita on to victory! I hope they won't be too disappointed.

MARY BETH'S VOICE: She seems to be making good time, Mel.

MEL'S VOICE: Yes, it takes all kinds to make a race. And it's a testimonial to the all-encompassing fairness . . . the greatness of this, the Wrigley Invitational Women's Swim to Catalina, where among all the professionals there is still room for the amateurs . . . like these, the simple people we see below us on the ragtag *La Havana*, taking their long-shot chance to victory. *Vaya con Dios!*

Helicopter sound fading as family, including Margarita, watch silently. Static as Simón turns radio off. Eduardo walks to bow of boat, looks out on the horizon.

EDUARDO: [*To himself.*] Amateurs.

AÍDA: Eduardo, that person insulted us. Did you hear, Eduardo? That he called us a simple people in a ragtag boat? Did you hear . . . ?

ABUELA [*Clenching her fist at departing helicopter.*]: *Mal-Rayo los parta!*

SIMÓN: [*Same gesture.*] Asshole!

Aída follows Eduardo as he goes to side of boat and stares at Margarita.

AÍDA: This person comes in his helicopter to insult your wife, your family, your daughter . . .

MARGARITA [*Pops her head out of the water.*]: *Papi?*

AÍDA: Do you hear me, Eduardo? I am not simple.

ABUELA: *Sí.*

AÍDA: I am complicated.

ABUELA: *Sí, demasiada complicada.*

AÍDA: Me and my family are not so simple.

SIMÓN: Mom, the guy's an asshole.

ABUELA [*Shaking her fist at helicopter.*]: Asshole!

AÍDA: If my daughter was simple, she would not be in that water swimming.

MARGARITA: Simple? *Papi* . . . ?

AÍDA: *Ahora,* Eduardo, this is what I want you to do. When we get to Santa Catalina, I want you to call the TV station and demand an apology.

EDUARDO: *Cállete mujer! Aquí mando yo.* I will decide what is to be done.

MARGARITA: *Papi,* tell me what's going on.

EDUARDO: Do you understand what I am saying to you, Aída?

SIMÓN [*Leaning over side of boat, to Margarita.*]: Yo Margo! You know that Mel Munson guy on TV? He called you a simple amateur and said you didn't have a chance.

ABUELA [*Leaning directly behind Simón.*]: *Mi hija, insultó a la familia. Desgraciado!*

AÍDA [*Leaning in behind Abuela.*]: He called us peasants! And your father is not doing anything about it. He just knows how to yell at me.

EDUARDO [*Through megaphone.*]: Shut up! All of you! Do you want to break her concentration? Is that what you are after? Eh?

Abuela, Aída, and Simón shrink back. Eduardo paces before them.

Swimming is rhythm and concentration. You win a race *aquí.* [*Pointing to his head.*] Now . . . [*To Simón.*] you, take care of the boat, Aída y *Mama* . . . do something. Anything. Something practical.

Abuela and Aída get on knees and pray in Spanish.

Hija, give it everything, eh? . . . *por la familia. Uno . . . dos.* . . . You must win.

Simón goes into cabin. The prayers continue as lights change to indicate bright sunlight, later in the afternoon.

Scene III

Tableau for a couple of beats. Eduardo on bow with timer in one hand as he counts strokes per minute. Simón is in the cabin steering, wearing his sunglasses, baseball cap on backward. Abuela and Aída are at the side of the boat, heads down, hands folded, still muttering prayers in Spanish.

AÍDA AND ABUELA: [*Crossing themselves.*] *En el nombre del Padre, del Hijo y del Espíritu Santo amén.*

EDUARDO: [*Through megaphone.*] You're stroking seventy-two!

SIMÓN: [*Singing.*] Mama's stroking, Mama's stroking seventy-two. . . .

EDUARDO: [*Through megaphone.*] You comfortable with it?

SIMÓN: [*Singing.*] Seventy-two, seventy-two, seventy-two for you.

AÍDA: [*Looking at the heavens.*] Ay, Eduardo, *ven acá,* we should be grateful that *Nuestro Señor* gave us such a beautiful day.

ABUELA: [*Crosses herself.*] *Sí, gracias a Dios.*

EDUARDO: She's stroking seventy-two, with no problem [*He throws a kiss to the sky.*] It's a beautiful day to win.

AÍDA: *Qué hermoso!* So clear and bright. Not a cloud in the sky. *Mira! Mira!* Even rainbows on the water . . . a sign from God.

SIMÓN: [*Singing.*] Rainbows on the water . . . you in my arms . . .

ABUELA AND EDUARDO: [*Looking the wrong way.*] *Dónde?*

AÍDA: [*Pointing toward Margarita.*] There, dancing in front of margarita, leading her on . . .

EDUARDO: Rainbows on . . . *Ay coño!* It's an oil slick! You . . . you . . . [*To Simón.*] Stop the boat. [*Runs to bow, yelling.*] Margarita! Margarita!

On the next stroke, Margarita comes up all covered in black oil.

MARGARITA: *Papi! Papi . . . !*

Everybody goes to the side and stares at Margarita, who stares back. Eduardo freezes.

AÍDA: *Apúrate,* Eduardo, move . . . what's wrong with you . . . *no me oíste,* get my daughter out of the water.

EDUARDO: [*Softly.*] We can't touch her. If we touch her, she's disqualified.

AÍDA: But I'm her mother.

EDUARDO: Not even by her own mother. Especially by her own mother. . . . You always want the rules to be different for you, you always want to be the exception. [*To Simón.*] And you . . . you didn't see it, eh? You were playing again?

SIMÓN: *Papi,* I was watching . . .

AÍDA: [*Interrupting.*] *Pues,* do something Eduardo. You are the big coach, the monitor.

SIMÓN: Mentor! Mentor!

EDUARDO: How can a person think around you? [*He walks off to bow, puts head in hands.*]

ABUELA: [*Looking over side.*] *Mira como todos los* little birds are dead. [*She crosses herself.*]

AÍDA: Their little wings are glued to their sides.

SIMÓN: Christ, this is like the La Brea tar pits.

AÍDA: They can't move their little wings.

ABUELA: *Esa niña tiene que moverse.*

SIMÓN: Yeah, Margo, you gotta move, man.

Abuela and Simón gesture for Margarita to move. Aída gestures for her to swim.

ABUELA: *Anda niña, muévete.*

AÍDA: Swim, *hija,* swim or the *aceite* will stick to your wings.

MARGARITA: *Papi?*

ABUELA: [*Taking megaphone.*] Your *papi* say "move it!"

Margarita with difficulty starts moving.

ABUELA, AÍDA AND SIMÓN [*Laboriously counting.*]: *Uno, dos . . . uno, dos . . . anda . . . uno, dos.*

EDUARDO: [*Running to take megaphone from Abuela.*] *Uno, dos . . .*

Simón races into cabin and starts the engine. Abuela, Aída and Eduardo count together.

SIMÓN: [*Looking ahead.*] *Papi,* it's over there!

EDUARDO: Eh?

SIMÓN: [*Pointing ahead and to the right.*] It's getting clearer over there.

EDUARDO: [*Through megaphone.*] Now pay attention to me. Go to the right.

Simón, Abuela, Aída and Eduardo all lean over side. They point ahead and to the right, except Abuela, who points to the left.

FAMILY: [*Shouting together.*] *Para yá! Para yá!*

Lights go down on boat. A special light on Margarita, swimming through the oil, and on Abuela, watching her.

ABUELA: *Sangre de mi sangre*, you will be another to save us. En Bolondron, where your great-grandmother Luz Suárez was born, they say one day it rained blood. All the people, they run into their houses. They cry, they pray, *pero* your great-grandmother Luz she had cojones like a man. She run outside. She look straight at the sky. She shake her fist. And she say to the evil one, "Mira . . . [*Beating her chest.*] *coño, Diablo, aquí estoy si me quieres.*" And she open her mouth, and she drunk the blood.

Blackout.

Scene IV

Lights up on boat. Aída and Eduardo are on deck watching Margarita swim. We hear the gentle, rhythmic lap, lap, lap of the water, then the sound of inhaling and exhaling as Margarita's breathing becomes louder. Then Margarita's heartbeat is heard, with the lapping of the water and the breathing under it. These sounds continue beneath the dialogue to the end of the scene.

AÍDA: *Dios mío.* Look how she moves through the water. . . .

EDUARDO: You see, it's very simple. It is a matter of concentration.

AÍDA: The first time I put her in water she came to life, she grew before my eyes. She moved, she smiled, she loved it more than me. She didn't want my breast any longer. She wanted the water.

EDUARDO: And of course, the rhythm. The rhythm takes away the pain and helps the concentration.

Pause. Aída and Eduardo watch Margarita.

AÍDA: Is that my child or a seal. . . .

EDUARDO: Ah, a seal, the reason for that is that she's keeping her arms very close to her body. She cups her hands, and then she reaches and digs, reaches and digs.

AÍDA: To think that a daughter of mine. . . .

EDUARDO: It's the training, the hours in the water. I used to tie weights around her little wrists and ankles.

AÍDA: A spirit, an ocean spirit, must have entered my body when I was carrying her.

EDUARDO: [To Margarita.] Your stroke is slowing down.

Pause. We hear Margarita's heartbeat with the breathing under, faster now.

AÍDA: Eduardo, that night, the night on the boat . . .

EDUARDO: Ah, the night on the boat again . . . the moon was . . .

AÍDA: The moon was full. We were coming to America. . . . *Qué romantico.*

Heartbeat and breathing continue.

EDUARDO: We were cold, afraid, with no money, and on top of every-thing, you were hysterical, yelling at me, tearing at me with your nails. [Opens his shirt, points to the base of his neck.] Look, I still bear the scars . . . telling me that I didn't know what I was doing . . . say-ing that we were going to die. . . .

AÍDA: You took me, you stole me from my home . . . you didn't give me a chance to prepare. You just said we have to go now, now! Now, you said. You didn't let me take anything. I left everything behind. . . . I left everything behind.

EDUARDO: Saying that I wasn't good enough, that your father didn't raise you so that I could drown you in the sea.

AÍDA: You didn't let me say even a good-bye. You took me, you stole me, you tore me from my home.

EDUARDO: I took you so we could be married.

AÍDA: That was in Miami. But that night on the boat, Eduardo. . . . We were not married, that night on the boat.

EDUARDO: *No pasó nada!* Once and for all get it out of your head, it was cold, you hated me, and we were afraid. . . .

AÍDA: *Mentiroso!*

EDUARDO: A man can't do it when he is afraid.

AÍDA: Liar! You did it very well.

EDUARDO: I did?

AÍDA: *Sí.* Gentle. You were so gentle and then strong . . . my passion for you so deep. Standing next to you . . . I would ache . . . looking at your hands I would forget to breathe, you were irresistible.

EDUARDO: I was?

AÍDA: You took me into your arms, you touched my face with your fingertips . . . you kissed my eyes . . . *la esquina de la boca y* . . .

EDUARDO: *Sí, Sí,* and then . . .

AÍDA: I look at your face on top of mine, and I see the lights of Havana in your eyes. That's when you seduced me.

EDUARDO: Shhh, they're gonna hear you.

Lights go down. Special on Aída.

AÍDA: That was the night. A woman doesn't forget those things . . . and later that night was the dream . . . the dream of a big country with fields of fertile land and big, giant things growing. And there by a green, slimy pond I found a giant pea pod and when I opened it, it was full of little, tiny baby frogs.

Aída crosses herself as she watches Margarita. We hear louder breathing and heartbeat.

MARGARITA: Santa Teresa. Little Flower of God, pray for me. San Martín de Porres, pray for me. Santa Rosa de Lima, *Virgencita de la Caridad del Cobre,* pray for me. . . . Mother pray for me.

Scene V

Loud howling of wind is heard, as lights change to indicate unstable weather, fog, and mist. Family on deck, braced and huddled against the wind. Simón is at the helm.

AÍDA: *Ay Dios mío, qué viento.*

EDUARDO: [*Through megaphone.*] Don't drift out . . . that wind is pushing you out. [*To Simón.*] You! Slow down. Can't you see your sister is drifting out?

SIMÓN: It's the wind, *Papi.*

AÍDA: Baby, don't go so far. . . .

ABUELA: [*To heaven.*] *Ay Gran Poder de Dios, quita este maldito viento.*

SIMÓN: Margo! Margo! Stay close to the boat.

EDUARDO: Dig in. Dig in hard . . . .Reach down from your guts and dig in.

ABUELA: [To heaven.] Ay Virgen de la Caridad del Cobre, por lo más tú quieres a pararla.

AÍDA: [Putting her hand out, reaching for Margarita.] Baby, don't go far.

Abuela crosses herself. Action freezes. Lights get dimmer, special on Margarita. She keeps swimming, stops, starts again, stops, then, finally exhausted, stops altogether. The boat stops moving.

EDUARDO: What's going on here? Why are we stopping?

SIMÓN: Papi, she's not moving! Yo Margo!

The family all run to the side.

EDUARDO: Hija! . . . Hijita! You're tired, eh?

AÍDA: Por supuesto she's tired. I like to see you get in the water, waving your arms and legs from San Pedro to Santa Catalina. A person isn't a machine, a person has to rest.

SIMÓN: Yo, Mama! Cool out, it ain't fucking brain surgery.

EDUARDO: [To Simón.] Shut up, you. [Louder to Margarita.] I guess your mother's right for once, huh? . . . I guess you had to stop, eh? . . . Give your brother, the idiot . . . a chance to catch up with you.

SIMÓN: [Clowning like Mortimer Snerd.] Dum dee dum dee dum ooops, ah shucks . . .

EDUARDO: I don't think he's Cuban.

SIMÓN: [Like Ricky Ricardo.] Oye, Lucy! I'm home! Ba ba lu!

EDUARDO: [Joins in clowning, grabbing Simón in a headlock.] What am I gonna do with this idiot, eh? I don't understand this idiot. He's not like us, Margarita. [Laughing.] You think if we put him into your bathing suit with a cap on his head . . . [He laughs hysterically.] You think anyone would know . . . huh? Do you think anyone would know? [Laughs.]

SIMÓN: [Vamping.] Ay, mi amor. Anybody looking for tits would know.

Eduardo slaps Simón across the face, knocking him down. Aída runs to Simón's aid. Abuela holds Eduardo back.

MARGARITA: Mía culpa! Mía culpa!

ABUELA: Qué dices hija?

MARGARITA: Papi, it's my fault, it's all my fault. . . . I'm so cold, I can't move. . . . I put my face in the water . . . and I hear them whispering . . . laughing at me. . . .

AÍDA: Who is laughing at you?

MARGARITA: The fish are all biting me . . . they hate me . . . they whisper about me. She can't swim, they say. She can't glide. She has no grace. . . . Yellowtails, bonita, tuna, man-o'-war, snub-nose sharks, *los baracudas* . . . they all hate me . . . only the dolphins care . . . and sometimes I hear the whales crying . . . she is lost, she is dead. I'm so numb, I can't feel. *Papi! Papi!* Am I dead?

EDUARDO: *Vamos*, baby, punch those arms in. Come on . . . do you hear me?

MARGARITA: *Papi . . . Papi . . .* forgive me. . . .

All is silent on the boat. Eduardo drops his megaphone, his head bent down in dejection. Abuela, Aída, Simón, all leaning over the side of the boat. Simón slowly walks away.

AÍDA: *Mi hija, qué tienes?*

SIMÓN: Oh, Christ, don't make her say it. Please don't make her say it.

ABUELA: Say what? *Qué cosa?*

SIMÓN: She wants to quit, can't you see she's had enough?

ABUELA: *Mira, para eso. Esta niña* is turning blue.

AÍDA: *Oyeme, mi hija.* Do you want to come out of the water?

MARGARITA: *Papi?*

SIMÓN: [*To Eduardo.*] She won't come out until *you* tell her.

AÍDA: Eduardo . . . answer your daughter.

EDUARDO: *Le dije* to concentrate . . . concentrate on your rhythm. Then the rhythm would carry her . . . ay, it's a beautiful thing, Aída. It's like yoga, like meditation, the mind over matter . . . the mind controlling the body . . . that's how the great things in the world have been done. I wish you . . . I wish my wife could understand.

MARGARITA: *Papi?*

SIMÓN: [*To Margarita.*] Forget him.

AÍDA: [*Imploring.*] Eduardo, *por favor.*

EDUARDO: [*Walking in circles.*] Why didn't you let her concentrate? Don't you understand, the concentration, the rhythm is everything. But no, you wouldn't listen. [*Screaming to the ocean.*] Goddamn Cubans, why, God, why do you make us go everywhere with our families? [*He goes to back of boat.*]

AÍDA: [*Opening her arms.*] Mi hija, ven, come to Mami. [*Rocking.*] Your *mami* knows.

Abuela has taken the training bottle, puts it in a net. She and Simón lower it to Margarita.

SIMÓN: Take this. Drink it. [*As Margarita drinks, Abuela crosses herself.*]
ABUELA: *Sangre de mi sangre.*

Music comes up softly. Margarita drinks, gives the bottle back, stretches out her arms, as if on a cross. Floats on her back. She begins a graceful backstroke. Lights fade on boat as special lights come up on Margarita. She stops. Slowly turns over and starts to swim, gradually picking up speed. Suddenly as if in pain she stops, tries again, then stops in pain again. She becomes disoriented and falls to the bottom of the sea. Special on Margarita at the bottom of the sea.

MARGARITA: *Ya no puedo* . . . I can't. . . . A person isn't a machine . . . *es mi culpa* . . . Father forgive me . . . *Papi! Papi!* One, two. *Uno, dos.* [*Pause.*] *Papi! A dónde estás?* [*Pause.*] One, two, one, two. *Papi! Ay, Papi!* Where are you . . . ? Don't leave me. . . . Why don't you answer me? [*Pause. She starts to swim, slowly.*] *Uno, dos, uno, dos.* Dig in, dig in. [*Stops swimming.*] *Por favor, Papi!* [*Starts to swim again.*] One, two, one, two. Kick from your hip, kick from your hip. [*Stops swimming. Starts to cry.*] Oh God, please. . . . [*Pause.*] Hail Mary, full of grace . . . dig in, dig in . . . the Lord is with thee. . . . [*She swims to the rhythm of her Hail Mary.*] Hail Mary, full of grace . . . dig in, dig in . . . the Lord is with thee . . . dig in, dig in. . . . Blessed art thou among women. . . . *Mami,* it hurts. You let go of my hand. I'm lost. . . . And blessed is the fruit of thy womb, now and at the hour of our death. Amen. I don't want to die, I don't want to die.

Margarita is still swimming. Blackout. She is gone.

Scene VI

Lights up on boat, we hear radio static. There is a heavy mist. On deck we see only black outline of Abuela with shawl over her head. We hear the voices of Eduardo, Aída, and Radio Operator.

EDUARDO'S VOICE: *La Havana!* Coming from San Pedro. Over.
RADIO OPERATOR'S VOICE: Right, DT6-6, you say you've lost a swimmer.
AÍDA'S VOICE: Our child, our only daughter . . . listen to me. Her name is Margarita Inez Suárez, she is wearing a black one-piece bathing suit cut high in the legs with a white racing stripe down the sides, a white bathing cap with goggles and her whole body covered with a . . . with a . . .

EDUARDO'S VOICE: With lanolin and paraffin.

AÍDA'S VOICE: *Sí ... con lanolin and paraffin.*

More radio static. Special on Simón, on the edge of the boat.

SIMÓN: Margo! Yo Margo! [*Pause.*] Man don't do this. [*Pause.*] Come on. . . . Come on. . . . [*Pause.*] God, why does everything have to be so hard? [*Pause.*] Stupid. You know you're not supposed to die for this. Stupid. It's his dream and he can't even swim. [*Pause.*] Punch those arms in. Come home. Come home. I'm your little brother. Don't forget what Mama said. You're not supposed to leave me behind. *Vamos,* Margarita, take your little brother, hold his hand tight when you cross the street. He's so little. [*Pause.*] Oh Christ, give us a sign. . . . I know! I know! Margo, I'll send you a message . . . like mental telepathy. I'll hold my breath, close my eyes, and I'll bring you home. [*He takes a deep breath; a few beats.*] This time I'll beep . . . I'll send out sonar signals like a dolphin. [*He imitates dolphin sounds.*]

The sound of real dolphins takes over from Simón, then fades into sound of Abuela saying the Hail Mary in Spanish, as full lights come up slowly.

Scene VII

Eduardo coming out of cabin, sobbing, Aída holding him. Simón anxiously scanning the horizon. Abuela looking calmly ahead.

EDUARDO: *Es mi culpa, sí, es mi culpa.* [*He hits his chest.*]

AÍDA: *Ya, ya viejo.* . . . it was my sin . . . I left my home.

EDUARDO: Forgive me, forgive me. I've lost our daughter, our sister, our granddaughter, *mi carne, mi sangre, mis ilusiones.* [*To heaven.*] *Dios mío,* take me . . . take me, I say . . . Goddammit, take me!

SIMÓN: I'm going in.

AÍDA AND EDUARDO: No!

EDUARDO [*Grabbing and holding Simón, speaking to heaven*]:   God, take me, not my children. They are my dreams, my illusions . . . and not this one, this one is my mystery . . . he has my secret dreams. In him are the parts of me I cannot see.

Eduardo embraces Simón. Radio static becomes louder.

AÍDA: I . . . I think I see her.

SIMÓN: No, it's just a seal.

ABUELA [*Looking out with binoculars.*]: *Mi nietacita, dónde estás?* [*She feels her heart.*] I don't feel the knife in my heart . . . my little fish is not lost.

Radio crackles with static. As lights dim on boat, Voices of Mel and Mary Beth are heard over the radio.

MEL'S VOICE: Tragedy has marred the face of the Wrigley Invitational Women's Race to Catalina. The Cuban swimmer, little Margarita Suárez, has reportedly been lost at sea. Coast Guard and divers are looking for her as we speak. Yet in spite of this tragedy the race must go on because . . .

MARY BETH'S VOICE: [*Interrupting loudly.*] Mel!

MEL'S VOICE: [*Startled.*] What!

MARY BETH'S VOICE: Ah . . . excuse me, Mel . . . we have a winner. We've just received word from Catalina that one of the swimmers is just fifty yards from the breakers . . . it's, oh, it's . . . Margarita Suárez!

Special on family in cabin listening to radio.

MEL'S VOICE: What? I thought she died!

Special on Margarita, taking off bathing cap, trophy in hand, walking on the water.

MARY BETH'S VOICE: Ahh . . . unless . . . unless this is a tragic . . . No . . . there she is, Mel. Margarita Suárez! The only one in the race wearing a black bathing suit cut high in the legs with a racing stripe down the side.

Family cheering, embracing.

SIMÓN: [*Screaming.*]Way to go, Margo!

MEL'S VOICE: This is indeed a miracle! It's a resurrection! Margarita Suárez, with a flotilla of boats to meet her, is now walking on the waters, through the breakers . . . onto the beach, with crowds of people cheering her on. What a jubilation! This is a miracle!

Sound of crowds cheering. Lights and cheering sounds fade.

Blackout.

—1984

YASMINA REZA ▓ (b. 1959)

A native Parisian, Reza combines in her ethnic background Hungarian, Iranian, and Jewish ancestry. She began her career as an actor but turned to writing in the late 1980s. Art *won a Tony Award for best play in 1998.* God of Carnage (Le Dieu du Carnage) *was first performed in Zurich. The London production, starring Ralph Fiennes and Janet McTeer, won the Laurence Olivier Award for best new comedy, and the New York production, starring James Gandolfini and Marcia Gay Harden, ran for over a year on Broadway, winning the 2009 Tony for best play. Reza has also published six novels, including* Dawn Evening or Night (L 'Aube le Soir ou la Nuit), *which drew on her experience following the political campaigns of Nicolas Sarkozy.*

The God of Carnage

Translated by Christopher Hampton

Characters

Véronique Vallon
Michel Vallon
Annette Reille
Alain Reille
All are in their forties

A living room. No realism. Nothing superfluous.

The Vallons and the Reilles, sitting down, facing one another. We need to sense right away that the place belongs to the Vallons and that the two couples have just met.

In the centre, a coffee table, covered with art books. Two big bunches of tulips in vases.

The prevailing mood is serious, friendly and tolerant.

VÉRONIQUE: So, this is our statement—you'll be doing your own, of course . . . 'At 5.30 p.m. on the 3rd November, in Aspirant Dunant Gardens, following a verbal altercation, Ferdinand Reille, eleven, armed with a stick, struck our son, Bruno Vallon, in the face. This action resulted in, apart from a swelling of the upper lip, the breaking of two incisors, including injury to the nerve in the right incisor.'

ALAIN: Armed?

VÉRONIQUE: Armed? You don't like 'armed'—what shall we say, Michel, furnished, equipped, furnished with a stick, is that all right?

ALAIN: Furnished, yes.

MICHEL: 'Furnished with a stick'.

VÉRONIQUE: (*making the correction*) Furnished. The irony is, we've always regarded Aspirant Dunant Gardens as a haven of security, unlike the Montsouris Park.

MICHEL: She's right. We've always said the Montsouris Park no, Aspirant Dunant Gardens yes.

VÉRONIQUE: Absolutely. Anyway, thank you for coming. There's nothing to be gained from getting stuck down some emotional cul-de-sac.

ANNETTE: We should be thanking you. We should.

VÉRONIQUE: I don't see that any thanks are necessary. Fortunately, there is still such a thing as the art of co-existence, is there not?

ALAIN: Which the children don't appear to have mastered. At least, not ours!

ANNETTE: Yes, not ours! . . . What's going to happen to the tooth with the affected nerve? . . .

VÉRONIQUE: We don't know yet. They're being cautious about the prognosis. Apparently the nerve hasn't been totally exposed.

MICHEL: Only a bit of it's been exposed.

VÉRONIQUE: Yes. Some of it's been exposed and some of it's still covered. That's why they've decided not to kill the nerve just yet.

MICHEL: They're trying to give the tooth a chance.

VÉRONIQUE: Obviously it would be best to avoid endodontic surgery.

ANNETTE: Well, yes . . .

VÉRONIQUE: So there'll be an interim period while they give the nerve a chance to recover.

MICHEL: In the meantime, they'll be giving him ceramic crowns.

VÉRONIQUE: Whatever happens, you can't have an implant before you're eighteen.

MICHEL: No.

VÉRONIQUE: Permanent implants can't be fitted until you finish growing.

ANNETTE: Of course. I hope . . . I do hope it all works out.

VÉRONIQUE: Let's hope so.

Slight hiatus.

ANNETTE: Those tulips are gorgeous.

VÉRONIQUE: It's that little florist's in the Mouton-Duvernet Market. You know, the one right up the top.

ANNETTE: Oh, yes.

VÉRONIQUE: They come every morning direct from Holland, ten euros for a bunch of fifty.

ANNETTE: Oh, really!

VÉRONIQUE: You know, the one right up the top.

ANNETTE: Yes, yes.

VÉRONIQUE: You know he didn't want to identify Ferdinand.

MICHEL: No, he didn't.

VÉRONIQUE: Impressive sight, that child, face bashed in, teeth missing, still refusing to talk.

ANNETTE: I can imagine.

MICHEL: He also didn't want to identify him for fear of looking like a sneak in front of his friends; we have to be honest, Véronique, it was nothing more than bravado.

VÉRONIQUE: Of course, but bravado is a kind of courage, isn't it?

ANNETTE: That's right . . . So how . . . ? What I mean is, how did you find out Ferdinand's name? . . .

VÉRONIQUE: Well, we explained to Bruno he wasn't helping this child by shielding him.

MICHEL: We said to him if this child thinks he can go on hitting people with impunity, why should he stop?

VÉRONIQUE: We said to him, if we were this boy's parents, we would definitely want to be told.

ANNETTE: Absolutely.

ALAIN: Yes . . .

His mobile vibrates.

Excuse me . . .

He moves away from the group; as he talks, he pulls a newspaper out of his pocket.

. . . Yes, Maurice, thanks for calling back. Right, in today's *Le Monde*, let me read it to you . . . 'According to a paper published in the *Lancet* and taken up yesterday in the *FT*, two Australian researchers have revealed the neurological side-effects of Antril, a hypertensive beta-blocker, manufactured at the Verenz-Pharma laboratories. These side-effects range from hearing loss to ataxia . . .' So who the hell is your media watchdog? . . . Yes, it's very bloody inconvenient . . . No, what's most inconvenient about it as far as I'm concerned is the AGM's in two weeks. Do you have an insurance contingency to cover litigation? . . . OK . . . Oh, and Maurice, Maurice, ask your DOC to find out if this story shows up anywhere else . . . Call me back.

He hangs up.

. . . Excuse me.

MICHEL: So you're . . .

ALAIN: A lawyer.

ANNETTE: What about you?

MICHEL: Me, I have a wholesale company, household goods, and Véronique's a writer and works part-time in an art-history bookshop.

ANNETTE: A writer?

VÉRONIQUE: I contributed to a collection on the civilisation of Sheba, based on the excavations that were restarted at the end of the Ethiopian–Eritrean war. And I have a book coming out in January on the Darfur tragedy.

ANNETTE: So you specialise in Africa.

VÉRONIQUE: I'm very interested in that part of the world.

ANNETTE: Do you have any other children?

VÉRONIQUE: Bruno has a nine-year-old sister, Camille. Who's furious with her father because last night her father got rid of the hamster.

ANNETTE: You got rid of the hamster?

MICHEL: Yes. That hamster made the most appalling racket all night. Then it spent the whole day fast asleep. Bruno was in a very bad way, he was driven crazy by the noise that hamster made. As for me, to tell you the truth, I've been wanting to get rid of it for ages, so I said to myself, right, that's it. I took it and put it out in the street. I thought they loved drains and gutters and so on, but not a bit of it, it just sat there paralysed on the pavement. Well, they're not domestic animals, they're not wild animals, I don't know where their natural habitat is. Dump them in the woods, they're probably just as unhappy. I don't know where you're meant to put them.

ANNETTE: You left it outside?

VÉRONIQUE: He left it there and tried to convince Camille it had run away. But she wasn't having it.

ALAIN: And had the hamster vanished this morning?

MICHEL: Vanished.

VÉRONIQUE: And you, what field are you in?

ANNETTE I'm in wealth-management.

VÉRONIQUE: Is it at all possible—forgive me for putting the question so bluntly—that Ferdinand might apologise to Bruno?

ALAIN: It'd be good if they talked.

ANNETTE: He has to apologise, Alain. He has to tell him he's sorry.

ALAIN: Yes, yes. Of course.

VÉRONIQUE: But is he sorry?

ALAIN: He realises what he's done. He just doesn't understand the implications. He's eleven.

VÉRONIQUE: If you're eleven, you're not a baby any more.

MICHEL: You're not an adult either! We haven't offered you anything —coffee, tea, is there any of that *clafoutis* left, Ronnie? It's an extraordinary *clafoutis!*

ALAIN: I wouldn't mind an espresso.

ANNETTE: Just some water.

MICHEL: (*to Véronique, on her way out*) Espresso for me too, darling, and bring the *clafoutis* anyway. (*After a hiatus.*) What I always say is, we're a lump of potter's clay and it's up to us to fashion something out of it. Perhaps it won't take shape till the very end. Who knows?

ANNETTE: Mm.

MICHEL: You have to taste the *clafoutis*. Good *clafoutis* is an endangered species.

ANNETTE: You're right.

ALAIN: What is it you sell?

MICHEL: Domestic hardware. Locks, doorknobs, soldering irons, all sorts of household goods, saucepans, frying pans . . .

ALAIN: Money in that, is there?

MICHEL: Well, you know, it's never exactly been a bonanza, it was pretty hard when we started. But provided I'm out there every day pushing my product, it rubs along. At least it's not seasonal, like textiles. Although we do sell a lot of *foie gras* pots in the run-up to Christmas!

ALAIN: I'm sure . . .

ANNETTE: When you saw the hamster sitting there, paralysed, why didn't you bring it back home?

MICHEL: Because I couldn't pick it up.

ANNETTE: You put it on the pavement.

MICHEL: I took it out in its cage and sort of tipped it out. I just can't touch rodents.

Véronique comes back with a tray. Drinks and the clafoutis.

VÉRONIQUE: I don't know who put the *clafoutis* in the fridge. Monica puts everything in the fridge, she won't be told. What's Ferdinand said to you? Sugar?

ALAIN: No, thanks. What's in the *clafoutis?*

VÉRONIQUE: Apples and pears.

ANNETTE: Apples and pears?

VÉRONIQUE: My own little recipe.

She cuts the clafoutis *and distributes slices.*

It's going to be too cold, shame.

ANNETTE: Apples and pears, this is a first.

VÉRONIQUE: Apples and pears, it's pretty textbook, but there's a trick to it.

ANNETTE: There is?

VÉRONIQUE: Pears need to be cut thicker than apples. Because pears cook faster than apples.

ANNETTE: Ah, of course.

MICHEL: But she's not telling you the real secret.

VÉRONIQUE: Let them try it.

ALAIN: Very good. It's very good.

ANNETTE: Tasty.

VÉRONIQUE: . . . Gingerbread crumbs!

ANNETTE: Brilliant!

VÉRONIQUE: It's a version of the way they make *clafoutis* in Picardy. To be quite honest, I got it from his mother.

ALAIN: Gingerbread, delicious . . . Well, at least all this has given us a new recipe.

VÉRONIQUE: I'd have preferred it if it hadn't cost my son two teeth.

ALAIN: Of course, that's what I meant.

ANNETTE: Strange way of expressing it.

ALAIN: Not at all, I . . .

His mobile vibrates, he looks at the screen.

I have to take this . . . Yes, Maurice . . . No, no, don't ask for right of reply, you'll only feed the controversy . . . Are you insured? . . . Mm, mm ... What are these symptoms, what is ataxia? ... What about on a standard dose? ... How long have you known about this? ... And all that time you never recalled it? ... What's the turnover? ... Ah, yes. I see ... Right.

He hangs up and immediately dials another number, scoffing clafoutis *all the while.*

ANNETTE: Alain, do you mind joining us?

ALAIN: Yes, yes, I'm coming ... *(To the mobile.)* Serge? ... They've known about the risks for two years ... An internal report, but it didn't formally identify any undesirable side-effects ... No, they took no precautions, they didn't insure, not a word about it in the annual report ... Impaired motor skills, stability problems, in short you look permanently pissed ... *(He laughs along with his colleague.)* ... Turnover, a hundred and fifty million dollars ... Blanket denial ... Idiot wanted to demand a right of reply. We certainly don't want a right of reply—on the other hand if the story spreads we could put out a press release, say it's disinformation put about two weeks before the AGM. ... He's going to call me back ... OK.

He hangs up.

Actually I hardly had any lunch.

MICHEL: Help yourself, help yourself.

ALAIN: Thanks. I'm incorrigible. What were we saying?

VÉRONIQUE: That it would have been nicer to meet under different circumstances.

ALAIN: Oh, yes, right.
So the *clafoutis*, it's your mother's?

MICHEL: The recipe is my mother's, but Ronnie made this one.

VÉRONIQUE: Your mother doesn't mix pears and apples!

MICHEL: NO.

VÉRONIQUE: Poor thing has to have an operation.

ANNETTE: Really? What for?

VÉRONIQUE: Her knee.

MICHEL: They're going to insert a rotatable prosthesis made of metal and polyethylene. She's wondering what's going to be left of it when she's cremated.

VÉRONIQUE: Don't be horrible.

MICHEL: She refuses to be buried next to my father. She wants to be cremated and put next to her mother who's all on her own down south. Two urns, looking out to sea, trying to get a word in edgeways. Ha, ha! . . .

Smiles all round. Hiatus.

ANNETTE: We're very touched by your generosity. We appreciate the fact you're trying to calm the situation down rather than exacerbate it.

VÉRONIQUE: Frankly, it's the least we can do.

MICHEL: Yes!

ANNETTE: Not at all. How many parents standing up for their children become infantile themselves? If Bruno had broken two of Ferdinand's teeth, I'm afraid Alain and I would have been a good deal more thin-skinned about it. I'm not certain we'd have been so broad-minded.

MICHEL: Course you would!

ALAIN: She's right. By no means certain.

MICHEL: Oh, yes. Because we all know very well it might easily have been the other way round.

Hiatus,

VÉRONIQUE: So what does Ferdinand have to say about it? How does he view the situation?

ANNETTE: He's not saying much. I think he's still slightly in shock.

VÉRONIQUE: He understands that he's disfigured his playmate?

ALAIN: No. No, he does not understand that he's disfigured his playmate.

ANNETTE: Why are you saying that? Ferdinand understands very well!

ALAIN: He understands he's behaved like a thug, he does not understand that he's disfigured his playmate.

VÉRONIQUE: You don't care for the word, but the word is unfortunately accurate.

ALAIN: My son has not disfigured your son.

VÉRONIQUE: Your son has disfigured my son. Come back at five and have a look at his mouth and teeth.

MICHEL: Temporarily disfigured.

ALAIN: The swelling on his lip will go down, and as for his teeth, take him to the best dentist—I'm prepared to chip in . . .

MICHEL: That's what the insurance is for. What we'd like is for the boys to make up so that this sort of thing never happens again.

ANNETTE: Let's arrange a meeting.

MICHEL: Yes. That's the answer.

VÉRONIQUE: Should we be there?

ALAIN: They don't need to be coached. Just let them do it man to man.

ANNETTE: Man to man? Alain, don't be ridiculous. Having said that, we don't necessarily have to be there. It'd probably be better if we weren't, wouldn't it?

VÉRONIQUE: The question isn't whether we should be there or not. The question is, do they want to talk to one another, do they want to have a reckoning?

MICHEL: Bruno wants to.

VÉRONIQUE: What about Ferdinand?

ANNETTE: It's no use asking his opinion.

VÉRONIQUE: But it has to come from him.

ANNETTE: Ferdinand has behaved like a hooligan, we're not interested in what mood he's in.

VÉRONIQUE: If Ferdinand is forced to meet Bruno in a punitive context, I can't see the results would be very positive.

ALAIN: Madame, our son is a savage. To hope for any kind of spontaneous repentance would be fanciful. Right, I'm sorry, I have to get back to the office. You stay, Annette, you'll tell me what you've decided, I'm no use whichever way you cut it. Women always think you need a man, you need a father, as if .they'd be the slightest use. Men are a dead weight, they're clumsy and maladjusted—oh, you can see a stretch of the overground metro, that's great!

ANNETTE: I'm really embarrassed, but I can't stay either . . . My husband has never exactly been a pushchair father!

VÉRONIQUE: What a pity. It's lovely, taking the baby for a walk. And it lasts such a short time. You always enjoyed taking care of the children, didn't you, Michel? You loved pushing the pushchair.

MICHEL: Yes, I did.

VÉRONIQUE: So what have we decided?

ANNETTE: Could you come by the house with Bruno about seven-thirty?

VÉRONIQUE: Seven-thirty? . . . What do you think, Michel?

MICHEL: Well . . . If I may . . .

ANNETTE: Go on.

MICHEL: I rather think Ferdinand ought to come here.

VÉRONIQUE: Yes, I agree.

MICHEL: I don't think it's for the victim to go traipsing around.

VÉRONIQUE: That's right.

ALAIN: Personally, I can't be anywhere at seven-thirty.

ANNETTE: Since you're no use, we won't be needing you.

VÉRONIQUE: All the same, it would be better if his father were here.

Alain's mobile vibrates.

ALAIN: All right, but then it can't be this evening. Hello? . . . There's no mention of this in the executive report. And no risk has been formally established. There's no evidence . . .

He hangs up.

VÉRONIQUE: Tomorrow?

ALAIN: I'm in The Hague tomorrow.

VÉRONIQUE: You're working in The Hague?

ALAIN: I have a case at the International Criminal Court.

ANNETTE: The main thing is that the children speak to one another. I'll bring Ferdinand here at seven-thirty and we can leave them to have their reckoning. No? You don't look very convinced.

VÉRONIQUE: If Ferdinand is not made aware of his responsibilities, they'll just look at each other like a pair of china dogs, it'll be a catastrophe.

ALAIN: What do you mean, madame? What do you mean, 'made aware of his responsibilities'?

VÉRONIQUE: I'm sure your son is not a savage.

ANNETTE: Of course Ferdinand isn't a savage.

ALAIN: Yes, he is.

ANNETTE: Alain, this is absurd, why say something like that?

ALAIN: He's a savage.

MICHEL: How does he explain his behaviour?

ANNETTE: He doesn't want to discuss it.

VÉRONIQUE: But he ought to discuss it.

ALAIN: He ought to do any number of things, madame. He ought to come here, he ought to discuss it, he ought to be sorry for it, clearly you have parenting skills that put us to shame, we hope to improve, but in the meantime, please bear with us.

MICHEL: Now, now! This is idiotic. Don't let's end up like this!

VÉRONIQUE: I'm only thinking of him, I'm only thinking of Ferdinand.

ALAIN: I got the message.

ANNETTE: Let's just sit down for another couple of minutes.

MICHEL: Another drop of coffee?

ALAIN: A coffee, OK.

ANNETTE: Then I'll have one too. Thanks.

MICHEL: That's all right, Ronnie, I'll do it.

Hiatus. Annette delicately shuffles some of the numerous art books dispersed around the coffee table.

ANNETTE: I see you're a great art-lover.

VÉRONIQUE: Art. Photographs. To some extent it's my job.

ANNETTE: I adore Bacon.

VÉRONIQUE: Ah, yes, Bacon.

ANNETTE: *(turning the pages)* . . . Cruelty. Majesty.

VÉRONIQUE: Chaos. Balance.

ANNETTE: That's right. . .

VÉRONIQUE: Is Ferdinand interested in art?

ANNETTE: Not as much as he should be . . . What about your children?

VÉRONIQUE: We try. We try to fill the gaps in the educational system.

ANNETTE: Yes . . .

VÉRONIQUE: We try to make them read. To take them to concerts and exhibitions. We're eccentric enough to believe in the pacifying abilities of culture!

ANNETTE: And you're right. . .

Michel comes back with the coffee.

MICHEL: *Clafoutis,* is it a cake or a tart? Serious question. I was just thinking in the kitchen—*Linzertorte,* for example, is that a tart? Come on, come on, you can't leave that one little slice.

VÉRONIQUE: *Clafoutis* is a cake. The pastry's not rolled out, it's mixed in with the fruit.

ALAIN: You really are a cook.

VÉRONIQUE: I love it. The thing about cooking is you have to love it. In my view, it's only the classic tart, that's to say on a pastry base, that deserves to be called a tart.

MICHEL: What about you, do you have other children?

ALAIN: A son from my first marriage.

MICHEL: I was wondering, not that it's at all important, what started the quarrel. Bruno won't say a blind word about it.

ANNETTE: Bruno refused to let Ferdinand join his gang.

VÉRONIQUE: Bruno has a gang?

ALAIN: He also called Ferdinand a grass.

VÉRONIQUE: Did you know Bruno had a gang?

MICHEL: No. Fantastic!

VÉRONIQUE: Why is it fantastic?

MICHEL: Because I had my own gang.

ALAIN: Me too.

VÉRONIQUE: And what does that entail?

MICHEL: There are five or six kids devoted to you and ready to sacrifice themselves. Like in *Spartacus*.

ALAIN: Absolutely, like in *Spartacus!*

VÉRONIQUE: Who knows about Spartacus these days?

ALAIN: They use a different model. Spiderman.

VÉRONIQUE: Anyway, clearly you know more than we do. Ferdinand hasn't been as silent as you led us to believe. And do we know why Bruno called him a grass? No, sorry, stupid, that's a stupid question. First of all, I couldn't care less, also it's beside the point.

ANNETTE: We can't get involved in children's quarrels.

VÉRONIQUE: And it's none of our business.

ANNETTE: No.

VÉRONIQUE: On the other hand, what is our business is what unfortunately happened. Violence is always our business.

MICHEL: When I was leader of my gang, when I was twelve, I fought Didier Leglu, who was bigger than me, in single combat.

VÉRONIQUE: What are you talking about, Michel? What's that got to do with it?

MICHEL: No, you're right, it's got nothing to do with it.

VÉRONIQUE: We're not discussing single combat. The children weren't fighting.

MICHEL: I know, I know. I just suddenly had this memory.

ALAIN: There's not that big a difference.

VÉRONIQUE: Oh, yes, there is. Excuse me, monsieur, there's a very big difference.

MICHEL: There's a very big difference.

ALAIN: What?

MICHEL: With Didier Leglu, we'd agreed to have a fight.

ALAIN: Did you beat the shit out of him?

MICHEL: Up to a point.

VÉRONIQUE: Right, shall we forget Didier Leglu? Would you allow me to speak to Ferdinand?

ANNETTE: By all means!

VÉRONIQUE: I wouldn't want to do it without your permission.

ANNETTE: Speak to him. What could be more natural?

ALAIN: Good luck.

ANNETTE: Stop it, Alain. I don't understand you.

ALAIN: Madame thinks . . .

VÉRONIQUE: Véronique. This will work out better if we stop calling each other 'madame' and 'monsieur'.

ALAIN: Véronique, you're motivated by an educational impulse, which is very sympathetic . . .

VÉRONIQUE: If you don't want me to speak to him, I won't speak to him.

ALAIN: No, speak to him, read him the riot act, do what you like.

VÉRONIQUE: I don't understand why you don't seem to care about this.

ALAIN: Madame . . .

MICHEL: Véronique.

ALAIN: Of course I care, Véronique, enormously. My son has injured another child . . .

VÉRONIQUE: On purpose.

ALAIN: See, that's the kind of remark that puts my back up. Obviously, on purpose.

VÉRONIQUE: But that makes *all the difference.*

ALAIN: The difference between what and what? That's what we're talking about. Our son picked up a stick and hit your son. That's why we're here, isn't it?

ANNETTE: This is pointless.

MICHEL: Yes, she's right, this kind of argument is pointless.

ALAIN: Why do you feel the need to slip in 'on purpose'? What kind of message is that supposed to be sending me?

ANNETTE: Listen, we're on a slippery slope, my husband is desperate about all sorts of other things. I'll come back this evening with Ferdinand and we'll let things sort themselves out naturally.

ALAIN: I'm not in the least desperate.

ANNETTE: Well, I am.

MICHEL: There's nothing to be desperate about.

ANNETTE: Yes, there is.

Alain's mobile vibrates.

ALAIN: Don't make any statement. . . No comment. . . No, of course you mustn't take it off the market! If you take it off the market, you become responsible . . . The minute you take Antril off the market, you're admitting liability! There's nothing in the annual accounts. If you want to be sued for falsifying the executive report and given the elbow in two weeks' time, take it off the market. . .

VÉRONIQUE: Last year, on Open Day, wasn't it Ferdinand who played Monsieur de . . .?

ANNETTE: Monsieur de Pourceaugnac.

VÉRONIQUE: Monsieur de Pourceaugnac.

ALAIN: We'll think about the victims later, Maurice . . . Let's see what the shares do after the AGM . . .

VÉRONIQUE: He was extraordinary.

ANNETTE: Yes . . .

ALAIN: We are not going to take the medicine off the market just because two or three people are bumping into the furniture! . . . Don't make any statements for the time being . . . Yes. I'll call you back . . .

He cuts him off and phones his colleague.

VÉRONIQUE: I remember him very clearly in *Monsieur de Pourceaugnac.* Do you remember him, Michel?

MICHEL: Yes, yes . . .

VÉRONIQUE: He was hilarious when he was in drag.

ANNETTE: Yes . . .

ALAIN: *(to his colleague)* . . . They're panicking, they've got the media up their arse, you have to prepare a press release, not something defensive, not at all, on the contrary, go out all guns blazing, you insist that Verenz-Pharma is the victim of a destabilisation attempt two weeks before its Annual General Meeting, where does this paper come from, why should it have fallen out of the sky just now, etcetera and so on . . . Don't say anything about health problems, just ask one question: who's behind this report? . . . Right.

He hangs up. Brief hiatus.

MICHEL: They're terrible, these pharmaceutical companies. Profit, profit, profit.

ALAIN: You're not supposed to be listening to my conversation,

MICHEL: You're not obliged to have it in front of me.

ALAIN: Yes, I am. I'm absolutely obliged to have it here. Not my choice, I can assure you.

MICHEL: They dump any old crap on you without giving it a second thought.

ALAIN: In the therapeutic field, every advance brings with it risk as well as benefit.

MICHEL: Yes, I understand that. All the same. Funny job you've got.

ALAIN: Meaning?

VÉRONIQUE: Michel, this is nothing to do with us.

MICHEL: Funny job.

ALAIN: And what is it you do?

MICHEL: I have an ordinary job.

ALAIN: What is an ordinary job?

MICHEL: I told you, I sell saucepans.

ALAIN: And doorknobs.

MICHEL: And toilet fittings. Loads of other things.

ALAIN: Ah, toilet fittings. Now we're talking. That's really interesting.

ANNETTE: Alain.

ALAIN: It's really interesting. I'm interested in toilet fittings.

MICHEL: Why shouldn't you be?

ALAIN: How many types are there?

MICHEL: Two different systems. Push-button or overhead flush.

ALAIN: I see.

MICHEL: Depending on the feed.

ALAIN: Well, yes.

MICHEL: Either the water comes down from above or up from under.

ALAIN: Yes.

MICHEL: I could introduce you to one of my warehousemen who specialises in this kind of thing, if you like. You'd have to leg it out to Saint-Denis la Plaine.

ALAIN: You seem to be very much on top of the subject.

VÉRONIQUE: Are you intending to punish Ferdinand in any way? You can carry on with the plumbing in some more appropriate setting.

ANNETTE: I'm not feeling well.

VÉRONIQUE: What's the matter?

ALAIN: Yes, you're very pale, sweetheart.

MICHEL: Palish, certainly.

ANNETTE: I feel sick.

VÉRONIQUE: Sick? . . . I have some Moxalon . . .

ANNETTE: No, no . . . It'll be all right. . .

VÉRONIQUE: What could we . . . ? Coke. Coke's very good.

She immediately sets off in search of it.

ANNETTE: It'll be all right. . .

MICHEL: Walk around a bit. Take a few steps.

She takes a few steps. Véronique comes back with the Coca-Cola.

ANNETTE: Really? You think so? . . .

VÉRONIQUE: Yes, yes. Small sips.

ANNETTE: Thank you . . .

Alain has discreetly called his office.

ALAIN: . . . Give me Serge, will you, please? . . . Oh, right. . . Ask him to call me back, ask him to call me back right away . . .

He hangs up.

It's good, is it, Coca-Cola? I thought it was just supposed to be for diarrhoea.

VÉRONIQUE: Not only for that. (*To Annette.*) All right?

ANNETTE: All right . . . Véronique, if we want to reprimand our child, we'll do it in our own way and without having to account to anybody.

MICHEL: Absolutely.

VÉRONIQUE: What do you mean, 'absolutely', Michel?

MICHEL: They can do whatever they like with their son, it's their prerogative.

VÉRONIQUE: I don't think so.

MICHEL: What do you mean, you don't think so, Ronnie?

VÉRONIQUE: I don't think it is their prerogative.

ALAIN: Really? Explain.

His mobile vibrates.

I'm sorry . . . (*To his colleague.*) Excellent. . . But don't forget, nothing's been proved, there's nothing definite . . . Get this straight, if anyone fucks up, Maurice is a dead man in two weeks, and us with him.

ANNETTE: That's enough, Alain! That's enough now with the mobile! Will you pay attention to what's going on here, shit!

ALAIN: Yes . . . Call me back and read it to me.

He hangs up.

What's the matter with you, have you gone mad, shouting like that? Serge heard everything.

ANNETTE: Good! Drives me mad, that mobile, endlessly!

ALAIN: Listen, Annette, I'm already doing you a big favour being here in the first place . . .

VÉRONIQUE: Extraordinary thing to say.

ANNETTE: I'm going to throw up.

ALAIN: No, you're not, you are not going to throw up.

ANNETTE: Yes, I am . . .

MICHEL: Do you want to go to the lavatory?

ANNETTE: *(to Alain)* No one's forcing you to stay.

VÉRONIQUE: No, no one's forcing him to stay.

ANNETTE: I'm feeling dizzy . . .

ALAIN: Stare at a fixed point. Stare at a fixed point, Woof-woof.

ANNETTE: Go away, leave me alone.

VÉRONIQUE: She would be better off in the lavatory.

ALAIN: Go to the lavatory. Go to the lavatory if you want to throw up.

MICHEL: Give her some Moxalon.

ALAIN: You don't suppose it could be the *clafoutis*?

VÉRONIQUE: It was made yesterday!

ANNETTE: *(to Alain)* Don't touch me! . . .

ALAIN: Calm down, Woof-woof.

MICHEL: Please, why get worked up about nothing?

ANNETTE: According to my husband, everything to do with house, school or garden is my department.

ALAIN: No, it's not!

ANNETTE: Yes, it is. And I understand why. It's deathly, all that. It's deathly.

VÉRONIQUE: If it's so deathly, why have children in the first place?

MICHEL: Maybe Ferdinand senses your lack of interest.

ANNETTE: What lack of interest?

MICHEL: You just said . . .

Annette vomits violently. A brutal and catastrophic spray, part of which goes over Alain. The art books on the coffee table are likewise deluged.

Go and fetch a bowl, go and fetch a bowl!

Véronique runs out to look for a bowl and Michel hands her the coffee tray, just in case. Annette retches again, but nothing comes out.

ALAIN: You should have gone to the lavatory, Woof-woof, this is ridiculous!

MICHEL: Your suit's definitely copped it!

Very soon, Véronique is back with a basin and a cloth. The basin is given to Annette.

VÉRONIQUE: Well, it's certainly not the *clafoutis*, it couldn't possibly be.

MICHEL: It's not the *clafoutis*, it's nerves. This is pure nerves.

VÉRONIQUE: *(to Alain)* Would you like to clean up in the bathroom? Oh, no, the Kokoschka! Oh, my God!

Annette vomits bile into the basin.

MICHEL: Give her some Moxalon.

VÉRONIQUE: Not now, she can't keep anything down.

ALAIN: Where's the bathroom?

VÉRONIQUE: I'll show you.

Véronique and Alain leave.

MICHEL: It's nerves. It's a panic attack. You're a mum, Annette. Whether you want to be or not. I understand why you feel desperate.

ANNETTE: Mmm.

MICHEL: What I always say is, you can't control the things that control you.

ANNETTE: Mmm . . .

MICHEL: With me, it's the cervical vertebrae. The vertebrae seize up.

ANNETTE: Mmm . . .

She brings up a little more bile. Véronique returns with another basin, containing a sponge.

VÉRONIQUE: What are we going to do about the Kokoschka?

MICHEL: Well, I would spray it with Mr Clean . . . The problem is how to dry it. . . Or else you could sponge it down and put a bit of perfume on it.

VÉRONIQUE: Perfume?

MICHEL: Use my Kouros, I never wear it.

VÉRONIQUE: It'll warp.

MICHEL: We could run the hair-dryer over it and flatten it out under a pile of other books. Or iron it like they do with banknotes.

VÉRONIQUE: Oh, my God . . .

ANNETTE: I'll buy you another one.

VÉRONIQUE: You can't find it! It went out of print years ago!

ANNETTE: I'm terribly sorry . . .

MICHEL: We'll salvage it. Let me do it, Ronnie.

She hands him the basin of water and the sponge, disgusted. Michel gets started on cleaning up the book.

VÉRONIQUE: It's a reprint of the catalogue from the '53 London exhibition, more than twenty years old! . . .

MICHEL: Go and get the hair-dryer. And the Kouros. In the towel cupboard.

VÉRONIQUE: Her husband's in the bathroom.

MICHEL: Well, he's not stark naked, is he?

She goes out as he continues to clean up.

. . . There, that's the worst of it. *The People of the Tundra* needs a bit of a wipe . . . I'll be back.

He goes out with the used basin. Véronique and Michel return more or less simultaneously. She has the bottle of perfume, he has the basin containing fresh water. Michel finishes cleaning up.

VÉRONIQUE: *(to Annette)* Feeling better?

ANNETTE: Yes . . .

VÉRONIQUE: Shall I spray?

MICHEL: Where's the hair-dryer?

VÉRONIQUE: He's bringing it when he's finished with it.

MICHEL: We'll wait for him. We'll put the Kouros on last thing.

ANNETTE: Can I use the bathroom as well?

VÉRONIQUE: Yes. Yes, yes. Of course.

ANNETTE: I can't tell you how sorry I am . . .

Véronique takes her out and returns immediately.

VÉRONIQUE: What a nightmare! Horrible!

MICHEL: Tell you what, he'd better not push me much further.

VÉRONIQUE: She's dreadful as well.

MICHEL: Not as bad.

VÉRONIQUE: She's a phoney.

MICHEL: Less irritating.

VÉRONIQUE: They're both dreadful! Why do you keep siding with them?

She sprays the tulips.

MICHEL: I don't keep siding with them, what are you talking about?

VÉRONIQUE: You keep vacillating, trying to play both ends against the middle.

MICHEL: Not at all!

VÉRONIQUE: Yes, you do. Going on about your triumphs as a gang leader, telling them they're free to do whatever they like with their son when the child is a public menace—when a child's a public menace, it's everybody's concern, I can't believe she puked all over my books!

She sprays the Kokoschka.

MICHEL: *(pointing)* Put some on *The People of the Tundra.*

VÉRONIQUE: If you think you're about to spew, you go to the proper place.

MICHEL: . . . And the Foujita.

VÉRONIQUE: *(spraying everything)* This is disgusting.

MICHEL: I was pushing it a bit with the shithouse systems.

VÉRONIQUE: You were brilliant.

MICHEL: Good answers, don't you think?

VÉRONIQUE: Brilliant. The warehouseman was brilliant.

MICHEL: What an arsehole. And what did he call her?! . . .

VÉRONIQUE: Woof-woof.

MICHEL: That's right, 'Woof-woof'!

VÉRONIQUE: Woof-woof!

They both laugh. Alain returns, hair-dryer in hand.

ALAIN: That's right, I call her Woof-woof.

VÉRONIQUE: Oh . . . I'm sorry, I didn't mean to be rude . . . It's so easy to make fun of other people's nicknames! What about us, what do we call each other, Michel? Far worse, isn't it?

ALAIN: Were you wanting the hair-dryer?

VÉRONIQUE: Thank you.

MICHEL: Thank you.

He takes the hair-dryer.

We call each other 'darjeeling', like the tea. Far more ridiculous, if you ask me!

Michel switches on the machine and starts drying the books.
Véronique flattens out the damp pages.

Smooth them out, smooth them out.

VÉRONIQUE: (*as she smooths out the pages, raising her voice above the noise*) How's the poor thing feeling, better?

ALAIN: Better.

VÉRONIQUE: I reacted very badly, I'm ashamed of myself.

ALAIN: Not at all.

VÉRONIQUE: I just steamrollered her about my catalogue, I can't believe I did that.

MICHEL: Turn the page. Stretch it out, stretch it out properly.

ALAIN: You're going to tear it.

VÉRONIQUE: You're right. . . That's enough, Michel, it's dry. Objects can become ridiculously important, half the time you can't even remember why.

Michel shuts the catalogue and they both cover it with a little cairn of heavy books. Michel finishes drying the Foujita, The People of the Tundra, etc. . . .

MICHEL: There we are! Good as new. Where does 'Woof-woof' come from?

ALAIN: 'How much is that doggie in the window?'

MICHEL: I know it! (*He sings.*) 'The one with the waggly tail.'

ALAIN: 'Woof-woof.'

MICHEL: Ha, ha! . . . Ours comes from our honeymoon in India. Idiotic, really!

VÉRONIQUE: Shouldn't I go and see how she is?

MICHEL: Off you go, darjeeling.

VÉRONIQUE: Shall I? . . .

Annette returns.

. . . Ah, Annette! I was worried about you . . . Are you feeling better?

ANNETTE: I think so.

ALAIN: If you're not sure, stay away from the coffee table.

ANNETTE: I left the towel in the bathtub, I wasn't sure where to put it.

VÉRONIQUE: Perfect.

ANNETTE: You've cleaned it all up. I'm so sorry.

MICHEL: Everything's great. Everything's in order.

VÉRONIQUE: Annette, forgive me, I've taken hardly any notice of you. I've been obsessed with my Kokoschka.

ANNETTE: Don't worry about it.

VÉRONIQUE: The way I reacted, very bad of me.

ANNETTE: Not at all . . . *(After an embarrassed hiatus.)* Something occurred to me in the bathroom . . .

VÉRONIQUE: Yes?

ANNETTE: Perhaps we skated too hastily over . . .

I mean, what I mean is . . .

MICHEL: Say it, Annette, say it,

ANNETTE: An insult is also a kind of assault.

MICHEL: Of course it is.

VÉRONIQUE: Well, that depends, Michel.

MICHEL: Yes, it depends.

ANNETTE: Ferdinand's never shown any signs of violence. He wouldn't have done that without a reason.

ALAIN: He got called a grass!

His mobile vibrates.

I'm sorry! . . .

He moves to one side, making elaborately apologetic signs to Annette.

. . . Yes . . . As long as there aren't any statements from victims. We don't want any victims. I don't want you being quoted alongside victims! . . . A blanket denial and if necessary attack the newspaper . . . They'll fax you a draft of the press release, Maurice.

He hangs up.

If anyone calls me a grass, I'm liable to get annoyed.

MICHEL: Unless it's true.

ALAIN: What did you say?

MICHEL: I mean, suppose it's justified?

ANNETTE: My son is a grass?

MICHEL: Course not, I was joking.

ANNETTE: Yours is as well, if that's to be the way of it.

MICHEL: What do you mean, ours is as well?

ANNETTE: Well, he did identify Ferdinand.

MICHEL: Because we insisted!

VÉRONIQUE: Michel, this is completely beside the point.

ANNETTE: What's the difference? Whether you insisted or not, he gave you the name.

ALAIN: Annette.

ANNETTE: Annette what? (*To Michel.*) You think my son is a grass?

MICHEL: I don't think anything.

ANNETTE: Well, if you don't think anything, don't say anything. Stop making these insinuations.

VÉRONIQUE: Let's stay calm, Annette. Michel and I are making an effort to be reasonable and moderate . . .

ANNETTE: Not that moderate.

VÉRONIQUE: Oh, really? What do you mean?

ANNETTE: Moderate on the surface.

ALAIN: I really have to go, Woof-woof . . .

ANNETTE: All right, go on, be a coward.

ALAIN: Annette, right now I'm risking my most important client, so this responsible parent routine . . .

VÉRONIQUE: My son has lost two teeth. Two incisors.

ALAIN: Yes, yes, I think we all got that.

VÉRONIQUE: One of them for good.

ALAIN: He'll have new ones, we'll give him new ones! Better ones! It's not as if he's burst an eardrum!

ANNETTE: We're making a mistake not to take into account the origin of the problem.

VÉRONIQUE: There's no origin. There's just an eleven-year-old child hitting someone. With a stick.

ALAIN: Armed with a stick.

MICHEL: We withdrew that word.

ALAIN: You withdrew it because we objected to it.

MICHEL: We withdrew it without any protest.

ALAIN: A word deliberately designed to rule out error or clumsiness, to rule out childhood.

VÉRONIQUE: I'm not sure I'm able to take much more of this tone of voice.

ALAIN: You and I have had trouble seeing eye to eye right from the start.

VÉRONIQUE: There's nothing more detestable than to be attacked for something you yourself consider a mistake. The word 'armed' was inappropriate, so we changed it. Although, if you stick to the strict definition of the word, its use is far from inaccurate.

ANNETTE: Ferdinand was insulted and he reacted. If I'm attacked, I defend myself, especially if I find myself alone, confronted by a gang.

MICHEL: Puking seems to have perked you up.

ANNETTE: Are you aware how crude that sounds?

MICHEL: We're people of good will. All four of us, I'm sure. Why let these irritants, these pointless aggravations push us over the edge? . . .

VÉRONIQUE: Oh, Michel, that's enough! Let's stop beating about the bush. If all we are is moderate on the surface, let's forget it, shall we!

MICHEL: No, no, I refuse to allow myself to slide down that slope.

ALAIN: What slope?

MICHEL: The deplorable slope those two little bastards have perched us on! There, I've said it!

ALAIN: I'm not sure Ronnie has quite the same outlook.

VÉRONIQUE: Véronique!

ALAIN: Sorry.

VÉRONIQUE: So Bruno's a little bastard' now, is he, poor child. That's the last straw!

ALAIN: Right, well, I really do have to leave you.

ANNETTE: Me too.

VÉRONIQUE: Go on, go, I give up.

The Vallon telephone rings.

MICHEL: Hello? . . . Oh, Mum . . . No, no, we're with some friends, but tell me about it . . . Yes, do whatever the doctor wants you to do . . . They've given you Antril?! Wait a minute, Mum, wait a minute, don't go away . . . (*To Alain.*) Antril's your crap, isn't it? My mother's taking it!

ALAIN: Thousands of people take it.

MICHEL: You stop taking that stuff right now. Do you hear what I'm saying, Mum? Immediately . . . Don't argue, I'll explain later . . . Tell Dr Perolo I'm forbidding you to take it. . . Why luminous? . . . So that you can be seen? . . . That's completely ridiculous . . . All right, we'll talk about it later. Lots of love, Mum. I'll call you back.

He hangs up.

She's hired luminous crutches, so she doesn't get knocked down by a truck. As if someone in her condition would be strolling down the motorway in the middle of the night. They've given her Antril for her blood pressure.

ALAIN: If she takes it and stays normal, I'll have her called as a witness. Didn't I have a scarf? Ah, there it is.

MICHEL: I do not appreciate your cynicism. If my mother displays the most minor symptom, I'll be initiating a class action.

ALAIN: Oh, that'll happen anyway.

MICHEL: So I should hope.

ANNETTE: Goodbye, madame . . .

VÉRONIQUE: Behaving well gets you nowhere. Courtesy is a waste of time, it weakens you and undermines you . . .

ALAIN: Right, come on, Annette, let's go, enough preaching and sermons for today.

MICHEL: Go on, go. But can I just say one thing: having met you two, it's pretty clear that for what's-his-name, Ferdinand, there are mitigating circumstances.

ANNETTE: When you murdered that hamster . . .

MICHEL: Murdered?!

ANNETTE: Yes.

MICHEL: I murdered the hamster?!

ANNETTE: Yes. You've done your best to make us feel guilty, but your virtue went straight out the window once you decided to be a killer.

MICHEL: I absolutely did not murder that hamster!

ANNETTE: Worse. You left it, shivering with terror, in a hostile environment. That poor hamster is bound to have been eaten by a dog or a rat.

VÉRONIQUE: It's true! That is true!

MICHEL: What do you mean, 'that is true'?

VÉRONIQUE: It's true. What do you expect me to say? It's appalling what must have happened to that creature.

MICHEL: I thought the hamster would be happy to be liberated. I thought it was going to run off down the gutter jumping for joy!

VÉRONIQUE: Well, it didn't.

ANNETTE: And you abandoned it.

MICHEL: I can't touch those things! For fuck's sake, Ronnie, you know very well, I'm incapable of touching that whole species!

VÉRONIQUE: He has a phobia about rodents.

MICHEL: That's right, I'm frightened of rodents, I'm terrified of snakes, anything close to the ground, I have absolutely no rapport with! So that's the end of it!

ALAIN: *(to Véronique)* And you, why didn't you go out and look for it?

VÉRONIQUE: Because I had no idea what had happened! Michel didn't tell us, me and the children, that the hamster had escaped till the following morning. I went out immediately, immediately, I walked round the block, I even went down to the cellar.

MICHEL: Véronique, I find it intolerable to be in the dock all of a sudden for this hamster saga that you've seen fit to reveal. It's a personal matter which is nobody else's business but ours and which has nothing to do with the present situation! And I find it incomprehensible to be called a killer! In my own home!

VÉRONIQUE: What's your home got to do with it?

MICHEL: My home, the doors of which I have opened' the doors of which I have opened wide in a spirit of reconciliation, to people who ought to be grateful to me for it!

ALAIN: It's wonderful the way you keep patting yourself on the back.

ANNETTE: Don't you feel any guilt?

MICHEL: I feel no guilt whatsoever. I've always found that creature repulsive. I'm ecstatic that it's gone.

VÉRONIQUE: Michel, that is ridiculous.

MICHEL: What's ridiculous? Have you gone crazy as well? Their son bashes up Bruno, and I get shat on because of a hamster?

VÉRONIQUE: You behaved very badly with that hamster, you can't deny it.

MICHEL: Fuck the hamster!

VÉRONIQUE: You won't be able to say that to your daughter this evening.

MICHEL: Bring her on! I'm not going to let myself be told how to behave by some nine-year-old bruiser.

ALAIN: Hundred per cent behind you there.

VÉRONIQUE: Pathetic.

MICHEL: Careful, Véronique, you be careful, I've been extremely restrained up to now, but I'm two inches away from crossing that line.

ANNETTE: And what about Bruno?

MICHEL: What about Bruno?

ANNETTE: Isn't he upset?

MICHEL: If you ask me, Bruno has other problems.

VÉRONIQUE: Bruno was less attached to Nibbles.

MICHEL: Grotesque name as well!

ANNETTE: If you feel no guilt, why do you expect our son to feel any?

MICHEL: Let me tell you this, I'm up to here with these idiotic discussions. We tried to be nice, we bought tulips, my wife passed me off as a lefty, but the truth is, I can't keep this up any more, I'm fundamentally uncouth.

ALAIN: Aren't we all?

VÉRONIQUE: No. No. I'm sorry, we are not all fundamentally uncouth.

ALAIN: Well, not you, obviously.

VÉRONIQUE: No, not me, thank the Lord.

MICHEL: Not you, darjee, not you, you're a fully evolved woman, you're skid-resistant.

VÉRONIQUE: Why are you attacking me?

MICHEL: I'm not attacking you. Quite the opposite.

VÉRONIQUE: Yes, you're attacking me, you know you are.

MICHEL: You organised this little get-together, I just let myself be recruited . . .

VÉRONIQUE: You let yourself be recruited?

MICHEL: Yes.

VÉRONIQUE: That's detestable.

MICHEL: Not at all. You stand up for civilisation, that's completely to your credit.

VÉRONIQUE: Exactly, I'm standing up for civilisation! And it's lucky there are people prepared to do that! (*She's on the brink of tears.*) You think being fundamentally uncouth's a better idea?

ALAIN: Come on now, come on . . .

VÉRONIQUE: (*as above*) Is it normal to criticise someone for not being fundamentally uncouth? . . .

ANNETTE: No one's saying that. No one's criticising you.

VÉRONIQUE: Yes, they are! . . .

She bursts into tears.

ALAIN: No, they're not!

VÉRONIQUE: What were we supposed to do? Sue you? Not speak to one another and try to slaughter each other with insurance claims?

MICHEL: Stop it, Ronnie . . .

VÉRONIQUE: Stop what?! . . .

MICHEL: You've got things out of proportion . . .

VÉRONIQUE: I don't give a shit! You force yourself to rise above petty-mindedness . . . and you finish up humiliated and completely on your own . . .

Alain's mobile has vibrated.

ALAIN: . . . Yes . . . 'Let them prove it!' . . . 'Prove it'. . . but if you ask me, best not to answer at all . . .

MICHEL: We're always on our own! Everywhere! Who'd like a drop of rum?

ALAIN: . . . Maurice, I'm in a meeting, I'll call you back from the office . . .

He cuts the line.

VÉRONIQUE: So there we are! I'm living with someone who's totally negative.

ALAIN: Who's negative?

MICHEL: I am.

VÉRONIQUE: This was the worst idea! We should never have arranged this meeting!

MICHEL: I told you.

VÉRONIQUE: You told me?

MICHEL: Yes.

VÉRONIQUE: You told me you didn't want to have this meeting?!

MICHEL: I didn't think it was a good idea.

ANNETTE: It was a good idea . . .

MICHEL: Oh, please! . . .

He raises the bottle of rum.

Anybody?

VÉRONIQUE: You told me it wasn't a good idea, Michel?!

MICHEL: Think so.

VÉRONIQUE: You think so!

ALAIN: Wouldn't mind a little drop.

ANNETTE: Didn't you have to go?

ALAIN: I could manage a small glass, now we've got this far.

Michel pours a glass for Alain.

VÉRONIQUE: You look me in the eye and tell me we weren't in complete agreement about this!

ANNETTE: Calm down, Véronique, calm down, this is pointless . . .

VÉRONIQUE: Who stopped anyone touching the *clafoutis* this morning? Who said, 'Let's keep the rest of the *clafoutis* for the Reilles'?! Who said it?!

ALAIN: That was nice.

MICHEL: What's that got to do with it?

VÉRONIQUE: What do you mean, 'what's that got to do with it'?

MICHEL: If you invite people, you invite people.

VÉRONIQUE: You're a liar, you're a liar! He's a liar!

ALAIN: You know, speaking personally, my wife had to drag me here. When you're brought up with a kind of John Wayne-ish idea of virility, you don't want to settle this kind of problem with a lot of yakking.

Michel laughs.

ANNETTE: I thought your model was Spartacus.

ALAIN: Same family.

MICHEL: Analogous.

VÉRONIQUE: Analogous! Are there no lengths you won't go to to humiliate yourself, Michel?

ANNETTE: Obviously it was pointless dragging you here.

ALAIN: What were you hoping for, Woof-woof? It's true, it's a ludicrous nickname—were you hoping for a glimpse of universal harmony? This rum is terrific.

MICHEL: It is, isn't it? *Coeur de Chauffe*, fifteen years old, direct from Santa Rosa.

VÉRONIQUE: And the tulips, whose idea was that? I said it's a shame the tulips are finished, I didn't say rush down to Mouton-Duvernet at the crack of dawn.

ANNETTE: Don't work yourself up into this state, Véronique, it's crazy.

VÉRONIQUE: The tulips were his idea! Entirely his idea! Aren't we allowed a drink?

ANNETTE: Yes, Véronique, and I would like one too. By the way, it's quite amusing, someone descended from Spartacus and John Wayne who can't even pick up a mouse.

MICHEL: Will you *shut up* about that hamster! Shut up! . . .

He gives Annette a glass of rum.

VÉRONIQUE: Ha, ha! You're right, it's laughable!

ANNETTE: What about her?

MICHEL: I don't think she needs any.

VÉRONIQUE: Give me a drink, Michel.

MICHEL: No.

VÉRONIQUE: Michel!

MICHEL: No.

Véronique tries to snatch the bottle out of his hands. Michel resists.

ANNETTE: What's the matter with you, Michel?!

MICHEL: All right, there you are, take it. Drink, drink, who cares?

ANNETTE: Is alcohol bad for you?

VÉRONIQUE: It's wonderful.

She slumps.

ALAIN: Right . . . Well, I don't know . . .

VÉRONIQUE: *(to Alain)* . . . Listen, monsieur . . .

ANNETTE: Alain.

VÉRONIQUE: Alain, we're not exactly soul-mates, you and me, but, you see, I live with a man who's decided, once and for all, that life is second rate, It's very difficult living with a man who comforts himself with that thought, who doesn't want anything to change, who can't work up any enthusiasm about anything . . .

MICHEL: He doesn't give a fuck. He doesn't give a fuck about any of that.

VÉRONIQUE: You have to believe . . . you have to believe in the possibility of improvement, don't you?

MICHEL: He's the last person you should be telling all this.

VÉRONIQUE: I'll talk to who I like, for fuck's sake!

The telephone rings.

MICHEL: Who the fuck's this now? . . . Yes, Mum . . . He's fine. I say he's fine, he's lost his teeth, but he's fine . . . Yes, he's in pain. He's in pain, but it'll pass. Mum, I'm busy, I'll call you back.

ANNETTE: He's still in pain?

VÉRONIQUE: No.

ANNETTE: Then why worry your mother?

VÉRONIQUE: He can't help himself. He always has to worry her.

MICHEL: Right, that's enough, Véronique! What is this psychodrama?

ALAIN: Véronique, are we ever interested in anything but ourselves?
Of course we'd all like to believe in the possibility of improvement.
Of which we could be the architect and which would be in no way
self-serving. Does such a thing exist? Some people drag their feet,
it's their strategy, others refuse to acknowledge the passing of
time, and drive themselves demented—what difference does it
make? People struggle until they're dead. Education, the miseries
of the world . . . You're writing a book about Darfur, fine, I can understand you saying to yourself, right, I'm going to choose a mas-
sacre, what else does history consist of, and I'm going to write
about it. You do what you can to save yourself.

VÉRONIQUE: I'm not writing the book to save myself. You haven't
read it, you don't know what it's about.

ALAIN: It makes no difference.

Hiatus.

VÉRONIQUE: Terrible stink of Kouros! . . .

MICHEL: Ghastly.

ALAIN: You certainly laid it on.

ANNETTE: I'm sorry.

VÉRONIQUE: Not your fault. I was the one spraying like a lunatic . . .
Anyway, why can't we take things more lightly, why does everything always have to be so exhausting? . . .

ALAIN: You think too much. Women think too much.

ANNETTE: There's an original remark, I bet that's thrown you for a
loop.

VÉRONIQUE: 'Think too much', I don't know what that means. And I
don't see the point of existence without some kind of moral conception of the world.

MICHEL: See what I have to live with?

VÉRONIQUE: Shut up! Will you shut up?! I detest this pathetic com-
plicity! You disgust me.

MICHEL: Come on, have a sense of humour.

VÉRONIQUE: I don't have a sense of humour. And I have no inten-
tion of acquiring one.

MICHEL: What I always say is, marriage: the most terrible ordeal God
can inflict on you.

ANNETTE: Great.

MICHEL: Marriage and children.

ANNETTE: There's no call for you to share your views with us, Michel. As a matter of fact, I find it slightly indecent.

VÉRONIQUE: That's not going to worry him.

MICHEL: You mean you don't agree?

ANNETTE: These observations are irrelevant. Alain, say something.

ALAIN: He's entitled to his opinions.

ANNETTE: Yes, but he doesn't have to broadcast them.

ALAIN: Well, yes, perhaps . . .

ANNETTE: We don't give a damn about their marriage. We're here to settle a problem to do with our children, we don't give a damn about their marriage.

ALAIN: Yes, but. . .

ANNETTE: But what? What do you mean?

ALAIN: There's a connection.

MICHEL: There's a connection! Of course there's a connection.

VÉRONIQUE: There's a connection between Bruno having his teeth broken and our marriage?!

MICHEL: Obviously.

ANNETTE: We're not with you.

MICHEL: Children consume and fracture our lives. Children drag us towards disaster, it's unavoidable. When you see those laughing couples casting off into the sea of matrimony, you say to yourself, they have no idea, poor things, they just have no idea, they're happy. No one tells you anything when you start out. I have an old school pal who's just about to have a child with his new girlfriend. I said to him, 'A child, at our age, are you insane?' The ten or a dozen good years left to us before we get cancer or a stroke, and you're going to bugger yourself up with some brat?

ANNETTE: You don't really believe what you're saying.

VÉRONIQUE: He does.

MICHEL: Of course I believe it. Worse, even.

VÉRONIQUE: Yes.

ANNETTE: You're demeaning yourself, Michel.

MICHEL: Is that right? Ha, ha!

ANNETTE: Stop crying, Véronique, you can see it only encourages him.

MICHEL: (to Alain, who's refilling his empty glass) Help yourself, help yourself—exceptional, isn't it?

ALAIN: Exceptional.

MICHEL: Could I offer you a cigar? . . .

VÉRONIQUE: No, no cigars!

ALAIN: Pity.

ANNETTE: You're not proposing to smoke a cigar, Alain!

ALAIN: I shall do what I like, Annette, if I feel like accepting a cigar, I shall accept a cigar. If I'm not smoking, it's because I don't want to upset Véronique, who's already completely lost it. She's right, stop snivelling, when a woman cries, a man is immediately provoked to the worst excesses. Added to which, Michel's point of view is, I'm sorry to say, entirely sound.

His mobile vibrates.

. . . Yes, Serge . . . Go ahead . . . Put Paris, the date . . . and the exact time . . .

ANNETTE: This is hideous!

ALAIN: *(moving aside and muffling his voice to escape her fury)* . . . Whatever time you send it. It has to look piping hot straight out of the oven . . . No, not 'We're surprised'. 'We condemn'. 'Surprised' is feeble . . .

ANNETTE: This goes on from morning to night, from morning to night he's glued to that mobile! That mobile makes mincemeat of our lives!

ALAIN: Er . . . Just a minute . . .

He covers the mobile.

Annette, this is very important! . . .

ANNETTE: It's always very important. Anything happening somewhere else is always more important.

ALAIN: *(resuming)* Go ahead . . . Yes . . . Not 'procedure', 'manoeuvre'. 'A manoeuvre, timed for two weeks before the annual accounts,' etc. . . .

ANNETTE: In the street, at dinner, he doesn't care where . . .

ALAIN: A 'paper' in inverted commas! Put the word 'paper' in inverted commas . . .

ANNETTE: I'm not saying another word. Total surrender. I want to be sick again.

MICHEL: Where's the basin?

VÉRONIQUE: I don't know.

ALAIN: . . . You just have to quote me: 'This is simply a disgraceful attempt to manipulate share prices . . .'

VÉRONIQUE: Here it is. Go on, off you go.

MICHEL: Ronnie . . .

VÉRONIQUE: Everything's all right. We're fully equipped.

ALAIN: '. . . share prices and to undermine my client,' confirms Maître
Reille, counsel for the Verenz-Pharma company'. . . AP, Reuters,
general press, specialised press, Uncle Tom Cobley and all. . .

He hangs up.

VÉRONIQUE: She wants to throw up again.

ALAIN: What's the matter with you?

ANNETTE: I'm touched by your concern.

ALAIN: It's upsetting me!

ANNETTE: I am sorry. I must have misunderstood.

ALAIN: Oh, Annette, please! Don't let us start now! Just because
they're quarrelling, just because their marriage is fucked, doesn't
mean we have to compete!

VÉRONIQUE: What right do you have to say our marriage is fucked?
Who gave you permission?

Alain's mobile vibrates.

ALAIN: . . . They just read it to me. We're sending it to you, Maurice
. . . 'Manipulation', 'manipulate share prices.' It's on its way.

He hangs up.

. . . Wasn't me who said it, it was François.

VÉRONIQUE: Michel.

ALAIN: Michel, sorry.

VÉRONIQUE: I forbid you to stand in any kind of judgement over our
relationship.

ALAIN: Then don't stand in judgement over my son.

VÉRONIQUE: That's got nothing to do with it! Your son injured ours!

ALAIN: They're young, they're kids, kids have always given each other
a good drubbing during break. It's a law of life.

VÉRONIQUE: No, no, it isn't!

ALAIN: Course it is. You have to go through a kind of apprenticeship
before violence gives way to what's right. Originally, let me remind
you, might was right.

VÉRONIQUE: Possibly in prehistoric times. Not in our society.

ALAIN: Our society? Explain 'society'.

VÉRONIQUE: You're exhausting me, these conversations are exhausting.

ALAIN: You see, Véronique, I believe in the god of carnage. He has ruled, uninterruptedly, since the dawn of time. You're interested in Africa, aren't you? . . . (*To Annette, who retches.*) . . . Feeling bad?

ANNETTE: Don't worry about me.

ALAIN: I am worried.

ANNETTE: Everything's fine.

ALAIN: As a matter of fact, I just came back from the Congo. Over there, little boys are taught to kill when they're eight years old. During their childhood, they may kill hundreds of people, with a machete, with a 12.7, with a Kalashnikov, with a grenade launcher, so you'll understand that when my son picks up a bamboo rod, hits his playmate and breaks a tooth, or even two, in Aspirant Dunant Gardens, I'm likely to be less disposed than you to horror and indignation.

VÉRONIQUE: You're wrong.

ANNETTE: (*mocking*) 12.7! . . .

ALAIN: Yes, that's what they're called.

Annette spits in the basin.

MICHEL: Are you all right?

ANNETTE: . . . Perfectly.

ALAIN: What's the matter with you? What's the matter with her?

ANNETTE: It's just bile! It's nothing!

VÉRONIQUE: Don't lecture me about Africa. I know all about Africa's martyrdom, I've been steeped in it for months . . .

ALAIN: I don't doubt it. Anyway, the Prosecutor of the International Criminal Court has opened an inquiry on Darfur . . .

VÉRONIQUE: You think I don't know about that?

MICHEL: Don't get her started on that! For God's sake!

Véronique throws herself at her husband and hits him several times, with an uncontrolled and irrational desperation. Alain pulls her off him.

ALAIN: You know what, I'm starting to like you!

VÉRONIQUE: Well, I don't like you!

MICHEL: She's a supporter of peace and stability in the world.

VÉRONIQUE: Shut up!

Annette retches. She picks up her glass of rum and lifts it to her mouth.

MICHEL: Are you sure about that?

ANNETTE: Yes, yes, it'll do me good.

Véronique follows suit.

VÉRONIQUE: We're living in France. We're not living in Kinshasa! We're living in France according to the principles of Western society. What goes on in Aspirant Dunant Gardens reflects the values of Western society! Of which, if it's all the same to you, I am happy to be a member.

MICHEL: Beating up your husband is one of those principles, is it?

VÉRONIQUE: Michel, this is going to end badly.

ALAIN: She threw herself on you in such a frenzy. If I were you, I'd be rather touched.

VÉRONIQUE: I'll do it again in a minute.

ANNETTE: He's making fun of you, you do realise?

VÉRONIQUE: I don't give a shit.

ALAIN: I'm not making fun, on the contrary. Morality decrees we should control our impulses, but sometimes it's good not to control them. You don't want to be singing 'Ave Maria' when you're fucking. Where can you find this rum?

MICHEL: That vintage, I doubt you can.

ANNETTE: 12.7! Ha, ha! . . .

VÉRONIQUE: *(same tone)* 12.7, you're right!

ALAIN: That's right. 12.7.

ANNETTE: Why can't you just say gun?

ALAIN: Because 12.7 is correct. You don't just say gun.

ANNETTE: Who's this 'you'?

ALAIN: That's enough, Annette. That's enough.

ANNETTE: The great warriors, like my husband, you have to give them some leeway, they have trouble working up an interest in local events.

ALAIN: It's true.

VÉRONIQUE: I don't see why. I don't see why. We're citizens of the world. I don't see why we should give up the struggle just because it's on our doorstep.

MICHEL: Oh, Ronnie! Do stop shoving these thoughts for the day down our throat.

VÉRONIQUE: I'm going to kill him.

Alain's mobile has vibrated.

ALAIN: . . . Yes, all right, take out 'regrettable'. . . 'Crude'. 'A crude attempt to . . .' That's it. . .

VÉRONIQUE: She's right, this is becoming unbearable!

ALAIN: . . . Otherwise he approves the rest? . . . Fine, fine. Very good.

He hangs up.

What were we saying? . . . 12.7 millimetre? . . .

VÉRONIQUE: I was saying, whether my husband likes it or not, that no one place is more important than another when it comes to exercising vigilance.

ALAIN: Vigilance . . . well . . . Annette, it's ridiculous to drink, the state you're in.

ANNETTE: What state? On the contrary.

ALAIN: Vigilance, it's an interesting idea . . .

His mobile. It's Serge.

. . . Yes, no, no interviews before the circulation of the press release.

VÉRONIQUE: That's it. I insist you break off this horrendous conversation!

ALAIN: . . . Absolutely not. . . The shareholders won't give a fuck . . . Remind him, the shareholder is king . . .

Annette launches herself at Alain, snatches the mobile and after a brief look-round to see where she can put it, shoves it into the vase of tulips.

Annette, what the . . .!

ANNETTE: So there.

VÉRONIQUE: Ha, ha! Well done!

MICHEL: *(horrified)* Oh, my God!

ALAIN: Are you completely insane? Fuck!!

He rushes towards the vase, but Michel, who has got in ahead of him, fishes out the dripping object.

MICHEL: The hair-dryer! Where's the hair-dryer?

He finds it and turns it on at once, directing it towards the mobile.

ALAIN: You need locking up, poor love! This is incomprehensible! . . . I had everything in there! . . . It's brand new, it took me hours to set up!

MICHEL: *(to Annette, above the infernal din of the hair-dryer)* Really, I don't understand you. That was completely irresponsible.

ALAIN: Everything's on there, my whole life . . .

ANNETTE: His whole life!. . .

MICHEL: *(still fighting the noise)* Hang on, we might be able to fix it . . .

ALAIN: No chance! It's fucked! . . .

MICHEL: We'll take out the battery and the SIM-card. Can you open it?

Alain tries to open it with no conviction.

ALAIN: I haven't a clue, I've only just got it.

MICHEL: Let's have a look.

ALAIN: It's fucked . . . And they think it's funny, they think it's funny! . . .

MICHEL: *(opening it easily)* There we are.

He goes back on the offensive with the hair-dryer, having laid out the various parts.

You, Véronique, you at least could have the manners not to laugh at this!

VÉRONIQUE: *(laughing heartily)* My husband will have spent his entire afternoon blow-drying!

ANNETTE: Ha, ha, ha!

Annette makes no bones about helping herself to more rum. Michel, immune to finding any of this amusing, keeps busy, concentrating intently.

For a moment, there's only the sound of the hair-dryer. Alain has slumped.

ALAIN: Leave it, mate. Leave it. There's nothing to be done . . .

Michel finally switches off the hair-dryer.

MICHEL: We'll have to wait a minute . . . *(Hiatus.)* You want to use our phone?

Alain gestures that he doesn't and that he couldn't care less.

I have to say . . .

ANNETTE: Yes, what is it you have to say, Michel?

MICHEL: No . . . I really can't think what to say.

ANNETTE: Well, if you ask me, everyone's feeling fine. If you ask me, everyone's feeling better. *(Hiatus.)* . . . Everyone's much calmer, don't you think? . . . Men are so wedded to their gadgets . . . It belittles them . . . It takes away all their authority . . . A man needs to keep his hands free . . . If you ask me. Even an attaché case is enough to put me off. There was a man, once, I found really attractive, then I saw him with a square shoulder-bag, a man's shoulder-bag, but that was it. There's nothing worse than a shoulder-bag. Although there's also nothing worse than a mobile phone. A man ought to give the impression that he's alone . . . If you ask me. I mean, that he's capable of being alone . . . ! I also have a John Wayne-ish idea of virility. And what was it he had? A Colt .45. A device for creating a vacuum . . . A man who can't give the impression that he's a loner has no texture . . . So, Michel, are you happy? It is somewhat fractured, our little . . . What was it you said? . . . I've forgotten the word . . . but in the end . . . everyone's feeling more or less all right . . . If you ask me.

MICHEL: I should probably warn you, rum drives you crazy.

ANNETTE: I've never felt more normal.

MICHEL: Right.

ANNETTE: I'm starting to feel rather pleasantly serene.

VÉRONIQUE: Ha, ha! That's wonderful! . . . 'Rather pleasantly serene'.

MICHEL: As for you, darjeeling, I fail to see what's to be gained by getting publicly pissed.

VÉRONIQUE: Get stuffed.

Michel goes to fetch the cigar box.

MICHEL: Choose one, Alain. Relax.

VÉRONIQUE: Cigars are not smoked in this house!

MICHEL: Those are Hoyo, those are Monte Cristo Number 3 and Number 4.

VÉRONIQUE: You don't smoke in a house with an asthmatic child!

ANNETTE: Who's asthmatic?

VÉRONIQUE: Our son.

MICHEL: Didn't stop you buying a fucking hamster.

ANNETTE: It's true, if somebody has asthma, keeping animals isn't recommended.

MICHEL: Totally unrecommended!

ANNETTE: Even a goldfish can prove counter-productive.

VÉRONIQUE: Do I have to listen to this fatuous nonsense?

She snatches the cigar box out of Michel's hands and slams it shut brutally.

I'm sorry, no doubt I'm the only one of us not feeling rather pleasantly serene. In fact, I've never been so unhappy. I think this is the unhappiest day of my life.

MICHEL: Drinking always makes you unhappy.

VÉRONIQUE: Michel, every word that comes out of your mouth is destroying me, I don't drink. I drank a mouthful of this shitty rum you're waving about as if you were showing the congregation the Turin Shroud. I don't drink and I bitterly regret it, it'd be a relief to be able to take refuge in a little drop at every minor setback.

ANNETTE: My husband's unhappy as well. Look at him. Slumped. He looks as if someone's left him by the side of the road. I think it's the unhappiest day of his life too.

ALAIN: Yes.

ANNETTE: I'm so sorry, Woof-woof.

Michel starts up the hair-dryer again, directing it at the various parts of the mobile.

VÉRONIQUE: Will you turn off the hair-dryer?! The thing is buggered.

The telephone rings.

MICHEL: Yes! . . . Mum, I told you we were busy . . . Because it could kill you! That medication is poison! Someone's going to explain it to you . . .

He hands the receiver to Alain.

Tell her.

ALAIN: Tell her what? . . .

MICHEL: Everything you know about that crap you're peddling.

ALAIN: . . . How are you, madame? . . .

ANNETTE: What can he tell her? He doesn't know the first thing about it!

ALAIN: Yes . . . And does it hurt? . . . Of course. Well, the operation will fix that . . And the other leg, I see. No, no I'm not an orthopaedist. . . (*Aside.*) She keeps calling me 'doctor'. . .

ANNETTE: Doctor, this is grotesque—hang up!

ALAIN: But you . . . I mean to say, you're not having any problems with your balance? . . . Oh, no. Not at all. Not at all. Don't listen to any of that. All the same, it'd probably be just as well to stop taking it for the moment. Until . . . until you've had a chance to get quietly through your operation . . . Yes, you sound as if you're on very good form . . .

Michel snatches the receiver from him.

MICHEL: All right, Mum, is that clear, stop taking the medication, why do you always have to argue, stop taking it, do what you're told, I'll call you back . . . Lots of love, love from us all.

He hangs up.

She's killing me. One pain in the arse after another!

ANNETTE: Right then, what have we decided? Shall I come back this evening with Ferdinand? No one seems to give a toss any more. All the same, I should point out, that's what we're here for.

VÉRONIQUE: Now I'm starting to feel sick. Where's the bowl?

Michel takes the bottle of rum out of Annette's reach.

MICHEL: That'll do.

ANNETTE: To my mind, there are wrongs on both sides. That's it. Wrongs on both sides.

VÉRONIQUE: Are you serious?

ANNETTE: What?

VÉRONIQUE: Are you aware of what you're saying?

ANNETTE: I am. Yes.

VÉRONIQUE: Our son Bruno, to whom I was obliged to give two Extra Strength Nurofen last night, is in the wrong?

ANNETTE: He's not necessarily innocent.

VÉRONIQUE: Fuck off! I've had quite enough of you.

She grabs Annette's handbag and hurls it towards the door.

Fuck off!

ANNETTE: My handbag! . . . (*Like a little girl.*) Alain! . . .

MICHEL: What's going on? They've slipped their trolley.

ANNETTE: (*gathering up her scattered possessions*) Alain, help! . . .

VÉRONIQUE: 'Alain, help!'

ANNETTE: Shut up! . . . She's broken my compact! And my atomiser! (To *Alain.*) Defend me, why aren't you defending me? . . .

ALAIN: We're going.

He prepares to gather up the parts of his mobile.

VÉRONIQUE: It's not as if I'm strangling her!

ANNETTE: What have I done to you?

VÉRONIQUE: There are not wrongs on both sides! Don't mix up the victims and the executioners!

ANNETTE: Executioners!

MICHEL: You're so full of shit, Véronique, all this simplistic claptrap, we're up to here with it!

VÉRONIQUE: I stand by everything I've said.

MICHEL: Yes, yes, you stand by what you've said, you stand by what you've said, your infatuation for a bunch of Sudanese coons is bleeding into everything now.

VÉRONIQUE: I'm appalled. Why are you choosing to show yourself in this horrible light?

MICHEL: Because I feel like it. I feel like showing myself in a horrible light.

VÉRONIQUE: One day you may understand the extreme gravity of what's going on in that part of the world and you'll be ashamed of this inertia and your repulsive nihilism.

MICHEL: You're just wonderful, darjeeling, you're the best of us all!

VÉRONIQUE: I am. Yes.

ANNETTE: Let's get out of here, Alain, these people are monsters!

She drains her glass and goes to pick up the bottle.

ALAIN: (*preventing her*) . . . Stop it, Annette.

ANNETTE: No, I want to drink some more, I want to get pissed out of my head, this bitch hurls my handbag across the room and no one bats an eyelid, I want to get drunk!

ALAIN: You already are.

ANNETTE: Why are you letting them call my son an executioner? You come to their house to settle things and you get insulted and bullied and lectured on how to be a good citizen of the planet—our son did well clout yours, and I wipe my arse with your charter of human rights!

MICHEL: A mouthful of grog and, bam, the real face appears.

VÉRONIQUE: I told you! Didn't I tell you?

ALAIN: What did you tell him?

VÉRONIQUE: That she was a phoney. This woman is a phoney. I'm sorry.

ANNETTE: *(upset)* Ha, ha, ha! . . .

ALAIN: When did you tell him?

VÉRONIQUE: When you were in the bathroom.

ALAIN: You'd known her for fifteen minutes but you could tell she was a phoney.

VÉRONIQUE: It's the kind of thing I pick up on right away.

MICHEL: It's true.

VÉRONIQUE: I have an instinct for that kind of thing.

ALAIN: And 'phoney', what does that mean?

ANNETTE: I don't want to hear any more! Why are you putting me through this, Alain?

ALAIN: Calm down, Woof-woof.

VÉRONIQUE: She's someone who tries to round off corners. Full stop. She's all front. She doesn't care any more than you do.

MICHEL: It's true.

ALAIN: It's true.

VÉRONIQUE: 'It's true'! Are you saying it's true?

MICHEL: They don't give a fuck! They haven't given a fuck since the start, it's obvious! Her too, you're right!

ALAIN: And you do, I suppose? *(To Annette.)* Let me say something, love. *(To Michel.)* Explain to me in what way you care, Michel. What does the word mean in the first place? You're far more authentic when you're showing yourself in a horrible light. To tell the truth, no one in this room cares, except for Véronique, whose integrity, it has to be said, must be acknowledged.

VÉRONIQUE: Don't acknowledge me! Don't acknowledge me!

ANNETTE: I care. I absolutely care.

ALAIN: We only care about our own feelings, Annette, we're not social crusaders, *(To Véronique.)* I saw your friend Jane Fonda on TV the other day, I was inches away from buying a Ku Klux Klan poster . . .

VÉRONIQUE: What do you mean, 'my friend'? What's Jane Fonda got to do with all this? . . .

ALAIN: You're the same breed. You're part of the same category of woman—committed, problem-solving. That's not what we like about women, what we like about women is sensuality, wildness, hormones. Women who make a song and dance about their intuition, women who are custodians of the world depress us—even him, poor Michel, your husband, he's depressed . . .

MICHEL: Don't speak for me!

VÉRONIQUE: Who gives a flying fuck what you like about women? Where does this lecture come from? A man like you, who could begin to give a fuck for your opinion?

ALAIN: She's yelling. She's a regimental sergeant major.

VÉRONIQUE: What about her, doesn't she yell?! When she said that little bastard had done well to clout our son?

ANNETTE: Yes, he did do well! At least he's not a snivelling little poof!

VÉRONIQUE: Yours is a grass, is that any better?

ANNETTE: Alain, let's go! What are we doing, staying in this dump?

She makes to leave, then returns towards the tulips which she lashes out at violently. Flowers fly, disintegrate and scatter all over the place.

There, there, that's what I think of your pathetic flowers, your hideous tulips! . . . Ha, ha, ha! *(She bursts into tears.)* . . . It's the worst day of my life as well.

Silence.

> *A long stunned pause.*
> *Michel picks something up off the floor.*

MICHEL: *(to Annette)* This yours?

Annette takes a spectacle case, opens it and takes out a pair of glasses.

ANNETTE: Thanks . . .

MICHEL: Not broken? . . .

ANNETTE: No . . .

Hiatus.

MICHEL: What I always say is . . .

Alain starts gathering up the stems and petals.

Leave it.

ALAIN: No . . .

The telephone rings. After some hesitation, Véronique picks up the receiver.

VÉRONIQUE: Yes, darling . . . Oh, good . . . Will you be able to do your homework at Annabelle's? . . . No, no, darling, we haven't found her . . . Yes, I went all the way to the supermarket. But you know, my love, Nibbles is very resourceful, I think you have to have faith in her. You think she was happy in a cage? . . . Daddy's very sad, he didn't mean to upset you . . . Of course you will. Yes, of course you'll speak to him again. Listen, darling, we're worried enough already about your brother . . . She'll eat. . . she'll eat leaves . . . acorns, conkers . . . she'll find things, she knows what food she needs . . . Worms, snails, stuff that drops out of rubbish bins, she's like us, she's omnivorous . . . See you soon, sweetheart.

Hiatus.

MICHEL: I dare say that creature's stuffing its face as we speak.
VÉRONIQUE: No.

Silence.

MICHEL: What do we know?

index of critical terms